A Perfectionist Theory of Justice

A Perfectionist Theory of Justice

COLLIS TAHZIB

Great Clarendon Street, Oxford, OX2 6DP,
United Kingdom

Oxford University Press is a department of the University of Oxford.
It furthers the University's objective of excellence in research, scholarship,
and education by publishing worldwide. Oxford is a registered trade mark of
Oxford University Press in the UK and in certain other countries

© Collis Tahzib 2022

The moral rights of the author have been asserted

Impression: 1

All rights reserved. No part of this publication may be reproduced, stored in
a retrieval system, or transmitted, in any form or by any means, without the
prior permission in writing of Oxford University Press, or as expressly permitted
by law, by licence or under terms agreed with the appropriate reprographics
rights organization. Enquiries concerning reproduction outside the scope of the
above should be sent to the Rights Department, Oxford University Press, at the
address above

You must not circulate this work in any other form
and you must impose this same condition on any acquirer

Published in the United States of America by Oxford University Press
198 Madison Avenue, New York, NY 10016, United States of America

British Library Cataloguing in Publication Data

Data available

Library of Congress Control Number: 2022933272

ISBN 978–0–19–284711–9

DOI: 10.1093/oso/9780192847119.001.0001

Printed and bound by
CPI Group (UK) Ltd, Croydon, CR0 4YY

Links to third party websites are provided by Oxford in good faith and
for information only. Oxford disclaims any responsibility for the materials
contained in any third party website referenced in this work.

Acknowledgements

During the writing of this book, I have incurred a number of debts of gratitude to both institutions and individuals.

I thank St John's College, Oxford University and the Clarendon Fund for generously supporting my doctoral research, which was on the topic of perfectionist political philosophy. I also owe thanks to Merton College, Oxford University, which subsequently provided marvellous conditions in which to continue this research at the post-doctoral level. I am very grateful as well to the University of Southern California for providing the support that enabled me to bring the book to its completion.

I also wish to thank participants of the various events at which I have presented ideas or chapters from this work: the Nuffield Political Theory Workshop in 2018; the Workshop in Honour of Matthew Kramer at Churchill College, Cambridge University in 2019; the Conference on Themes from the Political Philosophy of Gerald Gaus at Nuffield College, Oxford University in 2019; the 7th Annual Workshop for Oxford Studies in Political Philosophy at Syracuse University in 2019; a departmental colloquium at the University of Southern California in 2020; a conference at the University of Rijeka in 2020; and the Oxford Work in Progress in Political Theory Seminar in 2020. I was especially fortunate that in 2021 there were three events on the full manuscript of this book—an event as part of the Nuffield Political Theory Workshop at which Paul Billingham, Cécile Laborde, David Miller and Anthony Taylor provided terrific comments in their capacity as respondents; a two-day workshop within the Department of Philosophy at the University of Rijeka at which Elvio Baccarini, Iris Vidmar Jovanović, Marko Konjović, Chong-Ming Lim and Michal Sladeček gave illuminating presentations on the manuscript; and a highly instructive eleven-week reading group organized by Elvio Baccarini—and I extend my thanks to all involved in these events. In autumn 2021 I taught a graduate seminar at the University of Southern California based on themes explored in the manuscript, and I am grateful to the participants of that seminar for their insightful contributions and feedback.

I am very grateful to the following individuals for helpful conversations, comments or written feedback: Max Afnan, Elvio Baccarini, Jacob Barrett, Kristina Lekić Barunčić, Paul Billingham, David Birks, Giulia Bistagnino, Geertje Bol, Matthias Brinkmann, Samuel Bruce, Ivan Cerovac, Joseph Chan, Simon-Pierre Chevarie-Cossette, Jamie Draper, Emily Dyson, Sarah-Lea Effert, Jan Eijking, David Enoch, Cécile Fabre, Paul Garofalo, Gerald Gaus, Vafa Ghazavi, Simeon

vi ACKNOWLEDGEMENTS

Goldstraw, Jeremy Goodman, Laura Gurskey, John Hawthorne, Viktor Ivanković, Iris Vidmar Jovanović, Dominik Kobos, Marko Konjović, Matthew Kramer, Elsa Kugelberg, Henrik Kugelberg, Enes Kulenović, Visa Kurki, Cécile Laborde, Janet Levin, Chong-Ming Lim, Andrew Lister, Federica Liveriero, Harry Lloyd, Ruairí Maguire, Luca Malatesti, Franz Mang, Iva Martinić, Simon Căbulea May, Mark McBride, Jeff McMahan, David Miller, Ana Gavran Miloš, Alex Motchoulski, Daniel Pallies, Zeynep Pamuk, Fergus Peace, Jonathan Quong, Charlie Richards, Jacob Ross, Jay Ruckelshaus, Tom Sinclair, Michal Sladeček, Andrew Stewart, Valentina Marianna Stupnik, Anthony Taylor, Jonathan Turner, Kadri Vihvelin, Steven Wall, Ralph Wedgwood, Matthew Wiseman, Brian Wong, Kate Yoon and Nebojša Zelić. In addition, my thanks go to the anonymous reviewers for various journals who have provided comments on previously published work, parts of which have been revised for inclusion in this book. I am deeply grateful to Dominic Byatt at Oxford University Press for his wit and wisdom during the process of publication, and to Matthew Kramer and Steven Wall, who provided excellent comments and criticisms as the reviewers for OUP.

To a trio of these individuals I owe special thanks. I am greatly indebted to my doctoral supervisors Jeff McMahan and David Miller. When I asked Jeff whether he would be willing to supervise me, he said that he would be happy to—before warning that his comments would be 'unlikely to be penetratingly critical' both because the topic lay outside his area of expertise and because of his own sympathy for the sort of position I wanted to defend. After many a conversation in which he provided tremendously detailed and perceptive feedback on my work, I have been left wondering what it would be like to be supervised by Jeff on a project that falls *within* his area of expertise and that goes *against* his own political inclinations. David has been a continuous source of encouragement and insight. I am particularly grateful for his extensive and searching comments on a full draft of the manuscript—comments which led me to make a host of changes large and small. I also cannot thank enough Jonathan Quong, who has provided exceptionally generous and astute feedback on my work for several years. Indeed, it was over dinner in Venice, CA that some of the key ideas of Part II of this book began to fit together in my mind. That Jon, despite his own position in these debates, often sees better than I do how my argument will need to go is both dismaying and inspiring.

Finally, I am immensely grateful to my parents for their constant support and love, and to Raven, who daily fills me with an overwhelming sense of good fortune, love and admiration.

Contents

Introduction	1
Two Distinctive Features	5
Outline	11

I. THE FOIL: ANTI-PERFECTIONIST LIBERALISM

1. Comprehensive Liberalism	19
1.1 Two Kinds of Liberal Theory	20
1.2 Kantian Liberalism	23
1.3 Millian Liberalism	26
1.4 Dworkin's Challenge Model of Ethics	30
2. Political Liberalism	34
2.1 The Fact of Reasonable Disagreement	36
2.2 Public Justification	40
2.3 A Thin Normative Rationale	47
2.3.1 Respect	49
2.3.2 Stability	53
2.3.3 The Reactive Attitudes	56

II. PERFECTIONIST JUSTICE

3. A Perfectionist Conception of Society	63
3.1 The Rawlsian Conception of Society	64
3.2 Why the Rawlsian Conception of Society?	68
3.3 An Alternative Conception of Society	73
3.4 The Perfectionist Conception as Cultural Interpretation	77
3.5 The Perfectionist Conception in Reflective Equilibrium	86
4. Perfectionist Principles of Justice	89
4.1 Rawls's Original Position: The Set-Up	90
4.2 Rawls's Original Position: The Selection of Principles	94
4.3 A Perfectionist Original Position: The Set-Up	97
4.4 A Perfectionist Original Position: The Selection of Principles	110

viii CONTENTS

4.5 Are Judgements About Human Flourishing Especially
Controversial? 116
4.6 Is the Perfectionist Original Position Redundant? 120

5. A Provisional Conception of Human Flourishing 126
5.1 Three Conceptions Unfit for Political Purposes 131
5.2 The Enjoyment of Moral, Intellectual and Artistic
Excellence 133
5.3 Are the Three Excellences Too Abstract? 138
5.4 Provisionality 141
5.5 Arbitrariness 147
5.6 Are Enjoyment and Excellence Strictly Necessary? 151

6. Perfectionist Law and Public Policy 156
6.1 Preliminaries 158
6.2 Moral Excellence 160
6.3 Intellectual Excellence 164
6.4 Artistic Excellence 168
6.5 Indistinguishability: Doesn't Liberal Justice *Already* Give
Perfection Its Due? 170
6.6 Extensional Differences 175
6.6.1 Rawls's Arguments from Unanimous Consent and
Equality 177
6.6.2 Dworkin's Argument from Intergenerational Fairness 180
6.6.3 Wall's Argument from Equality and Fairness 182
6.6.4 Kramer's Argument from Warranted Self-Respect 184
6.7 Intensional Differences 189

III. OBJECTIONS

7. Public Justification 197
7.1 A Road Not Taken 199
7.2 Perfectionist Public Reason 205
7.3 Is the Marriage of Perfectionism and Constructivism
Well-Motivated? 213
7.4 Which Definition of Reasonableness is More Plausible? 218
7.5 Admissible Interpretations of the Excellences 225
7.6 A More Sectarian Definition of Reasonableness? 233
7.6.1 The Anti-Sectarian Desideratum 234
7.6.2 The Spirit of Public Reason Liberalism 236
7.6.3 Stability 238
7.6.4 Respect 240
7.6.5 Redundancy 241
7.7 An Overly Sectarian Definition of Reasonableness? 243

CONTENTS ix

8. Freedom	247
8.1 The Place of Freedom Within Perfectionist Justice	248
8.2 Four Freedom-Based Objections Defused	250
8.3 Libertarian Full Self-Ownership	256
8.3.1 Three Implausible Implications	258
8.3.2 Two Libertarian Responses	262
8.4 Pragmatic Concerns	267
9. Paternalism	273
9.1 Why Is Perfectionist State Action Necessary?	274
9.2 A Non-Paternalistic Justification for Perfectionist State Action?	278
9.3 Why Paternalism (in the Quongian Sense) Is Not Objectionable	280
10. The Village Busybody	294
10.1 What Is the Quidnunc Mentality?	295
10.2 How the Quidnunc Mentality Objection Begs the Question	300
10.3 A Substantive Argument Against Perfectionist Duties?	305
10.4 Indistinguishability Rides Again	310
10.5 Addendum	312
Conclusion	317
Justicitis?	319
References	323
Index	338

Introduction

This book is about one of the fundamental questions of political philosophy: for what purposes should we organize our collective lives? In the pursuit of what ends and ideals should the formidable powers and resources of the state be used? What is, and what is not, the proper business of government? In particular, should the state make and act on judgements about the worthiness of different ways of life or should it instead refrain from making and acting on any such judgements?

Many liberal theorists hold that the state has no business telling citizens how to live their lives. Such liberals are known as *anti-perfectionist liberals*.[1] While the nature of anti-perfectionist liberalism will be the subject of the first part of this book, it can initially be characterized as follows:

> *Anti-Perfectionist Liberalism*: The state should not seek to impose or even promote any particular ideal of the good life or human flourishing. It should not, for instance, enact laws and policies designed to elevate citizens' tastes, to refine their sensibilities or to perfect their characters. Indeed, it should, as far as possible, refrain altogether from forming judgements of this kind about the worthiness of different ways of life. So long as citizens do not harm others or violate other requirements of justice, their choices about what to do with their time and resources are none of the state's business. Instead, the state should restrict itself to establishing a fair framework of rights and opportunities within which citizens can pursue their own beliefs about what constitutes a valuable or flourishing life. To this end, the state should ensure that rights and liberties are protected, that all citizens receive a fair share of resources and opportunities, and that social cooperation proceeds on a footing of mutual respect. In this sense, there is an important asymmetry between values such as freedom, equality and fairness and values such as moral, intellectual and artistic excellence: the state should concern itself with the former values, but not with the latter.

Naturally, there are differences among the numerous versions of anti-perfectionist liberalism. Anti-perfectionist liberals disagree, for instance, over whether the

---

[1] Anti-perfectionist liberalism is also referred to as *neutralist* liberalism. I sometimes use the term 'neutrality' (or 'neutralist'), and when I do so I use it interchangeably with 'anti-perfectionism' (or 'anti-perfectionist'). But I generally prefer the term 'anti-perfectionism' as the term 'neutrality' has misleading connotations. For related comments on terminology, see Rawls, J., *Political Liberalism* (New York: Columbia University Press, 2005), p. 191; Matravers, M., 'What's "Wrong" in Contractualism?', in P. Kelly (ed.), *Impartiality, Neutrality and Justice: Re-reading Brian Barry's Justice as Impartiality* (Edinburgh: Edinburgh University Press, 2000), p. 115 n. 20.

A Perfectionist Theory of Justice. Collis Tahzib, Oxford University Press.
© Collis Tahzib (2022). DOI: 10.1093/oso/9780192847119.003.0001

2 A PERFECTIONIST THEORY OF JUSTICE

notion of a fair share of resources and opportunities should be interpreted in a more or less stringently egalitarian manner. Still, the view described above, or at least something in its vicinity, represents a dominant strand of contemporary liberal theory—one that encompasses many of the most impressive and influential exponents of liberalism in recent times, such as Brian Barry, Ronald Dworkin, Gerald Gaus, Charles Larmore, Martha Nussbaum, Jonathan Quong and John Rawls.[2]

This view of the state's legitimate domain of activity has deep roots in the liberal tradition, and something similar to it is memorably expressed by John Stuart Mill in *On Liberty*: 'the only freedom which deserves the name is that of pursuing our own good in our own way, so long as we do not attempt to deprive others of theirs or impede their efforts to obtain it. Each is the proper guardian of his own health, whether bodily or mental and spiritual. Mankind are greater gainers by suffering each to live as seems good to themselves than by compelling each to live as seems good to the rest.'[3] Arguably, in fact, it stretches back even further in the history of liberal thought to John Locke's *Letter Concerning Toleration*, in which Locke argues that the state should concern itself only with civil matters of life, liberty and property, and not with the 'care of souls', which should be left to the church.[4]

Anti-perfectionist liberalism also exerts an important influence on public policy, a clear illustration of which can be found in the 1978 report of the UK Royal Commission on Gambling:

> The objection that punters are wasting their time is a moral or possibly an aesthetic judgement. As it happens, none of us is attracted by the idea of spending an afternoon in a betting office. But the people who frequent betting offices have chosen to enjoy themselves in their own way and we think that in a free society it would be wrong to prevent them from doing so merely because others think that they would be better employed in digging the garden, reading to their children or playing healthy outdoor sports.[5]

And even outside of academic and public policy circles, the idea that the state has no business telling citizens how to live seems to form part of the public political

---

[2] See Barry, B., *Justice as Impartiality* (Oxford: Oxford University Press, 1995); Dworkin, R., *Sovereign Virtue: The Theory and Practice of Equality* (Cambridge, MA: Harvard University Press, 2000); Gaus, G., 'Liberal Neutrality: A Compelling and Radical Principle', in S. Wall and G. Klosko (eds), *Perfectionism and Neutrality: Essays in Liberal Theory* (Oxford: Rowman & Littlefield, 2003), pp. 137–65; Larmore, C., *Patterns of Moral Complexity* (Cambridge: Cambridge University Press, 1987); Nussbaum, M., 'Perfectionist Liberalism and Political Liberalism', *Philosophy & Public Affairs* 39 (2011), pp. 3–45; Quong, J., *Liberalism Without Perfection* (Oxford: Oxford University Press, 2011); Rawls, J., *Political Liberalism*.

[3] Mill, J. S., *On Liberty* (London: Penguin Books, 1985), p. 72.

[4] Locke, J., *Second Treatise of Government and a Letter Concerning Toleration* (Oxford: Oxford University Press, 2016), p. 129.

[5] *Royal Commission on Gambling: Final Report* (London: Her Majesty's Stationery Office, 1978), p. 68.

culture of modern societies, offering a picture of the proper role of government that is 'instantly recognizable' and that 'no contemporary Westerner can altogether escape'.[6]

By contrast, the view that I defend in this work emanates from the perfectionist tradition of political philosophy—though it will eventually converge with the liberal tradition on a number of important points. Perfectionist thought is animated by a different question from that which animates liberal thought. Whereas liberalism has traditionally been concerned with how best to protect and promote individual freedom, perfectionism has traditionally been concerned with how best to protect and promote human flourishing. In this spirit, I shall argue that one important role of a just state is to encourage citizens to pursue lives rich in the enjoyment of moral, intellectual and artistic excellence.

The debate between perfectionism and anti-perfectionist liberalism is of both practical and theoretical significance. On the practical side, this debate matters because it has implications for certain laws and public policies, such as state support for the arts and culture, that are standardly justified on the basis of claims about what constitutes a good or flourishing human life. If anti-perfectionist liberalism is true, then the standard justifications for these laws and policies are illegitimate. Of course, this does not mean that these laws and policies themselves are illegitimate. After all, there may be non-perfectionist justifications for these laws and policies— that is, justifications that avoid claims about the good life or human flourishing and that instead refer to quintessential liberal values such as freedom, equality and fairness. Rawls, for instance, explains that even though his 'principles of justice do not permit subsidizing universities and institutes, or opera and the theatre, on the grounds that these institutions are intrinsically valuable', they do permit taxation for these purposes on the grounds that these institutions advance 'directly or indirectly the social conditions that secure the equal liberties and [advance] in an appropriate way the long-term interests of the least advantaged'.[7] But, still, how we settle the debate between perfectionism and anti-perfectionist liberalism can be expected to have important and far-reaching implications for many areas of law and public policy.

On the theoretical side, this debate matters because it gets to the heart of some of the most basic and enduring questions of political philosophy. Over the years, anti-perfectionist liberals have levelled a number of powerful objections to perfectionism: that it relies on values and judgements that are controversial within modern pluralistic societies; that it is unduly restrictive of freedom and autonomy; that it treats citizens as if they are children, unable to run their own lives; that it

---

[6] Sher, G., *Beyond Neutrality: Perfectionism and Politics* (Cambridge: Cambridge University Press, 1997), p. 2.

[7] Rawls, J., *A Theory of Justice* (Cambridge, MA: Harvard University Press, 1971), p. 332. I explore this argument in Section 6.6.1.

4   A PERFECTIONIST THEORY OF JUSTICE

expresses the meddlesome mentality of a village busybody; that it mistakenly assumes that there are objective truths about human flourishing; and that it risks the abuse of power by incompetent, overzealous or corrupt state officials. These ideas represent some of the deepest, most vibrant and most powerful strains in liberal thought. In defending perfectionism against these charges, the arguments in this book connect with, and contribute to, influential and longstanding debates about the philosophical foundations of liberalism.

Before continuing, let me make a comment about the present state of the debate between perfectionists and anti-perfectionist liberals. Some may wonder whether another defence of perfectionism is needed. As long ago as 1998, after all, a reviewer of George Sher's defence of perfectionism wrote that 'as one finishes [this] book it is hard not to believe that the period of neutralist liberalism is now over', and by 2003 Richard Arneson had carried out anti-perfectionist liberalism's 'autopsy'.[8] So hasn't the debate between perfectionists and anti-perfectionists already between settled in favour of perfectionists?

Whatever the validity of these statements was in the late 1990s and early 2000s, however, they do not ring true as descriptions of the present state of the debate between perfectionists and anti-perfectionists. Indeed, if anything, it is anti-perfectionist liberalism that appears ascendant today. For in the last decade or so there has emerged a number of highly sophisticated and influential defences of liberal neutrality, as well as several novel and forceful critiques of leading perfectionist political theories.[9] Some theorists have also begun to argue that anti-perfectionist liberalism offers a promising political philosophy in the context of East Asian societies.[10] The suggestion that anti-perfectionism is dead is also belied by recent work that explores the implications of anti-perfectionist liberalism for various areas such as civic education, state recognition of marriage, and the functioning of the civil service.[11]

---

[8] Hurka, T., 'Book Review of George Sher's *Beyond Neutrality: Perfectionism and Politics*', *Ethics* 109 (1998), p. 190; Arneson, R., 'Liberal Neutrality on the Good: An Autopsy', in S. Wall and G. Klosko (eds), *Perfectionism and Neutrality*, pp. 191–218.

[9] For the defences of anti-perfectionist liberalism, see, for example, Nussbaum, M., 'Perfectionism Liberalism and Political Liberalism'; Quong, J., *Liberalism Without Perfection*; Patten, A., 'Liberal Neutrality: A Reinterpretation and Defense', *The Journal of Political Philosophy* 20 (2012), pp. 249–72. For the critiques of leading perfectionist theories, see, for example, Pallikkathayil, J., 'Neither Perfectionism Nor Political Liberalism', *Philosophy & Public Affairs* 44 (2016), pp. 171–96; Kramer, M., *Liberalism with Excellence* (Oxford: Oxford University Press, 2017), especially chs 5 and 6.

[10] See, for example, Li, Z., *Political Liberalism, Confucianism, and the Future of Democracy in East Asia* (New York: Springer, 2020).

[11] See, for example, Chambers, C., *Against Marriage: An Egalitarian Defence of the Marriage-Free State* (Oxford: Oxford University Press, 2017); Watson, L. and Hartley, C., *Equal Citizenship and Public Reason: A Feminist Political Liberalism* (Oxford: Oxford University Press, 2018); Schouten, G., *Liberalism, Neutrality, and the Gendered Division of Labor* (Oxford: Oxford University Press, 2019); Dietrich, F., 'Liberalism, Neutrality, and the Child's Right to an Open Future', *Journal of Social Philosophy* 51 (2020), pp. 104–28; Heath, J., *The Machinery of Government: Public Administration and the Liberal State* (Oxford: Oxford University Press, 2020), especially ch. 5.

In recent years, there has also been a proliferation of impressive contributions to the literature on public reason liberalism, and while theories of public reason differ in their details, they typically converge in their opposition to many, if not all, perfectionist laws and policies.[12] Indeed, Vallier and Muldoon suggest that since opposition to perfectionism is a common commitment of public reason liberals, 'one way for [different public reason views] to engage one another is to ask which view provides the better defense against perfectionist coercion'.[13] In this way, they suggest, anti-perfectionism can function as a kind of desideratum within the proliferating public reason literature, one that allows 'fruitful engagement' between different approaches and that means public reason liberals 'need not talk past one another'.[14]

More generally, the thumbnail sketch of anti-perfectionist liberalism that I offered at the outset of this chapter still also represents, or so it seems to me, the dominant outlook within contemporary political philosophy. A background assumption of many political philosophers, that is, seems to be that articulating the correct conception of social justice will be a matter of striking the appropriate balance between liberal values such as freedom and equality, and will not require recourse to perfectionist reasoning. In these and other ways, then, my sense is that reports of the death of anti-perfectionist liberalism have been much exaggerated, and that it remains a highly significant position within contemporary political philosophy.

Two Distinctive Features

The ways in which the view defended in this book differs from leading forms of anti-perfectionist liberalism will become apparent throughout the chapters that follow. Here, though, it is worth saying something about what distinguishes my form of perfectionism from other perfectionist views in the contemporary literature, such as those of Joseph Chan, Alexandra Couto, Thomas Hurka, Matthew Kramer, Joseph Raz, George Sher and Steven Wall.[15]

---

[12] See, for example, Gaus, G., *The Order of Public Reason: A Theory of Freedom and Morality in a Diverse and Bounded World* (Cambridge: Cambridge University Press, 2011); Lister, A., *Public Reason and Political Community* (London: Bloomsbury, 2013); Vallier, K., *Must Politics Be War? Restoring Our Trust in the Open Society* (Oxford: Oxford University Press, 2019).

[13] Vallier, K. and Muldoon, R., 'In Public Reason, Diversity Trumps Coherence', *The Journal of Political Philosophy* 29 (2021), p. 220.

[14] Ibid.

[15] See Chan, J., 'Legitimacy, Unanimity, and Perfectionism', *Philosophy & Public Affairs* 29 (2000), pp. 5–42; Couto, A., *Liberal Perfectionism* (Berlin: De Gruyter, 2014); Hurka, T., *Perfectionism* (Oxford: Oxford University Press, 1993); Kramer, M., *Liberalism with Excellence*; Raz, J., *The Morality of Freedom* (Oxford: Clarendon Press, 1986); Sher, G., *Beyond Neutrality*; Wall, S., *Liberalism, Perfectionism, and Restraint* (Cambridge: Cambridge University Press, 1998).

6   A PERFECTIONIST THEORY OF JUSTICE

In this book I develop a perfectionist theory of justice from within a Rawlsian methodological framework. More precisely, in fact, I develop a perfectionist theory of *social* justice from within a Rawlsian methodological framework, since there are other kinds of justice, such as criminal justice or reparative justice, that are not covered by this theory. There are two main distinctive features of this view: namely, that it presents perfectionism as a conception of social justice and that it is developed within a Rawlsian framework. Both features require some comment.

Most contemporary perfectionist theories are not theories of social justice.[16] Most contemporary perfectionists, that is, hold that perfectionist policies, such as state support for the arts and sin taxes on gambling, are permissible, or that they are legitimate, or that they are justified, or that there is a presumption in favour of them, or that there are reasons to pursue them—without going the extra step of saying that perfectionist policies are *required at the bar of justice*. Sher, for instance, advances the view that 'a government *may* legitimately promote the good' and that 'political agents often have ample *reason* to promote' flourishing lives.[17] In an influential article, Chan states that 'political perfectionism ... says that it is *permissible* for the state to design its political arrangement or policies with the aim of promoting what the state (or those citizens acting on the behalf of the state) thinks are worthwhile goods and ways of life'.[18] Couto argues for the view that 'the state is *permitted* and *justified* to protect and promote the opportunities for citizens to engage with intrinsically valuable goods on the basis of their intrinsic value'.[19] John Horton says that his 'claim is only a relatively weak one ... which is that there is nothing necessarily illiberal, unjust or disrespectful about a state supporting some activities because it attaches value to them or wishes to promote them rather than some other activities; it is not the stronger, but unsustainable, claim that any particular values or activities are *entitled* to such support'.[20] And Thaddeus Metz defends what he calls 'open perfectionism', which 'recognizes that there are conceptions of the good that could be significantly furthered with the use of state resources and that the potential for a majority to live a certain way can,

---

[16] The notable exception to this is Matthew Kramer's 'aspirational perfectionism'. See Kramer, M., *Liberalism with Excellence*, especially ch. 8. My view is importantly different from Kramer's, though, since it is what he would call an 'edificatory-perfectionist' theory of justice rather than an 'aspirational-perfectionist' theory of justice. Another difference between my view and Kramer's is that aspirational perfectionism 'does not amount to a full theory of justice; it is only one element therein' (p. 402), whereas the view defended here is intended to be a full theory of justice, one which explains how a distinctively perfectionist principle of justice integrates with other principles of justice. I evaluate Kramer's positive case for aspirational perfectionism in Section 6.6.4, and I evaluate his criticisms of edificatory perfectionism in Section 8.2 and Chapter 10.

[17] Sher, G., *Beyond Neutrality*, pp. 1, 245 (emphasis added).

[18] Chan, J., 'Legitimacy, Unanimity, and Perfectionism', p. 35 (emphasis added).

[19] Couto, A., *Liberal Perfectionism*, p. 33 (emphasis added).

[20] Horton, J., 'Why Liberals Should Not Worry About Subsidizing Opera', *Critical Review of International Social and Political Philosophy* 15 (2012), p. 444 (emphasis in original).

subject to certain constraints, *justify* such use'.[21] Of course, claiming that perfectionist policies are permissible, desirable, legitimate or justified is strictly speaking compatible with the more ambitious further claim that such policies are a requirement of justice. But the point is that the kinds of claims made by perfectionists typically fall short of establishing perfectionist duties of justice and are not supplemented and strengthened by further arguments that would establish any such duties.

Admittedly, some perfectionists, notably Raz and Wall, do endorse perfectionist duties, as opposed to merely perfectionist reasons and permissions. But even these perfectionists do not (or at any rate do not explicitly) endorse perfectionist duties *of justice*, such that a state that fails to enact perfectionist policies would count as pro tanto unjust. Wall, for instance, often describes his aim as that of articulating 'a perfectionist account of political morality' as opposed to a perfectionist account of social justice.[22] Elsewhere he says that 'while [perfectionism] is not unjust, it is not required by justice either'.[23] In other words, duty-based perfectionists such as Raz and Wall are not very forthcoming about what broader conception of social justice they endorse and about what role, if any, perfectionist considerations play within that conception. I try to correct for this imbalance by drawing out more explicitly and systematically the implications of conceiving of perfectionism as a doctrine of justice.

One reason why perfectionists have tended to regard perfectionist policies as justice-unrelated is, I suspect, dialectical. It is anti-perfectionist liberals who have set the tone of the neutrality-perfectionism debate and who have defined that debate as one about whether it is permissible for the state to act in pursuit of perfectionist ideals. Quong, for instance, follows Rawls in formulating the debate in terms of 'what liberal states can permissibly or legitimately do', and in particular whether 'it is permissible for a liberal state to promote or discourage some activities, ideals, or ways of life on grounds relating to their inherent or intrinsic value, or on the basis of other metaphysical claims'.[24] This formulation of the debate has, perhaps, put perfectionists on the back foot, and so most perfectionists have been content to show merely that perfectionist policies are permissible or legitimate—that they are *not impermissible or illegitimate*—without going the extra step of arguing that perfectionist policies are in fact required by justice.

The first distinctive feature of my view, then, is that it treats perfectionism as an integral component of justice and not merely a legitimate complement to justice.

---

[21] Metz, T., 'Respect for Persons and Perfectionist Politics', *Philosophy & Public Affairs* 30 (2001), p. 442 (emphasis added).

[22] See Wall, S., *Liberalism, Perfectionism, and Restraint*, pp. i, 1, 2, 125.

[23] Wall, S., 'The Good Society', in S. Olsaretti (ed.), *The Oxford Handbook of Distributive Justice* (Oxford: Oxford University Press, 2018), p. 196.

[24] Quong, J., *Liberalism Without Perfection*, pp. 15–16.

On this view, it is not just that there is no general exclusionary principle that forbids appeal to considerations about the good life and human flourishing when justifying political arrangements. Rather, the state is required at the bar of justice to encourage citizens to pursue worthy or flourishing ways of life and to discourage them from pursuing unworthy ways of life. The principles of social justice are, in this way, deeply shaped by specific claims about human flourishing. Perfectionist considerations partly define what constitutes fair terms. I thus reject the tendency to see perfectionism as the icing on the cake of social justice—as the policies added on once a state has established the fair terms of social cooperation. Instead, perfectionist policies form an essential part of what the rightful treatment of the citizenry by the state involves.

An important implication of this view is that even an ideal or well-ordered Rawlsian society fails to respect some of the moral rights of its citizens. Members of such a society who do not lead a flourishing life can feel legitimately aggrieved that the state did not do more to sustain an environment that was conducive to the best things in life and that it did not take more active steps to encourage the worthy and discourage the unworthy. Of course, the failure of these citizens to flourish is not *wholly* the state's fault. Like any credible theory of social or distributive justice, a perfectionist theory of justice incorporates an ideal of personal responsibility. But, still, such individuals retain an important justice-based grievance against the state for failing to give the claims of perfection their due in the design and operation of its main social and political institutions.

The second distinctive feature of my view is that it is developed within a methodological framework that echoes in various respects the framework within which Rawls developed his anti-perfectionist liberal theory of justice. For Rawls, liberal political philosophy begins with a conception of society as a fair system of social cooperation between free and equal citizens. We then ask what principles are most appropriate for regulating a society conceived of in this way. The device of the original position helps us to answer this question, yielding the equal basic liberties principle, the fair equality of opportunity principle and the difference principle. I take this methodology to be one of the most powerful aspects of Rawls's work. Yet no perfectionist has hitherto made use of this framework or explored whether it can be pressed in the service of perfectionism. Perfectionists have not, that is, explored what a 'perfectionist conception of society', a 'perfectionist original position' or even 'perfectionist principles of justice' might look like. In this way, perfectionists have tended to eschew not only Rawls's substantive conception of social justice but also his broader methodological innovations.

To illustrate: in his book-length defence of perfectionism, Sher develops a fairly traditional account of human flourishing according to which 'knowledge, excellence, and virtue make people's lives better', and he argues in light of this account that 'governments and individual political agents often have ample reason to promote such lives'.[25] From a Rawlsian perspective, however, Sher's view leaves a number of vital questions unanswered: what is the fundamental conception of society to which this political theory gives expression? Is Sher's view compatible with the attractive Rawlsian thought that, at least for political purposes, society ought to be conceived of as a fair system of social cooperation between free and equal persons? Or does it operate, implicitly, with an alternative conception of society? Is Sher's claim just that states have ample reason to promote flourishing lives, or is it, more strongly, that they are required to do so at the bar of justice? If the latter, what is the formulation of the specific perfectionist principle of justice that Sher defends? Would such a principle be selected in Rawls's original position by parties behind the veil of ignorance—and, if not, does that matter? How would this perfectionist principle of justice relate to other principles of justice, such as the equal basic liberties principle, the fair equality of opportunity principle and the difference principle?[26] Might it conflict with them? Or is it, say, additional and lexically posterior to them?

This is not intended as a criticism, as such, of Sher—or of the other perfectionists mentioned at the outset of this section, of whose views the same questions could also be asked. There are many possible frameworks for developing and expressing a political theory, and there is of course no obligation to operate within a Rawlsian framework. The point of posing these questions is rather to illustrate that thinking about perfectionist political theory from within a Rawlsian framework opens up a number of fruitful and neglected lines of inquiry. Whether these lines of inquiry are, in the end, sufficiently fruitful to assuage the serious reservations that many perfectionists have about the Rawlsian framework—whether, to put it differently, this methodologically Rawlsian yet substantively perfectionist theory fills a gap in the literature that is even *worth* filling—is not a question that can be settled at this stage in the exposition. My hope is that, once the whole theory is before us, the value of the Rawlsian framework for perfectionist theorizing will be evident. So while my version of perfectionism will differ from other versions in some of its conclusions about what the state should and should not do to promote human flourishing, the more important difference is in the nature of the argument used to reach those conclusions, and in particular in the mobilization of various Rawlsian devices to justify the promotion of perfectionist values by the state. This version of

[25] Sher, G., *Beyond Neutrality*, p. 245.
[26] Indeed, Sher himself admits that his view leaves various 'loose ends', one of which is the question of how his 'account of the good life can be woven into a more comprehensive scheme that also includes distributional' principles. (See Sher, G., *Beyond Neutrality*, p. 244; for similar disclaimers by other perfectionists, see, for example, Raz, J., *The Morality of Freedom*, pp. 2–3; Wall, S., *Liberalism, Perfectionism and Restraint*, p. 125; Kramer, M., *Liberalism with Excellence*, pp. 402–3.) One advantage of the Rawlsian methodology is that it impels us from the outset to weave the perfectionist principles into a broader conception of justice that has reasonably clear distributive implications.

10   A PERFECTIONIST THEORY OF JUSTICE

perfectionism illustrates that the debate need not be polarized between Rawlsian anti-perfectionists and perfectionist anti-Rawlsians.

A closely related way of putting this second distinctive feature is in terms of the distinction between 'comprehensive' and 'political' theories. It is, by now, widely recognized that there are two importantly different ways of conceptualizing liberalism: comprehensive liberalism and political liberalism. The distinction between comprehensive and political liberalism will be examined in Section 1.1 (and indeed in Part I more generally); but the basic idea is that comprehensive liberals, such as Kant and Mill, derive liberal conclusions from some comprehensive moral or philosophical doctrine (often a doctrine about the importance of personal autonomy), whereas political liberals, such as Larmore and Rawls, avoid presupposing any specific comprehensive doctrine and instead derive liberal conclusions in a more free-standing way from values and conceptions that all reasonable citizens can be expected to accept.

However, while liberals have paid close attention to the distinction between comprehensive liberalism and political liberalism, perfectionists have hardly availed themselves of this distinction. Almost all perfectionists are *comprehensive* perfectionists: that is, perfectionists who base their perfectionism in some comprehensive moral or philosophical doctrine. Thus, as I explain in more detail in Section 5.1, Hurka and Sher ground their perfectionisms in broadly Aristotelian ideas about human nature and human potentiality,[27] and Chan grounds his perfectionism in Confucianism.[28] And, of course, the paradigmatic historical example of perfectionism, namely 'the Catholic and Protestant states of the early modern period', was based squarely in Christian doctrine.[29]

But, as I explain more fully in Section 7.3, this neglects an important and plausible position in the conceptual space, namely *political perfectionism*.[30] According to political perfectionism, the state can and should promote the good life (hence the *perfectionism*) but it must avoid presupposing any specific comprehensive doctrine and must instead derive perfectionist conclusions in a more free-standing way from values and conceptions that all reasonable citizens can be expected to accept (hence the *political*). Thus, for political perfectionists, the perfectionist principles, laws and policies do not flow from some comprehensive moral or philosophical

---

[27] Hurka, T., *Perfectionism*; Sher, G., *Beyond Neutrality*.

[28] Chan, J., *Confucian Perfectionism: A Political Philosophy for Modern Times* (Princeton, NJ: Princeton University Press, 2014).

[29] Rawls, J., *Political Liberalism*, p. 195.

[30] In their two-by-two grid (which includes comprehensive liberalism, political liberalism, comprehensive perfectionism and political perfectionism), Mulhall and Swift leave the political perfectionism quadrant empty, saying, 'we know of no theorist, contemporary or otherwise, who could be described as a purely political perfectionist'. See Mulhall, S. and Swift, A., *Liberals and Communitarians* (Oxford: Blackwell Publishing, 1996), p. 252. Similarly, Quong, returning to the same grid, mentions a few philosophers who might qualify as political perfectionists before quickly adding, 'but it is not clear that any of them ... would endorse the political perfectionist label'. See Quong, J., *Liberalism Without Perfection*, p. 20.

doctrine (be it Aristotelian, Confucian, Christian or otherwise) but are instead determined by contractualist considerations about what is acceptable to suitably idealized citizens—where, in this work, 'suitably' idealized citizens are presumed to accept a perfectionist conception of society and a conception of human flourishing that are specially constructed for political purposes and with the fact of reasonable pluralism in mind. A perfectionism that is 'political not metaphysical' in this way can give us the best of both worlds by incorporating the central insights of political liberalism—that the terms of our common life should as far as possible be justifiable to all, and that political philosophers must show greater sensitivity to the fact of reasonable pluralism—while also avoiding its rather less appealing requirement that we 'cordon off political morality from our best understanding of human flourishing.'[31] Applying a 'political turn' to perfectionist theory thus emerges as a very natural and promising approach for those who wish to explore the most appropriate forms of perfectionist political action under conditions of reasonable pluralism.

So this work seeks to argue in support of both a neglected *family* of theories—a family of 'political perfectionisms' as opposed to 'comprehensive perfectionisms'— and a particular *member* of this family. The defence of the family of political perfectionisms is largely indirect, with the focus instead being on developing a particular first-order view. But the aim of opening up conceptual space for perfectionist thought remains operative throughout, and one could in principle reject the specific version of political perfectionism that I develop while endorsing some other view within the broader family of political perfectionisms. In this sense, one can expect there to be any number of ways for perfectionist theory to take a political turn, as the variegated fruits of the political turn within liberal theory amply demonstrate.

Outline

This book has three parts. In Part I, I set up the foil, namely anti-perfectionist liberalism. Because perfectionism is best understood in contrast to this brand of liberal theory, I spend some time exploring the nature of anti-perfectionist liberalism and the main motivations for this position. There are two major forms of anti-perfectionist liberalism: comprehensive liberalism, which is the subject of Chapter 1, and political liberalism, which is the subject of Chapter 2. Both views hold that the state should remain neutral between competing conceptions of the good or flourishing human life, but they differ in their justifications for this anti-perfectionist stance. For comprehensive liberals, anti-perfectionism flows from some ideal of personal autonomy. For instance, in *On Liberty* Mill sings the

---

[31] Wall, S., *Liberalism, Perfectionism and Restraint*, p. 123.

praises of individuality and 'experiments in living', and defends some kind of anti-perfectionism on the grounds that only an anti-perfectionist state would create the conditions necessary for such autonomous and experimental living and would prevent individuals being channelled into stultifying or conformist ways of life. By contrast, political liberals justify anti-perfectionism by reference to the fact of reasonable disagreement within modern societies and to a principle of public justification. For Rawls, for instance, the state should refrain from making and acting on judgements about the worthiness of different ways of life because 'in modern democratic society citizens affirm different, and indeed incommensurable and irreconcilable, though reasonable, comprehensive doctrines' and so perfectionist laws and policies could not be justified to all citizens in terms that they could reasonably be expected to endorse.[32]

Against this backdrop, I develop in Part II a perfectionist theory of justice. While no single component carries the entire burden of justification—after all, 'justification is a matter of the mutual support of many considerations, of everything fitting together into one coherent view'—the theory is shaped by a few fundamental ideas and conceptions set out in these chapters, including notably the perfectionist conception of society and the provisional conception of human flourishing.[33] These fundamental ideas and conceptions help to give structure to the whole perfectionist view. I begin, in Chapter 3, by arguing in favour of a perfectionist conception of society as a fair striving for human flourishing between free and equal citizens. This conception of society serves as an alternative and a competitor to Rawls's conception of society as a fair system of social cooperation between free and equal citizens. Echoing Rawls, I argue for the perfectionist conception of society as a fair striving for human flourishing partly on the grounds that this conception can be worked up from fundamental intuitive ideas embedded within the public political culture of modern societies and partly on the grounds that this conception helps to organize our considered convictions, at all levels of generality, into a state of reflective equilibrium.

I then consider, in Chapter 4, what principles of justice are most appropriate for regulating a society conceived of in these terms. Using an original position device, I argue that parties in a suitably revised original position—one that better models certain considerations that matter from the perfectionist point of view—would select the following principles:

(1) Each person has the same indefeasible claim to a fully adequate scheme of equal basic liberties compatible with the same scheme of liberties for all (the equal basic liberties principle);

---

[32] Rawls, J., *Justice as Fairness: A Restatement* (Cambridge, MA: Harvard University Press, 2001), p. 84.

[33] Rawls, J., *A Theory of Justice*, p. 579.

(2) Social and economic inequalities are to be attached to offices and positions open to all under conditions of fair equality of opportunity (the fair equality of opportunity principle);

(3) Social and economic inequalities are to be to the greatest benefit of the least advantaged members of society (the difference principle); and

(4) Social conditions promotive of and conducive to flourishing ways of life are to be established and maintained (the principle of perfection), where (1) is lexically prior to (2), (2) is lexically prior to (3) and (4), and (3) and (4) are not ordered in terms of lexical priority but must instead be intuitionistically balanced against each other.[34]

In Chapter 5, I consider the question of which conception of human flourishing should be plugged into the principle of perfection—the question, that is, of what counts as a 'flourishing' way of life. I first reject three prominent conceptions of human flourishing that have been defended by previous perfectionists—namely, Christian, Confucian and Aristotelian conceptions—on the grounds that they are subject to reasonable disagreement and so are not legitimate sources of political reasons under conditions of reasonable pluralism. I suggest that perfectionists should instead adopt a conception of human flourishing that is more free-standing and that is specially constructed for political purposes; in particular, I argue that, at least for political purposes, human flourishing should be taken to consist in the enjoyment of moral, intellectual and artistic excellence. But I stress in that chapter that this is a *provisional* conception of human flourishing: it is a reasonable approximation, but it is open to refinement and revision as a result of a broader process of philosophical inquiry into the nature of human flourishing. In brief, the idea is that we can theorize the distinctively political questions about the state's promotion of human flourishing without having in hand a fully worked-out conception of human flourishing, and so it makes sense to leave the finer details of this conception of human flourishing, such as the relative importance of the three excellences, to be figured out in due course. In this way, the provisional conception of human flourishing fixes ideas enough for us to be able to explore the main structural features of perfectionist justice, but not so much as to invite distracting quibbles about finer details.

In Chapter 6, I begin to explore what this perfectionist conception of justice might imply in terms of laws and public policies. While my discussion there is tentative and does not seek to make a definitive case for any particular legislative or policy programme, I suggest that moral excellence could be promoted through laws and policies designed to support the institution of friendship; that intellectual excellence could be promoted through informative and educational public broadcasting; and that artistic excellence could be promoted through the

---

[34] For principles (1)–(3), see Rawls, J., *Justice as Fairness*, pp. 42–3.

operation of publicly funded arts institutions and agencies. In this chapter I also address the concern that these laws and policies can already be justified on familiar liberal grounds, such as freedom, equality and fairness, and so the perfectionist conception of justice turns out to be practically indistinguishable from leading non-perfectionist conceptions of justice, such as those of Rawls and Dworkin. My response to this indistinguishability objection is twofold: first, many of the relevant non-perfectionist rationales do not succeed, and so in at least an interesting range of cases there will be genuine extensional differences between perfectionist and non-perfectionist conceptions of social justice; and second, even if these non-perfectionist rationales do succeed, this does not show that the perfectionist conception of justice is redundant or uninteresting since it may offer (among other things) more intrinsically plausible or straightforward rationales for these policies, thereby yielding the right policies for the right reasons.

In Part III, I defend this perfectionist conception of justice against a variety of objections. Although this part plays more defence than offence, many of the manoeuvres in these chapters serve to clarify, develop and apply ideas introduced in earlier chapters. In Chapter 7, I defend the perfectionist conception of justice against the objection that perfectionist laws and policies violate the public justification principle since they are premised on values or judgements that are subject to reasonable disagreement. I argue in favour of a perfectionist definition of reasonableness, according to which reasonableness is conditional not just on acceptance of certain liberal values such as freedom, equality and fairness (as political liberals tend to say) but also on acceptance of certain perfectionist values such as moral, intellectual and artistic excellence. Perfectionist laws and policies can thus be expected to pass the test of public justification because a citizen who rejects, say, the value of artistic excellence would count as unreasonable and so her veto would have no more normative force than that of a citizen who rejects the value of equality. This idea of 'perfectionist public reason' is defended against various objections, including the charge that it is excessively sectarian and so loses touch with the underlying motivations of the public reason project.

In Chapter 8, I consider the charge that perfectionist laws and policies are unduly restrictive of freedom or autonomy. My general response is that, on the one hand, perfectionist justice is compatible with many of the conceptions of freedom found within contemporary political philosophy and that, on the other hand, the conceptions of freedom with which perfectionist justice is incompatible (such as libertarian conceptions of freedom as full self-ownership) are not in any case independently plausible. In this chapter I also address a more pragmatic way of running the freedom-based objection: namely that, however hospitable to freedom perfectionism is *in theory*, any attempt to implement perfectionism *in practice* would risk the abuse of political power and the violation of individual liberties by incompetent or corrupt state officials, and so common sense dictates taking ideals of human flourishing off the political agenda as a kind of prophylactic measure. In response, I point out that officials of a modern anti-perfectionist liberal state also wield tremendous and potentially corrupting power, and so it remains unclear why we should expect perfectionist state officials to be *especially* prone to abuse their powers as compared with non-perfectionist state officials. I also argue that, even if perfectionist statecraft is at greater risk of backfiring than non-perfectionist statecraft, this poses a challenge more to the practical significance or feasibility of the perfectionist conception of justice than to its truth. Perhaps, that is, the perfectionist conception expresses the correct or true standards to which to hold social and political institutions, even if we are unlikely to live up to these standards.

In Chapter 9, I address the worry that perfectionist political action is paternalistic because it is premised on the belief that, when left to their own devices, citizens will fail to make sound choices about how to use their time and resources. I concede that perfectionist political action does involve the assumption that citizens are not *always* disposed to make rational decisions about their own good, but I deny that there is anything disrespectful about proceeding on the basis of such an assumption—especially given that, as a growing body of evidence from the fields of social psychology and behavioural economics suggests, this assumption is true of all human beings. To defend this position, I develop an alternative conception of what respect for the moral status of citizens requires—a conception that requires that the state treat citizens as if they are disposed *often*, but not *always*, to make rational decisions about their own good. Importantly, this alternative conception of respect is compatible with some degree of paternalism. I argue that until compelling reasons have been given for endorsing the view that respect requires treating citizens as if they are disposed always to make rational decisions about their own good, as opposed to the view that respect requires treating citizens as if they are disposed often to make rational decisions about their own good, it remains unclear why paternalism is incompatible with respect for the moral status of citizens.

Finally, in Chapter 10, I defend the perfectionist conception of justice against the charge that perfectionist regimes that seek the edification of the citizenry are guilty of an unappealingly meddlesome mentality—a mentality akin in important respects to that of a village busybody, a curtain-twitcher or a Nosey Parker. In response, I argue that this objection begs the question against perfectionist justice by assuming precisely what needs to be shown, namely that promoting the flourishing and edification of the citizenry falls outside the proper bounds of government. In other words, when one says that the perfectionist state meddles in matters that are none of its business or sticks its nose where it does not belong, one already assumes that the state has no duty to promote the flourishing and edification of the citizenry; but one cannot help oneself to this assumption because whether or not the state has a duty to promote the flourishing and edification of the citizenry is precisely what is at stake in the debate between perfectionists and anti-perfectionist liberals.

PART I

THE FOIL: ANTI-PERFECTIONIST LIBERALISM

1

Comprehensive Liberalism

The first part of this book is devoted to the elucidation of what is often called anti-perfectionist liberalism, as this strand of liberal theory provides a useful foil against which to develop a perfectionist theory of justice. Recall the thumbnail description of anti-perfectionist liberalism given in the Introduction:

> *Anti-Perfectionist Liberalism*: The state should not seek to impose or even promote any particular ideal of the good life or human flourishing. It should not, for instance, enact laws and policies designed to elevate citizens' tastes, to refine their sensibilities or to perfect their characters. Indeed, it should, as far as possible, refrain altogether from forming judgements of this kind about the worthiness of different ways of life. So long as citizens do not harm others or violate other requirements of justice, their choices about what to do with their time and resources are none of the state's business. Instead, the state should restrict itself to establishing a fair framework of rights and opportunities within which citizens can pursue their own beliefs about what constitutes a valuable or flourishing life. To this end, the state should ensure that rights and liberties are protected, that all citizens receive a fair share of resources and opportunities, and that social cooperation proceeds on a footing of mutual respect. In this sense, there is an important asymmetry between values such as freedom, equality and fairness and values such as moral, intellectual and artistic excellence: the state should concern itself with the former values, but not with the latter.

Why accept this position? There are two main variants of anti-perfectionist liberalism and each answers this question in a different way. The first variant is known as *comprehensive liberalism* and is the topic of this chapter; the second variant is known as *political liberalism* and is the topic of Chapter 2. Both comprehensive liberals and political liberals agree that the state should not favour certain ideals of the good life over others, but they disagree about what justifies this anti-perfectionist stance. Comprehensive liberals tend to argue for anti-perfectionism by appealing to the values of autonomy and individuality, whereas political liberals tend to argue for anti-perfectionism by appealing to the breadth and depth of reasonable disagreement within modern societies.

This is not to say that the autonomy-based arguments of comprehensive liberals and the disagreement-based arguments of political liberals exhaust the arguments that have been given for accepting anti-perfectionist liberalism. Other arguments

A Perfectionist Theory of Justice. Collis Tahzib, Oxford University Press.
© Collis Tahzib (2022). DOI: 10.1093/oso/9780192847119.003.0002

20 A PERFECTIONIST THEORY OF JUSTICE

for anti-perfectionist liberalism are also considered later in this book, such as arguments from scepticism about the existence of objective truths relating to human flourishing or about our ability to know any such truths, even assuming that they exist (Chapter 5); arguments from the insusceptibility of human flourishing to promotion by the state (Chapter 6); arguments from the risk of the abuse of power by incompetent or overzealous perfectionist state officials (Chapter 8); arguments from paternalism (Chapter 9); and arguments from the village busy-body mentality (Chapter 10). Nonetheless, the autonomy-based arguments of comprehensive liberals and the disagreement-based arguments of political liberals represent two of the most important and influential routes into anti-perfectionist liberalism.

In this chapter, I first offer (in Section 1.1) a brief characterization of the distinction between comprehensive liberalism and political liberalism. I then present some of the most prominent versions of comprehensive liberalism, namely Kantian liberalism (Section 1.2), Millian liberalism (Section 1.3) and Ronald Dworkin's 'challenge model of ethics' (Section 1.4), in a way that brings to the fore the anti-perfectionist implications of these conceptions of liberalism. I should stress that, throughout, my intention is not historical or exegetical. Indeed, any attempt to subsume Kant, Mill and Dworkin within a general theoretical category—be it 'comprehensive liberalism' or any other—is bound to involve a certain degree of anachronism and even distortion. Each of these thinkers, after all, writes within a specific context and is exercised by specific questions and concerns. Still, an emphasis on some idea of autonomy is central to all of these authors' conceptions of liberalism, and so the reception of these authors as comprehensive liberals does at least make sense and draws out this commonality in a helpful way.[1] With this in mind, the hope is that by considering some of the main features of these three views, we can build up a reasonably nuanced picture of comprehensive liberalism. With this picture in view, we can then compare comprehensive liberalism with political liberalism and, eventually, with the perfectionist theory developed in Part II.

1.1 Two Kinds of Liberal Theory

It is common to distinguish between two kinds of liberal theory: comprehensive liberalism and political liberalism. How exactly this distinction should be drawn—what, in other words, makes a given liberal theory an instance of comprehensive liberalism or political liberalism—turns out to be quite a contested

---

[1] For Rawls's references to Kant and Mill as 'comprehensive' liberals, see Rawls, J., *Political Liberalism* (New York: Columbia University Press, 2005), pp. 78, 98, 145, 159, 199, 211 n. 42, 375 n. 3, 400; Rawls, J., *Justice as Fairness: A Restatement* (Cambridge, MA: Belknap Press of Harvard University Press, 2001), pp. 33, 34, 156, 191, 198.

COMPREHENSIVE LIBERALISM   21

matter.[2] But for present purposes it suffices to say that comprehensive liberals tend to be concerned with the normative implications of autonomy, whereas political liberals tend to be concerned with the normative implications of reasonable disagreement. These commitments—to taking autonomy seriously and to taking reasonable disagreement seriously—capture sufficiently well the broad motivation of many of the writers typically classified as comprehensive liberals and political liberals, respectively.

A helpful way of thinking about this distinction is in terms of the question of who can be a wholehearted participant in the liberal project.[3] This distinction emerged in the 1980s, when a number of liberals, such as Charles Larmore and John Rawls, began to worry that traditional theories of liberalism, such as those influentially developed by Immanuel Kant and John Stuart Mill, were ill-suited to the highly pluralistic conditions of late modernity. In particular, these 'political liberals' worried that Kantian and Millian 'comprehensive liberalisms' could not be expected to command the allegiance of all reasonable citizens within modern societies and thus could not be expected to form the basis of a just and stable political order. Mill's liberalism, for instance, is premised on values such as individuality, experimental living and self-assertion. Yet many intelligent and good-willed citizens within liberal-democratic societies are sceptical of these values—or at least do not accord these values strong priority over other values such as tradition, belonging and community. Thus, as we shall see in Chapter 2, political liberals seek to develop theories of liberalism that take more seriously the depth and breadth of disagreement within modern liberal-democratic societies: they seek to show that one does not need to give pride of place in one's system of values to autonomy or individuality, as Mill does, in order to be a wholehearted participant in the liberal project.

Further insight into the nature of the distinction between comprehensive liberalism and political liberalism can be provided by noting that it is also sometimes referred to as the distinction between Enlightenment liberalism and Reformation liberalism.[4] These alternative labels shed light on this distinction by connecting each of these two kinds of liberal theory with a distinctive historical

---

[2] For analyses of this distinction, see, for example, Waldron, J., 'Liberalism, Political and Comprehensive', in G. Gaus and C. Kukathas (eds), *Handbook of Political Theory* (London: Sage, 2004), pp. 89–99; Gaus, G., 'The Diversity of Comprehensive Liberalisms', in G. Gaus and C. Kukathas (eds), *Handbook of Political Theory*, pp. 100–14; Young, S., 'The Concept of Political Liberalism', in S. Young (ed.), *Political Liberalism: Variations on a Theme* (Albany, NY: State University of New York Press, 2004), pp. 1–23; Quong, J., *Liberalism Without Perfection* (Oxford: Oxford University Press, 2011), pp. 15–21; Gaus, G., *Contemporary Theories of Liberalism: Public Reason as a Post-Enlightenment Project* (London: Sage, 2003), ch. 7; Easton, C., 'Two Types of Liberalism' (unpublished manuscript).

[3] This way of thinking about the distinction is suggested by Jonathan Quong in an interview with Jonathan Marshall. See 'Reasons for a Liberalism Without Perfection' at www.3-16am.co.uk/articles/reasons-for-a-liberalism-without-perfection, accessed 4 March 2021.

[4] See, for example, Galston, W., *Liberal Pluralism: The Implications of Value Pluralism for Political Theory and Practice* (Cambridge: Cambridge University Press, 2002), pp. 24–6.

22   A PERFECTIONIST THEORY OF JUSTICE

experience. Enlightenment liberalism is steeped in the convictions and ideals of the eighteenth-century European Enlightenment: that science and reason are the most reliable sources of knowledge and progress; that individuals should adopt a detached and questioning posture towards tradition, custom and faith; and that self-direction is preferable to external control. By contrast, Reformation liberalism grows out of an altogether different historical experience: the centuries-long European wars of religion, which were precipitated by the Protestant Reformation and the division of Western Christendom and which were eventually ended only by a series of compromises that crystallized into the modern understanding of freedom of conscience. Along these lines, Rawls explains that 'the historical origin of political liberalism ... is the Reformation and its aftermath, with the long controversies over religious toleration in the sixteenth and seventeenth centuries.'[5]

Of course, many comprehensive liberals are attuned to considerations of social pluralism and reasonable disagreement, and many political liberals are attuned to considerations of freedom and autonomy, and so it is often difficult to know exactly how a particular liberal theory should be classified. But this need not be too troubling, since the distinction between comprehensive and political liberalism is merely a convenient heuristic. It is meant to facilitate our study of liberal theory by bringing some order to what would otherwise be an unmanageably large and sprawling literature. Nothing of substance hangs on whether a theory is classified as an instance of political liberalism or comprehensive liberalism. Indeed, the distinction between comprehensive and political liberalism resembles, in this sense, the distinction between anti-perfectionist liberalism and perfectionism. 'Comprehensive liberalism' and 'political liberalism', like 'perfectionism' and 'anti-perfectionist liberalism', are not natural kinds. They are rather terms of art used by political philosophers, in inevitably stipulative ways, to classify families of political theories; and so, as I explain further in Section 6.5, it makes little sense to quarrel over the exact boundaries around these terms.

To serve its heuristic purpose, the distinction between comprehensive and political liberalism need not be perfect. For instance, perhaps the distinction lumps together theories that are importantly different and whose diversity more fine-grained distinctions would help to bring to light.[6] Alternatively, perhaps the distinction keeps apart theories that are importantly similar and whose commonalities would be illuminated by different typologies.[7] All of this is compatible with the distinction being sufficiently serviceable that it can facilitate our study of liberal theory by conveniently grouping together theories of liberalism based on a commitment to taking autonomy seriously and theories of liberalism based on a

---

[5] Rawls, J., *Political Liberalism*, p. xxiv.

[6] This criticism is made in Gaus, G., 'The Diversity of Comprehensive Liberalisms'.

[7] This criticism is made in Abbey, R. and Spinner-Halev, J., 'Rawls, Mill, and the Puzzle of Political Liberalism', *The Journal of Politics* 75 (2012), pp. 124–36.

commitment to taking reasonable disagreement seriously, thereby allowing us to speak about a large assortment of disparate ideas and perspectives in a reasonably systematic and orderly way.

1.2 Kantian Liberalism

At the heart of Kantian liberalism is a certain conception of freedom as independence.[8] Each person, says Kant, has 'only one innate right': the right to 'freedom (independence from being constrained by another's choice), insofar as it can coexist with the freedom of every other'.[9] This right 'is the only original right belonging to every man by virtue of his humanity'.[10] Ripstein offers the following gloss of this fundamental right to freedom as independence:

> You are independent if you are the one who decides what ends you will use your means to pursue, as opposed to having someone else decide for you. At the level of innate right, your right to freedom protects your purposiveness—your capacity to choose the ends you will use your means to pursue—against the choices of others, but not against your own poor choices or the inadequacy of your means to your aspirations. You remain independent if nobody else gets to tell you what purposes to pursue with your means; each of us is independent if neither of us gets to tell the other what purposes to pursue.[11]

When all citizens enjoy this right, a 'system of equal freedom' is said to obtain. Ripstein characterizes this idea as follows: 'a system of equal freedom is one in which each person is free to use his or her own powers, individually or cooperatively, to set his or her own purposes, and no one is allowed to compel others to use their powers in a way designed to advance or accommodate any other person's purposes'.[12] In a system of equal freedom, each citizen can possess what Kant calls the 'quality of being his own master'.[13]

Kantian liberalism gives rise to a distinctive account of the limits of legitimate state power. It holds that 'state power is only justified to create a system of equal

---

[8] My exposition of Kantian liberalism follows the influential reconstruction in Ripstein, A., *Force and Freedom: Kant's Legal and Political Philosophy* (Cambridge, MA: Harvard University Press, 2009), but there are of course many other interpretations of Kantian liberalism. For doubts about whether Kantian liberalism is aptly classified as a 'comprehensive' liberalism, see Pogge, T., 'Is Kant's *Rechtslehre* a "Comprehensive Liberalism"?', in M. Timmons (ed.), *Kant's Metaphysics of Morals: Interpretative Essays* (Oxford: Oxford University Press, 2002), pp. 133–58.

[9] Kant, I., *Practical Philosophy*, trans. and ed. M. Gregor (Cambridge: Cambridge University Press, 1996), p. 393.

[10] Ibid.

[11] Ripstein, A., *Force and Freedom*, pp. 33–4.

[12] Ibid., p. 33.

[13] Kant, I., *Practical Philosophy*, p. 394.

24   A PERFECTIONIST THEORY OF JUSTICE

freedom'—a system in which all citizens enjoy independence from the choices of others.[14] In this sense, the 'idea of independence carries the justificatory burden of [Kant's] entire argument' and all other liberal rights and duties 'must be derived from it'.[15] 'Freedom, understood as independence of another person's choice, is the only interest that matters' for political purposes.[16] Kantian political philosophy, at least on Ripstein's reconstruction of it, thus turns out to be highly unified and systematic: it is a matter of working out the implications of the innate right to freedom as independence.

The Kantian view vindicates many familiar liberal rights—such as freedom of expression, freedom of assembly, the right to bodily integrity, the right to private property and the legal presumption of innocence—because these are more or less immediate expressions of the innate right to freedom as independence. Moreover, despite its seemingly libertarian tendencies, Ripstein's Kantian liberalism also permits 'most of the familiar activities of modern states', such as a certain degree of redistributive taxation aimed at the relief of poverty.[17] The coercive imposition of redistributive taxation is consistent with, and indeed necessary for, the establishment of a system of equal freedom because otherwise 'the poor are completely subject to the choice of those in more fortunate circumstances'.[18] Only in a well-functioning liberal state, then, is each citizen free to use her own powers to set and pursue her own purposes without being constrained by the choices of others.

Kantian liberalism is strictly anti-perfectionist because perfectionist policies are not necessary for establishing or maintaining a system of equal freedom.[19] Indeed, on the contrary, perfectionist policies appear incompatible with a system of equal freedom, as they appear to involve some citizens telling other citizens what purposes to pursue with their time and resources. Thus, Ripstein explains that *private* 'charitable support for arts and culture, sports and recreation, and countless other activities to make other people happy is consistent with Kantian right', but such activities cannot legitimately be promoted through *public* action: the 'fact that a group of people are not able to coordinate to guarantee the production or preservation of something that they value does not entitle them to use the coercive apparatus of the state to compel others to join them in their efforts at producing it'.[20] Indeed, Kant at one point suggests that his conception

---

[14] Ripstein, A., *Force and Freedom*, p. 237.
[15] Ibid., pp. 14, 31.
[16] Ibid., p. 266.
[17] Ibid., p. 223.
[18] Ibid.
[19] For discussions that emphasize the anti-perfectionist aspects of Kantian liberalism, see Pallikkathayil, J., 'Neither Perfectionism Nor Political Liberalism', *Philosophy & Public Affairs* 44 (2016), pp. 171–96; Pallikkathayil, J., 'Resisting Rawlsian Political Liberalism', *Philosophy & Public Affairs* 45 (2017), pp. 413–26.
[20] Ripstein, A., *Force and Freedom*, pp. 260, 283.

of freedom as independence renders the idea of state perfectionism inherently self-contradictory:

> It is a contradiction for me to make another person's perfection my end and consider myself under obligation to promote this. For the perfection of another human being, as a person, consists just in this: that he *himself* is able to set his end in accordance with his own concepts of duty; and it is self-contradictory to require that I do (make it my duty to do) something that only the other himself can do.[21]

Similarly, Japa Pallikkathayil, another prominent exponent of Kantian liberalism, has this to say about a perfectionist state that bans tattoos on the grounds that they are degrading:

> A ban on tattoos justified in terms of how tattoos degrade those who have them would limit the ability of people to live their lives as they see fit, but not for the sake of enabling others to live their lives ... And so the Kantian holds that, insofar as the law is justified in this way, it is in tension with the requirement to treat others as independent. In the absence of some independence-based justification for banning tattoos, whether one has a tattoo or not is simply no one else's business.[22]

Kantian liberalism's opposition to perfectionism is thus different to, say, political liberalism's objection to perfectionism. As we shall see in Chapter 2, political liberals reject perfectionism because they maintain that perfectionist policies will not command the acceptance of all reasonable citizens. By contrast, the Kantian liberal's rejection of perfectionism is in a sense more principled and direct: it says that perfectionist policies are impermissible *regardless* of whether they are acceptable to all reasonable citizens because they exceed what is necessary to secure each citizen's right to freedom as independence. So 'even if citizens unanimously accept [a given perfectionist policy], they would not be entitled to use the state for what can be nothing other than a widely shared private purpose'—a purpose that is 'not itself immanent in the requirements of' a system of equal freedom.[23] 'Something has gone wrong', says Ripstein, 'when a legislative body considers questions about

---

[21] Kant, I., *Practical Philosophy*, pp. 517–18.

[22] Pallikkathayil, J., 'Neither Perfectionism Nor Political Liberalism', p. 178. It is worth noting here that Pallikkathayil's example of a perfectionist policy—a ban on tattoos—is somewhat unhelpful, since it is very difficult to believe that tattoos are in fact degrading or that this judgement could be publicly justified, even if true. For a more general discussion of the tendency in this literature for critics of perfectionism to attack tendentious versions of perfectionism that incorporate crude or excessively sectarian conceptions of human flourishing, see Section 5.4.

[23] Ripstein, A., 'Form and Matter in Kantian Political Philosophy: A Reply', *European Journal of Philosophy* 20 (2012), p. 493.

26 A PERFECTIONIST THEORY OF JUSTICE

what would be worth doing except from the point of view of purposes that make the state necessary', namely securing the independence of each citizen.[24]

1.3 Millian Liberalism

While Millian liberalism contains many strands and is amenable to different interpretations, its centrepiece is the value of individuality. In passionate and eloquent terms, Mill celebrates individuality as 'one of the principal ingredients of human happiness, and quite the chief ingredient of individual and social progress'.[25] As he similarly puts it, 'the free development of individuality is one of the leading essentials of well-being'.[26] Mill maintains that 'individuality is the same thing with development, and that it is only the cultivation of individuality which produces, or can produce, well-developed human beings'.[27] For each individual, says Mill, 'his own mode of laying out his existence is the best, not because it is the best in itself, but because it is his own mode'.[28] Mill praises 'individual spontaneity', 'peculiarity of taste' and 'eccentricity in conduct'.[29] And he contends that 'there should be different experiments of living' and that 'the worth of different modes of life should be proved practically'.[30]

In articulating the ideal of individuality, Mill explains that it is 'antagonistic to the sway of custom', which tends to produce a 'pinched and hidebound type of human character'.[31] He says that 'people should refus[e] to bend the knee to custom', that 'people should be eccentric' and that 'individuality should assert itself', so that 'new truths' and 'new practices' can be discovered.[32] In a famous analogy, Mill states that 'human nature is not a machine to be built after a model, and set to do exactly the work prescribed for it, but a tree, which requires to grow and develop itself on all sides, according to the tendency of the inward forces which make it a living thing'.[33] And Mill explains that his conception of individuality has roots in 'a Greek ideal of self-development' as well as 'Pagan self-assertion', and that it is most vigorously opposed to the 'Calvinistic theory', according to which 'the one great offence of man is self-will'.[34]

Like Kantian liberalism, Millian liberalism is quite strongly anti-perfectionist in character. Consider, for instance, Mill's statement of the harm principle:

---

[24] Ibid., p. 494.
[25] Mill, J. S., *On Liberty* (London: Penguin Books, 1985), p. 120.
[26] Ibid.
[27] Ibid., p. 128.
[28] Ibid., p. 133.
[29] Ibid., pp. 120, 126.
[30] Ibid., p. 120.
[31] Ibid., pp. 126, 136.
[32] Ibid., pp. 120, 129, 132.
[33] Ibid., p. 123.
[34] Ibid., pp. 126–7.

The object of this essay is to assert one very simple principle, as entitled to govern absolutely the dealings of society with the individual in the way of compulsion and control, whether the means used be physical force in the form of legal penalties or the moral coercion of public opinion ... That [principle holds that] the only purpose for which power can be rightfully exercised over any member of a civilized community, against his will, is to prevent harm to others. His own good, either physical or moral, is not a sufficient warrant. He cannot rightfully be compelled to do or forbear because it will be better for him to do so, because it will make him happier, because, in the opinions of others, to do so would be wise or even right. These are good reasons for remonstrating with him, or reasoning with him, or persuading him, or entreating him, but not for compelling him or visiting him with any evil in case he do otherwise.[35]

While this principle is most commonly taken to be an *anti-paternalistic* principle, it is also quite straightforwardly an *anti-perfectionist* principle—one that holds that claims about what constitutes a good or flourishing life are not valid reasons for coercive state action. Mill worries that interference by the state in questions of the good life would quash individuality: it would lead to a 'despotism of custom', render individuals 'inert and torpid instead of active and energetic', and 'maim by compression, like a Chinese lady's foot, every part of human nature which stands out prominently and tends to make the person markedly dissimilar in outline to commonplace humanity'.[36] Mill's anti-perfectionism also emerges in his statement, quoted in the Introduction, that 'the only freedom which deserves the name is that of pursuing our own good in our own way, so long as we do not attempt to deprive others of theirs or impede their efforts to obtain it. Each is the proper guardian of his own health, whether bodily or mental and spiritual. Mankind are greater gainers by suffering each to live as seems good to themselves than by compelling each to live as seems good to the rest'.[37]

More specifically, Mill's anti-perfectionism manifests itself in the positions he took on various social questions of his day. For instance, he discusses the United Kingdom Alliance, a temperance movement founded in 1853 to campaign for the prohibition of trade in alcohol in the United Kingdom. Participants in this movement emphasized the negative effect of alcohol on the mind and body, and criticized the spreading drunkenness and excess that they perceived in British society. Mill is wary about these attempts to use politics to advance Victorian middle-class ideals of respectability, self-restraint and temperance. He describes the outlook of this movement as 'monstrous', saying that it 'ascribes to all mankind a vested interest in each other's moral, intellectual, and even physical perfection'

---

[35] Ibid., p. 68.
[36] Ibid., pp. 123, 135, 136.
[37] Ibid., p. 72.

and that 'these intrusively pious members of society [should] mind their own business'.[38] He compares the 'considerable zeal' of such reformers to religious zeal and says that even if it 'has not the cruelty of the old persecutors, the state of mind indicated by it is fundamentally the same': namely, the intolerant urge 'to prohibit by law everything which it thinks wrong'.[39]

Mill's anti-perfectionism even appears to extend to more moderate and non-coercive sorts of measures. He considers the question of 'whether the State, while it permits, should nevertheless indirectly discourage conduct which it deems contrary to the best interests of the agent; whether, for example, it should take measures to render the means of drunkenness more costly'.[40] But he responds that 'to tax stimulants for the sole purpose of making them more difficult to be obtained is a measure differing only in degree from their entire prohibition, and would be justifiable only if that were justifiable'.[41] 'Every increase of cost is a prohibition to those whose means do not come up to the augmented price', he continues, 'and to those who do, it is a penalty laid on them for gratifying a particular taste'.[42] Other relatively moderate measures to discourage intemperance, apart from sin taxes, are similarly rejected: 'the limitation in number, for instance, of beer and spirit houses, for the express purpose of rendering them more difficult of access and diminishing the occasions of temptation ... is suited only to a state of society in which the labouring classes are avowedly treated as children or savages, and placed under an education of restraint, to fit them for future admission to the privileges of freedom'.[43]

Rawls thus explains that although 'Mill certainly recognizes the existence of the perfectionist values of the admirable and the excellent', it makes most sense to think of him as an anti-perfectionist liberal:

> In view of the content of the principle of liberty—its exclusion of perfectionist grounds for limiting individual liberty—these [perfectionist] values cannot be imposed by the sanctions of law and common moral opinion as coercive social pressure. It is up to each of us together with our friends and associates to settle this for ourselves. In this sense, his doctrine is not perfectionist ... If one were to object that he has left out the perfectionist values, he would reply, I suggest, that he has not left them out. Rather, he would say that he has taken them into account as they should be, namely, by setting out principles that, when realized in social arrangements, will be most effective in leading people freely ... to give those values a central place in their life. It is not necessary, I think he would say, to coerce

[38] Ibid., pp. 155, 157, 158.
[39] Ibid., pp. 156, 159.
[40] Ibid., p. 170.
[41] Ibid., pp. 170–1.
[42] Ibid., p. 171.
[43] Ibid., p. 172.

people to pursue activities that realize these values, and trying to do so when the institutions of justice and liberty are not in place does more injury than good. On the other hand, once these institutions are fully in place, the values of perfection will be realized in the most appropriate way in free lives and associations within the bounds of just and free institutions. The values of justice and liberty have a fundamental background role and in that sense a certain priority. Mill would say that he gives perfectionist values their due.[44]

The sketch I have provided can be challenged from at least two directions. On the one hand, one might accept that Mill's liberalism is comprehensive but deny that it is anti-perfectionist.[45] Is Mill an opponent of *all* forms of state perfectionism or merely of some crudely extreme and misguided instances thereof? Mill most commonly objects to highly coercive forms of perfectionism: he says that the state should not 'prohibit by law everything which it thinks wrong' and that it should not 'compel people to conform to its notions of personal [and] social excellence'.[46] But would Mill be similarly stringent in his opposition to a perfectionist state that encourages citizens to lead excellent lives through more moderate means such as education programmes, subsidies, incentives, sin taxes and the like? Similarly, Mill is opposed to the state's 'attempting to shape [citizens] all after one model'.[47] But might he nonetheless be open to a pluralistic perfectionism that recognizes the diversity of plausible forms of human flourishing and that steers citizens towards one or another of a wide variety of worthy models? And he laments social movements such as the temperance movement, which were aimed at 'the improvement of morals' and which conceived morality in terms of being 'moderate in inclinations' and 'without any marked character'.[48] But would Mill still be opposed to social and political movements aimed at the improvement of morals, if those movements were to conceive of morality in ways that have due regard for the value of individuality and eccentricity?

On the other hand, one might accept that Mill's liberalism is anti-perfectionist but deny that it is comprehensive.[49] Gerald Gaus, for instance, argues that Mill's appeal to individuality is only one part of a larger battery of arguments for anti-perfectionist liberalism, each designed to appeal to different constituencies, and

---

[44] Rawls, J., *Lectures on the History of Political Philosophy* (Cambridge, MA: Harvard University Press, 2007), p. 312.

[45] See, for example, Ryan, A., 'Mill in a Liberal Landscape', in J. Skorupski (ed.), *The Cambridge Companion to Mill* (Cambridge: Cambridge University Press, 1998), pp. 497–540; Brink, D., *Mill's Progressive Principles* (Oxford: Oxford University Press, 2013), pp. 255–9.

[46] Mill, J. S., *On Liberty*, pp. 72, 156.

[47] Ibid., p. 133.

[48] Ibid., pp. 134–5.

[49] See, for example, Rudisill, J., 'The Neutrality of the State and Its Justification in Rawls and Mill', *Auslegung* 23 (2000), pp. 153–68; Gaus, G., 'State Neutrality and Controversial Values in *On Liberty*', in C. L. Ten (ed.), *Mill's On Liberty: A Critical Guide* (Cambridge: Cambridge University Press, 2008), pp. 83–104; Abbey, R. and Spinner-Halev, J., 'Rawls, Mill, and the Puzzle of Political Liberalism'.

30 A PERFECTIONIST THEORY OF JUSTICE

that, in taking disagreement seriously in this way, Mill is most appropriately classified as a political, rather than a comprehensive, liberal.[50] Certainly Mill is aware that many of his contemporaries find it 'surprising' that 'so high a value [is] attached to individuality' within his thinking, and he endeavours to show why individuality should be valued even by those who choose to live in more traditional ways.[51]

These are interesting and important exegetical questions, but attempting to answer them is well beyond the scope of this brief discussion—a discussion that goes into only as much detail as is necessary to set up a reasonably nuanced foil for the perfectionist position that is developed in subsequent chapters. Far from settling any matters relating to Millian liberalism, then, this brief sketch only serves to illustrate the rough shape of one possible variety of comprehensive liberalism.

1.4 Dworkin's Challenge Model of Ethics

Although the liberalisms of Kant and Mill are the most influential versions of comprehensive liberalism, there are numerous other liberal theories that plausibly belong to this family. Many views could sensibly be discussed at this juncture, but one important version of comprehensive liberalism is found in the later work of Ronald Dworkin.[52] Dworkin's liberalism is anti-perfectionist: it maintains that 'government must be neutral' in the sense that 'it must not forbid or reward any private activity on the ground that one set of substantive ethical values, one set of opinions about the best way to lead a life, is superior or inferior to others'.[53] And his liberalism is comprehensive because it is based, if not exactly in the ideal of autonomy, then in an ideal with close affinities to autonomy.

To introduce his view, Dworkin draws a distinction between two models of ethics: the 'impact model' and the 'challenge model'.[54] These two models are general 'interpretations of ethical experience, attempts to organize the convictions or intimations of ethical value which most of us do have into a coherent picture'.[55] The impact model holds that 'the value of a good life consists in its product, that is, in

---

[50] Gaus, G., 'State Neutrality and Controversial Values in *On Liberty*'.

[51] Mill, J. S., *On Liberty*, p. 121.

[52] Where the transition from early Rawls to late Rawls marks a move from comprehensive to political liberalism, the transition from early Dworkin (of the 1978 essay 'Liberalism') to late Dworkin (of the 1990 essay 'Foundations of Liberal Equality') marks a move from political to comprehensive liberalism. The fullest statement of the challenge model of ethics is provided in Dworkin, R., 'Foundations of Liberal Equality', in G. Peterson (ed.), *The Tanner Lectures on Human Values* (Salt Lake City, UT: University of Utah Press, 1990), pp. 1–119, reprinted in S. Darwall (ed.), *Equal Freedom: Selected Tanner Lectures on Human Values* (Ann Arbor, MI: University of Michigan Press, 1995), pp. 190–306 and reprinted in abridged form in Dworkin, R., *Sovereign Virtue: The Theory and Practice of Equality* (Cambridge, MA: Harvard University Press, 2000), ch. 6.

[53] Dworkin, R., 'Foundations of Liberal Equality', in S. Darwall (ed.), *Equal Freedom*, p. 228.

[54] Ibid., pp. 240–5.

[55] Ibid., p. 241.

its consequences for the rest of the world.[56] Meanwhile, the challenge model holds that 'the value of a good life lies in the inherent value of a skillful performance of living.[57] The idea of a skilful performance, explains Dworkin, 'is perfectly familiar as a kind of value *within* lives', as when we admire the feats of a musician or a mountaineer.[58] The challenge model of ethics extends this idea by saying that 'living a life is *itself* a performance that demands skill, that it is the most comprehensive and important challenge we face, and that our critical interests consist in the achievements, events, and experiences that mean that we have met the challenge well.[59] These two models have a deliberately 'structural and philosophical rather than substantive character': they are broad models for organizing ideas about the good life and are compatible with a range of ways of fleshing out what exactly qualifies as a skilful performance or as a positive impact on the world.[60]

Both models, says Dworkin, have some grip on us. On the one hand, impact is clearly relevant to our considered judgements about what it means to lead a good life. We admire the lives of Alexander Fleming and Martin Luther King Jr, say, precisely because of the difference such individuals made in the world through discovering penicillin and advancing the cause of civil rights. The impact model 'generalizes from these examples; it holds that the ethical value of a life ... is entirely dependent on and measured by the value of its consequences for the rest of the world.[61] On the other hand, the challenge model is able to explain the value of pursuits and goals that may have little or no consequence at all for the objective state of the world—pursuits such as striving to acquire a basic grasp of the science of one's age, learning a musical instrument or spending time with one's grandchildren—and that would therefore seem 'silly and self-indulgent' in the vocabulary of impact.[62] The challenge model in this way recognizes that 'many of the ethical goals people regard as very important are not matters of consequence at all.[63]

In the end, Dworkin argues for the superiority of the model of challenge over the model of impact.[64] Though it would take us too far astray to review all of Dworkin's reasons for favouring the challenge model, one of the main considerations is that it can incorporate many of the insights of the impact model without being prone

---

[56] Ibid., pp. 240–1.
[57] Ibid., p. 241.
[58] Ibid., p. 244.
[59] Ibid.
[60] Ibid., pp. 207, 258.
[61] Ibid., p. 242.
[62] Ibid., p. 244.
[63] Ibid., p. 243.
[64] Of course, this only vindicates the challenge model on the further assumption—which Dworkin neither explicitly acknowledges nor defends—that the challenge model and the impact model exhaust the possible models of ethics. For a critique of this assumption, as well as of the challenge model more broadly, see Arneson, R., 'Cracked Foundations of Liberal Equality', in J. Burley (ed.), *Dworkin and His Critics* (Oxford: Blackwell, 2004), especially pp. 80–3.

32 A PERFECTIONIST THEORY OF JUSTICE

to its weaknesses. For instance, the challenge model is consistent with the thought that impact is relevant to the value of a life, since 'one way brilliantly to meet the challenge of living well is to reduce the world's suffering by conquering disease' or by otherwise having a positive impact on the world.

How does the challenge model of ethics get us to liberal principles, including in particular the principle of state neutrality? Why think that this model entails, or at least lends support to, anti-perfectionist liberalism? A crucial part of Dworkin's argument here is that one feature of the challenge model is an 'endorsement constraint'. He explains that 'on any plausible interpretation of that model ... my life cannot be better for me in virtue of some feature or component I think has no value'.[65] As he also puts this point: 'no component may even so much as contribute to the value of a person's life without his endorsement'.[66] 'A painter's artistic performance', for instance, 'is not improved when a master pushes his hand across the canvas, or drags it back from a stroke that would ruin what he has already done.'[67] By contrast, the impact model sees no objection to perfectionism, at least in principle. On the impact model, it could make sense that 'people's lives would go better if they were forced to pray, because in that case they might please God more and so have a better impact, even though they were atheists'.[68]

This feature of the challenge model rules out perfectionist laws and policies:

> The challenge view ... is suspicious of [perfectionism] because it rejects its root assumption: that a person's life can be improved just by forcing him into some act or abstinence he thinks valueless. Someone who accepts the challenge model might well think that religious devotion is an essential part of how human beings should respond to their place in the universe, and therefore that devotion is part of living well. But he cannot think that involuntary religious observance, prayer in the shadow of the rack, has any ethical value ... On the challenge model, that is, it is performance that counts, not mere external result, and the right motive or sense is necessary to the right performance.[69]

Here one might wonder whether the challenge model of ethics might be compatible with a more moderate and less coercive kind of perfectionism—a perfectionism that holds that 'people should be protected from choosing wasteful or bad lives not by flat prohibitions of the criminal law but by educational decisions and devices that remove bad options from people's view and imagination'.[70] But even this less coercive form of perfectionism is ruled out by the challenge model of ethics: 'a

---

[65] Dworkin, R., 'Foundations of Liberal Equality', in S. Darwall (ed.), *Equal Freedom*, p. 264.
[66] Ibid., p. 237.
[67] Ibid., p. 264.
[68] Ibid., p. 265.
[69] Ibid.
[70] Ibid., p. 270.

challenge cannot be more interesting, or in any other way a more valuable challenge to face, when it has been narrowed, simplified, and bowdlerized by others in advance, and that is as much true when we are ignorant of what they have done as when we are all too aware of it'.[71] Citizens cannot say that they responded skilfully to the challenge of life if they have selected options from a 'deliberately restricted menu', a 'culled list', a range of 'possibilities [that has been] filtered by wise collective rulers'.[72] A perfectionist state, in other words, 'usurp[s] the most important part of the challenge people face in leading a life, which is identifying life's values for themselves'.[73]

In short, then, those who 'take the challenge model seriously and give it a prominent if not exclusive role in ethical imagination' will arrive at anti-perfectionist liberal politics.[74] They will hold that the state 'must not forbid or reward any private activity on the ground that one set of substantive ethical values, one set of opinions about the best way to lead a life, is superior or inferior to others'.[75] They will resist the temptation to 'use whatever political power they have in a democratic society to improve the lives they and others lead, according to their best judgment about what a good life is', because doing so is ruled out by a model of ethics which focuses not on impact and outcomes but on living life as a 'skillful response to a complex challenge'.[76]

[71] Ibid., p. 271.
[72] Ibid.
[73] Dworkin, R., *Sovereign Virtue*, p. 277.
[74] Dworkin, R., 'Foundations of Liberal Equality', p. 241.
[75] Ibid., p. 228.
[76] Ibid., pp. 228, 275.

2

Political Liberalism

In the 1980s, a number of liberals—so-called 'political liberals'—began to worry that traditional theories of liberalism, such as those of Immanuel Kant and John Stuart Mill, were inadequate in an important respect.[1] In particular, these liberals argued that comprehensive liberalism did not take seriously enough the breadth and depth of *reasonable disagreement* within modern democratic societies. In modern societies, political liberals stressed, many citizens will reasonably reject the doctrines of comprehensive liberals such as Kant and Mill. Not everyone agrees with, say, Mill's claims that 'people should be eccentric', that 'individuality should assert itself' or that 'there should be different experiments of living'.[2] Many instead settle on more traditional or conventional ways of life—ways of life to which Mill's ideals are by his own admission 'antagonistic'.[3] Mill's arguments for liberal rights and principles thus cannot be expected to command the acceptance of all reasonable citizens. For Rawls, a liberalism based on Millian individuality or on some other 'comprehensive moral ideal' would be 'but another sectarian doctrine'—just another attempt to 'embody the whole truth in politics'.[4] Similarly, Larmore argues that, since in conditions of modernity there is no systematic agreement about the

[1] Political liberalism is often thought to originate with Rawls, J., 'Justice as Fairness: Political not Metaphysical', *Philosophy & Public Affairs* 14 (1985), pp. 223–51. Closely related views were expressed around the same time in Dworkin, R., 'Liberalism', in S. Hampshire (ed.), *Public and Private Morality* (Cambridge: Cambridge University Press, 1978), pp. 113–43; Ackerman, B., *Social Justice in the Liberal State* (New Haven, CT: Yale University Press, 1980); Larmore, C., *Patterns of Moral Complexity* (Cambridge: Cambridge University Press, 1987); Nagel, T., 'Moral Conflict and Political Legitimacy', *Philosophy & Public Affairs* 16 (1987), pp. 215–40; Waldron, J., 'Theoretical Foundations of Liberalism', *The Philosophical Quarterly* 147 (1987), pp. 127–50; Cohen, J., 'Moral Pluralism and Political Consensus', in D. Copp, J. Hampton and J. Roemer (eds), *The Idea of Democracy* (Cambridge: Cambridge University Press, 1989), pp. 270–91. Other influential articulations of political liberalism since then include Barry, B., *Justice as Impartiality* (Oxford: Oxford University Press, 1995); Gaus, G., *Justificatory Liberalism: An Essay on Epistemology and Political Theory* (Oxford: Oxford University Press, 1996); Klosko, G., *Democratic Procedures and Liberal Consensus* (Oxford: Oxford University Press, 2000); Rawls, J., *Political Liberalism* (New York: Columbia University Press, 2005); Weithman, P., *Why Political Liberalism? On John Rawls's Political Turn* (Oxford: Oxford University Press, 2010); Gaus, G., *The Order of Public Reason: A Theory of Freedom and Morality in a Diverse and Bounded World* (Cambridge: Cambridge University Press, 2011); Quong, J., *Liberalism Without Perfection* (Oxford: Oxford University Press, 2011); Nussbaum, M., 'Perfectionist Liberalism and Political Liberalism', *Philosophy & Public Affairs* 39 (2011), pp. 3–45; Vallier, K., *Must Politics Be War? Restoring Our Trust in the Open Society* (Oxford: Oxford University Press, 2019).

[2] Mill, J. S., *On Liberty* (London: Penguin Books, 1985), pp. 120, 132.

[3] Ibid., p. 136.

[4] Rawls, J., 'Justice as Fairness', pp. 245–6; Rawls, J., *Political Liberalism*, p. 442.

A Perfectionist Theory of Justice. Collis Tahzib, Oxford University Press.
© Collis Tahzib (2022). DOI: 10.1093/oso/9780192847119.003.0003

ends and purpose of human life, a 'liberalism come of age' will not be grounded in some general 'philosophy of man'.[5]

While political liberals reject comprehensive liberalism, it is important to be clear about the precise point at which these conceptions of liberalism diverge.[6] Political liberals need not reject the values that comprehensive liberals affirm, such as Kantian autonomy, Millian individuality or Dworkinian challenge. Nor need political liberals deny that these values *can* successfully justify liberal rights and institutions. Indeed, given that political liberals aim for an overlapping consensus on liberal rights and institutions, it is presumably their hope that the arguments of comprehensive liberalism do succeed in justifying liberal rights and institutions. Where political liberals part company with comprehensive liberals is when the latter claim that these values are the *only* or *best* way to justify liberal rights and institutions. Political liberals, that is, deny that one *must* endorse values such as Kantian autonomy, Millian individuality or Dworkinian challenge in order to be a wholehearted participant in the liberal project. For political liberals, the values to which comprehensive liberals appeal are not the only or best path to liberalism because they are disputed among reasonable people.

A central and distinctive commitment of political liberals, then, is the public justification principle. This principle holds that institutions, laws and policies must be in some sense justifiable, or acceptable, to all reasonable citizens. The public justification principle is typically taken to have quite strongly anti-perfectionist implications. So whereas comprehensive liberals justify anti-perfectionism in terms of some ideal of autonomy or individuality, political liberals justify anti-perfectionism in terms of the public justification principle in conjunction with the fact of reasonable disagreement. As Jonathan Quong puts this point:

> Governments should refrain from acting on judgements about human flourishing or value [because] such efforts cannot be justified to all the citizens in a liberal society. Liberal societies are crucially characterized by pluralism or disagreement regarding what makes a life good, or valuable, or worthwhile. Disagreement about the nature of human flourishing is a deep and permanent feature of free societies. This fact, when combined with the thesis that governments must be able to justify their actions to citizens, yields the conclusion that governments must refrain from acting on the basis of any particular conception of what makes for a valuable, flourishing, or worthwhile life. Because we disagree about what makes life worth living, it would be wrong for the government to take sides on this question. Instead, the government should remain *neutral* on the issue of the good life, and

---

[5] Larmore, C., *Patterns of Moral Complexity*, pp. 51, 129.
[6] For a clear discussion of this, see Quong, J., *Liberalism Without Perfection*, p. 22.

36 A PERFECTIONIST THEORY OF JUSTICE

restrict itself to establishing the fair terms within which citizens can pursue their own beliefs about what gives value to their lives.[7]

We can formulate political liberals' argument for anti-perfectionism as follows:

(P1) Reasonable citizens disagree in their judgements about what constitutes a good or flourishing human life (the fact of reasonable disagreement)
(P2) State action must be acceptable or justifiable to all reasonable citizens (the public justification principle)
(C) So, state action must not be premised on judgements about what constitutes a good or flourishing human life.

In this chapter, I elaborate this distinctive and influential argument for anti-perfectionist liberalism by examining each of the premises in greater depth. I first examine the nature and causes of the fact of reasonable disagreement (Section 2.1). I then expand on the nature of the public justification principle, exploring along the way the important question of how 'reasonable citizens' should be understood (Section 2.2) Finally, I explore several of the rationales that political liberals have given for why we should accept the public justification principle as a constraint on state action—rationales such as respect for persons and social stability (Section 2.3).

2.1 The Fact of Reasonable Disagreement

The arguments of political liberals typically take off from the observation that modern liberal-democratic societies are characterized by reasonable disagreement about the good life and human flourishing.[8] Modern societies, says Rawls, are marked by 'profound and irreconcilable differences in citizens' reasonable comprehensive religious and philosophical conceptions of the world, and in their views of the moral and aesthetic values to be sought in life'.[9] Such disagreement 'is

---

[7] Quong, J., *Liberalism Without Perfection*, p. 2.

[8] Rawls often refers to this as the fact of reasonable *pluralism* rather than the fact of reasonable *disagreement*, and many political liberals follow him in using this terminology. But the terminology of 'pluralism' can be misleading because it might be thought to imply the doctrine of value pluralism often associated with Isaiah Berlin: namely, that fundamental values are irreducibly plural and incommensurable. Since value pluralism is a thesis that is itself the object of reasonable disagreement, political liberalism must refrain from pronouncing on its truth or falsity. A liberalism based on value pluralism would face the same problems as the comprehensive liberalisms of Kant and Mill. What motivates political liberalism, then, is the quasi-sociological claim that reasonable people disagree about the nature of the good life, and not any metaphysical claim about the ultimate nature of value. For a helpful clarification in this regard, see Larmore, C., *The Morals of Modernity*, ch. 7; see also Rawls, J., 'The Domain of the Political and Overlapping Consensus', *New York University Law Review* 64 (1989), p. 237 n. 7.

[9] Rawls, J., *Justice as Fairness: A Restatement* (Cambridge, MA: Harvard University Press, 2001), p. 3.

not a mere historical condition that may soon pass away; it is a permanent feature of the public culture of democracy'.[10]

The most obvious example of disagreement about the good life, and the example with which political liberals often begin, is religious disagreement. In his introduction to *Political Liberalism*, for instance, Rawls explains that 'the historical origin of political liberalism (and of liberalism more generally) is the Reformation and its aftermath, with the long controversies over religious toleration in the sixteenth and seventeenth centuries'.[11] Rawls explains that these centuries saw a 'clash between salvationist, creedal, and expansionist religions'—a 'mortal conflict moderated only by circumstance and exhaustion'.[12] 'Political liberalism', he says, 'starts by taking to heart the absolute depth of that irreconcilable latent conflict.'[13] Indeed, one way of thinking about political liberalism is as the natural *generalization* of the principle of religious disestablishment: political liberalism generalizes that principle by calling for the liberal state to remain neutral not only among different religious conceptions of the good life but also among different conceptions of the good life in general (whether religious or non-religious).[14]

For political liberals, a particularly important instance of disagreement is disagreement about the values of autonomy and individuality, since these values play a central role in the thought of comprehensive liberals. As Larmore explains, a telling illustration of the controversy surrounding the ideals of autonomy and individuality is the enduring influence within Western culture of the Romantic tradition of thought—from Herder and Hegel to MacIntyre and Sandel—which has offered a powerful critique of Kant and Mill's individualist ideals.[15] This Romantic tradition places emphasis instead on the values of 'belonging and custom' and holds that some ways of life 'have a value we can appreciate only if we do not think of our allegiance to them as a matter of decision, but regard it instead as constitutive of what we hold to be valuable'.[16]

---

[10] Rawls, J., *Political Liberalism*, p. 36.

[11] Ibid., p. xxiv.

[12] Ibid., pp. xxv–xxvi.

[13] Ibid., p. xxvi.

[14] For recent discussions of anti-perfectionism as a generalization of religious disestablishment, see Laborde, C., *Liberalism's Religion* (Cambridge, MA: Harvard University Press, 2017), ch. 3; Koppelman, A., 'Neutrality and the Religion Analogy', in K. Vallier and M. Weber (eds), *Religious Exemptions* (Oxford: Oxford University Press, 2018), pp. 165–83.

[15] See Larmore, C., *Patterns of Moral Complexity*, ch. 5. For contemporary expressions of this tradition, see, for example, MacIntyre, A., *After Virtue* (Notre Dame, IN: University of Notre Dame Press, 1984); Sandel, M., *Liberalism and the Limits of Justice* (Cambridge: Cambridge University Press, 1998). See also Mulhall, S. and Swift, A., *Liberals and Communitarians* (Oxford: Blackwell Publishing, 1996).

[16] Larmore, C., 'Political Liberalism', *Political Theory* 18 (1990), p. 343. Larmore is keen to stress that Romanticism is a complex body of thought that defies any simple analysis, and that many Romantics did admittedly pursue the ideals of individuality and individualism. Nonetheless, he says, 'a new respect for tradition and belonging, along with a rejection of the supposedly shallow and dangerous individualism of the eighteenth century', was undeniably an important strand of German, French and English Romantic thought (p. 344).

38 A PERFECTIONIST THEORY OF JUSTICE

A leading contemporary exponent of this outlook is Michael Sandel. Many liberals, Sandel says, understate the centrality to our identities of communal bonds and allegiances—of 'those more or less enduring attachments and commitments which taken together define the person I am'.[17] Living by these commitments 'is inseparable from understanding ourselves as the particular persons we are—as members of this family or community or nation or people, as bearers of this history, as sons or daughters of that revolution, as citizens of this republic'.[18] So deep and so thoroughgoing are these ends and attachments that it makes little sense to think of them as objects of autonomous choice or affirmation by a self that is independent of and prior to them. There is, in this sense, no such thing as an 'unencumbered self'.[19] This thought is in tension with the emphasis by many comprehensive liberals on values such as autonomous choice, self-government and individuality, all of which introduce a certain 'distance' between a person and her ends:

> [The liberal self stands] always at a certain distance from the interests it has. One consequence of this distance is to put the self beyond the reach of experience, to make it invulnerable, to fix its identity once and for all. No commitment could grip me so deeply that I could not understand myself without it. No transformation of life purposes and plans could be so unsettling as to disrupt the contours of my identity. No project could be so essential that turning away from it would call into question the person I am. Given my independence from the values I have, I can always stand apart from them; my public identity as a moral person 'is not affected by changes over time' in my conception of the good.[20]

Larmore stresses that the most cogent Romantic thinkers do not say that *all* traditions and attachments are necessarily valuable. Rather, what they contend is that a 'distanced, questioning stance toward inherited ways of life' can 'blind us to the real merits of many ways of life'.[21] Whatever one ultimately thinks about the truth of these Romantic ideas, says Larmore, it is difficult to deny that these are 'views at which reasonable people can arrive'.[22] Given this, we cannot expect Kantian and Millian arguments for liberalism to be affirmed by all or even nearly all reasonable citizens. So 'the Kantian and Millian conceptions of liberalism are not adequate solutions to the political problem of reasonable disagreement about the good life [and] have themselves become simply another part of the problem'.[23]

---

[17] Sandel, M., *Liberalism and the Limits of Justice*, p. 179.
[18] Ibid. For a similar thought, see MacIntyre, A., *After Virtue*, p. 220.
[19] See Sandel, M., 'The Procedural Republic and the Unencumbered Self', *Political Theory* 12 (1984), pp. 81–96.
[20] Sandel, M., *Liberalism and the Limits of Justice*, p. 62.
[21] Larmore, C., 'Political Liberalism', p. 344.
[22] Ibid., p. 345.
[23] Ibid.

Larmore helpfully summarizes this point as follows:

Liberalism has always urged toleration for the diversity of ideals and forms of life, but almost as often it has sought to justify this position by appealing to some particular and controversial view of human flourishing. Such justifications are not improper to those who can accept their premises. It cannot be denied that these have been very influential rationales for a liberal political order ... But a liberalism come of age cannot rest content with these arguments. Its fundamental justification must be one that forgoes any appeal to the ideals whose controversial character sets the problem, after all, for political liberalism. It must be acceptable by reasonable people having different views of the good life, not just by those who share, for example, Mill's ideal of the person ... [Justifications of liberalism based on, say, the value of experimentation] will prove unacceptable to those holding different but still reasonable views about the human good ... who do not find the values of experiment and individual autonomy so important ... An experimental spirit may be alien and destructive to some forms of life, for example religious orthodoxies, whose claim is that in them one is to be brought up from infancy, acquiring habits and expectations that are to last a lifetime ... If liberals are to follow fully the spirit of liberalism, they must also devise a neutral justification of political neutrality.[24]

Political liberals view this kind of reasonable disagreement about the good life and human flourishing as 'the inevitable long-run result of the powers of human reason at work within the background of enduring free institutions'.[25] As Larmore puts this, 'people reasoning in good faith and to the best of their abilities disagree about the nature of the good'.[26] Reasonable disagreement is thus seen as a deep and permanent fact about human reasoning, even under favourable conditions.

Here it is natural to wonder: why take reasonable disagreement to be the inevitable long-run result of the exercise of human reason under conditions of freedom? Why not instead think that our conscientious attempts to reason with one another about the good life and human flourishing might in the end lead us to converge on the truth? As Rawls notes, convergence rather than divergence of opinion seems to be the case in natural science, at least in the long run.[27] So why should philosophical questions about the good life and human flourishing be any different?

Many political liberals answer this question by appealing to Rawls's account of the 'burdens of judgement'.[28] The burdens of judgement are the hazards or

[24] Larmore, C., *Patterns of Moral Complexity*, pp. 51–3.

[25] Rawls, J., *Political Liberalism*, p. 4.

[26] Larmore, C., 'Political Liberalism: Its Motivations and Goals', in D. Sobel, P. Vallentyne and S. Wall (eds), *Oxford Studies in Political Philosophy, Volume 1* (Oxford: Oxford University Press, 2015), p. 73.

[27] Rawls, J., *Political Liberalism*, p. 55.

[28] Ibid., pp. 54–8.

obstacles involved in the exercise of human reason in the ordinary course of political life. Rawls mentions six burdens of judgement: (1) that the relevant empirical and scientific evidence is often conflicting and complex; (2) that we disagree about the relative weight of different considerations; (3) that our concepts are vague and subject to borderline cases; (4) that how we assess evidence and weigh moral values is shaped by our total life experience, which differs from person to person; (5) that there are often different considerations on either side of an issue and it is difficult to make an all-things-considered assessment; and (6) that any social institution is limited in the range of values that it can realize and this gives rise to hard decisions about how to set priorities.[29] In light of these burdens, says Rawls, 'it is not to be expected that conscientious persons with full powers of reason, even after free discussion, will all arrive at the same conclusion' about what is good in human life.[30]

The burdens of judgement illustrate that when citizens disagree in their judgements about the good or flourishing human life, they need not be being *unreasonable*. Such disagreements need not be rooted 'in ignorance and perversity, or else in the rivalries for power, status, or economic gain'.[31] We need not say that such disagreements occur because 'people are often irrational and not very bright'.[32] Rather, the burdens of judgement help us to see that when citizens disagree about important matters, their disagreements are very often eminently *reasonable*: their disagreements stem from the complexity of the issues and from the tendency of intelligent, good-willed, morally serious reasoners to 'draw inferences, weigh evidence, and balance competing considerations' differently.[33] In this sense, 'the fact of reasonable pluralism is not an unfortunate condition of human life, as we might say of pluralism as such, allowing for doctrines that are not only irrational but mad and aggressive'; it is instead 'the inevitable outcome of free human reason' and is thus something that liberals should take seriously and seek to accommodate politically.[34]

2.2 Public Justification

But what would it mean to 'take seriously' the fact of reasonable disagreement? A central claim of political liberals is that—for reasons I go on to discuss in Section 2.3—the appropriate way to respond to the fact of reasonable disagreement is to adhere to the public justification principle. This principle holds that the state's exercise of political power must be justifiable, or acceptable, to all reasonable

[29] Ibid., pp. 56–7.
[30] Ibid., p. 58.
[31] Ibid.
[32] Ibid., p. 55.
[33] Ibid.
[34] Ibid., pp. 37, 144.

citizens.[35] As Thomas Nagel puts this, 'we should not impose arrangements, institutions, or requirements on other people on grounds that they could reasonably reject (where reasonableness is not simply a function of the independent rightness or wrongness of the arrangements in question, but genuinely depends on the point of view of the individual to some extent).'[36] In this way, the public justification principle functions as a kind of 'filter' or 'gatekeeper' for the sorts of reasons that can be invoked in favour of political action.[37] It says that laws and policies cannot, for instance, be justified in terms of religious or theological values, as these are subject to controversy among reasonable citizens; instead, laws and policies must be justified in terms of values such as freedom and equality, which all reasonable citizens can be expected to endorse.[38]

Many political liberals have sung the praises of the public justification principle. For Stephen Macedo, 'the moral lodestar of liberalism ... is the project of public justification.'[39] For Bruce Ackerman, it is 'the organizing principle of liberal thought.'[40] Jeremy Waldron explains that the 'demand that the social order should in principle be capable of explaining itself at the tribunal of each person's

---

[35] It is common in this literature to distinguish between 'consensus' and 'convergence' models of public justification. See, for example, Vallier, K., *Liberal Politics and Public Faith: Beyond Separation* (New York: Routledge, 2014), ch. 4. However, I largely gloss over this distinction in this section, since it is not relevant to the present discussion. Both consensus and convergence models of public justification will, after all, converge in their opposition to most, if not all, perfectionist laws and policies. I say more about the consensus/convergence distinction at the outset of Chapter 7.

[36] Nagel, T., 'Moral Conflict and Political Legitimacy', p. 221.

[37] These images are found respectively in Quong, J., *Liberalism Without Perfection*, p. 137 and in Pallikkathayil, J., 'Neither Perfectionism Nor Political Liberalism', *Philosophy & Public Affairs* 44 (2016), p. 179.

[38] Early political liberals restricted the scope of the public justification principle: they held that it is not *all* laws and policies that must be publicly justified but rather only 'constitutional essentials and matters of basic justice' (*Political Liberalism*, passim; see also Barry, B., *Justice as Impartiality*, pp. 160–1; Larmore, C., 'The Moral Basis of Political Liberalism', *The Journal of Philosophy* 96 (1999), p. 606 n. 8). But since then, many have questioned the distinction between the essential and non-essential, both on grounds of conceptual tenability (see, for example, Greenawalt, K., 'On Public Reason', *Chicago-Kent Law Review* 69 (1994), especially pp. 686–7; Wall, S., *Liberalism, Perfectionism and Restraint* (Cambridge: Cambridge University Press, 1998), pp. 41–2) and of normative significance (see, for example, Quong, J., *Liberalism Without Perfection*, pp. 273–89). Critics have argued, in other words, that there is no clear criterion for drawing the distinction between the constitutional and the legislative in a principled and non-arbitrary way, and that even if such a criterion were forthcoming, there is no plausible rationale for why public justification should apply to the former but not the latter. Contemporary political liberals thus tend to interpret the scope of public justification more broadly: some, such as Quong, take public justification to apply to all laws and policies, and others, such as Gaus and Vallier, take it to apply even to aspects of interpersonal life. (Indeed, despite his official scope restriction, Rawls himself also says that 'it is usually highly desirable to settle political questions' generally, rather than constitutional questions specifically, in terms of public reason; he elsewhere says that 'constitutional essentials, basic institutions *and public policies* should be justifiable to all citizens.' See *Political Liberalism*, p. 215; *Justice as Fairness*, p. 89, emphasis added.) In what follows, I assume that the public justification principle has fairly broad scope, applying to all laws and policies. In part this is because I agree with contemporary political liberals that a scope restriction is not well-motivated and in part it is because this assumption helps to bring into relief the anti-perfectionist implications of the public justification principle.

[39] Macedo, S., *Liberal Virtues* (Oxford: Clarendon Press, 1990), p. 78.

[40] Ackerman, B., *Social Justice in the Liberal State*, p. 10.

42   A PERFECTIONIST THEORY OF JUSTICE

understanding', or at least something in the vicinity of this demand, 'underpins many of the most characteristic and distinctive liberal positions', and so the discovery of the public justification principle by political liberals opens the way for a rational 'reconstruction of the foundations of liberalism'.[41] Larmore says that the public justification principle is the 'abiding moral heart of liberal thought' and Vallier describes it as 'focus[ing] like a laser on the core aim of the liberal tradition: justifying coercion to all'.[42] And Rawls says that the proposition that 'a legitimate regime is such that its political and social institutions are justifiable to all citizens— to each and every one—by addressing their reason, theoretical and practical' is a good 'candidate for the central thesis of liberalism'.[43]

Of course, the vital question for political liberals is: what are the criteria of reasonableness? Who counts as a 'reasonable' citizen? Who belongs to the justificatory constituency—the constituency of normatively or epistemically idealized citizens to whom justification is owed? After all, the question of what laws and policies will pass the public justification test will largely, and perhaps entirely, depend on how reasonable citizens are defined.

Different political liberals draw the circle of the reasonable more or less widely. Gaus, for instance, has a fairly inclusive account of the justificatory constituency, according to which laws and policies must be justified not to all citizens as they actually are but to all citizens who have engaged in a 'respectable amount' of reasoning.[44] But other political liberals such as Quong have argued that this account of reasonableness cannot rule out the possibility of individuals who, even after a respectable amount of good reasoning, still hold racist and sexist views.[45] To avoid making the legitimacy of liberal laws and policies hostage to the views of racists and sexists, argues Quong, political liberals need to build substantive liberal values into the definition of reasonableness. On Quong's view, then, acceptance of certain fundamental liberal values such as freedom, equality and fairness, and acceptance of the 'deliberative priority' of these liberal values over other values, is part of the very definition of reasonableness.[46]

On either of these definitions of reasonableness, perfectionist laws and policies can be expected to fail the test of public justification. Consider a perfectionist state that subsidizes opera on the grounds that artistic appreciation is a component of human flourishing. For Quong, reasonableness is a matter of endorsing freedom, equality and fairness—and so, insofar as a citizen could reject the claim that artistic

---

[41] Waldron, J., 'Theoretical Foundations of Liberalism', pp. 128, 149.

[42] Larmore, C., 'The Moral Basis of Political Liberalism', p. 606; Vallier, K., *Liberal Politics and Public Faith*, p. 261.

[43] Rawls, J., *Lectures on the History of Political Philosophy* (Cambridge, MA: Harvard University Press, 2007), p. 13.

[44] Gaus, G., *The Order of Public Reason*, especially ch. 13.

[45] Quong, J., 'What Is the Point of Public Reason?', *Philosophical Studies* 170 (2014), pp. 545–53.

[46] See Quong, J., *Liberalism Without Perfection*; Quong, J., '*Liberalism Without Perfection*: Replies to Gaus, Colburn, Chan, Bocchiola', *Philosophy and Public Issues* 2 (2012), pp. 53–6.

appreciation is a component of human flourishing without thereby rejecting freedom, equality or fairness, this judgement is not one that all reasonable citizens
could be expected to endorse. Similarly, for Gaus, reasonableness is a matter of
having engaged in a respectable amount of reasoning—and so, insofar as a citizen
could engage in such reasoning and yet still see no reason to think that artistic appreciation is a component of human flourishing, this judgement is not one that all
reasonable citizens could be expected to endorse. Either way, then, the state's support for opera violates the public justification principle: when the state coercively
extracts tax money for use on opera subsidies on the grounds that artistic appreciation is a component of human flourishing, it acts in a way that is not justifiable
to all reasonable citizens.

One rather strong way in which political liberals have put this point is that even
a moderate perfectionist state is analogous, at least in one respect, to a theocratic
state. Those who would use the power of the state to promote artistic conceptions
of the good life are, in one way, no different from those who would use the power
of the state to promote Christian or Muslim conceptions of the good life. Both advance ideals of human flourishing that some citizens not unreasonably reject. It
just happens that in one case the favoured ideals of human flourishing are secular rather than religious. Rawls, for instance, states that 'government can no more
act ... to advance human excellence, or the values of perfection (as in perfectionism), than it can act to advance Catholicism or Protestantism, or any other religion.
None of these views of the meaning, value, and purpose of human life ... is affirmed
by citizens generally, and so the pursuit of any one of them through the basic institutions gives political society a sectarian character'.[47] Elsewhere he explains that
'the human perfections are to be pursued within the limits of the principle of free
association' and that 'persons join together to further their cultural and artistic
interests in the same way that they form religious communities'.[48] A similar point
is made by Ackerman:

> For liberals like myself, the case for state-supported opera [is] complicated. What-
> ever else liberalism may be about, it has always stood for the separation of church
> and state. Given this commitment, subsidy for the opera raises an obvious ques-
> tion: If liberals are opposed to the establishment of religion, how can they justify
> supporting the establishment of one of the great totems of secular humanism—
> the operas of Mozart, Beethoven, Wagner, and other lesser saints in the secular
> canon? ... As much as possible the liberal state should be neutral on such mat-
> ters, leaving it to each citizen to determine whether he should give his financial
> support to the Church of Rome or the one at Bayreuth.[49]

[47] Rawls, J., *Political Liberalism*, pp. 179–80.
[48] Rawls, J., *A Theory of Justice* (Cambridge, MA: Harvard University Press, 1971), pp. 328–9.
[49] Ackerman, B., 'Should Opera Be Subsidized?', *Dissent* 46 (1999), pp. 89–90.

Of course, moderate perfectionists will want to say that there are plenty of important disanalogies between using state power to promote opera and using state power to promote religion, and so fixating on a single structural similarity, or insisting that support for art and support for religion stand or fall together, is at best misleading and at worst simply mistaken. Political liberals are unlikely to deny these disanalogies. Still, political liberals will likely stress that while moderate perfectionism and theocracy are not the same in all respects, they remain analogous in one highly significant respect: both involve the pursuit by the state of ideals of human flourishing that all citizens cannot reasonably be expected to endorse. This shared property is especially significant from the point of view of liberal political morality, which has traditionally emphasized toleration and respect for diversity.

In light of this, political liberals tend to be quite strongly anti-perfectionist. According to Ronald Dworkin, for instance, 'liberalism takes as its constitutive political morality' the requirement of 'official neutrality amongst theories of what is valuable in life'.[50] 'Political decisions', he explains, 'must be, so far as is possible, independent of any particular conception of the good life, or of what gives value to life'.[51] And he goes so far as to say that the principle of state neutrality is 'the nerve of liberalism'.[52] For Ackerman, no citizen may assert that 'her own ideal of the good life is worthy of special endorsement by the political community as superior to the ideals affirmed by others'.[53] Quong states that the 'main thesis' of his book is that 'the government should remain neutral on the issue of the good life, and restrict itself to establishing the fair terms within which citizens can pursue their own beliefs about what gives value to their lives'.[54] Rawls says that 'all conceptions of the good (consistent with justice) are regarded as equally worthy, not in the sense that there is an agreed public measure of intrinsic value or satisfaction with respect to which all these conceptions come out equal, but in the sense that they are not evaluated at all from a social standpoint'.[55] Similarly, Brian Barry contends that 'nobody is to be allowed to assert the superiority of his own conception of the good over those of other people as a reason for building into the framework for social cooperation special advantages for it'.[56] For Gerald Gaus, 'liberal neutrality' is a 'compelling and radical principle', one that prohibits using state power to make others 'more perfect in our eyes'.[57] And Will Kymlicka contends that 'the state should not reward or penalize particular conceptions of the good life but,

[50] Dworkin, R., 'Liberalism', in S. Hampshire (ed.), *Public and Private Morality*, pp. 127, 142.
[51] Ibid., p. 127.
[52] Ibid., p. 115.
[53] Ackerman, B., 'Neutralities', in R. B. Douglass et al. (eds), *Liberalism and the Good* (London: Routledge, 1990), p. 37.
[54] Quong, J., *Liberalism Without Perfection*, p. 2.
[55] Rawls, J., 'Social Unity and Primary Goods', in his *Collected Papers*, ed. S. Freeman (Cambridge, MA: Harvard University Press, 1999), p. 373.
[56] Barry, B., *Justice as Impartiality*, p. 160.
[57] Gaus, G., 'Liberal Neutrality: A Compelling and Radical Principle', in S. Wall and G. Klosko (eds), *Perfectionism and Neutrality: Essays in Liberal Theory* (Oxford: Rowman & Littlefield, 2003), p. 162.

rather, should provide a neutral framework within which different and potentially conflicting conceptions of the good can be pursued'.[58]

It should now be clear why political liberalism has been described as a 'liberalism come of age'. It lowers the barriers of entry into the liberal project in a way that makes liberalism more consistent with its own underlying motivations. Political liberalism says that, to be a liberal, one does not need to believe, with Mill, that individuality is 'the chief ingredient of individual and social progress' or that 'there should be different experiments of living'.[59] One can reject these claims, as do many more traditional yet still reasonable citizens within pluralistic societies, without thereby repudiating liberalism. As Larmore puts it, 'Romantics can also be liberals'.[60] When liberalism is conceived in this 'political not metaphysical' manner, it emerges as not 'just another sectarian doctrine, one that competes alongside others to use the state to promote its particular views about value and human flourishing', but instead as a more impartial and mutually acceptable public perspective from which the competing claims of different individuals and social groups can be fairly adjudicated.[61]

At this point, it is natural to wonder what *would* pass the public justification test. Given the depth of disagreement among sincere, good-willed, intelligent citizens in modern pluralistic societies, would anything pass this test? In particular, aren't ideals of justice just as subject to reasonable disagreement as ideals of human flourishing? Don't people 'reasoning in good faith and to the best of their abilities' also disagree in profound and pervasive ways about questions of justice, such as taxation, health care, affirmative action, capital punishment and freedom of expression?[62] Don't the burdens of judgement apply to these questions just as much as they do to questions of human flourishing? So isn't the public justification requirement a recipe not just for anti-perfectionism but also for libertarianism or perhaps even anarchism?

Some are willing to embrace this conclusion, or something like it.[63] Gaus, for instance, notes that a flirtation with anarchy 'seems like the right sort of challenge for a liberal theory'.[64] It reminds us, he says, of an important insight familiar to classical social contract liberals such as Hobbes and Locke but often forgotten by contemporary theorists who 'call themselves liberal [but whose theories] are often modified forms of socialism or collectivism': namely, that 'liberalism is at the

---

[58] Kymlicka, W., 'Liberal Individualism and Liberal Neutrality', *Ethics* 99 (1989), p. 883.

[59] Mill, J. S., *On Liberty*, pp. 120, 132.

[60] Larmore, C., 'Political Liberalism', p. 354.

[61] Quong, J., '*Liberalism Without Perfection*: A Précis', *Philosophy and Public Issues* 2 (2012), p. 1.

[62] Larmore, C., 'Political Liberalism: Its Motivations and Goals', p. 73.

[63] See especially Gaus, G., 'Liberal Neutrality: A Compelling and Radical Principle'; Gaus, G., 'Coercion, Ownership, and the Redistributive State: Justificatory Liberalism's Classical Tilt', *Social Philosophy & Policy* 27 (2010), pp. 233–75.

[64] Gaus, G., 'Liberal Neutrality: A Compelling and Radical Principle', p. 155.

46 A PERFECTIONIST THEORY OF JUSTICE

edge of anarchy' and that, for liberals, who take individual freedom to be funda-mental, the question must always be that of why state coercion is justified.[65] This is why classical social contract liberals 'begin with the state of nature and seek to justify the creation of a state'.[66] On this view, public justification is a radical prin-ciple which, when faithfully applied, tilts towards a purer, more minimal kind of liberalism.

Other political liberals, however, have tried to resist this libertarian tilt and to maintain that, while perfectionist laws and policies fail the public justification test, laws and policies aimed at realizing liberal justice survive this test. The standard way of doing this is to idealize the constituency of citizens to whom justification is owed. Rawls, for instance, accepts that there is reasonable disagreement not only about the good life but also about justice, but he maintains that reasonable disagreement about justice is significantly more limited than reasonable disagree-ment about the good life.[67] In particular, he explains that there is 'a family of reasonable liberal political conceptions of justice': reasonable citizens will disagree about many aspects of justice but they will all at least accept that justice (a) guaran-tees certain basic rights and freedoms, (b) assigns these rights and freedoms special priority over other values and (c) assures all citizens adequate all-purpose means to make effective use of these rights and freedoms.[68] These ideas can of course be interpreted in different ways, but all reasonable citizens would affirm only princi-ples of justice that satisfy these three conditions. Many versions of libertarianism, for instance, do not count as reasonable conceptions of social justice, since they vi-olate condition (c).[69] In this sense, there is reasonable disagreement about justice, but such disagreement must fall 'within a certain more or less narrow range'.[70]

Similarly, we have seen that Quong holds that acceptance of three basic liberal values (namely freedom, equality and fairness), and acceptance of the deliberative priority of these values over perfectionist values, is part of the very definition of reasonableness. For Quong, 'the constituency of the reasonable is defined by ask-ing what beliefs, attitudes, or values ideal citizens in a well-ordered liberal society

---

[65] Ibid., pp. 155–6. For the view that Rawls's theory could only be realized by socialist institutions, see Edmundson, W., *John Rawls: Reticent Socialist* (Cambridge: Cambridge University Press, 2017).

[66] Gaus, G., 'Liberal Neutrality: A Compelling and Radical Principle', p. 161.

[67] Here it is worth noting that only in his very late writings (the 1996 preface to the paperback edition of *Political Liberalism* and the 1997 essay 'The Idea of Public Reason Revisited') did Rawls come to a full recognition the existence of reasonable disagreement about justice; thus even some parts of *Political Liberalism*, unrevised from 1993 to 1996, continue to define the well-ordered society as 'a society in which everyone accepts, and knows that everyone else accepts, *the very same principles of justice*' (see Rawls, J., *Political Liberalism*, p. 35, emphasis added; see also pp. 39, 201).

[68] Rawls, J., *Political Liberalism*, p. xlvi. See also pp. 6, 223, 226, 450–2.

[69] See, for example, ibid., p. lvi; see also Reidy, D., 'Reciprocity and Reasonable Disagreement: From Liberal to Democratic Legitimacy', *Philosophical Studies* 132 (2007), pp. 287–8 n. 40; Freeman, S., 'Il-liberal Libertarians: Why Libertarianism Is Not a Liberal View', *Philosophy & Public Affairs* 30 (2001), pp. 105–51.

[70] Rawls, J., *Political Liberalism*, p. 164.

would necessarily have to share'.[71] Someone could not deny the value of freedom, equality or fairness while still remaining an ideal citizen of a well-ordered liberal society. By contrast, Quong argues, someone could deny the value of artistic excellence, say, without thereby being 'impaired from doing all the things citizens would need to do in a perfectly well-ordered liberal society'.[72] Thus, he says, reasonable citizens 'would have to be committed to certain liberal egalitarian values' but would not also have to 'share any substantive views about religion or the good life'.[73]

By stipulating certain commitments about social justice into reasonable citizens in this way, without similarly stipulating commitments about human flourishing into reasonable citizens, it becomes clearer how the public justification principle rules out the state's pursuit of human flourishing without simultaneously ruling out its pursuit of social justice. Political liberals can thus argue that a suitable interpretation of the principle of public justification will thus justify neither more nor less than an anti-perfectionist liberal state: suitably interpreted, the public justification principle prohibits the state's promotion of ideals of human flourishing but does not similarly prohibit its promotion of ideals of social justice.

2.3 A Thin Normative Rationale

Let us return to the argument formulated at the outset of this chapter:

(P1) Reasonable citizens disagree about what constitutes a good or flourishing human life (the fact of reasonable disagreement)
(P2) State action must be acceptable or justifiable to all reasonable citizens (the public justification principle)
(C) So, state action must not be premised on claims about what constitutes a good or flourishing human life.

So far, I have discussed the nature of the fact of reasonable disagreement and the nature of the public justification principle. But I have not yet explained *why* we should accept the public justification principle. What makes (P2) true? Certainly, the public justification principle is not self-evident. For political liberals, reasonableness is a 'deliberately loose' category: the category of reasonable beliefs is meant to be much wider than the category of true beliefs, in the sense that many false beliefs are nonetheless reasonable.[74] As Rawls puts this, political liberalism 'counts many [views] as reasonable even though we could not seriously entertain

[71] Quong, J., 'On Laborde's Liberalism', *Criminal Law and Philosophy* 15 (2021), p. 53.
[72] Ibid.
[73] Ibid.
[74] Rawls, J., *Political Liberalism*, p. 59.

them for ourselves'.[75] But given that reasonable citizens can hold false beliefs in this way, why should we care about whether laws and policies are acceptable to reasonable citizens? Why should their objections matter if they may be based on claims that are false or that cannot be seriously entertained? Why should the legitimate use of state power be hostage to what such individuals do or do not accept? Shouldn't we instead seek to implement the laws and policies that are *true* or *correct*—or at least that are most likely to be true or correct—regardless of whether those laws and policies could be reasonably rejected by some citizens?[76] Moreover, even if some explanation can be given for why justification to all reasonable citizens matters, we would need to know why it matters *so much* that we should treat public justification as a constraint of 'very great and normally overriding weight'.[77] Why should public justification hold sway in the normal run of cases of political disagreement? Why not instead think that acceptability to all reasonable citizens is simply a pro tanto value—just another item on the long and dense list of political desiderata, and not an especially weighty item at that?[78]

Political liberals have answered these questions in various ways. After all, although political liberals are wary of basing liberalism, as comprehensive liberals do, on thick moral values such as individuality and experimental living—because these values are subject to reasonable disagreement in free societies—they equally do not say that liberalism is a mere modus vivendi in which citizens are self-interestedly or strategically, rather than morally, committed to liberal rights and institutions. Political liberals thus offer a range of rationales for the public justification principle: respect for persons,[79] civic friendship,[80] stability,[81] social trust,[82]

---

[75] Ibid., pp. 59–60.

[76] For similar questions, see Nagel, T., 'Moral Conflict and Political Legitimacy', p. 222. For the contrast between public justification and truth- or correctness-based justification, see Wall, S., 'Is Public Justification Self-Defeating?', *American Philosophical Quarterly* 39 (2002), p. 386; Pallikkathayil, J., 'Neither Perfectionism Nor Political Liberalism', pp. 185–8.

[77] Rawls, J., *Political Liberalism*, p. 241.

[78] See Enoch, D., 'Against Public Reason', in D. Sobel, P. Vallentyne and S. Wall (eds), *Oxford Studies in Political Philosophy, Volume 1* (Oxford: Oxford University Press, 2015), especially pp. 138–40. For similar thoughts, see Wall, S., *Liberalism, Perfectionism and Restraint* (Cambridge: Cambridge University Press, 1998), pp. 75–91; Wendt, F., 'Rescuing Public Justification from Public Reason Liberalism', in D. Sobel, P. Vallentyne and S. Wall (eds), *Oxford Studies in Political Philosophy, Volume 5* (Oxford: Oxford University Press, 2019), pp. 39–64.

[79] Nagel, T., 'Moral Conflict and Political Legitimacy'; Larmore, C., 'The Moral Basis of Political Liberalism'; Boettcher, J., 'Respect, Recognition, and Public Reason', *Social Theory and Practice* 33 (2007), pp. 223–49; Nussbaum, M., 'Perfectionist Liberalism and Political Liberalism'; van Wietmarschen, H., 'Political Liberalism and Respect', *The Journal of Political Philosophy* 29 (2021), pp. 353–74.

[80] Ebels-Duggan, K., 'The Beginning of Community: Politics in the Face of Disagreement', *The Philosophical Quarterly* 60 (2010), pp. 50–71; Lister, A., *Public Reason and Political Community*; Leland, R. J. and van Wietmarschen, H., 'Political Liberalism and Political Community', *Journal of Moral Philosophy* 14 (2017), pp. 151–75; Leland, R. J., 'Civic Friendship, Public Reason', *Philosophy & Public Affairs* 47 (2019), pp. 72–103.

[81] Weithman, P., *Why Political Liberalism? On John Rawls's Political Turn*.

[82] Vallier, K., *Must Politics Be War?*

egalitarian justice,[83] political autonomy[84] and our everyday reactive attitudes.[85] One important feature of these rationales is that they all refer to quite *thin* normative values: they offer what Larmore calls a 'minimal moral conception of liberalism'.[86] The hope of political liberals is thus that even those who do not accept comprehensive liberalism—for instance, those who do not believe, with Mill, that individuality is 'the chief ingredient of individual and social progress'—can still recognize the value of respect for persons, stability, and so on, and on this basis can still commit to the public justification of political power.

In the remainder of this chapter, I shall briefly discuss three prominent attempts by political liberals to provide a normative foundation or rationale for the public justification principle: the argument from respect (Section 2.3.1), the argument from stability (Section 2.3.2) and the argument from the reactive attitudes (Section 2.3.3). The purpose of this discussion is not to demonstrate decisively which, if any, of these arguments for the public justification principle succeed. Rather, it is meant to complete this exposition of political liberalism by illustrating the sorts of ways in which political liberals typically go about defending their commitment to public justification.

2.3.1 Respect

The traditional rationale for the public justification principle refers to the idea of respect for persons. There are different ways of developing an argument from respect to public justification, but an impressive and influential rendition of this argument can be found in the work of Larmore.[87]

Larmore's argument for the public justification principle relies on two fundamental norms, which he calls the 'norm of rational dialogue' and the 'norm of equal respect'.[88] He explains the norm of rational dialogue as follows: 'when two people disagree about some specific point, but wish to continue talking about the more general problem they wish to solve, each should prescind from the beliefs that the other rejects, (1) in order to construct an argument on the basis of his

---

[83] Quong, J., 'On the Idea of Public Reason', in J. Mandle and D. Reidy (eds), *The Blackwell Companion to Rawls* (Oxford: Wiley Blackwell, 2013), pp. 265–80; Quong, J., 'Disagreement, Equality, and the Exclusion of Ideals: A Comment on *The Morality of Freedom*', *Jerusalem Review of Legal Studies* 14 (2016), pp. 135–46; Kugelberg, H., 'Civic Equality as a Democratic Basis for Public Reason', *Critical Review of International Social and Political Philosophy* (forthcoming).

[84] Weithman, P., 'In Defence of a Political Liberalism', *Philosophy & Public Affairs* 45 (2017), pp. 397–412; Neufeld, B., 'Shared Intentions, Public Reason, and Political Autonomy', *Canadian Journal of Philosophy* 49 (2019), pp. 776–804.

[85] Gaus, G., *The Order of Public Reason*.

[86] Larmore, C., 'Political Liberalism', p. 341.

[87] Larmore develops this argument in several places. See his *Patterns of Moral Complexity*, pp. 50–68; 'Political Liberalism', pp. 347–52; *The Morals of Modernity*, pp. 134–44; 'Political Liberalism: Its Motivations and Goals', pp. 74–80.

[88] Larmore, C., 'Political Liberalism', p. 348.

other beliefs that will convince the other of the truth of the disputed belief, or (2) in order to shift to another aspect of the problem, where the possibilities of agreement seem greater.'[89] In so doing, one manages to 'keep the conversation going, in order to achieve some reasoned agreement about how to solve the problem at hand'.[90] In support of this norm of rational dialogue, Larmore points to the distinction between proof and justification.[91] Whereas proof is a matter of logical relations between propositions, a justification is 'a proof directed at those who disagree with us to show them that they should join us in believing what we do'.[92] As Rawls similarly puts it, 'justification is not simply valid reasoning, but argument addressed to others'.[93] Justification 'can fulfil this pragmatic role', Larmore continues, 'only by appealing to what [others] already believe, thus to what is common ground between us'.[94]

But the norm of rational dialogue is not by itself a sufficient basis for the public justification principle. It 'tells us what to do, *if* we want to talk together about what political principles to establish'.[95] But it does not tell us *why* it is so important to 'talk together' or to 'keep the conversation going'. Why shouldn't we resort to other means, such as force or deceit, rather than dialogue, to reach political decisions? This is where the norm of equal respect for persons comes in. This norm has close connections to the Kantian requirement that we should never treat other persons merely as means, or as tools of our will, but should rather treat them also always as ends. Larmore goes on to say that 'if we try to bring about conformity to a political principle simply by threat, we will be treating people solely as means, as objects of coercion' and 'we will not also be treating them as ends, engaging directly their distinctive capacity as persons'—which is 'the capacity of thinking and acting on the basis of reasons'.[96] Thus, says Larmore, 'to respect another person as an end is to insist that coercive or political principles be as justifiable to that person as they are to us'.[97]

Larmore explains that 'the special virtue' of his argument from these two basic norms is that it is a 'minimal' argument.[98] It can be accepted even by those, such as communitarians and other Romantics, who have serious doubts about the high premium placed by comprehensive liberals on ideals such as autonomy and individuality. Of course, Larmore recognizes that not *everyone* accepts the norm of equal respect; virulent forms of racism, for instance, clearly reject this norm. But,

---

[89] Larmore, C., *Patterns of Moral Complexity*, p. 53.
[90] Ibid.
[91] See also Quong, J., 'Justification vs. Proof', in J. Mandle (ed.), *The Cambridge Rawls Lexicon* (Cambridge: Cambridge University Press, 2014), pp. 390–1.
[92] Larmore, C., 'Political Liberalism', p. 347.
[93] Rawls, J., *Political Liberalism*, p. 465. See also Rawls, J., *A Theory of Justice*, pp. 580–1.
[94] Larmore, C., 'Political Liberalism', p. 347.
[95] Ibid., p. 348.
[96] Ibid., pp. 348–9.
[97] Ibid., p. 349.
[98] Ibid., p. 347.

POLITICAL LIBERALISM 51

while there are limits to the allegiance that equal respect enjoys within contemporary societies, it nonetheless represents a far less controversial basis for liberalism than that given by comprehensive liberals—and in particular it is a basis that remains 'neutral with regard to the dispute between individualism and tradition'.[99] The broad appeal of Larmore's argument thus makes it 'a more fitting response to the basic political problems which liberalism has sought to solve'.[100] In this regard, Larmore helpfully explains that political liberalism can be understood as being situated between two extremes: at one extreme are comprehensive liberals, such as Kant and Mill, who base liberalism on controversial moral ideals such as individuality and experimentation, and at the other extreme are modus vivendi liberals, such as Hobbes, who base liberalism on solely strategic considerations of self-interest.[101] A political liberalism based on the norms of rational dialogue and equal respect occupies a middle ground: it is more moral than Hobbesian modus vivendi liberalism but more minimal than Kantian and Millian comprehensive liberalism.

Over the years, Larmore's argument has been criticized in at least two ways. The first objection is that respect does not in fact require public justification. Even if offering others reasons they accept is *one* way of showing them respect, why think that this is the *only* way of showing them respect? In other words, critics of public reason need not reject the idea of equal respect; they simply hold a different *interpretation* of what equal respect requires. To press this objection, one needs to articulate a well-developed alternative conception of what respect requires—a conception that does not make the public justification of political power a necessary condition of respect for persons. One such alternative conception of respect is suggested by William Galston:

> While the (general) concept of equal respect may be relatively uncontroversial, the (specific) conception surely is not. To treat an individual as person rather than object is to offer him an explanation. Fine; but *what kind* of explanation? Larmore seems to suggest that a properly respectful explanation must appeal to beliefs already held by one's interlocutors; whence the need for [public justification]. This seems arbitrary and implausible. I would suggest, rather, that we show others respect when we offer them, as explanation, what we take to be our true and best reasons for acting as we do.[102]

---

[99] Ibid., p. 349.

[100] Ibid., p. 347.

[101] See ibid., p. 346.

[102] Galston, W., *Liberal Purposes: Goods, Virtues, and Diversity in the Liberal State* (Cambridge: Cambridge University Press, 1991), p. 109. For related arguments, see Raz, J., *The Morality of Freedom* (Oxford: Clarendon Press, 1986), p. 157; Chan, J., 'Legitimacy, Unanimity, and Perfectionism', *Philosophy & Public Affairs* 29 (2000), pp. 21–2; Arneson, R., 'Liberal Neutrality on the Good: An Autopsy', in S. Wall and G. Klosko (eds), *Perfectionism and Neutrality*, pp. 213–14; Wall, S., 'Perfectionism', in G.

Eberle provides a more developed and sophisticated alternative conception of respect in the form of his 'ideal of conscientious engagement'.[103] This ideal is constituted by a variety of moral constraints. One of these constraints is that a citizen should only advance laws and policies that enjoy a 'high degree of rational justification' (understood in terms of considering the relevant evidence, discharging various epistemic obligations governing belief formation, and so on).[104] Another is that a citizen should not support a law or policy that 'denies the dignity of her compatriots'.[105] A third constraint is that, during political deliberation, a citizen should 'listen to her compatriots ... with the intention of learning from them'.[106] Fourth, the ideal of conscientious engagement even requires a citizen to '*pursue* public justification for her favoured coercive policies'.[107] But crucially—and this is what distinguishes the ideal of conscientious engagement from the ideal of public justification—citizens need not withhold their support for policies if, after looking for reasons that are acceptable to other citizens, no such reasons are ultimately forthcoming.

For Eberle, what respect requires is compliance with the ideal of conscientious engagement rather than compliance with the ideal of public justification. The ideal of conscientious engagement does not appear, in any obvious sense, to be disrespectful: it does not involve (in Larmore's words) 'try[ing] to bring about conformity to a political principle simply by threat' and it does not treat people 'solely as means, as objects of coercion'. Insofar as it prescribes honest and open dialogue, the ideal of conscientious engagement recognizes (again in Larmore's words) that citizens possess 'the capacity of thinking and acting on the basis of reasons'. In light of this, Eberle argues that while Larmore may well succeed in demonstrating that *some* models of political decision-making that depart from public justification would be disrespectful (such as making decisions simply by threat or force), he has not demonstrated that *all* models of political decision-making short of public justification (such as the ideal of conscientious engagement) are incompatible with respect for persons.[108]

Gaus and F. D'Agostino (eds), *The Routledge Companion to Social and Political Philosophy* (London: Routledge, 2013), pp. 346–7.

[103] See Eberle, C., *Religious Conviction in Liberal Politics* (Cambridge: Cambridge University Press, 2002), chs 4 and 5.

[104] Ibid., p. 104.

[105] Ibid., p. 105.

[106] Ibid.

[107] Ibid.

[108] Interestingly, Rawls himself was quite reluctant to say that political liberalism is grounded in an idea of respect for persons (see Rawls, J., 'Justice as Fairness: Political not Metaphysical', p. 236 n. 19) and the reason for this may well have been that (as the arguments from Galston, Eberle and others illustrate) there are as many conceptions of respect as there are principles of political morality. In other words, if respect for persons is just a matter of treating persons in accordance with the appropriate principles of political morality, then respect cannot offer independent grounds for selecting a given principle of political morality (such as the public justification principle) over others (such as the ideal

POLITICAL LIBERALISM   53

A second objection to Larmore's argument is that even if it could be shown that the failure to publicly justify is disrespectful in some sense, this does not look like an especially *grievous* kind of disrespect. As Lott puts it, 'respect comes in shades': 'it is disrespectful to cut in front of someone for the last spot on an elevator, it is more disrespectful to spit on someone whose jokes annoy you, and it is even more disrespectful to shoot someone for the same reason'.[109] The kind of disrespect involved in the failure to offer reasons that are acceptable to all reasonable citizens looks fairly slight. Public justification, that is, looks to be at the periphery of our concept of respect rather than a paradigmatic instance of respect.[110] This worry about weightiness becomes particularly acute once we observe that there are other important dimensions of respect (such as that mentioned by Galston earlier) that are in tension with the dimension of respect picked out by proponents of public justification. So, in order to ground the kind of robust public justification principle they are after—a principle of 'very great and normally overriding weight'—political liberals need to explain why we should care so much about the specific kind of respect (or disrespect) expressed in giving (or failing to give) public justifications.[111] Why does this highly specific and seemingly peripheral kind of respect generally take priority over (a) other senses or dimensions of respect and (b) other values in general?

Here is not the place to assess the success of these two objections. The important point for our purposes is that traditional arguments from respect to public justification have been subjected to powerful criticisms, and thus it is natural that political liberals have since searched for alternative yet similarly minimal rationales for public justification, such as stability and the reactive attitudes.

2.3.2 Stability

Another rationale for the public justification principle is that it is required by considerations of stability. Rawls himself can be read as arguing from stability to public justification. As we have seen, in his introduction to *Political Liberalism*

---

of conscientious engagement), as Larmore hopes, because the content of respect is itself already determined by reference to the appropriate principles of political morality. Respect thus cuts little or no dialectical ice in this context. Similarly, at the end of *A Theory of Justice*, Rawls explains that he does not derive his principles of justice from a principle of respect or human dignity because 'it is precisely these ideas that call for interpretation'. Prior to the principles of justice, the meaning of respect is indeterminate; it is only 'once the conception of justice is on hand [that] the ideas of respect and of human dignity can be given a more definite meaning'. Thus a 'theory of justice provides a *rendering* of these ideas but we cannot *start out* from them'. See Rawls, J., *A Theory of Justice*, pp. 585–6. See also Larmore, C., 'Political Liberalism: Its Motivations and Goals', p. 79 n. 24.

[109] Lott, M., 'Restraint on Reasons and Reasons for Restraint: A Problem for Rawls' Ideal of Public Reason', *Pacific Philosophical Quarterly* 87 (2006), p. 87.

[110] Ibid., p. 95 n. 36.

[111] Rawls, J., *Political Liberalism*, p. 241.

Rawls posits that 'the historical origin of political liberalism (and of liberalism more generally) is the Reformation and its aftermath, with the long controversies over religious toleration in the sixteenth and seventeenth centuries'.[112] He states that these centuries saw a 'clash between salvationist, creedal, and expansionist religions', that this was a 'mortal conflict moderated only by circumstance and exhaustion' and that 'political liberalism starts by taking to heart the absolute depth of that irreconcilable latent conflict'.[113]

Rawls explains that the shift towards a 'political' liberalism was motivated by his coming to realize that comprehensive liberalisms—such as the liberalisms of Kant and Mill, as well as the liberalism he earlier articulated in *A Theory of Justice*—would not be stable under conditions of reasonable pluralism.[114] He expresses his puzzlement that 'the problem of stability has played very little role in the history of moral philosophy' and that theorists of justice have not often enough considered whether a society regulated by their favoured principles could be expected to stably endure over time. At least for the foreseeable future, he says, a political order could not be stably based on one or another comprehensive doctrine, such as the Millian doctrine of individuality and experimental living, since these doctrines 'rest in large part on ideals and values that are not generally, or perhaps even widely, shared in a democratic society'.[115] Rather, a political order can only be stable over time if it is based on values which can be expected to command the allegiance of all reasonable citizens despite their differing comprehensive doctrines and around which an 'overlapping consensus' can be expected to form.

There are different ways of understanding the argument that public justification is necessary for stability. On the one hand, some read Rawls as advancing what is primarily an *empirical* claim.[116] On this view, when the state exercises its coercive power in ways that are acceptable to all reasonable citizens, this fosters trust and cooperation, reduces frustration and violence, and has other stabilizing effects, and vice versa when the state fails to achieve public justification. Rawls certainly sometimes uses empirical language of this kind; he says, for instance, that 'the common sense political sociology of democratic societies' tells us that 'an enduring and stable democratic regime, one not divided into contending factions and hostile classes, must be willingly and freely supported by a substantial majority of at least its politically active citizens'.[117] But one problem with this interpretation of the stability argument is that it is unclear that the relevant empirical claim is true: it is unclear, that is, that in the absence of public justification society would fall

---

[112] Ibid., p. xxiv.

[113] Ibid., pp. xxv–xxvi.

[114] Ibid., pp. xv–xvi.

[115] Rawls, J., 'The Idea of an Overlapping Consensus', *Oxford Journal of Legal Studies* 7 (1987), p. 6.

[116] For an interpretation along these lines, see, for example, Klosko, G., 'Rawls's "Political" Philosophy and American Democracy', *The American Political Science Review* 87 (1993), pp. 348–59.

[117] Rawls, J., 'The Idea of an Overlapping Consensus', p. 4 n. 7.

into a state of conflict, hostility or social instability. After all, most modern liberal democracies are not Rawlsian 'well-ordered societies' or 'orders of public reason', and yet they are not marred by instability. Very many factors contribute to stability: a culture of civility and toleration, respect for rights, checks and balances on political institutions, national sentiment and community ties, economic development, a system of sanctions and punishments, and so on.[118] So even if commitment to the principle of public justification is one factor that contributes to social stability, is it really a *necessary* condition thereof, such that, in the absence of public justification, these other factors would not be jointly sufficient to sustain a stable society?

On the other hand, some read Rawls as advancing what is primarily a *normative* claim.[119] This is reinforced by the fact that Rawls refers to his conception of stability as 'stability for the right reasons'. Stability for the right reasons is achieved if all citizens growing up within a society whose major institutions are regulated by principles of justice come to freely endorse and affirm these principles in wide and general reflective equilibrium, and all citizens know that all other citizens also endorse and affirm these principles in this way. As Rawls puts this, 'the kind of stability required of justice as fairness is based, then, on its being a liberal political view, one that aims at being acceptable to citizens as reasonable and rational, as well as free and equal, and so as addressed to their public reason'.[120] He further says that a political order is stable for the right reasons when 'it can win its support by addressing each citizen's reason'.[121] But one problem with this interpretation of the stability argument is that it makes the stability story into another way of telling the public justification story.[122] If a society is stable for the right reasons when its major institutions are 'acceptable to citizens as reasonable and rational', then stability for the right reasons amounts merely to a restatement of, rather than an independent justification for, the public justification principle.

Perhaps this is put too strongly. Even if stability for the right reasons does not provide a fully independent justification for the public justification principle, perhaps it helps to clarify certain aspects of public justification and to cast them in a favourable light. Still, it remains the case that when the argument from stability to public justification is interpreted in this heavily moralized way, the justificans is so close to the justificandum that it does little, if anything, to persuade those who are not antecedently persuaded of the public justification principle.

---

[118] See Wendt, F., *Compromise, Peace and Public Justification: Political Morality Beyond Justice* (London: Palgrave Macmillan, 2016), pp. 145–6.

[119] For an interpretation along these lines, see, for example, Weithman, P., *Why Political Liberalism?*

[120] Ibid, p. 143.

[121] Ibid.

[122] A number of theorists have made this criticism of stability for the right reasons. See, for example, Mulhall, S. and Swift, A., *Liberals and Communitarians*, pp. 184–8, 240–2; Quong, J., *Liberalism Without Perfection*, pp. 166–70.

None of this is meant to show that there cannot be a sound argument from considerations of stability, or considerations in the vicinity of stability, to the public justification principle. Recently, for instance, Vallier has developed an argument from social trust to public justification, and this might be understood as falling within the family of stability-based rationales.[123] Vallier's key claim is that 'publicly justified moral rules have the unique power to sustain a system of trust' in an appropriate way within large-scale and diverse societies.[124] Vallier explains that 'when a moral [or political] rule is publicly justified, complying with it flows from one's personal convictions'.[125] This means that 'persons see themselves as having reason to be trustworthy by complying with the rule' and so 'social trust forms through the perception of this properly incentivized trustworthiness'.[126] Whether Vallier's argument in the end succeeds is beyond the scope of the present discussion, but it represents an interesting, important and sophisticated attempt to ground public justification on an empirical-cum-normative value that is closely related to stability.[127]

2.3.3 The Reactive Attitudes

A third argument for public justification is Gaus's argument from the reactive attitudes. On Gaus's view, one should not make an authoritative demand on others unless those subject to the demand 'have sufficient reasons' to accept it—where one 'has sufficient reasons' to accept a demand if one would, after a 'respectable amount of good reasoning', accept the demand.[128] For Gaus, this is a principle that applies both to the activity of states and to that of individuals.

Gaus's argument from the reactive attitudes to this version of the public justification principle has two key premises. The first is that our everyday reactive attitudes of blame and resentment presuppose public justification. To see why this might be, it is helpful to get clearer on the nature of the reactive attitudes. The term 'reactive attitudes' was introduced by Strawson in his seminal essay 'Freedom and Resentment'.[129] For Strawson, the reactive attitudes are the 'attitudes belonging to involvement or participation with others in interpersonal human relationships'.[130] Paradigmatic examples of such reactive attitudes are resentment, indignation and gratitude. What makes these attitudes *reactive*, says Strawson, is

---

[123] See Vallier, K., *Must Politics Be War?*
[124] Ibid., p. 118.
[125] Ibid., p. 79.
[126] Ibid.
[127] For some doubts about Vallier's argument, see Tahzib, C., 'Does Social Trust Justify the Public Justification Principle?', *The Journal of Applied Philosophy* 38 (2021), pp. 461–78.
[128] Gaus, G., *The Order of Public Reason*, pp. 250, 263.
[129] Strawson, P. F., 'Freedom and Resentment', *Proceedings of the British Academy* 48 (1962), pp. 187–211. Reprinted in G. Watson (ed.), *Free Will* (Oxford: Oxford University Press, 2003), pp. 72–93.
[130] Strawson, P. F., 'Freedom and Resentment', in G. Watson (ed.), *Free Will*, p. 79.

that they are 'reactions to the quality of others' wills towards us'—to their good will or ill will.[131]

A crucial point made by both Strawson and Gaus is that these reactive attitudes have certain 'appropriateness conditions'.[132] For instance, while it makes perfect sense to be indignant if my brother bites me, it seems quite inappropriate to be indignant if my *dog* bites me. Perhaps I can in such moments appropriately experience *non-reactive* attitudes such as frustration and annoyance. But insofar as my dog is incapable of *ill will* towards me, it seems misplaced and inappropriate to direct at it the *reactive* attitudes of resentment, blame and indignation.

Under what conditions, then, are the reactive attitudes appropriate? Insofar as reactive attitudes are responses to the quality of others' wills towards us, we can put this question in terms of quality of will: under what conditions can individuals be understood to possess a good or ill will?

For Gaus, there are two appropriateness conditions for the reactive attitudes. The first is that the individual to whom the reactive attitudes are directed must be 'capable of caring for a moral rule even when it does not promote her wants, ends, or goals'.[133] We can call this the *Capacity Condition*.[134] This condition explains the common belief that young children, psychopaths, dogs and others who lack minimal capacities for moral motivation should not be the targets of blame and resentment.

Gaus's second condition for the appropriateness of the reactive attitudes can be termed the *Sufficient Reason Condition*.[135] To introduce this second condition, Gaus notes that sometimes the reactive attitudes are inappropriate even when the first condition is met. Consider the case of systematic indoctrination, such as that of Winston Smith at the end of *1984*. Even though he is a fully fledged moral agent, capable of putting aside his own wants and acting on the basis of moral reasons, it is still inappropriate to feel resentment and indignation towards Smith when he embraces Big Brother because the relevant moral reasons 'are now beyond his comprehension'.[136] The Sufficient Reason Condition, then, says that the reactive attitudes are appropriately directed towards an individual who violates a moral rule only if that individual 'has sufficient reasons to endorse the relevant rule'.[137] To motivate this condition, Gaus imagines making a moral demand on an individual:

> However, I know that she does not see that it is the moral thing to, and suppose I think her lack of appreciation is quite genuine. I demand "Φ!" and she does not see

---

[131] Ibid., p. 83.
[132] Gaus, G., *The Order of Public Reason*, p. 206.
[133] Ibid., p. 211.
[134] I take this label from Taylor, A., 'Public Justification and the Reactive Attitudes', *Politics, Philosophy & Economics* 17 (2018), p. 103.
[135] This label also comes from ibid.
[136] Gaus, G., *The Order of Public Reason*, p. 218.
[137] Ibid., p. 222.

why she is obligated to Φ. She is puzzled that anyone would think Φ is obligatory. If I think this, then again I cannot reasonably feel resentment or indignation that she fails to Φ, any more than I can feel indignation at a four-year-old who is unable to detach himself from what he most wants to do and so steals some favourite candy. She just cannot see how "Φ!" has any internal authority over her.[138]

As he puts the same point in a more recent paper:

If I say to Betty "You must do this, though of course given your view, you cannot be expected to see why", and she fails to do it, I cannot see her action as manifesting ill-will to me. I have admitted that she cannot see that what I am on about gives her any reasons, nor do I think it is reasonable to expect her to see such reasons. So where is her ill-will? And if there is no ill-will, the Strawsonian reactive attitudes do not get a grip.[139]

In short, then, the first premise of Gaus's argument is that the reactive attitudes of resentment and indignation presuppose public justification because these attitudes can be appropriately harboured towards an individual who violates a moral rule only if that individual has sufficient reasons to accept the rule. The distinctive political-liberal ideal of justification *to* others, in other words, turns out on reflection to be implicit in our everyday reactive attitudes.

Suppose we accept the first premise of Gaus's argument. We accept, that is, that anyone committed to the reactive attitudes of resentment and indignation is thereby committed to public justification. Still, for this to be a compelling argument for public justification—an argument that explains why public justification is not merely a pro tanto value but a weighty constraint—we need to know more about our commitment to the reactive attitudes. In particular, we need to know why the reactive attitudes matter so much. The second premise of Gaus's argument, then, is that the reactive attitudes cannot be rationally renounced or repudiated. In making this argument, Gaus follows Strawson, who similarly claims that our commitment to the reactive attitudes is 'too thoroughgoing and deeply rooted for us to take seriously the thought' that these attitudes should be repudiated.[140] Such a thought, says Strawson, 'is, for us as we are, practically inconceivable'.[141] As Gaus put this Strawsonian point:

We are embedded in certain sorts of practices, with certain beliefs and emotions. They form part of the reasons from which we must judge, criticize, and propose

---

[138] Ibid., p. 219.
[139] Gaus, G., 'On Being Inside Social Morality and Seeing It', *Criminal Law and Philosophy* 9 (2015), p. 145.
[140] Strawson, P. F., 'Freedom and Resentment', p. 81.
[141] Ibid.

changes. A practice such as social morality is deeply embedded in our view of the world; it affects our understanding of interpersonal relations, including love and friendship, and so of what sort of life is worth living. If the presuppositions of our moral practices are so deep a part of the way we see the world, then to renounce the practice would be to renounce most of what we care for and value. But how could we have reason to do *that*? How can we survey all that matters to us and come to the conclusion that our reasons lead us to give it up, by renouncing the view of the world on which our reasons depend? Where would *that* reason come from? It is, I think, as difficult to argue a moral person out of her moral practices as it would be to argue the psychopath into them; given who they are, they do not have reasons to change their view of the world.[142]

This is a powerful passage, but one that is not easy to interpret. In particular, it is not easy to say precisely what makes it the case that we cannot rationally renounce the reactive attitudes. Is the rational non-renounceability of the reactive attitudes a claim about what is *psychologically* possible—in the same way that some hold that, given our innate selfishness, we just cannot abide by the utilitarian requirement that 'as between [our] own happiness and that of others' we be 'as strictly impartial as a disinterested and benevolent spectator'?[143] Or is it a claim about what is *conceptually* possible—in the same way that some hold that we cannot prove the legitimacy of the laws of logic without presupposing the laws of logic themselves?[144]

Regardless, the two crucial steps in Gaus's reactive attitudes argument for public justification should now be clear. If the reactive attitudes presuppose public justification, and if we cannot rationally renounce the reactive attitudes, then it follows that the public justification principle cannot be rationally renounced. Together, these two premises make up a strong case for the public justification principle: they show how a commitment to public justification follows from our unsheddable commitment to the reactive attitudes.[145]

---

[142] Gaus, G., *The Order of Public Reason*, p. 192.

[143] Mill, J. S., *Utilitarianism* (Oxford: Oxford University Press, 1998), p. 64.

[144] These two readings of Gaus correspond to the two main ways in which Strawson's original essay has been interpreted. See, for example, McKenna, M., 'Where Frankfurt and Strawson Meet', *Midwest Studies in Philosophy* 29 (2005), pp. 166–7.

[145] For critiques of this argument, though, see Taylor, A., 'Public Justification and the Reactive Attitudes'; Tahzib, C., 'Do the Reactive Attitudes Justify Public Reason?', *European Journal of Political Theory* 21 (2022), pp. 423–44.

PART II
PERFECTIONIST JUSTICE

3
A Perfectionist Conception of Society

In addition to defending a specific anti-perfectionist theory of justice, Rawls also pioneered a general framework within which to construct political theories. This framework recommends beginning with an abstract conception of society and then employing certain theoretical devices such as the original position in order to derive, from this conception of society, certain more definite principles of justice that can then be applied to specific practical problems. Notwithstanding my disagreements with Rawls and Rawlsians regarding the place of perfectionism in politics, this framework still strikes me as one of the most powerful and systematic frameworks available for expressing political ideas and thoughts. As I hope to show in the following chapters, it is a framework that can profitably be pressed in the service of perfectionist political philosophy.

We must begin, then, with the most fundamental and abstract question of all: what is the conception of society which serves as the basis of perfectionist political philosophy and to which perfectionist principles, laws and policies give expression? To answer this question, I begin by sketching the Rawlsian conception of society as a fair system of social cooperation between free and equal citizens (Section 3.1). I then ask why we should accept the Rawlsian conception of society. For Rawls, I explain (Section 3.2), the conception of society as a fair system of social cooperation between free and equal citizens recommends itself on two main grounds: first, it is a plausible and recognizable interpretation of widely accepted basic beliefs and values implicit in the public political culture of liberal-democratic societies; and second, it helps to organize our considered convictions, at all levels of generality, into a state of reflective equilibrium. I then develop an alternative perfectionist conception of society, according to which society is to be viewed for political purposes as a fair striving for human flourishing between free and equal persons (Section 3.3). I argue (in Sections 3.4 and 3.5) that this perfectionist conception of society fares at least as well as, if not better than, the Rawlsian conception of society in terms of the interpretive criterion and the justificatory criterion spelled out in Section 3.2.

A Perfectionist Theory of Justice. Collis Tahzib, Oxford University Press.
© Collis Tahzib (2022). DOI: 10.1093/oso/9780192847119.003.0004

3.1 The Rawlsian Conception of Society

A political theory often assumes, implicitly or explicitly, a particular conception of society.[1] As Rawls puts this, 'the various conceptions of justice are the outgrowth of different notions of society'.[2] Whether they are liberal, conservative, communitarian, socialist or libertarian, that is, political theories are frequently derivable from, or expressive of, some or another view about how society ought to be understood. This is especially true of Rawls, whose distinctive conception of society lies behind both his rejection of other political theories and his elaboration of his own political theory.[3] For instance, apart from his arguments from the original position, Rawls rejects classical utilitarianism on the grounds that it presupposes an unappealing conception of society, one according to which society is viewed as a kind of group agent. Classical utilitarianism, says Rawls, should be rejected because it 'adopt[s] for society as a whole the principle of rational choice for one man' and 'conflat[es] all persons into one through the imaginative acts of the impartial sympathetic spectator'.[4] Utilitarianism views society in terms of 'the efficient administration of social resources to maximize the satisfaction of the system of desire constructed by the impartial spectator from the many individual systems of desires'.[5] 'On this conception of society', Rawls explains, 'separate individuals are thought of as so many different lines along which rights and duties are to be assigned and scarce means of satisfaction allocated in accordance with rules so as to give the greatest fulfilment of wants.'[6]

Rawls's rejection of libertarian theories of justice, such as that of Robert Nozick, also appears to derive as much from ideas about the nature of society as from ideas about justice and fairness.[7] For instance, Rawls argues that citizens' prospects are affected by various kinds of contingencies, such as their upbringing and their genetic endowments, and that these contingencies are ignored by libertarian theories. 'Yet', continues Rawls, 'if we ignore the inequalities in people's prospects in life arising from these contingencies and let those inequalities work themselves out while failing to institute the regulations necessary to preserve background justice, we would not be taking seriously the idea of society as a fair system of cooperation between citizens as free and equal.'[8] Rawls also explains that a theory of justice

---

[1] For a brief but interesting analysis of some of the dominant metaphors that have been used to describe society within the history of political philosophy, see Kukathas, C., *The Liberal Archipelago: A Theory of Diversity and Freedom* (Oxford: Oxford University Press, 2003), pp. 8–9, 20–2.

[2] Rawls, J., *A Theory of Justice* (Cambridge, MA: Harvard University Press, 1971), pp. 9–10.

[3] For a discussion of this, see Pettit, P., 'Rawls's Political Ontology', *Politics, Philosophy & Economics* 4 (2005), pp. 157–74.

[4] Rawls, J., *A Theory of Justice*, pp. 26–7.

[5] Ibid., p. 33.

[6] Ibid., p. 27.

[7] See Nozick, R., *Anarchy, State, and Utopia* (New York: Basic Books, 1974).

[8] Rawls, J., *Justice as Fairness: A Restatement* (Cambridge, MA: Harvard University Press, 2001), p. 56.

must provide 'an account not only of the just initial state and of fair agreements, but also of *just social conditions* under which fair agreements are to be reached'.[9] Libertarianism, however, does not secure these 'just social conditions': 'even though the initial state may have been just, and subsequent social conditions may also have been just for some time, the accumulated results of many separate and seemingly fair agreements entered into by individuals and associations are likely over an extended period to undermine the background conditions required for free and fair agreements'.[10]

Similarly, in elaborating his own view, Rawls explains that certain of its ideas 'are more basic than others' and that most basic of all is its conception of society:

> The fundamental organizing idea of justice as fairness, within which the other basic ideas are systematically connected, is that of society as a fair system of co-operation over time, from one generation to the next. We start the exposition with this idea, which we take to be implicit in the public culture of a democratic society. In their political thought, and in the discussion of political questions, citizens do not view the social order as a fixed natural order, or as an institutional hierarchy justified by religious or aristocratic values.[11]

Having said this, Rawls is at pains to stress that his conception of society serves a very specific purpose: it is an account of how we should view society 'from the political point of view' or 'for political purposes'.[12] This conception of society is thus compatible with understanding society differently from other points of view and for other purposes. For instance, ecological conceptions of society might be premised on the holistic interconnectedness of all living beings; sociological or psychological conceptions of society might portray society as a kind of theatrical performance in which individuals are engaged in constant acts of face-saving, role-playing and self-presentation; and religious conceptions of society might view society as a fallen people in need of redemption.[13] The Rawlsian conception of society as a fair system of social cooperation does not preclude holding these other views and perspectives. The point is just that, for political purposes, these other perspectives are bracketed; a conception of society suitable for political purposes must be 'expounded apart from, or without reference to' these other doctrines and points of view.[14] As Rawls puts this point:

---

[9] Ibid., p. 53 (emphasis added).

[10] Ibid.

[11] Rawls, J., *Justice as Fairness: A Restatement*, p. 5; Rawls, J., *Political Liberalism* (New York: Columbia University Press, 2005), p. 15.

[12] Rawls, J., *Political Liberalism*, pp. 126, 200, *et passim*.

[13] For these three conceptions, see, for example, Lovelock, J., *Gaia: A New Look at Life on Earth* (Oxford: Oxford University Press, 1979); Goffman, E., *The Presentation of the Self in Everyday Life* (London: Penguin, 1990); Eliot, T. S., *The Idea of a Christian Society* (London: Faber & Faber, 1939).

[14] Rawls, J., *Political Liberalism*, p. 12.

The religious doctrines that in previous centuries were the professed basis of society have gradually given way to principles of constitutional government that all citizens, whatever their religious view, can endorse. Comprehensive philosophical and moral doctrines likewise cannot be endorsed by citizens generally, and they also no longer can, if they ever could, serve as the professed basis of society.[15]

Rawls's hope thus seems to be that his conception of society as a fair system of social cooperation can constitute a minimally acceptable basis for thinking about, and making progress on, the questions and controversies that arise within liberal-democratic politics—a basis that citizens can affirm for these political purposes, even if they conceive of society very differently in other contexts and for other purposes.

To complete the exposition of Rawls's conception of society, it is necessary to spell out his conception of the person. Indeed, Rawls explains that his conception of society 'is worked out in conjunction with' a 'companion' conception of the person:

> Since our account of justice as fairness begins with the idea that society is to be conceived as a fair system of cooperation over time between generations, we adopt a conception of the person to go with this idea. Beginning with the ancient world, the concept of the person has been understood, in both philosophy and law, as the concept of someone who can take part in, or who can play a role in, social life, and hence exercise and respect its various rights and duties. Thus, we say that a person is someone who can be a citizen, that is, a normal and fully cooperating member of society over a complete life ... Since we start within the tradition of democratic thought, we also think of citizens as free and equal.[16]

Again, Rawls stresses that his conception of persons as free and equal citizens is not intended to exclude other ways of thinking about persons. 'There are', Rawls clarifies, 'many aspects of human nature that can be singled out as especially significant, depending on our point of view. This is witnessed by such expressions as "homo politicus" and "homo oeconomicus", "homo ludens" and "homo faber".'[17] The Rawlsian conception of the person as a free and equal citizen is not meant to supply a complete description of human nature, as might be given by natural science, social theory or religion. Endorsing the Rawlsian conception of the person in political contexts does not preclude one from seeing human beings in other contexts through the lens of, say, Freudian psychoanalysis. Rather, and similarly to the Rawlsian conception of society, this is a deliberately minimal conception of the person—one that, it is hoped, can constitute a suitable basis for addressing the various political questions and controversies confronting modern liberal-democratic societies.

---

[15] Ibid., p. 10.
[16] Rawls, J., *Justice as Fairness*, p. 5; Rawls, J., *Political Liberalism*, pp. 18–19.
[17] Rawls, J., *Political Liberalism*, p. 18.

A PERFECTIONIST CONCEPTION OF SOCIETY   67

Still, while deliberately thin and designed to acknowledge the depth of disagreement within society, the Rawlsian conception of persons as free and equal citizens is not vacuous or devoid of content. Free and equal citizens are understood to have what Rawls calls 'two moral powers'—namely, the capacity for a sense of justice and the capacity for a conception of the good.[18] The capacity for a sense of justice is 'the capacity to understand, to apply, and to act from the public conception of justice.'[19] And the capacity for a conception of the good is 'the capacity to form, to revise, and rationally to pursue a conception of one's rational advantage or good'.[20] The conception of persons as free and equal citizens who participate in a fair system of social cooperation thus involves viewing persons as possessing these two moral powers to some requisite minimum degree.[21]

Rawls is aware, of course, that this conception of society as a fair system of social cooperation between free and equal citizens involves 'very considerable idealization' and abstraction.[22] It is a normative ideal, not a descriptively accurate account of society. Some citizens, for instance, lack one or both of the two moral powers. But Rawls defends the use of this abstract ideal on the grounds that it can offer a 'clear and uncluttered view' of the fundamental questions of political justice:

> The work of abstraction is not gratuitous: not abstraction for abstraction's sake. Rather, it is a way of continuing public discussion when shared understandings of lesser generality have broken down. We should be prepared to find that the deeper the conflict, the higher the level of abstraction to which we must ascend to get a clear and uncluttered view of its roots. Since the conflicts in the democratic tradition about the nature of toleration and the basis of cooperation for a footing of equality have been persistent, we may suppose they are deep. Seen in this context, formulating idealized, which is to say abstract, conceptions of society and person ... is essential to finding a reasonable political conception of justice.[23]

Pulling all of this together, we can say that the Rawlsian conception of society views society as a fair system of social cooperation between free and equal citizens who are regarded as possessing the capacity for a sense of justice and the capacity for a conception of the good. This conception of society defines the questions that Rawlsian political philosophy asks, and it motivates and constrains the answers in important ways. Understanding why we should conceive of society in this way,

---

[18] Ibid., p. 19.
[19] Ibid.
[20] Ibid.
[21] I analyse the idea of free and equal citizenship, including the two moral powers that are constitutive of such citizenship, in more depth in Section 9.3. While these ideas are incorporated into the perfectionist conception of society, they are interpreted and specified differently, as I explain in that section.
[22] Rawls, J., *Justice as Fairness*, p. 9.
[23] Rawls, J., *Political Liberalism*, pp. 45–6.

68　A PERFECTIONIST THEORY OF JUSTICE

and examining the merits of alternative conceptions of society more congenial to perfectionism, are thus vital tasks for those seeking to defend a perfectionist conception of social justice.

3.2 Why the Rawlsian Conception of Society?

Why, then, accept the Rawlsian conception of society as a fair system of social co-operation between free and equal citizens? This view of society is not, after all, self-evident. While it will strike some as morally compelling, it will likely strike others as overstating certain aspects of society and understating others. So why take it to be the conception of society of choice for political purposes—the conception of society that is uniquely suitable, or at least that is most suitable, as a basis for thinking about the political questions and controversies that confront modern liberal-democratic societies?

Rawls suggests two related criteria by which a conception of society is to be judged, which I will refer to as the *interpretive criterion* and the *justificatory criterion*:

(1) *Interpretive Criterion*: a conception of society must be a plausible and recognizable interpretation of widely accepted basic beliefs and values implicit in the public political culture of liberal-democratic societies.

(2) *Justificatory Criterion*: a conception of society must help to organize our considered convictions, at all levels of generality, into a state of reflective equilibrium.

At least two important questions arise at this point. Why ought a conception of society be judged against these criteria? And how does the Rawlsian conception of society satisfy these criteria? In this section, I shall address each of these questions in turn.

First, then, why ought a conception of society be judged against these criteria? The justificatory criterion, I take it, is fairly uncontroversial. Within moral and political philosophy, general normative principles, ideals and conceptions are frequently tested against considered convictions. But the interpretive criterion is more peculiar to Rawls, and it is natural to wonder why it matters whether a conception of society fits with the public political culture of our society. Doesn't this risk making political philosophy parochial, ethnocentric or relativistic?

While it is not possible to provide a full analysis of the interpretive or contextualist aspects of Rawls's later writings here, two points should be stressed.[24]

---

[24] For instructive discussions of these aspects of Rawls's later writings, see, for example, Baier, K., 'Justice and the Aims of Political Philosophy', *Ethics* 99 (1989), pp. 771–90; Hampton, J., 'Should Political Philosophy Be Done Without Metaphysics?', *Ethics* 99 (1989), pp. 791–814; Raz, J., 'Facing

A PERFECTIONIST CONCEPTION OF SOCIETY 69

The first is that, for Rawls, political philosophy has a 'practical role'.[25] Modern constitutional democracies, says Rawls, are marked by 'deep and sharp conflict and it seems difficult if not impossible to find any reasoned common ground for political agreement'.[26] In light of this, one of the most important roles of political philosophy is 'to focus on deeply disputed questions and to see whether, despite appearances, some underlying basis of philosophical and moral agreement can be uncovered'.[27] Political philosophers should seek to present 'a political conception of justice that can not only provide a shared public basis for the justification of political and social institutions but also helps ensure stability from one generation to the next'.[28] So, for Rawls, the proper role of political philosophy is not merely epistemic but also practical: it should seek to uncover appropriate bases for social unity and stability.

Related to this point about the proper *role* of political philosophy is a point about the proper *methods* of political philosophy. For Rawls, the methods employed by political philosophers must be suited to its practical role. A promising method for achieving social unity and stability, thinks Rawls, is to look to our political history and traditions for the fundamental ideas on which to base a conception of justice. By 'drawing upon citizens' fundamental intuitive ideas about their society and their place in it', a conception of justice has a chance of 'gaining the support of an overlapping consensus [between] the opposing religious, philosophical and moral doctrines' within modern societies.[29] As Rawls also puts this, 'what justifies a conception of justice is not its being true to an order antecedent to and given to us, but its congruence with our deeper understanding of ourselves and our aspirations, and our realization that, given our history and the traditions embedded in our public life, it is the most reasonable doctrine for us'.[30]

In short, then, the interpretive criterion is dictated by a broader view about the practical role of political philosophy and the method best suited to serve this role under conditions of reasonable pluralism. Of course, it is possible to challenge both (a) the claim that political philosophy should be oriented towards the practical aim of uncovering bases for social unity and stability and (b) the claim

---

Diversity: The Case of Epistemic Abstinence', *Philosophy & Public Affairs* 19 (1990), pp. 3–46; Rorty, R., 'The Priority of Democracy to Philosophy', in his *Objectivity, Relativism, and Truth: Philosophical Papers* (Cambridge: Cambridge University Press, 1991), pp. 175–96; Lloyd, S. A., 'Relativizing Rawls', *Chicago-Kent Law Review* 69 (1994), pp. 709–35; Neal, P., *Liberalism and Its Discontents* (New York: New York University Press, 1997), chs 5 and 6; James, A., 'Constructing Justice for Existing Practice: Rawls and the Status Quo', *Philosophy & Public Affairs* 33 (2005), pp. 281–316; Sangiovanni, A., 'Justice and the Priority of Politics to Morality', *The Journal of Political Philosophy* 16 (2008), pp. 137–64.

[25] Rawls, J., *Justice as Fairness*, p. 1.
[26] Ibid.
[27] Ibid., p. 2.
[28] Rawls, J., 'The Idea of an Overlapping Consensus', *Oxford Journal of Legal Studies* 7 (1987), p. 1.
[29] Rawls, J., 'The Idea of an Overlapping Consensus', pp. 1, 25.
[30] Rawls, J., 'Kantian Constructivism in Moral Theory', *The Journal of Philosophy* 77 (1980), p. 519.

70 A PERFECTIONIST THEORY OF JUSTICE

that constructing conceptions of justice from the resources latent in the public political culture is the method best suited to this practical aim. In relation to (a), for
instance, Rawls notes that some may worry that this 'detaches political philosophy
from philosophy and makes it into politics'.[31] As Jean Hampton puts this worry,
'politicians only want *acceptance* of ideas they (for whatever reason) are pushing; philosophers are supposed to want *truth*'.[32] Rawls's response to this charge is:
'yes and no'.[33] While it is true that 'political philosophy ... must be concerned, as
moral philosophy need not be, with practical political possibilities', political philosophy differs from politics insofar as it 'takes the longest view, looks to society's
permanent historical and social conditions, and tries to mediate society's deepest
conflicts'.[34] 'The politician', Rawls says, 'looks to the next election, the statesman
to the next generation, and philosophy to the indefinite future'.[35] In any case, my
purpose here is not to offer a full defence of Rawls's picture of the proper roles and
methods of political philosophy; the discussion is only meant to give some initial
motivation for the inclusion of the interpretive criterion.

We can turn, now, to our next question: how does the Rawlsian conception of
society satisfy these criteria? For Rawls, the idea that society should be conceived
of as a fair system of social cooperation between free and equal citizens recommends itself, in the first instance, because it is an interpretation or distillation of
basic values and principles latent in our political traditions and culture. As Rawls
explains:

> These fundamental intuitive ideas [of society as a fair system of social cooper-
> ation and of citizens as free and equal] are viewed as being familiar from the
> public political culture of a democratic society. Even though such ideas are not
> often expressly formulated, nor their meanings clearly marked out, they may play
> a fundamental role in society's political thought and in how its institutions are
> interpreted, for example, by courts and in historical or other texts regarded as
> being of enduring significance. That a democratic society is often viewed as a
> system of social cooperation is suggested by the fact that from a political point
> of view, and in the context of the public discussion of basic questions of political
> right, its citizens do not regard their social order as a fixed natural order, or as an
> institutional structure justified by religious doctrines or hierarchical principles
> expressing aristocratic values. Nor do they think a political party may properly,
> as a matter of its declared program, work to deny any recognized class or group
> its basic rights and liberties.[36]

---

[31] Rawls, J., 'The Idea of an Overlapping Consensus', p. 24.
[32] Hampton, J., 'Should Political Philosophy Be Done Without Metaphysics?', p. 807.
[33] Rawls, J., 'The Idea of an Overlapping Consensus', p. 24.
[34] Ibid.
[35] Ibid.
[36] Rawls, J., *Justice as Fairness*, pp. 5–6.

As Rawls says elsewhere, his conception of society can be 'worked up from' the way in which citizens and society are regarded in our culture's 'shared fund of implicitly recognized basic ideas and principles' and in 'the historical tradition of the interpretation' of a democratic society's 'basic political texts', such as the Declaration of Independence, the Constitution and the Bill of Rights.[37] Rawls continues: 'for these interpretations we look not only to courts, political parties, and statesmen, but also to writers on constitutional law and jurisprudence, and to the more enduring writings of all kinds that bear on a society's political philosophy'.[38] Rawls thus argues for this conception of society by citing what is common ground between us in our role as citizens of a liberal democracy, with some knowledge of or at least familiarity with its political history, its constitutional rules, its official documents, its main institutions, and so forth. In this way, the Rawlsian ideal of society is presented as being, if not explicitly endorsed, then 'at least familiar and intelligible to the educated common sense of citizens generally'.[39]

However, fit with public political culture cannot be a sufficient reason for endorsing some particular conception of society. The reason for this is fairly straightforward: namely, that the beliefs, ideas and principles found within our public political culture may be indefensible or undesirable. It is hardly philosophically satisfying to assert that *if* our historically contingent and culturally relative beliefs and values are taken for granted, *then* a certain conception of society follows. 'This', says Lloyd, may be 'a fine procedure for articulating, clarifying, and systematizing what we *already* believe. But how could such a procedure fulfill the philosophical function of justifying, or alternatively of correcting, our beliefs? And unless it fulfills that function, how could we have philosophical confidence in the conception of [society] that flows from those beliefs?'[40] Galston says that 'if someone argues that we ought to do something because it corresponds to the best interpretation of the shared understandings that constitute our culture, it is always open to me to ask why I should consider myself bound by those understandings'.[41] Why should the 'sheer factuality of culture' matter in this way?[42] Quong likewise states that developing a political theory is 'a justificatory project, not an interpretive one, and so it need not take certain facts about our public culture as static or given'.[43] In short, then, while correspondence with political culture might show that we already *do* endorse (explicitly or implicitly) a particular conception of society, it does not show that we *ought* to endorse this conception of society.

---

[37] Rawls, J., *Political Liberalism*, p. 8; Rawls, J., *Justice as Fairness*, p. 19.
[38] Rawls, J., *Justice as Fairness*, p. 19.
[39] Rawls, J., *Political Liberalism*, p. 14.
[40] Lloyd, S. A., 'Relativizing Rawls', p. 714.
[41] Galston, W., *Liberal Purposes: Goods, Virtues, and Diversity in the Liberal State* (Cambridge: Cambridge University Press, 1991), p. 158.
[42] Ibid.
[43] Quong, J., *Liberalism Without Perfection* (Oxford: Oxford University Press, 2011), p. 155.

Particularly important in this context is the concern that the public political culture of modern societies is distorted, perhaps even in deep and systematic ways, by past and present injustice. What counts as belonging to 'the more enduring writings of all kinds that bear on a society's political philosophy', for instance, is no doubt shaped by historical forces of exclusion and marginalization, which have played a significant role in the construction of the canon. Tailoring a conception of society to the most dominant or most enduring ideas within a society's public political culture, then, may simply amount to a rationalization of or an apology for an unjust status quo.[44] As Raz similarly explains, unless we are to be 'essentially complacent' about our culture and traditions, 'any moral and political theory must be open to the possibility that the societies to which it applies are fundamentally defective. Radical criticism of common institutions and common beliefs is, at least in principle, part of the function of such theories'.[45] The bare appeal to public political culture and other interpretive considerations thus runs the risk of reproducing existing patterns of injustice.

The second kind of argument, then, for the Rawlsian conception of society is that conceiving of society in this way leads to an overall theory that 'accord[s] with our considered convictions, at all levels of generality, on due reflection, or in what I have called elsewhere "reflective equilibrium"'.[46] These 'considered convictions' about social justice are the convictions 'in which we have the greatest confidence' and which are formed 'under conditions in which our capacity for judgment is most likely to have been fully exercised and not affected by distorting influences'.[47] By employing the method of reflective equilibrium in this way, we do not take the public political culture at face value: we seek to retain the finest and most worthy ideas within the public political culture while filtering out its more problematic elements. Thus, for instance, we say that citizens are to be conceived of as free and equal, despite the existence of racist elements within our public political culture, because these racist elements do not survive the auditing process of reflective equilibrium; for this reason, the Rawlsian conception of society and citizenship is superior to a racist conception of society and citizenship, even if both

---

[44] Rawls is not unaware of this worry, saying in an intriguing footnote: 'Political philosophy is always in danger of being used corruptly as a defense of an unjust and unworthy status quo, and thus of being ideological in Marx's sense. From time to time we must ask whether justice as fairness, or any other view, is ideological in this way; and if not, why not? Are the very basic ideas it uses ideological? How can we show they are not?' See *Justice as Fairness*, p. 4 n. 4. For the view that justice as fairness is indeed ideological in this way, at least in its neglect of gender and race, see, for example, Pateman, C. and Mills, C., *Contract and Domination* (Cambridge: Polity, 2007). Similarly, several early critics dismissed Rawls's view on the grounds that it is little more than an apology for late capitalism. See, for example, Wolff, R. P., *Understanding Rawls: A Reconstruction and Critique of A Theory of Justice* (Princeton, NJ: Princeton University Press, 1977).

[45] Raz, J., 'Facing Diversity', p. 19.

[46] Rawls, J., *Political Liberalism*, p. 8.

[47] Rawls, J., *A Theory of Justice*, p. 19; Rawls, J., *Justice as Fairness*, p. 29.

A PERFECTIONIST CONCEPTION OF SOCIETY   73

have deep roots in the public political culture.[48] As Rawls explains, then, the fact that his conception of society is implicit in the public political culture is not by itself sufficient to establish its validity:

> Because the exposition begins with these ideas does not mean that the argument for justice as fairness simply assumes them as a basis. Everything depends on how the exposition works out as a whole and whether the ideas and principles of this conception of justice, as well as its conclusions, prove acceptable on due reflection.[49]

A clarification is in order here: the method of reflective equilibrium does not involve merely moving back and forth between general principles and particular considered judgements, revising each until they become maximally consistent and mutually reinforcing. We also have to look to see if a view's guiding values and principles have for us what Rawls calls 'a certain intrinsic reasonableness'.[50] Consider a general principle that says that my moral duties to others are a function of their distance from me.[51] It may well be that this principle accords well with our particular considered judgements: this principle accords with, say, the intuition that we have stronger duties to a child who is drowning in a nearby pond than we do to a far-off stranger who is in similarly dire circumstances. Yet when we abstract away from these particular judgements and reflect on this principle in a more detached or theoretical manner, we begin to doubt its intrinsic reasonableness or plausibility. For while one's distance from someone in need might *correlate* with something of intrinsic moral significance (such as special relationships of co-nationality or the possibility and costliness of providing aid), it is difficult to see how, these other things equal, a person's physical location could *itself* possibly be the kind of property that possesses intrinsic and non-derivative moral significance. An important consideration in favour of the Rawlsian conception of society is thus that it expresses an ideal of society and of citizenship that has considerable intrinsic appeal and plausibility, independently of the plausibility of its more concrete implications.

3.3 An Alternative Conception of Society

Despite many decades of critical engagement with Rawls's thought, few if any have questioned his organizing conception of society in the way that one might expect:

---

[48] For more detail on how problematic elements can be filtered out of the public political culture, see Lloyd, S. A., 'Relativizing Rawls', especially pp. 716–18.

[49] Rawls, J., *Justice as Fairness*, p. 5 n. 5.

[50] Ibid., p. 30.

[51] This example is used in a related context in Ramakrishnan, K., 'Treating People as Tools', *Philosophy & Public Affairs* 44 (2016), p. 161.

namely, by articulating alternative conceptions of society, by considering how each of these alternative conceptions might generate different principles of justice and different public policies, and finally by comparing in reflective equilibrium each conception and its associated principles and policies. Instead, most commentators and critics have seemed to operate under the assumption that to deny the Rawlsian conception of society is to abandon liberalism itself. In a recent discussion, for instance, Jonathan Quong mentions the possibility of rejecting Rawls's conception of society as a fair system of social cooperation between free and equal citizens, before quickly dismissing it in one sentence: 'This seems a deeply counter-intuitive move.'[52]

It is difficult to account for this unswerving devotion to the Rawlsian conception of society. After all, the claim that society ought to be viewed for political purposes as a fair system of social cooperation between free and equal citizens is not obvious. Indeed, this conception of society is not even particularly familiar outside of academic political philosophy. As Rawls himself recognizes, this conception of society is rather 'abstract and unworldly' and is 'not often expressly formulated' in political discourse and debate.[53] A 'great shift in perspective' is required, explains Rawls, in order to take us from our everyday personal understandings of society to an understanding of society that could function as a suitable basis from which to develop a political theory applicable to modern liberal-democratic regimes.[54] None of this, of course, is a criticism of the Rawlsian conception of society. It is merely to say that we should be sceptical of any attempt to present this conception of society as a hallmark of liberalism or as a non-negotiable commitment of any political philosophy worth taking seriously.

To develop a perfectionist political theory in a compelling and systematic way, it is helpful to articulate some alternative conception of society—a *perfectionist conception of society* that could function as a fundamental organizing idea within which other more specific ideas and principles can be systematically connected and related. As with the Rawlsian conception of society, this perfectionist conception of society would then gradually be developed into a perfectionist conception of justice that has more determinate shape and content.

One might wonder whether articulating an alternative perfectionist conception of society in this way is strictly necessary in order to argue for perfectionism. After all, the Rawlsian conception of society as a fair system of social cooperation between free and equal citizens is very general, and arguably is consistent with both perfectionism and anti-perfectionism. So isn't it possible to begin the case for perfectionism at a lower level of abstraction by arguing that perfectionist politics represents the best way of working out the details of the Rawlsian conception

---

[52] Quong, J., *Liberalism Without Perfection*, p. 220.
[53] Rawls, J., *Political Liberalism*, p. lx; Rawls, J., *Justice as Fairness*, p. 6.
[54] Rawls, J., 'Kantian Constructivism in Moral Theory', p. 551.

of society?[55] As I explain in Sections 3.4 and 3.5, however, there is a case to be made that conceiving of society as a fair system of social cooperation is not entirely adequate from a perfectionist perspective. Moreover, as I argue in Sections 6.6 and 6.7, many of the existing arguments for perfectionist policies that appeal to the values implicit in the Rawlsian conception of society—values such as freedom, equality and fairness—are not convincing. I am thus inclined to think that articulating an alternative perfectionist conception of society is indeed necessary in order to make a persuasive case for perfectionism. But even if articulating such a conception is not in the end strictly necessary, it still remains a fruitful way to develop a perfectionist political theory on strong and distinctive normative foundations—or so I hope to show.

In articulating a perfectionist conception of society, one need not reject outright the Rawlsian conception of society. Perfectionists might argue that Rawls's conception of society as a fair system of social cooperation between free and equal citizens is not so much mistaken as incomplete. Many options are available here. Perhaps, for instance, society ought to be conceived of as a fair system of social cooperation *and a striving for human flourishing* between free and equal citizens.[56] Or perhaps we should say that society is a fair system of social cooperation between citizens regarded as free and equal *and pursuers of human flourishing*. Regardless of the specifics, the thought here is that perfectionist political philosophy begins with an amplified conception of society—one that makes essential reference to the idea of human flourishing, thus bringing to the fore what is for perfectionists a central and unignorable aspect of society omitted by the Rawlsian conception.

In particular, the perfectionist theory of justice developed in this work is based on a conception of society as *a fair striving for human flourishing between free and equal citizens*. This is the fundamental normative ideal from which we derive the perfectionist principles of justice as well as perfectionist laws and public policies. As Rawls rightly states, there are many aspects of individual and collective life that can be singled out as especially significant depending on our point of view. But whereas Rawls takes human flourishing to be an aspect of society that is unnecessary and even unhelpful for political purposes—whereas Rawls takes it that we can construct acceptable political principles and policies out of a conception of society that makes no essential reference to human flourishing—from a perfectionist point of view this aspect of society is of such primacy that it cannot be ignored for political purposes and must be baked directly into our organizing conception of society.

---

[55] I thank Steven Wall for pressing me on this point.

[56] In earlier work, I defended this view: see Tahzib, C., 'Perfectionism: Political not Metaphysical', *Philosophy & Public Affairs* 47 (2019), pp. 144–78. But the conception of society that I now favour (as discussed in the main text) strikes me as synthesizing perfectionist and liberal elements in a simpler and more principled way. I thank Jeremy Goodman, Henrik Kugelberg, Janet Levin, Jake Ross and Kadri Vihvelin for helpful feedback and discussion of this point.

Here it is worth stressing that, in moving away from the Rawlsian conception of society as a fair system of social cooperation, I do not mean to deny the importance of cooperation between citizens. It is certainly not being suggested, for instance, that society ought to be viewed as some sort of competitive power struggle between individuals or groups. The point is simply that the perfectionist conception of society places primary emphasis on the idea of a fair striving for human flourishing and not on the idea of a fair system of social cooperation. Other ideas, including that of social cooperation, are to be explained and specified later in terms of the fundamental perfectionist conception of society.

What exactly does it mean to say that society is to be conceived of as a fair striving for human flourishing between free and equal citizens? In what ways does a society that reflects this perfectionist ideal differ, practically speaking, from one that reflects the Rawlsian ideal? How do we know that these aren't just different labels applied to the same tin? Couldn't anti-perfectionist liberals argue that their favoured principles of justice already give adequate expression to the ideal of society as a fair striving for human flourishing between free and equal citizens? These questions will be answered throughout Part II as the content of this conception of society is progressively unfolded, but, even at this stage, it is possible to point to one important difference between the perfectionist and Rawlsian conceptions of society—a difference that may well raise eyebrows among anti-perfectionist liberals. In particular, the perfectionist conception of society takes human flourishing to be a final end or goal of society, and this influences in important ways the perfectionist theory that follows. In this regard, the perfectionist conception of society aligns with Joseph Chan's remark that 'the purpose of living together in a complex community is precisely to enable people to pursue a better life in material, social, and cultural terms. In the course of pursuing better lives, no doubt justice needs to be observed—physical security needs to be protected, opportunities distributed fairly, and rights respected—but we should not lose sight of the fundamental point that people live together not for justice but for pursuing better lives'.[57]

By contrast, Rawls stresses that within his theory 'society has no final ends and aims in the way that persons or associations do'.[58] The only ends that Rawls is willing to attribute to society are 'constitutionally specified' ends such as 'the blessings of liberty [and] the common defence'.[59] He is also prepared to say that justice is itself the goal of social cooperation. Rawls explains that citizens 'cooperate to achieve their common shared end of justice' and that 'their cooperation is to assure one another political justice'.[60] In restricting the final ends or goals of society

---

[57] Chan, J., 'Political Authority and Perfectionism: A Response to Quong', *Philosophy and Public Issues* 2 (2012), p. 40.
[58] Rawls, J., *Political Liberalism*, p. 41.
[59] Ibid.
[60] Ibid., p. 42 n. 44.

A PERFECTIONIST CONCEPTION OF SOCIETY 77

in this way, says Rawls, a properly liberal state distinguishes itself from perfectionist societies of the past, which 'pursued as final ends religion and empire, dominion and glory'.[61] The examples of perfectionist ends that Rawls provides, however, are unfortunate because they give the misleading impression that a perfectionist conception of society must be theocratic or imperialistic in nature. Perfectionists can readily accept that modern societies have no final ends or aims of the kind that Rawls mentions. Their only contention is that this does not rule out some other perfectionist ideal that has broader appeal and that is more at home in modern thought, such as human flourishing, from serving as one of the final ends of a liberal-democratic society.

The political theory developed in this work is therefore not 'rights-based' (as in the case of Dworkin's theory of liberal equality, which holds that all individuals have a right to equal concern and respect from their government), or 'duty-based' (as in the case of Kantian deontology, which holds that all individuals are under a duty to treat other persons as ends and not as mere means), or 'goal-based' (as in the case of classical utilitarianism, which holds that right action is that which maximizes overall welfare), to invoke Dworkin's scheme for classifying political theories.[62] It does not give pride of place to any one of these concepts, treating other rights, duties and goals as derivative therefrom. I agree with Rawls that this typology is 'too narrow and leaves out important possibilities'.[63] Rather, the view developed in this work is an instance of what Rawls calls a 'conception-based' view: a view that treats as fundamental a certain conception of society and that seeks to relate other ideas to this conception in a systematic and mutually reinforcing way. Rights, duties and goals all enter later in the story as elements of this conception of society. In this way, the perfectionist theory defended in this work differs from most contemporary perfectionist theories, which have tended to have a goal-based or consequentialist structure.[64]

3.4 The Perfectionist Conception as Cultural Interpretation

In order to adjudicate between these rival conceptions of society—society as a fair system of social cooperation between free and equal citizens, and society as a fair striving for human flourishing between free and equal citizens—we have to return to the criteria outlined in Section 3.2. In particular, we have to ask whether the

---

[61] Ibid., p. 41.

[62] Dworkin, R., *Taking Rights Seriously* (Cambridge, MA: Harvard University Press, 1978), especially pp. 169–77.

[63] Rawls, J., 'Justice as Fairness: Political not Metaphysical', *Philosophy & Public Affairs* 14 (1985), p. 236 n. 19.

[64] See, for example, Hurka's defence of agent-neutral consequentialist perfectionism in *Perfectionism* (Oxford: Oxford University Press, 1993), especially ch. 5. Hurka suggests (esp. pp. 55–6) that most historical perfectionists have also been consequentialist perfectionists.

perfectionist conception of society fares as well as, or perhaps even better than, the Rawlsian conception of society in terms of the interpretive and justificatory criteria.

Let us begin, then, by considering the perfectionist conception of society in light of the interpretive criterion. Is the perfectionist conception of society as a fair striving for human flourishing between free and equal citizens a plausible and recognizable interpretation of widely accepted basic beliefs and values implicit in the public political culture of liberal-democratic societies? How, to put it differently, does the perfectionist conception of society fare as cultural interpretation?

This is a very difficult question to answer. We first need to know the answer to a number of other questions about how exactly to understand Rawls's interpretive criterion: what is the 'public political culture' of a democratic society? How is the political culture of a society to be distinguished from *other* forms of culture within that society? What, in other words, is the mark of the 'political'? Given that, as Rawls admits, 'the public political culture may be of two minds even at a very deep level', is it even appropriate to talk of *the* public political culture?[65] Shouldn't we instead think in terms of public political cultures? If, as Rawls suggests, the public political culture includes historical texts 'of enduring significance', then which historical texts count? How far back into our history should we look? If the public political culture includes the pronouncements of 'courts', then which courts and which pronouncements? If it includes the speeches of 'statesmen', then which statesmen and which speeches? What percentage of citizens must actually endorse a given idea or value, and over how many generations must it have been endorsed in this way, in order for it to count as 'part of' the public political culture?

Reading a conception of society off the public political culture—saying that one or another conception of society is 'implicit in' or 'familiar from' the public political culture of liberal-democratic societies, as Rawls does—is thus a very complicated exercise, one that raises a multitude of sociological, historical and philosophical questions. Without an answer to these questions, it is difficult to see how we can decide, in a rigorous and non-impressionistic way, either (i) whether a given conception of society really is a plausible and recognizable interpretation of widely accepted basic beliefs and values implicit in the public political culture of liberal-democratic societies or (ii) which of two rival conceptions of society does this to a superior degree.

At this point, one might think that a natural and helpful place to turn to for insight would be Rawls. Does Rawls offer a well-developed theory of cultural interpretation? What reasons does Rawls give to establish that his own conception of society is implicit in the public political culture? Perfectionists might then be able to consider whether these reasons apply to the perfectionist conception of society too.

---

[65] Rawls, J., 'Justice as Fairness', pp. 228–9.

Unfortunately, however, Rawls is surprisingly breezy and speculative when seeking to demonstrate that his conception of society as a fair system of social cooperation between free and equal citizens is an interpretation of values and principles implicit in the public political culture of liberal-democratic societies. As Aaron James puts this point, Rawls 'does not explicitly carry out the dirty work of interpretive argument'.[66] Rawls's most extensive discussion of this vital issue appears to be in the one short paragraph quoted in Section 3.2. It is worth reproducing that passage here:

> These fundamental intuitive ideas are viewed as being familiar from the public political culture of a democratic society. Even though such ideas are not often expressly formulated, nor their meanings clearly marked out, they may play a fundamental role in society's political thought and in how its institutions are interpreted, for example, by courts and in historical or other texts regarded as being of enduring significance. That a democratic society is often viewed as a system of social cooperation is suggested by the fact that from a political point of view, and in the context of the public discussion of basic questions of political right, its citizens do not regard their social order as a fixed natural order, or as an institutional structure justified by religious doctrines or hierarchical principles expressing aristocratic values. Nor do they think a political party may properly, as a matter of its declared program, work to deny any recognized class or group its basic rights and liberties.[67]

Rawls appears to adduce three distinct reasons here for thinking that his conception of society as a fair system of social cooperation between free and equal citizens is implicit in the public political culture of modern liberal-democratic societies. All of them, however, suffer from a common problem: while these reasons rule out *certain* alternative conceptions of society (for instance, racist, authoritarian or theocratic conceptions of society), they do not rule out *all* alternatives and thus do not uniquely pick out the Rawlsian conception of society as a fair system of social cooperation between free and equal citizens. In particular, these reasons do not rule out the specific alternative conception developed in Section 3.3—namely, society as a striving for human flourishing on fair terms between free and equal citizens. Here is another way of putting this point: if showing that a conception of society can accommodate ideas found in 'texts regarded as being of enduring significance', or that it does not see society as an aristocratic or religious 'fixed natural order', or that it respects 'basic rights and liberties' is all it takes to show that a conception of society is implicit in the public political culture of liberal-democratic societies, then not only the Rawlsian conception of society

---

[66] James, A., 'Constructing Justice for Existing Practice', p. 305.
[67] Rawls, J., *Justice as Fairness*, pp. 5–6.

80 A PERFECTIONIST THEORY OF JUSTICE

but also the perfectionist conception of society will qualify as implicit in our public political culture.

To show this more clearly, let us consider Rawls's three reasons in greater depth. First, Rawls says that his conception of society has its roots in court decisions and historical texts 'of enduring significance'—by which he presumably has in mind the Declaration of Independence, the Constitution and the Bill of Rights, as well as the decisions of the Supreme Court. Though he does not explicitly connect his conception of society with a close reading of these historical texts or court opinions, Rawls presumably means that his conception of society makes direct reference to values such as freedom, equality and fairness and that, correspondingly, these texts of enduring significance speak of 'the blessings of liberty' (in the Preamble to the Constitution), of 'equal protection' (in the Fourteenth Amendment to the Constitution) and of the need to 'establish justice' (in the Preamble to the Constitution). But the problem with this argument is that the same can be said of the perfectionist conception of society: after all, insofar as it regards society as a *fair* striving for human flourishing between *free* and *equal* citizens, it, too, makes direct reference to values such as freedom, equality and fairness and corresponds with the language of these texts. So while consistency with texts of enduring significance might tell against an authoritarian conception of society that rejects the values of freedom, equality and fairness, it does not tell against the perfectionist conception of society.

Second, Rawls says that the implicitness-in-public-culture of his conception of society is supported by the fact that most citizens do not regard their social order as 'an institutional structure justified by religious doctrines or hierarchical principles expressing aristocratic values'. But, again, while this consideration casts doubt on religious or aristocratic conceptions of society, it does not tell against the perfectionist conception of society articulated above. The perfectionist conception of society does not make reference to God, the Church or the salvation of souls; nor does it refer to nobility, class or hereditary rank. Of course, this conception does refer to the idea of human flourishing, and one might worry that this idea, when concretized, could open the doors to religious or aristocratic values. I address this sort of worry later on—in particular in Sections 4.4 and 5.1 and in Chapter 7—when this conception of society is given more determinate content. But, for the moment, it suffices to say that there is no clear reason why the perfectionist conception of society must be inconsistent with the belief of the majority of citizens in modern liberal democracies that society is not 'an institutional structure justified by religious doctrines or hierarchical principles expressing aristocratic values'. Again, then, this reason for thinking that the Rawlsian conception of society is a plausible and recognizable interpretation of widely accepted basic beliefs and values implicit in the public political culture of liberal-democratic societies applies equally well to the perfectionist conception of society.

Third, Rawls argues that the fact that most people do not think that a political party may 'work to deny any recognized class or group its basic rights and liberties' supports the claim that his conception of society is implicit in public political culture. But, as before, while this fact gives us reason to doubt the implicitness-in-public-culture of racist or authoritarian conceptions of society (which can be expected to lead to political arrangements that deny basic rights and liberties), it gives us no reason to doubt that the perfectionist conception of society is implicit in the public political culture of liberal-democratic societies. For, to repeat, the perfectionist conception of society sees society as a striving for human flourishing on *fair* terms between *free* and *equal* citizens—where the inclusion of the values of freedom, equality and fairness gives rise to principles of social justice that are respectful of basic rights and liberties, as I go on to explain in Chapters 4 and 8.

In short, even if Rawls's three reasons do rule out some conceptions of society, they *underdetermine* the choice between the Rawlsian and the perfectionist conceptions of society: these three reasons do not tell us why we should regard the Rawlsian conception of society as any more plausible or recognizable an interpretation of the beliefs and values implicit in the public political culture of liberal-democratic societies than the perfectionist conception of society. So until we are given more details about how to read conceptions of society off the public political culture in a non-impressionistic way, it seems reasonable to say that the reasons Rawls gives in support of his own conception of society's implicitness or embeddedness within the public political culture of liberal-democratic societies can carry over unproblematically in support of the perfectionist conception of society's implicitness or embeddedness within the public political culture of liberal-democratic societies.[68]

---

[68] One might try to rescue Rawls's arguments by distinguishing between consistency and coherence. Even if the perfectionist conception of society is consistent with the public political culture, perhaps the Rawlsian conception of society is more coherent with this culture, in the sense that the public political culture stands in a stronger and more direct relation to the Rawlsian conception of society. The thought here is that while the ideas within the public political culture that Rawls identifies—such as that society is not a fixed natural order and that political parties may not work to deny any group its basic rights and liberties—might not *exclude* the perfectionist conception of society, they *fit better*, in some sense, with the Rawlsian conception of society as a fair system of social cooperation between free and equal citizens. (I thank Elvio Baccarini for putting this objection to me.) It is unclear to me, however, what basis there is for saying that the public political culture stands in a stronger or more direct relation to, or fits better with, the Rawlsian conception of society than the perfectionist conception of society—and thus what basis there is for saying that the Rawlsian conception is coherent with the public political culture, whereas the perfectionist conception is merely consistent therewith. The ideas of freedom, equality and fairness are, after all, essential elements of the perfectionist conception of society. There is a very strong and direct relation between the perfectionist conception of society and the ideas that society is not a fixed natural order and that political parties may not work to deny any group its basic rights and liberties. All that differs between the conceptions is an emphasis on human flourishing rather than social cooperation—and, as I shall go on to explain in the rest of this section, it is possible to argue, on this basis, that it is in fact the perfectionist conception of society that stands in a stronger or more direct relation to, or fits better with, the public political culture.

82   A PERFECTIONIST THEORY OF JUSTICE

It is possible to go further still. So far, I have argued that, for all Rawls has said, the perfectionist conception of society is *as* plausible and recognizable an interpretation of the values and beliefs implicit in our public political culture as the Rawlsian conception of society. I have argued, in other words, that Rawls's reasons for thinking that his conception of society grows out of the public political culture apply *equally well* to the perfectionist conception of society. But it is possible to argue that, if anything, the perfectionist conception of society is even *more* implicit and embedded within public political culture than the Rawlsian conception of society, since the perfectionist conception accommodates important parts of the public political culture that the Rawlsian conception leaves out.

To see this, it is helpful to examine two examples of statements, by individuals who presumably qualify as having enduring significance, about how society ought to be viewed from the political point of view. Both of these passages align much more naturally with the view of society as a fair striving for human flourishing than with the view of society as a fair system of social cooperation.

Consider, first, the understanding of society expressed by James Wilson, one of the Founding Fathers of the United States and one of the signatories of the Declaration of Independence and of the Constitution:

> Society ought to be preserved in peace; most unquestionably. But is this all? Ought it not to be improved as well as protected? Look at individuals: observe them from infancy to youth, from youth to manhood. Such is the order of Providence with regard to society. It is in a progressive state, moving on towards perfection. How is this progressive state to be assisted and accelerated? Principally by teaching the young 'ideas how to shoot', and the young affections how to move. What intrinsically can be more dignified, than to assist in preparing tender and ingenuous minds for all the great purposes, for which they are intended! What, I repeat it, can intrinsically be more dignified, than to assist in forming a future Cicero, or a future Bacon, without the vanity of one, and without the meanness of the other![69]

Consider, next, the following more recent statement from a speech of Robert F. Kennedy while on the campaign trail in 1968:

> Too much and too long, we seemed to have surrendered community excellence and community values in the mere accumulation of material things. Our gross national product is now over eight hundred billion dollars a year, but that GNP ... counts the destruction of our redwoods and the loss of our natural wonder in chaotic sprawl. It counts napalm and the cost of a nuclear warhead, and armored

---

[69] Wilson, J., *The Works of James Wilson, Volume 1*, ed. R. McCloskey (Cambridge, MA: Harvard University Press, 1967), p. 84.

cars for police who fight riots in our streets. It counts Whitman's rifle and Speck's knife, and the television programs which glorify violence in order to sell toys to our children. Yet gross national product does not allow for the health of our children, the quality of their education, or the joy of their play. It does not include the beauty of our poetry or the strength of our marriages; the intelligence of our public debate or the integrity of our public officials. It measures neither our wit nor our courage; neither our wisdom nor our learning; neither our compassion nor our devotion to our country; it measures everything, in short, except that which makes life worthwhile.[70]

Both of these passages, despite the span of time that separates them, make a similar point. They begin by rejecting the thought that some or another end (peace in Wilson's case and total economic activity in Kennedy's case) is sufficient for a society. However important these values are, they do not by themselves get to the core of a society's rightful self-conception. Each individual then goes on to state what, in addition, is fundamental to, or constitutive of, society. In doing so, neither mentions social cooperation. Both instead speak to the moral, intellectual and artistic dimensions of human flourishing: poetry, wit, courage, wisdom, learning and the avoidance of vanity and meanness are among the ideas referred to. These are presented as ineliminable features of society; a proper understanding of society simply cannot be 'expounded apart from, or without reference to', these ideas.[71] The suggestion in both passages, in other words, seems to be that conceiving of society merely as a fair system of social cooperation is not a minimally adequate description of society, even (and perhaps especially) for political purposes. Wilson and Kennedy appear to suggest instead that something more like the perfectionist conception of society is needed—a conception that includes the striving for human flourishing as a constitutive and essential feature of society.

Of course, one might want to object here that the passages I have cited are cherry-picked to align with the perfectionist conception of society—that these passages are little more than self-serving anecdotes. To some extent, this objection is valid. To convincingly and rigorously establish that the perfectionist conception of society fares better than the Rawlsian conception of society by the lights of the interpretive criterion, we need a well-developed account of cultural interpretation, one that addresses the sociological, historical and philosophical questions mentioned at the outset of this section. But, still, the passages quoted above do strike me as suggestive: they come from individuals of enduring cultural and political significance, and they do appear to indicate a rich and deep

---

[70] Guthman, E. and Allen, C. (eds), *RFK: His Words for Our Times* (New York: Harper Collins, 2018), pp. 333–4.
[71] Rawls, J., *Political Liberalism*, p. 12.

strain of perfectionism within our public political culture as it relates to the question of how society ought to be understood. Moreover, Rawls and Rawlsians have not provided noticeably more systematic and empirically informed arguments for the implicitness-in-public-political-culture of the Rawlsian conception of society. So it seems reasonable to maintain that the perfectionist and Rawlsian conceptions of society are roughly on a par so far as implicitness in and coherence with public political culture is concerned, and that, if anything, the perfectionist conception of society coheres even better with that culture as it is sensitive to distinctively perfectionist strains within the public political culture of liberal-democratic societies.

Let me close this section with a comment on what may initially seem an unrelated topic—namely, the stability of a perfectionist conception of justice. An important issue for perfectionists to consider is whether a well-ordered society regulated by their preferred perfectionist principles can be expected to be appropriately stable over time. After all, for Rawls an important virtue of political liberalism is that it would be 'stable for the right reasons', since it would 'gain the support of an overlapping consensus [between the] opposing religious, philosophical, and moral doctrines likely to persist over generations and to gain a sizable body of adherents in a more or less just constitutional regime'.[72] Indeed, as we saw in Section 3.2, Rawls regards it as one of the fundamental aims of political philosophy to present a conception of justice that can 'help [to] ensure stability from one generation to the next'.[73] So can a perfectionist conception of justice be expected similarly to command the sort of overlapping consensus necessary for stability (or stability for the right reasons)?[74]

Some perfectionists may respond by denying that a society's being stable (or stable for the right reasons) depends on it seeing some sort of overlapping consensus between comprehensive doctrines. As was mentioned in Section 2.3.2, very many factors contribute to the stability of society: a culture of civility and toleration, respect for rights, checks and balances on political institutions, national sentiment and community ties, economic development, and so on.[75] So even if overlapping consensus is one factor that contributes to social stability, is it really a *necessary* condition thereof, such that, in the absence of overlapping consensus, these other factors would not be jointly sufficient to sustain social stability (or stability for the right reasons)?

Here, though, we will set aside this response and say, with Rawls, that stability (or stability for the right reasons) does depend in some way on there being

---

[72] Ibid., p. 15.

[73] Rawls, J., 'The Idea of an Overlapping Consensus', p. 1.

[74] I thank Giulia Bistagnino, Federica Liveriero and Tom Sinclair for pressing me on the question of perfectionism's stability.

[75] See Wendt, F., *Compromise, Peace and Public Justification: Political Morality Beyond Justice* (London: Palgrave Macmillan, 2016), pp. 145–6.

an overlapping consensus between comprehensive doctrines. There are different ways of interpreting Rawls's reflections on stability and overlapping consensus. In particular, there are different interpretations of what the *subject* of overlapping consensus must be. But on Quong's interpretation, which I find compelling, 'the subject of the consensus should be the fundamental idea of society as a fair system of cooperation between free and equal people, rather than any specific principles or conception of justice'.[76] On this view, the Rawlsian ideal of society 'provides the initial common ground' and 'the normative material' from which free-standing arguments proceed, but there need not be any direct congruence between those further free-standing arguments and comprehensive doctrines in order for the free-standing arguments to be fully justified. There is no 'second stage' test of stability—no 'group which has the normative power to veto or modify valid free-standing arguments'.[77] Rather, 'overlapping consensus represents the beginning, not the end, of political justification'.[78]

Assuming that this is the right way to interpret Rawls's stability argument, the question about perfectionism's stability (or its stability for the right reasons) becomes a question about whether the fundamental perfectionist ideal of society as a fair striving for human flourishing between free and equal citizens can be expected to be the subject of an overlapping consensus between the comprehensive doctrines that would be likely to persist over generations and to gain a sizeable body of supporters in a more or less just regime. For the reasons given in this section, among others, I am inclined to think that the perfectionist ideal of society is a plausible candidate for overlapping consensus of this kind. The evidence for the perfectionist conception of society's implicitness within our public political culture, that is, plausibly doubles up as evidence for this conception's prospects of commanding an overlapping consensus among different comprehensive doctrines. Moreover, many of the reasons given by Rawlsians for why we can expect there to be congruence between the Rawlsian ideal of society and comprehensive doctrines—for instance, the fact that the Rawlsian ideal of society is pitched at a high level of abstraction and the fact that most comprehensive doctrines contain what Rawls calls 'a certain looseness' and 'slippage' that allows them to be understood in ways that support the Rawlsian ideal of society—apply equally well to the perfectionist ideal of society.[79]

Of course, as it stands, this is little more than speculation. A full assessment of the question of stability (or stability for the right reasons) would require an analysis of the compatibility of the contents of numerous specific comprehensive doctrines with the perfectionist conception of society, as well as an analysis of a great deal of evidence from political sociology and moral psychology. But here

---

[76] Quong, J., *Liberalism Without Perfection*, p. 163.
[77] Ibid., p. 186.
[78] Ibid., p. 163.
[79] See, for example, ibid., p. 185; Rawls, J., *Political Liberalism*, pp. 159–60.

86   A PERFECTIONIST THEORY OF JUSTICE

it seems only fair to recall that Rawls's stability argument is also by his own admission 'speculative'.[80] He does not spend much time looking inside the various comprehensive doctrines, one by one, in order to see whether they contain the resources to support his conception of society and instead relies to a large extent on 'educated conjecture' and 'hope'.[81]

3.5 The Perfectionist Conception in Reflective Equilibrium

Let us now consider the perfectionist conception of society in light of the justificatory criterion. Does the perfectionist conception of society as a fair striving for human flourishing between free and equal citizens help to organize our considered convictions, at all levels of generality, into a state of reflective equilibrium?

We cannot, yet, provide a full answer to this question. We can only determine whether the perfectionist conception of society helps to make sense of our considered convictions at all levels of generality once we have put forward a fully worked-out perfectionist theory of justice—a theory that begins with this abstract perfectionist conception of society but that goes on to derive therefrom certain more specific principles of justice and that then considers the application of these principles of justice to some specific questions of law and public policy. This is the work of subsequent chapters; only at the end of the day can we decide whether reflective equilibrium has been attained. Everything depends on how the view hangs together in its totality. In a sense, then, this work as a whole is a sustained attempt to show that conceiving of society as a fair striving for human flourishing between free and equal citizens survives the auditing process of reflective equilibrium: that this conception of society leads to an overall political outlook that organizes our considered convictions at all levels of generality into a consistent, mutually reinforcing and morally attractive system.

Still, although a full answer to the question of whether the perfectionist conception of society satisfies the justificatory criterion must await the arguments of later chapters, it is possible to make some initial comments at this stage. In particular, we can comment on whether the abstract perfectionist conception of society accords with the considered convictions we have at the highest level of generality. Recall that, for Rawls, we have to consider whether a political theory's fundamental organizing ideals possess 'a certain intrinsic reasonableness'.[82] And when we reflect on the perfectionist conception of society as a fair striving for human flourishing between free and equal citizens in a detached and theoretical manner, it does possess, or so it seems to me, considerable intrinsic appeal and plausibility—at least as

---

[80] Rawls, J., *Political Liberalism*, p. 15.
[81] Ibid., pp. 15, 40, 65, 172, 246, 252, 392.
[82] Rawls, J., *Justice as Fairness*, p. 30.

much intrinsic appeal and plausibility as the Rawlsian conception of society. Even before we consider whether the perfectionist conception of society yields verdicts at lower levels of generality that match our considered judgements, that is, it seems to express an ideal that is plausible and attractive in its own right.

It is difficult to say anything especially precise or sophisticated by way of substantiating these sorts of reflections about intrinsic reasonableness. Nonetheless, two supporting considerations are worth noting here. The first is that something akin to the perfectionist conception of society has a rich heritage within perfectionist thought and has been defended by historically significant thinkers of the past, including those mentioned in Section 3.4. Aristotle, for instance, holds that 'the political fellowship must ... be deemed to exist for the sake of noble actions, not merely for living in common'.[83] He says that 'the good life then is the chief aim of society, both collectively for all its members and individually'.[84] Of course, showing that the perfectionist conception of society is continuous with a long tradition of thought does not by itself prove its intrinsic reasonableness or plausibility. But what it does do is dispel the worry that the perfectionist conception of society lacks deep motivation and has merely been artificially constructed as an ad hoc device for critiquing Rawls and other anti-perfectionists—a worry which, if true, might cast doubt on the intrinsic plausibility of the perfectionist conception of society.

The second supporting consideration comes from reflecting on a society that satisfies the Rawlsian conception yet fails to realize various components of human flourishing. Consider the following case:

> *Degradia*: Degradia is a society with impeccable liberal credentials. All citizens treat each other in accordance with the requirements of freedom, equality and fairness. The state protects the rights and liberties of all citizens. People pay their taxes, vote in elections, and perform other civic duties. In this sense, Degradia functions as a fair system of social cooperation between free and equal citizens. However, beyond this, the citizens in Degradia live hollow lives because the vast majority of them spend the vast majority of their free time playing videogames. For many, this means playing videogames from morning until night, with only small breaks. The overall result of this societal obsession with videogames is that Degradia lacks artistic excellence, intellectual feats, bonds of community and other dimensions of human flourishing.

There is, I claim, something deeply troubling about the society depicted here— something troubling not just from the point of view of a personal morality but also from the political point of view. It is important to be clear about the nature of this claim. I am not here saying anything about the justness or unjustness of

---

[83] Aristotle, *The Politics*, trans. H. Rackham (Cambridge, MA: Harvard University Press, 1990), p. 219.
[84] Ibid., p. 201.

Degradia. Principles of justice are the subject of Chapter 4. Rather, at this point, we are adjudicating between two rival normative ideals of society—the Rawlsian ideal and the perfectionist ideal. So the claim I am making is specifically a normative evaluation of Degradia *as a society*: it is that Degradia is unappealing as a society, or that it does not function as a society should, or something in this vicinity. For someone who conceives of society as a fair striving for human flourishing between free and equal citizens, this judgement is easy to accommodate. After all, Degradia does not plausibly instantiate a striving for human flourishing. But it is much less clear how a defender of the Rawlsian conception of society can accommodate this judgement, since ex hypothesi Degradia functions as a fair system of social cooperation between free and equal citizens.

Of course, it may be that, in the end, defenders of the Rawlsian conception of society have an adequate response to the case of Degradia. Perhaps Degradia is under-described and once its details are fully spelled out, we will notice that members of this society do not, after all, realize a fair system of social cooperation between free and equal citizens. By spending so much time playing videogames, for instance, members of Degradia may neglect duties that they owe to others qua members of a fair system of social cooperation. In this sense, the stipulation that Degradia functions as a fair system of social cooperation between free and equal citizens may turn out to be incompatible with the other stipulations of the case, and so what is troubling about Degradia may ultimately be explainable in terms of the Rawlsian conception of society and the values implicit within it, such as freedom, equality, fairness and the social bases of self-respect. Alternatively, perhaps one ought to bite the bullet: if this society truly does realize a fair system of social cooperation between free and equals, then whether citizens choose generally to spend the vast majority of their free time playing videogames should not be troubling. Perhaps, for instance, our intuitions about what features of society should be regarded as unappealing or problematic from the political point of view are polluted by our intuitions about what features of a society should be regarded as problematic from the point of view of personal morality—and that, from the strictly political point of view, there is nothing amiss if a free society chooses to organize itself along the lines of Degradia.

Here is not the place to try to evaluate these responses, for, in a sense, they are ways of expressing thoughts and arguments that will be considered under more precise guises later in this work. Cases that are structurally similar to *Degradia* therefore recur at several junctures, such as the case of *Betty of Mediocria* in Section 6.6.4 and the cases of *Anna*, *Barry* and *Callum* in Section 7.4. For now, the important point is that reflection on the case of *Degradia* can serve to motivate an abstract and high-level judgement about the intrinsic plausibility of the perfectionist conception of society as a fair striving for human flourishing between free and equal citizens.

4

Perfectionist Principles of Justice

In Chapter 3, I argued for a perfectionist conception of society as a fair striving for human flourishing between free and equal citizens, as an alternative and a competitor to the Rawlsian conception of society as a fair system of social cooperation between free and equal citizens. But this perfectionist conception of society is pitched at a high level of generality and abstraction, and so it is still unclear how the perfectionist conception of society comes apart from the Rawlsian conception. What we now need to do is to work this perfectionist conception of society into principles of justice that have more definite content. In other words, we need to answer the question: what principles are the most appropriate for regulating a society conceived of as a fair striving for human flourishing between free and equal citizens?

There are many ways of tackling this difficult question. It turns out, however, that perfectionists can profitably employ an original position device in order to move from an abstract perfectionist conception of society to more determinate perfectionist principles of justice—just as Rawls employed an original position device in order to move from his conception of society to his principles of justice. On this approach, we make progress on the question of what principles are most appropriate for regulating a society conceived of as a fair striving for human flourishing between free and equal citizens by considering the hopefully more manageable question of what principles would be agreed upon by parties in a suitably specified contractual situation.

To get a feel for the contractualist style of argument, I begin by reviewing Rawls's use of the original position—the details of its set-up (Section 4.1) and the argument for why parties in Rawls's original position would agree to the principles that they do (Section 4.2). I then show (in Section 4.3) how the original position can be reinterpreted so that it better models and represents considerations that are important from the point of view of perfectionist political philosophy. I argue (in Section 4.4) that parties in this perfectionist original position would select a principle of justice according to which social conditions promotive of and conducive to flourishing ways of life are to be established and maintained, and I explain how this distinctively perfectionist principle of justice integrates with other principles of justice. Finally, I defend this argument against two objections: that considerations of human flourishing are too controversial to shape the principles of social justice (Section 4.5) and that the argument from the perfectionist original position is in some way redundant or needlessly convoluted (Section 4.6).

A Perfectionist Theory of Justice. Collis Tahzib, Oxford University Press.
© Collis Tahzib (2022). DOI: 10.1093/oso/9780192847119.003.0005

90 A PERFECTIONIST THEORY OF JUSTICE

4.1 Rawls's Original Position: The Set-Up

Conceiving of society as a fair system of social cooperation between free and equals only gets Rawlsians so far. For, as Rawls recognizes, the question naturally arises as to what this conception of society looks like in more specific terms:

> Once we view a democratic society as a fair system of social cooperation between citizens regarded as free and equal, what principles are most appropriate to it? Alternatively: which principles are most appropriate for a democratic society that not only professes but wants to take seriously the idea that citizens are free and equal, and tries to realize that idea in its main institutions?[1]

Elsewhere, Rawls describes his principles of justice as being an 'unfoldment' of his conception of society: 'we must keep in mind that we are trying to show how the idea of society as a fair system of social cooperation can be *unfolded*, so as to find principles specifying the basic rights and liberties and the forms of equality most appropriate to those cooperating, once they are regarded as citizens, as free and equal persons.'[2]

To move from his abstract conception of society to more determinate principles of justice, Rawls famously employs the device of the original position. The original position is a thought experiment in which we imagine parties coming to an agreement about principles of justice from behind a 'veil of ignorance' that deprives them of information about their race, religion, gender, socioeconomic status, and so on. Whatever principles would be agreed to from the perspective of the original position—a perspective that is designed to 'situate free and equal persons fairly'—we can suppose to be the most appropriate principles for regulating a society conceived of as a fair system of social cooperation between free and equal citizens.[3]

The style of reasoning that Rawls uses to derive principles of justice from his conception of society is thus distinctively contractualist. It involves translating a justificatory question (namely, what are the fair terms of social cooperation between free and equal persons?) into a deliberative question (namely, what terms would be selected by parties in an original position that situates free and equal persons fairly?). As Rawls puts this, 'the question of justification is settled by working out a problem of deliberation: we have to ascertain which principles it would be rational to adopt given the contractual situation.'[4]

---

[1] Rawls, J., *Justice as Fairness: A Restatement* (Cambridge, MA: Harvard University Press, 2001), p. 39.
[2] Rawls, J., *Political Liberalism* (New York: Columbia University Press, 2005), p. 27 (emphasis added).
[3] Rawls, J., *Justice as Fairness*, p. 15.
[4] Rawls, J., *A Theory of Justice* (Cambridge, MA: Harvard University Press, 1971), p. 17.

Of course, it is natural to wonder what the point is of re-casting the justificatory question in these deliberative terms. Why not work out the principles of justice more directly, rather than going to the trouble of imagining what parties in the original position would or would not agree to? Whether anything is indeed gained from the contractualist reasoning of the original position is a complex matter that I address at the end of this chapter, in Section 4.6. But before we can assess this worry, we need to consider in more detail the set-up of the original position and the argument from the original position to the principles of justice.[5]

One element of the set-up of the original position that is especially important is the specification of the parties. The most striking feature of the parties in the original position is that they are situated behind a 'veil of ignorance':

> One of our considered convictions, I assume, is this: the fact that we occupy a particular social position is not a good reason for us to propose, or to expect others to accept, a conception of justice that favours those in this position. Similarly, the fact that we affirm a particular religious, philosophical, or moral comprehensive doctrine with its associated conception of the good is not a reason for us to propose, or to expect others to accept, a conception of justice that favours those of that persuasion. To model this conviction in the original position, the parties are not allowed to know the social position of those they represent, or the particular comprehensive doctrine of the person each represents. The same idea is extended to information about people's race and ethnic group, sex and gender, and their various native endowments such as strength and intelligence, all within the normal range. We express these limits on information figuratively by saying the parties are behind a veil of ignorance.[6]

However, while the veil of ignorance deprives parties in the original position of certain kinds of knowledge, this does not mean they lack all knowledge whatsoever. For otherwise it would be unclear on what basis parties in the original position could rationally decide between principles of justice. If they knew nothing at all, the choice of the parties would be 'reduced to mere guessing'.[7] To solve this problem, Rawls introduces the idea of 'primary goods'. These are very general all-purpose goods, such as health and wealth and self-respect, that every rational person is presumed to want:

> [Primary goods] are things which it is supposed a rational man wants whatever else he wants. Regardless of what an individual's rational plans are in detail, it

---

[5] For a more in-depth discussion of these matters, see, for example, Freeman, S., *Rawls* (London: Routledge, 2007), ch. 4; Hinton, T. (ed.), *The Original Position* (Cambridge: Cambridge University Press, 2015).

[6] Rawls, J., *Political Liberalism*, pp. 24–5.

[7] Rawls, J., *A Theory of Justice*, p. 142.

92   A PERFECTIONIST THEORY OF JUSTICE

is assumed that there are various things which he would prefer more of rather than less. With more of these goods men can generally be assured of greater success in carrying out their intentions and in advancing their ends, whatever these ends may be. The primary goods, to give them in broad categories, are rights and liberties, opportunities and powers, income and wealth.[8]

In addition to knowing about the primary goods, the parties in the original position are specified to know certain other general facts. They understand that the 'circumstances of justice'—the circumstances without which there would be no need for principles of justice—obtain. These circumstances include, say, the condition of moderate scarcity, according to which 'natural and other resources are not so abundant that schemes of cooperation become superfluous'.[9] The parties in the original position also know certain other 'general facts about human society'.[10] As Rawls explains, 'they understand political affairs and the principles of economic theory; they know the basis of social organization and the laws of human psychology'.[11] There is no harm in general facts and laws of this kind being known in the original position because parties cannot exploit such knowledge to their own advantage.

Despite being situated behind the veil of ignorance, then, the parties know enough to make rational choices. Guided by a preference for more primary goods rather than less, by an awareness of the circumstances of justice and by other general facts about human beings and human society, they are able to select principles in a manner that does not reduce to mere guesswork.

A second significant element of the set-up of the original position is the specification of the alternatives. Rawls explains that we do not try to say what principles the parties would think of as available alternatives because to do so 'would be a complicated business and a distraction from our practical aim'.[12] Instead, 'we simply hand the parties a list of principles, a menu, as it were'.[13] This menu includes the major principles of justice found in the history of political philosophy as well as any further principles that occur to us. In practice, Rawls's primary concern is to challenge 'the dominant utilitarianism of the tradition' and so his most detailed arguments from the original position involve pairwise comparisons between his principles of justice and various utilitarian principles of justice.[14] But the important point is that the original position is to be construed as a 'selection device' that operates on a menu of traditional principles of justice rather than as a device

---

[8] Ibid., p. 92.
[9] Ibid., p. 127.
[10] Ibid., p. 137.
[11] Ibid.
[12] Rawls, J., *Justice as Fairness*, p. 83.
[13] Ibid.
[14] Rawls, J., *A Theory of Justice*, p. viii.

PERFECTIONIST PRINCIPLES OF JUSTICE   93

for constructing principles of justice directly out of the assumptions built into the original position.[15]

Significantly, Rawls includes on this menu his own two principles of justice:

(1) Each person has the same indefeasible claim to a fully adequate scheme of equal basic liberties, which scheme is compatible with the same scheme of liberties for all (the 'equal basic liberties principle');

(2a) Social and economic inequalities are to be attached to offices and positions open to all under conditions of fair equality of opportunity (the 'fair equality of opportunity principle'); and

(2b) Social and economic inequalities are to be to the greatest benefit of the least advantaged members of society (the 'difference principle').[16]

To briefly clarify: the equal basic liberties principle guarantees the familiar list of basic rights and liberties, such as freedom of expression, freedom of religion or belief, freedom of assembly, the right to vote, the right to bodily integrity, the right to privacy, and so on. The fair equality of opportunity principle is meant to go beyond a formal equality of opportunity principle (which requires that careers and other social positions be open to talents) by requiring, among other things, equal educational opportunities regardless of family income. And the difference principle is a demanding principle that tells us to compare alternative political arrangements by how the least advantaged group fares in each and to select the alternative in which the least advantaged group does best— where the 'least advantaged' group is the group with the smallest share of primary goods.

These principles are ordered by 'lexical priority': the equal basic liberties principle is lexically prior to the fair equality of opportunity principle, and the fair equality of opportunity principle is lexically prior to the difference principle. This lexical priority means that we apply a given principle only once the prior principles are fully satisfied. Thus, a person's equal basic liberties may not be sacrificed for the sake of advancing fair equality of opportunity or the position of the least advantaged, and a person's fair equality of opportunity may not be sacrificed for the sake of advancing the position of the least advantaged.[17]

---

[15] Rawls, J., *Justice as Fairness*, p. 83.

[16] Ibid., pp. 42–3. Rawls explains that this statement of the two principles, in *Justice as Fairness*, revises and supersedes his earlier statement of these principles in *A Theory of Justice* (pp. 302–3), and that these revisions were forced primarily by the objections raised in Hart, H. L. A., 'Rawls on Liberty and Its Priority', *University of Chicago Law Review* 40 (1973), pp. 534–55.

[17] See Rawls, J., *A Theory of Justice*, pp. 40–5.

94 A PERFECTIONIST THEORY OF JUSTICE

4.2 Rawls's Original Position: The Selection of Principles

Having explained the set-up of the original position (both the specification of the parties and the specification of the alternatives), let us turn to the argument from the original position to the principles of justice. Though these arguments are very familiar—celebrated, in fact—it is important to spell them out in at least a little detail because they will be relevant later on, in Section 4.4, when making a case for the perfectionist principles of justice.

Rawls explains that the reasoning of the parties in the original position for the two principles of justice can be organized into 'two fundamental comparisons'.[18] Doing so helps to separate the parties' reasons for selecting the first principle of justice from their reasons for selecting the second principle of justice. The two principles of justice are first compared with *the principle of average utility*. This first fundamental comparison serves to illustrate the reasons that particularly favour the selection of the equal basic liberties principle. The two principles are then compared with *the principle of average utility with a social minimum*. This latter principle is a version of what Rawls calls a 'mixed conception' of justice, since it blends utilitarian and non-utilitarian elements.[19] Because the reasons that particularly favour the equal basic liberties principle underdetermine the choice between Rawls's two principles of justice and the principle of average utility with a social minimum, this second fundamental comparison serves to illustrate the reasons that particularly favour the selection of the difference principle. It is worth noting, though, that Rawls concedes that the comparisons are not equally decisive: 'the first comparison, which gives the reasoning for the first principle, is, I think, quite conclusive; the second comparison, which gives the reasoning for the difference principle, is less conclusive'.[20] He adds that the second comparison 'turns on a more delicate balance of less decisive considerations'.[21]

Let us begin by considering the first comparison, in which the two principles of justice are compared with the principle of average utility. This principle says that political institutions and laws 'are to be arranged so as to maximize the average welfare of the members of society'.[22] Rawls explains that a significant problem with this principle is that 'there are realistic social circumstances, even with reasonably favorable conditions, under which the principle of utility would require, or allow, that the basic rights and liberties of some be in various ways restricted, or even denied altogether, for the sake of greater benefits for others or for society as a whole'.[23] Such examples need not be as extreme as slavery or religious persecution

---

[18] Rawls, J., *Justice as Fairness*, p. 94.
[19] See Rawls, J., *A Theory of Justice*, pp. 315–25.
[20] Rawls, J., *Justice as Fairness*, p. 95.
[21] Ibid.
[22] Ibid., p. 96.
[23] Ibid., p. 100.

PERFECTIONIST PRINCIPLES OF JUSTICE   95

and may instead simply involve the limiting by a strong majority of a weak minority's political liberties or religious freedoms. Parties in the original position would regard these possibilities as intolerable. They would thus reject the principle of average utility because they would not want 'to gamble with [their] basic rights and liberties'.[24]

Of course, it is true that parties might get a better deal under the principle of average utility, if they turn out not to belong to the group whose basic rights and liberties are infringed. But a crucial element of the parties' reasoning in the original position is that a society regulated by the two principles of justice is already 'a highly satisfactory political and social world'.[25] It is a world in which even the least advantaged members of society have a fully adequate scheme of equal basic liberties, enjoy fair equality of opportunity and receive an adequate share of primary goods that enables them to develop and exercise their two moral powers, one of which is the power to form, revise and pursue a conception of the good. It is also a world that can be expected to have a desirable political climate: by taking the basic rights and liberties 'off the political agenda of political parties', by not viewing them as 'subject to political bargaining or to the calculus of social interests' and by treating them instead as 'settled once and for all', the two principles of justice lower the stakes of political controversy, reduce the insecurity and hostility of public life, and allow for social cooperation to proceed on a footing of mutual respect and civility.[26] In light of this, the parties in the original position would rationally select the two principles of justice over the principle of average utility: they would not 'put their basic rights and liberties in jeopardy' when there exists a 'readily available and satisfactory alternative' in the form of Rawls's two principles of justice.[27]

Let us now turn to the second fundamental comparison, in which the two principles of justice are compared with the principle of average utility with a social minimum. This principle imports the equal basic liberties principle and the fair equality of opportunity principle, but, in the place of the difference principle, it puts the principle of average utility. As Rawls explains, the principle of average utility with a social minimum says that political institutions and laws 'are to be arranged so as to maximize average utility consistent, first, with guaranteeing the equal basic liberties (including their fair value) and fair equality of opportunity, and second, with maintaining a suitable social minimum'.[28]

The kind of maximin reasoning that leads parties to select the equal basic liberties cannot adjudicate between the difference principle and the principle of average utility with a social minimum, because in neither case is the hardship seriously

[24] Ibid., p. 102.
[25] Ibid., p. 100.
[26] Rawls, J., *A Theory of Justice*, p. 4; Rawls, J., *Justice as Fairness*, pp. 115, 119.
[27] Rawls, J., *Justice as Fairness*, p. 102.
[28] Ibid, p. 120.

intolerable if the parties turn out to be among the least advantaged members of society. Rawls thus explains that the argument for the difference principle involves 'no appeal at all' to maximin reasoning and that parties are instead led to the difference principle on the basis of a more delicate balance of considerations.[29]

The most important of these considerations is the idea of reciprocity. The principle of average utility with a social minimum, says Rawls, has 'no inherent tendency towards either equality or reciprocity'.[30] Any such tendency is purely contingent. By contrast, Rawls explains that an idea of reciprocity is built into the difference principle at a deep level insofar as the difference principle satisfies 'the following reciprocity condition: those who are better off at any point are not better off to the detriment of those who are worse off at that point'.[31] Rawls admits that this is not the only way of specifying the idea of reciprocity. But he says that 'it is hard to imagine' what other form the reciprocity condition might take.[32]

A second consideration relates to stability. Principles of justice are said to be stable if citizens growing up in a society regulated by these principles can be expected to support them and 'usually have no desire either to violate or to renegotiate the terms of social cooperation, given their present or prospective social position'.[33] Of course, as Rawls recognizes, no principles of justice can possibly eliminate *all* tendencies to violate or renegotiate social terms, at least if such tendencies arise whenever gains to one or another social group are possible and if we assume moderate scarcity of resources. But such tendencies need not undermine stability if the principles of justice do not ask too much of any one group and if citizens are given countervailing reasons in favour of usually complying with the current terms of social life. In the second fundamental comparison, the more advantaged stand to gain from a renegotiation of the difference principle and the least advantaged stand to gain from a renegotiation of the principle of utility with a social minimum. But, says Rawls, 'the principle of utility asks more of the less advantaged than the difference principle asks of the more advantaged'.[34] This is because the principle of utility asks the least advantaged to accept less satisfactory social terms in order that the most advantaged may become even more advantaged—which, says Rawls, is an 'extreme' demand.[35] By contrast, the difference principle makes the more moderate demand of the most advantaged that, when availing themselves of the opportunity to better their situation, they ensure that they do not do so at the expense of the least advantaged members of society.

---

[29] Ibid., p. 43; see also pp. xvii, 95, 96.
[30] Ibid., p. 122.
[31] Ibid., p. 124.
[32] Ibid.
[33] Ibid., p. 125.
[34] Ibid., p. 127.
[35] Ibid.

A further related consideration concerns the 'strains of commitment'. Parties in the original position must take into account the strains of commitment in the sense that they cannot in good faith enter into an agreement without being reasonably confident that they would be able to honour and affirm the terms of that agreement.[36] Here Rawls draws a distinction between two senses of affirmation. He concedes that, in one sense, citizens could be expected to affirm the principle of average utility with a social minimum: these terms would not be so miserable for the least advantaged that they would feel the need to resort to 'violent action' to improve their condition.[37] Yet, in another 'milder' sense of affirmation, citizens might plausibly fail to affirm the principle of average utility with a social minimum: the least advantaged could be expected to 'grow distant from political society and retreat into [their] social world', to 'feel left out' and to become 'withdrawn and cynical'.[38] Once again, then, the difference principle promises to offer the most reciprocal and stable basis for social cooperation.

4.3 A Perfectionist Original Position: The Set-Up

Just as Rawls asks the question of what his conception of society looks like in more specific terms, the following question naturally arises for an advocate of the perfectionist conception of society defended in Chapter 3:

> Once we view a democratic society as a fair striving for human flourishing between free and equal citizens, what principles are most appropriate to it? Alternatively: which principles are most appropriate for a democratic society that not only professes but wants to take seriously the idea that society is a fair striving for human flourishing between free and equal citizens, and that tries to realize this idea in its main institutions?

And, just as Rawls did, perfectionists can profitably employ an original position device in order to derive these more determinate principles of justice. In doing so, however, certain modifications will need to be made to the set-up of the original position in order better to model certain considerations that matter from a perfectionist point of view—considerations that are implicit in the perfectionist conception of society as a fair striving for human flourishing between free and equal citizens. These modifications to the set-up concern the *specification of the alternatives* and *the specification of the parties*. Let us consider these in order.

As Rawls admits, one significant limitation of his argument from the original position to the two principles of justice is that it proceeds only 'relative to a given

[36] Ibid., p. 128.
[37] Ibid.
[38] Ibid.

list' of alternatives.[39] He shows, perhaps, that the selection device of the original position favours the two principles of justice over the alternative principles of justice that he considers, which are primarily utilitarian principles. But how do we know that other plausible principles of justice have not been overlooked? Can we be sure that Rawls's principles would still be selected from a more comprehensive menu of alternatives? Rawls's most detailed and celebrated arguments from the original position involve a coarse-grained comparison between his two principles of justice and fairly crude forms of utilitarianism—forms of utilitarianism that will strike many political philosophers today as non-starters. In this sense, Rawls succeeds, I think, in his aim of articulating a systematic alternative to the 'dominant utilitarianism of the tradition' and of challenging the tendency for the maximization of utility to 'hold sway by default' in our practical thought and public policy.[40] But, as Rawls himself concedes, once more moderate and sophisticated principles of justice (principles that do not allow the infringement of basic rights and liberties) are on the table, the superiority of justice as fairness is far less obvious. Indeed, one is tempted to say that the real work in the original position only begins at that point—namely, once the equal basic liberties principle and the fair equality of opportunity principle (or something in their vicinity) are taken as given and the difference principle is being compared in a focused and fine-grained way, and likely on the basis of a delicate balance of considerations, with moderate and plausible rival principles drawn from the tradition of political philosophy.

In particular, we need to consider whether there are attractive principles of justice drawn from the perfectionist tradition of political philosophy that could make their way onto the menu presented to the parties in the original position. In *A Theory of Justice*, after comparing his two principles with various utilitarian principles of justice, Rawls does consider some candidate perfectionist principles.[41] He first considers an extreme form of perfectionism according to which society is 'to arrange institutions and to define the duties and obligations of individuals so as to maximize the achievement of human excellence in art, science, and culture.'[42] Rawls traces this view to Nietzsche, who says that an individual can realize his full value only by 'living for the good of the rarest and most valuable specimens' and that 'mankind must work continually to produce individual great human beings—this and nothing else is the task.'[43] As Rawls rightly notes, this extreme and maximizing form of perfectionism would be rejected by parties in the

---

[39] Ibid., p. 95.

[40] Rawls, J., *A Theory of Justice*, pp. viii, 586.

[41] See ibid., pp. 325–32. For an instructive analysis of Rawls's discussion here, see Sheppard, S., 'The Perfectionisms of John Rawls', *Canadian Journal of Law and Jurisprudence* 11 (1998), pp. 383–416.

[42] Rawls, J., *A Theory of Justice*, p. 325.

[43] Ibid., citing Hollingsdale, J. R., *Nietzsche: The Man and His Philosophy* (Baton Rouge, LA: Louisiana State University Press, 1965), p. 127. For discussion of Nietzsche's perfectionism, see, for example, Hurka, T., 'Nietzsche: Perfectionist', in B. Leiter and N. Sinhababu (eds), *Nietzsche and Morality* (Oxford: Oxford University Press, 2007), pp. 9–31.

original position for similar reasons to those for which the principle of average utility was rejected in the first fundamental comparison, namely that it 'might lead to a lesser religious or other liberty, if not to a loss of freedom altogether to advance many of one's spiritual ends'.[44]

But this still leaves open a second and more moderate form of perfectionism.[45] Just as Rawls imagines a 'mixed conception' of utilitarianism in which the principle of utility is subordinated to the equal basic liberties principle and the fair equality of opportunity principle, we can imagine what could be called a 'mixed conception of perfectionism' in which a principle of perfection is subordinated to these other lexically prior principles of justice. This principle of perfection would require the establishment and maintenance of social conditions promotive of and conducive to flourishing ways of life. On this mixed conception, once everyone has equal basic liberties and fair equality of opportunity, social resources are intuitionistically balanced between the further pursuit of equality (as dictated by the difference principle) and the pursuit of various dimensions of human flourishing (as dictated by the principle of perfection).

On this view, then, social justice is about more than the distribution of the primary goods. It is also about the encouragement of the good and the discouragement of the bad, and this calls for an additional and independent principle of justice. There can be stronger and weaker forms of this mixed conception of perfectionism, depending on how much weight is assigned to the principle of perfection as compared to the difference principle at the intuitionistic balancing stage. But even the strongest form of the mixed conception of perfectionism would respect basic rights and liberties as well as fair equality of opportunity. In other words, the perfectionist imperative kicks in only once the equal basic liberties principle and fair equality of opportunity principle are fully satisfied, at which point the perfectionist imperative is balanced against an egalitarian imperative.

The parties in the original position would therefore be presented with a menu that includes the following perfectionist principles of justice:

(1) Each person has the same indefeasible claim to a fully adequate scheme of equal basic liberties compatible with the same scheme of liberties for all (the equal basic liberties principle);

---

[44] Rawls, J., *A Theory of Justice*, p. 327.

[45] In fairness, Rawls is aware of the possibility of more moderate, non-Nietzschean perfectionist principles similar to those I develop in the main text. But he maintains that even these more moderate perfectionist principles would be rejected by parties in the original position. I discuss his reason for thinking so in Section 4.5. Peter de Marneffe also sketches (but does not endorse) a similar position which he calls 'limited moral majoritarianism'; see 'The Possibility and Desirability of Neutrality', in R. Merrill and D. Weinstock (eds), *Political Neutrality: A Re-evaluation* (New York: Palgrave Macmillan, 2014), pp. 48–50.

(2) Social and economic inequalities are to be attached to offices and positions open to all under conditions of fair equality of opportunity (the fair equality of opportunity principle);

(3) Social and economic inequalities are to be to the greatest benefit of the least advantaged members of society (the difference principle); and

(4) Social conditions promotive of and conducive to flourishing ways of life are to be established and maintained (the principle of perfection),
    where (1) is lexically prior to (2), (2) is lexically prior to (3) and (4), and (3) and (4) are not ordered in terms of lexical priority but must instead be intuitionistically balanced against each other.[46]

Before continuing, let me address a worry that arises immediately at this point. The objection is that by building perfectionist justice atop of Rawls's justice as fairness in this way, perfectionist justice inherits any weaknesses of justice as fairness. Rawls's lexical priority rules, for instance, are notoriously difficult to defend and have been sharply criticized: Brian Barry calls them 'outlandishly extreme' and H. L. A. Hart calls them 'dogmatic'.[47] The lexical priority of the basic liberties seems to imply that a minor, one-off violation of the basic liberties (for example, the restriction in a single election of a single randomly selected citizen's right to vote) cannot be offset by astronomical gains in wealth and well-being for society as a whole, including for the individual whose right to vote was restricted. Similarly, the difference principle contains within it a lexical priority for the least advantaged members of society, and this makes it a highly demanding principle. The difference principle appears to imply, for instance, that we ought to give a single penny to those who are worst-off at the cost of giving thousands of pounds to those who are badly off (but not *as* badly off as the worst-off).[48] Many theorists of justice thus reject the strong medicine of this distributive principle in favour of sufficientarian, prioritarian or egalitarian alternatives. In light of all of this, how wise is it to tie perfectionist justice so closely to the details of justice as fairness? Would it not be better to avoid taking on board all these Rawlsian trappings?[49]

The rationale for mirroring justice as fairness is that any acceptable conception of social justice will in my view need to include some kind of liberty principle and

---

[46] Two presentational points are in order here. First, I have for the sake of perspicuity renumbered Rawls's principles from 1 to 3 (instead of numbering them 1, 2a and 2b, as Rawls does). Second, I refer to these four principles, collectively, as the *perfectionist principles of justice* (even though only the last principle is a distinctively perfectionist principle), so as to mark the contrast with Rawls's principles of justice; when referring to the last principle specifically, I talk of the *principle of perfection*.

[47] Barry, B., 'John Rawls and the Priority of Liberty', *Philosophy & Public Affairs* 2 (1973), p. 276; Hart, H. L. A., 'Rawls on Liberty and Its Priority', p. 554.

[48] See, for example, Arneson, R., 'Rawls Versus Utilitarianism in the Light of *Political Liberalism*', in V. Davion and C. Wolf (eds), *The Idea of a Political Liberalism* (Oxford: Rowman & Littlefield, 2000), pp. 237–9.

[49] I thank Cécile Fabre, David Miller and Steven Wall for putting this sort of objection to me.

some kind of equality principle—and so, rather than reinvent the wheel, it makes sense to import the leading and most impressive liberal conception of social justice at this point, even if, like all such conceptions, justice as fairness contains controversial features. In doing so, I do provide, in Sections 4.1 and 4.2, *some* defence of Rawls's principles of justice. But I recognize that I have not mounted anything like a comprehensive, self-standing defence of the distributive principles that I import from justice as fairness, including a detailed cost-benefit analysis that demonstrates the superiority of these principles to sufficientarian, prioritarian and egalitarian alternatives—an endeavour that would, in any case, be well beyond the scope of this work.

The failure to mount such a defence is not, however, as glaring an omission as it might at first appear because this work fights for the most part on a particular dialectical front: it is primarily in dialogue with anti-perfectionist liberals, as opposed to, say, utilitarians or libertarians. Since my main interlocutors, such as Rawls and Dworkin and Quong, are already on board with some kind of liberal-egalitarian principles of justice, what stands in most urgent need of defence, dialectically speaking, is not the liberal-egalitarian component of perfectionist justice but rather its perfectionist component. Anti-perfectionist liberals, in other words, are likely to be willing to bracket their intramural differences and to overlook concerns about the more controversial features of justice as fairness, since their main bone of contention with perfectionist justice will not be with its Rawlsian imports.

There are different ways of arguing for these perfectionist principles of justice. One way is to say that, once these principles are added to the menu, they would be selected by parties in the Rawlsian original position. Here the set-up of the original position remains fairly close to Rawls's set-up—while the specification of the *alternatives* is changed, the specification of the *parties* remains unchanged—and a detailed comparison is made within that set-up between the perfectionist principles of justice and Rawls's two principles of justice. I am unsure about the prospects this strategy, and I mention it only to draw attention to its possibility.

My preferred way of arguing for the perfectionist principles of justice is to change the set-up of the original position more extensively. On this approach, we say not just that, in presenting parties with a menu of options, Rawls has omitted plausible perfectionist principles of justice but also that, in specifying the parties themselves, Rawls has failed to represent important considerations—or at least has failed to represent considerations that are important from the perfectionist point of view. Here the set-up of the perfectionist original position differs from the set-up of the Rawlsian original position in terms of both the specification of the alternatives and the specification of the parties.

102 A PERFECTIONIST THEORY OF JUSTICE

In particular, there are two differences between the parties in the perfectionist original position and the parties in the Rawlsian original position.[50] These differences consist in two further stipulations—stipulations that the Rawlsian original position does without but that are called for by the perfectionist conception of society as a fair striving for human flourishing:

(a) The parties in the perfectionist original position are presumed to want to flourish to a greater rather than lesser degree.
(b) The parties in the perfectionist original position are presumed to know that some ways of life realize a higher level of flourishing than others; alternatively put, they are presumed to know that not all ways of life realize the same level of flourishing.[51]

The first stipulation is an amplification of the rationality of the parties in the original position. Recall the question of how, given the veil of ignorance condition, the choice of the parties in the original position can possibly be rational rather than mere guesswork. Rawls's answer was to stipulate that parties want primary goods and that they select between principles of justice by reference to their expected share of primary goods. These primary goods, such as wealth and the social bases of self-respect, are things that 'every rational man is presumed to want', and the parties in the original position are stipulated to 'prefer more rather than less primary goods'.[52] In the perfectionist original position, however, parties are assumed to want not just a greater rather than lesser share of the primary goods but also a greater rather than lesser degree of flourishing. Of course, they are not presumed to want to flourish in the specific manner recommended by any particular comprehensive doctrine. They are not presumed, for instance, to want to flourish in the specific sense recommended by Christian doctrine or by a Millian ideal of individuality. Stipulating such specific moral content into the parties in the original position would defeat the purpose of using the original position device. Rather, a deliberately much weaker and thinner stipulation is made of the parties in the perfectionist original position, namely that they want to flourish to a greater rather than lesser degree.

The second stipulation also amplifies the account of the rationality of the parties in the original position—though in this case by adjusting their beliefs rather than their desires. Alongside the other things that the parties know—for instance, that

---

[50] I thank Simon Căbulea May for very helpful discussions about the specification of the parties in the perfectionist original position.

[51] In both stipulations I assume, as seems plausible, that flourishing is a property that comes in degrees. But nothing hangs on this. If one insists that flourishing is an all-or-nothing property, the arguments that follow could be made, mutatis mutandis, with the stipulations that (a) parties want to flourish rather than to fail to flourish and (b) parties know that some ways of life involve flourishing whereas others do not.

[52] Rawls, J., *A Theory of Justice*, pp. 62, 93.

society is subject to a condition of moderate scarcity, and general facts and laws about human psychology—the parties are presumed to know that not all ways of life realize the same level of flourishing. This stipulation, like the first stipulation, is deliberately weak. We do not suppose that parties in the perfectionist original position know *which* ways of life are more flourishing than others. Parties are not stipulated to think, for instance, that Christian ways of life are superior to Millian ways of life, or vice versa. Again, a stipulation along these highly specific lines would undermine the whole point of employing the original position device. So parties are instead presumed to know the much weaker and more general proposition that *some* ways of life, whatever they may be, realize a higher degree of human flourishing than others.

A natural objection at this point is that these two stipulations are in some sense too thick or too strong—that specifying the parties in this way somehow undermines the point of the original position. Indeed, the objections I consider later, in Sections 4.5 and 4.6, can be understood as ways of expressing precisely this worry. Before exploring this issue, however, an even more immediate question arises: are these stipulations defensible? Do they suitably model our considered convictions? Do they express and embody values that really matter to us?

Recall that, for Rawls, the various specifications of the parties in the original position are not haphazard. He explains that 'each aspect of the contractual situation can be given supporting grounds' and plays an important role within a broader theoretical structure.[53] As we saw in Section 4.1, for instance, Rawls gives a clear rationale for imposing the veil of ignorance condition on the parties:

> One of our considered convictions, I assume, is this: the fact that we occupy a particular social position is not a good reason for us to propose, or to expect others to accept, a conception of justice that favours those in this position ... To model this conviction in the original position, the parties are not allowed to know the social position of those they represent, or the particular comprehensive doctrine of the person each represents ... We express these limits on information figuratively by saying the parties are behind a veil of ignorance.[54]

As Rawls forcefully puts this point: '"To persons according to their threat advantage" (or their de facto political power, or wealth, or native endowments) is not the basis of political justice.'[55] Elsewhere, Rawls explains that this condition prevents distributive shares from being 'improperly influenced by ... factors so arbitrary

---

[53] Ibid., p. 21.
[54] Rawls, J., *Political Liberalism*, pp. 24–5.
[55] Rawls, J., *Justice as Fairness*, p. 16.

from a moral point of view', such as natural and social endowments and other 'chance contingencies'.[56]

More needs to be said, then, to justify each of the two stipulations mentioned above. Let us consider them in reverse order. So consider, first, the stipulation that parties know that some ways of life realize a higher level of flourishing than others—or, put differently, that parties know that not all ways of life realize the same level of flourishing. I offer a fuller discussion of these issues in Chapter 5, but for now let us motivate this stipulation by considering some judgements about ways of life. Imagine a person 'whose only pleasure is to count blades of grass in various geometrically shaped areas such as park squares and well-trimmed lawns'.[57] Or imagine a person who 'has the project of knocking down as many icicles as he can before they melt. He hires a crew of workers and a fleet of trucks, so that he can reach icicles hanging from tall buildings; and this is how he spends his winters'.[58] Most people, I take it, would agree that these individuals do not lead flourishing lives. Or, to put the point comparatively, the ways of life of the grass-counter and icicle-smasher are less worthy, meaningful or flourishing than the way of life of someone with family, friends and a career in scientific research. In light of judgements of this kind, it seems difficult to deny the assumption that some ways of life realize a higher level of flourishing than others.

Of course, this does not mean that it is always *clear* whether one way of life realizes a higher level of flourishing than another, or even that there is always a *fact of the matter* about whether one way of life realizes a higher level of flourishing than another. Perhaps it is not clear—or perhaps there is no fact of the matter about—whether the way of life of an astronaut realizes a higher or lower level of flourishing than the way of life of a family man. In this sense, there might be plenty of vagueness, incommensurability or indeterminacy surrounding the relative merits of different ways of life. But this hardly undermines the judgement stipulated into the parties in the perfectionist original position, namely that *some* ways of life realize a higher level of flourishing than others.

Indeed, it is worth noting here that even Rawls accepts the plausibility of the claim that some ways of life are more flourishing than others. He emphasizes that he does 'not contend that the criteria of excellence lack a rational basis'.[59] He continues: 'Clearly there are standards in the arts and sciences for appraising creative

---

[56] Rawls, J., *A Theory of Justice*, p. 72. For a reading of Rawls that emphasizes the luck-egalitarian strand in his thought, see Kymlicka, W., *Contemporary Political Philosophy* (Oxford: Oxford University Press, 2002), ch. 3. See also Freeman, S., *Justice and the Social Contract: Essays on Rawlsian Political Philosophy* (Oxford: Oxford University Press, 2007), ch. 4; Lippert-Rasmussen, K., 'Rawls and Luck Egalitarianism', in J. Mandle and S. Roberts-Cady (eds), *John Rawls: Debating the Major Questions* (Oxford: Oxford University Press, 2020), pp. 133–47.

[57] Rawls, J., *A Theory of Justice*, p. 432.

[58] Kraut, R., 'Desire and the Human Good', *Proceedings and Addresses of the American Philosophical Association* 68 (1994), p. 42.

[59] Rawls, J., *A Theory of Justice*, p. 328.

efforts ... Very often it is beyond question that the work of one person is superior to that of another. Indeed, the freedom and well-being of individuals, when measured by the excellence of their activities and works, is vastly different in value ... Comparisons of intrinsic value can obviously be made.'[60] The point is just that Rawls denies the need to appeal to the truth of these claims or to build them into the original position. He chooses to develop his theory of justice while 'doing without a standard of perfection', but he does not deny the plausibility or defensibility of such a standard.[61]

One might object to my defence of this stipulation by biting the bullet and insisting that, despite appearances to the contrary, individuals who engage in apparently pointless pursuits such as grass-counting and icicle-smashing do in fact flourish. Donald Bruckner has recently offered an interesting defence of this sort of hard-line position.[62] Bruckner contends that we are reluctant to say that the grass-counter or icicle-smasher flourishes because grass-counting and icicle-smashing seem 'incomprehensible'. We cannot imagine what anyone could possibly find appealing about endlessly counting blades of grass or smashing icicles. But perhaps this is simply a failure of imagination on our part. If we could somehow be helped to understand what the grass-counter *sees* in counting blades of grass, then we might be more willing to accept that counting blades of grass can contribute to a person's flourishing. Bruckner then suggests various things that a grass-counter or icicle-smasher might say in order to render these activities 'comprehensible to others'—in order to 'make it clear to others what one sees in the object of one's desire.'[63] He proposes that the grass-counter might say, 'It's soothing, like walking on the beach' or 'You would think all the blades of grass were the same, but when you set your mind to counting them, you have the wonderful aesthetic experience of appreciating their individual differences!'[64] Similarly, Bruckner proposes that the icicle-smasher might say, 'I love hearing them crash to the ground' or 'I see the pursuit as challenging, as bowlers see it as challenging to knock down as many pins as possible with the fewest possible throws.'[65] Bruckner suggests that even if these statements fail to convince us of the value of grass-counting and icicle-smashing, they nonetheless may succeed in rendering these activities comprehensible in a way that makes it plausible (or at least less implausible) to think that they contribute to a person's flourishing.

---

[60] Ibid.

[61] Ibid., p. 331.

[62] See Bruckner, D., 'Quirky Desires and Well-Being', *Journal of Ethics & Social Philosophy* 10 (2016), pp. 1–34. Strictly speaking, Bruckner holds that satisfying pointless desires such as counting blades of grass or smashing icicles can contribute to a person's *well-being* rather than to a person's *flourishing*, so it is possible that he would not endorse my application of his argumentative strategy in this context.

[63] Ibid., pp. 5, 7.

[64] Ibid., p. 8.

[65] Ibid., p. 9.

106 A PERFECTIONIST THEORY OF JUSTICE

However, there are at least two problems with Bruckner's 'incomprehensibility defence' of the claim that grass-counters and icicle-smashers do in fact flourish. First, the simple description of grass-counting as 'soothing, like walking on the beach' or icicle-smashing as 'challenging, like bowling' does not suffice to render these activities comprehensible to others. After all, it is likely to remain entirely mysterious to others *how* someone could possibly find counting blades of grass to be soothing or smashing icicles to be challenging. Perhaps we can just about make sense of the claim that, say, spending a few hours or a few days counting blades of grass is soothing. But can we really make sense of the claim that spending one's entire life counting blades of grass is soothing? So grass-counters and icicle-smashers would, I think, need to provide much more extensive explanations in order to make it even dimly clear to others what they see in these activities.

The second and more important problem is that our reluctance to say that the grass-counter or icicle-smasher flourishes does not seem to me to stem from the *incomprehensibility* of grass-counting or icicle-smashing (though these activities certainly *are* incomprehensible); rather, it stems from the *pointlessness* of grass-counting and icicle-smashing. So even if these descriptions of grass-counting and icicle-smashing ('it's soothing', 'it's challenging', and so on) *did* suffice to render these activities comprehensible to others, this would do little if anything to show that these activities contribute to our flourishing. In other words, while Bruckner is quite correct that grass-counting and icicle-smashing are 'difficult to under-stand' and even 'downright inscrutable', the features of incomprehensibility and inscrutability are *orthogonal*—or at least not at all central—to the intuition that these activities do not contribute to a person's flourishing.[66] What is central to the intuitive force of these thought experiments is instead the fact that grass-counting and icicle-smashing are *intrinsically pointless* or *a waste of time*. And grass-counting and icicle-smashing remain intrinsically pointless even if we can understand why grass-counters and icicle-smashers partake in these activities. The project of trying to render pointless activities comprehensible to others by imag-ining how grass-counters and icicle-smashers might explain to others what they see in these activities is thus largely irrelevant to the project of showing that these activities contribute to a person's flourishing.[67]

---

[66] Ibid., p. 2.
[67] Bruckner considers this sort of objection in a footnote; see ibid., pp. 9 n. 12, 30–1. In reply, he says, 'I take the charge of incomprehensibility just to be the charge of pointlessness'. In other words, the considerations that demonstrate that an activity is comprehensible *just are* the considerations that demonstrate that it is not pointless. Specifically, 'the grass-counter ... appeals to aesthetic experience. Counting the grass has that point, so it is not a waste of time'. However, incomprehensibility and point-lessness seem to be fundamentally distinct notions—and thus the charge of incomprehensibility and the charge of pointlessness seem to be fundamentally distinct charges. Of course, here it would be helpful to have a well-developed account of the conditions under which an activity is pointless. Such an account would illuminate the relationship between pointlessness and incomprehensibility, and in particular it would make clear how an activity could be comprehensible yet pointless. But I shall not

PERFECTIONIST PRINCIPLES OF JUSTICE   107

Let me close the defence of this stipulation with a more general point. One would, I think, need to subscribe to a fairly extreme form of subjectivism or scepticism in order to deny that the grass-counter or the icicle-smasher fails to lead a flourishing life. It is revealing, for instance, that Bruckner's defence of grass-counters and icicle-smashers is part of a broader defence of 'a subjective view according to which things are valuable because they are valued, not the other way around. There is no objective value or to-be-pursued-ness in objects themselves or the fabric of the world'.[68] This is important because many prominent anti-perfectionist liberals such as Rawls and Quong are at pains to stress that one need not be a subjectivist or sceptic about human flourishing in order to be an anti-perfectionist liberal.[69] Rawls, for instance, says that political liberalism 'does not argue that we should be hesitant or uncertain, much less sceptical, about our own beliefs'.[70] Indeed, he adds that 'it would be fatal to the idea of a political conception to see it as sceptical about, or indifferent to, truth' because 'such scepticism or indifference would put political philosophy in opposition to numerous comprehensive doctrines, and thus defeat from the outset its aim of achieving an overlapping consensus'.[71] For these political liberals, it is vital that what justifies anti-perfectionism is not subjectivism or scepticism about standards of perfection and flourishing but rather the recognition of reasonable disagreement about those standards in conjunction with a commitment to the public justification of political power.

Consider, next, the defensibility of the stipulation that people want to flourish to a greater rather than lesser degree. This claim is admittedly false as an empirical matter: there are no doubt some individuals who have no such desire. Some individuals, that is, surely do abjure the values of human flourishing and excellence, and instead revel in ways of life that they themselves know to have little value or merit. But the fact that this stipulation is not a universal empirical generalization does not tell against it, for the stipulation is intended as a normative construction rather than an empirical fact. In this, the stipulations of the perfectionist original position are no different from the stipulations of the Rawlsian original position, which also fail as universal empirical generalizations. Rawls, for

---

take up this task, since our intuitive grip on the notion of pointlessness seems sufficient for present purposes. In particular, incomprehensibility has more descriptive connotations, whereas pointlessness has more normative connotations. At the most general level, then, what Bruckner's argument appears to lack is a persuasive way of bridging the gap between the descriptive property of 'being comprehensible to others' and the normative properties of 'having a point' and 'being capable of contributing to a person's flourishing'.

[68] Ibid., p. 25.

[69] This is not true of all anti-perfectionist liberals, though. Brian Barry famously rests his anti-perfectionism on scepticism about the good life. See his *Justice as Impartiality* (Oxford: Oxford University Press, 1995), especially pp. 168–73. I discuss subjectivism and scepticism about human flourishing in Chapter 5.

[70] Rawls, J., *Political Liberalism*, p. 63.

[71] Ibid., p. 150.

108   A PERFECTIONIST THEORY OF JUSTICE

instance, stipulates that parties 'prefer more rather than less primary goods', where primary goods include freedoms, wealth and the social bases of self-respect.[72] Yet there are no doubt some individuals who do not harbour this preference. For instance, there are likely some monks who have taken a vow of poverty and would prefer to have less rather than more wealth, seeing wealth as a distraction from spiritual devotion and contemplation.[73]

Here it might be argued that if the relevant Rawlsian primary good is viewed not as the actual *possession* of wealth per se but instead as the *entitlement* to wealth, then it will indeed be true that people in the real world will prefer more rather than less of the Rawlsian primary goods.[74] An entitlement to wealth, Kramer explains in this vein, 'will be serviceable for the realization of [a person's] ends regardless of what those ends might be', even if this is not the case for the actual possession of wealth.[75] 'Because such entitlements can be waived', Kramer continues, 'the assignment of them to individuals under principles of justice will not retard anyone's pursuit of his or her conception of the good. Indeed, those waivable entitlements can contribute to the realization of anyone's conception of the good even if that conception is highly abstemious.'[76] The self-denial of a monk, for instance, might 'carry special cogency and probity because of his disowning of the fortune to which he could have laid claim'.[77] However, there may well be individuals who lack not only a desire actually to possess wealth but also a desire even to be entitled to wealth. The monk may believe, for instance, that, far from investing his strivings with special cogency and probity, his retaining an entitlement to wealth constitutes a vestigial form of worldly attachment and temptation that detracts from, rather than contributes to, his quest for full severance from the world. To be clear: none of this is intended to be a critique of Rawls's inclusion of wealth (or an entitlement to wealth) as a primary good. The point is simply that it is no objection to the stipulation of the perfectionist original position to say that people in the real world do not always want to flourish to a greater rather than lesser degree—since this stipulation, like Rawls's stipulations, is meant to be a normative construction rather than an exceptionless empirical generalization.

Still, even if the stipulations of the Rawlsian and perfectionist original positions are matters of normative construction rather than empirical fact, it remains true that those normative constructions must reproduce something of importance in the real world. It is one thing to say that the stipulation that parties want to flourish

---

[72] Rawls, J., *A Theory of Justice*, p. 93.

[73] A number of early critics of Rawls objected to his account of primary goods on the grounds that it is biased in favour of certain ways of life. See, for example, Nagel, T., 'Rawls on Justice', *The Philosophical Review* 82 (1973), pp. 228–9; Schwartz, A., 'Moral Neutrality and Primary Goods', *Ethics* 83 (1973), pp. 294–307; Arneson, R., 'Primary Goods Revisited', *Noûs* 24 (1990), pp. 429–54.

[74] I thank Matthew Kramer for pressing me on this point.

[75] Kramer, M., *Liberalism with Excellence* (Oxford: Oxford University Press, 2017), p. 328.

[76] Ibid., p. 330.

[77] Ibid., p. 331.

to a greater rather than lesser degree is not *purely* empirical; it is another to say that this stipulation has no relation at all to the cares and wants of people in real-world settings. In the latter case, this stipulation would not model our considered convictions and would fail to embody and express values that really matter to us. So the question we have to ask here is: even if this stipulation about what the parties in the perfectionist original position want is not meant to perfectly track empirical facts about what actual people want, is there a sufficiently strong correlation between the two? How plausible is it to presume that individuals want to flourish to a greater rather than lesser degree?

This is a difficult question to answer, but my sense is that there is a sufficiently strong correlation between the stipulation about what parties in the perfectionist original position want and the empirical facts about what people in the real world want. After all, the vast majority of people in the real world do actually want to flourish to a greater rather than lesser degree, in the same way that the vast majority of people in the real world do actually prefer a greater rather than lesser share of the primary goods of wealth, freedom and self-respect. For now, then, it seems reasonable to stipulate this desire into parties in the original position—though, like all stipulations, this stipulation will need eventually to be assessed by reference to the whole theory to which it belongs.[78]

At this point, one might object as follows:

> Even if it is plausible to suppose that the vast majority of people want to flourish to a greater rather than lesser degree, is it plausible to suppose that they want to flourish in this way *at the expense of primary goods*? And isn't the latter (less plausible) stipulation the stipulation that is needed in the context of an argument for the perfectionist principles of justice, since any allocation of public funds towards the establishment and maintenance of social conditions conducive to human flourishing, such as subsidies for museums and art galleries, could always instead have been put directly into the pockets of citizens to spend as they see fit?[79]

However, the whole point of the original position is to show how strong moral principles can be derived from weaker assumptions, and so the parties in the original position are to be described in the normatively thinnest way possible. This idea is emphasized at numerous junctures by Rawls. For instance, he considers the question of why we do not postulate *benevolence* rather than mutual disinterestedness plus the veil of ignorance—especially given that the former is 'at first sight [a] morally more attractive assumption'.[80] His reply is that 'there is no need

---

[78] See Rawls, J., *A Theory of Justice*, pp. 95, 578.
[79] I thank Henrik Kugelberg for putting this objection to me.
[80] Rawls, J., *A Theory of Justice*, p. 149.

for so strong a condition' and that assuming this condition would 'defeat the purpose of grounding the theory of justice on weak stipulations'.[81] Similarly, it is worth noting that Rawls assumes that parties in the original position 'prefer more rather than less primary goods'.[82] He does not assume that parties in the original position prefer more rather than less primary goods *but only if not at the expense of the equal basic liberties.* For, again, that would be to over-specify: it would be to stipulate more into parties than is needed here.

Of course, whether parties in the original position would in fact select this perfectionist conception of justice—or whether, instead, parties in the original position would regard perfectionist principles as objectionably inegalitarian, paternalistic or intrusive—is another matter, and one that resurfaces in various guises throughout this work. The present point is just that, at this stage in the construction of the theory, the most appropriate stipulation is the thinner one: we should start with the weak assumption that parties want to lead more rather than less flourishing ways of life and see whether it can be combined with other similarly weak assumptions in order to yield, in a possibly unexpected way, plausible perfectionist principles of justice.

4.4 A Perfectionist Original Position: The Selection of Principles

We have seen how the perfectionist original position is set up: parties are described inter alia as wanting to flourish to a greater rather than lesser degree and as knowing that some ways of life realize a higher level of flourishing than others; and parties are given an expanded menu of principles which includes the perfectionist principles of justice articulated in Section 4.3. We have seen, too, that the description of the parties is not ad hoc; the perfectionist stipulations are well-motivated and morally defensible. The question that now arises is: would the parties thus specified select the perfectionist principles of justice over Rawls's two principles of justice?

It should be noted at the outset that—like the comparison between the principle of average utility with a social minimum and Rawls's two principles of justice— the comparison between the perfectionist principles of justice and Rawls's two principles of justice is likely to turn on a delicate balance of less-than-decisive considerations. As I shall seek to show, this balance of considerations seems to favour the perfectionist principles of justice, but I recognize that (like Rawls's own argument for the difference principle) this balance of considerations is not decisive and inevitably rests on judgement.

---

[81] Ibid.
[82] Ibid., p. 93.

The main line of reasoning that would lead parties in the perfectionist original position to the perfectionist principles of justice in some ways resembles the reasoning in the first fundamental comparison, though of course the stakes are lower in this case. Here is an intuitive way of thinking through this line of reasoning. Suppose that people lead only one of two ways of life: people are grass-counters or they are scientists. Suppose that you do not know which of these ways of life you will end up leading. Suppose that you know that one of these ways of life realizes a high degree of flourishing and the other realizes a low degree of flourishing: you know that either the way of life of a scientist realizes a high degree of flourishing and the way of life of a grass-counter realizes a low degree of flourishing, or vice versa, but you do not know which. And suppose, finally, that you want to flourish to a greater rather than lesser degree. Then you would be very fearful of ending up in the way of life that realizes a low degree of flourishing—just as you would be fearful of ending up in a group whose basic liberties are infringed or a group who suffer great economic disadvantage. So just as it would be rational for you to select social institutions that insure against these outcomes, it would also be rational for you to select institutions that insure against your ending up as a grass-counter if that is the less flourishing way of life, or as a scientist if that is the less flourishing way of life. The perfectionist principles of justice, which call for the establishment and maintenance of social conditions promotive of and conducive to flourishing ways of life, insure against these eventualities in a way that the difference principle simply does not.

This point generalizes beyond the case in which there are only two ways of life within a society. Of the many possible ways of life, parties know that some of these ways of life realize a higher level of flourishing than others, and they want their life to be among the more rather than less flourishing possibilities. So the more general point is that it is rational for parties in the perfectionist original position to select institutions that insure against their ending up in less rather than more flourishing ways of life. The perfectionist principles of justice provide such insurance in a way that the difference principle does not, since they call for laws and policies that encourage citizens to pursue flourishing ways of life.

Both of the assumptions made of parties in the perfectionist original position are necessary for this argument. After all, if parties wanted to flourish to a greater rather than lesser degree, but failed to recognize that not all ways of life realize the same level of flourishing, then it would not occur to them that they might end up as someone who leads a way of life that realizes a low degree of flourishing. Parties would know no better than to view the property of being flourishing as a property that all ways of life realize equally well. At the same time, if parties recognized that not all ways of life realize the same level of flourishing, but did not have a desire to flourish to a greater rather than lesser degree, then, while it would occur to them that they might end up as someone who leads a way of life that realizes a low degree of flourishing, they would not fear this outcome or care about avoiding

112 A PERFECTIONIST THEORY OF JUSTICE

it. Such an eventuality, while it would occur to the parties, would utterly fail to move them.

So there is, from the perspective of parties in the perfectionist original position, something to be gained from selecting a principle of justice that would see the establishment and maintenance of social conditions promotive of and conducive to flourishing ways of life. Selecting this principle would protect and promote interests that the parties are presumed to have. The question is: is there also something to be lost by selecting the perfectionist principles of justice? And if so, which principles of justice do the competing considerations favour on balance?

Here it is helpful to return to the considerations that, according to Rawls in the second fundamental comparison, particularly favour the difference principle as compared to the principle of average utility with a social minimum. The main such consideration is that of reciprocity. Recall that the principle of average utility with a social minimum has 'no inherent tendency' towards reciprocity and makes what Rawls calls an 'extreme' demand on the least advantaged, namely that they accept less satisfactory social terms in order that the most advantaged may become more advantaged still.[83] By contrast, the difference principle satisfies 'the following reciprocity condition: those who are better off at any point are not better off to the detriment of those who are worse off at that point.'[84] So how do the perfectionist principles of justice fare with respect to reciprocity? Do they satisfy a plausible reciprocity condition? Or do they, like the principle of average utility with a social minimum, come at the cost of reciprocity?

In my view, the perfectionist conception of justice does express an idea of reciprocity. The principle of perfection decidedly does not ask the least advantaged to accept less satisfactory social terms in order that the most advantaged may become more advantaged still. Rather, it satisfies the following reciprocity condition: departures from a benchmark of equal division are permitted only on condition that they are necessary to establish and maintain social conditions that encourage *everyone*, including the least advantaged, to lead flourishing ways of life. As I go on to discuss below, the perfectionist principles of justice are admittedly less egalitarian than Rawls's principles, since they can call for the promotion of art and culture, say, even when this is not the most effective way to benefit the least advantaged. Nonetheless, the justification given to the least advantaged for using public funds in this way is not that this is a means of providing further advantages to those who are already most advantaged—an 'extreme' demand that would indeed be inimical to the idea of reciprocity—but that this is a means of sustaining social conditions that encourage everyone, including the least advantaged, to lead flourishing ways of life.

---

[83] Rawls, J., *Justice as Fairness*, pp. 122, 127.
[84] Ibid., p. 124.

One might object that the reciprocity condition alleged to be implicit in the principle of perfection sounds suspiciously similar to the principle of perfection itself. But the same could be said of the reciprocity condition alleged to be implicit in the difference principle. After all, isn't the claim that 'those who are better off at any point are not better off to the detriment of those who are worse off at that point' suspiciously similar to, and perhaps even a mere restatement of, the difference principle itself?[85] It seems, then, that the best way of thinking about the satisfaction of a reciprocity condition is not as some kind of independently defined condition that can adjudicate between the difference principle and the principle of perfection. Rather, we are to try to see whether it is possible to re-describe each principle of justice in terms that bring out more vividly the way in which it is in some way expressive of the idea of reciprocity. Understood thus, both principles appear roughly on a par so far as satisfying a plausible reciprocity condition is concerned.

Recall another consideration that Rawls says would lead parties to choose the difference principle in the second fundamental comparison: namely, that the strains of commitment are greater under the principle of average utility with a social minimum than under the difference principle. So it is worth considering at this juncture whether the perfectionist principles of justice might involve significant strains of commitment.

Two potential kinds of strains are worth considering in this regard. First, one might worry that the perfectionist principles of justice would involve significant strains of commitment for the worst-off members of society. The perfectionist principles of justice, after all, are less egalitarian than Rawls's principles of justice. Once equal basic liberties and fair equality of opportunity are in place, the perfectionist principles call for intuitionistic trade-offs between the pursuit of further equality (as dictated by the difference principle) and the pursuit of excellence (as dictated by the principle of perfection). This means that the perfectionist principles of justice might require, say, that available tax revenues be used to provide funding for museums instead of income supplements for low-income workers. Yet those low-income workers may have no interest at all in frequenting museums. In these instances, then, perfectionist justice appears to involve a kind of reverse Robin Hood effect, whereby the better-off gain at the expense of the worse-off. Wouldn't this create significant strains of commitment for the worst-off members of society, who are in effect forced to subsidize the cultural and artistic pursuits of the better-off?[86]

In reply, it is important to note that, although the perfectionist principles of justice are less egalitarian than Rawls's principles of justice, they are still strongly egalitarian: the equal liberties principle and the fair equality of opportunity

---

[85] Ibid.
[86] I thank David Miller for putting this objection to me.

114 A PERFECTIONIST THEORY OF JUSTICE

principle are quite demanding principles that would significantly constrain permissible social and economic inequalities, and the influence of the difference principle at the intuitionistic balancing stage would constrain these inequalities even further.[87] Many of the most disturbing social and economic inequalities that characterize contemporary societies would be eliminated in a well-ordered society that is effectively regulated by the perfectionist conception of justice. It seems unlikely that the remaining inequalities would be so great that the worst-off within such a society would be unable to honour and affirm the terms of perfectionist justice. This is bolstered by the observation that contemporary practices of state support for museums—which take place against a background of greater inequalities than would be present in a well-ordered perfectionist society—have not tended to create significant strains of commitment for the worst-off. Certainly, these moderately perfectionist policies do not appear to have caused the worse-off to 'grow distant from political society', to 'retreat into [their] social world' or to become 'withdrawn and cynical' to any noticeable degree. So whatever the plausibility of Rawls's sociological speculations about the strains on the worst-off so far as a society regulated by the principle of average utility with a social minimum is concerned, they do not seem likely to apply to a society regulated by the perfectionist principles of justice.[88]

It is true that other conceptions of justice, such as Rawls's justice as fairness, would go further in reducing inequality. But, in general, a conception of social or distributive justice must do more than promote equality to the greatest extent possible. Equality is only part of social justice, even if it is a major part thereof. A conception of justice must strike an appropriate balance between a world of competing claims—the claims of liberty, the claims of equality, the claims of efficiency, the claims of stability, the claims of community and, or so I am suggesting, the claims of perfection. Indeed, one of the most important criticisms of Rawls's theory of justice is precisely that he is too willing to tolerate departures from equality for the sake of other values such as freedom and efficiency.[89] So we have to consult our considered convictions to assess whether the perfectionist conception of justice makes the right trade-offs between equality and excellence on due reflection—whether the value of great works of art, historic treasures, architectural wonders and cultural heritage, as well as other forms of excellence whose existence would be

---

[87] See Rawls, J., *Justice as Fairness*, p. 46 n. 10 on the 'important distributive effects' of the prior principles of justice.

[88] It is also worth noting here that, even if some perfectionist policies (e.g. museums) would disadvantage the worst-off, other perfectionist policies (e.g. gambling restrictions) may advantage the worst-off. An argument to this effect from Steven Wall is discussed in Section 6.6.3. While I do not agree with Wall's contention that perfectionism would be *overall* advantageous to the worst-off, his argument is relevant here because it reveals the egalitarian tendency of some elements of a programme of perfectionist law and public policy, thereby mitigating to some extent the worry that perfectionist justice involves a reverse Robin Hood effect.

[89] See Cohen, G. A., *Rescuing Justice and Equality* (Cambridge, MA: Harvard University Press, 2008).

put in jeopardy without state support, is worth the limited albeit real costs in terms of equality. A contention of this work as a whole is that the perfectionist conception of justice does strike the most reasonable balance between these competing demands.

Second, one might worry that the perfectionist principles of justice would involve significant strains of commitment for those who reject the ideals of human flourishing favoured by the perfectionist state. A tempting example here concerns religious perfectionism. Would parties select the perfectionist principles of justice, knowing that they might turn out to be atheists in a state that promotes a specifically Christian conception of human flourishing? Religious perfectionism is not, however, the best example because, as I shall explain in Section 5.1 and Chapter 7, religious ideals are subject to reasonable disagreement and so would be ruled out as legitimate sources of political reasons by the public justification principle. In this sense, I endorse a version of what Steven Wall calls a 'restricted neutrality principle', one which holds that even though the perfectionist state should promote many ideals of human flourishing, it should remain neutral with respect to other such ideals about which there is reasonable disagreement, including religious ideals.[90] Still, an important version of the challenge remains: would parties agree to the perfectionist principles of justice, knowing that they might turn out to be hermits in a state that promotes friendship or that they might turn out to be art-haters in a state that promotes artistic excellence? Wouldn't they worry that the perfectionist contract looks too much like a blank cheque—one whose central provisions are specified *after* the parties have signed on the dotted line?[91]

Whereas the previous worry was about the strains of commitment on the worse-off, here the worry is about the strains of commitment on the dissenter, for whom perfectionist laws and policies represent unacceptable impositions of alien values. Objections of this kind are important and recur at various points and in various guises in this work, especially in Section 4.5 and Chapter 7. At this point, then, I shall only make a brief response—one which echoes my response to the egalitarian challenge by bringing out certain features of the perfectionist principles of justice under consideration by the parties. In this regard, what must be remembered is that the art-hater (or the hermit) would still enjoy the following benefits: he would be guaranteed the basic liberties (including freedom of belief, freedom of expression, bodily integrity, and so on), he would enjoy fair equality of opportunity, and he would receive a suitably equal share of primary goods (including wealth, income and the social bases of self-respect). Whatever policies are advocated in the name of perfection cannot infringe on any of this. He would therefore still live under highly favourable social and political conditions. The state would,

---

[90] See Wall, S., 'Neutralism for Perfectionists: The Case of Restricted State Neutrality', *Ethics* 120 (2010), pp. 232–56.

[91] I thank Cécile Laborde for putting this objection to me.

116 A PERFECTIONIST THEORY OF JUSTICE

of course, promote the enjoyment of artistic excellence through a range of public policies, and these policies can be expected to raise somewhat the level of his taxes. But these perfectionist policies would be moderate and heavily constrained by prior principles of justice, and so it is difficult to see how they would give rise to significant strains of commitment.

Here again it is helpful to observe that the well-established practice of state support for the arts within contemporary societies does not appear to have caused great strains for those who are indifferent or opposed to art. There are admittedly furores from time to time about government involvement in the arts. A clear illustration of this is the controversy over the purchase in 1973 of Jackson Pollock's abstract expressionist painting *Blue Poles* by Prime Minister Gough Whitlam for the Australian National Gallery at a cost of $1.3 million to the taxpayer.[92] Many citizens publicly complained about being made to contribute to an artwork that they regarded as a gimmick—as being totally bereft of artistic merit or value. One opposition senator, Condor Laucke, held a special press conference to condemn the purchase, saying that 'the government had been taken for a ride' and that the purchase of *Blue Poles* reflected Whitlam's 'complete irresponsibility in the outlay of public monies'.[93] Still, this outcry blew over relatively quickly and does not appear to have left lasting cleavages within Australian society. In general, moderately perfectionist policies have not tended to cause high levels of alienation and cynicism on the part of dissenters. Given the other features of the perfectionist principles of justice, as well as the constraints imposed by the 'restricted neutrality principle' discussed in Sections 5.1 and 7.3, then, it is not implausible to suppose that the parties in the perfectionist original position would sign the perfectionist contract, even without knowing whether they will agree with all the details of its conception of human flourishing once the veil of ignorance is lifted.

4.5 Are Judgements About Human Flourishing Especially Controversial?

As I alluded to above, Rawls is aware of the possibility of more moderate perfectionist principles not dissimilar to those I defend, and he admits that this mixed view is 'not easy to argue against'.[94] In an interesting anticipation of his later work, Rawls's main worry appears to be about the disagreement surrounding perfectionist considerations:

---

[92] For an interesting exploration of this episode, see Barrett, L., *The Prime Minister's Christmas Card: Blue Poles and Cultural Politics in the Whitlam Era* (Sydney: Power Publications, 2001).
[93] Quoted in ibid., p. 18.
[94] Rawls, J., *A Theory of Justice*, p. 330.

PERFECTIONIST PRINCIPLES OF JUSTICE 117

> Criteria of excellence are imprecise as political principles, and their application to public questions is bound to be unsettled and idiosyncratic, however reasonably they may be invoked and accepted within narrower traditions and communities of thought ... Appeal to perfectionist criteria [is often made] in an ad hoc manner. When it is said, for example, that certain kinds of sexual relationships are degrading and shameful, and should be prohibited on this basis, if only for the sake of the individuals in question irrespective of their wishes, it is often because a reasonable case cannot be made in terms of the principles of justice. Instead we fall back on notions of excellence. But in these matters we are likely to be influenced by subtle aesthetic preferences and personal feelings of propriety; and individual, class, and group differences are often sharp and irreconcilable. Since these uncertainties plague perfectionist criteria and jeopardize individual liberty, it seems best to rely entirely on the principles of justice which have a more definite structure. Thus even in its intuitionistic form, perfectionism would be rejected as not defining a feasible basis of social justice.[95]

I briefly touched on one version of this objection in Section 4.4, and I address the objection in a general way in Chapter 7, and so my full response must await that chapter. Nonetheless, let me make three comments here on the specific rendition of this objection found in this important passage from Rawls.

The first point is that although Rawls is meant to be considering a more moderate kind of perfectionism at this point, he talks as if the perfectionism is far more extreme and Nietzschean in kind. For instance, he suggests that the perfectionist view in question may 'jeopardize individual liberty' and that it may say that certain kinds of relationships 'should be prohibited' on the grounds that they are degrading. But, to repeat, on the perfectionist principles of justice that I am proposing, the provision of an environment that is promotive of and conducive to flourishing ways of life is *conditional* on the other lexically prior principles of justice being met (including, in particular, the principle that each person has the same indefeasible claim to a fully adequate scheme of equal basic liberties compatible with the same scheme of liberties for all). So, as I explain further in Chapter 8, prohibited relationships and jeopardized liberty are not in fact risks of these perfectionist principles of justice rightly understood.

The second point is that Rawls's brief consideration of one specific class of perfectionist judgements (namely, judgements about sexual morality) is insufficient to establish some *general asymmetry* between the controversiality of non-perfectionist and perfectionist judgements, such that the former but not the latter could shape social terms.[96]

---

[95] Ibid., pp. 330–1.
[96] This point is connected to the so-called asymmetry objection to political liberalism. See, for example, Caney, S., 'Liberal Legitimacy, Reasonable Disagreement, and Justice', *Critical Review of International Social and Political Philosophy* 1 (1998), pp. 19–36; Sandel, M., *Liberalism and the Limits of*

On the one hand, many perfectionist judgements are *not* deeply controversial. As I suggested in Section 4.3, for instance, it seems likely that very many people—at least as many people as would accept comparable non-perfectionist judgements— would agree that someone who devotes his life to counting blades of grass does not lead a flourishing life. More generally, it is unclear why appeal to a handful of core perfectionist values that have broad appeal and that are pitched at a high level of generality, such as moral, intellectual and artistic excellence, would be too 'ad hoc', 'idiosyncratic' or 'uncertain' to feasibly be part of social justice. Here one might object that these abstract perfectionist values will become more controversial as they are made more concrete. I consider a version of this objection in detail in Section 7.5. For now, though, it suffices to say that the same is true of abstract liberal values such as freedom, equality and fairness. So to insist that the concretization of abstract perfectionist values will incur more controversy than the concretization of abstract liberal values does not *vindicate* the asymmetry between perfectionist and non-perfectionist judgements but instead only *relocates* that asymmetry. In brief, while Rawls is no doubt correct that judgements about sexual morality are too idiosyncratic or controversial to be a feasible basis of social justice, it is doubtful that this is true of perfectionist judgements generally.[97]

On the other hand, many non-perfectionist judgements *are* deeply controversial. For instance, many people disagree heatedly about what equality of opportunity requires in relation, say, to employment practices. For some, it requires only non-discrimination along morally arbitrary lines, such as race and gender; for others, it requires us to 'wrestle with counterfactuals about what the [applicants] would have been like if they had had each other's backgrounds';[98] and for yet others, it requires us to take into account the unearned effects not only of the social lottery but also of the genetic lottery. So deep are these disagreements that some wonder whether there is any remaining shared ground: 'the fact that we all converge on a certain form of words [i.e. "equality of opportunity"] does not mean we actually agree on anything substantial'.[99] Indeed, the fact that non-perfectionist judgements are controversial in this way should hardly come as a surprise. After all, Rawls's influential explanation of why disagreement about perfectionist questions

---

Justice (Cambridge: Cambridge University Press, 1998), pp. 202–10. For an important defence of this asymmetry, see Quong, J., *Liberalism Without Perfection*, ch. 7. As Quong recognizes, the success of his response depends on the correctness of a particular conception of reasonableness—one that 'define[s] reasonableness in a way that leads reasonable persons to accept a principle of liberal neutrality' (p. 218). In Chapter 7, I challenge this anti-perfectionist definition of reasonableness, and so my rebuttal of Quong's defence of this asymmetry must await that chapter. For a different rebuttal of Quong's argument, see Fowler, T. and Stemplowska, Z., 'The Asymmetry Objection Rides Again: On the Nature and Significance of Justificatory Disagreement', *Journal of Applied Philosophy* 32 (2015), pp. 133–46.

[97] For a more general discussion of the tendency in this literature for critics of perfectionism to falsely generalize from versions of perfectionism that incorporate crude or excessively sectarian conceptions of human flourishing, see Section 5.4.

[98] Richards, J., 'Equality of Opportunity', in A. Mason (ed.), *Ideals of Equality* (Oxford: Blackwell, 1998), p. 56.

[99] Cavanagh, M., *Against Equality of Opportunity* (Oxford: Clarendon Press, 2002), pp. 1–2.

is 'the inevitable long-run result of the powers of human reason at work within the background of enduring free institutions'—which, as we saw in Section 2.1, has to do with the six 'burdens of judgement' involved in the exercise of human reason—applies equally well to non-perfectionist questions.[100] Questions about taxation, immigration, affirmative action, abortion, capital punishment, freedom of speech, just war and health care, that is, all involve the assessment of complex empirical evidence, the application of vague concepts, the balancing of conflicting normative considerations, and so on. So why should we expect the powers of human reason at work within the background of enduring free institutions to produce in the long run disagreement about ideals of human flourishing but not about ideals of social justice too?

In short, then, Rawls's suggestion that there is some interestingly general asymmetry between the controversiality of perfectionist and non-perfectionist judgements relies on a false generalization: it draws a conclusion about all instances of perfectionist claims on the basis of only one instance thereof. In reality, perfectionist and non-perfectionist judgements appear to be roughly on a par in terms of how controversial they are. We are thus left with the question: what is the basis for thinking that the distinction between perfectionist and non-perfectionist judgements tracks the distinction between what is and what is not a matter of controversy within contemporary societies? 'One wonders', Arneson rightly says in this regard, 'whether the bar of rational acceptability is being raised and lowered arbitrarily when one moves from the domain of the right to the domain of the good, so that the standard cannot be met when we are debating what is good but can be met when we are debating what is right.'[101]

The third point is that, as Rawls himself says elsewhere, it is also impossible to make highly precise judgements and measurements of non-perfectionist values such as freedom, equality, fairness and self-respect. Our judgements '[need] not be very exact', Rawls explains, and only need to be 'accurate enough to guide the main decisions' concerning the provision of fair social terms.[102] So the question is: can we make *sufficiently* determinate assessments about the good life to guide certain important political decisions? Yet, as Rawls himself concedes, many (though of course not all) perfectionist judgements do appear to pass this test: 'clearly there are standards in the arts and sciences for appraising creative efforts' and 'very often it is beyond question that the work of one person is superior to that of another'.[103] Rawls further states that 'comparisons of intrinsic value can obviously be made'

---

[100] See Rawls, J., *Political Liberalism*, pp. 4, 54–7. This point is recognized by both perfectionists (see, e.g., Caney, S., 'Liberal Legitimacy, Reasonable Disagreement and Justice', p. 23) and anti-perfectionists (see, e.g., Quong, J., *Liberalism Without Perfection*, pp. 196–8).

[101] Arneson, R., 'Neutrality and Political Liberalism', in R. Merrill and D. Weinstock (eds), *Political Neutrality*, p. 27.

[102] Rawls, J., *A Theory of Justice*, p. 327.

[103] Ibid., p. 328.

120   A PERFECTIONIST THEORY OF JUSTICE

and that 'judgments of value have an important place in human affairs'.[104] 'They are not necessarily so vague', Rawls admits, 'that they must fail as a workable basis for assigning rights.'[105]

Pulling together these three points, Rawls's reply gives us no reason to doubt the main thrust of the perfectionist conception of justice. Rawls's reply, that is, gives us no reason to doubt that *certain* abstract and widely shared perfectionist values such as moral, intellectual and artistic excellence (as opposed to highly specific claims about sexual morality) are *sufficiently* precise and determinate (as opposed to perfectly precise and determinate) to shape social terms in a manner *consistent* with the other principles of justice (as opposed to doing so in a manner that jeopardizes liberties and prohibits relationships).

4.6 Is the Perfectionist Original Position Redundant?

For some, the argument from the perfectionist original position to the perfectionist principles of justice may seem in some way redundant or needlessly convoluted:

> Suppose it is true that parties in the perfectionist original position would select the perfectionist principles of justice. As we saw in Section 4.4, when we ask *why* the parties would select these principles over other principles, the answer involves a delicate balance of reasons having to do with the importance of flourishing, the nature of reciprocity, the strains of commitment, and so on. But then aren't *these* the reasons that do the fundamental moral work here? What does the agreement of the parties add to these reasons? Once those reasons are on the table, hasn't the case already been made for the perfectionist principles of justice? Acceptability to the parties in the perfectionist original position, it appears, is not what *makes* it the case that the perfectionist principles of justice are correct but is instead merely a *by-product* of the reasons in virtue of which the perfectionist principles of justice are correct. So why not dispense with the original position machinery altogether? Why not appeal directly to the morally fundamental reasons themselves, rather than going through the superfluous and distracting process of imagining which principles of justice would be selected by parties in the perfectionist original position?[106]

---

[104] Ibid.
[105] Ibid.
[106] For an influential early version of this charge as applied to Rawls's use of the original position, see Dworkin, R., 'The Original Position', in N. Daniels (ed.), *Reading Rawls: Critical Studies on Rawls' A Theory of Justice* (Stanford, CA: Stanford University Press, 1989), pp. 16–53. See also Kymlicka, W., 'The Social Contract Tradition', in P. Singer (ed.), *A Companion to Ethics* (Oxford: Blackwell, 1991), p. 193. Similar redundancy objections have been directed against Scanlon's contractualist moral theory as developed in his *What We Owe to Each Other* (Cambridge, MA: Harvard University Press, 1998). For early examples, see Thomson, J. J., *The Realm of Rights* (Cambridge, MA: Harvard University Press,

PERFECTIONIST PRINCIPLES OF JUSTICE   121

This is a well-known objection to contractualist arguments within moral and political philosophy, and it applies to Rawls's use of the original position too. So it is helpful, in the first instance, to consider what Rawls says in response to this concern about redundancy. Doing so helps us to gain a clearer understanding of the nature and purpose of original position arguments.

As Rawls stresses at various points, the original position should be understood as a 'device of representation'.[107] 'The original position', he says, 'serves to keep track of all our assumptions and to bring out their combined force by uniting them into one framework so that we can more easily see their implications'.[108] The original position is 'economical and suggestive' and 'a natural guide to intuition'.[109] It 'brings out certain essential features that otherwise one might easily overlook'.[110] By imposing restrictions on what the parties know, the original position specifies a standpoint for reasoning about justice that is to a high degree objective and impartial, that 'enables us to envision our [situation] from afar', and that makes it 'impossible to tailor principles' to our own advantage.[111] At its best, Rawls explains, the original position offers us a highly rigorous method for the analysis of principles of justice. Noting that the various specifications of the parties are to feature as premises in the description of the original position, he explains:

> Clearly arguments from such premises can be fully deductive, as theories in politics and economics attest. We should strive for a kind of moral geometry with all the rigor which this name connotes. Unhappily the reasoning I shall give will fall far short of this, since it is highly intuitive throughout. Yet it is essential to have in mind the ideal one would like to achieve.[112]

The objector is thus entirely correct that the agreement of the parties in the perfectionist original position is not what does 'fundamental moral work' in justifying the perfectionist principles of justice. But the objector is incorrect to conclude, thereby, that the original position device is pointless. For the sorts of reasons given by Rawls, the perfectionist original position can still play an important heuristic role within a perfectionist political theory. It can function as a valuable philosophical tool for representing or modelling certain ideas in a vivid, objective and focused way. The perfectionist original position thus helps us to unfold or operationalize

---

1990), pp. 30 n. 19, 188 n. 5; McGinn, C., 'Reasons and Unreasons', *The New Republic*, 24 May 1999, pp. 34–8. For a helpful overview of such redundancy objections, see Southwood, N., *Contractualism and the Foundations of Morality* (Oxford: Oxford University Press, 2010), ch. 7. Related worries appear, of course, in many areas of moral and political philosophy, including in connection with public justification (see the discussion in Section 7.6.5).

[107] Rawls, J., *Justice as Fairness*, p. 86 *et passim*.
[108] Ibid., p. 39.
[109] Rawls, J., *A Theory of Justice*, pp. 138–9.
[110] Ibid., p. 138.
[111] Ibid., pp. 18, 22.
[112] Ibid., p. 121.

122   A PERFECTIONIST THEORY OF JUSTICE

the perfectionist conception of society as a fair striving for human flourishing between free and equal persons and to identify the principles of justice most fitting to that conception of society.

So even if the perfectionist original position is explanatorily redundant in the sense that it is possible fully to articulate the case for the perfectionist principles of justice without any reference to what the parties in the perfectionist original position would or would not accept, it does not follow that the perfectionist original position is redundant in a broader philosophical sense: for it can still be highly fruitful as a device for presenting this case in a concise and persuasive manner. There is thus still an important role for the original position apparatus to play, even if it 'does not take us to rock bottom'.[113]

At this point, however, the objector might respond as follows: even if the argument from the Rawlsian original position is strictly speaking redundant too, isn't there something *distinctively* redundant or pointless about the argument from the perfectionist original position? Rawls's anti-perfectionist liberalism is the kind of view that in some sense *lends itself* to being represented through the heuristic device of the original position. But perfectionism—so this objection goes—does not similarly lend itself to being represented in this way. In the perfectionist original position, for instance, fairly substantive moral claims about human flourishing are stipulated into the parties—stipulations that make it more difficult for us to imaginatively relate to our heuristic counterparts in the perfectionist original position and that might even 'defeat the purpose' of the original position (to use Rawls's phrase).[114] In short, then, is it really the case that perfectionist thought is *as* well-suited to being expressed within the framework of the original position as Rawlsian liberal thought? Doesn't the original position device provide less illumination in the perfectionist context than it does in the anti-perfectionist liberal context?[115]

I find it hard, though, to see why perfectionist ideas and commitments cannot be aptly expressed in terms of the original position. Everything that Rawls says in support of the heuristic value of his original position carries over to the perfectionist original position: the perfectionist original position helps to keep track of all our assumptions; it brings out their combined force by uniting them into a single manageable idea; it is economical and suggestive and a natural guide to intuition; it brings out considerations that one might easily overlook; it specifies an objective standpoint for reasoning about justice; it makes it impossible to tailor principles to one's own advantage; and it promises a strictly deductive ideal of argument.

The objector might press that the assumptions in the perfectionist original position are thicker or more controversial than the assumptions in the Rawlsian

---

[113] Pettit, P., 'Can Contract Theory Ground Morality?', in J. Dreier (ed.), *Contemporary Debates in Moral Theory* (Oxford: Blackwell, 2006), p. 95.

[114] Rawls, J., *A Theory of Justice*, p. 149.

[115] I thank Matthew Kramer and Cécile Laborde for pressing me on this point.

original position. Rawls is keen to stress that the original position 'must be characterized by stipulations that are widely accepted' and that 'one must try to avoid introducing into it any controversial ethical elements.'[116] Yet aren't the stipulations in the perfectionist original position significantly more controversial than the stipulations in the Rawlsian original position and to this extent less suited to being modelled using the original position device?

But there are two problems with this rejoinder. First, it is unclear that the elements introduced into the perfectionist original position really are significantly more controversial than those introduced into the Rawlsian original position. The beliefs and desires about human flourishing that are stipulated into the parties in the perfectionist original position are deliberately thin and abstract. As was stressed in Section 4.3, it is not assumed that parties believe any specific comprehensive doctrine such as Christianity or Confucianism to be correct, nor is it assumed that parties desire to flourish in the sense recommended by any specific doctrine of this kind. Such assumptions would indeed be too controversial to be introduced into the original position. Instead, the beliefs and desires about human flourishing that are stipulated into the parties—namely, that individuals want to flourish to a greater rather than lesser degree and that not all ways of life are equally flourishing—are widely accepted, even within pluralistic societies. The second problem is that, even if the assumptions of the perfectionist original position are more controversial than the assumptions of the Rawlsian original position, it is unclear that they are *too* controversial to rule out the apt or suitable employment of the original position device. To establish this, the objector would need to provide answers to difficult questions such as these: how controversial is too controversial? At what point does an assumption become so thick or controversial that it could not aptly feature as part of the description of an original position? How is this degree of controversiality to be specified in a principled way?

In short, then, without a more precise and fleshed-out account of when and why the original position is (and is not) a useful heuristic device, it remains unclear to me why the original position is any less illuminating or suitable for perfectionist purposes than it is for Rawlsian purposes. Indeed, for what it is worth, it is interesting to note here that Rawls himself does not seem to think that anti-perfectionist liberalism is the only political philosophy that is amenable to being expressed in terms of the original position. Far from jealously guarding the original position heuristic as the exclusive preserve of a certain kind of liberal theorist, Rawls is open to the idea of there being 'many possible' original positions, each of which would correspond to a tradition of political philosophy, such as utilitarianism, perfectionism and libertarianism:

---

[116] Rawls, J., *A Theory of Justice*, p. 14.

124 A PERFECTIONIST THEORY OF JUSTICE

There are ... many possible interpretations of the initial situation. This conception varies depending upon how the contracting parties are conceived, upon what their beliefs and interests are said to be, upon which alternatives are available to them, and so on. In this sense, there are many different contract theories. Justice as fairness is but one of these.[117]

As Rawls explains in a deep and important passage, part of the power of the original position is precisely that it offers a highly general method for formulating and evaluating rival conceptions of justice:

We may conjecture that for each traditional conception of justice there exists an interpretation of the initial situation in which its principles are the preferred solution. Thus, for example, there are interpretations that lead to the classical as well as the average principle of utility ... The procedure of contract theories provides, then, a general analytic method for the comparative study of conceptions of justice. One tries to set out the different conditions embodied in the contractual situation in which their principles would be chosen. In this way one formulates the various underlying assumptions on which these conceptions seem to depend. But if one interpretation is philosophically most favoured, and if its principles characterize our considered judgments, we have a procedure for justification as well.[118]

This thought can be put slightly more specifically. Responding to libertarian critics such as Robert Nozick, Rawls makes the following point:

If it is objected that certain principles are not on the list [that is presented to parties], say libertarian principles of justice, those principles must be added to it. Justice as fairness then argues that the two principles of justice would still be agreed to. Should this argument succeed, libertarians must object to the setup of the original position itself as a device of representation. For example, they must say that it fails to represent considerations they regard as essential, or that it represents them in the wrong way. The argument continues from there.[119]

The arguments of this chapter—in which I add a perfectionist principle of justice to the list presented to the parties and in which I object to the set-up of the original position by arguing that it fails to represent considerations that perfectionists regard as essential—can thus be understood as the pursuit by a perfectionist of the project that Rawls here recommends to libertarians. So, far from dismissing the marriage of perfectionism and the original position device as inapt or

---

[117] Ibid., p. 121.
[118] Ibid., pp. 121–2.
[119] Rawls, J., *Justice as Fairness*, p. 83.

ill-motivated, it is not unreasonable to think that Rawls would himself have welcomed the arguments of this chapter as exactly the right sort of way to develop a perfectionist theory of justice, even if he were to remain ultimately unconvinced by them.

5
A Provisional Conception of Human Flourishing

I have argued that for political purposes society ought to be conceived of as a fair striving for human flourishing between free and equal citizens (Chapter 3) and that the principles most appropriate for regulating a society conceived of in this way would include the establishment and maintenance, in a manner consistent with other principles of justice, of social conditions promotive of and conducive to flourishing ways of life (Chapter 4). But, so far, the idea of 'human flourishing' has been left fairly non-specific. This naturally raises the question: what is a flourishing way of life? Which conception of human flourishing—or, more pointedly, *whose* conception of human flourishing—should social conditions be promotive of and conducive to?

Supplying a plausible conception of human flourishing at this point is especially important because some sort of subjectivism or scepticism about human flourishing has traditionally been an important part of the case for anti-perfectionist liberalism.[1] For many, that is, the appeal of anti-perfectionist liberalism derives precisely from uncertainty about our answers to the deepest questions of human life. Subjectivists question the *existence* of objective truths about human flourishing and sceptics question our ability to *know* such truths, assuming they exist. But either subjectivism or scepticism, if correct, threatens to undercut perfectionism as a political project.

In relation to subjectivism, Bruce Ackerman suggests that doubting 'the reality of transcendent meaning' is one of the four 'main highways' that lead to anti-perfectionist liberalism.[2] As Ackerman puts it, perhaps 'the hard truth is this: there

---

[1] At the same time, of course, many anti-perfectionist liberals have been at pains to stress that their anti-perfectionism does not in any way rest on subjectivist or sceptical premises. Indeed, as we saw in Section 4.3, subjectivism or scepticism have often been seen as highly inappropriate bases for anti-perfectionist liberalism. For the disavowal of subjectivism or scepticism by anti-perfectionist liberals, see, for example, Dworkin, R., 'Liberalism', in S. Hampshire (ed.), *Public and Private Morality* (Cambridge: Cambridge University Press, 1978), p. 142; Rawls, J., *Political Liberalism* (New York: Columbia University Press, 2005), pp. 62–3, 150–4; Larmore, C., *Patterns of Moral Complexity* (Cambridge: Cambridge University Press, 1987), pp. 51–2; Kymlicka, W., *Liberalism, Community and Culture* (Oxford: Oxford University Press, 1989), pp. 17–18; Nagel, T., *Equality and Partiality* (Oxford: Oxford University Press, 1991), p. 157; Quong, J., *Liberalism Without Perfection* (Oxford: Oxford University Press, 2011), pp. 33, 243–55.

[2] Ackerman, B., *Social Justice in the Liberal State* (New Haven, CT: Yale University Press, 1980), p. 369. The other three highways are scepticism (which I discuss below), 'realism about the corrosiveness of power' and 'respect for the autonomy of persons' (both of which I discuss in Chapter 8). Similarly,

---

A Perfectionist Theory of Justice. Collis Tahzib, Oxford University Press.
© Collis Tahzib (2022). DOI: 10.1093/oso/9780192847119.003.0006

is no moral meaning hidden in the bowels of the universe. All there is is you and I struggling in a world that neither we, nor any other thing, created.[3] On this view, there are no objectively correct answers to questions about human flourishing—only personal opinions, tastes and preferences. These sorts of arguments from subjectivism about human flourishing to anti-perfectionist liberalism (or to some predecessor of this view) play an important role in the liberal tradition and go back at least to John Locke:

> The Mind has a different relish, as well as the Palate; and you will as fruitlesly endeavour to delight all Men with Riches or Glory, (which yet some Men place their Happiness in,) as you would to satisfy all Men's Hunger with Cheese or Lobsters; which, though very agreeable and delicious fare to some, are to others extremely nauseous and offensive: And many People would with Reason preferr the griping of an hungry Belly, to those Dishes, which are a Feast to others. Hence it was, I think, that the Philosophers of old did in vain enquire, whether *Summum bonum* consisted in Riches, or bodily Delights, or Virtue, or Contemplation: And they might have as reasonably disputed, whether the best Relish were to be found in Apples, Plumbs, or Nuts; and have divided themselves into Sects upon it. For as pleasant Tastes depend not on the things themselves, but their agreeableness to this or that particular Palate, wherein there is great variety: So the greatest Happiness consists, in the having those things, which produce the greatest Pleasure; and in the absence of those, which cause any disturbance, any pain. Now these, to different Men, are very different things ... Men may chuse different things, and yet all chuse right.[4]

And in relation to scepticism, Brian Barry contends that 'the sheer weight of the evidence in favour of scepticism [about human flourishing] seems overwhelming'.[5] As he explains: 'it is hard not to be impressed by the fact that so many people have devoted so much effort over so many centuries to a matter of the greatest moment [namely, the identification of sound ideals of human flourishing] with so little success in the way of securing rational conviction among those not initially predisposed in favour of their conclusions'.[6] Barry thus concludes that 'no conception

---

Sarah Conly argues against perfectionism partly on the grounds that all objective conceptions of human flourishing 'fail the test for intuitive plausibility'. See Conly, S., *Against Autonomy: Justifying Coercive Paternalism* (Cambridge: Cambridge University Press, 2013), pp. 107–10.

[3] Ackerman, B., *Social Justice in the Liberal State*, p. 368.

[4] Locke, J., *An Essay Concerning Human Understanding*, ed. P. Nidditch (Oxford: Clarendon Press, 1975), pp. 269–70.

[5] See Barry, B., *Justice as Impartiality* (Oxford: Oxford University Press, 1995), especially pp. 168–73. Ackerman also takes scepticism to be one of the 'highways' to anti-perfectionist liberalism, saying that 'while everybody has an opinion about the good life, none can be known to be superior to any other' (see *Social Justice in the Liberal State*, p. 11). A related sceptical argument for anti-perfectionist liberalism is found in Peter, F., 'Epistemic Foundations of Political Liberalism', *Journal of Moral Philosophy* 10 (2013), pp. 598–620.

[6] Barry, B., *Justice as Impartiality*, p. 171.

128 A PERFECTIONIST THEORY OF JUSTICE

of the good can justifiably be held with a degree of certainty that warrants its imposition on those who reject it'.[7]

If one of these possibilities turns out to be true, the perfectionist position would be in danger of collapsing, or at least of becoming entirely indistinguishable from anti-perfectionist liberalism. Take a subjectivist view according to which a flourishing life for an individual is one in which she has a fair share of resources (as defined by the appropriate non-perfectionist theory of justice, such as Rawls's justice as fairness) and uses those resources to pursue her preferred plan of life free from outside interference. There is certainly something appealing about this view. What could possibly be better for a person, we may well wonder, than the pursuit of a plan of life that seems good to her? Yet if this turns out to be the correct conception of human flourishing, then perfectionist justice seems to end up resembling anti-perfectionist liberalism in all but name. So until these subjectivist and sceptical possibilities are ruled out, how can we be sure that perfectionism is a viable and distinctive political theory?

One way to respond to these subjectivist and sceptical arguments is to try to rebut them one by one. In response to the subjectivist view according to which human flourishing is a matter of the satisfaction of desires, one might point out that this offends against many of our considered convictions. Purely subjective conceptions of human flourishing, after all, have the highly implausible implication that the satisfaction of *ill-informed* desires (such as the desire to cross a bridge that one mistakenly believes to be safe), of *pointless* desires (such as the desire to endlessly count blades of grass) and of *sadistic* desires (such as the desire to see others in pain) contributes to our flourishing.

Of course, defenders of a subjective conception of human flourishing might reply by shifting to *idealized* desires: what is constitutive of human flourishing, they may say, is not the satisfaction of what we *actually* desire (which may indeed be ill-informed, pointless, sadistic, and so on) but rather the satisfaction of what we *would* desire under suitable idealizing conditions (such as full information and full rationality).[8] But this reply invites at least two further problems. First, while these idealizing conditions might deal with some of the cases (such as the person who has a desire to cross a bridge that she mistakenly believes to be safe), do they really eliminate *all* problematic desires? Isn't it possible for someone who is fully informed and fully rational still to desire what is pointless or sadistic? Second, even if these idealizing conditions succeed in eliminating all problematic desires,

---

[7] Ibid., p. 169.

[8] For views along these lines, see, for example, Rawls, *A Theory of Justice* (Cambridge, MA: Harvard University Press, 1971), pp. 407–24; Railton, P., 'Facts and Values', *Philosophical Topics* 14 (1986), pp. 5–29; Sobel, D., *From Valuing to Value: A Defense of Subjectivism* (Oxford: Oxford University Press, 2017). Alternatively, defenders of a subjective conception can adopt a more hard-line reply, insisting that, despite appearances to the contrary, the satisfaction of ill-informed, pointless or sadistic desires does contribute to a person's flourishing. I critique a version of this position in Section 4.3.

it is unclear that the appeal to ideal desires is philosophically well-motivated.[9] Why think that only ideal desires contribute to a person's flourishing? The most natural answer here is that our suitably idealized counterparts will desire what is objectively good. But that, of course, is not something that a subjectivist can say. So is there a reason, from within a recognizably subjectivist framework, for privileging idealized desires over actual desires? The worry here is that, even if it secures extensional adequacy, the appeal to ideal desires is an ad hoc manoeuvre for fending off counterexamples, rather than something that is driven by, or at least is consistent with, the basic motivations of the subjectivist project.[10]

Similarly, in response to Barry's sceptical argument we might point out that it is also the case that so many people have devoted so much effort over so many centuries to another matter of similarly great historical moment—namely, the identification of sound ideals of *justice*—with so little success in the way of securing rational conviction among those not initially predisposed in favour of their conclusions. The truth about social justice is enormously complex, and heated disagreements about taxation, immigration, affirmative action, abortion, capital punishment, freedom of speech, just war, and so on still persist. Barry's own conception of justice, 'justice as impartiality', hardly seems to put an end to this centuries-long disputation.[11] But it is difficult to believe that the right lesson to draw from this is that no conception of justice can rightly be believed with a high degree of confidence. So Barry's argument proves too much: if taken seriously, it entails scepticism not just about matters of human flourishing but also about matters of social and distributive justice, thereby undercutting the foundations of anti-perfectionist liberalism.[12] It thus remains unclear what the rationale is for the highly selective and asymmetrical sort of scepticism—a scepticism that applies to questions of human flourishing but not to questions of social justice—that would be needed to justify anti-perfectionist liberalism.

These sorts of responses are fine so far as they go, but it is unclear where they leave perfectionism. Even if we succeed in parrying subjectivist and sceptical arguments in this way, we will hardly have vindicated perfectionism. To refute certain arguments *against* the existence or knowability of objective truths about human

---

[9] See Enoch, D., 'Why Idealize?', *Ethics* 115 (2005), pp. 759–87.

[10] This is plainly a mere sketch of some of the many issues here; for a more detailed discussion, see, for example, Heathwood, C., 'Desire-Fulfillment Theory', in G. Fletcher (ed.), *The Routledge Handbook of Philosophy of Well-Being* (London: Routledge, 2016), pp. 135–47; Fletcher, G., *The Philosophy of Well-Being* (Oxford: Routledge, 2016), ch. 2.

[11] For some critical responses to Barry's theory of justice, see P. Kelly (ed.), *Impartiality, Neutrality and Justice: Re-reading Brian Barry's Justice as Impartiality* (Edinburgh: Edinburgh University Press, 2000).

[12] For related critical discussions of Barry's sceptical argument for anti-perfectionist liberalism, see, for example, Caney, S., 'Impartiality and Liberal Neutrality', *Utilitas* 8 (1996), pp. 273–93; Wall, S., *Liberalism, Perfectionism and Restraint*, pp. 94–100; Clarke, S., 'Contractarianism, Liberal Neutrality, and Epistemology', *Political Studies* 47 (1999), pp. 634–7; Quong, J., *Liberalism Without Perfection*, pp. 33, 251–3.

flourishing is not to provide a positive case *for* the existence or knowability of such truths. A better way to respond to these subjectivist and sceptical possibilities, then, is to articulate a conception of human flourishing that has a significant objective component and that on due reflection seems appealing and worth promoting. Of course, there will still be numerous objections to the promotion of this conception of human flourishing through political action, and I try to respond to some of these objections in Part III. But the articulation of an appealing objective conception of human flourishing would at least go some way towards dispelling the distinctively subjectivist and sceptical objections to the perfectionist project.

In this chapter, then, I seek to defend a provisional free-standing conception of human flourishing, which can be plugged into the perfectionist principles of justice. I first set out three prominent conceptions of human flourishing that have been defended by previous perfectionists—namely, Christian, Confucian and Aristotelian conceptions of human flourishing. I argue that even if these conceptions of human flourishing are true, they are subject to reasonable disagreement and so are not legitimate sources of political reasons under conditions of reasonable pluralism (Section 5.1). I then suggest that perfectionists should instead adopt a conception of human flourishing that is more *free-standing* and that is specially constructed for political purposes; in particular, I contend that for political purposes human flourishing should be understood to consist in the enjoyment of moral, intellectual and artistic excellence (Section 5.2). A somewhat more specific and informative version of the principle of perfection articulated in Chapter 4 is thus that justice requires the establishment and maintenance of social conditions promotive of and conducive to ways of life rich in the enjoyment of moral, intellectual and artistic excellence.

I then defend this conception against the charge that the values of moral, intellectual and artistic excellence are too abstract and need to be specified further if the perfectionist conception of social justice is to deliver determinate verdicts about law and public policy (Section 5.3). I then explain (in Section 5.4) what is meant by saying that this is a *provisional* conception of human flourishing. In brief, the idea is that we can theorize the distinctively political questions about the state promotion of human flourishing without having in hand a fully worked-out conception of human flourishing, and so it makes sense to leave the finer details of this conception of human flourishing, such as the relative importance of the three excellences, to be figured out in due course. Finally, I address two important objections to this conception of human flourishing: that the list of excellences is arbitrary because no mention is made of the deeper feature that explains why all and only these items contribute to human flourishing (Section 5.5); and that enjoyment and excellence are not strictly necessary conditions of human flourishing because excellence devoid of enjoyment and enjoyment devoid of excellence can both contribute to human flourishing (Section 5.6).

5.1 Three Conceptions Unfit for Political Purposes

Perfectionist political theorists advance two distinctive claims: (1) that the state can or should promote human flourishing and (2) that human flourishing has a significant objective component.[13] Despite their shared commitment to (2), however, perfectionists have offered a wide variety of conceptions of human flourishing.

Some perfectionists understand human flourishing in explicitly religious terms. John Finnis, for instance, states that 'one of the basic human values is the establishment and maintenance of proper relationships between oneself (and the orders one can create and maintain) and the divine.'[14] 'One's life and actions are in fundamental disorder', he argues, 'if they are not brought, as best one can, into some sort of harmony with whatever can be known or surmised about that transcendent other and its lasting order.'[15] Similarly, Robert George holds that 'religion is a basic human good, an intrinsic and irreducible aspect of the well-being and flourishing of human persons' and thus that the state should 'encourage and support religious reflection, faith, and practice.'[16] And of course one of the major historical examples of perfectionism, namely 'the Catholic and Protestant states of the early modern period', was based squarely in a Christian conception of human flourishing.[17]

Other perfectionists defend conceptions of human flourishing rooted in Confucian thought. Sungmoon Kim, for instance, argues that the conception of human flourishing fit for promotion by the state is shaped by 'a constellation of Confucian values such as, but not limited to, filial piety, respect for elders, ancestor worship, ritual propriety, harmony within the family, and social harmony.'[18] Likewise, Joseph Chan regards 'material well-being, moral self-cultivation, and virtuous social relationships as constituents of "the good life" for a normal human being, with

---

[13] For these two commitments, see, for example, Wall, S., 'Perfectionist Politics: A Defense', in T. Christiano and J. Christman (eds), *Contemporary Debates in Political Philosophy* (Oxford: Blackwell, 2009), pp. 99–105. Recently, Steven Wall, despite not being a subjectivist, has relaxed the assumption that perfectionism must be wedded to an objective conception of human flourishing and has provided an interesting arm's-length exploration of what it might look like to combine perfectionism with a subjective conception of human flourishing. See 'Subjective Perfectionism', *The American Journal of Jurisprudence* 63 (2018), pp. 109–31. One way of understanding many versions of paternalism, I suppose, is as instances of a subjective perfectionism of this sort. But since I am not sure about what to make of subjective perfectionism, and in particular about whether subjective perfectionism would meaningfully differ from anti-perfectionist liberalism, I will adopt Wall's earlier (and more traditional) taxonomy, namely that a belief that human flourishing has a significant objective component is a constitutive commitment of perfectionism.

[14] Finnis, J., *Natural Law and Natural Rights* (Oxford: Oxford University Press, 2011), p. 89.

[15] Ibid., p. 90.

[16] George, R., *Making Men Moral: Civil Liberties and Public Morality* (Oxford: Oxford University Press, 1993), pp. 221, 225.

[17] Rawls, J., *Political Liberalism*, p. 195.

[18] Kim, S., *Public Reason Confucianism: Democratic Perfectionism and Constitutionalism in East Asia* (Cambridge: Cambridge University Press, 2016), p. 87.

132   A PERFECTIONIST THEORY OF JUSTICE

the ideal of sagehood as the highest good'.[19] Among the central Confucian virtues are 'respect, reverence, sincerity, lenience, truthfulness, industry, and beneficence', as well as a distinctive kind of civility that involves 'yielding, conceding, compromising, and deferring for the sake of maintaining a good relationship with others or for the greater good of all'.[20]

Yet other perfectionists, taking their inspiration from Aristotle, conceive of human flourishing in terms of the development and exercise of certain distinctively or essentially human capacities.[21] Thomas Hurka, for instance, argues that 'what is good, ultimately, is the development of human nature', where this is to be understood in terms of an 'Aristotelian theory of human nature, one in which human rationality, both theoretical and practical, plays a central role'.[22] Similarly, George Sher argues that 'some activities, traits, and types of relationship are inherently valuable because they are implicated in certain very abstract goals that (virtually) all humans unavoidably seek'.[23] Richard Kraut can also be understood to endorse a broadly Aristotelian conception of human flourishing.[24] He argues that 'when we consider the good of any living thing'—be it a plant, an animal or a human—'we should look to the process of growth and development that best suits things of its kind'.[25] So to say what is good for human beings specifically, 'we must in some way reckon with human nature'.[26] In light of this, Kraut argues that 'a flourishing human being is one who possesses, develops, and enjoys the exercise of cognitive, affective, sensory, and social powers (no less than physical powers)'.[27]

In my view, none of these conceptions of human flourishing can appropriately belong within the perfectionist theory of justice. The reason for this will only become fully clear in Chapter 7, but, in brief, it is that none of these conceptions of human flourishing can satisfy a plausible specification of the public justification principle. As I hinted at in Section 4.4, and as I will explain in Chapter 7, I

---

[19] Chan, J., *Confucian Perfectionism: A Political Philosophy for Modern Times* (Princeton, NJ: Princeton University Press, 2014), p. 44. It should be noted, however, that in an earlier article Chan also develops a more free-standing conception of human flourishing that is based on a list of objective goods and that is closer to the sort of view I develop in Section 5.2. See Chan, J., 'Legitimacy, Unanimity, and Perfectionism', *Philosophy & Public Affairs* 29 (2000), pp. 5–42.

[20] Chan, J., *Confucian Perfectionism*, pp. 93, 196.

[21] Views of this kind are also sometimes called 'perfectionist' views. Rather unfortunately, then, the label 'perfectionism' can refer both to a position within political theory and a position within ethical theory. Whereas Hurka and Sher endorse perfectionism in both senses, I endorse perfectionism in the former sense but not in the latter sense. To avoid confusion, in this work I use 'perfectionism' exclusively to denote a position within political theory and I use 'Aristotelianism' to denote the relevant position within ethical theory.

[22] Hurka, T., *Perfectionism* (Oxford: Oxford University Press, 1993), pp. 3, 6.

[23] Sher, G., *Beyond Neutrality: Perfectionism and Politics*, p. 11.

[24] For Kraut's conception of human flourishing, see Kraut, R., *What Is Good and Why: The Ethics of Well-Being* (Cambridge, MA: Harvard University Press, 2007). And for his defence of perfectionism, see Kraut, R., 'Politics, Neutrality, and the Good', in E. Paul, F. Miller and J. Paul (eds), *Human Flourishing* (Cambridge: Cambridge University Press, 1999), pp. 315–32.

[25] Kraut, R., *What Is Good and Why*, p. 136.

[26] Ibid., p. 4.

[27] Ibid., p. 137.

A PROVISIONAL CONCEPTION OF HUMAN FLOURISHING   133

endorse a version of the public justification principle, according to which laws and policies must be justifiable, or acceptable, to all reasonable citizens. Unlike political liberals, I believe that many ideals of human flourishing can satisfy the public justification principle; but nonetheless I do accept that *certain* ideals of human flourishing are too controversial to plausibly satisfy this principle. Another way of putting this is that I endorse a version of what Steven Wall calls a 'restricted neutrality principle', one which holds that even though the perfectionist state should promote many ideals of human flourishing, it should remain neutral with respect to other such ideals about which there is reasonable disagreement.[28]

In particular, the Christian, Confucian and Aristotelian conceptions of human flourishing all seem to me too controversial to satisfy a plausible specification of the public justification principle. It would strain credulity to assert that under conditions of freedom all reasonable citizens must converge on one or another of these highly specific conceptions of human flourishing—to assert, say, that all reasonable citizens must agree that 'religion is a basic human good', must recognize the importance of 'filial piety, respect for elders [and] ancestor worship', or must endorse an 'Aristotelian theory of human nature'.[29] Even if the Christian, Confucian or Aristotelian conceptions of human flourishing are true, they are subject to reasonable disagreement and so are not legitimate sources of political reasons under conditions of reasonable pluralism. For this principled reason, the conceptions of human flourishing just canvassed are not suitable to be plugged into the perfectionist principles of justice; even if they are true, these conceptions are not appropriate for political purposes and cannot plausibly be expected to form the basis of a just and stable political order within modern pluralistic societies. The fact of reasonable disagreement thus significantly constrains what sort of conception of human flourishing can form part of the perfectionist theory of justice. In this way, the perfectionist theory of justice developed here takes the fact of reasonable disagreement much more seriously than previous perfectionist theories have done.

5.2 The Enjoyment of Moral, Intellectual and Artistic Excellence

A better way to proceed, I believe, is to refrain from affiliating the conception of human flourishing with any particular comprehensive doctrine or tradition of

---

[28] See Wall, S., 'Neutralism for Perfectionists: The Case of Restricted State Neutrality', *Ethics* 120 (2010), pp. 232–56.
[29] Interestingly, Sher at one point raises the related objection that his theory is 'too abstruse to achieve general currency' and that 'it is a dissociated fantasy to suppose that any public figure will couch his reasoning in terms of notions such as teleology, essentialism, or the fact-value gap'—notions he relies on in making the case for perfectionism (see *Beyond Neutrality*, p. 245 n. 1). But he does not take this to be a decisive reason to adopt instead some philosophically thinner conception of human flourishing.

134   A PERFECTIONIST THEORY OF JUSTICE

thought—Christian, Confucian, Aristotelian or otherwise—and instead to adopt a more free-standing conception of human flourishing that is specially constructed for political purposes and that does not purport to embody the full meta-ethical truth about human flourishing. I explain some of the motivations for this move more fully in Chapter 7, and in particular in Section 7.3, but the basic idea is that applying a 'political turn' to perfectionist theory offers a natural and promising approach for those who wish to explore the most appropriate forms of perfectionist political action under conditions of reasonable pluralism.

In developing a suitably free-standing conception of human flourishing to be plugged into the perfectionist principles of justice, it makes sense to work from a list of objective goods or excellences that are, in some sense, fairly thin or generic. This is the approach taken by Richard Arneson and by Alexandra Couto. Arneson expresses sympathy for a list of objective goods that includes the following items: 'pleasurable experience and especially enjoyment of the excellent, satisfaction of reasonable life aims, relationships of friendship and love, intellectual and cultural achievement, meaningful work, athletic excellence, living one's life according to autonomously embraced values and norms, [and] systematic understanding of the causal structure of the world'.[30] And Couto defends the following list of objective goods: 'empathy, rational activity, knowledge, understanding, craft, physical (bodily) skills, deep personal relationships, the awareness of beauty, pleasure and the absence of pain, autonomy, artistic and technological creativity, awareness of the human condition (or wisdom), [and] awareness of nature'.[31]

In other branches of philosophy, similar lists abound. Admittedly, these lists are often presented as conceptions of *well-being*, not conceptions of *human flourishing*, which is the subject matter of this chapter and which is the operative notion in perfectionist political theory. But there is presumably considerable overlap between these notions and so these lists still offer numerous insights into the notion of human flourishing. Derek Parfit, for instance, famously illustrates what he calls 'the objective list theory' by suggesting that 'the good things might include moral goodness, rational activity, the development of one's abilities, having children and being a good parent, knowledge, and the awareness of true beauty'—though he does not address the question of whether or not it would be permissible for the state to seek to promote this list of goods.[32] So here perfectionists could also import one of the lists of objective goods developed by those philosophers working outside of the debate between perfectionists and anti-perfectionist liberals.

In formulating a conception of human flourishing to be plugged into the perfectionist principles of justice, I am inclined towards a briefer list of objective goods

---

[30] Arneson, R., 'Liberal Neutrality on the Good: An Autopsy', in S. Wall and G. Klosko (eds), *Perfectionism and Neutrality: Essays in Liberal Theory* (New York: Rowman & Littlefield, 2003), p. 215.
[31] Couto, A., *Liberal Perfectionism* (Berlin: De Gruyter, 2014), pp. 43–4.
[32] Parfit, D., *Reasons and Persons* (Oxford: Oxford University Press, 1984), p. 499.

than the lists of Arneson, Couto and Parfit—brevity being an important virtue for a conception of human flourishing, given what was just mentioned about the need for this conception to satisfy a public justification condition. In particular, I contend that, at least for political purposes, human flourishing should be understood in terms of moral, intellectual and artistic excellence.

How exactly these three excellences should be interpreted and specified is an important question that we will consider at various junctures in this work—including in Section 5.3, in Sections 6.2 to 6.4, and in Section 7.5. For now, though, we can fix ideas by noting that moral excellence can encompass many of the familiar virtues such as generosity, courage and friendliness; intellectual excellence can encompass many of the endeavours within the familiar fields of academic inquiry and scholarship, such as the sciences and humanities; and artistic excellence can encompass many of the familiar forms and expressions of art and culture such as music, literature, poetry and theatre. These examples are by no means exhaustive; they are merely illustrative of some of the diverse ways in which moral, intellectual and artistic excellence can be interpreted and instantiated.

The selection of the three ideals of moral, intellectual and artistic excellence is not haphazard. These excellences appear to match, and to provide a reasonably unifying explanation for, many of our considered convictions about human flourishing. When we think about what makes a person flourish, we often point towards the achievement of moral, intellectual and artistic excellence—or, at least, we often point towards the achievement of specific instantiations of these excellences. For instance, it is often thought that it is good for a person to be kind, altruistic, courageous; that it is good for a person to have wide and deep knowledge of important truths about the world and the human condition; that it is good for a person to create beautiful artworks or to contemplate and appreciate those of others. If these more specific claims about human flourishing are not quite truisms, they are at least close to truisms and appear to be widely shared. Moreover, the three excellences seem to capture many of the central convictions of perfectionist writers of the past and present. These three ideals can be understood as core axioms of perfectionist thought, rather in the way that freedom, equality and fairness are sometimes taken to be three core axioms of liberal thought. It is thus hoped that many plausible conceptions of human flourishing will agree that moral, intellectual and artistic excellences are constituents of human flourishing, even if they diverge on a number of other points and even if they diverge on the relative weight to be accorded to each of these excellences.

As it stands, this conception of human flourishing is vulnerable to the charge that it allows for individuals to be radically alienated from their own good. It leaves open the possibility that artistic excellence, say, could contribute to my flourishing, even though I have no interest in or desire for artistic excellence— even though the prospect of artistic excellence leaves me cold. But surely 'it would be an intolerably alienated conception of someone's good to imagine that it might

136 A PERFECTIONIST THEORY OF JUSTICE

fail in any way to engage him.'[33] Surely 'what is intrinsically valuable for a person must have a connection with what he would find in some degree compelling or attractive, at least if he were rational and aware.'[34] If someone attains objective goods such as moral, intellectual and artistic excellence, yet feels no resonance with these excellences, does she really thereby lead a flourishing life?[35] Along similar lines, Ronald Dworkin says of objective-list conceptions of the good life: 'whether someone lives well cannot just be a question of how many tick marks he scores, one by one, on some long list—how could that matter just on its own?—but of what his life as a whole *comes to*, of whether it has achieved, in the common phrase, a *meaning*, and this must be a matter of integrating discrete experiences and achievements in some way that he himself finds to have value in some dimension.'[36]

To overcome this problem of alienation or lack of resonance, we must build a significant subjective component into our conception of human flourishing. There are various ways to do this (as we shall see in Section 5.6), but I shall adopt the simplest approach: namely, that in order for moral, intellectual and artistic excellence to contribute to one's flourishing, one must take *enjoyment* in these excellences.[37] To fully develop this idea, one would need to explain more precisely what 'enjoyment' is and how it relates to other nearby attitudes and states such as pleasure, desire and appreciation. But for the reasons that will be given in Section 5.4, clarification of these sorts of matters is neither necessary nor desirable at this stage. The key point is that, once this move is made, the individual we are being invited to consider—someone who achieves moral, intellectual and artistic excellence, yet fails to be affectively engaged by these excellences—no longer registers as flourishing by the lights of this conception of human flourishing. Her failure to enjoy the excellences means that they do not contribute to her flourishing. A certain kind of

---

[33] Railton, P., 'Facts and Values', p. 9.

[34] Ibid.

[35] For discussions of this issue in relation to theories of well-being, see, for example, Rosati, C., 'Internalism and the Good for a Person', *Ethics* 106 (1996), pp. 297–326; Sarch, A., 'Internalism About a Person's Good: Don't Believe It', *Philosophical Studies* 152 (2011), pp. 161–84; Fletcher, G., *The Philosophy of Well-Being*, pp. 65–75; Dorsey, D., 'Why Should Welfare "Fit"?', *The Philosophical Quarterly* 67 (2017), pp. 685–708. See also the related literature on the so-called 'endorsement constraint', which is defended by Ronald Dworkin (see 'Foundations of Liberal Equality' in S. Darwall (ed.), *Equal Freedom: Selected Tanner Lectures on Human Values* (Ann Arbor, MI: University of Michigan Press, 1995), pp. 237, 264) and Will Kymlicka (see *Liberalism, Community and Culture* (Oxford: Clarendon Press, 1989), pp. 12–13, 18–19) and which is analysed and criticized in Hurka, T., 'Indirect Perfectionism: Kymlicka on Liberal Neutrality', *Journal of Political Philosophy* 3 (1995), pp. 40–50; Wall, S., *Liberalism, Perfectionism and Restraint* (Cambridge: Cambridge University Press, 1998), pp. 189–97; Arneson, R., 'Human Flourishing Versus Desire Satisfaction', *Social Philosophy and Policy* 16 (1999), pp. 135–41; Wilkinson, T., 'Against Dworkin's Endorsement Constraint', *Utilitas* 15 (2003), pp. 175–93.

[36] Dworkin, R., 'Ronald Dworkin Replies', in J. Burley (ed.), *Dworkin and His Critics* (Oxford: Blackwell, 2004), p. 354.

[37] This idea is suggested by Parfit (see *Reasons and Persons*, pp. 501–2) and is developed more fully in, for example, Adams, R., *Finite and Infinite Goods: A Framework for Ethics* (Oxford: Oxford University Press, 1999), pp. 93–101; Kagan, S., 'Well-Being as Enjoying the Good', *Philosophical Perspectives* 23 (2009), pp. 253–72.

strong internal resonance is in this way a necessary condition of this conception of human flourishing.

The introduction of this enjoyment condition moves the conception of human flourishing in a more subjective direction. It may be most appropriate to classify the provisional conception as a *hybrid* conception of human flourishing, one that takes human flourishing to involve a blend of subjective and objective elements.[38] And one might worry that inner states such as enjoyment are simply not susceptible to political promotion—or, as Locke puts it, 'confiscation of estate, imprisonment, torments, nothing of that nature can have any such efficacy as to make men change the inward judgment that they have framed of things.'[39] But while the question of how exactly the state would go about fostering enjoyment of the excellent is important, it need not detain us here since I shall take it up in Chapter 6. For now, what matters is not whether this conception is susceptible to state promotion but whether it aligns with our considered convictions about human flourishing.

In short, what I shall call *the provisional conception of human flourishing* holds that, at least for political purposes, human flourishing consists in the enjoyment of moral, intellectual and artistic excellence. A person flourishes to the extent that she leads a life rich in the enjoyment of these excellences—where the way in which these excellences are concretely realized within a life can of course differ greatly from person to person. The subjective state of enjoyment and the objective state of excellence are individually necessary and jointly sufficient conditions for human flourishing. The achievement of moral, intellectual or artistic excellence does not contribute to a person's flourishing if she does not take enjoyment in these excellences, and the enjoyment of some activity or pursuit does not contribute to a person's flourishing if that activity or pursuit is devoid of moral, intellectual or artistic excellence. Only when both the subjective and objective conditions are present—only when a person takes enjoyment in what is truly excellent—does a person flourish.

---

[38] On Steven Wall and David Sobel's important recent taxonomy, though, this still counts as an objective conception, rather than a hybrid conception, since it does not grant the attitudes (e.g. enjoyment) 'the power to turn objectively valueless or neutral objects into prudential value for the agent' (p. 2832). For Wall and Sobel, granting attitudes this sort of 'free play to create value for the agent wherever they go' is what 'carves the subjective/objective distinction at the [most] philosophically important joint' (p. 2834). See Wall, S. and Sobel, D., 'A Robust Hybrid Theory of Well-Being', *Philosophical Studies* 178 (2021), especially pp. 2831–7.

[39] Locke, J., *Second Treatise of Government and a Letter Concerning Toleration* (Oxford: Oxford University Press, 2016), p. 129. Relatedly, Dworkin and Kymlicka defend the endorsement constraint (see footnote 35) and take this to have politically anti-perfectionist implications. But anti-perfectionism only follows on the further, largely empirical assumption that the state cannot influence what people endorse or enjoy, and in particular that the state cannot influence citizens to endorse or enjoy various kinds of excellences. My discussion in Chapter 6 is meant to cast doubt on this assumption. The assumption is also challenged in Hurka, T., 'Indirect Perfectionism: Kymlicka on Liberal Neutrality', pp. 44–50 and in Sher, G., *Beyond Neutrality*, pp. 61–71.

5.3 Are the Three Excellences Too Abstract?

At this point, one might worry that this conception of human flourishing is excessively abstract. Even if the appeal to moral, intellectual and artistic excellence adds *some* degree of specificity and informativeness to the idea of human flourishing—even if the appeal to these excellences is an improvement on untutored intuition and rules out some ways of thinking about human flourishing—these excellences are still amenable to a wide variety of different interpretations and so they still under-determine many specific questions of public policy. And while I have above offered some illustrative examples of moral, intellectual and artistic excellence, I have not provided any general criteria or standards for determining whether a given ideal or activity counts as a bona fide instance of one of these excellences. So, if the perfectionist conception of social justice is to have determinate and testable implications for law and public policy, wouldn't we need to say much more here about what exactly moral, intellectual and artistic excellence each consist in?

This is an important issue, and I shall return to it at several junctures: in Sections 6.2 to 6.4, I provide some potential (if rather stipulative) interpretations of moral, intellectual and artistic excellence and suggest laws and public policies that would promote the excellences so interpreted; and in Section 7.5, I tentatively place some bounds on the family of admissible interpretations of these three excellences. Here, though, let me offer a broader reply by making a methodological point about how much specificity we should, in general, expect from a political theory. A good theory defines an illuminating perspective from which to think about and understand a particular question or problem. It clears our vision and focuses our reflections on the most relevant and basic considerations. To do this, it need not single out any particular answer; it only needs to establish a manageable range within which the answer should fall. In this way, a good political theory will lessen our reliance on intuition and judgement but it can never eliminate such reliance altogether.[40]

Of course, this characterization itself relies on several vague ideas, such as the idea of a 'manageable' range of possible answers. But it suffices for our purposes, and it seems to suggest that the provisional conception achieves as much as one can reasonably expect from a conception of human flourishing. After all, the provisional conception narrows in important ways the range of possible conceptions of human flourishing. It rules out subjective conceptions of human flourishing according to which a person flourishes insofar as she uses her fair share of resources (as defined by the appropriate non-perfectionist theory of justice) to pursue a plan of life that seems good to her. It similarly rules out sceptical views that say that 'while everybody has an opinion about the good life, none can be known to

---

[40] These general methodological remarks follow similar remarks in Rawls, J., *A Theory of Justice*, pp. 53, 364, 391.

be superior to any other'.[41] The provisional conception also rules out, as unsuitable for political purposes, certain other conceptions of human flourishing—such as Christian, Confucian and Aristotelian conceptions—that have been championed by previous perfectionists. It clears our vision and focuses our reflections on moral, intellectual and artistic excellence as three of the most relevant and basic considerations for perfectionist law and public policy. And while the provisional conception still leaves a role for interpretation and judgement in specifying the three excellences, much of this can occur during the application of the theory at later stages, such as at the legislative or administrative stages, and need not be built into the foundations of the theory itself.[42]

Of course, there is a sense in which it would be desirable to flesh out in greater detail the content of the three excellences, since this would narrow even further the range of possible answers. However, as I shall go on to explain, there is also a sense in which adding greater specificity is undesirable—which is why this conception is deliberately provisional in the sense explained in Section 5.4. It is thus hoped that, even at this level of abstraction, the three excellences are sufficiently informative for us to begin to get a feel for the content of this conception of human flourishing and for the likely practical implications of the perfectionist conception of social justice.

Finally, as a dialectical point, it is worth noting that a similar charge of abstractness or under-specificity can and has also been levelled against Rawls's account of the primary goods.[43] Of course, Rawls only intends the primary goods to be part of a 'thin theory of the good', and not a conception of human flourishing of the thicker kind developed here, but the primary goods play a related role within Rawls's theory since they are the basis for 'interpersonal comparisons of citizens' well-being' and so consideration of the relative abstractness of this element of Rawls's theory is apt in this context.[44] There are at least three ways in which the primary goods might be too abstract or in need of further specification. First, exactly what goods belong on the index of primary goods? Rawls explains that the primary goods are 'things citizens need as free and equal persons' and he says that the 'basic list of primary goods' includes rights and liberties, powers and opportunities, income and wealth, and the social bases of self-respect.[45] But Rawls is keen to stress that this list is 'provisional': 'provided due precautions are taken, we can, if need be, expand the list to include other goods'.[46] And, indeed, in response to certain objections to his theory, Rawls states that he is willing to include leisure in the index of primary

---

[41] Ackerman, B., *Social Justice in the Liberal State*, p. 11.

[42] See Rawls's discussion of the 'four-stage sequence' in *A Theory of Justice*, pp. 195–201.

[43] I thank Paul Billingham for helpful discussion of this point.

[44] Rawls, J., 'The Priority of Right and Ideas of the Good', in S. Freeman (ed.), *John Rawls: Collected Papers* (Cambridge, MA: Harvard University Press, 1999), p. 453.

[45] Rawls, J., *Political Liberalism*, p. 181.

[46] Rawls, J., *A Theory of Justice*, p. 397; Rawls, J., *Political Liberalism*, p. 181.

goods.[47] But one might wonder what basis there is for stopping there. Why not also include, say, health as a primary good to be distributed in accordance with the difference principle? Health, after all, certainly appears to be something that citizens need as free and equal persons.[48]

Second, assuming that we have settled on an appropriate index of primary goods, what do each of these primary goods consist in? Offhand, it might seem obvious what 'income' and 'wealth', say, consist in, but the reality is more complicated. Private income and wealth can take many forms—employment wages, bonuses, investments, dividends from investments, capital gains, fixed interest, rental income, rights in a pension, and so on—and there is likely to be significant disagreement about how to aggregate these components of wealth and income into a single measure.[49] A further complication is that, as Rawls himself notes, we have access to income and wealth not only as individuals but also as members of groups. For instance, 'members of a faculty have some control over a university's wealth viewed as a means for carrying out their aims of scholarship and research'.[50] Judgements about whether one citizen is more or less wealthy than another are therefore not as straightforward as one might unreflectively suppose.

Third, assuming that we have settled on an appropriate index of primary goods, and assuming that we know what each of these goods consists in, how are the different goods on this index to be balanced against each other? Rawls does not squarely address this question because he often uses income and wealth as an approximation for the whole index—and when he does employ the whole index he relies on the simplifying assumption that the primary goods 'tend to be associated', such that the better-off 'frequently have more of *every* primary good' and vice versa for the worse-off.[51] But it is not at all unrealistic to suppose that one citizen could have much wealth but little self-respect and that another citizen could have much self-respect but little wealth. In cases like this in which primary goods are not correlated, there appears to be no principled basis for determining which citizen is better off and instead we need to 'rely upon our intuitive capacities'.[52]

There are, then, several ways in which Rawls's account of the primary goods remains highly abstract: it does not say what the final index of primary goods is; it does not say what these goods consist in; and it does not say what the relative

---

[47] See Rawls, J., *Political Liberalism*, pp. 181–2; Rawls, J., *Justice as Fairness: A Restatement* (Cambridge, MA: Harvard University Press, 2001), p. 179.

[48] For Rawls's reluctance to treat health as a social primary good, see *Justice as Fairness*, p. 173; for a similar reluctance, see Daniels, N., 'Health-Care Needs and Distributive Justice', *Philosophy & Public Affairs* 10 (1981), pp. 163–4. But for a recent argument that the 'social bases of health' should be considered a social primary good, see Kniess, J., 'Justice in the Social Distribution of Health', *Social Theory and Practice* 45 (2019), especially pp. 405–12.

[49] This point is made in Barry, B., *The Liberal Theory of Justice: A Critical Examination of the Principal Doctrines in A Theory of Justice by John Rawls* (Oxford: Clarendon Press, 1973), pp. 43–4.

[50] Rawls, J., *Justice as Fairness*, p. 171.

[51] Rawls, J., *A Theory of Justice*, p. 94 (emphasis added).

[52] Ibid.

A PROVISIONAL CONCEPTION OF HUMAN FLOURISHING   141

importance of these goods is. These three points are not intended as criticisms of Rawls's account of the primary goods. As I indicated above, we should not in general expect too much specificity from a political theory. Not every question needs to be settled within the foundations of a political theory, and some degree of reliance on intuition and reflective judgement in the application of the theory at the legislative and administrative stages is inevitable. My point here is simply about dialectical double standards: it is unfair to hold the provisional conception of human flourishing to a standard of specificity and determinacy that leading anti-perfectionist liberal theories do not themselves appear to meet.

5.4 Provisionality

The conception given in Section 5.2 falls short of a fully worked-out conception of human flourishing. Many questions remain unanswered:

Why these particular excellences and not others? Why doesn't athletic excellence, say, belong on the list of objective goods? Is there a deeper rationale that explains why all and only these three excellences contribute to human flourishing? Why is enjoyment necessary? Can't an excellent activity (such as writing a great work of fiction) contribute to a person's flourishing even if she does not enjoy this activity? And why is excellence necessary? Can't an enjoyable activity (such as eating ice cream) contribute to a person's flourishing even if this activity is not excellent? Why focus on 'excellence' as opposed to satisfactoriness? Mightn't the vigorous pursuit of moral excellence, say, make for an obsessive or overzealous character?[53] What do each of these excellences involve? How exactly are moral, intellectual and artistic excellence to be interpreted and specified? What is the relative importance of each of these excellences? Do moral, intellectual and artistic excellence contribute equally to human flourishing? Or do some have priority over others? How does the level of flourishing realized by someone who enjoys much intellectual excellence but little moral excellence, say, compare with the level of flourishing realized by someone who enjoys little intellectual excellence but much moral excellence? Should we care about the 'shape' of a life? Does a life that starts out badly but then improves (as measured by enjoyment of these three excellences) realize a higher level of flourishing than a life that starts out well but then worsens (as measured by enjoyment of these three excellences)—even if both lives contain the same overall amount of enjoyment of moral, intellectual and artistic excellence? In other words, does an 'uphill curve' itself contribute to human flourishing?

---

[53] See Wolf, S., 'Moral Saints', *The Journal of Philosophy* 79 (1982), pp. 419–39.

142 A PERFECTIONIST THEORY OF JUSTICE

Perhaps surprisingly, I shall not attempt to address all of these questions and concerns—though I do begin to address some of them in the subsequent sections. In this sense, the conception of human flourishing given in Section 5.2 is *provisional*: it is a reasonable approximation, and is serviceable for the time being, but it is open to clarification, refinement and revision as a result of a broader process of philosophical inquiry into the nature of human flourishing. Any revisions would need to satisfy a plausible specification of the public justification constraint, as indicated in Section 5.1; but it may be, for instance, that in the end one or two other items, say athletic excellence, need to be added to the list of objective goods. So this conception of human flourishing helps to fix ideas—it helps to give a feel for the likely practical upshots of perfectionism so that the debate between perfectionists and anti-perfectionists can come alive—but it is by no means meant to be the full story or final word on the topic of human flourishing.[54]

The rationale for treating this conception of human flourishing as merely provisional is that doing so allows us to zero in on certain distinctively political questions that confront a perfectionist theory of social justice. The focus of this work, after all, is on a fundamental question within *political* philosophy: namely, should the state promote sound ideals of human flourishing? The focus is not on the further question within *moral* philosophy: namely, what *are* the sound ideals of human flourishing? Offering a provisional, rather than fully worked-out, conception of human flourishing allows us to retain a focus on the former, rather than the latter, question.

---

[54] This aspect of my argumentative strategy resembles, in some ways, a recent argument of Jason Hanna, who defends the claim that there is nothing distinctively objectionable about paternalistic interventions in a person's affairs so long as these interventions are *actually* in that person's interests, but who remains officially agnostic on the question of how a person's interests are best understood. Hanna, that is, treats 'interests' as a *placeholder* or *blank* to be filled in by whatever turns out to be the best account of interests. See Hanna, J., *In Our Best Interest: A Defense of Paternalism* (Oxford: Oxford University Press, 2018), especially pp. 8–14. Hanna's approach contrasts with that of other paternalists, who tend to yoke their views to a subjective account of interests, often precisely out of a concern to avoid the more perfectionist forms of paternalism; see, for example, Conly, S., *Against Autonomy*, especially pp. 102–12. One could imagine transposing this strategy from the debate about paternalism to the debate about perfectionism: perfectionists could treat 'human flourishing' as a placeholder or blank to be filled in by whatever turns out to be the best account of human flourishing after a broader process of philosophical inquiry. However, I am inclined to think that—at least in the perfectionist context, and perhaps in the paternalist context too—the placeholder approach faces significant problems. For one thing, certain important possibilities (such as subjectivism and scepticism about human flourishing) have to be ruled out before perfectionism can even get off the ground. For another, the placeholder approach would leave large parts of the perfectionist theory under-determined, thus stymying efforts to compare perfectionist and anti-perfectionist theories at all levels of generality using the method of reflective equilibrium. Still, even if it is not helpful to theorize the question of whether the state should promote human flourishing in *total* abstraction from the question of what human flourishing actually consists in, I believe that it is quite helpful to theorize the question of whether the state should promote human flourishing in *relative* abstraction from the question of what human flourishing actually consists in. In this sense, my strategy of treating moral, intellectual and artistic excellence as elements of a provisional conception of human flourishing is meant to be attuned to some of the insights of Hanna's more thoroughgoingly agnostic approach.

To clarify, the kinds of distinctively political questions addressed in this work are as follows: is the promotion of flourishing ways of life a requirement of justice? If so, how does the promotion of the flourishing ways of life relate to, and integrate with, other principles of justice? Does the fact that in free societies there is deep and pervasive disagreement surrounding questions of the good life call into question the legitimacy of perfectionist politics? Does state promotion of the good life threaten freedom and autonomy? Is it motivated by the paternalistic belief that citizens when left to their own devices will fail to make sound choices about how to run their own lives? Does it manifest the meddlesome mentality of a village busybody?

What is important to note about all of these questions is that they can be explored in the absence of a fully worked-out conception of human flourishing. Consider, for instance, Matthew Kramer's objection that when the perfectionist state seeks to edify citizens it expresses thereby the 'quidnunc mentality' of a village busybody. This objection will be explored in considerable detail in Chapter 10, but consider here Kramer's important clarification about the nature of this objection:

> Profound and important though the affinities are between an edificatory-perfectionist system of governance and a busybody, the analogy between them would be misleading if it were taken to imply that every edificatory-perfectionist system of governance will very likely blunder in its evaluative judgments ... My critique can grant *arguendo* the rather implausible proposition that systems of governance which pursue edificatory objectives will usually be correct—or even always be correct—in their identifying of evaluative standards that are to be drawn upon for the realization of those objectives ... [It] maintains that, whether or not the officials in such systems will tend to identify standards of goodness correctly, their interaction with citizens is both overbearingly meddlesome and debasingly dependent on the citizens' choices of lifestyles. Even if the evaluative inclinations of the officials in some society are sound, their operations tarnish the moral integrity of their system of governance by placing that system in the posture of a busybody.[55]

Similarly, none of the other distinctively political questions I posed above—which raise the possibility that perfectionism is insensitive to reasonable disagreement, that it is invasive of autonomy and that it treats citizens like children—relies essentially on the claim that perfectionist states are promoting the wrong conception of the good. They are generally meant to show the impermissibility of perfectionist politics even in circumstances in which the perfectionist state is acting in pursuit of sound ideals of human flourishing. We thus do not need to have on hand a fully worked-out conception of human flourishing—one that explains what the three

---

[55] Kramer, M., *Liberalism with Excellence* (Oxford: Oxford University Press, 2017), pp. 279–80.

excellences involve more specifically, that explains the relative importance of these excellences, that explains the relevance of the 'shape' of a life, and so on—in order to explore the important questions about perfectionist political theory.

In fact, the case for provisionality can be put more strongly. It is not just that we *need not* provide a fully worked-out conception of human flourishing in order to answer the question of whether the state can and should promote flourishing ways of life. We also have *positive reasons to avoid* trying to provide such a conception because doing so would introduce needless distractions: it would inevitably invite anti-perfectionists to focus on and quibble with the finer details of this conception of human flourishing rather than considering the moral bearings of perfectionism as a more general matter and in some or another form. Treating the conception of human flourishing as provisional removes this hazard and puts us in a better position to explore in a systematic and uncluttered way the main structural features of perfectionist political morality.

Suppose, for instance, we were to say that the 'shape' of a life matters—in particular, that an 'uphill curve' contributes non-derivatively to human flourishing. On this view, a life that starts out badly but then improves (as measured by enjoyment of the three excellences) realizes a higher level of flourishing than a life that starts out well but then worsens (as measured by enjoyment of the three excellences)— even though both lives contain the same overall amount of enjoyment of moral, intellectual and artistic excellence. Inevitably, saying this would invite a range of familiar objections. Those who live uphill lives often exhibit certain moral excellences, such as determination and grit. So, even though it is stipulated that the uphill and downhill lives contain the same overall amount of excellence, can we really be sure that we have internalized this stipulation when forming intuitions about the case? Isn't it possible that our intuition that the uphill life realizes a higher level of flourishing is being inadvertently influenced by the thought that the uphill life contains a greater amount of moral excellence? Moreover, if an uphill curve makes an independent contribution to human flourishing, over and above the contribution made by the three excellences, doesn't this mean that parents have reasons to bring it about that their child's life starts out somewhat badly (in terms of enjoyment of the three excellences), thus giving the child's life an uphill curve? Perhaps defenders of the shape-of-a-life thesis will reply here that, while an uphill curve does contribute to human flourishing to some degree, this contribution is almost always insufficient to offset a somewhat bad start in life. But then how significant is the shape-of-a-life thesis? If the contribution of the uphill curve rarely tips the scales of decision, mightn't we begin to wonder whether it does any real work at all?[56]

---

[56] For discussion of these issues, see, for example, Rosati, C., 'The Story of a Life', *Social Philosophy and Policy* 30 (2013), pp. 21–50; Dorsey, D., 'The Significance of a Life's Shape', *Ethics* 125 (2015), pp. 303–30; Fletcher, G., *The Philosophy of Well-Being*, ch. 7.

What makes this line of questioning needlessly distracting is that, even if it succeeds in undermining the claim that the shape of a life matters, it would not thereby undermine the claim that the state should seek to promote flourishing ways of life, where flourishing lives are conceived of in terms of the enjoyment of moral, intellectual and artistic excellence. All it would show is that one specific proposal for how to work out the details of the provisional conception of human flourishing—a proposal according to which it matters how enjoyment of the three excellences is distributed over the span of a life—fails. Perfectionists could go on being perfectionists. All they would need to do is to yoke the perfectionist principles of justice to some other more plausible proposal about how to work out the finer details of the provisional conception of human flourishing.

Indeed, my suspicion is that the relative unpopularity of perfectionist political philosophy can be accounted for in terms of the fact that the question of whether the state should promote human flourishing has not been theorized in sufficient abstraction from the question of what human flourishing consists in. On the one hand, this is the doing of proponents of perfectionism, who have not typically argued for perfectionism at the levels of generality that best demonstrate its philosophical power and flexibility, and who have instead moved hastily to the defence of particular and often fairly idiosyncratic varieties of perfectionism. On the other hand, this is the doing of critics of perfectionism, who frequently speak as if the shortcomings of specific instances of perfectionism, such as highly conservative religious versions of perfectionism, impugn perfectionism as a general thesis.

Here it is instructive to examine in more detail an example of this tendency of critics of perfectionism to infer from the shortcomings of a particular instance of perfectionism—typically, an instance of perfectionism that incorporates a crude or excessively sectarian conception of human flourishing—that perfectionism as a general thesis must fail. Consider, then, Ronald Dworkin's characterization of perfectionism in the following passage:

> Government must be neutral in matters of personal morality, [and] must leave people free to live as they think best so long as they do not harm others. But the Reverend Jerry Falwell, and other politicians who claim to speak for some 'moral majority', want to enforce their own morality with the steel of the criminal law. They know what kind of sex is bad, which books are fit for public libraries, what place religion should have in education and family life, when human life begins, that contraception is sin, and that abortion is capital sin. They think the rest of us should be forced to practice what they preach.[57]

---

[57] Dworkin, R., 'Neutrality, Equality, and Liberalism', in D. MacLean and C. Mills (eds), *Liberalism Reconsidered* (Totowa, NJ: Rowman and Allanheld, 1983), p. 1. As we saw in Sections 1.2 and 4.5, anti-perfectionists such as Japa Pallikkathayil and John Rawls also target versions of perfectionism

146 A PERFECTIONIST THEORY OF JUSTICE

Dworkin's argumentation here strikes me as uncharitable: it saddles perfectionism with a conception of human flourishing that is not independently attractive (presumably Dworkin himself does not regard this conception as plausible) and that does not satisfy a plausible specification of the public justification principle.[58] What makes this unhelpful is that, even if we can agree with Dworkin that the specific form of perfectionism he considers should be rejected, this still does not tell us whether we should reject *all* forms of perfectionism. How, in other words, can we be sure whether our reservations about Falwell's perfectionism are based on its being perfectionist or on its being the wrong *kind* of perfectionism? How can we be sure that Dworkin hasn't thrown out the perfectionist baby with the Falwellian bathwater?[59] For anti-perfectionist liberals, the case against Falwell's perfectionism is morally overdetermined. To properly evaluate the moral bearings of perfectionism per se, then, we should screen off these distractions and extraneous factors and try to hold before us a form of perfectionism that has lots going for it and thus that gives perfectionism its fairest hearing: say, by combining moderate perfectionist principles of justice that respect basic rights and that give some sort of distributive priority to the worst-off (such as the principles articulated in Section 4.3) with a conception of human flourishing that is independently appealing and that satisfies a plausible specification of the public justification principle (such as the conception articulated in Section 5.2). If this fine-tuned form of perfectionism *still* faces decisive problems, then that would be very strong evidence in favour of anti-perfectionist liberalism. By contrast, the fact that Falwell's view faces decisive problems provides little or no support for anti-perfectionist liberalism because, to put it mildly, Falwell's view hardly exhausts the logical space of perfectionist views—and so there are plenty of plausible alternative forms of perfectionism that Dworkin's arguments against Falwell's perfectionism leave untouched.

Of course, I do not mean to suggest that the question of whether the state should promote human flourishing can be theorized in *total* abstraction from the question of what human flourishing actually consists in. As has been mentioned, subjectivist and sceptical possibilities—that is, the possibility that there are no objective truths about human flourishing and the possibility that such

---

that incorporate crude or excessively sectarian conceptions of human flourishing. See Pallikkathayil, J., 'Neither Perfectionism Nor Political Liberalism', *Philosophy & Public Affairs* 44 (2016), pp. 171–96; Rawls, J., *A Theory of Justice*, pp. 330–1.

[58] This passage is also uncharitable in another way, namely that it plugs this conception of human flourishing into extreme perfectionist principles of justice rather than plugging it into more moderate perfectionist principles of justice which treat the promotion of flourishing ways of life as lexically posterior to other familiar liberal principles of justice, such as the equal basic liberties principle. But here my focus is primarily on matters of human flourishing.

[59] For related points, see Eberle, C., *Religious Conviction in Liberal Politics* (Cambridge: Cambridge University Press, 2002), pp. 109–15.

truths exist but are unknowable—have to be ruled out in order for perfectionism to get off the ground. Conceptions of human flourishing such as Falwell's also need to be ruled out—and, as I suggested in Section 5.1, one way to do this is to point out that these conceptions do not plausibly satisfy a public justification condition in a free society. But what I do mean to say is that the question of whether the state should promote human flourishing can be theorized in *relative* abstraction from the question of what human flourishing actually consists in. Once we have on hand a conception of human flourishing that does a reasonable job of approximating our considered convictions, we need not worry too much about finessing this conception and can proceed to the more distinctively political questions about the state's promotion of this conception (or something in its vicinity).

In short, because there is no need to answer in great detail the question of what constitutes human flourishing in order to answer the question of whether the state should promote human flourishing, and because answering in great detail the former question can in fact often distract from answering the latter question, I do not attempt to provide a fully worked-out conception of human flourishing. Instead, I provide a provisional free-standing conception of human flourishing, leaving many of its specifics, such as the relative weight of the three excellences or the relevance of the shape of a life, to be worked out in due course through a broader process of philosophical inquiry. In this way, the hope is that the provisional conception of human flourishing fixes ideas enough for us to be able to systematically explore the main structural features of perfectionist political morality but not so much as to invite distracting quibbles about finer details.

5.5 Arbitrariness

In this section and Section 5.6, I defend the provisional conception of human flourishing against objections. The objection considered in this section is that the provisional conception of human flourishing is unacceptably arbitrary. The provisional conception says that the enjoyment of moral, intellectual and artistic excellence contributes to human flourishing. But it does not explain *why* all and only these excellences figure on the list. This can make the provisional conception seem theoretically unsatisfying or ad hoc—a mere 'unconnected heap'. Why this particular list of excellences rather than some other list that contains more or fewer items? Why not think that athletic excellence, say, also contributes to human flourishing? To the extent that these questions remain unanswered, one might worry that we have not been given anything like a genuine philosophical *theory* or *conception* of human flourishing, as those terms are customarily understood. We finish our reflections with not much more insight into the nature of human flourishing than we had going into them. As Ben Bradley puts this, 'we wanted enlightenment, but we are provided instead with a list, and are told not to look any deeper. This is not theorizing, but a refusal to theorize.'[60]

It is unfair, however, to suggest that nothing can be said in favour of including moral, intellectual and artistic excellence on the list of goods that contribute to human flourishing. The provisional conception, I suggested above, coheres with our considered convictions about human flourishing on due reflection. One way to see this is to consider what Fred Feldman calls the 'crib test', whereby one imagines gazing lovingly into the crib of one's newborn child and being filled with hopes for how her life might turn out.[61] This heuristic is meant to elicit our deepest convictions about the good life, since a parent in this situation tends to hope for what is good for the child. Insofar as enjoyment of moral, intellectual and artistic excellence would figure prominently in one's thoughts as one looks down on one's child, there is some basis for specifying the list of objective goods in this way rather than in some other way. Moreover, the provisional conception approximates our convictions in a reasonably unifying or systematic way, even if it is not as unifying or systematic as, say, hedonist or desire-satisfaction conceptions. It is, for instance, considerably more unifying and systematic than the lengthier objective lists of Parfit, Arneson and Couto mentioned in Section 5.2, which have six, eight and thirteen entries, respectively. Of course, a conception of human flourishing has to do more than cohere with and systematize our ideas about human flourishing. Such a conception needs explanatory depth as well as explanatory breadth. But, still, even if a fully justified conception needs to have more going for it than coherence and systematization, these considerations do at least lend some support to the provisional conception of human flourishing.

It is true that I have not given any 'deeper' explanation of why enjoyment of all and only these three excellences contributes to human flourishing. But here it is, I think, perfectly appropriate to point out that it is true of *all* philosophical conceptions that their basic claims are incapable of being explained or justified by reference to any further fact or principle. Explanations must stop somewhere. We can see this by noting that a similar challenge of arbitrariness can equally well be put to defenders of rival conceptions of human flourishing.[62] Suppose one adopts a desire-satisfaction view, whereby human flourishing consists in the satisfaction of actual or idealized desires. We can always ask the question: but *why* does the satisfaction of actual or idealized desires contribute to our flourishing? What *explains* why this, and only this, contributes to our flourishing? Or suppose one adopts an Aristotelian view, whereby human flourishing consists in the development of

---

[60] Bradley, B., *Well-Being and Death* (Oxford: Oxford University Press, 2009), pp. 16–17, quoted in Fletcher, G., *The Philosophy of Well-Being*, p. 58.

[61] See Feldman, F., *Pleasure and the Good Life: Concerning the Nature, Varieties and Plausibility of Hedonism* (Oxford: Oxford University Press, 2004), pp. 9–10.

[62] This point is made in Fletcher, G., *The Philosophy of Well-Being*, pp. 56–7 and in Bradford, G., 'Problems for Perfectionism', *Utilitas* 29 (2017), pp. 354–64.

distinctive human capacities. Again, we can ask: but *why* does the development of distinctive human capacities contribute to our flourishing? What *explains* why this, and only this, contributes to our flourishing? Or suppose, finally, one adopts a hedonist view, whereby human flourishing consists in experiencing pleasure. Once again, we can ask: but *why* does experiencing pleasure contribute to our flourishing? What *explains* why this, and only this, contributes to our flourishing? In each case, these questions look impossible to answer in an informative and non-circular way. The provisional conception of human flourishing, then, does not seem to fare much worse than rival conceptions—which similarly reach a point at which deeper explanations run out and a less-than-fully-satisfying appeal to brute facts must be made.

Perhaps, in the face of this tu quoque reply, the objector would seek to develop the charge of arbitrariness in a way that tells *especially* against the provisional conception. There are at least three ways in which this might be done. On the first rendition, the objector might point out that other conceptions of human flourishing posit only *one* brute fact—that desire satisfaction contributes to human flourishing, or that the development of distinctive human capacities contributes to human flourishing, or that the experience of pleasure contributes to human flourishing—whereas the provisional conception is pluralistic. It posits *three* brute facts: that enjoyment of moral excellence contributes to human flourishing, that enjoyment of intellectual excellence contributes to human flourishing, and that enjoyment of artistic excellence contributes to human flourishing. It might seem particularly strange that there is a plurality of fundamental facts about human flourishing. We should (other things equal) prefer explanations that posit fewer brute facts. The appeal to brute facts, that is, is a kind of explanatory last resort. So we should (other things equal) prefer desire-satisfaction conceptions, Aristotelian conceptions and hedonist conceptions over the provisional conception of human flourishing. Or so one might argue.[63]

I accept that, for the reason just given, the provisional conception of human flourishing may come with some unique costs in terms of arbitrariness. But the question we would then have to ask is: how *much* of a cost is this? In the above rendition of the objection, it was said that *other things equal* we should prefer more parsimonious explanations. But other things are not equal between these rival conceptions of human flourishing, and so we now have to ask whether, over-all, the benefits of the provisional conception offset the costs. These sorts of overall plausibility assessments are notoriously difficult to defend. Here I can only report my sense that considerations of arbitrariness do not upset, or even nearly upset,

---

[63] An argument along these lines is suggested in Bradley, B., *Well-Being* (Cambridge: Polity Press, 2015), pp. 68–9 and in Fletcher, G., *The Philosophy of Well-Being*, p. 57. One advantage of the provisional conception of human flourishing, as compared with the lengthier objective lists of Arneson, Couto and Parfit mentioned in Section 5.2, is that it appeals to fewer brute facts and as such is less vulnerable to this rendition of the arbitrariness objection.

the case for the provisional conception: we should not reject the provisional conception of human flourishing, that is, just because it appeals to three brute facts rather than one.

A second rendition of the arbitrariness objection such that it applies specifically to the provisional conception contends that pleasure and desire satisfaction, say, strike us as more immediately self-evident starting points for a conception of human flourishing than the three excellences.[64] On this rendition, what makes the provisional conception particularly arbitrary is not that the brute facts to which it appeals are *greater in number* than those appealed to by alternative conceptions but rather that the brute facts to which it appeals are *less immediately self-evident in kind* than those appealed to by alternative conceptions. It is difficult to know what to make of this argument, since there is no way to rigorously evaluate claims about relative degrees of immediate self-evidence. But suffice it to say that a moment's reflection on the possibility of sadistic pleasures and sadistic desires seems to me to significantly dent the immediate self-evidence of pleasure and desire satisfaction as starting points for a conception of human flourishing. This way of running the arbitrariness objection, then, also fails to undermine, or even nearly undermine, the case for the provisional conception of human flourishing.

A third rendition of the arbitrariness objection such that it tells especially against the provisional conception might begin by pointing out that the ideals of moral, intellectual and artistic excellence smack of a certain privileged class outlook. One might find it suspicious—even elitist or ideological—that the provisional conception of human flourishing fits so comfortably with a middle-class, materially comfortable academic's worldview. So when it is said that the provisional conception offers a reasonable approximation of 'our' considered convictions about human flourishing on due reflection, *whose* convictions exactly are being accounted for? Or when we apply Feldman's crib test as a heuristic for eliciting convictions about the good life, *who* exactly is gazing into the crib? On this rendition, then, the provisional conception is especially arbitrary neither because it makes more brute assumptions nor because its assumptions are less immediately self-evident, but because its assumptions reflect and favour the outlook of people who belong to a specific class in a way that other conceptions of human flourishing do not.[65]

This is an important objection, and it requires more discussion than I can give it here, but let me make two initial points in reply. First, my sense is that its force depends a great deal on how the details of the provisional conception of human flourishing are filled in—in particular, on how capaciously moral, intellectual and artistic excellence are understood. If these excellences are understood

---

[64] For a similar idea, see Bradford, G., 'Problems for Perfectionism', p. 363.
[65] I thank Jonathan Quong and Tom Sinclair for putting to me this version of the arbitrariness objection.

very narrowly, then the claim that they are strongly correlated with some specific class outlook seems plausible.[66] But if, as I maintain, these excellences can be interpreted and specified in a diversity of ways, then the claim that they are strongly correlated with some specific class outlook seems much less plausible. Perhaps opera and ballet, for instance, have niche appeal to the privileged classes; but when artistic excellence is understood more broadly to include musical, theatrical, literary and poetic forms, as well as the many forms of visual art such as painting, sculpture, architecture, ceramics, printmaking and photography, it becomes much less plausible to suppose that a commitment to the value of artistic excellence is peculiar to any specific social class. Once we construe the three excellences suitably broadly, then, it seems unlikely that they favour the more privileged social classes.[67]

Second, even if some degree of correlation remains between suitably capacious interpretations of the three excellences and the outlook of a particular social class, it is unclear that this shows that the excellences are unsound or unworthy. After all, liberal values such as freedom, equality and fairness might also turn out to be correlated to some comparable degree with the outlook of one or another social class. Probably these sorts of sociological correlations, if they exist, should make one wonder: it is plausible that they would provide a reason to re-examine one's values and to reflect carefully on whether they might be influenced by class bias. But it is difficult to believe that such correlations should always undermine or even significantly dent one's confidence in these values (be they liberal or perfectionist). At the least, then, there remains much more work to do before deploying an ideological critique of the provisional conception of human flourishing: one would need to provide (i) compelling sociological evidence that suitably capacious interpretations of the three excellences really do correlate strongly with a specific class outlook and (ii) some strong independent reason for thinking that this correlation debunks the excellences, as opposed to simply giving us some pause for thought.[68]

5.6 Are Enjoyment and Excellence Strictly Necessary?

According to the provisional conception of human flourishing, the subjective state of enjoyment and the objective state of excellence are individually necessary

---

[66] For an interesting analysis of the interaction between social class and certain narrow conceptions of morality and the good life, see Lamont, M., *Money, Morals, and Manners: The Culture of the French and American Upper-Middle Class* (Chicago, IL: University of Chicago Press, 1992). For related themes, see Fraser, R., 'Aesthetic Injustice' (unpublished manuscript).

[67] In the context of this worry about bias or elitism, it is also important to bear in mind that the provisional conception of human flourishing is to be embedded within a broader conception of social justice that is quite strongly egalitarian in character and that would prohibit many of the social and economic inequalities and stratifications that characterize contemporary societies.

[68] I thank Jeff McMahan for helpful discussion of this response.

152   A PERFECTIONIST THEORY OF JUSTICE

conditions for human flourishing: the achievement of moral, intellectual or artistic excellence does not contribute to a person's flourishing if she does not take enjoyment in these excellences, and the enjoyment of some activity or pursuit does not contribute to a person's flourishing if that activity or pursuit is devoid of moral, intellectual or artistic excellence. Only when both the subjective and objective conditions are present—only when a person takes enjoyment in what is truly excellent—does a person flourish.

Both of these necessity conditions, however, can be challenged. On the one hand, it is possible to argue that excellence devoid of enjoyment can contribute to human flourishing. And on the other hand, it is possible to argue that enjoyment devoid of excellence can contribute to human flourishing. So even if the presence of both the subjective component of enjoyment and the objective component of excellence is the ideal, the presence of either of these components in isolation is arguably sufficient to contribute (if only to a limited extent) to a person's flourishing.

To motivate this objection, let us consider a case in each direction. Consider, first, a case in which excellence devoid of enjoyment appears to contribute to human flourishing.[69] Suppose Ava, a scientist, discovers the cure to cancer, but takes no enjoyment in this and goes to her grave thinking that her scientific career was a waste of time. Isn't it implausible to think that Ava's outstanding achievements do not at all contribute to her flourishing just because she does not take enjoyment in them? Of course, we might think it would be *better* for Ava if she enjoyed or endorsed her accomplishments. But this is compatible with thinking that her failure to take enjoyment in her accomplishments does not entirely *nullify* their value for her—such that discovering the cure to cancer is, in the absence of enjoyment, no better for Ava than counting blades of grass. Another way of putting this is that the provisional conception conflicts with the following plausible general principle: 'if one is to do something that one does not like or value, it is better for one if what one does at least realizes something of objective value'.[70] In short, then, the objection is that even if enjoyment is *relevant* to human flourishing, it does not function as a strictly *necessary* condition of human flourishing.

Consider, next, a case in which enjoyment devoid of excellence appears to contribute to human flourishing.[71] In particular, consider the value to people of

---

[69] For similar cases, see, for example, Hurka, T., 'Indirect Perfectionism: Kymlicka on Liberal Neutrality', pp. 42–3; Wall, S., *Liberalism, Perfectionism and Restraint*, p. 196; Arneson, R., 'Human Flourishing Versus Desire Satisfaction', pp. 136–7; McCabe, D., *Modus Vivendi Liberalism: Theory and Practice* (Cambridge: Cambridge University Press, 2010), p. 36; Hooker, B., 'The Elements of Well-Being', *Journal of Practical Ethics* 3 (2015), pp. 30–1.

[70] Wall, S. and Sobel, D., 'A Robust Hybrid Theory of Well-Being', p. 18.

[71] For similar cases, see, for example, Arneson, R., 'Human Flourishing Versus Desire Satisfaction', p. 120; Hooker, B., 'The Elements of Well-Being', pp. 31–3; Sobel, D., 'The Case for Stance-Dependent Reasons', *Journal of Ethics and Social Philosophy* 15 (2019), pp. 146–74; Wall, S. and Sobel, D., 'A Robust Hybrid Theory of Well-Being', pp. 10–11, 15.

so-called 'cheap thrills'—that is, the pleasure or enjoyment taken in activities (such as eating ice cream or smelling freshly baked bread) that are neither objectively valuable nor objectively disvaluable but instead matters of mere taste.[72] Suppose that Billy and Clara have lives that are equally flourishing in terms of the enjoyment of moral, intellectual and artistic excellence, but that Billy's life also contains numerous cheap thrills whereas Clara's does not. Billy's life is not so full of cheap thrills that he becomes distracted from engagement with the objective goods—by stipulation, his life is equivalent to Clara's in terms of the enjoyment of moral, intellectual and artistic excellence—but still it contains a healthy number of cheap thrills. The provisional conception of human flourishing implies that Billy and Clara flourish to an equal degree; since Billy's cheap thrills do not realize moral, intellectual or artistic excellence, the pleasure or enjoyment he takes in them does not at all contribute to his flourishing. Yet isn't it clear that Billy flourishes to a higher degree than Clara? For Arneson, 'the world being as it is, and human nature being what it is, [cheap thrills] seem to me to be significant sources of enjoyment that significantly enhance many people's lives in ways for which there is no practical substitute ... if these pleasures were to disappear without replacement, the world would be immensely worse and most human lives would be significantly blighted.'[73] Perhaps Arneson goes too far here. But even if cheap thrills are not major contributors to human flourishing, don't they at least make *some* contribution to the flourishing of a life? Once again, then, the objection is that even if excellence is *relevant* to human flourishing, it does not function as a strictly *necessary* condition of human flourishing.

There are various ways in which a defender of the provisional conception of human flourishing might respond to this objection. One option is to bite the bullet. Here the defender of the provisional conception simply denies the intuitive judgements that drive this objection. This might be accompanied by an effort to cast doubt on the strength or reliability of these intuitive judgements. Consider, for instance, the intuition that Ava's finding the cure to cancer is still good for her, even if she goes to her grave thinking that her scientific career was a waste of time. A defender of the provisional conception of human flourishing might point out that if Ava finds the cure to cancer, then this is clearly good *in some sense*. Finding the cure to cancer increases the levels of well-being of others, for instance. But saying this is very different from saying that if Ava finds the cure to cancer, then this is good *for her*. So it is possible that when forming intuitions about whether, in the absence of enjoyment, Ava's finding the cure to cancer is good for her, we are sensitive to other questions in the picture (for instance, whether Ava's finding the cure to cancer is good) which are similar to, and thus conflatable with, but strictly distinct from, the question of whether Ava's finding the cure to cancer is good *for*

---

[72] Arneson uses this term in this context in 'Human Flourishing Versus Desire Satisfaction', p. 120.
[73] Ibid.

Ava. Once we realize this, perhaps we ought to become less confident that our intuitions about this case are sufficiently fine-grained and are really tracking what they are meant to.

In any event, I myself favour a different and more concessive response to this objection—a response that is more in line with the spirit of Section 5.4. This response reiterates that the conception of human flourishing developed in this chapter is only supposed to be provisional. It is meant to be a reasonable approximation of our considered judgements about human flourishing for the purposes of developing a perfectionist theory of social justice, but it is by no means meant to be the final word on the topic of human flourishing. This conception is open to clarification, refinement and revision in due course as a result of a broader process of philosophical inquiry into the nature of human flourishing. Treating enjoyment and excellence as hard constraints on human flourishing is a simple way of relating the subjective and objective components of human flourishing. Ultimately, though, it may turn out that it is too extreme to say that excellence without enjoyment and enjoyment without excellence each contribute *nothing* to our flourishing. Perhaps we should instead say that excellence without enjoyment and enjoyment without excellence each contribute *something* to our flourishing but contribute (much) *less* to our flourishing than the combination of enjoyment and excellence. Or perhaps we should espouse an 'asymmetrical hybrid' conception.[74] One version of this view says that excellence without enjoyment contributes nothing to our flourishing but enjoyment without excellence contributes something to our flourishing; a second says that excellence without enjoyment contributes something to our flourishing but enjoyment without excellence contributes nothing to our flourishing; a third says that excellence without enjoyment and enjoyment without excellence each contribute something to our flourishing but that excellence without enjoyment contributes more than enjoyment without excellence (but still not as much as the combination of enjoyment and excellence); and a fourth says that excellence without enjoyment and enjoyment without excellence each contribute something to our flourishing but that enjoyment without excellence contributes more than excellence without enjoyment (but still not as much as the combination of enjoyment and excellence).

These are just some of the many possible ways of specifying the precise relationship between the subjective and objective components of human flourishing— and, importantly, they represent alternative ways of accommodating the resonance and anti-alienation intuitions that motivated the hybrid structure of the provisional conception in the first place.[75] But adjudicating between these options is

---

[74] This possibility is mentioned in Hurka, T., 'On "Hybrid" Theories of Personal Good', *Utilitas* 31 (2019), p. 453.

[75] For examination of the possible structures of a hybrid conception, see, for example, Kagan, S., 'Well-Being as Enjoying the Good'; Sarch, A., 'Multi-Component Theories of Well-Being and Their Structure', *Pacific Philosophical Quarterly* 93 (2012), pp. 439–71; Woodard, C., 'Hybrid Theories', in G.

precisely the kind of task that, I argued in Section 5.4, should be set aside for the moment. The distinctively political questions confronting the perfectionist conception of social justice can be theorized in abstraction from how these finer details are worked out. So even if the rather simple account of the interaction between subjective and objective components needs to be finessed or revised, this does not threaten perfectionist justice: any such revisions can be easily incorporated into the conception of human flourishing that is plugged into the perfectionist principles of justice without thereby disrupting the case for perfectionist justice.

Fletcher (ed.), *The Routledge Handbook of Philosophy of Well-Being*, especially pp. 167–9; Wall, S. and Sobel, D., 'A Robust Hybrid Theory of Well-Being'.

6

Perfectionist Law and Public Policy

So far, I have argued that at least for political purposes society ought to be conceived of as a fair striving for human flourishing between free and equal citizens, and that the perfectionist principles of justice are the most appropriate principles for regulating a society conceived of in this way. These principles of justice call for the establishment and maintenance of social conditions promotive of and conducive to flourishing ways of life, where flourishing ways of life, I have argued, are to be understood as ways of life rich in the enjoyment of moral, intellectual and artistic excellence.

However, this picture still remains quite abstract, and so the next step is to begin to explore what it might imply in terms of laws and public policies. What are the distinctive practical implications of the perfectionist conception of social justice? What would a programme of perfectionist law and public policy look like in at least a reasonable degree of detail? Until we have an answer to these questions—until we have in clear view some concrete policy or policies that perfectionist justice calls for but that other views cannot sign onto—it is difficult to get a grip on the ways in which the perfectionist theory of social justice is meant to come apart from leading anti-perfectionist liberal theories of social or distributive justice. And without a grip on these differences, it is difficult to determine which theory best 'accord[s] with our considered convictions, at all levels of generality, on due reflection'.[1]

Exploring the practical upshots of perfectionist justice is particularly important for two reasons. The first is that many ideals of human flourishing—for instance, ideals of friendship, aesthetic appreciation and moral virtue—do not appear to be readily susceptible to promotion by the state. We are quite familiar with social institutions, laws and public policies designed to advance, say, ideals of public health, economic equality and national defence. But what social institutions, laws and public policies would be suitable for advancing perfectionist ideals? If friendship is a component of the good life, should the state act as a matchmaker for the loveless or the friendless? Surely perfectionists would not countenance 'the formation of a new state agency, the Department of Love, whose duty it would be to assist anyone who has fallen below some putative affection line, construed on the model of a poverty line'?[2] If literary appreciation is a component of the good

---

[1] Rawls, J., *Political Liberalism* (New York: Columbia University Press, 2005), p. 8.

[2] Carroll, N., 'Can Government Funding of the Arts Be Justified Theoretically?', *Journal of Aesthetic Education* 21 (1987), p. 26. For similar points, see Ackerman, B., *Social Justice in the Liberal State* (New Haven, CT: Yale University Press, 1980), p. 362; Barry, B., 'Something in the Disputation Not

---

A Perfectionist Theory of Justice. Collis Tahzib, Oxford University Press.
© Collis Tahzib (2022). DOI: 10.1093/oso/9780192847119.003.0007

PERFECTIONIST LAW AND PUBLIC POLICY   157

life, surely the state should not enforce a 'mandatory George Eliot reading hour across the nation'?[3] In this light, Bruce Ackerman appeals to the inherent insusceptibility of many ideals of human flourishing to state promotion as part of his case for anti-perfectionist liberalism: 'you may have scaled Mount Olympus only to discover the blazing truth that the good is of a kind that cannot—conceptually cannot—be imposed on another.'[4] Can we really be confident, then, that the perfectionist objectives of moral, intellectual and artistic excellence lend themselves to a meaningful and viable programme of political action?

The second reason why it is particularly important to spell out some likely practical implications of perfectionism is that, in making the case for perfectionist justice, I appealed at several points to hypothetical cases featuring individuals with rather bizarre psychologies, such as the individual who is obsessed with counting blades of grass. But how far can these fanciful cases take us? What are the politically relevant implications of recognizing that the grass-counter does not lead a flourishing life? After all, few citizens in the real world are particularly attracted to counting blades of grass, and so the perfectionist state will presumably not need to enact laws and policies designed to prohibit or discourage grass-counting. So, again, what *does* buying into the perfectionist project mean in practical terms?

In this chapter, I seek to address these questions about perfectionist law and public policy. After some preliminary remarks (in Section 6.1), I consider various laws and public policies that might be expected to promote the enjoyment of moral, intellectual and artistic excellence within the citizenry. I suggest that moral excellence could be promoted through laws and policies designed to support the institution of friendship (Section 6.2); that intellectual excellence could be promoted through informative and educational public broadcasting (Section 6.3); and that artistic excellence could be promoted through the operation of publicly funded arts institutions and agencies (Section 6.4). Throughout these three sections, the discussion is tentative, since the implementation of perfectionist justice depends on a complex array of empirical contingencies that vary from setting to setting.

I then introduce (in Section 6.5) the objection that most, if not all, of these policies can already be justified on standard liberal grounds such as freedom, equality and fairness, and so the resort to perfectionism is unnecessary. My response is twofold: first, many of the relevant non-perfectionist rationales do not succeed, and so in at least an interesting range of cases there will be genuine extensional

---

Unpleasant', in P. Kelly (ed.), *Impartiality, Neutrality and Justice* (Edinburgh: Edinburgh University Press, 2000), pp. 231–2.

[3] Conly, S., *Against Autonomy: Justifying Coercive Paternalism* (Cambridge: Cambridge University Press, 2013), p. 110.

[4] Ackerman, B., *Social Justice in the Liberal State*, p. 367. See also Ogien, R., 'Neutrality Toward Non-Controversial Conceptions of the Good Life', in R. Merrill and D. Weinstock (eds), *Political Neutrality: A Re-evaluation* (New York: Palgrave Macmillan, 2014), pp. 100–1.

158 A PERFECTIONIST THEORY OF JUSTICE

differences between perfectionist and non-perfectionist conceptions of social justice (Section 6.6); and second, even if the non-perfectionist rationales do succeed,
this does not show that perfectionism is redundant or uninteresting since it may
offer (among other things) more intrinsically plausible or straightforward rationales for these policies, thereby yielding the right policies for the right reasons
(Section 6.7).

6.1 Preliminaries

Before exploring the subject of perfectionist law and public policy, four preliminary remarks are in order. The first is that throughout the following three sections
the discussion will be tentative and exploratory. My aim is not to make a definitive
case for any particular legislative or policy programme. Identifying which of the
many possible legislative or policy programmes best answers to the perfectionist
conception of justice is not something that can be done at the level of philosophical abstraction. Instead, the implementation of perfectionist justice in the context
of a given society depends on an array of empirical contingencies. Assessing these
sorts of nuts-and-bolts considerations is beyond the scope of this work and is not,
in any case, a task that political philosophers are typically best placed to perform.
As stressed in Section 5.3, then, we should not expect too much specificity from
the perfectionist theory of justice; even if it does not single out any particular
answer, we should be pleased if the theory defines an illuminating perspective
from which to think about questions of law and public policy, clearing our vision
and focusing our reflections on the most relevant and basic considerations. For
these reasons, my aim in the following three sections is simply to give a feel for the
potential practical upshots of the perfectionist conception of justice by indicating
the sorts of laws and policies that this conception might be expected to support in
the context of societies like ours. The suggestions advanced in the following three
sections are not, however, strictly speaking part of the perfectionist theory of justice. So even if it turns out that the particular laws and policies I consider should be
rejected—perhaps because they would be impracticable or counterproductive—
it does not follow that the perfectionist theory of justice should be
rejected.

The second preliminary remark is that in order to determine what kinds of laws
and public policies promote the enjoyment of moral, intellectual and artistic excellence, we will first have to come to a more specific view about what each of
these excellences consists in. As I indicated in Section 5.3, the values of moral,
intellectual and artistic excellence are quite abstract and can be specified and interpreted in a diversity of ways. However, since my intention here is merely to fix
ideas and to give a feel for the kinds of laws and public policies that perfectionist
justice might yield, and not to make a definitive case for this or that policy, I shall

not offer an extended argument for how these excellences are to be understood. Instead, I shall rely on fairly stipulative, but hopefully not too implausible, claims about what moral, intellectual and artistic excellence each consist in.

The third preliminary remark is about the *degree* to which the enjoyment of moral, intellectual and artistic excellence is susceptible to promotion by the state. In order for perfectionism to be of practical interest, the values of moral, intellectual and artistic excellence must be *to some degree* susceptible to state promotion. I try to demonstrate such susceptibility in the following three sections. But it is worth stressing that, for perfectionism to be of practical interest, the three excellences need not be *fully* susceptible to state promotion. For instance, perhaps wittiness is one of the virtues that falls under the rubric of moral excellence, occupying the golden mean between dourness and buffoonery; and perhaps wittiness cannot be taught, in the sense that state subsidization of comedy classes and stand-up shows will not tend to make people wittier. Perfectionists can readily admit that, in such instances, there simply does not exist a social institution or policy mechanism capable of effectively promoting this aspect of human flourishing. They just maintain that these instances are the exception rather than the norm. When thinking about the practical implications of perfectionist justice, then, it is important to bear in mind that all the perfectionist needs is the relatively moderate claim that the enjoyment of moral, intellectual and artistic excellence is *to some interesting degree* or *in some interesting ways* susceptible to promotion by the state.

Finally, an important concern with perfectionist laws and public policies is that they run the risk of sending a message of official condemnation or denigration towards some citizens and their ways of life. Since state action has a significant expressive dimension, and since perfectionist state action is premised on the view that certain ways of life are objectively better than others, isn't there a danger that perfectionist laws and policies might erode the sense of self-worth of those citizens who lead disfavoured ways of life?[5]

There is something to be said for this argument, but my impression is that whether perfectionist laws and public policies carry expressive harms will depend to a large extent on contingent facts about how those laws and policies are formulated and implemented. Of course, if the perfectionist state goes out of its

---

[5] I thank Jonathan Quong, Charlie Richards and Tom Sinclair for putting this sort of objection to me. For different responses to this sort of objection, see Wall, S., 'Neutralism for Perfectionists: The Case of Restricted State Neutrality', *Ethics* 120 (2010), pp. 246–55; Wall, S., 'Enforcing Morality', *Criminal Law and Philosophy* 7 (2013), pp. 460–5. In considering this objection, it is also important to bear in mind that non-perfectionist laws and public policies can also run the risk of denigrating citizens. See, for example, Jonathan Wolff's influential critique of various luck-egalitarian theories on the grounds that, at the level of implementation, they would require the worst-off members of society to make 'shameful revelations' about themselves in order to demonstrate that they are entitled to welfare support. (See Wolff, J., 'Fairness, Respect, and the Egalitarian Ethos', *Philosophy & Public Affairs* 27 (1998), pp. 97–122.) In Chapter 9, I consider a related yet distinct worry about the denigration, insult or disrespect of status that is said to accompany perfectionist laws and policies.

160   A PERFECTIONIST THEORY OF JUSTICE

way to insult its citizens or their ways of life, then this could indeed be expected to damage citizens' sense of self-worth. But the perfectionist state need not be, and should not be, gratuitously insulting in this way, and as such many instances of perfectionism are likely to avoid the worry about expressive harm. A perfectionist state that allocates scarce public funds to one activity over another, on the basis of claims about the relative value of the former activity, does not express messages of condemnation or denigration in any straightforward way. Certainly, moderate perfectionist policies within actual societies, such as public funding of the arts, have not typically been interpreted as expressing such messages and have not typically damaged the sense of self-worth of those who are indifferent or opposed to art. So it is unclear that there is anything *inherently* expressively harmful about perfectionist state action: everything depends on context and on the sensitivity with which perfectionist laws and policies are formulated and implemented. In the following three sections, I seek to identify laws and policies that would involve little if any expressive harm. These examples, it is hoped, point towards the possibility of a programme of laws and public policies that promote the enjoyment of moral, intellectual and artistic excellence without expressing messages of denigration or damaging citizens' sense of self-worth.

6.2 Moral Excellence

Let us consider, first, the enjoyment of moral excellence as a component of human flourishing. How might the state go about establishing and maintaining social conditions promotive of and conducive to morally excellent ways of life? Through what kinds of laws and public policies might the state promote the enjoyment of moral excellence among the citizenry?

To answer these questions, we have to start with some more specific claims about what moral excellence consists in. In particular, I shall say, stipulatively but hopefully not too implausibly, that the virtues constitutive of or associated with friendship—such as trustworthiness, empathy, generosity and loyalty—are components of moral excellence. This is not to say that these virtues are the only components of moral excellence. As I have indicated at various junctures, there is a diversity of plausible ways of interpreting and specifying the three excellences. Nor is this to say that these virtues are only realizable through having friends. The point is just that one way of interpreting moral excellence is in terms of virtues such as trustworthiness, empathy, and so on, and one way of realizing these virtues is through forming and sustaining friendships.

Assuming this to be the case, the promotion of moral excellence could occur, in part, through laws and public policies designed to support the institution of friendship. This is particularly important, since a number of sociologists have warned that for various reasons—including longer working hours, suburban sprawl, and technology and social media—the institution of friendship is in decline in many contemporary societies.[6] This decline can be detected across diverse indicators such as participation in bowling leagues, bird-watching groups, choirs, book clubs, picnics and barbecues.

Offhand, it is difficult to envisage how friendship could be promoted through the blunt instrument of the law and public policy. Recall the question posed above: surely perfectionists are not proposing 'the formation of a new state agency, the Department of Love, whose duty it would be to assist anyone who has fallen below some putative affection line, construed on the model of a poverty line'?[7] Similarly, Ackerman states that 'love, friendship and the like are not readily susceptible of mass production. A vital communal life will not flourish under the watchful gaze of bureaucrats dispatched from the imperial center'.[8] But many of these reservations strike me as rhetorically overblown. With enough creativity and resourcefulness, it is possible to devise laws and public policies that support and strengthen the institution of friendship. As Christine Sypnowich puts it, 'the state cannot find friends for the friendless, but a robust conception of the public good will involve an imaginative approach to the problem of community in modern, complex societies, facilitating local communities, clubs, societies, public lectures, festivals, and so on, as well as attending to social handicaps and problems of alienation'.[9]

Particularly interesting in this regard is the 'pro-friendship policy agenda' developed by Ethan Leib.[10] Leib first provides a multifactor test for determining whether someone counts as a friend—rather like the multifactor tests used in other areas of law to determine, say, whether a worker counts as an 'employee' or an 'independent contractor'. This test includes factors such as voluntariness, intimacy, trust, exclusivity, reciprocity, warmth, mutual assistance, equality, duration over time, and modalities of conflict resolution.[11] Though he does not endorse them, preferring instead a more organic approach, Leib even hints at the possibility of establishing registers and ceremonies and 'legal rituals to solidify friendships just as we solemnize the status of marriage and citizenship ... through public oaths and legal documents'.[12] Leib recognizes that his definition of friendship may need some finessing and indeed he states that 'each domain of the law or public policy may need to operate with a slightly different definition to stay true to the needs of

---

[6] See, for example, Putnam, R., *Bowling Alone: The Collapse and Revival of American Community* (New York: Simon & Schuster, 2000).

[7] Carroll, N., 'Can Government Funding of the Arts Be Justified Theoretically?', p. 26.

[8] Ackerman, B., *Social Justice in the Liberal State*, p. 362.

[9] Sypnowich, C., *Equality Renewed: Justice, Flourishing and the Egalitarian Ideal* (London: Routledge, 2017), p. 182.

[10] Leib, E., *Friend v. Friend: The Transformation of Friendship—And What the Law Has to Do with It* (Oxford: Oxford University Press, 2011).

[11] Ibid., pp. 19–24.

[12] Ibid., p. 82.

162   A PERFECTIONIST THEORY OF JUSTICE

particularized areas of the legal and political system.[13] Still, he contends that the multifactor test delineates the notion of friendship sufficiently well as a starting point for discussion, as indicated by the fact that similar tests for friendship have already been used in other contexts, such as health-care proxy decision-making.

Leib then argues that friendship so understood should be facilitated and supported 'through legislative initiatives, public policy sensitivity, or judicial decisions.'[14] Many of his proposals for state support for the institution of friendship are modelled on, and involve extensions of, state support for the institutions of marriage and family. These proposals are designed to incentivize people to develop and deepen their friendships, in a way that is fairly indirect and that does not intrude too far into the internal dynamics of friendship:

- *Friendship Expenditures*: Many countries already have tax deductions for married couples and for charities, so mightn't there similarly be a case for expenses related to friendship activities to be tax deductible at least in part? Such deductions could be very broad (such that cinema tickets, say, are included) or they could be quite narrow (such that only expenses incurred in connection with the provision of care, such as driving a friend to hospital, are included), and they could be subject to a cap.
- *Health-Care Proxy Decision-Making*: In many countries, doctors consult families to determine what a patient might have wanted, if a patient is unable to make medical decisions for themselves, so mightn't there similarly be a case for including friends in health-care proxy decision-making? After all, individuals are often more comfortable speaking to friends than to family members about sensitive end-of-life matters.
- *Extension to Friends of Loss of Consortium*: Many countries already allow spouses to sue for loss of consortium or companionship in a wrongful death claim, so mightn't there similarly be a case for allowing friends to collect for loss of consortium? After all, for many people friends are just as important a source of companionship and fellowship as spouses are.
- *Friendship Leave*: Many countries already require employers to treat employees without reprisal when they need to leave the workplace to care for close family members, so mightn't there similarly be a case for allowing friends to be guaranteed leave to care for one another in times of illness? This would be especially important for individuals who do not have close family members and who need their friends urgently in serious illnesses.
- *Pro-Friendship Urban Planning*: Cities and towns could be designed with friendship in mind. This might involve more public spaces for people to gather and converse face to face. Foot traffic might be incentivized over car

[13] Ibid., p. 24.
[14] Ibid., p. 38.

traffic. The problem of suburban sprawl might also be tackled. Policies of integration, for the purpose of promoting economic and racial equality, might be pursued in ways that enable friendship groups to remain together.

- *Smile Zones*: Signs could be posted to encourage people to smile at one another so as to create an environment that is more conducive to the formation of new friendships. A policy of this kind was implemented in the municipality of Port Phillip in Australia, which posted signs telling people that they were entering a '10 smiles per hour zone'.[15]

Leib notes that some of these proposals are already pursued in an ad hoc way, as the example from Port Phillip illustrates. In this sense, there is already some latent understanding of the importance of friendship within the law and public policy in some settings. However, current practices towards friendship are not consistent, systematic or self-conscious. These practices are not placed on a firm normative foundation. 'There is something haphazard', says Leib, 'about the law's approach to friendship that invites further study [into] the ways law makes friendship matter, why it makes friendship matter in the ways it does, and whether there are particular areas within the law that are especially appropriate (or inappropriate) for the promotion of friendship'.[16]

Of course, there are pressing questions about the *moral bearings* of this pro-friendship policy agenda: we may wonder whether it passes the test of public justification, whether it is too restrictive of autonomy, whether it is paternalistic, and so on. But here we are not concerned with these principled objections to perfectionism; they will be discussed in Part III. At this point, we are instead concerned with how, in practice, the state might go about promoting the ideal of friendship. More pertinent in this context, then, are the questions that might be asked about the *practical workability* of this pro-friendship policy agenda: Mightn't the existence of tax exemptions and other regulatory privileges introduce perverse incentives for people to befriend others? Is it not a pitiful friend who needs to be financially incentivized to go to the cinema or to provide care? In this way, how can we be sure that the pro-friendship agenda isn't counterproductive, inadvertently corrupting or undermining the institution of friendship? Even if these laws and policies would increase the *quantity* of friendships, can we be confident that they would also increase the *quality* of friendships and thereby foster the sorts of virtues and character traits that were said to be cultivated through friendship, such as trustworthiness, empathy and generosity? Moreover, how do we know these policies won't lead to too much friendship and associated problems such as cronyism and old boys' networks, thereby entrenching

---

[15] These examples are all drawn, almost verbatim, from the instructive discussion in ibid., pp. 79–81; for a broader discussion of these issues, see chs 4–6.

[16] Ibid., p. 105.

gender-, race- and class-based stratifications and damaging the ideal of impartiality upon which much of public life rests? And how realistic is it, in any case, to think that friendship can be adequately defined for legal purposes? Isn't the concept of friendship too radically indeterminate to be captured even by a broad multifactor test?[17]

While these questions are important, what they illustrate more than anything else is that there is an interesting conversation to be had about promoting friendship through political action—a conversation that will need to draw on research from the social sciences as well as other fields. These questions show that perfectionist laws and policies are likely to have costs as well as benefits and that perfectionist state officials will need to engage in careful and empirically informed cost-benefit calculations on a case-by-case basis. But there is no reason to assume, a priori, that the costs of perfectionist laws and policies will always or even typically outweigh the benefits. It seems unwarranted to shut down the conversation before it has even begun by dismissing out of hand the possibility of a workable and effective pro-friendship legal and policy agenda. At the very least, then, the ball has been thrown back into the court of the anti-perfectionist liberal, who must now offer not simply an armchair hunch but rather a persuasive and empirically informed argument for why we should expect the costs of these sorts of pro-friendship policies to always, or at least typically, outweigh the benefits.

6.3 Intellectual Excellence

Let us turn, next, to the enjoyment of intellectual excellence as a component of human flourishing. How might the state go about establishing and maintaining social conditions promotive of and conducive to intellectually excellent ways of life? Through what kinds of laws and public policies might the state promote the enjoyment of intellectual excellence among the citizenry?

In order to answer these questions, we will, as in Section 6.2, need to make some more specific claims about what intellectual excellence consists in. In particular, I shall say, once again stipulatively but hopefully not too implausibly, that possessing a healthy curiosity and a knowledge and understanding of diverse fields of human endeavour, such as science and natural history and psychology, is a component of intellectual excellence.[18] As before, this does not mean that the only way to understand and specify the idea of intellectual excellence is in terms of a healthy curiosity and a knowledge and understanding of diverse fields of human

---

[17] Some of these objections are raised in Eric Posner's review of Leib's book. See 'Huck and Jim and Law', *The New Republic*, 21 February 2011. For Leib's reply, see 'Friendship and the Law: A Response', *The New Republic*, 22 February 2011.

[18] For a defence of this stipulation, see, for example, King, N., *The Excellent Mind: Intellectual Virtues for Everyday Life* (Oxford: Oxford University Press, 2021), ch. 3.

endeavour. Perhaps someone who achieves a mastery of a single specialized domain, such as Greek poetry, still realizes intellectual excellence. The point is just that one way of interpreting intellectual excellence is in terms of a healthy curiosity and a wide and deep knowledge of important truths about the world and the human condition.

How might intellectual excellence so understood be promoted among the general public? One way in which this might occur is through informative and educational public broadcasting. An interesting example in this regard is the BBC, the world's oldest and largest national broadcaster, which is publicly funded by licence fees, and whose mission, in the famous words of its first director-general Lord Reith, is to 'inform, educate and entertain'.[19] This core cultural mission is part of what distinguishes the BBC from private commercial broadcasters and media companies, and has been described by Huw Wheldon, a former managing director of BBC TV, as 'making the good popular and the popular good'.[20] In his 1924 manifesto, *Broadcast Over Britain*, Reith explained that broadcasting should 'carry into the greatest possible number of homes everything that is best in every department in human knowledge, endeavour and achievement'.[21]

Reith was aware that this might appear paternalistic—'we are apparently setting out to give the public what we think they need, and not what they want'—but he rejected any simple market model in which demand shapes supply, suggesting that supply can also shape demand through a process of habituation:

> We tend to take our pleasures in water-tight compartments. We often dislike things intensely, or rather persuade ourselves that we do, when we have actually never been brought into contact with them, and really know nothing whatever about them. On the first occasion when, perforce, we are brought up against them, we are quite sure that our antipathy was justified, but next time perhaps they do not seem so bad, and so gradually we may even come to appreciate them.[22]

As Reith also puts this point, 'the more one gets, the more one wants'.[23] On this sort of basis, it is not implausible to suppose that over time informative and educational public broadcasting could foster the enjoyment of intellectual excellence among the citizenry.

---

[19] For an interesting exploration of the history, present state and future prospects of the BBC, see Higgins, C., *This New Noise: The Extraordinary Birth and Troubled Life of the BBC* (London: Faber & Faber, 2015). Lord Reith's motto is discussed on pp. 37, 52–3. For a discussion of the different strands of 'Reithianism', see Hendy, D., *Public Service Broadcasting* (Basingstoke: Palgrave Macmillan, 2013), pp. 20–6.

[20] Quoted in Higgins, C., *This New Noise*, p. 52.

[21] Reith, J., *Broadcast Over Britain* (London: Hodder and Stoughton, 1924), p. 34.

[22] Ibid., pp. 34, 123.

[23] Ibid., p. 27.

166 A PERFECTIONIST THEORY OF JUSTICE

Many of the BBC's most celebrated television programmes—such as Kenneth Clark's *Civilisation*, a thirteen-part history of Western art aired in 1969, which attracted 2.5 million viewers in Britain and led to a significant upsurge of visitors to museums and art exhibits; Bryan Magee's interviews with philosophers on the radio and television in the 1970s and 1980s, which achieved the 'near-impossible feat of presenting to a mass audience recondite issues of philosophy without compromising intellectual integrity';[24] David Attenborough's two *Blue Planet* documentaries in 2001 and 2017, which were on the subject of marine life and had 12 and 14 million viewers, respectively; and Mary Beard's three-part documentary series *Meet the Romans* in 2012, which had 2 million viewers per programme—have had a significant influence on the intellectual and cultural life of British society. Discussing the way in which programmes such as these have broadened horizons, Alasdair Milne, BBC director-general from 1982 to 1987, states: 'had [audiences] been asked *before* seeing any of these [programmes] whether they were interested in Ramses the Second, or the mating habits of frogs, or black holes, they might have, ever so politely, sent you packing', yet because of well-conceived public broadcasting these topics 'gripped the attention of millions of people' and became 'national talking points'.[25]

The capacity of this kind of broadcasting to contribute to the intellectual enrichment of the general public is nicely brought out by award-winning writer and radio producer Armando Iannucci, who describes the impact of the BBC on his childhood: 'I loved that I could glide from *Fawlty Towers* to a Horizon documentary on *Voyager*'s trip past Saturn ... British television said this: that everything, the whole world of knowledge and of creativity is on offer, is for you, all of you'.[26] Similarly, the British screenwriter Dennis Potter explains that, although the BBC of his childhood and youth was 'paternalistic and often stuffily pompous' and 'saw itself in an almost priestly role', it nonetheless 'threw open the "magic casement" on great sources of mindscape at a time when books were hard to come by, and when I had never stepped into a theatre or even a concert hall, and would have been scared to do so even if given the chance'.[27] That the BBC is delivering on its Reithian mission to inform, educate and entertain is also supported by a study conducted by the UK's independent broadcasting regulator Ofcom in 2019, which found that 66 per cent of respondents agreed that the BBC provides 'informative and educational content which is inspiring and challenging and [which] supports learning for all ages'.[28]

---

[24] Obituaries, *The Telegraph*, 26 July 2019.
[25] Quoted in Hendy, D., *Public Service Broadcasting*, pp. 83–4.
[26] Quoted in Barwise, P. and York, P., *The War Against the BBC* (London: Penguin Books, 2020), p. xii.
[27] Quoted in Higgins, C., *This New Noise*, pp. 63–4.
[28] *Ofcom's Annual Report on the BBC*, 24 October 2019, p. 30; see also Barwise, P. and York, P., *The War Against the BBC*, pp. 240–5.

Two fine-grained anecdotes illustrate these points. The first comes from a friend of Kenneth Clark, who recounts that in a Covent Garden pub he once 'found two of the market porters discussing Caravaggio; he thought he was suffering from a hallucination. The railway porters at Charing Cross used to sit up with their children long after bedtime to listen to talks on Michelangelo'.[29] The second anecdote concerns one of David Attenborough's programmes, in which he was pursuing a rare bald-headed rock crow called the *picathates gymnocephalus*. Attenborough 'doubted this creature would be alluring enough [to hold the attention of viewers], but when his cameraman Charles Lagus was driving him down Regent Street in an open-top sports car and a bus driver leaned out of his cab and asked him, in a neat piece of tmesis, if he was ever going to catch "that *picafartees gymno-bloody-cephalus*", he knew it had lodged itself in the public mind'.[30]

Of course, the BBC's pursuit of informative and educational broadcasting has come in for criticism. Some have contended that its programmes are marked by an air of self-important intellectualism. According to one common jibe, BBC programmes consist of 'dons talking to dons'. Another common criticism is that, at least until recently, the BBC has been heavily London-centric, neglecting or marginalizing the diversity of regional traditions within Wales, Scotland and Ireland as well as within England itself.

But, again, this does not seem to show that any attempt by the perfectionist state to promote enjoyment of intellectual excellence through informative and educational public broadcasting is doomed to failure. What it shows is that any such attempt would need to be sensitive and nuanced: it would need to strike a delicate balance between the niche and the popular, the serious and the relaxed, the old and the new, the challenging and the entertaining, and it would need to avoid pomposity, snobbery and elitism. Public service broadcasters must balance 'the need to show cultural leadership—to be, as it were, in advance of public taste—and the equally powerful need to ensure audience figures don't fall below a critical level by being *too far* in advance of the public'.[31] These considerations give an indication of the complexities involved in devising effective perfectionist public policies, and they illustrate that the implementation of perfectionist justice depends on a variety of empirical contingencies. But they do not appear to present an insurmountable obstacle to the promotion by the state of intellectual excellence through suitable public broadcasting. So, once again, the ball has at least been thrown back into the court of the anti-perfectionist liberal, who must now offer persuasive and empirically informed arguments for why we should expect efforts to foster intellectual excellence through informative and educational public broadcasting to be always or typically futile.

---

[29] Moran, J., *Armchair Nation: An Intimate History of Britain in Front of the TV* (London: Profile Books, 2013), p. 110.
[30] Ibid., pp. 98–9.
[31] Hendy, D., *Public Service Broadcasting*, p. 56.

6.4 Artistic Excellence

Let us turn, finally, to the enjoyment of artistic excellence as a component of human flourishing. How might the state go about establishing and maintaining social conditions promotive of and conducive to artistically excellent ways of life? Through what kinds of laws and public policies might the state promote the production and consumption of excellent works of art?

One way in which the enjoyment of artistic excellence can be promoted is through the operation of publicly funded institutions and agencies dedicated to the encouragement of artistic excellence in its various forms—including musical, operatic, theatrical, literary and poetic forms, as well as the many forms of visual art such as painting, sculpture, architecture, ceramics, printmaking and photography. Arts institutions can encourage these forms of artistic expression through grants, awards, prizes and scholarships.

Institutions of this kind already exist in many countries. In the UK, for instance, the Arts Council of Great Britain was established by Royal Charter in 1946 to 'develop and improve the knowledge, understanding and practice of the arts'.[32] A particularly interesting and important example in this regard is the National Endowment for the Arts (NEA), an independent agency of the US federal government which was established in 1965 with a mandate to 'promote progress and scholarship in the humanities and arts', to support the 'great branches of scholarly and cultural activity', to 'provide models of excellence to the American people' and to assist citizens 'to recognize and appreciate the aesthetic dimensions of our lives, the diversity of excellence that comprises our cultural heritage, and artistic and scholarly expression'.[33] This founding legislation explains that 'the encouragement and support of national progress and scholarship in the humanities and the arts' are 'appropriate matters of concern to the federal government', and that 'while no government can call a great artist or scholar into existence', the state can nonetheless create and sustain conditions that 'facilitat[e] the release of this creative talent'.[34]

However, the budget given to the NEA by the federal government has over the years been very limited. A comparative analysis of public arts spending in 1998 found that in the US per capita public spending on the arts was only £3.80 and public spending on the arts was only 0.13 per cent of total public spending—as compared with Finland, say, where per capita public spending on the arts was £59.20 and public spending on the arts was 2.1 per cent of total public

---

[32] See the 'Our Royal Charter' page on the website of the Arts Council of England (www.artscouncil.org.uk), accessed 19 February 2021.
[33] See the 'Founding Legislation' page on the website of the NEA (www.arts.gov), accessed 19 February 2021.
[34] Ibid.

spending.[35] And still today the NEA's current budget constitutes only a miniscule fraction (0.004 per cent) of the total federal budget. In light of this, there is a strong case to be made that if the state really is under a duty of justice to promote the enjoyment of artistic excellence, then the current level of federal support extended to the NEA is unacceptably low. Perfectionist justice, then, would not simply replicate the model of the NEA or other similar arts agencies. Rather, it can be expected to recommend a legislative and institutional framework that expresses a much more profound commitment on the part of government to the advancement of the arts.

As with previous examples of perfectionist laws and public policies, there are plenty of critics of the NEA. Many recurring criticisms were in fact prefigured in the lively debates during the passage of the NEA's founding legislation in the House of Representatives in 1965. In those debates, Congressman John Rhodes contended that the consequences of state control of the arts in the Soviet Union should be 'a sufficient warning against experiments of this nature in this country' and that the arts would not thrive if subjected to 'the deadening hand of the federal bureaucracy'; Congressman Paul Findley argued that art is undefinable, saying that 'the language presently before us is broad enough to cover' federal subsidies for anything 'from Tchaikovsky to cheesecake'; and Congressman Robert Duncan similarly attacked the idea that the concept of artistic excellence was amenable to definition, saying that 'artistic excellence to one is often absurd nonsense to another' and that the state 'has no business setting arts standards or attempting to influence them' because doing so would merely amount to government 'financing its judgments and prejudices with the public's money'.[36]

Perfectionist state officials will, of course, need to be attentive to these sorts of hazards. Perhaps some can be mitigated by ensuring that decisions about specific grants are made not by politicians but by an independent public body composed of individuals drawn from a diverse range of backgrounds, who have a proven appreciation of the arts and who are instructed to give special attention to the initiatives of historically underrepresented groups. In any event, there is no reason to assume, a priori, that these hazards spell doom for efforts to promote the enjoyment of artistic excellence through the operation of publicly funded arts institutions. After all, the NEA does appear to have done a reasonable job of encouraging a wide cross-section of society to take enjoyment in the arts while avoiding many of these pitfalls.[37]

---

[35] Policy Research and Planning Department of the Arts Council of England, *International Data on Public Spending on the Arts in Eleven Countries* (London: Arts Council of England, 1998), p. 166.

[36] All of these quotations are drawn from the account in Taylor, F. and Barresi, A., *The Arts at a New Frontier: The National Endowment for the Arts* (New York: Plenum Press, 1984), pp. 44–7.

[37] For an account of the impact of the NEA in the areas of dance, literature, media arts, museums and visual arts, music and opera, and theatre, see M. Bauerlein and E. Grantham (eds), *National Endowment for the Arts: A History 1965–2008* (Washington, DC: National Endowment for the Arts, 2009), pp. 171–253.

Pulling things together, the state could go about promoting the enjoyment of moral, intellectual and artistic excellence through a range of measures, including pro-friendship policies, informative and educational public broadcasting, and public arts institutions and agencies. Far from it being the case that ideals of human flourishing do not lend themselves to a meaningful legal and public policy programme—or that, if they do, they pale in comparison to the much weightier non-perfectionist values at stake—we have seen that moral, intellectual and artistic excellence can be expected to have significant and far-reaching political consequences. This is nicely brought out by Sher:

> If we should not expect perfectionist values to dominate, we also should not consign them to a marginal role. We may be tempted to do this if we concentrate too exclusively on a few stock examples, such as the criminalization of pornography and prostitution, which are indeed tangential to most people's main concerns. But when we [reflect on the nature of perfectionist values] we realize that they are potentially relevant to virtually every aspect of human life. Thus, once perfectionist considerations are admitted at all, they can be expected to play a role in many areas of political decision-making. They are, for instance, often relevant to decisions about public assistance, educational policy, the criminal and civil justice system, the prison system, city planning and land use, transportation policy, the tax code, support for cultural institutions, regulation of the entertainment industry, investment incentives, and the structure of institutions such as the military—to name just a few of the more obvious candidates. If perfectionist reasons rarely exclude others, they are also rarely absent from any list of relevant factors.[38]

While my goal has not been to recommend any particular legislative or policy prescription—since a proper assessment of these matters would depend on a range of empirical contingencies and contextual factors—the laws and public policies discussed in the previous sections hopefully give a feel for the possible practical upshots of perfectionist justice and indicate that effective state promotion of various ideals of human flourishing is not beyond the realms of possibility.

6.5 Indistinguishability: Doesn't Liberal Justice *Already* Give Perfection Its Due?

An important objection to the arguments so far is that the kinds of policies that perfectionists want to pursue can in fact be justified on the basis of standard liberal values such as freedom, equality and fairness, and so when all is said

[38] Sher, G., *Beyond Neutrality: Perfectionism and Politics* (Cambridge: Cambridge University Press, 1997), p. 246.

PERFECTIONIST LAW AND PUBLIC POLICY   171

and done perfectionism and anti-perfectionist liberalism turn out to be largely indistinguishable. Here is one way of putting this thought:

> The perfectionist laws and public policies mentioned in the previous sections can all be adequately justified from within the leading non-perfectionist theories of social or distributive justice, such as those of Ronald Dworkin and John Rawls. State support for the arts—to take just one example—can be justified on the basis of claims about equality of opportunity. The best forms of anti-perfectionist liberalism can thus be expected to provide fair access to a rich variety of cultural and educational activities. So once one properly appreciates the power and flexibility of the conceptual resources internal to leading non-perfectionist theories, the resort to perfectionist reasoning—to claims about moral, intellectual and artistic excellence—turns out to be unnecessary. In this sense, wouldn't an ideal or well-ordered liberal society already give the claims of perfection their due? Wouldn't it already have ample grounds for enacting many of the policies that perfectionists favour? So isn't the perfectionist theory of justice practically indistinguishable from its main rivals? Why does the promotion of the various dimensions of human flourishing call for some separate principle of perfection, one that goes above and beyond leading liberal principles of justice?[39]

This objection reminds us that the debate between perfectionists and anti-perfectionist liberals is not about the *consequences* of state action but rather about the *reasons* that can justify state action. Anti-perfectionist liberals often make this point by saying that they endorse 'neutrality of justification', not 'neutrality of effect'.[40] On Quong's telling, for instance, the debate between perfectionists and anti-perfectionists concerns whether judgements about the good life or human flourishing 'can serve as valid reasons for state action, not whether state action can ever have the effect of favouring some conceptions of the good over others'.[41] Insofar as anti-perfectionist liberalism is defined by a view about what reasons for state action are legitimate, and not by a view about what laws and policies are legitimate, it is possible that most, if not all, of the laws and policies that perfectionists favour can be justified in terms of the reasons that anti-perfectionist liberals regard

---

[39] I thank Max Afnan, Zeynep Pamuk and Anthony Taylor for putting to me this sort of worry. For discussions of the indistinguishability of perfectionist and non-perfectionist theories, see Weinstock, D., 'Neutralizing Perfection: Hurka on Liberal Neutrality', *Dialogue* 38 (1999), pp. 53–7; Quong, J., *Liberalism Without Perfection* (Oxford: Oxford University Press, 2011), pp. 122–6; Arneson, R., 'Neutrality and Political Liberalism', in R. Merrill and D. Weinstock, *Political Neutrality: A Re-evaluation* (New York: Palgrave Macmillan, 2014), pp. 30–3; Kramer, M., *Liberalism with Excellence* (Oxford: Oxford University Press, 2017), pp. 294–5. I also discuss a different version of this indistinguishability worry in Section 10.4.

[40] I discuss these and other conceptions of neutrality in Tahzib, C., 'Pluralist Neutrality', *Journal of Political Philosophy* 26 (2018), pp. 508–32. My arguments in this work do not, however, rely on the positive account of pluralist neutrality that I defend therein.

[41] Quong, J., *Liberalism Without Perfection*, p. 18.

172   A PERFECTIONIST THEORY OF JUSTICE

as legitimate. In this case, perfectionism would turn out to be indistinguishable, practically speaking, from anti-perfectionist liberalism.

There are two main ways of responding to this indistinguishability objection. The first is to argue that many of the relevant non-perfectionist rationales for the policies typically favoured by perfectionists are unsuccessful, and so in at least an interesting range of cases there will be genuine extensional differences between perfectionist and non-perfectionist theories of social justice. The second response is to argue that even if perfectionist and non-perfectionist theories are largely or wholly extensionally equivalent, this does not show that perfectionism is redundant or uninteresting since these theories may agree for importantly different reasons. Perfectionism might still recommend itself, for instance, on the grounds that it yields the right policies for the right reasons. I think that both of these responses have merit, and so in what follows I shall elaborate both.

Before doing so, however, a caveat is in order. In exploring what laws and policies anti-perfectionist liberalism can and cannot support, it is vital not to set up a straw man by underestimating the justificatory resources available to anti-perfectionist liberals. We should not conclude that anti-perfectionist liberalism cannot account for a given law or policy until we have considered the resources and rationales available to the most promising and sophisticated articulations of anti-perfectionist liberalism on offer.

The importance of this caveat can be illustrated by briefly considering Richard Kraut's arguments against anti-perfectionist liberalism.[42] Kraut seeks 'to show by means of a series of examples that this thesis [i.e. anti-perfectionist liberalism] is radically at odds with' familiar political practices, and that if anti-perfectionist liberalism were to be followed our 'political life would become badly disfigured'.[43] He first considers the issue of assisted suicide in the case of 'someone who is old, gravely ill, in great pain [and] utterly dependent on others'.[44] Kraut says that, because 'the thesis of neutrality holds that the state has no business addressing the issue of when a life is worth leading', the 'defender of neutrality must say that these features of the case' (namely, grave illness, great pain, and so on) are politically irrelevant.[45] As such, 'the neutralist holds that assisted suicide must be allowed not just in the case of those who are terminally ill and in great pain, but in all cases whatsoever (so long as the decision to commit suicide is fully voluntary)'.[46] However, the values that Kraut suggests are unavailable to anti-perfectionist liberals—such as health and the avoidance of pain—are not, in the relevant sense, perfectionist values at all. Leading anti-perfectionist liberals recognize certain very 'thin' or 'all-purpose' goods, such as health and the avoidance of pain, as legitimate

---

[42] See Kraut, R., 'Politics, Neutrality, and the Good', in E. Paul, F. Miller and J. Paul (eds), *Human Flourishing* (Cambridge: Cambridge University Press, 1999), pp. 315–32.
[43] Ibid., p. 319.
[44] Ibid., p. 320.
[45] Ibid.
[46] Ibid.

sources of political reasons.[47] To pay attention to these values in formulating assisted suicide legislation is not to violate the requirement of liberal neutrality as that requirement has typically been understood.

Kraut also considers the issue of democracy. He says that democracy is 'best interpreted as a way of supporting a substantive conception of the good'.[48] In particular, democracy 'encourages the development of a certain kind of person, someone who is thoughtful, fair-minded, and public-spirited'.[49] Even assuming that Kraut is right that democracy is best justified in terms of these considerations (as opposed to considerations of freedom, equality, fairness or self-respect, which plainly are available rationales for anti-perfectionist liberals), however, these considerations are again not, in the relevant sense, perfectionist considerations. After all, leading anti-perfectionist liberals recognize the importance of many of these traits. Rawls, for instance, explains that 'justice as fairness includes an account of certain political virtues' and he includes 'civility', 'tolerance', 'fair-mindedness' and 'a readiness to meet others halfway' among these political virtues.[50] Indeed, Rawls is at pains to stress that 'if a constitutional regime takes certain steps to strengthen the virtues of toleration and mutual trust ... it does not thereby become a perfectionist state' because 'the political virtues are tied to the principles of political justice and to the forms of judgment and conduct essential to sustain fair social cooperation over time'.[51]

Particularly perplexing is Kraut's treatment of the issue of dignity and humiliation. He imagines 'an act in which one person publicly humiliates and cruelly degrades another—for example, by assaulting him, insulting him, [or] spitting on him'.[52] In this case, the victim 'is not being deprived of a physical capacity or of money. Rather, the injury consists in the very fact that his dignity as a human being, the honor he is due as a member of the human community, his claim to equality of respect, is being denied'.[53] 'In describing the case in this way', says Kraut, 'we are presupposing that one of the things that makes a human life go well is the recognition received by the person who lives it that he is fully human', and so 'the importance of this form of justice cannot be recognized' by anti-perfectionist liberals.[54] Once again, however, the values to which Kraut refers—namely, dignity, honour, equality of respect, recognition of others' full humanity—are not, in the relevant sense, perfectionist values at all. To suppose that anti-perfectionist liberals cannot consistently appeal to these values to condemn humiliation and degradation—or to suppose that anti-perfectionist liberals can only understand the wrongness of humiliation and degradation in terms of the

---

[47] See, for example, Rawls, J., *Justice as Fairness*, p. 179.
[48] Kraut, R., 'Politics, Neutrality, and the Good', p. 326.
[49] Ibid., p. 327.
[50] Rawls, J., *Political Liberalism*, pp. 139, 163, 194.
[51] Ibid., pp. 194–5.
[52] Kraut, R., 'Politics, Neutrality, and the Good', p. 328.
[53] Ibid.
[54] Ibid., p. 329.

174   A PERFECTIONIST THEORY OF JUSTICE

deprivation of a physical capacity or of money—is to caricature anti-perfectionist liberalism. Indeed, Rawls explains that within his theory 'perhaps the most important primary good is that of self-respect', and so it is unclear why Rawlsian anti-perfectionists should feel any tension in affirming, with Kraut, that 'one of the things that makes a human life go well is the recognition received by the person who lives it that he is fully human'.[55]

In short, Kraut's arguments illustrate the importance of not constructing a straw man when trying to compare the practical implications of perfectionist and anti-perfectionist liberal theories. Anti-perfectionist liberalism offers a far richer and more flexible account of political morality than it is sometimes given credit for. In particular, the broad and rich set of considerations to which Kraut refers in the course of his discussion—the importance of health, the badness of pain, the need to encourage certain political virtues and traits in citizens, dignity, honour, equality of respect, recognition of others' full humanity—can all be coherently and comfortably placed within leading anti-perfectionist liberal theories. Indeed, these considerations are not just consistent with these anti-perfectionist liberal theories but in fact often already quite central to them. So these considerations are not aptly construed as perfectionist considerations at all, despite the fact that they draw on some broad ideas of the good. The state can, that is, act on the basis of these considerations without thereby 'mak[ing] assumptions about what the constituents of a flourishing life are' or 'operat[ing] with a substantive conception of what is intrinsically good and bad' in life, as those phrases have normally been understood in the context of the debate between perfectionists and anti-perfectionist liberals.[56]

It is worth noting that I have been speaking as if there is a bright line between 'perfectionist' and 'non-perfectionist' rationales for laws and public policies. For instance, I have said that the considerations to which Kraut refers are not 'in the relevant sense' perfectionist at all. But, although in Part I I described some typical features of anti-perfectionist liberalism, I have not provided any general criteria for drawing the distinction between perfectionism and anti-perfectionist liberalism.[57] The reason for this, as I suggested in Section 1.1, is that 'perfectionism' and 'anti-perfectionist liberalism' are not natural kinds but instead terms of art used by political philosophers, in stipulative ways, to classify and study political theories and so it makes little sense to get too caught up in demarcating the exact boundaries of these terms.

Without an analysis of the distinction between perfectionist and non-perfectionist rationales, one might wonder how we can know whether or not a putative rationale for a law or policy remains within the theoretical bounds

---

[55] Rawls, J., *A Theory of Justice* (Cambridge, MA: Harvard University Press, 1971), p. 440; see also p. 396.

[56] Kraut, R., 'Politics, Neutrality, and the Good', pp. 315, 324.

[57] For a helpful analysis of this taxonomical issue, see de Marneffe, P., 'The Slipperiness of Neutrality', *Social Theory and Practice* 32 (2006), pp. 17–34.

of anti-perfectionist liberalism. When an anti-perfectionist liberal advances a justification for, say, state support for the arts, how are we to decide whether this justification relies on resources 'internal' to anti-perfectionist liberalism (and thus illustrates the flexibility and explanatory power of anti-perfectionist liberalism) or whether instead it relies on resources 'external' to anti-perfectionist liberalism (and thus amounts to jumping ship and becoming a perfectionist in all but name)? At what point does an attempt to justify a given law or policy involve such significant reshaping of the inner workings of an anti-perfectionist liberal theory that it is more aptly classified as an abandonment of anti-perfectionist liberalism than a modification or amplification thereof?

However, we seem to be able to apply the distinction between perfectionist and non-perfectionist rationales even without knowing what exactly this distinction consists in. Some rationales are clearly recognizable as 'perfectionist' (such as those based on a certain conception of artistic excellence) and others are clearly recognizable as 'non-perfectionist' (such as those based on a certain conception of equality). As Sher rightly says, 'the extension of [this distinction] is better understood than its intension'.[58] In particular, many of the rationales that I shall go on to consider appeal to values such as equality, fairness and self-respect, which have been at the heart of leading non-perfectionist theories and are as such quite clearly and uncontroversially classifiable as non-perfectionist values. In short, then, the lack of an underlying analytic account of the distinction between 'perfectionism' and 'anti-perfectionist liberalism' is not as damning as it might at first appear: we seem perfectly capable of determining whether a given rationale is 'external' or 'internal' to anti-perfectionist liberalism—whether or not it counts as perfectionist 'in the relevant sense'—despite not having in hand a precise account of how to demarcate these boundaries.

6.6 Extensional Differences

Let us begin with the first response to the indistinguishability charge. According to this response, there would be genuine differences in the practical implications of perfectionist and non-perfectionist theories. I do not doubt that it is possible to find plausible non-perfectionist rationales for *certain* laws and policies called for by perfectionists. The question is how *many* of the laws and policies that perfectionists want to pursue are amenable to this kind of non-perfectionist

[58] Sher, G., *Beyond Neutrality*, p. 38; see also p. 15.

176 A PERFECTIONIST THEORY OF JUSTICE

justification. Instead of going through particular perfectionist laws and policies one by one and assessing whether each could plausibly be supported by a non-perfectionist rationale, I shall consider some of the most prominent *general* attempts to justify standard perfectionist policies (often policies of state support for the arts) in terms of the values and commitments internal to anti-perfectionist liberalism: Rawls's attempts to justify perfectionist policies in terms of unanimous consent and equality (Section 6.6.1); Dworkin's attempt to justify perfectionist policies in terms of intergenerational fairness (Section 6.6.2); Wall's attempt to justify perfectionist policies in terms of equality and fairness (Section 6.6.3); and Kramer's attempt to justify perfectionist policies in terms of the social bases of warranted self-respect (Section 6.6.4). My conclusion will be that, despite their ingenuity and resourcefulness, none of these arguments succeeds. Whatever else may be said of perfectionist justice, then, one cannot contend that it is extensionally equivalent to leading non-perfectionist theories of justice.[59]

It is true that this conclusion goes against the self-understanding of some anti-perfectionist liberals, who profess their approval of public funding for the arts and culture. For instance, in conversation in the 1990s Rawls was reportedly 'surprised that others thought that *Theory* committed him to denying a democratic society the authority to publicly support perfectionist cultural institutions.'[60] But whether anti-perfectionist liberalism really does approve of perfectionist cultural institutions is plainly not something that can be settled by the say-so of this or that anti-perfectionist liberal. Anti-perfectionist liberals must employ the resources internal to their theories in order to justify their approval of public funding for the arts and culture. Of course, as we have just mentioned, it is not straightforward to determine whether a given argument employs resources 'internal' or 'external' to anti-perfectionist liberalism. But the general point remains that anti-perfectionist liberals need to show that there is a compelling rationale for arts funding from within a recognizably anti-perfectionist liberal framework. My contention in Sections 6.6.1–6.6.4 will thus be that, Rawls's and others' say-so to the contrary notwithstanding, no compelling non-perfectionist rationale for arts funding is available: the existing rationales either (i) are compelling but do not remain recognizably within the confines of anti-perfectionist liberalism or (ii) do remain recognizably within the confines of anti-perfectionist liberalism but are not compelling.

[59] For similarly pessimistic conclusions about the prospects of a non-perfectionist justification of state support for art and culture, see Carroll, N., 'Can Government Funding of the Arts Be Justified Theoretically?', *Journal of Aesthetic Education* 21 (1987), pp. 21–35; Brighouse, H., 'Neutrality, Publicity, and State Funding of the Arts', *Philosophy & Public Affairs* 24 (1995), pp. 35–63.

[60] See Freeman, S., *Rawls* (London: Routledge, 2007), p. 511 n. 15.

6.6.1 Rawls's Arguments from Unanimous Consent and Equality

Rawls is clear and uncompromising in his rejection of perfectionist justice:

> Human perfections are to be pursued within the limits of the principle of free association. Persons join together to further their cultural and artistic interests in the same way that they form religious communities. They do not use the coercive apparatus of the state to win for themselves a greater liberty or larger distributive shares on the grounds that their activities are of more intrinsic value. Perfectionism is denied as a political principle. Thus the associations dedicated to advancing the arts and sciences and culture generally are to be won as a fair return for services rendered, or from such voluntary contributions as citizens wish to make, all within a regime regulated by the two principles of justice.[61]

Yet, in an important and more concessive passage, Rawls explains that 'eventually of course we would have to check whether the consequences of doing without a standard of perfection are acceptable, since offhand it may seem as if justice as fairness does not allow enough scope for ideal-regarding considerations'.[62] Rawls then goes on to make two points to try to assuage the worry that anti-perfectionist liberalism would not give perfection its due.

The first point is that 'public funds for the arts and sciences may be provided through the exchange branch' of government.[63] Rawls explains that the exchange branch is a branch of government that is established to 'provide for government activities independent from what justice requires'.[64] Because of this justice-unrelatedness, though, and unlike other branches of government, the taxes imposed to fund the projects of the exchange branch must be 'agreed upon, if not unanimously, then approximately so'.[65] Rawls calls this requirement 'Wicksell's unanimity criterion'.[66] When perfectionist policies are delivered through the exchange branch, 'no one is taxed without his consent'.[67]

To support the conjecture that there would be unanimous (or near-unanimous) support for perfectionist policies, Rawls might appeal to the 'Aristotelian Principle'.[68] This principle holds that 'other things equal, human beings enjoy the exercise of their realized capacities (their innate or trained abilities), and this enjoyment increases the more the capacity is realized, or the greater its complexity'.[69]

---

[61] Rawls, J., *A Theory of Justice*, pp. 328–9.
[62] Ibid., p. 331.
[63] Ibid. For discussion of the exchange branch, see pp. 282–4.
[64] Ibid., p. 282.
[65] Ibid.
[66] Ibid.
[67] Ibid., p. 331.
[68] See ibid., pp. 424–33. I thank Elvio Baccarini for suggesting that I consider the Aristotelian Principle in this context.
[69] Ibid., p. 426.

'The intuitive idea here', Rawls continues, 'is that human beings take more pleasure in doing something as they become more proficient at it, and of two activities they do equally well, they prefer the one calling on a larger repertoire of more intricate and subtle discriminations.'[70] This principle explains, for instance, why many people prefer chess to checkers. Elaborating on this principle, Rawls explains that more complex activities 'satisfy the desire for variety and novelty of experience, and leave room for feats of ingenuity and invention'; they permit and even require 'individual style and personal expression' in a way that simpler activities do not; they also 'evoke the pleasures of anticipation and surprise, and often the overall form of the activity, its structural development, is fascinating and beautiful.'[71] There is of course something vaguely 'perfectionist' about this principle, but Rawls is clear that it is an empirical principle about what people do desire, not a normative principle about what people should desire or should be induced to desire, and as such invoking this principle is entirely consistent with anti-perfectionist liberalism. Appealing to the Aristotelian Principle, then, Rawls might argue that in a well-ordered society the free and cooperative association of individuals can be expected to tend increasingly towards the kinds of complex, creative and excellent activities and forms of life that perfectionist policies typically support, leading to unanimous (or near-unanimous) consent for these policies.

However, Rawls's argument here does little to assuage the worry that his view fails to give the claims of perfection their due. The reason for this is that unanimous (or near-unanimous) consent is an extremely strong requirement. While it is difficult to forecast such things with precision, it seems unlikely, even under highly idealized conditions, that unanimous (or near-unanimous) consent for perfectionist policies will typically be forthcoming in large-scale, pluralistic societies. Certainly, the Aristotelian Principle does not imply in any straightforward way there will be such consent. After all, the Aristotelian Principle is only a psychological tendency or empirical generalization and it does not hold in all or even nearly all cases. Rawls describes it as a 'deep psychological fact' that 'seems to be borne out by many facts of everyday life', but he recognizes that it is 'not an invariable pattern of choice, and like all tendencies it may be overridden.'[72] Presumably there are *other* principles of human psychology—say, the inclination towards passive amusement, the desire to stay in one's comfort zone, the tendency to procrastinate or the profit motive—that compete with, and not infrequently defeat, the tendency identified by the Aristotelian Principle. So, without a more thorough empirical analysis of the relative strength of the Aristotelian Principle as compared

[70] Ibid.
[71] Ibid., p. 427.
[72] Ibid., pp. 429, 431, 432.

PERFECTIONIST LAW AND PUBLIC POLICY   179

with other countervailing principles of human psychology, it remains unclear exactly what pattern of desires would emerge within a society regulated by Rawlsian principles of justice.[73]

Of course, Rawls could relax the kind of unanimity required by saying that the projects of the exchange branch must enjoy *widespread endorsement* rather than unanimity or near-unanimity. At one point, Rawls does suggest something along these lines, saying that the exchange branch can use public funds 'if a *sufficiently large number*' of citizens consent to such use.[74] But this looks troublingly ad hoc. What is the motivation from within the Rawlsian framework for relaxing Wicksell's unanimity criterion in this way? Given Rawls's other commitments, it is difficult to see how widespread endorsement could be a morally acceptable substitute for unanimity in ideal conditions. A relaxed condition would be inconsistent, for instance, with Rawls's claim that once a fair distribution of primary goods is in place, 'there is no more justification for using the state apparatus to compel some citizens to pay for unwanted benefits that others desire than there is to force them to reimburse others for their private expenses.'[75]

The second point that Rawls makes, in an attempt to assuage the worry that justice as fairness does not allow enough scope for ideal-regarding considerations, is that some perfectionist policies can be justified in terms of equality. Rawls explains that 'the principles of justice do not permit subsidizing universities and institutes, or opera and the theatre, on the grounds that these institutions are intrinsically valuable' and that 'taxation for these purposes can be justified only as promoting directly or indirectly the social conditions that secure the equal liberties and as advancing in an appropriate way the long-term interests of the least advantaged.'[76]

The problem with this argument, however, is that it is unclear what exactly the *link* is between perfectionist policies on the one hand and the liberties and interests of the least advantaged members of society on the other. What is the mechanism by which the policies that perfectionists favour, such as subsidies for opera and art galleries, are meant systematically to secure the equal liberties or the long-term interests of the least advantaged? Here it is crucial to recall that, instead of spending its resources to promote art and other dimensions of perfection, the state can always distribute these resources directly to citizens in the form of cash for them to do with what they will. So the proper question to put to Rawls is even more difficult

---

[73] I have assumed that the Aristotelian Principle is a genuine tendency of human psychology, questioning only whether it is sufficiently strong relative to other such tendencies to secure unanimous (or near-unanimous) consent for perfectionist policies. But it is worth noting here that not everyone is convinced that the Aristotelian Principle is even a genuine psychological tendency in the first place. Brian Barry, for instance, believes it to be 'false for most people most of the time'. See Barry, B., *The Liberal Theory of Justice: A Critical Examination of the Principal Doctrines in A Theory of Justice by John Rawls* (Oxford: Oxford University Press, 1973), p. 29.

[74] Rawls, J., *A Theory of Justice*, p. 282 (emphasis added).

[75] Ibid., p. 283.

[76] Ibid., p. 332.

180 A PERFECTIONIST THEORY OF JUSTICE

to answer: what is the mechanism by which the policies that perfectionists favour, such as subsidies for opera and art galleries, are meant systematically to secure the equal liberties or the long-term interests of the least advantaged, in a manner that is at least as effective as a direct redistribution of wealth to the least advantaged? Surely, if one cares about improving the condition of the least advantaged members of society (or something in this distinctively egalitarian vicinity), the most obvious way to do this would be to redistribute resources directly to the worst-off members of society in the form of cash to spend as they see fit, rather than to use those resources to subsidize opera and other such activities that the worst-off may very well not enjoy or choose to pursue?[77] Rawls never addresses this question—though one way of understanding the arguments that I shall consider in Sections 6.6.2–6.6.4 is as attempts to improve on Rawls's arguments by spelling out, in a more precise and less speculative way, this link between perfectionist policies and egalitarian concern for the worst-off.

6.6.2 Dworkin's Argument from Intergenerational Fairness

In a well-known discussion of whether the liberal state can support art, Dworkin argues from the value of intergenerational fairness to perfectionist policies.[78] Before developing this argument, Dworkin considers a distinctively perfectionist argument for arts subsidies. The perfectionist approach, says Dworkin, 'turns its back on what the people think they want' and 'concentrates instead on what it is good for people to have'.[79] It 'insists that art and culture must reach a certain degree of sophistication, richness, and excellence in order for human nature to flourish, and that the state must provide this excellence if the people will not or cannot provide it for themselves'.[80] But Dworkin firmly rejects this 'haughtily paternalistic' view:

> Orthodox liberalism holds that no government should rely, to justify its use of public funds, on the assumption that some ways of life are more worthy than others, that it is more worthwhile to look at Titian on the wall than watch a football game on television. Perhaps it is more worthwhile to look at Titian; but that is not the point. More people disagree with this judgement than agree with it, so it must be wrong for the state, which is supposed to be democratic, to use its monopoly of taxing and police power to enforce judgements only a minority accepts.[81]

---

[77] This is a point that Quong makes at various junctures in *Liberalism Without Perfection*, especially chs 2 and 3. See also Brighouse, H., 'Neutrality, Publicity, and State Funding of the Arts', p. 45.

[78] Dworkin, R., 'Can a Liberal State Support Art?', in *A Matter of Principle* (Cambridge, MA: Harvard University Press, 1985), pp. 221–33.

[79] Ibid., p. 221.

[80] Ibid.

[81] Ibid., p. 222.

Instead, Dworkin argues that art contributes to a 'rich cultural structure', one that 'multiplies distinct possibilities or opportunities of value' and that makes available forms of life of 'complexity and depth'.[82] Dworkin then goes on to argue that 'we should act as trustees for the future of the complexity of our own culture'.[83] We must 'count ourselves trustees for protecting the richness of our culture for those who will live their lives in it after us'.[84] As he also puts this point: 'we inherited a cultural structure, and we have some duty, out of simple justice, to leave that structure at least as rich as we found it'.[85] This is done by publicly funding activities such as art and opera, which would languish if left to the rigours of the market. Thus, argues Dworkin, the policies standardly associated with perfectionism need not and should not be justified on the grounds that some activities are worthier than others; rather, they are to be justified on the grounds that intergenerational fairness requires us to protect and preserve a rich cultural structure so that future generations can have varied opportunities for deep and complex forms of life.

It is unclear, however, that Dworkin's argument really manages to avoid relying on 'the [perfectionist] assumption that some ways of leading one's life are more worthy than others'.[86] To see why, it is helpful to observe that Dworkin does not squarely address the following crucial question: what makes a given activity part of the 'rich cultural structure' of a society? Dworkin uses the example of opera on several occasions. But what *makes* opera part of the rich cultural structure? Why should opera form part of this structure, yet mudwrestling or monster truck racing fail to form part of the structure (as Dworkin presumably wants to say)? Why are future generations owed a cultural structure that includes opera but not owed a cultural structure that includes mudwrestling?

For Dworkin's argument to entail state subsidies for the arts but not for these other activities too, some explanation will need to be given for why they fail to form part of the rich cultural structure of which we are required at the bar of intergenerational fairness to act as trustees. Yet the natural answer to this question—namely, that activities like opera are more worthwhile than activities like mudwrestling—is not available to Dworkin. After all, this amounts to 'the [perfectionist] assumption that some ways of leading one's life are more worthy than others, that it is more worthwhile to look at Titian on the wall than watch a football game on television'.

---

[82] Ibid., p. 229.
[83] Ibid., p. 232.
[84] Ibid., p. 229.
[85] Ibid., p. 233.
[86] Ibid., p. 222. This critique has been made by numerous writers. See, for example, Carroll, N., 'Can Government Funding of the Arts Be Justified Theoretically?', p. 33; Sinopoli, R., 'Liberalism and Contested Conceptions of the Good: The Limits of Neutrality', *The Journal of Politics* 55 (1993), p. 648; Nathan, D., 'Liberal Principles and Government Support for the Arts', *Public Affairs Quarterly* 8 (1994), pp. 143, 149; Macleod, C., 'Liberal Neutrality or Liberal Tolerance?', *Law and Philosophy* 16 (1997), pp. 536–8.

182 A PERFECTIONIST THEORY OF JUSTICE

Dworkin's argument for state support for the arts thus appears inconsistent with his commitment to anti-perfectionist liberalism.[87]

A clear way of putting this point is that, in talking of the need to protect a 'rich cultural structure', Dworkin appears to equivocate on the word 'rich', which can be construed either quantitatively or qualitatively.[88] If, on the one hand, a rich cultural structure is one that exhibits a large *quantity* of ideals, activities or pursuits, then while protecting a rich cultural structure for future generations might provide grounds for arts subsidies, it also appears, implausibly, to provide grounds for subsidizing mudwrestling and monster truck racing. Yet if, on the other hand, a rich cultural structure is one that exhibits ideals, activities or pursuits of high *quality*, then while the argument no longer implies state support for mudwrestling and monster trucks, it violates the principle of liberal neutrality by assuming that some ways of leading one's life are more valuable or worthy than others.

6.6.3 Wall's Argument from Equality and Fairness

In a recent discussion, Steven Wall advances a brief yet interesting argument from the values of equality and fairness to perfectionist policies.[89] Though Wall is himself a perfectionist, his argument offers a way in which an anti-perfectionist liberal could argue from liberal principles of justice to perfectionist conclusions, and so it merits consideration at this juncture. Using the term 'moral environmentalism' for a position that resembles what we have been calling perfectionism, Wall presents the following argument:

> People differ with respect to decision-making competence. Some are disposed to make good decisions about their lives, others poor decisions. Naturally, and speaking generally, those who are bad decision-makers will tend to be less well off overall than those who are good decision-makers. This reality has a significant upshot for our discussion. Moral environments that offer their inhabitants bad

[87] The argument in this paragraph also, I believe, tells against the internal consistency of another argument that anti-perfectionist liberals sometimes offer in support of state subsidies for the arts: namely, that state subsidies for the arts are necessary for reasons of *fair access* or *equality of opportunity*. After all, such an argument needs to explain why there should be fair access to, or equality of opportunity for, *these specific activities* (such as opera, museums, and so on) *as opposed to other activities* (such as mudwrestling, monster truck racing, and so on). Why is it important that there be access to and opportunity for the arts, but not important that there be access to and opportunity for mudwrestling? To differentiate between these activities, it looks like one will need to breach anti-perfectionism and say that the former activities are more worthwhile or edifying than the latter.

[88] Here I follow Mendus, S., *Toleration and the Limits of Liberalism* (London: Macmillan, 1989), pp. 137–8.

[89] Wall, S., 'Moral Environmentalism', in C. Coons and M. Weber (eds), *Paternalism: Theory and Practice* (Cambridge: Cambridge University Press, 2013), pp. 98–100. As Wall explains (p. 99 n. 10), his argument draws on a similar fairness-based argument for paternalism developed in Arneson, R., 'Paternalism, Utility, and Fairness', *Revue Internationale de Philosophie* 43 (1989), pp. 409–37.

PERFECTIONIST LAW AND PUBLIC POLICY 183

options, when compared to the available alternatives, will tend to disadvantage those who are less well off. The failure to engage in moral environmentalism thus comes at the expense of those who fare least well. Now suppose that we think that, when the interests of different persons conflict, fairness sometimes requires that, holding other things constant, we should favour those who are less well off over those who are better off. Call this the minimal priority claim. If we accept this claim, as I believe we should, then we have a fairness-based case for moral environmentalism.[90]

We can formulate this argument as follows:

- (P1) Bad decision-makers tend to be worse-off
- (P2) The presence of bad options tends to disadvantage bad decision-makers
- (C1) So, the presence of bad options tends to disadvantage the worse-off
- (P3) Perfectionist laws and policies remove bad options
- (C2) So, perfectionist laws and policies are in the interests of the worse-off
- (P4) Fairness requires that laws and policies give priority to the interests of the worse-off
- (C3) So, fairness requires the implementation of perfectionist laws and policies.

We can grant that (P1), (P2), (P3) and (P4) are true. Still, the argument does not succeed because (C1) and (P3) do not entail (C2). This is because perfectionist laws and policies do not *merely* involve the *removal of bad options*; a major part of a perfectionist programme of law and policy is the *provision of good options*. In this sense, (P3) presents only half of the truth. By Wall's own logic, it would seem that the better-off (insofar as they are better decision-makers) will be more likely to take advantage of these good options, whereas the worse-off (insofar as they are worse decision-makers) will be more likely to ignore them. Consider, for instance, Quong's list of standard perfectionist laws and policies: 'performance art, art galleries, public parks, works of literature, sights of cultural significance, education programmes for adults, and athletic events.'[91] One might think that these laws and policies are likely to be most advantageous to the better-off. Indeed, this is why, as we saw in Section 4.4, it is sometimes suggested that, far from being *required* by fairness, perfectionist laws and policies are in fact highly *unfair*, since they involve a kind of reverse Robin Hood effect whereby the worse-off are in effect forced to subsidize the cultural and artistic pursuits of the better-off.

So once a broad range of perfectionist laws and policies is on the table—both policies that remove bad options and policies that provide good options—it is not

---

[90] Wall, S., 'Moral Environmentalism', p. 99.
[91] Quong, J., *Liberalism Without Perfection*, p. 89.

184   A PERFECTIONIST THEORY OF JUSTICE

clear why we should think that any particular segment of society would stand to gain more or less from perfectionism than any other. Assuming the truth of Wall's premises, some perfectionist policies (namely, those that remove bad options) can be expected to be of most benefit to the worse-off (qua worse decision-makers); other perfectionist policies (namely, those that provide good options) can be expected to be of most benefit to the better-off (qua better decision-makers). How do all these benefits wash out? It is difficult, if not impossible, to say from the armchair. What is needed here is some robust, empirically informed sociological model that explains why we should expect the worse-off to be greater beneficiaries of perfectionist laws and policies overall. In the absence of this, the argument from fairness to perfectionist policies does not go through.

6.6.4 Kramer's Argument from Warranted Self-Respect

Recently, Kramer has developed an important and sophisticated argument from the value of warranted self-respect to perfectionist policies.[92] Although Kramer describes his position as a form of perfectionism, his argument, like Wall's, is highly pertinent at this juncture because it offers a way of justifying perfectionist policies by reference to 'a value at the heart of Rawlsian liberalism', thereby undercutting the need for some separate principle of perfection that goes above and beyond Rawls's liberal principles of justice.[93]

Kramer draws a distinction between two forms of perfectionist political theory: 'edificatory perfectionism' (which is the form of perfectionism espoused by all contemporary perfectionists, including myself) and 'aspirational perfectionism' (which is Kramer's preferred form of perfectionism and which, he explains, 'has not heretofore been espoused by anyone').[94] Both views largely converge on the bottom line insofar as they both call for public policies that promote excellence

---

[92] Kramer, M., *Liberalism with Excellence*, especially ch. 8. For a related argument, see Wall, S., 'Enforcing Morality', pp. 460–5.

[93] Kramer, M., *Liberalism with Excellence*, p. 344. A taxonomical quibble: in my view, Kramer's view is more aptly classified as a species of anti-perfectionist liberalism than as a species of perfectionism. The fact that Kramer endorses many policies standardly associated with perfectionism, such as state support for the arts, does not suffice to make his view perfectionist. After all, and as we have seen in Sections 6.6.1 and 6.6.2, paradigmatic anti-perfectionist liberals such as Rawls and Dworkin readily concede that there can be non-perfectionist arguments for the policies that perfectionists typically favour. As I intimated at the outset of Section 6.5, the distinction between perfectionists and anti-perfectionist liberals is best captured in terms of a view about what reasons for state action are legitimate, not in terms of a view about what laws and public policies are legitimate. Yet, as will be discussed in Chapter 10, Kramer denies that promoting the edification of the citizenry is a legitimate reason for state action. Insofar as promoting the edification of the citizenry has been central to most contemporary perfectionist theories, it seems to me more natural to classify Kramer's view as a species of anti-perfectionist liberalism—albeit one that seeks to reveal the surprisingly far reach of the reasons for state action that anti-perfectionist liberals regard as legitimate (in particular, warranted self-respect). But nothing substantive turns on these taxonomical matters.

[94] Ibid., p. 36.

in a range of areas of human endeavour.[95] However, they differ 'in the *ratio-nales* that generate their respective verdicts on matters of public policy'.[96] Whereas edificatory perfectionists justify perfectionist policies on the grounds that these policies promote the edification of the citizenry—on the grounds that they 'steer people toward ways of life that are more flourishing or upright or wholesome or successful'—an aspirational perfectionist eschews this 'edificatory impulse' and instead justifies perfectionist policies on the grounds that 'the attainment of excellence by a society through the emergence of impressive feats within it is a necessary condition for the warrantedness of a robust sense of self-respect on the part of each individual who belongs to that society'.[97] Kramer's aspirational perfectionism contends, in other words, that 'the social bases of warranted self-respect are more expansive than Rawls allowed' and as such perfectionist policies can be justified in terms of their contribution to the social bases of warranted self-respect.[98]

The contrast between edificatory perfectionism and aspirational perfectionism can be illustrated and illuminated by considering how each of these forms of perfectionism approaches the question of state support for the arts. From the *edificatory*-perfectionist point of view, says Kramer, 'public subventions for the arts are morally justifiable insofar as those disbursals are effective in inclining people to attend events that will stretch their sensibilities and elevate their perceptions'.[99] By contrast, from the *aspirational*-perfectionist point of view, such subventions are advocated 'as a policy that can promote the occurrence of outstanding achievements and thereby help to bring about the conditions under which every citizen can be warranted in feeling a strong sense of self-respect'.[100] On the aspirational-perfectionist view, 'any enhancement of the aesthetic sensibilities of the citizenry is a byproduct rather than a justificatory factor'.[101]

Having set out the nature of the distinction between edificatory perfectionism and aspirational perfectionism, let us consider Kramer's case for aspirational perfectionism. What grounds are there for saying that 'the attainment of excellence by a society through impressive feats within it is a necessary condition for the warrantedness of a robust sense of self-respect on the part of each individual who belongs to that society'?[102] Why, in the absence of a 'sumptuous assortment of activities that are worthy of admiration', must citizens lack grounds for harbouring a solid sense of self-respect?[103]

---

[95] See ibid., pp. 49, 55, 278–9.
[96] Ibid., p. 49 (emphasis added).
[97] Ibid., p. 36.
[98] Ibid., p. 340.
[99] Ibid., p. 348.
[100] Ibid., p. 349.
[101] Ibid., pp. 350–1.
[102] Ibid., p. 36.
[103] Ibid., p. 285. Kramer uses a variety of adjectives to characterize the kind of sense of self-respect the warrantedness of which is conditional on the occurrence of societal excellences, including 'solid',

To answer this question, Kramer considers an individual, P, who belongs to a society that lacks societal excellences:

> Suppose that the country to which P belongs is drably mediocre, or suppose that it is worse than mediocre (perhaps because it has long been convulsed by a civil war with atrocities on all sides). In that event, given the connection between P and her country is an important constituent of the overall trajectory of her life ... she will be warranted in lowering her sense of how well her life has gone. Of course, if P has managed to attain success in many of her endeavors, any warranted lowering of her self-esteem in response to the mediocrity or depravity of her country will most likely leave her warranted level of self-esteem at quite a high pitch. Nevertheless, the level would have been even higher and more solid if it had not been held down by the failings of the society to which P belongs. Had her country been a place of excellence in which she could warrantedly have taken pride instead of warrantedly feeling abashed or dismayed about her connection to it, her warrantedness in feeling good about herself and in pursuing her projects with gusto would have been strengthened. Thus, even for a successful person like P, the full warrantedness of her experiencing a strong sense of self-respect depends partly on the flourishing of her society.[104]

Kramer goes on to clarify that if P is a 'towering genius such as Shakespeare or Beethoven or Albert Einstein', then she could still have grounds for harbouring a solid sense of self-respect despite the drably mediocre nature of her society.[105] Yet 'the vast majority of people are not even close to the rank of towering geniuses' and so for them the existence of societal excellences is necessary for the warrantedness of their harbouring a solid level of self-respect.[106] And since 'aspirational perfectionism is centered on bringing about the socioeconomic and political conditions under which *every* citizen can be warranted in feeling a strong sense of self-respect', aspirational perfectionists advocate state support for various forms of societal excellence.[107]

We can grant Kramer's claim that societal excellences *contribute* to each citizen's grounds for harbouring a solid sense of self-respect. However, I remain unconvinced by his significantly stronger claim that societal excellences are *necessary* for each citizen to have grounds for harbouring a solid sense of self-respect. One

---

'hearty', 'robust' and 'ample'. For comments on this, see Stemplowska, Z., 'Should I Be Proud of *Liberalism with Excellence*? On the Collective Grounds of Self-Respect', *The American Journal of Jurisprudence* 63 (2018), p. 83; Kramer, M., 'Replies to the Symposium Articles on *Liberalism with Excellence*', *The American Journal of Jurisprudence* 63 (2018), pp. 137, 169. In my discussion, I shall refer invariably to a *solid* sense of self-respect.

[104] Kramer, M., *Liberalism with Excellence*, pp. 365–6.

[105] Ibid., p. 366.

[106] Ibid.

[107] Ibid., p. 345 (emphasis added).

important reason for this is that, as Kramer recognizes, liberal democracy is itself 'a mode of excellence in which every generally law-abiding citizen can warrantedly take pride.'[108] In light of this, it is natural to wonder why the attainment of excellence in art, music, sport and other areas of human endeavour—as distinct from, and over and above, the attainment of the excellence of liberal democracy—is necessary for citizens to be warranted in harbouring a solid sense of self-respect. Why isn't the excellence of liberal-democratic institutions *itself* sufficient to constitute the conditions under which all citizens can be warranted in harbouring a solid sense of self-respect?[109]

In response to an earlier rendition of this worry by Paul Billingham and Anthony Taylor, Kramer makes two points. The first is to concede that there may be some countries—he suggests the examples of Taiwan and Israel—for which 'the sustainment of vibrantly liberal-democratic institutions in the face of extreme external threats is such a monumental achievement that it renders superfluous the pursuit of any other distinctively aspirational-perfectionist policies.'[110] But he is keen to stress that such cases are rare exceptions: '*normally*, a society will fall short of satisfying [the necessary conditions for every citizen to be warranted in harbouring a solid sense of self-respect] if its striving for excellence is confined to the sustainment of a liberal-democratic system of governance.'[111]

The second response Kramer makes in response to the earlier rendition of this worry is to re-emphasize the egalitarian character of aspirational perfectionism:

> One thing which [aspirational perfectionism] shares with Rawlsian liberalism is its egalitarian insistence that the primary natural goods are to be promoted ... for everyone alike ... In a typical situation, some of the members of the society will be much more accomplished than others, and most members will be at intermediate degrees of accomplishment. For the people toward the top end of the scale of personal achievement, the fostering of excellence beyond the sustainment of a liberal-democratic system of governance will very likely be icing on the cake. Significantly further down that scale, however, the level of self-respect that is warranted for each person will require more and more bolstering from the general excellence of the society if that level is to remain ample ... [T]o supply the political and economic and social conditions under which the prospect of being warranted in enjoying a hearty sense of self-respect is meaningfully available to

---

[108] Ibid., pp. 368–73, at pp. 371–2.

[109] This question is posed in Billingham, P. and Taylor, A., 'Liberal Perfectionism, Moral Integrity, and Self-Respect', *The American Journal of Jurisprudence* 63 (2018), pp. 74–5. For a response, see Kramer, M., 'Replies to the Symposium Articles', pp. 149–51. For a related objection, see Bird, C., 'Review of Matthew Kramer, *Liberalism with Excellence*', *Political Theory* 47 (2019), pp. 290–1.

[110] Kramer, M., 'Replies to the Symposium Articles', p. 151.

[111] Ibid., p. 150 (emphasis added).

188 A PERFECTIONIST THEORY OF JUSTICE

every citizen [an aspirational-perfectionist] system of governance has to take into account the likely spread of personal achievements.[112]

These two considerations do not, however, succeed in defusing the force of the objection. To see this, consider the following case:

> *Betty of Mediocria*: Betty is a citizen of a society called Mediocria. Mediocria is a well-functioning liberal democracy. It is in a relatively peaceful part of the world and its liberal-democratic institutions have not faced any great threats either internally or externally. However, beyond the excellence of its liberal-democratic political institutions, Mediocria has scant further modes of societal excellence. From its musicians to its writers, from its athletes to its restauranteurs, all are relentlessly middling and pedestrian. Betty is an ordinary individual. She is located exactly in the middle of the (limited) spread of personal achievements within her society. She is an accountant and a mother of two children in whom she takes great pride. She is a kind and friendly person. From time to time, she takes part in peaceful marches in support of environmental causes. Betty feels happy about her life and enjoys a solid sense of self-respect.

Given that Mediocria lacks societal excellences—and given that Mediocria is not a society like Israel whose liberal democracy faces 'extreme external threats' and that Betty is not 'toward the top end of the scale of personal achievement', either of which would make this case fall outside of the proper scope of Kramer's thesis—aspirational perfectionism implies that Betty lacks adequate grounds for harbouring a solid sense of self-respect. Betty, in other words, must be *deluded* to respect herself in this way. Now while I certainly agree that there is *something* troubling about Mediocria, this judgement strikes me as implausibly harsh. It is difficult to see why Betty's endeavours in relation to work and family and environmental activism, together with the excellence of her liberal-democratic political institutions, cannot together suffice to furnish her with a sufficient warrant for harbouring a solid sense of self-respect. Must we really conclude that Betty is deluded to harbour a solid sense of self-respect just because her society lacks a 'sumptuous assortment of activities that are worthy of admiration'?[113]

Of course, Kramer might stress that Betty's level of warranted self-respect would be 'even higher and more solid' if her society had more admirable activities and impressive feats.[114] But this does not establish that, without these admirable activities and impressive feats, Betty would be unwarranted in harbouring a solid sense of self-respect. To establish this, we would need to be told why alternative paths to a solid sense of self-respect—including in particular one's work and family and the

[112] Ibid., pp. 149–50.
[113] Kramer, M., *Liberalism with Excellence*, p. 285.
[114] Ibid., p. 366.

PERFECTIONIST LAW AND PUBLIC POLICY 189

excellence of one's liberal-democratic political institutions—are inadequate bases for a solid sense of self-respect for ordinary people like Betty. It thus remains unclear why the existence of societal excellences is a strictly necessary condition for every citizen to be warranted in harbouring a solid sense of self-respect, as opposed to a merely contributory factor.

At this point, Kramer might emphasize that he is interested not in self-respect as an empirical or psychological property but in *warranted* self-respect as a norma-tive property. So even though Betty feels a solid sense of self-respect on account of her work, family, activism and the liberal-democratic institutions of her society, it is nevertheless *inappropriate* for her to feel this way given the mediocrity of her society. But we have to tread carefully here because if the notion of 'warrantedness' carries too much of the justificatory burden, then the argument from warranted self-respect to perfectionist laws and policies loses its intuitive persuasiveness.

This is not to deny that warrantedness can and should play *some* role in Kramer's argument. Consider Cathy, who takes part in marches and protests in support of white supremacy. Cathy is not warranted in harbouring a solid sense of self-respect, however she feels about the matter, because she is in the grip of a deeply objectionable ideology. Or consider Demi, who is hooked up to a Nozickian 'experience machine' and who takes pride in having written a success-ful novel, alongside a host of other illusory accomplishments.[115] Again, Demi is not warranted in harbouring a solid sense of self-respect because she is in the grip of a systematic illusion. If warrantedness does too much moral work be-yond this, however, much of the intuitive force and dialectical reach of the value of warranted self-respect is lost. In such a case, those who are not antecedently convinced that the state should support excellent accomplishments in sundry areas of human endeavour are likely to respond that, while they care about war-ranted as opposed to merely empirical self-respect in *some* sense (in particular, where warrantedness plays only the fairly minimal role needed to deal with cases like those of Cathy and Demi), they simply do not care about *this* specific and heavily moralized account of warranted self-respect—an account that feels very custom-built, even ad hoc, and that functions like a Trojan horse for perfectionist policies.

6.7 Intensional Differences

Even if the first line of response to the indistinguishability objection fails—even, in other words, if perfectionist and non-perfectionist theories turn out to be ex-tensionally equivalent—it does not follow that perfectionist justice is redundant or uninteresting. After all, these theories might recommend the same laws and

---

[115] See Nozick, R., *Anarchy, State, and Utopia* (New York: Basic Books, 1974), pp. 42–5.

policies for importantly different reasons. In this sense, there might still be significant *intensional* differences between perfectionist and non-perfectionist theories. In this section, I shall mention three of the various ways in which these intensional differences matter.

First and perhaps most importantly, one or another of these theories might offer a *more intrinsically plausible* justification for perfectionist laws and policies. So even if perfectionist and non-perfectionist theories yield substantially the same policies, perfectionism might still recommend itself on the grounds that it yields the right policies for the right reasons. Consider a parallel issue in the debate between paternalists and anti-paternalists. Very often, one can construct non-paternalistic rationales for the laws and policies that paternalists favour. For instance, seatbelt laws can be justified on the grounds that those who drive without a seatbelt are more likely to sustain injuries that require more medical attention, thereby imposing a greater cost on other taxpayers. However, these sorts of non-paternalistic rationales strike many as artificial and beside the point. After all, those who support seatbelt laws tend to do so independently of any grasp of the empirical data about the aggregate effects of driving without a seatbelt on the tax burden. By contrast, the paternalistic rationale for seatbelt laws—namely, that these laws protect drivers' own health and well-being—seems much more natural and direct. It is responsive to what is on due reflection the most morally relevant feature of seatbelt laws. In this way, we can make judgements about the relative intrinsic plausibility of different proposed rationales for a law by carefully reflecting on which rationale most closely tracks the considerations that actually drive our intuitions about the justifiability of the law in question.

Now consider again Rawls's response to the worry that his view rules out state support for the arts and culture:

> The principles of justice do not permit subsidizing universities and institutes, or opera and the theatre, on the grounds that these institutions are intrinsically valuable ... Taxation for these purposes can be justified only as promoting directly or indirectly the social conditions that secure the equal liberties and as advancing in an appropriate way the long-term interests of the least advantaged.[116]

As he similarly explains:

> [Justice as fairness] puts in question whether society can allocate great public resources to pure science—to mathematics and theoretical physics, say—or to philosophy, or to the arts of painting and music, solely on the grounds that their study and practice realizes certain great excellences of thought, imagination, and

---

[116] Rawls, J., *A Theory of Justice*, p. 332.

feeling. No doubt their study does this, but it is far better to justify the use of public funds to support them by reference to political values. Some public support of art and culture and science, and funding museums and public performances, is certainly vital to the public political culture: to a society's sense of itself and its history, and an awareness of its political traditions. But a large fraction of the social product for the advancement of mathematics and science requires a basis in advancing the good of citizens generally, say by the expected benefits to public health and preserving the environment, or to the needs of (justified) national defense.[117]

As I explained in the preceding sections, I am doubtful that the kind of political values to which Rawls appeals—the protection of equal liberties, the advancement of the long-term interests of the least advantaged, and so on—yield the full package of perfectionist policies that perfectionists typically want to implement. But, even if they do, this strikes me as a highly artificial, strained and roundabout justification for public funding of the arts and culture. Here anti-perfectionist liberalism supports the right policy for wholly the wrong kind of reason. The non-perfectionist argument for arts funding on the basis of claims about equal liberty resembles the non-paternalistic argument for seatbelt laws on the basis of claims about costs to taxpayers. The best and most direct justification for arts funding—the justification that most closely tracks the considerations that on due reflection actually drive our intuitions about the justifiability of arts funding—is the perfectionist justification. So the fact that the set of concrete policies recommended by anti-perfectionist liberalism is coextensive with the set of concrete policies recommended by perfectionism does not show that both views are indistinguishable or equally good, since the perfectionist view appears to offer a more attractive and intrinsically plausible underlying account of political morality.

The second way in which the intensional differences between perfectionist and non-perfectionist theories matter is that they tell us something important about the *strength* of the case for a given law or policy. Consider the conditions of work in highly competitive markets such as the US. Suppose non-perfectionist reasons are given for regulating or reforming these conditions—say, reasons having to do with freedom, equality, fairness or self-respect. And suppose perfectionist reasons are also given for regulating or reforming these conditions—say, reasons having to do with the effect of long working hours and of routinized labour on the ability of individuals to develop their moral, intellectual and artistic powers. Even if the non-perfectionist reasons in favour of economic regulations are just as intrinsically plausible as the perfectionist reasons, the perfectionist reasons still matter because they change the balance of reasons by providing additional force to the case for

---

[117] Rawls, J., *Justice as Fairness*, p. 152.

these regulations. Sometimes, the normative contribution these perfectionist reasons make will be decisive: sometimes, that is, the non-perfectionist reasons for economic regulations will be insufficient because of the presence of countervailing reasons, and so the perfectionist reasons will be what tips the scales in favour of these regulations. But even when the non-perfectionist reasons are by themselves sufficient to justify the relevant regulations, the perfectionist reasons can still earn their keep by telling us something about the urgency of these regulations and the extent to which they should be prioritized.[118]

The third way in which the intensional differences between perfectionist and non-perfectionist theories matter relates to what Rawls says when contrasting utilitarianism's commitment to the equal liberties with justice as fairness's commitment to the equal liberties.[119] Utilitarians often maintain that the nature of society and of human beings is such that the denial of basic liberties will rarely, if ever, promote utility on balance. Rawls's first response to this is that these 'actuarial calculations' may well admit of exceptions.[120] But his second (and for our purposes more important) response is that 'there is a real advantage in persons' announcing to one another once and for all that even though theoretical computations of utility always happen to favor the equal liberties (assuming that this is indeed the case here), they do not wish that things had been different'.[121] The choice of justice as fairness 'is, in effect, such an announcement'.[122] In this way, there are often 'good reasons for embedding convictions of justice more directly into first principles than a theoretically complete grasp of the contingencies of the world may actually require'.[123] Similarly, even if perfectionist laws and policies can be justified on non-perfectionist grounds, there may well remain good reasons for embedding perfectionist ideals more directly into the fundamental principles of justice than the contingencies of the world actually require, since in doing so we bypass various calculations and make a clear announcement of our commitment to the values of moral, intellectual and artistic excellence.

In short, even if perfectionist and non-perfectionist theories turn out to be extensionally equivalent, this does not show that perfectionism is redundant or uninteresting. After all, the intensional differences between these theories can still matter—perhaps because one or another theory offers more intrinsically appealing rationales for the relevant laws and policies, or perhaps because the intensional differences reveal the full range and weight of the reasons that bear on a given political question, or perhaps because there is value to the 'embedding of ideals

---

[118] I thank Joseph Chan and Vafa Ghazavi for discussion of this point.
[119] See Rawls, J., *A Theory of Justice*, pp. 160–1.
[120] Ibid., p. 161.
[121] Ibid.
[122] Ibid.
[123] Ibid.

PERFECTIONIST LAW AND PUBLIC POLICY   193

into first principles'.[124] In these three ways, among others, a perfectionist theory of justice can be of theoretical or philosophical interest, even if it is not of immediate practical interest.

At this point, one might object that, assuming perfectionism and anti-perfectionist liberalism really do converge on the bottom line, the intensional differences between these theories lack even theoretical or philosophical interest (let alone immediate practical interest). To see this, consider the following two kinds of extensional indistinguishability:

> *Shallow Extensional Indistinguishability*: Perfectionist and non-perfectionist theories have the same implications in the here and now, but have different implications in realistic alternative circumstances.
> *Deep Extensional Indistinguishability*: Perfectionist and non-perfectionist theories have the same implications in all possible worlds.

Perhaps, this objection continues, if it is the case that perfectionist and non-perfectionist theories are extensionally indistinguishable in the shallow sense, then the intensional differences between them would still be of theoretical interest. But if these theories are extensionally indistinguishable in the deep sense, wouldn't the intensional differences between them lose even theoretical interest? We come to political philosophy, after all, because we care about what we ought to do, and not because we care about particular theoretical labels in and of themselves. So if these theories are deeply extensionally indistinguishable, wouldn't this debate cease to connect with the concerns and worries that motivate our political theorizing in the first place? Wouldn't there be nothing of interest at stake in the debate? Wouldn't it become a kind of purely verbal dispute?[125]

I accept that if perfectionism and anti-perfectionist liberalism turned out to be extensionally indistinguishable in the deep sense, then any intensional differences between these theories would indeed cease to be of even theoretical or philosophical interest. But it is difficult to see why the verdicts of perfectionism and anti-perfectionist liberalism would coincide in all possible worlds or even in nearly all possible worlds. Of course, perfectionist and non-perfectionist theories of justice might look like they are headed towards deep indistinguishability if the correct conception of human flourishing turns out to say that a flourishing life for an individual is one in which she has a fair share of primary goods (as defined by the appropriate non-perfectionist theory of justice) and uses that share to pursue her preferred plan of life free from interference. But in Chapter 5 I argued against subjectivist views of this kind and in favour of a conception of human flourishing that

---

[124] Ibid., p. 160.
[125] I thank Anthony Taylor for putting to me this objection, including the distinction between different kinds of extensional indistinguishability. See more generally Chalmers, D., 'Verbal Disputes', *The Philosophical Review* 120 (2011), pp. 515–66.

has a significant objective component. Assuming that something in the vicinity of the provisional conception of human flourishing articulated in that chapter is correct, the charge of deep indistinguishability does not stick. The inner workings of perfectionist and non-perfectionist theories, including their underlying conceptions of society and principles of justice, are just too different for that kind of counterfactually robust convergence on the bottom line.

My sense, then, is that there are realistic social circumstances in which perfectionism and anti-perfectionist liberalism diverge in their practical implications—for instance, circumstances in which state support for the arts is not an effective way of advancing 'the long-term interests of the least advantaged' or circumstances in which state support for the arts is not necessary for 'every citizen [to] be warranted in feeling a strong sense of self-respect'.[126] Even if these theories are extensionally indistinguishable in the here and now (something I questioned in Sections 6.6.1–6.6.4), their extensional indistinguishability is shallow rather than deep. The situation is not one in which there is agreement about all the relevant facts of political morality and disagreement merely about the language used to describe those facts. As such, the intensional differences between perfectionist and anti-perfectionist theories remain theoretically or philosophically interesting.

---

[126] Rawls, J., *A Theory of Justice*, p. 332; Kramer, M., *Liberalism with Excellence*, p. 349.

PART III
OBJECTIONS

7
Public Justification

Many liberals are struck by the fact that in free societies there is no systematic agreement about the ends and purpose of human life. Modern liberal democracies, says Rawls, are characterized by 'profound and irreconcilable differences in citizens' reasonable comprehensive religious and philosophical conceptions of the world, and in their views of the moral and aesthetic values to be sought in life'.[1] Such disagreement 'is not a mere historical condition that may soon pass away; it is a permanent feature of the public culture of democracy'.[2] It is 'the inevitable long-run result of the powers of human reason at work within the background of enduring free institutions'.[3] As we saw in Chapter 2, political liberals respond to this feature of modern societies by arguing that laws and policies must satisfy a principle of public justification. The public justification principle holds that laws and policies must be in some sense justifiable, or acceptable, to all reasonable citizens.[4]

A perfectionist state appears to violate the public justification principle. After all, judgements about the good life and human flourishing are controversial. Good-willed, intelligent people disagree about what constitutes a flourishing way of life.

---

[1] Rawls, J., *Justice as Fairness: A Restatement* (Cambridge, MA: Harvard University Press, 2001), p. 3.

[2] Rawls, J., *Political Liberalism* (New York: Columbia University Press, 2005), p. 36.

[3] Ibid., p. 4.

[4] It is common in this literature to distinguish between 'consensus' and 'convergence' models of public justification. See, for example, Vallier, K., *Liberal Politics and Public Faith: Beyond Separation* (New York: Routledge, 2014), ch. 4. However, it is unclear that this distinction properly captures what is at stake between different public reason liberals. Consider the claim that the convergence model has a 'classical tilt', whereas the consensus model does not. What makes this true is not the consensus/convergence distinction per se but rather the fact that defenders of the convergence model typically favour weaker idealizations, whereas defenders of the consensus model typically favour stronger idealizations. The consensus model would also have a classical tilt if it were to employ weaker idealizations, and the convergence model would lose its classical tilt if it were to employ stronger idealizations. The consensus/convergence distinction thus misses where the action is: the real debate between consensus and convergence theorists is about the appropriate level of idealization to employ within a public reason theory. Put differently, the disagreements between consensus and convergence theorists are driven more by disagreements about who should be included in the justificatory constituency than by disagreements about the structure of public justification. (This diagnosis of the consensus/convergence distinction follows the discussion in Billingham, P. and Taylor, A., 'A Framework for Analyzing Public Reason Theories', *European Journal of Political Theory* (forthcoming), pp. 16–17.) So, although for expository purposes I couch my arguments in terms of the consensus model, I still engage with many of the substantive concerns that convergence theorists are likely to have about perfectionist public reason (e.g. the concern that perfectionist idealizations fail to take reasonable disagreement seriously or are objectionably sectarian). As such, my defence of perfectionist public reason in this chapter does not talk past those who develop their views within the convergence model of public justification; it just locates the disagreement with convergence theorists in a question about what the right justificatory constituency is.

A Perfectionist Theory of Justice. Collis Tahzib, Oxford University Press.
© Collis Tahzib (2022). DOI: 10.1093/oso/9780192847119.003.0008

198   A PERFECTIONIST THEORY OF JUSTICE

So wouldn't perfectionist justice involve the imposition of values and judgements that cannot be justified to all reasonable citizens? Couldn't the claim that states have a duty to promote artistic excellence through the subsidization of art galleries, say, be reasonably rejected by the average Joe who prefers to stay at home and watch TV? Given the depth and breadth of disagreement about the good life, how many perfectionist laws and policies could be expected to survive the public justification test?

'The deeply objectionable characteristic' of perfectionist politics, says Gerald Gaus in a forceful rendition of this worry, is that it makes the terms of our common life 'dictated by the conscience of some, demanding that others simply obey'.[5] He continues:

> Social interaction is to be on their terms, directed by their conscience and their convictions about moral truth [or human flourishing]. Those who do not share this conscience must submit to the truth. It is precisely this imperious claim of private conscience that the social contract-liberal tradition has rejected. Hobbes saw that it was fundamentally hostile to cooperative social life for each conscience to claim not only to know, but in the name of truth assert its authority to impose its view of proper behavior on others ... A social morality on these terms must be one in which power supplants justified authority as the core social moral relation ... Surely the great liberal lesson, first glimpsed in the sixteenth century, is that successful large-scale cooperative social orders are precisely those in which people do come to 'bracket' their rationally controversial first-personal convictions about the truth when these convictions are about how others must live.[6]

Broadly speaking, there are two ways in which perfectionists can reply to this sort of objection: the hard-line response, which simply rejects the public justification principle as a valid principle of political morality; and the conciliatory response, which accepts the public justification principle but maintains that many perfectionist laws and policies would pass the test of public justification. In this chapter, I first consider the hard-line response (Section 7.1). While I do not favour this approach, it is by far the most common perfectionist response to the public justification objection, and so it is worth exploring in order to give a full picture of the responsive strategies available to perfectionists. I then defend a version of the conciliatory response (Section 7.2). On this view, certain perfectionist commitments—in particular, moral, intellectual and artistic excellence—are baked into the notion of reasonableness in much the same way that many political liberals make reasonableness conditional on acceptance of certain liberal commitments such as freedom, equality and fairness. Only those who recognize

---

[5] Gaus, G., *The Order of Public Reason: A Theory of Freedom and Morality in a Diverse and Bounded World* (Cambridge: Cambridge University Press, 2011), p. 230.

[6] Ibid., pp. 230–2.

these perfectionist values count as reasonable. Perfectionist laws and policies can thus be expected to pass the public justification test because a citizen who rejects, say, the value of artistic excellence would count as unreasonable and so her veto would have no more normative force than that of a citizen who rejects the value of equality.

I then address the question of whether the marriage of perfectionism and constructivism is coherent and well-motivated (Section 7.3). Next, I begin to argue that this perfectionist definition of reasonableness is more plausible than the rival anti-perfectionist definition of reasonableness (Section 7.4). I then defend perfectionist public reason against three objections: that the relationship between the abstract perfectionist values that all reasonable citizens are said to endorse and the more specific interpretations of those values that justify laws and policies is too 'loose' for perfectionist public reason to plausibly offer citizens a shared framework for reasoning and mutual justification (Section 7.5); that the perfectionist definition of reasonableness should be rejected because it is *more* sectarian than the anti-perfectionist definition of reasonableness (Section 7.6); and that the perfectionist definition of reasonableness should be rejected because it is *excessively* sectarian (Section 7.7).

7.1 A Road Not Taken

The most common response among perfectionists to the public justification objection is simply to reject the public justification principle as a valid principle of political morality. Perfectionists who pursue this hard-line response might begin by pointing out that (as mentioned in Section 2.3) for political liberals reasonableness is a 'deliberately loose' category: the category of reasonable beliefs is meant to be much wider than the category of true beliefs, in the sense that many false beliefs are nonetheless reasonable.[7] As Rawls puts this, political liberalism 'counts many [views] as reasonable even though we could not seriously entertain them for ourselves.'[8] But given that reasonable citizens can hold false beliefs in this way, why should we care about whether laws and policies are acceptable to reasonable citizens? Why should their objections matter, if they may be based on claims that are false or that cannot be seriously entertained? Why should the legitimate use of state power be hostage to what such individuals do or do not accept? Shouldn't we instead seek to implement the laws and policies that are *true* or *correct*—or at least that are most likely to be true or correct—regardless of whether those laws and policies could be reasonably rejected by some citizens?[9] Moreover, even if some

---

[7] Rawls, J., *Political Liberalism*, p. 59.
[8] Ibid., pp. 59–60.
[9] For similar questions, see Nagel, T., 'Moral Conflict and Political Legitimacy', p. 222. For the contrast between public justification and truth- or correctness-based justification, see Wall, S., 'Is Public

200 A PERFECTIONIST THEORY OF JUSTICE

explanation can be given for why justification to all reasonable citizens matters, we would need to know why it matters *so much* that we should treat public justification as a constraint of 'very great and normally overriding weight'.[10] Why should public justification hold sway in the normal run of cases of political disagreement? Why not instead think that acceptability to all reasonable citizens is simply a pro tanto value—just another item on the long and dense list of political desiderata, and not an especially weighty item at that?[11]

Of course, defenders of the public justification principle have sought to provide answers to these important questions, as we saw in Section 2.3. For some, public justification is required by *respect for persons*. Charles Larmore, for instance, argues that 'if we try to bring about conformity to a rule of conduct solely by the threat of force [and not by offering reasons that others recognize as valid], we shall be treating persons merely as a means, as objects of coercion, and not also as ends, engaging directly their distinctive capacity as persons'.[12] For others, public justification is required by *civic friendship*. Andrew Lister argues that 'public reason makes possible civic friendship despite deep disagreement'.[13] For yet others, public justification is required by *social trust*. Kevin Vallier argues that 'publicly justified moral rules have the unique power to sustain a system of trust'.[14] And for still others, public justification is required by *egalitarian justice*. 'Part of what political equality necessarily requires', Jonathan Quong argues, 'is that the substantive grounds supporting certain laws be reasonably acceptable to each person—to reject this idea risks reducing the democratic process to a competition for power, rather than a process of reasoning among equals about the fair terms of social cooperation.'[15]

It is not possible here to assess, on its own terms and in great detail, each of these attempts to justify the public justification principle. These rationales have in any case been subjected to some critical scrutiny in Section 2.3. But in the remainder of this section I indicate a fairly general and schematic way in which perfectionists might respond to these various attempts to justify the public justification principle. What follows, then, is the sketch of an argumentative strategy available to

---

Justification Self-Defeating?', *American Philosophical Quarterly* 39 (2002), p. 386; Pallikkathayil, J., 'Neither Perfectionism Nor Political Liberalism', pp. 185–8.

[10] Rawls, J., *Political Liberalism*, p. 241.

[11] See Enoch, D., 'Against Public Reason', in D. Sobel, P. Vallentyne and S. Wall (eds), *Oxford Studies in Political Philosophy, Volume 1* (Oxford: Oxford University Press, 2015), especially pp. 138–40. For similar thoughts, see Wall, S., *Liberalism, Perfectionism and Restraint* (Cambridge: Cambridge University Press, 1998), pp. 75–91; Wendt, F., 'Rescuing Public Justification from Public Reason Liberalism', in D. Sobel, P. Vallentyne and S. Wall (eds), *Oxford Studies in Political Philosophy, Volume 5* (Oxford: Oxford University Press, 2019), pp. 39–64.

[12] Larmore, C., 'The Moral Basis of Political Liberalism', *The Journal of Philosophy* 96 (1999), p. 607.

[13] Lister, A., *Public Reason and Political Community* (London: Bloomsbury, 2013), p. 105.

[14] Vallier, K., *Must Politics Be War? Restoring Our Trust in the Open Society* (Oxford: Oxford University Press, 2019), p. 118.

[15] Quong, J., 'On the Idea of Public Reason', in J. Mandle and D. Reidy (eds), *The Blackwell Companion to Rawls* (Oxford: Wiley Blackwell, 2013), p. 274.

perfectionists who want to deny the public justification principle—a sketch that abstracts from many of the finer details that would need to be filled in during any particular application of this strategy.

The persuasiveness of the arguments from respect, civic friendship, social trust and egalitarian justice to public justification depends, to a large extent, on the way in which the *alternative* to public reason liberalism is characterized. One very common strategy in this literature is to motivate the public justification principle by portraying alternative approaches in tendentious or unsympathetic ways.[16] Often it is suggested that if one rejects public justification, then one must be some kind of theocrat or imperialist. Thus Rawls defends his view, in his *Commonweal* interview, by suggesting that we have to choose between either public reason liberalism or the wars of religion:

> How many religions are there in the United States? How are they going to get on together? One way, which has been the usual way historically, is to fight it out, as in France in the sixteenth century. That's a possibility. But how do you avoid that? See, what I should do is to turn around and say, What's the better suggestion, what's your solution to it? And I can't see any other solution ... Again, what's the alternative?[17]

Similarly, recall from Section 5.4 the way in which Dworkin seeks to bolster the plausibility of political liberalism by contrasting it with the practice of inflammatory conservative evangelists such as Jerry Falwell, as if to reject the former is to accept the latter:

> Government must be neutral in matters of personal morality, [and] must leave people free to live as they think best so long as they do not harm others. But the Reverend Jerry Falwell, and other politicians who claim to speak for some 'moral majority', want to enforce their own morality with the steel of the criminal law. They know what kind of sex is bad, which books are fit for public libraries, what place religion should have in education and family life, when human life begins, that contraception is sin, and that abortion is capital sin. They think the rest of us should be forced to practice what they preach.[18]

More recently, Lister contrasts public reason liberalism with a modus vivendi regime—a regime in which citizens 'agree on policy for strategic reasons based on a persistent balance of forces' and which remains stable because no one social

---

[16] For a discussion of this point, which I have drawn upon and generalized in this section, see Eberle, C., *Religious Conviction in Liberal Politics* (Cambridge: Cambridge University Press, 2002), pp. 109–15.

[17] Rawls, J., *Collected Papers*, ed. S. Freeman (Cambridge, MA: Harvard University Press, 1999), p. 620.

[18] Dworkin, R., 'Neutrality, Equality, and Liberalism', in D. MacLean and C. Mills (eds), *Liberalism Reconsidered* (Totowa, NJ: Rowman and Allanheld, 1983), p. 1.

group 'is large enough or strong enough to be confident of its ability to dominate the others over the long term'.[19] And Gaus trades on a characterization of violators of the public justification principle as dictatorial and priestly: 'a morality for our democratic age', he says, 'takes seriously that people of good will in a diverse society have differing views of what constitutes an acceptable way of living together, and there is no priestly class who can dictate to the rest how we are to live together'.[20]

The arguments from respect, civic friendship, social trust and egalitarian justice to public justification look plausible if we take these portrayals as paradigms of non-public reasoning. A politics modelled on Jerry Falwell, to take just one of these examples, would indeed plausibly undermine respect, civic friendship, social trust and egalitarian justice. But it is unclear whether our judgement that respect, civic friendship, social trust and egalitarian justice would be undermined is elicited by Falwell's failure to publicly justify his views per se or instead by a range of other factors present in the description of the case that are strictly distinct from, but easily conflatable with, such failure: for instance, that Falwell's conclusions are substantively unsound, that he expresses himself in an insensitive way, that he shows disregard for the perspectives of others, that he makes no *attempt* to publicly justify, and so on. Can we really be confident that our judgement that a politics modelled on Jerry Falwell would undermine respect, civic friendship, social trust and egalitarian justice is a product of his failure to reason publicly and not a product of these other contingently associated factors?[21]

Another way of putting this point is that to reject public justification is not to say that 'politics is war', that 'anything goes' or that there are no moral constraints at all on political discourse and decision-making. Those who reject public justification do not in general claim that citizens may engage in rabid sectarianism, flagrantly disregard other citizens' perspectives, base their decisions on considerations of naked self-interest and power, or browbeat and ostracize others. So once we consider more sympathetic and attractive alternatives to public justification, it becomes less clear why all alternative models short of public justification must be incompatible with respect, civic friendship, social trust and egalitarian justice.

There are many plausible alternative models of political discourse and decision-making that would fit the bill here, but for illustrative purposes let us consider Eberle's 'ideal of conscientious engagement', which was briefly discussed in Section 2.3.1.[22] Indeed, Eberle develops his ideal of conscientious engagement explicitly as

---

[19] Lister, A., *Public Reason and Political Community*, p. 115.

[20] Gaus, G., 'On Theorizing About Public Reason', *European Journal of Analytic Philosophy* 9 (2013), p. 84.

[21] See Eberle, C., *Religious Conviction in Liberal Politics*, pp. 110–14.

[22] See ibid., ch. 4. Other models that are deliberately designed to acknowledge social pluralism and disagreement, and that could therefore more plausibly realize respect or civic friendship or social trust or egalitarian justice, yet that eschew a public justification requirement, can be found in Wolterstorff, N., *Understanding Liberal Democracy: Essays in Political Philosophy* (Oxford: Oxford University Press, 2012), ch. 5; Pallikkathayil, J., 'Disagreement and the Duties of Citizenship',

part of a critique of public reason liberals' argument from respect to public justification: respect does not require public justification, Eberle argues, because citizens who adhere to the ideal of conscientious engagement adequately express respect for their fellow citizens. Eberle's ideal of conscientious engagement is constituted by a variety of moral constraints. One of these constraints is that a citizen should only advance laws and policies that enjoy a 'high degree of rational justification' (understood in terms of considering the relevant evidence, discharging various epistemic obligations governing belief formation, and so on).[23] Another is that a citizen should not support a law or policy that 'denies the dignity of her compatriots'.[24] A third constraint is that, during political deliberation, a citizen should 'listen to her compatriots ... with the intention of learning from them'.[25] Fourth, the ideal of conscientious engagement even requires a citizen to '*pursue* public justification for her favoured coercive policies'.[26] But crucially—and this is what distinguishes the ideal of conscientious engagement from public reason liberalism—citizens need not withhold their support for policies if, after looking for reasons that are acceptable to other citizens, no such reasons are ultimately forthcoming. 'So long as a ... citizen sincerely and conscientiously *attempts* to articulate a rationale for his favoured coercive policies that will be convincing to his compatriots, then he has thereby discharged his obligation to respect them—even if his attempt ends in failure.'[27]

With the ideal of conscientious engagement in view, we can more accurately test whether the failure to abide by public justification would undermine respect, civic friendship, social trust and egalitarian justice. In characterizing those who fail to abide by public justification as supporting policies that we have independent reasons to think are wrong or as exhibiting unattractive character traits, public reason liberals introduce rhetorical distractions. To properly test the claim that respect, civic friendship, social trust and egalitarian justice require public justification, we should screen off these extraneous factors and imagine instead someone who, while failing to abide by public justification, is sympathetic and admirable in other respects—someone, in other words, who abides by the ideal of conscientious engagement.[28]

American Philosophical Quarterly 56 (2019), pp. 71–82; Wendt, F., 'Rescuing Public Justification from Public Reason Liberalism'; Turner, J., 'Politics, Truth, and Respect', in D. Sobel, P. Vallentyne and S. Wall (eds), *Oxford Studies in Political Philosophy, Volume 7* (Oxford: Oxford University Press, 2021), pp. 100–23.

[23] Eberle, C., *Religious Conviction in Liberal Politics*, p. 104.
[24] Ibid., p. 105.
[25] Ibid.
[26] Ibid.
[27] Ibid., p. 82.
[28] See ibid., p. 112.

Consider, then, the following portrait:

Edwin's Carbon Tax: Edwin subscribes to an unorthodox ecological philosophy according to which the Earth is regarded 'not as an inanimate globe of rock, liquid and gas driven by geological processes, but as a sort of biological superorganism, a single life-form, a living planetary body that adjusts and regulates the conditions in its surroundings'.[29] This philosophy leads Edwin to support and campaign for very heavy carbon taxes to reduce environmental degradation. He is aware that some reasonable citizens reject this philosophy and the environmental policies that flow from it. He has tried his best to justify this policy in terms that his fellow citizens accept, but it turns out that the environmental policy he favours depends *ineliminably* on acceptance of this controversial ecological doctrine. Edwin regards this situation as tragic: he wishes he did not have to impose his views on citizens who from their point of view lack sufficient reasons to accept the carbon tax.[30]

The question we have to ask is: could a political community populated by citizens like Edwin achieve respect, civic friendship, social trust and egalitarian justice? It is difficult to see why not—or so a perfectionist might argue. Edwin is conscientious and engaged. The policies he supports are not mere hunches. He spends long hours thinking deeply about environmental issues and only supports policies after careful consideration of the relevant evidence. He ensures that the policies he supports do not deny the dignity of his compatriots. He is cooperative, deliberative, civil and polite. He takes no joy in imposition and tries his best to inhabit the distinctive perspectives of his fellow citizens and to find justifications that they will find convincing.

Edwin's behaviour is thus nothing like various examples that public reason liberals distractingly use to portray the violator of public justification: Edwin is not infused with apocalyptic fervour to 'fight it out'; he does not follow either the substantive policies or the fulminatory style of sectarian evangelists such as Jerry Falwell; he is morally and not merely 'strategically' committed to his society's main social and political institutions; he does not regard himself as belonging to any superior 'priestly class'. Why, then, must the presence of people like Edwin within society undermine the values of respect, civic friendship, social trust and egalitarian justice?

In short, once we test the public reason liberal's claim against the proper alternative—the comparison with all the morally relevant variables appropriately controlled—it becomes much less clear why respect, civic friendship, social trust

---

[29] Huggett, R., *Physical Geography: The Key Concepts* (Oxford: Routledge, 2010), p. 84.
[30] The case of Edwin is based on Eberle's case of Elijah. See Eberle, C., *Religious Conviction in Liberal Politics*, pp. 112–15.

and egalitarian justice require public justification. Even if *some* alternatives to public justification would be incompatible with these values, it is unclear why general adherence to the ideal of conscientious engagement could not realize these values.

7.2 Perfectionist Public Reason

The second and more conciliatory response to the public justification objection is to accept that public justification is a genuine principle of political morality but to argue that many perfectionist laws and policies would nonetheless survive the public justification test. Despite the general argumentative strategy I offered in Section 7.1 as an option for some perfectionists, this rather neglected conciliatory response is in fact the approach that I myself favour.[31] The discussion in the rest of this chapter, then, not only charts a relatively novel avenue of response to a traditional objection to perfectionism; it also opens up independently interesting theoretical questions about the flexibility and generalizability of the public reason framework.

According to this conciliatory response, there are certain claims about human flourishing that all reasonable citizens can be expected to endorse—just as there are, or so say political liberals, certain claims about social justice that all reasonable citizens can be expected to endorse. Perfectionist laws and policies that are justified in terms of these claims about human flourishing could thus be expected to pass the test of public justification because anyone who rejects the claims in question would count as unreasonable. In this way, perfectionists need not rely on any particular comprehensive doctrine that is put forward as the full truth about human flourishing. Instead, they can derive political conclusions from a free-standing conception of human flourishing that belongs within the domain of the political and that is adopted for political purposes. A perfectionism that is 'political not metaphysical' in this way involves the idea of 'perfectionist public reason': the shared fund of public reasons is expanded to include not just liberal reasons such as freedom, equality and fairness but also certain perfectionist reasons. On this view, the framework of public justification is highly versatile; it is amenable to the expression of perfectionist thought as well as anti-perfectionist liberal thought.

Of course, strictly speaking political liberals do already recognize that, in addition to accepting liberal values such as freedom, equality and fairness, reasonable citizens must accept certain very minimal claims about the good life—for instance, the claim that it is better to have more rather than less of the primary goods of health, wealth and self-respect. Rawls accounts for this in terms of what he calls the

---

[31] I have previously elaborated this strategy in 'Perfectionism: Political not Metaphysical', *Philosophy & Public Affairs* 47 (2019), pp. 144–78, though my argument here is different in several respects.

206   A PERFECTIONIST THEORY OF JUSTICE

'thin theory of the good' and explains that it is impossible to construct a political theory without at least some thin theory of the good along these lines.[32] But these claims about what makes people better off are not, in the relevant sense, perfectionist claims at all. What is being proposed in this chapter goes considerably beyond Rawls's thin theory of the good—a theory of the good that is 'deliberately restricted to the bare essentials'—for it involves stipulating into reasonable citizens much 'thicker' claims about the good life and human flourishing than political liberals such as Rawls and Quong are willing to do.[33]

The important question is how to determine the content of the perfectionist definition of reasonableness. How should we determine the claims about human flourishing that all reasonable persons must accept? There are two main ways of proceeding at this point: the empirical approach and the constructivist approach.[34] Though I favour the constructivist approach, let us begin by considering the suggestion that the perfectionist definition of reasonableness is to be determined through empirical investigation.

On the empirical approach, we study the beliefs held by actual citizens in liberal-democratic societies and look to see if there are claims about the good life that almost everyone seems to accept. The content of reasonableness is then determined by the results of this empirical investigation. This empirical approach appears to be the approach pursued in the writings of the 'moderate perfectionists', namely Simon Caney, Joseph Chan and Franz Mang, who are the only perfectionists to date to defend an idea of perfectionist public reason.[35]

---

[32] Rawls, J., *Political Liberalism*, p. 176. See also Section 4.1.

[33] Rawls, J., *A Theory of Justice* (Cambridge, MA: Harvard University Press, 1971), p. 396. See also Quong, J., *Liberalism Without Perfection*, p. 215.

[34] These two approaches are considered by Quong, who is the only political liberal to explore the possibility of a perfectionist definition of reasonableness. See *Liberalism Without Perfection*, pp. 216–17. As Quong also notes, these are of course the two main approaches for any proponent of a public reason view, and not just proponents of a perfectionist public reason view, to determine the content of reasonableness. The contrast between the empirical approach and the constructivist approach should not, however, be overdrawn. As will become clear in the remainder of this chapter, there are at least three ways in which the constructivist approach (at least as I employ it) is still sensitive to empirical facts. First, what most people actually care about is relevant to assessing the plausibility in reflective equilibrium of a justificatory constituency that has been determined through normative construction rather than empirical investigation, because a normatively constructed justificatory constituency must still embody values that matter to us. Second, as I explain in Section 7.5, the perfectionist values that are baked into reasonableness must be interpreted in ways that enjoy 'broad and enduring appeal', where this condition is to be understood in empirical terms. Third, as I explain in Section 7.7, a satisfactory definition of reasonableness must not be excessively 'sectarian', where sectarianism is also to be understood in empirical terms. However, to acknowledge these ways in which the constructivist approach is sensitive to empirical facts is not to adopt the empirical approach to determining the content of reasonableness.

[35] See Caney, S., 'Thomas Nagel's Defence of Liberal Neutrality', *Analysis* 52 (1992), pp. 41–5; Caney, S., 'Impartiality and Liberal Neutrality', *Utilitas* 8 (1996), pp. 273–93; Caney, S., 'Liberal Legitimacy, Reasonable Disagreement, and Justice', *Critical Review of International Social and Political Philosophy* 1 (1998), pp. 19–36; Chan, J., 'Legitimacy, Unanimity, and Perfectionism', *Philosophy & Public Affairs* 29 (2000), pp. 5–42; Mang, F., 'Liberal Neutrality and Moderate Perfectionism', *Res Publica* 19 (2013), pp. 297–315. See also the brief but instructive discussion in Macleod, C., 'Neutrality, Public Reason and Deliberative Democracy', in R. Merrill and D. Weinstock (eds), *Political Neutrality: A Re-evaluation* (New York: Palgrave Macmillan, 2014), pp. 167–8.

This attribution is made tentatively because these moderate perfectionists have not always been very clear about the contractualist details that political liberals have agonized over—they do not, for instance, draw the distinction between the empirical and the constructivist approach to determining the constituency of reasonable citizens—and so it is difficult to know exactly how to read their arguments. One illustration of this is that moderate perfectionists typically focus on isolated judgements about human flourishing that almost everyone accepts, such as the judgement that a drug addict does not lead a flourishing life. But what moderate perfectionists have not offered, or at any rate not explicitly, is a systematic and general conception of reasonableness that accommodates these more specific perfectionist judgements—a conception that is not a mere conjunction of piecemeal judgements about human flourishing, that is coherent and appealing, and that could compete with the Rawlsian conception of reasonableness.[36] In what follows, I attempt to offer just such general criteria for a perfectionist conception of reasonableness.

In any case, what these moderate perfectionists point out is that, even if comprehensive religious and moral doctrines are indeed subject to considerable controversy among thoughtful and reflective people, there are plenty of other judgements about human flourishing that are shared by virtually everyone in contemporary societies. To put this point in Rawlsian terms, there appear to be many (or at least an interesting number of) claims about human flourishing that are the subject of overlapping consensus among the comprehensive religious, moral and philosophical doctrines found within modern societies. Candidate perfectionist judgements of this kind include:

- that 'Scrooge's ... life went better when he renounced his callous, miserly, misanthropic ways';[37]
- that 'someone whose whole outlook on life is focused simply on acquiring power, money, and status, and mixing with the rich and famous' thereby leads a less flourishing life;[38]
- that 'a life dedicated to counting blades of grass' is 'meaningless';[39]
- that someone 'who is wise, upright, [and] talented in music and philosophy' has a 'more worthwhile' life than someone who 'spends all his time chasing after elusive drug pleasures at the expense of all other goods';[40]
- that 'deep personal relations' of love and friendship 'contribute to the good life.'[41]

[36] For a similar criticism, see Quong, J., 'Disagreement, Asymmetry, and Liberal Legitimacy', *Politics, Philosophy & Economics* 4 (2005), pp. 322–3.
[37] Caney, S., 'Impartiality and Liberal Neutrality', p. 278.
[38] Ibid.
[39] Caney, S., 'Thomas Nagel's Defence of Liberal Neutrality', p. 45.
[40] Chan, J., 'Legitimacy, Unanimity, and Perfectionism', pp. 13–14.
[41] Mang, F., 'Liberal Neutrality and Moderate Perfectionism', p. 302.

There are two main problems, however, with this empirical or inductive approach to determining the content of the perfectionist definition of reasonableness.[42] The first is that gathering the relevant information about the prevalence of various beliefs about human flourishing would be a very complex and demanding undertaking. So far, moderate perfectionists have tended to make armchair speculations about what is 'widely accepted by many people' and what 'many people would sincerely agree [to]' when it comes to matters of human flourishing.[43] These speculations are not implausible, but nor is it immediately obvious that they are true. After all, a good number of people do appear, say, to focus primarily on acquiring power, money and status, and mixing with the rich and famous, and it is unclear that such people do so against their better judgement. So, to rigorously defend the view that all, most or even many actual citizens within modern societies do endorse these local perfectionist judgements, one would need to leave the armchair and engage with a significant amount of empirical evidence and research.

The second and more serious problem with the empirical approach is that it is overly contingent or relativistic. On the empirical approach, state action that encourages friendship and discourages misanthropy is permissible only because people happen to believe that friendship is superior to misanthropy. If people believed differently—if, say, they believed that misanthropy is superior to friendship—then the empirical approach would say that state action that encourages friendship is impermissible (because a matter of reasonable disagreement). Even more worryingly, the empirical approach implies that the perfectionist state's protection of basic liberal values such as freedom and equality would be impermissible (because a matter of reasonable disagreement) if there was no widespread consensus on these values within contemporary societies. The empirical approach thus makes laws and policies hostage to citizens as we actually find them, however implausible, bizarre or unjust their beliefs may be. It takes disagreement *too* seriously and makes our normative theory 'political in the wrong way'.[44] So even if perfectionist theory should rely on empirical claims *in some way*, the empirical approach seems to make it rely on empirical claims in a way that it should not.[45]

---

[42] In spelling out these two problems, I follow the discussion in Quong, J., *Liberalism Without Perfection*, p. 216. See also Quong's arguments against the 'external conception' in *Liberalism Without Perfection*, ch. 5. Other problems with this approach can be found in Kugelberg, H., 'Can Local Comparative Judgements Justify Moderate Perfectionism?' *Philosophia* 50 (2022), pp. 595–604.

[43] Chan, J., 'Legitimacy, Unanimity, and Perfectionism', p. 17; Mang, F., 'Liberal Neutrality and Moderate Perfectionism', p. 303.

[44] Rawls, J., *Political Liberalism*, p. 40.

[45] See Quong, J., *Liberalism Without Perfection*, p. 200 n. 20.

In my view, a more promising avenue for perfectionists is the constructivist approach.[46] On this view, the values that are endorsed by the constituency of reasonable citizens are determined not by empirical investigation but rather by normative construction. This is the approach pursued by political liberals such as Rawls and Quong when determining the content of their definitions of reasonableness. Rawls, for instance, explains that the values that reasonable citizens affirm are not meant to be the values that 'strike some kind of balance of forces between ... the various comprehensive doctrines actually found in society ... so as to be near to those doctrines' center of gravity, so to speak.'[47] Rather, the content of reasonableness is constructed out of 'the fundamental idea of society as a fair system of cooperation and its companion ideas.'[48] Similarly, for Quong the content of reasonableness 'at no point depends on the beliefs of real people' and 'does not rest on any empirical claim about substantive agreement between actual citizens ... at any level of abstraction.'[49] It is instead a matter of moral construction: 'to say that certain principles of justice could be endorsed by all reasonable people is to say that those principles can be validly constructed from a normative ideal of society as a fair system of social cooperation between free and equal citizens.'[50] 'Reasonable citizens', he continues, 'are a hypothetical constituency defined in terms of their acceptance of this ideal.'[51] Elsewhere, Quong states that laws and policies are publicly justified just in case they 'are justifiable to the hypothetical constituency of persons who endorse the values of freedom, equality, and fairness.'[52]

---

[46] The application of the constructivist approach to perfectionism is explored in an instructive discussion by Paul Billingham (see 'Liberal Perfectionism and Quong's Internal Conception of Political Liberalism', Social Theory and Practice 43 (2017), pp. 99–105), though there are two differences between our arguments. First, and most importantly, Billingham gives no positive reason for thinking that there is perfectionist content to the idea of the reasonable. Indeed, he does not actually endorse or argue for the 'perfectionist internal conception' and only postulates it as a critical tool to contend that Quong lacks grounds for preferring anti-perfectionist over perfectionist definitions of reasonableness. By contrast, I seek to develop a positive case for thinking that reasonableness includes perfectionist content. The perfectionist definition of reasonableness that I defend thus grows out of a deeper normative theory. This is important because (as I go on to explain in the main text) until some positive rationale has been given for thinking that the perfectionist definition of reasonableness is the right definition, anti-perfectionists can legitimately say in response to Billingham that pointing to the *mere possibility* of a 'perfectionist internal conception' is too undermotivated and underpowered an argumentative strategy to cast real doubt on the more deeply theorized anti-perfectionist definitions of Rawls and Quong. (A similar point applies, I believe, to Andrew Lister's related arguments in 'Public Reason and Perfectionism: Comments on Quong's *Liberalism Without Perfection*', Philosophy and Society 25 (2014), pp. 26–32.) A second difference is that Billingham makes reasonableness conditional on acceptance of a thin claim about the value of autonomy, whereas I make reasonableness conditional on acceptance of the more full-bloodedly perfectionist values of moral, intellectual and artistic excellence.

[47] Rawls, J., Political Liberalism, p. 39.

[48] Ibid., p. 40.

[49] Quong, J., Liberalism Without Perfection, pp. 144, 214.

[50] Ibid., p. 144.

[51] Ibid.

[52] Ibid., p. 149.

On the approach I favour, certain perfectionist commitments, namely moral, intellectual and artistic excellence, are baked into the notion of reasonableness in much the same way that many political liberals make reasonableness conditional on acceptance of certain liberal commitments such as freedom, equality and fairness. In other words, a reasonable citizen must accept the basic liberal values of freedom, equality and fairness, as well as the basic perfectionist values of moral, intellectual and artistic excellence. More precisely, in fact, a reasonable citizen must accept the *political relevance* of these values—since a citizen who personally endorses moral, intellectual and artistic excellence, but who denies that these excellences can play a justificatory role in politics, does not count as reasonable from the perspective of perfectionist public reason.[53] Many (though of course not all) perfectionist laws and policies could thus be expected to pass the public justification test because a citizen who rejects, say, the value of artistic excellence (or who accepts the value of artistic excellence but denies its political relevance) would count as unreasonable, and so her veto would have no more normative force than that of a free rider who rejects the value of fairness or that of a racist who rejects the value of equality.

Just as proponents of liberal public reason say that laws and policies must be justified in terms of a plausible interpretation and balance of the abstract liberal values, proponents of perfectionist public reason can say that laws and policies must be justified in terms of a plausible interpretation and balance of the abstract perfectionist values (as well as any relevant non-perfectionist values). In this way, there is an analogy between perfectionist public reason and Rawlsian accounts of public reason—an analogy that is examined in more detail in Section 7.5. Rawlsian public reason theorists hold that there is a 'family' of reasonable conceptions of justice, each of which offers an interpretation of the abstract liberal values that all reasonable citizens are presumed to accept (namely, freedom, equality and fairness), and that laws are legitimate so long as they are justified by appeal to some member of this family. Analogously, the perfectionist view holds that there is a family of reasonable conceptions of human flourishing, each of which offers an interpretation of the abstract perfectionist values that all reasonable citizens are presumed to accept (namely, moral, intellectual and artistic excellence), and that laws are legitimate so long as they are justified by appeal to some member of this family.

This perfectionist conception of reasonableness can be connected with some of the main ideas introduced in Part II. Most obviously, the construction of the perfectionist conception of reasonableness is strongly influenced by the provisional

---

[53] For ease of exposition, I shall not hereafter draw much attention to the distinction between acceptance of the perfectionist values and acceptance of the political relevance of the perfectionist values. I will illustrate the implications of perfectionist public reason by considering citizens who reject one or more of the three excellences, since it is the imposition of alien values on these citizens that presumably most exercises anti-perfectionist liberals. But what is said about these citizens applies equally well to citizens who accept the three excellences but deny their political relevance.

free-standing conception of human flourishing developed in Chapter 5.[54] We take reasonableness to be conditional on acceptance of moral, intellectual and artistic excellence, rather than on acceptance of other perfectionist claims, because these three excellences make up the provisional conception of human flourishing— a conception of human flourishing that was deliberately designed for political purposes and with the fact of reasonable disagreement in mind, as explained in Sections 5.1 and 5.2. Speaking more generally, we can now see that although society is to be understood as a fair striving for human flourishing between free and equal citizens, citizens reasonably disagree about what constitutes human flourishing, and so (for the sorts of reasons mentioned in Section 7.1, such as respect, civic friendship, social trust and egalitarian justice) the perfectionist state may not act on the basis of highly specific conceptions of human flourishing such as Christianity or Confucianism, even if these conceptions are true, and must instead only act on the basis of moral, intellectual and artistic excellence (as well as any relevant non-perfectionist values), since these are values that all reasonable citizens can be expected to endorse.

Since I have working within the 'constructivist' approach to public reason (or, as Quong also calls it, the 'internal conception' of public reason), it is worth closing this section by considering an important objection to this approach—namely, that it involves *preaching to the converted*. On the constructivist approach, the values of moral, intellectual and artistic excellence are defined into reasonableness by the theorist as a matter of normative construction rather than empirical investigation. But unless some compelling independent reasons are given for accepting these three excellences and their political relevance, the perfectionist definition of reasonableness is at risk of being convincing only to card-carrying perfectionists. Isn't it unsurprising that perfectionist policies pass the test of public justification, since they need only be justified to those who are already perfectionists?

The arguments in Part II, however, are supposed to offer the requisite independent reasons for the perfectionist definition of reasonableness. Those arguments support the perfectionist definition by showing how that definition grows out of a deeper normative theory. Even putting this point aside, though, we can respond

---

[54] The fact that the provisional conception of human flourishing influences the construction of the perfectionist definition of reasonableness means that this definition of reasonableness is also provisional in some sense. For instance, if after a broader process of philosophical inquiry it becomes necessary to add athletic excellence as a fourth component of human flourishing (alongside moral, intellectual and artistic excellence), then athletic excellence will also need to be added to the perfectionist definition of reasonableness. As I stressed in Sections 5.1 and 5.2, however, the influence goes in both directions, because whatever conception of human flourishing is settled on must satisfy a plausible specification of the public justification principle. The need to leave intact the underlying public reason motivations, that is, constrains in important ways what sort of conception of human flourishing can form part of the perfectionist theory of justice. So political perfectionists must go back and forth between their conception of human flourishing and their conception of reasonableness, making revisions to each in turn until everything hangs together in reflective equilibrium as a coherent and appealing whole.

212   A PERFECTIONIST THEORY OF JUSTICE

to the preaching-to-the-converted objection by noting that it is a very *general* objection to the constructivist approach to public reason. It applies just as well to the efforts of Rawls, Quong and others to defend an anti-perfectionist definition of reasonableness using the constructivist approach as to my effort to defend a perfectionist definition of reasonableness using this approach.[55] After all, for anti-perfectionist liberals such as Rawls and Quong, the values of freedom, equality and fairness are defined into reasonableness by the theorist as a matter of normative construction rather than empirical investigation. So the anti-perfectionist definition of reasonableness is similarly at risk of being convincing only to those who are already card-carrying liberals.

Of course, this tu quoque reply does not by itself defuse the preaching-to-the-converted objection. Proponents of this objection might say that if the theories of Rawls and Quong also merely preach to the converted, then so much the worse for those theories. Indeed, some might interpret my use of the constructivist approach to argue for perfectionist public reason to be itself a *reductio ad absurdum* of the constructivist approach, rather than a novel way to develop and defend a perfectionist theory.[56] But what the tu quoque reply does show is that the worry about preaching to the converted does not signal anything *distinctively* objectionable about the perfectionist application of the constructivist approach. So far as the preaching-to-the-converted objection goes, perfectionist and anti-perfectionist applications of the constructivist approach stand or fall together. So the best perfectionist response to the worry about preaching to the converted would, I think, simply overlap with the best response to this worry from political liberals who defend the constructivist approach—namely, that unless reasonable citizens are understood to accept the values of freedom, equality and fairness, we cannot be confident that the public justification principle will yield minimally acceptable outcomes. Put differently, alternatives to the constructivist approach to public reason make the legitimacy of laws and policies 'hostage' to those who are unjust or illiberal (such as racists, sexists and free riders) and so such alternatives are 'political in the wrong way'.[57]

---

[55] This is acknowledged by Quong, who regards this as one of the 'most serious' objections to his view. See *Liberalism Without Perfection*, p. 218; see also van Schoelandt, C., 'Justification, Coercion, and the Place of Public Reason', *Philosophical Studies* 172 (2015), pp. 1037–41.

[56] I thank Elvio Baccarini for putting this point to me. A similar point is made in Vallier, K. and Muldoon, R., 'In Public Reason, Diversity Trumps Coherence', *The Journal of Political Philosophy* 29 (2021), p. 225.

[57] See, for example, Rawls, J., *Political Liberalism*, pp. 39–40; Quong, *Liberalism Without Perfection*, ch. 5; Quong, J., '*Liberalism Without Perfection*: Replies to Gaus, Colburn, Chan, Bocchiola', *Philosophy and Public Issues* 2 (2012), pp. 51–8; Quong, J., 'What Is the Point of Public Reason?', *Philosophical Studies* 170 (2014), pp. 545–53. Recently, Vallier and Muldoon defend what they call the 'diversity' view of public reason against the charge that it does not *guarantee* liberal outcomes, saying 'we do not think that's a significant problem, since the [constructivist] view pursues the guarantee through arguments we consider circular and stipulative'. See Vallier, K. and Muldoon, R., 'In Public Reason, Diversity Trumps Coherence', pp. 226–7. But this does not address a modified version of the original charge: namely that the diversity view does not make liberal outcomes *sufficiently likely* when applied to

PUBLIC JUSTIFICATION   213

For the remainder of this chapter, then, I shall focus on the question of whether there is anything distinctively objectionable about using the constructivist approach to defend a perfectionist definition of reasonableness. I shall focus, in other words, on the following question: is there a compelling argument available to someone who is happy to grant that reasonableness is conditional on acceptance of certain liberal commitments such as freedom, equality and fairness, but who wishes to deny that reasonableness is *also* conditional on acceptance of certain perfectionist commitments such as moral, intellectual and artistic excellence? This does not mean that I shall entirely ignore broader questions about the constructivist approach itself, including the preaching-to-the-converted objection. After all, as we shall see in the following sections, the more specific question of whether the constructivist approach can be used to defend a perfectionist definition of reasonableness intersects with, and sheds light on, the more general question of the viability of that approach itself. So in what follows I do offer a defence of sorts of the constructivist approach to public reason more broadly—the point is just that this defence is indirect, emerging as a result of my defence of the application of this approach to perfectionism in particular.

7.3 Is the Marriage of Perfectionism and Constructivism Well-Motivated?

Quong is aware of the possibility of constructing a perfectionist conception of reasonableness, but he explains in a brief yet important passage that he has 'serious doubts as to whether a marriage of constructivism and perfectionism is feasible or plausible':

> I cannot understand why a perfectionist would want to pursue this strategy. Political liberals who take the fact of reasonable pluralism as an essential premise in political philosophy have a clear rationale for seeking to construct a free-standing conception of political justice that could be the subject of agreement amongst an idealized constituency of persons who agree only on some abstract political values. But it is unclear what would motivate a perfectionist to pursue a contractualist strategy of this sort. Once particular claims about what is intrinsically valuable are assumed to be true and to be the legitimate source of political reasons, the main impetus behind seeking a free-standing conception—the fact of reasonable pluralism—seems to have been jettisoned. I don't see why such perfectionists wouldn't simply prefer to make direct appeals to what they take to be

large-scale modern societies, which almost always contain at least some citizens with unjust or illiberal views. Admittedly, one would have to do more to develop this sort of objection, including specifying at what point exactly a liberal theory's vindication of liberal outcomes becomes insufficiently likely or excessively contingent, but filling in these details is beyond the scope of this discussion.

true claims about the good life or human flourishing (which is, of course, what most contemporary perfectionists do).[58]

Quong is correct that most contemporary perfectionists to date, such as Thomas Hurka, Matthew Kramer, Joseph Raz, George Sher and Steven Wall, 'jettison' the fact of reasonable pluralism—or, at least, do not take the fact of reasonable pluralism to be an essential premise in political philosophy, one that significantly constrains the sorts of claims that count as legitimate sources of political reasons. Most contemporary perfectionists, in other words, have been *comprehensive* perfectionists. These perfectionists have not generally tended to see any problem— from the point of view of respect, civic friendship, social trust, justice, stability, legitimacy and so on—with promoting laws and policies that are not publicly justifiable. Indeed, some even *define* perfectionism in terms of its rejection of the public justification principle. Wall, for instance, states that 'perfectionist political morality is committed to four claims', one of which is that 'there is no general moral principle that forbids the state from favouring sound ideals of human flourishing, as well as enforcing conceptions of political morality informed by them, when these ideals are controversial and subject to reasonable disagreement'.[59]

But it is unclear why, in principle, perfectionists *must* jettison the fact of reasonable pluralism or *must* assume that true claims about what is intrinsically valuable are always a legitimate source of political reasons. As I suggested in Section 5.1, perfectionists can and should accept that many perfectionist values—including Christian, Confucian and Aristotelian values—are subject to reasonable disagreement and so cannot be invoked to justify political decisions, even if true. It would strain credulity to assert that all reasonable citizens must converge on one or another of these highly specific conceptions of human flourishing under liberal conditions, and so, even if these conceptions are true, they are not legitimate sources of political reasons. Perfectionists' only contention is that not *all* claims about the good life and human flourishing are subject to reasonable disagreement in this way. Certain thinner perfectionist values—including in particular moral, intellectual and artistic excellence—are beyond reasonable rejection and so can legitimately figure in political reasoning. So perfectionists can and should wholeheartedly accept that reasonable disagreement about human flourishing exists; they just offer an alternative interpretation of the boundaries of reasonable disagreement and maintain that reasonable disagreement is not as *extensive* as political liberals suggest. In this way, political perfectionists take the fact of reasonable pluralism to be an essential premise in political philosophy, one that significantly

---

[58] Quong, J., *Liberalism Without Perfection*, p. 217; Quong, J., '*Liberalism Without Perfection*: Replies to Lister, Kulenović, Zoffoli, Zelić, and Baccarini', *Philosophy and Society* 25 (2014), p. 101. See also Stephen Mulhall and Adam Swift's doubts about the prospects of political perfectionism in *Liberals and Communitarians* (Oxford: Blackwell Publishing, 1996), p. 252.

[59] Wall, S., *Liberalism, Perfectionism and Restraint*, p. 8.

constrains the sorts of claims that count as legitimate sources of political reasons, and so they have precisely the same 'clear rationale' as political liberals for constructing a free-standing conception of human flourishing.[60]

Beyond recognition of the fact of reasonable disagreement, some further premise is needed in order to get to the public justification principle. As we saw in Sections 2.3 and 7.1, political liberals have appealed to ideas such as respect, civic friendship, social trust and egalitarian justice in order to explain why in the face of reasonable disagreement laws and policies must satisfy the public justification principle. But, crucially, there is no reason why perfectionists should not be troubled by precisely the same considerations and concerns that motivate political liberals, and moved therefore to explore the extent to which perfectionist policies can be compatible with a framework of public justification that is itself adopted as a response to those considerations and concerns. As Quong recognizes, perfectionists are not 'committed to the view that *only* perfectionist reasons are valid in political debate: they can accept that there are non-perfectionist considerations (e.g. considerations of fairness or natural rights) that are also relevant in reaching valid political judgements'.[61] So perfectionists can very plausibly import the political liberals' arguments that under conditions of reasonable pluralism the imposition of a law or policy that fails to secure public justification would not be respectful, or would compromise civic friendship, or would damage social trust, or would constitute an egalitarian injustice.[62]

So the rationale for constructing a public reason view—namely, recognition of the fact of reasonable pluralism in conjunction with some further premise about, say, respect, civic friendship, social trust or egalitarian justice—coheres perfectly well with the perfectionist framework. Perfectionists have every reason to seek to derive political conclusions from a free-standing conception of human flourishing that is specially constructed for political purposes and that does not purport to embody the full truth about human flourishing. A perfectionism that is 'political not metaphysical' in this way can give us the best of both worlds by incorporating the central insights of political liberalism—that political philosophers must show greater sensitivity to the fact of reasonable pluralism and that the terms of our common political life should as far as possible be justifiable to all—while also avoiding its rather less appealing requirement that we 'cordon off political morality from our best understanding of human flourishing'.[63] Far from being unmotivated or paradoxical—or, at least, some sort of intellectual curiosity—applying a 'political turn' to perfectionist theory emerges as a very natural and promising approach

---

[60] For further discussion of this point, see Billingham, P., 'Liberal Perfectionism and Quong's Internal Conception of Political Liberalism', pp. 99–100.

[61] Quong, J., *Liberalism Without Perfection*, p. 29.

[62] I thank Jonathan Quong and Tom Sinclair for helpful discussions of the ideas in this paragraph.

[63] Wall, S., *Liberalism, Perfectionism and Restraint*, p. 123.

for those who wish to explore the most appropriate forms of perfectionist political action under conditions of reasonable pluralism. Adapting a phrase of Larmore, one might even say that political perfectionism represents a perfectionism come of age.[64]

Of course, there are limits to the sorts of claims about human flourishing that can be baked into the notion of reasonableness while remaining faithful to the basic public reason motivations. For instance, and as I explain further in Section 7.7, it would clearly make a mockery of the public justification apparatus if we held a view such as 'Opus Dei: Political Not Metaphysical', according to which reasonableness is conditional on acceptance of Opus Dei doctrine. A view that defines 'reasonable disagreement' in a way that bears no relation at all to the folk concept of reasonable disagreement is not aptly characterized as a 'public reason' view. To affirm 'Opus Dei: Political Not Metaphysical' would amount to denying the very possibility of reasonable disagreement: it would, in Quong's language, 'jettison' the fact of reasonable disagreement. Similarly, as I just mentioned and as I suggested in Section 5.1, Christian, Confucian and Aristotelian doctrines cannot plausibly be thought to satisfy a public justification condition in a free society. None of these comprehensive doctrines can aptly be piped through the public reason framework.

It is difficult, however, to see why these limits of fidelity are necessarily co-extensive with liberal neutrality. In particular, why can't the view articulated in Section 7.2 be faithful to the basic public reason motivations? After all, the ideals of moral, intellectual and artistic excellence are deliberately thin and abstract. A justificatory constituency defined in terms of acceptance of these excellences would still leave plenty of room for disagreements about a range of other important religious and philosophical matters. Justifications phrased in terms of moral, intellectual and artistic excellence can plausibly be said to involve 'forms of reasoning and argument available to citizens generally'.[65] So even if some forms of perfectionist public reason would make a mockery of the public justification apparatus or would amount to denying the very possibility of reasonable disagreement, it is difficult to see why this is true of the specific form of perfectionist public reason developed in Section 7.2.

Of course, in order to convincingly establish that this conception of perfectionist public reason leaves intact the underlying motivations of the public reason project, we would need a more precise articulation of what exactly those 'motivations' are. To this end, it is helpful to consider two ways in which leading public reason liberals have sought to describe what is so attractive about a public reason view. Consider, first, Kevin Vallier's observation that 'the reason many accept political liberalism is because they seek a truly non-sectarian conception' of politics.[66]

---

[64] See Larmore, C., *Patterns of Moral Complexity*, p. 51.
[65] Rawls, J., *Political Liberalism*, p. 162.
[66] Vallier, K., 'On Jonathan Quong's Sectarian Political Liberalism', *Criminal Law and Philosophy* 11 (2017), p. 185.

Yet while it would no doubt be objectionably sectarian to suppose that all reasonable persons must accept, say, Christian, Confucian or Aristotelian doctrines, it is much less clear that there is anything objectionably sectarian about supposing that all reasonable persons must accept moral, intellectual and artistic excellence—or so I go on to argue in Sections 7.6 and 7.7. Or consider, second, David Estlund's statement that 'even if the pope has a pipeline to God's will, it does not follow that atheists may permissibly be coerced on the basis of justifications drawn from Catholic doctrine [because] some non-Catholic views should count as [reasonable] even if they are mistaken'.[67] Proponents of perfectionist public reason can and should fully agree that Catholic ideals (and religious ideals more generally), even if true, are subject to reasonable disagreement and as such are not a legitimate source of political reasons.[68] They simply resist the attempt to *generalize* from religious ideals to all ideals of human flourishing, including in particular moral, intellectual and artistic excellence. In these ways, the conception of perfectionist public reason articulated in Section 7.2 appears to be fully capable of cashing in on some important specifications of the underlying 'motivations' for the public reason project, namely non-sectarianism and principled secularism.

More generally, the compatibility of this conception of perfectionist public reason with the basic motivations of the public reason project can be supported by observing that this conception gives rise to a plausible specification of the notion of neutrality. As I hinted at in Sections 4.4 and 5.1, the arguments in this chapter entail a version of what Steven Wall calls a 'restricted neutrality principle': they entail that although the perfectionist state should promote *some* ideals of human flourishing, it should remain neutral with respect to *other* ideals of human flourishing about which there is reasonable disagreement, such as ideals of salvation, piety and spiritual fulfilment.[69] Neutrality remains an important principle in certain domains. So there is a principled rationale for rejecting objectionably sectarian forms of perfectionism without rejecting perfectionism wholescale. In this sense,

[67] Estlund, D., *Democratic Authority: A Philosophical Framework* (Princeton, NJ: Princeton University Press, 2008), p. 5.

[68] Political perfectionists differ in this respect from mainstream comprehensive perfectionists, who hold that *truth* (rather than *reasonable acceptability*) is the relevant standard of political justification and who therefore face some pressure to reject Estlund's statement. Richard Arneson, for instance, responds to Estlund by insisting that 'if the pope *really* did have a pipeline to God, this would be a proper basis for religious establishment'. It is just that the pope has no such pipeline: 'so far as we can tell, Christianity is not true'. See Arneson, R., 'Political Liberalism, Religious Liberty, and Religious Establishment', in H. Dagan, S. Lifshitz and Y. Stern (eds), *Religion and the Discourse of Human Rights* (Jerusalem: The Israel Democracy Institute, 2014), p. 141. Political perfectionism's commitment to secularism is in this sense more principled than the commitment to secularism of many forms of comprehensive perfectionism, since (like political liberalism's commitment to secularism) it does not hinge on the truth or falsity of religious doctrines.

[69] See Wall, S., 'Neutralism for Perfectionists: The Case of Restricted State Neutrality', *Ethics* 120 (2010), pp. 232–56. An important difference between Wall's restricted neutrality principle and the restricted neutrality principle that I favour, though, is that his is justified on the basis of claims about value pluralism, whereas mine is justified on the basis of claims about the normative significance of reasonable disagreement.

7.4 Which Definition of Reasonableness Is More Plausible?

The vital question that arises at this point is this: is the perfectionist justificatory constituency the *right* justificatory constituency? Is it more or less plausible than the justificatory constituency defended by political liberals such as Rawls and Quong? What justifies the claim that reasonableness is conditional not only on acceptance of liberal values (such as freedom, equality and fairness) but also on acceptance of perfectionist values (such as moral, intellectual and artistic excellence)? In particular, should a person who accepts freedom, equality and fairness, but who rejects, say, the value of artistic excellence, really thereby be excluded as 'unreasonable'? Is such a person really beyond the justificatory pale, in the way that a racist who rejects the value of equality is beyond the justificatory pale? Without a clear answer to these questions, the strategy of baking perfectionist content into the constituency of reasonable citizens looks ad hoc and gerrymandered—and thus unconvincing in comparison to the more deeply theorized anti-perfectionist definitions of reasonableness of political liberals such as Rawls and Quong.

These questions shall occupy us for the remainder of this chapter. To begin to explore them, it is helpful to have before us some specific cases. Consider the following three individuals, each of whom rejects one of the three perfectionist axioms:

Anna: Anna is influenced by the philosophical thought of Ayn Rand and gives pride of place in her system of values to the pursuit of self-interest. She works as a high-flying investment banker and uses her earnings to buy herself mansions, sports cars and other luxuries. She is willing to abide by the liberal conception of the fair terms of social cooperation; she is not so extreme in her self-interestedness that she rejects the values of freedom, equality and fairness. But, beyond this, she rejects the ideal of moral excellence and most of the familiar virtues such as generosity, friendship and forgiveness.

Barry: Barry spends most of his free time watching television. Despite not having given it much explicit thought, he is willing to abide by the liberal conception of the fair terms of social cooperation; he does not reject the values of freedom, equality and fairness. But he does reject the ideal of intellectual excellence. In his view, academics and other intellectual types are wasting their time: they overcomplicate life with their pedantic hair-splitting and interminable debates.

Callum: Callum belongs to a religious order focused centrally on the cultivation of humility. He is willing to abide by the liberal conception of the fair terms of social cooperation; nothing in his religious convictions leads him to reject the values of freedom, equality and fairness. But he does reject the ideal of artistic excellence (in all of its musical, dramatic, visual and other forms), as he regards art as a means of self-expression that awakens problematic feelings of vanity and superiority.

Anna, Barry and Callum each resent being coercively taxed by the state in order to fund policies aimed at the realization of moral, intellectual and artistic excellence—perfectionist ideals that conflict not just with their raw preferences but also with their conceptions of what is good in human life (however simple or unarticulated this conception is in Barry's case).

For political liberals such as Rawls and Quong, these characters count as reasonable. Since Anna, Barry and Callum affirm basic liberal values, they belong to the idealized constituency of citizens to whom laws and policies must be justified, and so they are entitled to exercise a veto over perfectionist laws and policies. By contrast, on the view I am suggesting, these characters count as unreasonable and have no such entitlement. So the disagreements that matter are more circumscribed on the perfectionist view than they are on the political-liberal view.

Two related points should be stressed at this juncture. The first is that, as Quong puts it, whether a particular citizen counts as reasonable 'is not something we work out by appeal to intuitions about the colloquial use of the term "reasonable", or by appeal to empirical evidence about what people might deem to be a reasonable position. "The reasonable" is a technical term within a larger theoretical structure, and the boundaries of reasonable disagreements must be determined by appeal to its technical definition'.[70] So to say that Anna, Barry and Callum are 'unreasonable' in the technical sense that they deny certain components of a perfectionist theory, such as the political relevance of the values of moral, intellectual and artistic excellence, is not to say that these individuals are 'unreasonable' in a more colloquial or everyday sense. The second point is that, even though unreasonable citizens have no entitlement to veto laws and public policies with which they do not agree, such individuals are still entitled to the full range of rights, resources and opportunities accorded to citizens generally.[71] Being unreasonable, in other words, does not affect one's political status: the unreasonable enjoy the same rights and benefits of citizenship as the reasonable, such as freedom of speech and the right to vote. It is just that the specific contours of these rights and benefits can be determined by considerations that are unacceptable to the unreasonable.

---

[70] Quong, J., 'On Laborde's Liberalism', *Criminal Law and Philosophy* 15 (2021), p. 54.
[71] On this point, see Quong, J., *Liberalism Without Perfection*, ch. 10.

To answer the question of whether individuals such as Anna, Barry and Callum should be deemed reasonable or unreasonable, it is helpful first to consider where the orthodox Rawlsian definition of reasonableness comes from. What justifies the claim of political liberals that reasonableness is conditional on acceptance of liberal values such as freedom, equality and fairness? For Rawls, the bounds of reasonableness are set by 'a fundamental organizing idea within which all ideas and principles can be systematically connected and related. This organizing idea is of society as a fair system of social cooperation between free and equal persons'.[72] Rawls also says that 'citizens are reasonable when, viewing one another as free and equal in a system of social cooperation over generations, they are prepared to offer one another fair terms of cooperation'.[73] As we saw above, the same goes for Quong: 'to say that certain principles of justice could be endorsed by all reasonable people is to say that those principles can be validly constructed from a normative ideal of society as a fair system of social cooperation between free and equal citizens. Reasonable citizens are a hypothetical constituency defined in terms of their acceptance of this ideal'.[74] And what, in turn, justifies this organizing idea of society? As we saw in Chapter 3, the Rawlsian conception of society as a fair system of social cooperation between free and equal persons recommends itself on two main grounds: first, it is a plausible and recognizable interpretation of widely accepted basic beliefs and values implicit in the public political culture of liberal-democratic societies; and second, it helps to organize our considered convictions, at all levels of generality, into a state of reflective equilibrium.

I agree that the bounds of reasonableness are to be set by some fundamental organizing conception of society and that this conception of society must be selected on the basis of how it fares as cultural interpretation and as a means of attaining reflective equilibrium. But, as I argued in Chapter 3, I am doubtful that the political-liberal conception of society—a fair system of social cooperation between free and equal citizens—is the only, let alone the best, such conception available. In particular, a plausible and arguably superior alternative conception of society, I have argued, is that of society as a fair striving for human flourishing between free and equal citizens. It is this perfectionist conception of society that sets the bounds of the perfectionist definition of reasonableness. So on the view I am suggesting, and to adapt Quong's turn of phrase, to say that perfectionist laws and policies could be endorsed by all reasonable people is to say that those laws and policies can be validly constructed from a normative ideal of society as a fair striving for human flourishing between free and equal citizens. Reasonable citizens are a hypothetical constituency defined in terms of their acceptance of this fundamental

[72] Rawls, J., *Political Liberalism*, p. 9.
[73] Ibid., p. 446.
[74] Quong, J., *Liberalism Without Perfection*, p. 144.

idea of society as well as its companion ideas such as the provisional conception of human flourishing.

As I argue in Sections 3.4 and 3.5, this perfectionist conception of society is appealing in a number of respects. Indeed, the perfectionist conception of society is arguably superior to the Rawlsian conception because it better accommodates our considered convictions. For while both conceptions recognize that citizens are free and equal and that social terms must be fair, the perfectionist conception is in addition sensitive to certain distinctly perfectionist convictions shared by a good many citizens in contemporary liberal democracies. Most ordinary people, after all, are not anti-perfectionists. They see nothing wrong with, say, state support for the arts. Using US survey data from 1990 to 2016, for instance, one recent study finds that 'a strong majority favours keeping government funding of the arts at least at current levels'—a finding that 'mesh[es] well with previous studies that indicate that Americans have a "reservoir of goodwill" towards the arts'.[75] Of course, one complication here is that we do not know *why* these individuals are in favour of government funding of the arts. As was discussed in Section 6.6, there might be non-perfectionist rationales for arts funding, such as securing equality of opportunity or the social bases of warranted self-respect. Still, this sort of survey data is suggestive and does, I think, lend some degree of support to the perfectionist position. It is an advantage of the perfectionist conception of society as a fair striving for human flourishing between free and equal citizens that it coheres with and accommodates these distinctly perfectionist strains within ordinary moral and political thought.

In short, those who deny the political relevance of moral, intellectual and artistic excellence count as unreasonable because they rebel against the fundamental ideal of society as a fair striving for human flourishing between free and equal citizens— just as a Rawlsian would justify the exclusion of racists and free riders from the constituency of the reasonable on the grounds that they fail to honour the ideal of society as a fair system of social cooperation between free and equal citizens. The exclusion of citizens like Anna, Barry and Callum from the constituency of reasonable citizens, then, is not an ad hoc fix but rather flows from deeper ideas about the nature of society which set the bounds of reasonableness. So while the exclusion of these sorts of citizens may be stipulative, it is not *arbitrarily* stipulative. These stipulations are well-motivated and driven by other theoretical commitments; there are deeper reasons for making these particular stipulations rather than others.

Let us close this section by considering an argument given by some political liberals in favour of the anti-perfectionist definition of reasonableness. We can call this the *argument from practical necessity*. The basic idea is that what justifies the anti-perfectionist specification of reasonableness is the fact that society needs to

---

[75] Jacobsmeier, M., 'Public Opinion on Government Funding of the Arts in the United States: Demographic and Political Factors', *International Journal of Cultural Policy* 27 (2021), p. 476.

222 A PERFECTIONIST THEORY OF JUSTICE

reach a common agreement on the liberal values, but it does not similarly need to reach a common agreement on the perfectionist values. Moral, intellectual and artistic excellence, in other words, go beyond the minimum necessary commitments of citizenship. This sort of argument is made by Rawls, who explains that that 'the aspects of our view that we assert should not go beyond what is *necessary* for the political aim of consensus'.[76] As he also says:

> This account of reasonable comprehensive doctrines is deliberately loose. We avoid excluding doctrines as unreasonable without strong grounds based on clear aspects of the reasonable itself. Otherwise our account runs the danger of being arbitrary and exclusive. Political liberalism counts many familiar and traditional doctrines—religious, philosophical, and moral—as reasonable even though we could not seriously entertain them for ourselves, as we think they give excessive weight to some values and fail to allow for the significance of others. A tighter criterion is not, however, *needed* for the purposes of political liberalism.[77]

Quong develops a similar argument:

> The constituency of the reasonable is defined by asking what beliefs, attitudes, or values ideal citizens in a well-ordered liberal society would necessarily *have* to share. Such citizens, I argue, would have to be committed to certain liberal egalitarian values, and a very thin theory of the good [i.e. health, wealth and the social bases of self-respect]. But there's no reason to assume citizens in a well-ordered liberal society would [need to] agree on anything else ... so I don't assume any further level of agreement in designing my theory ... A citizen with this view about human flourishing [i.e. that drug addiction is a worthwhile way of life] isn't impaired from doing all the things citizens would need to do in a perfectly well-ordered liberal society, and so there is no basis to assume that reasonable persons share a particular view about the badness of addiction.[78]

But why think that it is necessary for citizens to accept liberal values but not necessary for citizens to accept perfectionist values? Given that, in general, things are necessary *for* some end or purpose, we can put this question slightly differently by asking: *for what purpose* is citizens' acceptance of liberal values necessary but citizens' acceptance of perfectionist values unnecessary? Here it is helpful to draw a distinction between two ways in which the appeal to practical necessity can be interpreted:

---

[76] Rawls, J., 'The Idea of an Overlapping Consensus', *Oxford Journal of Legal Studies* 7 (1987), p. 14 (emphasis added).

[77] Rawls, J., *Political Liberalism*, pp. 59–60 (emphasis added). See also the related argument in Nagel, T., *Equality and Partiality* (Oxford: Oxford University Press, 1991), pp. 164–5.

[78] Quong, J., 'On Laborde's Liberalism', p. 53 (emphasis added).

(1) *Empirical Necessity*: citizens' acceptance of moral, intellectual and artistic excellence is not necessary for the purpose of sustaining a society over time.

(2) *Normative Necessity*: citizens' acceptance of moral, intellectual and artistic excellence is not necessary for the purpose of sustaining a just and well-ordered society over time.[79]

Anti-perfectionists are correct that a commitment to perfectionist values among citizens is not necessary in the empirical sense. A society in which only a small percentage of citizens are committed to the values of moral, intellectual and artistic excellence can nonetheless be expected to sustain itself over time. Such a society would not inevitably collapse. But the problem with this version of the argument from practical necessity is that it proves too much. After all, a society in which only a small percentage of citizens are committed to the values of freedom, equality and fairness can also be expected to sustain itself over time—as is illustrated by the persistence of certain illiberal, inegalitarian and aristocratic societies in the past and present. So if we work out the content of reasonableness by asking ourselves what commitments citizens need to share in the empirical sense, this threatens to undermine the claim that reasonableness is conditional on acceptance of freedom, equality and fairness.

In response, anti-perfectionist liberals might instead appeal to the normative interpretation of necessity and say that these illiberal, inegalitarian and aristocratic states do not function *as they ought to*. On this approach, we work out the content of reasonableness by asking ourselves what commitments citizens would need to share in a just and well-ordered liberal-democratic society. Anti-perfectionists can argue that this approach supports neither more nor less than the anti-perfectionist definition of reasonableness. It supports nothing less because a society in which only a small percentage of citizens are committed to freedom, equality and fairness cannot be expected to be just and well-ordered. And it supports nothing more because a society in which only a small percentage of citizens are committed to moral, intellectual and artistic excellence can be expected to be just and well-ordered.

However, the problem with appealing to the idea of normative necessity in this way is that it begs the question against the perfectionist conception of justice. After all, the perfectionist conception of justice incorporates a concern with moral, intellectual and artistic excellence; and so, from the perspective of this conception, a society cannot be expected to be fully just and well-ordered without a commitment to these excellences on the part of citizens. For proponents of perfectionist justice, policies such as subsidies for the arts are not merely beneficial public policies. They

---

[79] For similar distinctions, see Caney, S., 'Thomas Nagel's Defence of Liberal Neutrality', pp. 42–3; Chan, J., 'Legitimacy, Unanimity, and Perfectionism', pp. 25–7.

are not the cherry on the top of an already just and well-ordered society. Rather, such policies are an indispensable feature of a just and well-ordered society; they are essential if the fundamental perfectionist ideal of society as a fair striving for human flourishing between free and equal persons is to be taken seriously. So, in the absence of some deeper explanation of why citizens' acceptance of moral, intellectual and artistic excellence is unnecessary for the purpose of sustaining a just and well-ordered society over time, this version of the argument from practical necessity amounts to little more than a denial of precisely what perfectionist justice affirms.[80]

Let us pull together the argument of this chapter so far. A common objection to perfectionism is that some citizens reject the value of, say, artistic excellence. Art-hating citizens of this kind may protest: '*Who says* that artistic excellence is a genuine value? Insofar as laws based on claims about artistic excellence cannot be justified *to me*, such laws represent raw power rather than legitimate authority.' The problem with this objection, of course, is that some citizens also reject the value of, say, racial equality. Racist citizens of this kind may protest: '*Who says* that racial equality is a genuine value? Insofar as laws based on claims about racial equality cannot be justified *to me*, such laws represent raw power rather than legitimate authority.' So, to level the original objection without also undercutting the political pursuit of liberal goals such as equality, the anti-perfectionist needs to say that there is an important asymmetry between these two citizens: the first citizen's objection is *reasonable*, whereas the second citizen's objection is *unreasonable*. This would explain why the first citizen gets a veto, whereas the second citizen does not. But here perfectionists can retort that on their favoured conception of reasonableness, all reasonable citizens must accept certain ideals of human flourishing, including the ideal of artistic excellence. So, without further argument, the anti-perfectionist's contention that the art-hater is reasonable whereas the racist is unreasonable simply begs the question against the perfectionist conception of reasonableness—a conception which places both citizens in the unreasonable camp and which grants neither of them a veto.

---

[80] Here one might argue that the appeal to a well-ordered society doesn't need to be so specific—*so driven by our preferred conception of justice*—to play some role in helping us to determine the content of reasonableness. Without having any detailed theory of justice in hand, we can still make some assumptions about what citizens would and would not need to share in a well-ordered liberal-democratic society. To this extent, it needn't beg the question to say that it is implausible to suppose that citizens in a well-ordered society would need to share a commitment to moral, intellectual and artistic excellence. (I thank Jonathan Quong for putting this objection to me.) But it is not clear to me that we do in fact have a strong pre-theoretical grip on the notion of a 'well-ordered society'. After all, the 'well-ordered society' is a term of art in political philosophy rather than a notion used widely in everyday thought and speech. It is in this sense unlike 'stability', 'justice' and so on. So how much independent work can the appeal to a well-ordered society do? How much intuitive pressure is there to say that citizens in a well-ordered society needn't share a commitment to moral, intellectual and artistic excellence?

7.5 Admissible Interpretations of the Excellences

A natural objection to the perfectionist definition of reasonableness is that, when considering concrete matters of public policy, citizens are bound to disagree about the interpretation of the basic perfectionist values of moral, intellectual and artistic excellence. Even if it is plausible that perfectionist ideals such as moral, intellectual and artistic excellence are beyond reasonable rejection when articulated at this coarse-grained level, is it still plausible that they are beyond reasonable rejection when articulated at a more fine-grained level? Isn't any particular interpretation or concretization of these abstract perfectionist ideals bound to be vigorously disputed?

But, as it stands, this objection cannot tell against the perfectionist definition of reasonableness, since it is equally true of the anti-perfectionist definition of reasonableness. After all, when considering concrete matters of public policy, citizens are bound to disagree about the interpretation of the basic liberal values of freedom, equality and fairness. In the arena of real-world politics, there are vigorous disputes about what freedom, equality and fairness imply for issues such as taxation, immigration, abortion, affirmative action, capital punishment, freedom of speech, just war and health care. And in the arena of political philosophy, attempts to interpret these values give rise to a diverse array of political theories. In this way, any particular interpretation or concretization of the abstract liberal values is similarly bound to be subject to disagreement and controversy.

In light of this, political liberals typically say that the public justification principle, if it is to be at all plausible, must operate at a suitably high level of abstraction.[81] Public justification, that is, is not plausibly construed as requiring that all reasonable citizens reach the same conclusions 'down to the last details' on specific political issues.[82] Rather, public justification requires something more coarse-grained: it requires that political action can be justified to citizens in terms of an

---

[81] It is true that some do take the public justification principle to apply at a much more specific level. Gaus, for instance, holds that 'to publicly justify a state action or policy it is not sufficient to show that we all accept these values or goods, but that there is a trade-off rate or ranking that all fully rational citizens would accept'. Giving the example of mandatory motorcycle helmet laws, he explains that 'many motorcyclists prefer the freedom to choose—to run the risk of a serious accident and brain damage, to ride with the wind in the hair—and so resent these laws because they ... simply [reflect] the trade-off rate of middle-class, middle-aged people, who are risk-averse'. See Gaus, G., 'Liberal Neutrality: A Compelling and Radical Principle', in S. Wall and G. Klosko (eds), *Perfectionism and Neutrality: Essays in Liberal Theory* (Oxford: Rowman & Littlefield, 2003), p. 158. But if it is applied at this very specific level, the public justification principle is not a plausible principle of political morality. One way to see this is to observe that this interpretation of the public justification principle is extremely difficult to satisfy and would rule out all but the most minimal state. Gaus, though, readily embraces this libertarian implication; he explains that public justification is 'a radical principle [that] severely limits what policies a state can pursue' (p. 159). So a less question-begging way to argue against this interpretation of the public justification principle is to argue against its derivation or rationale. I do this elsewhere; see Tahzib, C., 'Do the Reactive Attitudes Justify Public Reason?', *European Journal of Political Theory* 21 (2022), pp. 423–44.

[82] Rawls, J., *Political Liberalism*, p. 226.

226 A PERFECTIONIST THEORY OF JUSTICE

interpretation of certain basic values that all citizens can be reasonably expected to endorse, such as freedom, equality and fairness.[83] When this condition is met, no citizen 'can reasonably think that the collectivity's decisions aim at fundamentally alien values', even if she does not always agree with those decisions and would have preferred alternative decisions.[84]

Similarly, then, perfectionists can say that public justification does not require that everyone reaches the same fine-grained conclusions about how the perfectionist values bear on specific political issues. All it requires is that political action can be justified to citizens in terms of an interpretation of certain basic values that all citizens can be reasonably expected to endorse (namely, the liberal values of freedom, equality and fairness, and the perfectionist values of moral, intellectual and artistic excellence). So perfectionists, too, can lay claim to ensuring that no citizen subject to the perfectionist state can reasonably think that the collectivity's decisions aim at fundamentally alien values, even if such a citizen does not always agree with those decisions and would have preferred alternative decisions.

Here, though, the objector might push back with the following very important concern:

> There remains a significant disanalogy or asymmetry between perfectionist public reason and liberal public reason. This asymmetry centres on the relationship between the abstract values that all reasonable citizens are said to endorse and the specific interpretations of those values that justify laws and policies. This relationship is much 'looser' within perfectionist public reason than it is within liberal public reason, and this creates trouble for the claim that a justification that appeals to the abstract perfectionist values (namely moral, intellectual and artistic excellence) counts as a public justification.
>
> To see this, we can note that liberal public reason does not remain merely at the level of the abstract liberal values of freedom, equality and fairness. Rawls, for instance, provides some *specification* of what each of these values involves: he explains that the abstract liberal values of freedom, equality and fairness also include somewhat more specific principles and ideas, such as basic liberal rights (for example, freedom of expression, freedom of religion, bodily integrity), principles of non-discrimination, a social minimum that is guaranteed for all citizens, the importance of values such as education, public health and security, and so

---

[83] Another way of putting this is that state action on the basis of judgements that are subject to 'justificatory disagreement' is legitimate, whereas state action on the basis of judgements that are subject to 'foundational disagreement' is illegitimate. For this distinction, see Quong, J., *Liberalism Without Perfection*, ch. 7. Once the perfectionist definition of reasonableness is in place, many perfectionist laws and policies will be subject to merely justificatory, rather than foundational, disagreement because the values of moral, intellectual and artistic excellence will provide a common 'fundamental normative framework' and will supply a set of shared 'premises which can serve as a mutually acceptable standard of justification' (pp. 204, 206).

[84] Lister, A., *Public Reason and Political Community*, p. 106.

on. There are, in other words, some *bounds* on what Rawls calls the 'family' of admissible interpretations of the abstract liberal values of freedom, equality and fairness.[85] Of course, Rawls recognizes that reasonable citizens will disagree about how to understand and weigh these somewhat more specific principles and ideas. Reasonable citizens will disagree, for instance, about whether a particular anti-discrimination law strikes the most appropriate balance between freedom of association and equality of opportunity. But, still, disagreements are subject to quite tight bounds and occur 'within a certain more or less narrow range'.[86] Many forms of libertarianism, for instance, would fall outside of this family of admissible interpretations of freedom, equality and fairness, despite claiming to reflect these values. All this matters because it means that within liberal public reason all citizens can recognize the normative force of others' arguments: all citizens can recognize laws and policies justified by liberal public reason as justified *to them*. So, within liberal public reason, the specific interpretations that justify laws and policies are tied to the abstract values in a way that gives them a unity and similarity, and this is crucial to the plausibility of the claim that liberal public reason offers citizens a shared framework for reasoning and mutual justification.

By contrast, perfectionist public reason remains very abstract. No specification is given of what moral, intellectual and artistic excellence each involves. No bounds are placed on the family of admissible interpretations of these abstract perfectionist values. This means that interpretations of these abstract values could be extremely diverse. Consider Diana, who is a devotee of modern abstract and conceptual art, and who deems Italian artist Maurizio Cattelan's *Comedian* (which consists of a banana stuck to a wall with a piece of duct tape) to be the epitome of artistic excellence. Diana's idea of what makes for artistic excellence is diametrically opposed to that of Ethan, who in fact does not even recognize the art that Diana considers excellent as *being art at all*. And it is precisely this looseness in the relationship between the abstract perfectionist values and the specific interpretations of those values that makes it implausible to say that an argument that appeals to Diana's interpretation of artistic excellence counts as providing a justification *to Ethan*, in the way required by public reason theorists. Or consider Felix, who holds an idiosyncratic, highly demanding, secular ascetic interpretation of what moral excellence involves. On this basis, Felix justifies a range of policies designed to promote and incentivize ascetic practices—for instance, promotional campaigns and state subsidies for retreat centres in which participants spend prolonged periods fasting, being silent, performing manual labour and engaging in contemplation. How plausible is it to say that Felix provides a justification *to Gemma*—a fun-loving, outgoing person who, though she

---

[85] See Rawls, J., *Political Liberalism*, pp. xlvi, 6, 223, 226, 450–2.
[86] Ibid., p. 164.

228 A PERFECTIONIST THEORY OF JUSTICE

endorses moral excellence, finds Felix's interpretation of moral excellence utterly alien and wholly lacking in normative force—simply because he happens to invoke an abstract value that they both endorse in some verbal sense?

So insofar as the abstract liberal values are more tightly connected to the more specific claims that support political proposals than the abstract perfectionist values are, liberal public reason more plausibly offers a 'common currency of discussion' in politics.[87] While perfectionist public reason does involve agreement at some very high level of abstraction, this is not sufficient to plausibly conclude that it offers citizens a shared framework for reasoning and mutual justification in the sense that matters for public reason theorists. Agreement at a somewhat more specific level is needed for that conclusion to be plausible and for the analogy with liberal public reason to be sustained. In short, then, some further specification or bounding of the shape of the abstract perfectionist values is necessary in order for it to be plausible to suppose that justification in terms of abstract perfectionist values really constitutes justification to all reasonable citizens.[88]

I am not convinced that cases like those of Diana and Felix arise only or especially within perfectionist public reason. We can see this by noting that Felix might justify ascetic policies on the basis of an abstract liberal value (such as equality) or on the basis of some admissible interpretation of an abstract liberal value (such as public health). Of course, defenders of liberal public reason might argue that these ascetic policies do not represent a *plausible* balance of liberal values.[89] But defenders of perfectionist public reason can similarly argue that these policies do not represent a plausible balance of perfectionist values. So without a more detailed account of what constitutes a 'plausible' balance of values, the appeal to plausibility does not explain why liberal public reason is any less vulnerable to these sorts of cases than perfectionist public reason. The general point is that the public justification principle is a constraint on *reasons*, not a constraint on *policies*, and so it remains true on *all* versions of the public justification principle that seemingly sectarian policies can, in principle, be sincerely defended at the legislative and administrative stages on the basis of public reasons. It is thus difficult to see how perfectionist public reason and liberal public reason are asymmetrical in terms of their vulnerability to cases like those of Diana and Felix in which intuitively sectarian policies pass the public justification test.

Still, even if vulnerability to cases like those of Diana and Felix cannot itself *be* the asymmetry between perfectionist public reason and liberal public reason,

---

[87] Ibid., p. 165.

[88] I thank Paul Billingham for developing this objection over the course of eleven exceptionally penetrating pages (personal correspondence, 15 January 2021).

[89] See, for example, Quong, J., *Liberalism Without Perfection*, pp. 134, 137, 185, 207. For an interesting discussion of Quong's appeal to plausibility in this sort of context, see Fowler, T. and Stemplowska, Z., 'The Asymmetry Objection Rides Again: On the Nature and Significance of Justificatory Disagreement', *Journal of Applied Philosophy* 32 (2015), pp. 139–41.

these cases may well help to *illustrate* some more general or structural asymmetry. In particular, I accept that, as it stands, the structure of perfectionist public reason is looser than the structure of liberal public reason and that this casts some degree of doubt on the plausibility of the claim that justifications phrased in terms of abstract perfectionist values really do constitute public justifications. Put differently, it is less clear within perfectionist public reason that the specific interpretations that justify laws and policies are tied to the abstract values in a way that gives them a sufficient degree of unity and similarity to plausibly constitute a shared framework for reasoning and mutual justification in the sense that matters for public reason theorists.

To overcome this problem, we need to offer at least the beginnings of an account of how the bounds on the family of admissible interpretations of the abstract values of moral, intellectual and artistic excellence are set. One promising bound in this regard is that these excellences must be specified in a way that has broad and enduring appeal within liberal-democratic societies. To this extent, reasonable citizens do not have unlimited latitude in how they interpret moral, intellectual and artistic excellence. This bound seems well-motivated in this context, since perfectionists who endorse the idea of public reason—unlike the perfectionists who take truth, rather than reasonable acceptability, to be the relevant standard of political justification and who pursue the more hard-line strategy outlined in Section 7.1— will naturally be attuned to the importance of avoiding excessive sectarianism within their theory, as I explore in greater depth in Sections 7.6 and 7.7.

Of course, it is difficult to say exactly what broad and enduring appeal consists in, but I take it that this condition would be satisfied by the interpretations of the perfectionist values mentioned for illustrative purposes in Section 5.2—namely, in the case of moral excellence, many of the familiar virtues such as generosity, courage and friendliness; in the case of intellectual excellence, many of the endeavours within the familiar fields of academic inquiry and scholarship, such as the sciences and humanities; and in the case of artistic excellence, many of the familiar forms and expressions of art and culture such as music, literature, poetry and theatre. All of these activities and ideals enjoy, in some sense, broad and enduring appeal and widespread endorsement within modern liberal-democratic societies. This condition will also, I believe, be satisfied by the interpretations of moral, intellectual and artistic excellence put forward, if rather stipulatively, in Sections 6.2, 6.3 and 6.4—such as the claim that possessing a healthy curiosity and a knowledge and understanding of diverse fields of human endeavour is a component of intellectual excellence—when exploring some potential perfectionist laws and public policies.

By contrast, Diana's interpretation of artistic excellence (according to which Cattelan's *Comedian* exemplifies artistic excellence) and Felix's interpretation of moral excellence (according to which an idiosyncratic brand of asceticism exemplifies moral excellence) are quite extreme and would not appear to satisfy the

230 A PERFECTIONIST THEORY OF JUSTICE

condition of broad and enduring appeal. To put it simply, neither what Diana judges to be artistically excellent nor what Felix judges to be morally excellent are widely held to be excellent by citizens of contemporary societies. So these interpretations of artistic and moral excellence would not be admissible, despite Diana's and Felix's nominal appeal to the abstract perfectionist values. These specifications are not part of the shared fund of perfectionist public reason and are not a legitimate source of political reasons under conditions of reasonable pluralism.[90]

Clearly, there is no bright line between interpretations of the excellences that do enjoy broad and enduring appeal and interpretations of the excellences that do not enjoy such appeal. Consider Howard Gardner's theory of multiple intelligences, according to which there are nine distinct 'modalities' of intelligence: linguistic, logical-mathematical, musical, spatial, bodily-kinaesthetic, interpersonal, intrapersonal, naturalistic and existential.[91] In relation to naturalistic intelligence, for instance, Gardner says that 'it seems to me that the individual who is able readily to recognize flora and fauna, to make other consequential distinctions in the natural world, and to use this ability productively (in hunting, in farming, in biological science) is exercising an important intelligence'.[92] Which of these nine interpretations of the abstract perfectionist value of intellectual excellence enjoy 'broad and enduring appeal'? There may be no determinate answer to this question. But, for the sorts of reasons given in Section 5.3, this should come as no embarrassment.

---

[90] But what if Felix were to justify the ascetic policies on the grounds that they would promote generosity or courage or one of the other interpretations of moral excellence that I have said would satisfy the broad-and-enduring-appeal condition? Wouldn't this mean that these policies could pass the public justification test? There are at least three things to say in reply here. First, the exercise of public reason must be sincere. As Rawls says, public reasons 'are not puppets manipulated from behind the scenes' by non-public reasons. (See Rawls, J., *Political Liberalism*, p. 454.) So if Felix is dissimulating—if he does not really believe that this policy will promote generosity or courage but uses these arguments as a smokescreen for his ascetic ideals—then his justification does not in fact constitute a bona fide public justification. Of course, if Felix *is* sincere, then it may be true that this policy could pass the public justification test. But here it is important to remember—and this is the second responsive point—that similar results can also occur within liberal public reason, as I stressed above. After all, one can imagine a citizen who sincerely believes that state subsidies for retreat centres would promote admissible interpretations of the liberal values of freedom, equality and fairness. Indeed, it has often been pointed out that it is possible to provide a public justification for certain forms of religious establishment—that is, a justification that appeals not to the truth of a particular religion but to neutral values such as social stability. (See, e.g., Kramer, M., *Liberalism with Excellence* (Oxford: Oxford University Press, 2017), pp. 17–18, 23–4; Miller, D., 'What's Wrong with Religious Establishment?', *Criminal Law and Philosophy* 15 (2021), pp. 75–89; see also Rawls's remarks on public reason and school prayer in *Political Liberalism*, pp. li–lii, 474–6.) Given that the public justification principle is a constraint on reasons, rather than a constraint on policies, it remains true on *all* versions of the public justification principle that seemingly sectarian policies can, in principle, be sincerely defended on the basis of public reasons. Third, even if the policy Felix favours passes the public justification test, it does not follow that it is morally legitimate. After all, public justification is a necessary rather than sufficient condition of legitimacy, and so this policy can still be rejected either in principle (because it is ruled out by other values or principles within the perfectionist theory of justice) or in practice (because it is likely to be counterproductive).

[91] Gardner, H., *Multiple Intelligences* (New York: Basic Books, 2006).

[92] Gardner, H., 'Reflections on Multiple Intelligences: Myths and Messages', *The Phi Delta Kappan* 77 (1995), p. 206.

Almost all of the concepts used in political theories are indeterminate to some extent. These concepts narrow the range of possible options, but they do not typically single out any particular option as uniquely superior. Indeed, there may similarly be no determinate answer to the question of whether a particular interpretation of the abstract liberal values satisfies the bounds that Rawls places on the 'family' of admissible interpretations of those values, because what counts as providing all citizens with 'adequate all-purpose means' to make effective use of their liberties, say, is to some degree indeterminate.[93] So for the broad-and-enduring-appeal criterion to succeed, it need not be fully determinate; what is important is that there are at least clear cases either side of a blurry line.

The introduction of this broad-and-enduring-appeal bound tightens up the structure of perfectionist public reason, and it rules out certain problematic cases. But does it tighten up the structure enough? In all likelihood, we will need more than one bound on the family of admissible interpretations of the abstract perfectionist values. These further bounds would constrain free-standing perfectionist reasoning and argumentation by requiring that reasonable citizens' interpretations of the three excellences have a particular kind of shape or content. These bounds would also provide a basis for saying that not everything that is widely held to be excellent automatically constitutes an admissible interpretation of excellence. Though I shall not try to identify these further bounds, it is evident that they will need to be quite thin, for otherwise they would raise a worry about sectarianism— an issue I discuss in Sections 7.6 and 7.7. So we cannot, for instance, insist that any admissible interpretation of artistic excellence must agree that Rembrandt was the greatest of the Old Masters. This would clearly be excessively sectarian. Instead, the bounds that are imposed on the family of admissible interpretations will need to have a fairly structural and generic character. Various possibilities of this kind suggest themselves: perhaps whatever is properly said to be an interpretation of the abstract perfectionist values must involve a certain degree of subtlety, complexity and rigour; perhaps it must involve the development or exercise of certain important capacities; or perhaps it must conform in the appropriate way to the standards and judgements of those with expertise in the relevant domains, such as art critics and those with specialized scientific training.

Each of these bounds is unhappily vague, nor has a deeper rationale for each of these bounds been suggested. But this is not too much of a problem since the main goal of this chapter is quite modest and exploratory. It is to chart some of the simplest and most general features of perfectionist public reason—a hitherto almost wholly unexplored territory—as a way of opening up conceptual space, of showing that the public justification framework is highly flexible and is amenable to the expression of perfectionist ideas, and thus of indicating that objections from public

---

[93] Rawls, J., *Political Liberalism*, p. xlvi.

justification need not be fatal to the perfectionist project. Insofar as this discussion is only meant to begin the rescue of public justification from anti-perfectionist liberalism, it is neither necessary nor desirable to offer a fully worked-out account of the bounds of the family of admissible interpretations of the abstract perfectionist values. The key point for our purposes is just that these sorts of conditions promise to significantly delimit the shape and content of the abstract perfectionist values, thereby eliminating much of the looseness within perfectionist public reason.

After the relevant bounds are imposed, there will still remain a significant role for intuition and judgement in determining what does and does not count as moral, intellectual and artistic excellence for political purposes. But this should come as no surprise. As I suggested in Section 5.3, judgements about how to interpret moral, intellectual and artistic excellence need not be built into the foundations of the perfectionist theory and can instead be made at the legislative and administrative stages. So while the objection from looseness requires us to place *some* substantive constraints on admissible interpretations, many questions of interpretation and specification can nonetheless be left open by the theory. Reliance on intuition is lessened, not eliminated. A degree of indeterminacy remains. In this regard, a suitably bounded perfectionist public reason resembles liberal public reason: it offers a general framework that can guide and discipline political argument and justification, but it does not try to fix the precise content of public reason prior to actual democratic debate.

In brief, then, while I see the force of the worry about the looseness of the structure of perfectionist public reason, I reject what appears to be its underlying assumption—namely, that the abstract perfectionist values of moral, intellectual and artistic excellence are by their nature so hopelessly subjective or open-textured that there is little prospect of imposing plausible, non-sectarian constraints on how these excellences are to be interpreted and understood for the purposes of political argument and justification. Even if the abstract perfectionist values of moral, intellectual and artistic excellence are amenable to different interpretations, it is difficult to believe that these values are a matter of interpretation *all the way down*. Certainly, this is not the view of Rawls, who is keen to stress that he does 'not contend that the criteria of excellence lack a rational basis' and who states that 'clearly there are standards in the arts and sciences for appraising creative efforts'.[94] My own sense is that the abstract perfectionist values of moral, intellectual and artistic excellence function in roughly the same way as the abstract liberal values of freedom, equality and fairness, insofar as there is a fairly stable set of core or paradigmatic cases as well as a range of borderline cases in which it is unclear whether or not the relevant value is exemplified. For both sets of values, there are easy cases and hard cases. It thus remains difficult to see why justifications phrased in terms of suitably bounded interpretations of the abstract perfectionist values of

[94] Rawls, J., *A Theory of Justice*, p. 328.

moral, intellectual and artistic excellence cannot have a sufficient degree of unity and similarity to plausibly belong within a shared framework for reasoning and mutual justification in the sense that matters for public reason theorists.

7.6 A More Sectarian Definition of Reasonableness?

In my view, the most compelling objection to perfectionist public reason concerns the *sectarianism* of the perfectionist definition of reasonableness. Indeed, I suspect that the sectarianism objection is a more philosophically powerful and precise way of deploying the sort of undermotivation objection considered in Section 7.3. In this section and Section 7.7, then, I defend the perfectionist conception of reasonableness against two ways of running this sectarianism-based objection.

According to the first way of running the objection from sectarianism, the perfectionist definition of reasonableness is problematic because it is *more* sectarian than the anti-perfectionist definition of reasonableness. On this view, which has been advanced forcefully and influentially by a number of public reason theorists in recent years, we should prefer a public reason view whose justificatory constituency more closely approximates the constituency of citizens as we actually find them in contemporary liberal-democratic societies.[95] The intuitive idea here is that, as more normative content is baked into the definition of reasonableness, the constituency of the reasonable increasingly resembles (in Gaus's words) a kind of 'sect', one that 'excludes a great many good-willed and sensible people'.[96] Yet wasn't the whole point of the public reason project to transcend the conflict between sectarian doctrines and creeds? Given that one of the underlying motivations for the public reason project is to show how laws and policies can be legitimate in the face of the deep and pervasive disagreements that characterize modern democratic societies, one might think that public reason theorists should prefer more rather than less inclusive accounts of the justificatory constituency.

The perfectionist constituency of reasonable citizens, so this objection goes, is far more of an exclusive club—far more of a sect—than the anti-perfectionist constituency of reasonable citizens. After all, the perfectionist constituency excludes all those excluded by the anti-perfectionist constituency (that is, it excludes all those who reject freedom, equality or fairness) *plus more*. For it *also* excludes

[95] See, for example, Gaus, G., 'Sectarianism Without Perfection? Quong's Political Liberalism', *Philosophy and Public Issues* 2 (2012), pp. 7–15; Vallier, K., 'On Jonathan Quong's Sectarian Political Liberalism'. For an instructive recent treatment of this topic, see Wong, B., 'Is It Sectarian for a Rawlsian State to Coerce Nozick? On Political Liberalism and the Sectarian Critique', *Philosophia* (forthcoming). Wong's central contention is that the sectarian critique can be overcome if state officials engage in 'reasoning from conjecture' with those deemed to be unreasonable. Though I offer a different response to the sectarian critique, there is of course no reason why perfectionist state officials cannot also employ the practice of reasoning from conjecture insofar as this overcomes the charge of sectarianism.

[96] Gaus, G., 'Sectarianism Without Perfection?', p. 10.

those who reject moral, intellectual or artistic excellence. Moreover, as we saw in Section 7.5 in response to the worry about the relative 'looseness' of perfectionist public reason, the perfectionist view turns out to say not only that reasonable citizens must accept the abstract perfectionist values of moral, intellectual and artistic excellence but also that they must interpret these excellences in ways that fall within some definite bounds. Reasonable citizens must hold views about moral, intellectual and artistic excellence that have some particular kind of shape or content. So it is not only someone like Anna (who rejects moral excellence) who is excluded from the perfectionist justificatory constituency but also someone like Felix (who accepts moral excellence but who interprets this value in terms of an idiosyncratic brand of asceticism) who is excluded. The anti-perfectionist definition of reasonableness commonly employed by political liberals is thus preferable, at least in one respect, to the more sectarian definition of reasonableness being proposed on behalf of perfectionists. Or so this objection alleges.

I grant that the perfectionist definition of reasonableness is more sectarian than the anti-perfectionist definition. But I deny that this makes the perfectionist definition worse, even in one respect. Substantiating this claim requires us to delve fairly deeply into the theory of public reason, so let me provide a roadmap of the argument. I first offer a more precise definition of 'Sectarianism' and of the 'Anti-Sectarian Desideratum' (Section 7.6.1). I then consider the case for the Anti-Sectarian Desideratum. Despite being used to tremendous effect to motivate certain theories of public reason and to criticize others, public reason liberals do not typically offer explicit arguments for the Anti-Sectarian Desideratum, and so a certain degree of reconstruction is required to identify and disentangle the possible reasons for accepting it. I reconstruct and reject four potential rationales for the Anti-Sectarian Desideratum: that less sectarian views are more in keeping with the *spirit* of public reason liberalism (Section 7.6.2), that less sectarian views do a better job of realizing the value of *stability* (Section 7.6.3), that less sectarian views are more *respectful* (Section 7.6.4) and that less sectarian views are less at risk of *redundancy* (Section 7.6.5). In the end, I find that there is no good reason to regard less sectarian public reason views as pro tanto better than more sectarian public reason views.[97]

7.6.1 The Anti-Sectarian Desideratum

To sharpen the discussion, let us offer some definitions:

> *Sectarianism*: A public reason view is more sectarian if its account of the constituency of reasonable citizens excludes more members of the actual constituency of citizens in democratic societies.[98]

---

[97] I develop these lines of argument in greater detail in Tahzib, C., 'Is Anti-Sectarianism a Desideratum of a Public Reason View?', *Public Affairs Quarterly* 35 (2021), pp. 228–46.

[98] See also Gaus, G., 'Sectarianism Without Perfection?', p. 8.

The Anti-Sectarian Desideratum: If a public reason view X is less sectarian than a public reason view Y, then X is a better public reason view than Y in at least one respect.[99]

The Anti-Sectarian Desideratum has arguably always played a role in the background of debates over public reason. Early political liberals such as Charles Larmore appear to be sympathetic to the Anti-Sectarian Desideratum, saying that public reason liberalism must offer 'a conception that as many people as possible can affirm, despite their inevitable differences about the worth of specific ways of life'.[100] Similarly, George Klosko says that 'if the principles we seek are to be acceptable to widely diverse liberal citizens, there is a presumption against additional restrictions [on reasonableness] which could lead to large numbers of people not recognizing or accepting resultant principles'.[101] Elsewhere, he writes that 'we can posit a continuum, ranging from the intensely shared convictions of a sectarian group to broader principles that can be accepted by a large percentage of a given population, in spite of many other points of issues about which they continue to disagree. I believe the principles that political liberalism seeks should be closer to the latter than the former'.[102]

In recent years, however, the Anti-Sectarian Desideratum has begun to play an increasingly pivotal role at the forefront of debates over public reason. Vallier explicitly appeals to the Anti-Sectarian Desideratum in arguing that since Quong's public reason view 'dramatically shrinks the justificatory public' in a way that his does not, his own view should be preferred to Quong's.[103] In a recent discussion, Vallier and Muldoon argue against what they call the 'coherence' approach to public reason partly on the grounds that it 'label[s] a broader swath of (otherwise reasonable) persons as unreasonable' and 'shrinks the scope of liberal justification'.[104] And they defend instead what they call the 'diversity' approach to public reason partly on the grounds that it 'count[s] a wider range of people as reasonable'.[105] And along similar lines, Gaus states that 'public reason liberalism [should aim] not to develop a controversial ideological position that seeks to exclude large parts of our society as "unreasonable", but to press the bounds of inclusiveness as far as possible'.[106]

The statements of Gaus, Klosko, Larmore, Muldoon, Vallier and others are not, however, typically supplemented by detailed arguments for why we should care about anti-sectarianism in this way—for why we should think that less sectarian

---

[99] See also Vallier, K., 'On Jonathan Quong's Sectarian Political Liberalism', p. 185.

[100] Larmore, C., 'Political Liberalism', *Political Theory* 18 (1990), p. 341.

[101] Klosko, G., *Democratic Procedures and Liberal Consensus* (Oxford: Oxford University Press, 2000), p. 25.

[102] Klosko, G., 'An Empirical Approach to Political Liberalism', in S. Young (ed.), *Political Liberalism: Variations on a Theme* (Albany, NY: State University of New York Press, 2004), p. 132.

[103] Vallier, K., 'On Jonathan Quong's Sectarian Political Liberalism', p. 176.

[104] Vallier, K. and Muldoon, R., 'In Public Reason, Diversity Trumps Coherence', p. 212.

[105] Ibid., p. 222.

[106] Gaus, G., 'Public Reason Liberalism', in S. Wall (ed.), *The Cambridge Companion to Liberalism* (Cambridge: Cambridge University Press, 2015), p. 134.

public reason views are in one way better than more sectarian public reason views. This is an important omission because there is a compelling argument *against* the Anti-Sectarian Desideratum: namely, that public reason theorists should be aiming for the *right* account of reasonableness, not the *least sectarian* account of reasonableness per se.[107] We should not, that is, be trying to make the constituency accommodate more of the views of actual citizens in modern democratic societies unless we have prior reasons for thinking that the views of actual citizens ought to be accorded normative authority. *Any* remotely plausible conception of reasonableness, after all, will be sectarian with respect to some individuals within contemporary democratic societies, such as racists and murderers. Yet this hardly counts, in any respect, against these conceptions of reasonableness. Given our normative commitments, we should expect no less than that these individuals are excluded from the constituency that gets to shape the content of justice. The same applies in less extreme cases. So, for public reason theorists, the sheer *volume* of exclusion should be irrelevant (at least up to a point, as I explain in Sections 7.6.2 and 7.7). Bigger is not always better; less is sometimes more. Instead, what matters is whether the *right* individuals are being excluded. What we need to ensure is that those whom we *ought* to deem reasonable—those whose beliefs *ought* to shape the content of social justice—are not being excluded.

7.6.2 The Spirit of Public Reason Liberalism

One argument for the Anti-Sectarian Desideratum is that it is dictated by the 'spirit' of public reason liberalism. More sectarian public reason views, so this thought goes, miss the point of the public reason project or lose contact with its basic motivations. This idea has recently been developed by Vallier:

> There is a strong case to be made that political liberalism must avoid being sectarian insofar as it can. The case is relatively simple. Political liberals generally acknowledge that one point of public reason is to avoid the sectarianism of alternative approaches to political legitimacy. Theological conceptions are the subject of reasonable contestation, so imposing them on those who disagree would be sectarian. Similarly, comprehensive liberal conceptions are the subject of reasonable contestation, so imposing them on those who disagree would also be sectarian. The reason many accept political liberalism is because they seek a truly non-sectarian conception of liberalism. So it seems safe to say that if an interpretation A of political liberalism is less sectarian than interpretation B, then all else equal, A is superior to B.[108]

---

[107] See the discussion in Quong, J., '*Liberalism Without Perfection*: Replies to Gaus, Colburn, Chan, Bocchiola', pp. 53–6; see also Quong, J., *Liberalism Without Perfection*, p. 149 n. 28.
[108] Vallier, K., 'On Jonathan Quong's Sectarian Political Liberalism', p. 185.

Gaus makes a similar point about sectarian accounts of reasonableness and the spirit of public reason liberalism:

> Rather than helping us devise a public social world all can live with, [sectarian public reason views] valorize the social world of some as *the* social world. In response, those excluded either oppose public reason liberalism as a sectarian project, or draw back, alienated, into their own social worlds. The promise of public reason as providing a common world in the midst of diversity goes unfulfilled. More than that: it becomes a screen for the dominance of a controversial secular social world, focusing on a restricted set of eligible moral categorizations. In the end, such public reason views are very similar to traditional moral theories, which are based on claims to correctly understand the moral realm and social world as they truly are.[109]

Gaus and Vallier are surely right that the avoidance of sectarianism is an important aim of the public reason project. But there are ways of accommodating this aim without going so far as to accept the Anti-Sectarian Desideratum. One can, that is, readily accept that the avoidance of sectarianism matters *in some sense*, without accepting the specific sense in which the Anti-Sectarian Desideratum cashes this out. In particular, a plausible alternative interpretation of the idea that the avoidance of sectarianism is an aim of the public reason project is that sectarianism functions as a kind of *threshold* or *constraint* on a public reason view. On this interpretation, to which I am sympathetic, and which I discuss further in Section 7.7, a public reason view should not be *excessively* sectarian—it should count *enough* actual citizens as reasonable—even if a public reason view need not be *less* sectarian than other views.

Consider an analogy. Vanilla extract is an ingredient of a good vanilla ice cream. But this does not mean that more vanilla extract necessarily makes for a better vanilla ice cream. There comes a point after which each additional increment of vanilla extract does not at all enhance the taste of the ice cream and may in fact spoil the taste. Instead, what it means for vanilla extract to be an ingredient of a good vanilla ice cream is that a good vanilla ice cream must contain enough vanilla extract. Similarly, we can agree with Gaus and Vallier that anti-sectarianism is an ingredient of a good public reason view. But this does not mean that more anti-sectarianism necessarily makes for a better public reason view. There comes a point after which each additional increment of anti-sectarianism is not at all better and may even spoil the shape of political justice. Instead, what it means for anti-sectarianism to be an ingredient of a good public reason view is that a good public reason view must contain enough anti-sectarianism.

---

[109] Gaus, G., 'Is Public Reason a Normalization Project? Deep Diversity and the Open Society', *Social Philosophy Today* 33 (2017), p. 46.

238 A PERFECTIONIST THEORY OF JUSTICE

In short, then, those who reject the Anti-Sectarian Desideratum can still whole-heartedly accept that the avoidance of sectarianism is essential to the spirit of the public reason project and that it is highly relevant to the choice of justificatory constituency, insofar as the avoidance of sectarianism functions as a threshold that all public reason views must pass in order to stay in contact with the folk concept of reasonable disagreement and in order to avoid collapsing into 'traditional moral theories, which are based on claims to correctly understand the moral realm and social world as they truly are'.

7.6.3 Stability

A second possible argument for the Anti-Sectarian Desideratum appeals to the value of stability. This sort of argument is suggested by Gaus:

> Because [sectarian] principles would not appeal to the reason of many, it is likely that they could only be upheld by the oppressive use of coercion, 'with all its official crimes and the inevitable brutality and cruelties'. To the extent liberalism fails to resolve the problem of ineffective endorsement, widespread state coercion will be required to stabilize liberal practices; to the extent that the problem of defeated endorsement cannot be solved, in the name of reasonableness, the liberal state will force its citizens to act against their consciences. Such a regime will not be enduring or secure.[110]

We can state the argument from stability to the Anti-Sectarian Desideratum as follows: (1) less sectarian public reason views are more stable than more sectarian public reason views; (2) it is in one way better for a view to be more rather than less stable; so (3) less sectarian public reason views are in one way better than more sectarian public reason views.

Neither of the premises in this argument, however, seems to me to be true. In relation to the premise that less sectarian views are more stable than more sectarian views, it is unclear how the inclusion of racists, murderers and psychopaths in the justificatory constituency (such that these individuals are given a veto over liberal justice and rights) would lead to a more stable society than if such individuals are excluded from the justificatory constituency. Of course, *some* expansions of the justificatory constituency—expansions that do not give a veto to these extreme types—might increase stability. But there is no reason to think that bigger is *always* more stable.

---

[110] Gaus, G., 'A Tale of Two Sets: Public Reason in Equilibrium', *Public Affairs Quarterly* 25 (2011), p. 311. The quotation is from Rawls, J., *Justice as Fairness*, p. 34.

But even granting the premise that each additional increment of anti-sectarianism contributes to stability, it is not always in one way better for a view to be more rather than less stable. To see this, consider a stable racist regime. This regime enjoys widespread support from the citizenry: there is no problem of defeated endorsement and the state need not use coercion to stabilize its racist practices, and so the regime is enduring and secure. But because racism is morally unsound, the regime's stability in this instance not only fails to be a desirable feature but is also in fact positively undesirable.[111]

This point applies equally well to the justificatory constituency of a public reason view. Consider two rival accounts of the constituency of reasonable citizens. The first view defines reasonableness in terms of acceptance of the value of equality, and the second view defines reasonableness in terms of acceptance of the values of equality and fairness. The first view is less sectarian than the second because it includes all the citizens in the second view plus more (namely, those citizens who accept equality but not fairness). Let us grant that the first view, because less sectarian, is more stable. The question is: does the greater stability of the first view thereby make it in one respect a better public reason view? It is difficult to see why it should unless we are antecedently persuaded that reasonableness need not be conditional on acceptance of the value of fairness. Indeed, it may well be that it is pro tanto bad, rather than pro tanto good, for this view to be stable—just as it is pro tanto bad, rather than pro tanto good, for the racist regime to be stable.

In short, what we seem to care about is not that a public reason view achieves non-moralized empirical stability, but rather that a public reason view achieves stability for the right reasons *among the right constituency*. So stability cannot be a factor that determines the correct conception of reasonableness but is rather something downstream from the conception of reasonableness.[112]

---

[111] Here one might object that it is not the *stability* of a stable racist regime that is undesirable but the *racism* of a stable racist regime that is undesirable. Stability is always pro tanto good because chaos and disorder are always pro tanto bad. It is just that the badness of accommodating racists outweighs the goodness of stability, and so a stable racist regime, though pro tanto good (because stable), is all-things-considered bad (because racist). If we understand things this way, premise (2) of the argument from stability to the Anti-Sectarian Desideratum remains true. (I thank an anonymous reviewer for putting this objection to me.) In my view, however, it is both the racism and the stability of a stable racist regime that are undesirable. In other words, and though I cannot defend this view in full here, stability has only *conditional* value: the stability of a practice is desirable only if that practice is itself desirable (or at least not undesirable). Viewing stability as having only conditional value in this way appears necessary in order to make sense of the idea that we should hope that injustice lacks persistence. How could we hope that injustice does not persist—that injustice gives way to justice, that justice prevails in the end, and so on—if we took stability to be a good-making feature of unjust practices?

[112] I thank Jonathan Quong for helpful discussion of the argument in this section. Of course, one might accept that stability does not justify the Anti-Sectarian Desideratum but still wonder whether perfectionist justice can be expected to achieve stability through commanding an overlapping consensus between the comprehensive doctrines likely to gain a sizeable body of adherents under a regime regulated by its principles. I consider this question in Section 3.4.

7.6.4 Respect

A third possible argument for the Anti-Sectarian Desideratum takes off from the value of respect. The argument here is: (1) it is pro tanto disrespectful to impose laws and policies on individuals who see themselves as having no reason to comply with those laws and policies; (2) less sectarian public reason views engage in less of this kind of disrespectful imposition; so (3) less sectarian public views are in one way preferable to more sectarian views.[113]

However, the main problem with this argument is that premise (1) is not plausible. As we have seen in Sections 2.3.1 and 7.1, there are debates about what respect requires so far as political justification is concerned. Many defenders of public reason argue that respect requires that laws and policies be acceptable to all reasonable citizens. Critics of public reason deny this and instead typically hold that 'we show others respect when we offer them, as explanation, what we take to be our true and best reasons for acting as we do' (or at least something in this non-contractualist vicinity).[114] But despite their differences about whether respect requires acceptability to the reasonable, both sides in this debate typically agree that respect does not require acceptability to the *unreasonable*. And rightly so: it is difficult to believe that respect requires that laws and policies be acceptable to racists, murderers, psychopaths, and so on. Surely laws against racism and murder are not disrespectful, *even in one respect*, in virtue of the fact that they are unacceptable to murderers and racists? Or, if such laws are disrespectful in some sense, then surely this is not a sense of disrespect that we should be worried about morally? The proposed argument for the Anti-Sectarian Desideratum thus rests on an implausibly extreme conception of what respect for persons requires—a conception that goes well beyond the already quite controversial view that respect requires justification to all reasonable citizens.

Of course, one might insist in response that insofar as laws against murder and racism cannot be justified to murderers and racists, these laws are pro tanto disrespectful; it is just that this disrespect pales in comparison to the overwhelming reasons in favour of laws against murder and racism. But this does not seem right because it implies that the legitimacy of laws against murder and racism is based on an 'on-balance' judgement. The legitimacy of these laws is not, however, based on this sort of judgement. As Lister puts it, 'we do not weigh the benefit of being safe from murder [or racism] against the cost of losing one's freedom to murder [or to be racist]; we do not count frustrated desires to murder [or to be racist] as having *any* value.'[115]

---

[113] I thank Alex Motchoulski for putting this argument to me.

[114] Galston, W., *Liberal Purposes: Goods, Virtues, and Diversity in the Liberal State* (Cambridge: Cambridge University Press, 1991), p. 109.

[115] See Lister, A., 'Public Justification and the Limits of State Action', *Politics, Philosophy & Economics* 9 (2010), p. 164. In a response to Lister, Gaus seems to maintain that the legitimacy of laws against

7.6.5 Redundancy

Another argument for the Anti-Sectarian Desideratum that is implicit in certain remarks of Gaus and Vallier is that more sectarian public reason views are at greater risk of redundancy or circularity. As Gaus and Vallier respectively put this, a view that is too sectarian risks a 'victory by definition' and risks making 'the main conclusions of political liberalism [or political perfectionism] true by stipulation'.[116] This objection is quite closely related to the objection considered at the end of Section 7.2—namely, that the constructivist approach to public reason involves preaching to the converted, that it merely reproduces the commitments defined into reasonableness by the theorist and that its vindication of perfectionist political action is hardly surprising or philosophically interesting—and so this clearly is an area in which my defence of the application of the constructivist approach to perfectionism doubles up as an indirect defence of the constructivist approach itself.

The worry here is that if laws and policies are permissible when they are acceptable to reasonable citizens, and if reasonable citizens are defined in terms of endorsement of certain perfectionist values, then isn't the public justification machinery redundant? Isn't all the fundamental moral work being done by the perfectionist values? Hasn't the distinctive and interesting idea of 'justification-to' or 'acceptability-to' simply dropped out of the picture? What is the point of the constituency move? Why not cut out the middleman and just derive laws and policies directly from the values of moral, intellectual and artistic excellence?

At some level, I think this charge is accurate. More sectarian views do have a greater tendency towards 'redundancy', in some sense of that term. But the charge is unduly pejorative. For while it is indeed possible to frame this objection in terms of redundancy—more sectarian views make public justification into a 'spare wheel'; this is a 'victory by stipulation'; we have 'definitional fiat' from start to finish—there are also more charitable ways of understanding and describing what is going on. In particular, I view the idea of public justification, like the idea of the

---

murder and racism is in fact based on an 'on-balance' judgement. (See *The Order of Public Reason*, pp. 482–3.) More generally, Gaus might be an important exception to my claim that both proponents and critics of public reason agree that respect does not require acceptability to the unreasonable. He suggests that the imposition of laws against murder on a murderer is permissible but still pro tanto disrespectful: '*in extremis* we must act as we must' but when enforcing these laws on a murderer 'we do not treat him as a free and equal moral reasoner'. (See Gaus, G., 'The Good, the Bad, and the Ugly: Three Agent-Type Challenges to *The Order of Public Reason*', *Philosophical Studies* 170 (2014), p. 574.) He describes these as cases in which 'we justifiably coerce [yet] do so with a certain regret'. (See Gaus, G., *The Order of Public Reason*, p. 483.) It is not possible to offer a full analysis and evaluation of Gaus's general conception of respect; suffice it to say that this conception is rooted in a broader account of the role of the reactive attitudes in social life, and I express doubts about that account elsewhere. See Tahzib, C., 'Do the Reactive Attitudes Justify Public Reason?'.

[116] Gaus, G., 'A Tale of Two Sets', p. 310; Vallier, K., 'On Jonathan Quong's Sectarian Political Liberalism', p. 190. See also Van Schoelandt, C., 'Justification, Coercion, and the Place of Public Reason', pp. 1037–41

original position, essentially as a heuristic device—a framework for setting out in an attractive and systematic way certain basic thoughts and commitments, and not something that was ever expected to exist, let alone 'do moral work', at the morally fundamental level. Public justification is meant to model or represent certain deep normative commitments, and thus to say that some policy is justified to all reasonable persons is no more, and no less, than to say that this policy can be derived from the fundamental idea of society as a fair striving for human flourishing between free and equal persons and the values implicit within it. Since derivations in political philosophy, unlike those in mathematics, are not an exact science, the point of introducing the constituency move is to make things as vivid and pellucid as possible. So, while strictly speaking dispensable, the process of considering whether a given policy could be reasonably rejected helps us to focus intuitions, to organize ideas and to make more transparent derivations and extrapolations. In this sense, my response to this redundancy objection parallels my response to the redundancy objection considered in Section 4.6.

Often, public reason liberals seem to want more than this from the public justification principle. Indeed, public reason liberals often speak as if the principle of public justification is a fundamental principle of political morality. Macedo trumpets public justification as being the 'moral lodestar of liberalism' and Ackerman refers to it as 'the organizing principle of liberal thought'.[117] Nozick even identifies something in this vicinity as being a 'candidate for a fundamental self-subsuming principle of morality'.[118]

However, it is difficult to see how the public justification principle could possibly be fundamental in this way because it involves justification to a *normatively* defined constituency: the constituency of reasonable citizens. This constituency might be defined in terms of acceptance of certain substantive moral values (such as freedom, equality and fairness, or moral, intellectual and artistic excellence) or in terms of acceptance of a certain conception of society (such as society as a fair system of social cooperation between free and equal persons, or society as a fair striving for human flourishing between free and equal persons). But, irrespective of the specifics, it is *those* values and conceptions that do fundamental 'moral work' and are more likely candidates for moral lodestars. Public justification is just a way of representing or modelling those values and conceptions in an attractive and intuitive way.[119]

---

[117] Macedo, S., *Liberal Virtues* (Oxford: Clarendon Press, 1990), p. 78; Ackerman, B., *Social Justice in the Liberal State*, p. 10.

[118] Nozick, R., *Philosophical Explanations* (Oxford: Clarendon Press, 1981), p. 541.

[119] Of course, public reason liberals could try to define the justificatory constituency in non-normative terms. But then it would be mysterious why justification to that constituency could *matter* in the way that public reason liberals say it does. Gaus comes closest to offering a non-normative definition of the justificatory constituency. See *The Order of Public Reason*. I critique Gaus's view in Tahzib, C., 'Do the Reactive Attitudes Justify Public Reason?'.

There is a parallel here with the harm principle. Many liberals speak as if the harm principle is a fundamental principle of liberal political morality—as if the harm principle plays a more or less fundamental role within the liberal order of explanation. But, again, it is difficult to see how the harm principle could possibly function in this way because it makes essential reference to a normative notion, namely harm. After all, on a plausible view what is 'harmful' just is a matter of what violates positive and negative duties.[120] Mill, for instance, says that an action is harmful if it 'violate[s] a distinct and assignable obligation to any other person or persons'.[121] For Mill, then, the justification for the state's inference with an individual's course of action cannot ultimately consist in facts about harmfulness because facts about harmfulness are themselves parasitic on prior facts about what duties we owe to others. Of course, once these duties to others have been established, we can choose to speak primarily in terms of harm—perhaps because, as Mill may have thought, the language of harm provides a memorable or systematic or otherwise useful language for representing those claims about our duties to others. But this should not mislead us into thinking that the harm principle itself plays a fundamental explanatory role within the justificatory structure of liberalism.

In short, once we recognize the level of fundamentality at which the public justification principle is most plausibly thought to operate, the claim that more sectarian views have a greater tendency towards redundancy ceases to be surprising or troubling: it is just a pejorative way of saying that sectarian public reason views do not treat public justification as a fundamental principle of political morality and instead treat it, rather like the harm principle, as a mid-level principle that represents more basic commitments in a vivid or systematic way.

7.7 An Overly Sectarian Definition of Reasonableness?

In Section 7.6, I defended the perfectionist definition of reasonableness against the charge that it is more sectarian than the anti-perfectionist definition of reasonableness by arguing that there is no good reason for thinking that more sectarian definitions of reasonableness are necessarily in one respect worse than less sectarian definitions of reasonableness. But this does not mean that the perfectionist definition is in the clear with respect to sectarianism. After all, the Anti-Sectarian Desideratum is not the only way in which the broader idea of anti-sectarianism can be interpreted and factored into the theory of public reason. In particular, even if each additional increment of anti-sectarianism is not always better, it might be that anti-sectarianism functions as a threshold or constraint of some kind on a public

---

[120] As with attempts to define the justificatory constituency in non-normative terms, there have been attempts to define harm in non-normative terms. But, for the reasons given in Section 10.3, these also do not strike me as promising.

[121] Mill, J. S., *On Liberty* (London: Penguin, 1985), p. 148.

244 A PERFECTIONIST THEORY OF JUSTICE

reason view. Indeed, as I hinted at in Section 7.6.2, I am sympathetic to this way of understanding the role of anti-sectarianism within the theory of public reason. So even if the perfectionist definition of reasonableness is not to be rejected because it is *more* sectarian than the anti-perfectionist definition, perhaps it nonetheless ought to be rejected because it is *overly* or *excessively* sectarian.[122]

Consider a view that we can call 'Opus Dei: Political Not Metaphysical', according to which the state can only act on the basis of values that reasonable citizens affirm, where reasonableness is conditional on acceptance of Opus Dei doctrine. This view would clearly be defective as a public reason view. And one important reason for this has to do with its sectarianism—not because it is *more* sectarian than other views but because it is *too* sectarian. Given that only a tiny fraction of the actual constituency of citizens in contemporary democratic societies subscribes to Opus Dei, this view violates some kind of constraint on the level of sectarianism that a public reason view can have. Its account of what constitutes a reasonable disagreement is insufficiently inclusive and so it loses contact with the folk concept of reasonable disagreement and with the basic motivations of the public reason project.

In this sense, when Quong strikingly states that, on his view, 'the justification of liberal principles at no point depends on the beliefs of real people'—a statement that critics have pounced on as indicating his abandonment of public reason

---

[122] There is yet a third way to run a sectarianism-style objection to the perfectionist definition of reasonableness. This rendition holds that *within some bounds* each additional increment of anti-sectarianism is pro tanto good. These bounds are designed to exclude citizens with dangerously extreme views, such as racists, psychopaths and murderers. So the anti-perfectionist's argument would be neither 'the anti-perfectionist justificatory constituency is less sectarian than, and thus superior to, the perfectionist constituency' (as per the argument considered in Section 7.6) nor 'the anti-perfectionist constituency meets the threshold for anti-sectarianism, and is thus superior to the perfectionist constituency, which does not meet this threshold' (as per the argument considered in this section) but rather 'we are within the bounds that less sectarianism is better, and the anti-perfectionist justificatory constituency is less sectarian than, and thus superior to, the perfectionist constituency'. (I thank an anonymous reviewer for suggesting this possibility.) However, this argument will face the same general problem faced by the original Anti-Sectarian Desideratum in Section 7.6: namely, that we should not be trying to make the constituency accommodate more of the views of actual citizens (even within certain bounds) unless we have independent reasons for thinking that the views of those citizens ought to be accorded normative authority. The imposition of bounds makes this less dramatic—since it eliminates the cases of racists, murderers and psychopaths that were used to illustrate this problem in a vivid way—but it does not make the theoretical problem go away. To see this, suppose that we have imposed some bounds that screen off citizens with dangerously extreme views. Now consider two rival justificatory constituencies within these bounds. These constituencies are the same except for the fact that the first constituency (C_1) defines reasonableness in a way that includes libertarians and the second constituency (C_2) defines reasonableness in a way that excludes libertarians. So C_1 is less sectarian than C_2 because it includes all the citizens in C_2 plus more. Is C_1 thereby better in one respect? It is difficult to see why, unless we have independent reasons to think that libertarians *ought* to be deemed reasonable and *ought* to shape the content of social justice. Indeed, it may well be pro tanto bad, rather than pro tanto good, to give libertarians a veto. This point generalizes to the choice between other justificatory constituencies within these bounds, including the choice between the anti-perfectionist and perfectionist constituencies. Even within certain bounds, then, what public reason theorists should be aiming for is the *right* account of reasonableness, not the least sectarian account of reasonableness per se.

liberalism's distinctively interpersonal form of justification in favour of comprehensive liberalism's impersonal form of justification[123]—he perhaps goes too far, or puts things in unnecessarily and misleadingly strong terms.[124] The 'beliefs of real people' constitute the folk concept of reasonable disagreement, and this folk concept in turn constrains the technical or theoretical concept of reasonable disagreement. As the case of 'Opus Dei: Political Not Metaphysical' demonstrates, a public reason view must include *enough* of the beliefs of real people on pain of excessive sectarianism. As such, the justification of liberal principles does depend on the beliefs of real people, albeit in a mediated and indirect way. In other words, it is not that there is some clearly defined notion of 'reasonable disagreement' that can be specified completely independently of facts about what real people believe. The social distribution of views is not completely irrelevant to how we understand what is reasonable. Those facts constitute general background conditions that inform and constrain our theorizing about reasonable disagreement, even if not in the exact way dictated by the Anti-Sectarian Desideratum.[125]

The second way, then, of running a sectarianism-based objection to the perfectionist definition of reasonableness is by analogy to excessively sectarian views such as 'Opus Dei: Political Not Metaphysical'. Isn't the perfectionist definition of reasonableness—with its requirement that citizens accept not only the abstract perfectionist values of moral, intellectual and artistic excellence but also an interpretation of these values that has some particular kind of shape or content—likewise too sectarian? Doesn't it violate some constraint on the level of sectarianism that a public reason view can have? Isn't its account of what constitutes a reasonable disagreement insufficiently inclusive and thereby at risk of losing contact with the folk concept of reasonable disagreement and with the basic motivations of the public reason project?

An objection along these lines to the perfectionist definition of reasonableness is certainly possible. But there is, intuitively, an importance difference between the level of sectarianism of the perfectionist definition of reasonableness and the level of sectarianism of 'Opus Dei: Political Not Metaphysical'. Whereas it is obvious that the latter denies the very existence of reasonable disagreement, it is not obvious that the former does. So, to deploy this sort of objection in a persuasive way, one would need to answer a number of very difficult questions. Among these are the following: what makes a definition of reasonableness 'too' sectarian? How sectarian is too sectarian? At what point, that is, is there is an

---

[123] See Van Schoelandt, C., 'Justification, Coercion, and the Place of Public Reason', pp. 1037–41.

[124] Quong, J., *Liberalism Without Perfection*, p. 144. Similarly, Quong states at several points that reasonable disagreement is not 'a fact about the world, like scarce resources, to which liberal theory must accommodate itself' but rather is a construct of liberal theory (ibid., p. 142; see also pp. 6, 138, 139). But I think reasonable disagreement is better regarded as *both* a fact about the world *and* a construct of liberal theory, in the sense I go on to explain in the main text.

[125] I thank an anonymous reviewer for helping me to formulate this point.

insufficiently close resemblance between a public reason view's constituency of reasonable citizens and the actual constituency of citizens in contemporary democratic societies? Must the idealized constituency citizens include 50 per cent of the actual constituency? 75 per cent? More? How can this point be specified in a principled and non-arbitrary way? What is the deeper rationale for this specification of the anti-sectarian constraint as opposed to some alternative possible specification? And where is the empirical evidence that the perfectionist justificatory constituency fails to satisfy this constraint, whereas the anti-perfectionist justificatory constituency does satisfy it?

Needless to say, the answer to these queries cannot be that a definition of reasonableness counts as 'too' sectarian whenever it includes acceptance of claims about human flourishing, since at this point in the dialectic that would flatly beg the question against the proponent of perfectionist public reason. While it is not impossible for an anti-perfectionist liberal to non-question-beggingly answer these queries, none has yet come close to doing so. Allegations of sectarianism have not hitherto been made with a high degree of precision. At least for the time being, then, it is difficult to see what principled grounds there are for saying that the perfectionist definition of reasonableness is overly sectarian. So even if there are limits to how much normative content can be baked into the definition of reasonableness while remaining true to the spirit of the public reason project and its underlying aim of avoiding excessive sectarianism, it is difficult to see why these limits are necessarily coextensive with anti-perfectionism, in the way that would be required to deploy a public-justification-based objection to perfectionism.

In closing, let me comment on the wider significance of the lines of argument developed in this chapter. Beyond its relevance to the debate over the legitimacy of perfectionist laws and policies, the idea of 'perfectionist public reason' merits consideration because it opens up independently interesting theoretical questions about the flexibility and generalizability of the public justification framework. Perfectionist public reason can, I believe, serve as a foil to help us sharpen our understanding of various big-picture questions about public justification, including: what is fundamentally at stake in the debate between defenders and critics of public justification? Is the disagreement largely presentational, one about the best way to express or represent certain first-order political commitments? Or is it about those first-order commitments themselves? If the debate is about first-order commitments, such as a commitment to taking reasonable disagreement seriously or a commitment to avoiding sectarianism, what exactly do these commitments amount to? And if the debate is largely presentational, when is public justification an apt or suitable framework for representing political commitments and when is it not?

8

Freedom

Whereas political liberals are likely to object to perfectionism on the grounds that judgements about human flourishing are too controversial to play a significant role in politics, comprehensive liberals are likely to object to perfectionism on the grounds that perfectionist laws and policies are unduly restrictive of freedom. As we saw in Chapter 1, comprehensive liberals such as Immanuel Kant, John Stuart Mill and Ronald Dworkin have mounted influential arguments against perfectionism based on the value of freedom or on some value in this vicinity, such as autonomy, individuality, independence, personal sovereignty or self-ownership.

In this chapter, I seek to defend perfectionism against several different renditions of the objection that it fails to give the claims of liberty their due. Since these renditions are somewhat miscellaneous, it is helpful at the outset to articulate explicitly the general ideal of freedom that is embedded in the perfectionist conception of social justice articulated in Part II (Section 8.1). Doing this serves to illustrate the strong liberal credentials of perfectionist justice and provides a principled basis for responding to many of the more specific renditions of the charge that perfectionism is unduly restrictive of freedom. I then consider and reject four freedom-based arguments against perfectionism, contending that perfectionist justice is compatible with the conceptions of freedom upon which these arguments are premised (Section 8.2). Admittedly, however, there are some conceptions of freedom with which perfectionist justice is incompatible, notably the libertarian conception of freedom as full self-ownership. But as I go on to argue (in Section 8.3), the libertarian conception of freedom is not in any case independently plausible or attractive. So the fact perfectionist justice conflicts with libertarian full self-ownership should come as no embarrassment to the perfectionist. Finally, I defend (in Section 8.4) perfectionist justice against a more pragmatic way of running the freedom-based objection: namely that, however hospitable to freedom perfectionism is *in theory*, any attempt to implement perfectionism *in practice* would risk the abuse of power and the violation of individual liberties by incompetent, corrupt or overzealous state officials, and so common sense dictates taking ideals of human flourishing off the political agenda as a kind of prophylactic measure.

A Perfectionist Theory of Justice. Collis Tahzib, Oxford University Press.
© Collis Tahzib (2022). DOI: 10.1093/oso/9780192847119.003.0009

8.1 The Place of Freedom Within Perfectionist Justice

I have not classified the perfectionist conception of justice as a species of 'liberal perfectionism'. The main reason for this is that the term 'liberal perfectionism' is normally used to refer to views that hold that (a) the state should promote the good life, that (b) autonomy is a central constituent of the good life and thus that (c) the state should promote autonomous lives.[1] This kind of view is closely associated with Joseph Raz and Steven Wall.[2] By contrast, and contra (b), the conception of human flourishing that I favour does not give autonomy 'pride of place' or 'a special standing' (in Wall's phrases) and emphasizes instead the values of moral, intellectual and artistic excellence.[3]

Nonetheless, the perfectionist conception of justice has strong liberal credentials. In view of the significance it accords to individual liberty, it would not be at all inapt to describe this conception as a form of liberal perfectionism. In particular, and as explained in Chapter 4, perfectionist justice incorporates the equal basic liberties principle, according to which each person has the same indefeasible claim to a fully adequate scheme of equal basic liberties compatible with the same scheme of liberties for all. These basic liberties include the familiar liberal rights and freedoms, such as freedom of thought and conscience, freedom of expression, freedom of association, the right to privacy and the right to bodily integrity. Perfectionist justice also incorporates the fair equality of opportunity principle, according to which social and economic inequalities are to be attached to offices and positions open to all under conditions of fair equality of opportunity. This principle helps to ensure that liberties do not remain merely formal; rather, citizens are guaranteed the means necessary to make effective use of their liberties. Importantly, perfectionist justice assigns these two principles lexical priority over the principle of perfection, which calls for the establishment of conditions conducive to flourishing ways of life. Prior principles of justice thus far-reachingly constrain what can be done in the name of promoting human flourishing. In these ways, the claims of freedom are enshrined within the fundamentals of this perfectionist conception

---

[1] See, for example, Wall, S., *Liberalism, Perfectionism and Restraint* (Cambridge: Cambridge University Press, 1998), p. 2 n. 3.

[2] See Raz, J., *The Morality of Freedom* (Oxford: Oxford University Press, 1986), especially ch. 14; Wall, S., *Liberalism, Perfectionism and Restraint*, especially ch. 6.

[3] See Wall, S., *Liberalism, Perfectionism and Restraint*, pp. 125, 162. One way of seeing why autonomy is not privileged is to consider again Feldman's 'crib test' heuristic, whereby one imagines gazing lovingly into the crib of one's newborn child and being filled with hopes for how her life might turn out. (See Feldman, F., *Pleasure and the Good Life: Concerning the Nature, Varieties and Plausibility of Hedonism* (Oxford: Oxford University Press, 2004), pp. 9–10; see also Section 5.5.) While it is certainly plausible that as one looks down on one's child one would hope that she becomes autonomous, how plausible is it that this would be one's exclusive or predominant hope? Mightn't other hopes— for instance, that she turns out to take enjoyment in moral, intellectual and artistic excellence—figure just as prominently, if not even more prominently, in one's thoughts? The provisional conception thus offers, I believe, a closer-to-the-ground view of what it means to flourish than that given by liberal perfectionists.

of justice. And none of this should come as any surprise, since the perfectionist principles of justice are meant to be expressive of a normative ideal of society as a striving for human flourishing on fair terms between citizens conceived of as *free* and *equal*.

This background picture of the place of freedom within perfectionist justice is crucial to understanding its approach to trade-offs between liberty and excellence. Like any political theory, perfectionist justice prescribes non-trivial restrictions on individual freedom. In particular, perfectionist justice requires the establishment and maintenance of social conditions that are promotive of and conducive to morally, intellectually and artistically excellent ways of life—and this will clearly restrict the non-basic liberties of citizens in certain ways. I have explored some of the potential practical implications of perfectionist justice in Chapter 6, but in general perfectionist law and public policy can be thought of as proceeding along two tracks: the encouragement of the worthy and the discouragement of the unworthy. In terms of the encouragement of the worthy, the perfectionist state might offer generous subsidies for museums, art galleries and adult education classes. This will clearly impinge on the freedom of citizens, who will be required on pain of punishment to pay taxes to fund these subsidies. In terms of the discouragement of the unworthy, the perfectionist state might disincentivize, regulate and perhaps even prohibit activities such as gambling and the use of recreational drugs. This, too, will clearly impinge on the freedom of citizens, who will find it more difficult or expensive (and in some cases altogether impossible) to engage in these pursuits. Both in its encouragement of the worthy and its discouragement of the unworthy, then, the perfectionist state clearly restricts or diminishes the freedom of its citizens.

These restrictions of freedom, however, are moderate and are heavily constrained by lexically prior principles of justice. They involve restrictions only of non-basic liberties. And they use only minimal forms of coercion, such as the coercion involved in the collection of taxes. Citizens are not forced into any highly specific ways of life. So moderate perfectionist laws and policies do not in any straightforward sense threaten the status of citizens as free persons. As Raz puts it, a moderate perfectionist state is a far cry from 'the threatening popular image of imprisoning people who follow their religion, express their views in public, grow long hair, or consume harmless drugs'.[4] Perfectionist justice seems in this way to provide sufficient room for freedom. The kinds of concrete laws and public policies that it recommends, such as those discussed in Chapter 6, seem to trade off liberty and excellence in a reasonable way. So while perfectionist justice is of course restrictive of freedom, it is not *unduly* restrictive of freedom.

This perfectionist political theory thus differs significantly from the theories championed by previous perfectionists. Patrick Devlin, for instance, is well known

---

[4] Raz, J., *The Morality of Freedom*, p. 161.

250 A PERFECTIONIST THEORY OF JUSTICE

for defending a particularly illiberal form of perfectionism.[5] On his view, 'it is not possible to set theoretical limits to the power of the state to legislate against immorality'.[6] In arguing in this way, Devlin appears to deny the existence of liberal rights, at least at the level of philosophical principle, if not at the level of political practice. Other perfectionists, despite disagreeing in important ways with Devlin's specific views about what constitutes 'immorality', nonetheless appear to agree with his denial of liberal rights at the level of philosophical principle. Thomas Hurka, for instance, states that he 'do[es] not see how we can expect [perfectionist] theory to provide anything more than an *in-practice* guarantee of liberal institutions'.[7] And even those perfectionists who do endorse liberal rights at the level of philosophical principle have not systematically explored how exactly these rights are to constrain perfectionist state action. As mentioned in the Introduction, there is little exploration of how liberal principles relate to perfectionist principles and whether this relationship might be illuminated by, say, the idea of lexical priority. George Sher, for instance, rightly explains that a 'government can both acknowledge many substantive rights and still leave much latitude for nonneutral legislation'; but he says little about the principles by reference to which we should determine in any given case whether a putative piece of perfectionist legislation is in breach of a liberal right.[8]

Unlike these other perfectionist theories, perfectionist justice explicitly holds that the equal basic liberties principle and the fair equality of opportunity principle specify a scheme of rights and liberties that have lexical priority over other considerations and thus function as theoretical limits on the power of the state to promote the enjoyment of moral, intellectual and artistic excellence through perfectionist law and public policy. In this way, perfectionist justice still leaves ample room for citizens to be authors of their own lives, and so is fully compatible with a wide range of conceptions of freedom, as we shall see in Section 8.2.

8.2 Four Freedom-Based Objections Defused

In this section, I consider in turn four objections to perfectionism—respectively from John Stuart Mill, Ronald Dworkin, Matthew Kramer and Jonathan Quong—all of which are united by an emphasis on some broad idea of freedom. I will argue that, whatever the merits of these arguments against other perfectionist

[5] See Devlin, P., *The Enforcement of Morals* (Oxford: Oxford University Press, 1970).

[6] Ibid., p. 12.

[7] Hurka, T., 'Critical Notice of Vinit Haksar, *Equality, Liberty and Perfectionism*', *Canadian Journal of Philosophy* 13 (1983), p. 469 (emphasis added). See also Hurka's comments on the distinction between 'pure' and 'impure' perfectionism in his *Perfectionism* (Oxford: Oxford University Press, 1993), pp. 6, 27–8, 32, 55, 75, 77–8, 83, 183, 190–1.

[8] Sher, G., *Beyond Neutrality: Perfectionism and Politics* (Cambridge: Cambridge University Press, 1997), p. 7.

FREEDOM 251

theories, they do not tell against the perfectionist conception of social justice articulated in Part II, thus illustrating the compatibility of perfectionist justice with a wide range of conceptions of freedom.[9]

Consider, in the first instance, Mill's argument from the value of individuality to anti-perfectionism, as discussed in Section 1.3. Recall that Mill identifies 'the free development of individuality' as 'one of the leading essentials of well-being'.[10] He praises 'individual spontaneity', 'peculiarity of taste' and 'eccentricity in conduct'.[11] He contends that 'there should be different experiments of living' and that 'the worth of different modes of life should be proved practically'.[12] Individuality is 'antagonistic to the sway of custom', which tends to produce a 'pinched and hidebound type of human character'.[13] And he states that 'human nature is not a machine to be built after a model, and set to do exactly the work prescribed for it, but a tree, which requires to grow and develop itself on all sides, according to the tendency of the inward forces which make it a living thing'.[14]

The important point to note about Mill's argument here is that little in what he says is threatened by perfectionist justice. Perhaps more extreme and coercive forms of perfectionism, such as that defended in the past by Devlin, would undermine Mill's ideal of individuality. If the law was used without limits to criminalize certain ways of life, then this might plausibly compromise the free development of individuality and the ability of citizens to conduct experiments of living. But it is difficult to see how the more moderate sorts of perfectionist laws and public policies such as those discussed in Chapter 6 are incompatible with Millian individuality. In a society regulated by the perfectionist principles of justice, citizens would still have the space necessary for individual spontaneity, peculiarity of taste and eccentricity in conduct. The free development of individuality would be safeguarded. Moderate perfectionist policies such as state support for the arts and sin taxes on gambling would not plausibly undermine the ability of citizens to conduct experiments in living, or produce a pinched and hidebound type of human character, or inhibit the healthily organic growth and development of individuals. Indeed, if anything, a perfectionist state may well *increase* the possibilities for individuality and experimentation by sponsoring valuable activities and ways of life that might otherwise have disappeared if their fate were left to the rigours of the market within an anti-perfectionist liberal state. In these ways, perfectionist justice appears to leave the Millian ideal of individuality substantially intact.

---

[9] For defences of perfectionism against other freedom-based objections, see, for example, Sher, G., *Beyond Neutrality*, chs 3 and 4; Wall, S., *Liberalism, Perfectionism and Restraint*, ch. 8; Wall, S., 'Moral Environmentalism', in C. Coons and M. Weber (eds), *Paternalism: Theory and Practice* (Cambridge: Cambridge University Press, 2013), pp. 93–114.

[10] Mill, J. S., *On Liberty* (London: Penguin Books, 1985), p. 120.

[11] Ibid., pp. 120, 126.

[12] Ibid., p. 120.

[13] Ibid., pp. 126, 136.

[14] Ibid., p. 123.

252   A PERFECTIONIST THEORY OF JUSTICE

Consider, next, Dworkin's argument from the challenge model of ethics to anti-perfectionism, as discussed in Section 1.4. Recall that, according to the challenge model, 'the value of a good life lies in the inherent value of a skillful performance of living'.[15] The challenge model of ethics says that 'living a life is itself a performance that demands skill, that it is the most comprehensive and important challenge we face, and that our critical interests consist in the achievements, events, and experiences that mean that we have met the challenge well'.[16] The challenge model rules out state perfectionism, says Dworkin, because it 'rejects its root assumption: that a person's life can be improved just by forcing him into some act or abstinence he thinks valueless'.[17] 'Someone who accepts the challenge model might well think that religious devotion is an essential part of how human beings should respond to their place in the universe, and therefore that devotion is part of living well'.[18] 'But', says Dworkin, 'he cannot think that involuntary religious observance, prayer in the shadow of the rack, has any ethical value'.[19]

As before, Dworkin's argument may tell against a more extreme and illiberal form of perfectionism, such as that defended by Devlin, which countenances the use of the criminal law in order to 'force' people into one or another way of life. But it is much less clear why the challenge model is incompatible with the sorts of moderate perfectionist policies discussed in Chapter 6, such as informative and educational public broadcasting and public funding of the arts. Here the argument is much less persuasive because no one is being made to do anything 'in the shadow of the rack' and because plenty of options remain for citizens to select between. Is it really plausible to say that life would be rendered uninteresting and unchallenging, or even appreciably *less* interesting and *less* challenging, if subsidies were provided to the arts or if sin taxes were levied on gambling? In what sense is someone who lives in a society regulated by the perfectionist principles of justice thereby deprived of the opportunity to engage in a skilful performance of living by responding admirably to the complex challenges of life? Once again, then, perfectionist justice appears to leave intact much if not all of Dworkin's challenge model of ethics.[20]

---

[15] Dworkin, R., 'Foundations of Liberal Equality', in S. Darwall (ed.), *Equal Freedom: Selected Tanner Lectures on Human Values* (Ann Arbor, MI: University of Michigan Press, 1995), p. 241.

[16] Ibid.

[17] Ibid., p. 265.

[18] Ibid.

[19] Ibid.

[20] In fairness, Dworkin does offer an argument against more moderate kinds of perfectionism: namely, that 'a challenge cannot be more interesting, or in any other way a more valuable challenge to face, when it has been narrowed, simplified, and bowdlerized by others [i.e. perfectionist state officials] in advance' (ibid., p. 271; see also Section 1.4). But an obvious objection here is that Dworkin's language is exaggerated or rhetorical. Again, we can ask: even if *certain* extreme forms of perfectionism would render the challenge of life 'narrowed, simplified, and bowdlerized', how persuasive a description is this of the effects of *moderate* perfectionist policies, such as state support for the arts and sin taxes on gambling, that leave sufficiently many options for citizens to choose between? So, while Dworkin is free to say that moderate perfectionist policies 'bowdlerize' the challenge of life in the *descriptive* sense

FREEDOM 253

Consider, thirdly, Kramer's recent argument that proponents of perfectionism are 'prone to obscure or neglect the value of freedom'.[21] One argument that perfectionists sometimes make is that since (a) freedom is only valuable when it is used in the pursuit of worthwhile ends and activities, and since (b) the perfectionist state restricts the freedom of citizens to pursue ends and activities that are worthless, it follows that (c) the perfectionist state's restrictions on the freedom of citizens are not morally problematic. As Raz puts this point, 'since autonomy is valuable only if it is directed at the good it supplies no reason to provide, nor any reason to protect, worthless let alone bad options'.[22] Kramer rejects this argument on the grounds that premise (a) is false. For Kramer, freedom has 'content-independent value'. That is to say, the freedom to φ is valuable even when φ-ing is not itself valuable.

Kramer explains that there are three kinds of content-independent value ascribable to freedom: 'instrumental', 'intrinsic' and 'constitutive' content-independent value.[23] Being free to φ has *instrumental* content-independent value because we are fallible and so cannot rule out coming to want to φ in the future. Being free to φ has *intrinsic* content-independent value because our ability to imprint our will upon the world is a function of how many options we decline: if Amy chooses to ψ rather than to φ, she 'impresse[s] her will on the world more', is 'more expansively an agent' and acts with more 'declinatory force' than if she merely chooses to ψ without having had φ as an option to decline, even if φ-ing is a worthless activity that Amy would not in any case have contemplated pursuing.[24] And being free to φ has *constitutive* content-independent value because it is an essential ingredient of autonomy. In these three ways, having the freedom to engage in activities that the perfectionist state deems worthless may nonetheless be of great importance.

Unlike Raz's perfectionist theory, however, perfectionist justice is not committed to the claim that freedom is only valuable when it is used in the pursuit of worthwhile ends and activities. That premise forms no part of the justification of

---

of reducing the absolute number of available choices, this does little to show that moderate perfectionist policies bowdlerize the challenge of life *in any morally significant sense*. For this point, see Neal, P., 'Dworkin on the Foundations of Liberal Equality', pp. 222–3.

[21] Kramer, M., *Liberalism with Excellence* (Oxford: Oxford University Press, 2017), ch. 5, at p. 193. Strictly speaking, Kramer is opposed to what he calls 'edificatory perfectionism', rather than to perfectionism per se, since he defends a form of perfectionism that he refers to as 'aspirational perfectionism', as explained in Section 6.6.4. But I drop the qualifier 'edificatory', since edificatory perfectionism is the only form of perfectionism under consideration here.

[22] Raz, J., *The Morality of Freedom*, p. 411.

[23] Here Kramer follows Carter, I., *A Measure of Freedom* (Oxford: Oxford University Press, 1999), ch. 2. Kramer also argues that freedom has deontological value and thus that the perfectionist state's restrictions on the freedom of citizens are manifestations of disrespect (see Kramer, M., *Liberalism with Excellence*, pp. 200–1, 211–12, 217, 223, 231, 235); I consider this kind of objection to perfectionism in Chapter 9.

[24] This case originally comes from Hurka: see Hurka, T., 'Why Value Autonomy?', *Social Theory and Practice* 13 (1987), pp. 366–7. The locution of being 'more expansively an agent' is from Hurka (p. 366); the other two locutions in this sentence are from Kramer (*Liberalism with Excellence*, pp. 204–5).

perfectionist politics given in Part II. What renders freedom-restricting perfectionist laws and public policies morally justified is not any specific thesis about the conditions under which freedom is valuable, but rather the fact that these policies flow from principles that would be chosen in a suitably specified contractual scenario and that are as such expressive of the idea of society as a fair striving for human flourishing between free and equal citizens. In this sense, Kramer's contention that freedom has instrumental, intrinsic and constitutive forms of content-independent value is perfectly compatible with perfectionist justice.

What perfectionist justice contends is simply that the three forms of content-independent value ascribable to freedom that Kramer identifies are insufficiently *weighty* to justify a blanket prohibition on perfectionist laws and policies.[25] They do not block all trade-offs between freedom and edification. In this regard, Kramer does concede that the content-independent value of freedom is not 'invariably supreme in the sense that it *always* surpasses the value of every other desideratum with which it might compete'.[26] But can we be confident that the content-independent value of freedom will even *generally* (let alone always) surpass the value of competing desiderata, such as the edification produced by perfectionist policies? One reason to doubt this is that the properties that Kramer cites—such as acting with more or less 'declinatory force'—can appear quite intricate and esoteric. Another is that, for all Kramer has said, the content-independent value of freedom may well exhibit diminishing marginal value, and so when an agent already has an adequate range of options the added value of being free to φ (when φ-ing is not itself valuable) may be only very slight. It thus remains unclear why the content-independent value ascribable to freedom is sufficiently weighty to ground anything approaching a generally overriding prohibition on perfectionist laws and public policies.

Fourth and finally, consider Quong's argument that 'perfectionist subsidies are a form of autonomy intrusion'.[27] Quong states this argument as follows:

> The choice for citizens is between having the money to spend themselves, or having the government take it from them and then spend it on subsidizing opera tickets. Since the latter option simply reduces what you can do with your resources, it would be irrational to prefer it ... We must thus assume ... that citizens would prefer the status quo (keep their resources) over the post-subsidy situation where the government taxes them and uses those funds to subsidize opera. By putting citizens in the post-subsidy situation, the government thus does attempt

---

[25] For similar doubts about the weightiness of the content-independent value of freedom, see Sher, G., 'Confessions of a Quidnunc', *The American Journal of Jurisprudence* 63 (2018), pp. 50–3; Billingham, P. and Taylor, A., 'Liberal Perfectionism, Moral Integrity, and Self-Respect', *The American Journal of Jurisprudence* 63 (2018), pp. 66–7.

[26] Kramer, M., *Liberalism with Excellence*, p. 204 (emphasis added).

[27] Quong, J., *Liberalism Without Perfection* (Oxford: Oxford University Press, 2011), ch. 2, at p. 65.

FREEDOM   255

to subject the will of citizens to its own perfectionist judgement. Perfectionist sub-sidies are not like the offers one person might make to another: they involve the government taking funds from citizens in order to restrict the ways in which citizens can spend those resources ... Perfectionist subsidies are a form of autonomy intrusion since, under normal conditions, they represent the government placing citizens in a choice situation in which they would not have chosen to place themselves, and so citizens' subsequent choices would be ... not fully their own: they represent an attempt to subject citizens to the will of the perfectionist state.[28]

However, an important problem with this argument against perfectionist subsidies is that one could imagine someone running the same line of argument against *any* state subsidy, including those that anti-perfectionist liberals typically endorse. Consider subsidies for public education. Mightn't some citizens prefer the status quo (in which they keep their resources) over the post-subsidy situation (in which the government taxes them and uses those funds to subsidize education)? By putting citizens in the post-subsidy situation, doesn't the state subject the will of citizens to its own *liberal* judgement? In this way, Quong's argument against perfectionism threatens to pave a road to libertarianism.

Here Quong would no doubt reply that being forced to pay taxes towards public education is not a form of autonomy intrusion because we are under a *duty of justice* to contribute towards the provision of public education. What threatens the autonomy of citizens, in other words, is not the mere fact that a tax-funded subsidy puts some citizens in a post-subsidy choice situation that they disprefer relative to a pre-subsidy situation in which the resources remain with the individual citizens to spend as they see fit. Rather, what threatens the autonomy of citizens is that a tax-funded subsidy puts some citizens in a post-subsidy choice situation that they disprefer relative (as Quong elsewhere puts it) to a *'morally justified status quo'*—a morally justified pre-subsidy situation in which the resources remain with the individual citizens to spend as they see fit.[29]

But when this feature of Quong's argument—that is, its presupposition of a specific 'morally justified status quo'—is brought to the fore, its powerlessness against perfectionist justice becomes clear. After all, a defender of perfectionist justice will want to say about perfectionist policies what Quong presumably wants to say about policies such as public education. For such perfectionists, we are under a duty of justice to contribute towards the provision of amenities like opera that incline citizens towards flourishing ways of life. Since the provision of such amenities is entailed by the perfectionist principles of justice—since, in other words, the failure to provide such amenities would be inconsistent with the perfectionist conception

[28] Ibid., pp. 65–6.
[29] Ibid., p. 66 (emphasis added).

of society as a fair striving for human flourishing between free and equal persons—citizens never had any right in the first place to the money that the perfectionist state takes from them and uses to subsidize these amenities. So the perfectionist state does not place citizens in a situation that they rationally disprefer relative to a morally justified status quo, since in the absence of perfectionist policies the status quo is not morally justified.

Another way of putting this is that Quong's argument begs the question against perfectionist justice by assuming that a pre-subsidy situation in which citizens do not contribute towards perfectionist policies is morally justified.[30] Yet whether or not a situation without perfectionist policies is morally justified is precisely what is at stake in the debate between perfectionists and anti-perfectionists, and so an affirmative (or negative) answer to this question is not something that can be assumed without supporting argumentation. Quong's freedom-based argument thus appears to presuppose the truth of anti-perfectionist liberalism rather than calling forth independent considerations or intuitions that could be expected to sway someone who was not antecedently convinced of anti-perfectionist liberalism.

In brief, various freedom-based objections to perfectionism, while possibly valid criticisms of other perfectionist theories, fail against the perfectionist conception of justice. Perfectionist justice, in other words, is fully compatible with the following plausible thoughts about freedom that derive from Mill, Dworkin, Kramer and Quong and that motivate their respective objections to perfectionism: namely, that citizens should have ample room for individual spontaneity, peculiarity of taste, eccentricity in conduct, experiments in living and other expressions of individuality; that citizens should have the opportunity to engage in a skilful performance of living; that freedom has content-independent value in the sense that the freedom to φ is valuable even when φ-ing is not itself valuable; and that the state should not subject citizens to its will by placing them in a choice situation that they rationally disprefer relative to a morally justified status quo. In this sense, as well as in the sense described in Section 8.1, perfectionist justice has strong liberal credentials and can be understood to give the claims of freedom their due.

8.3 Libertarian Full Self-Ownership

So far, I have argued that perfectionist justice is compatible with the conceptions of freedom that underwrite various objections to perfectionism. But perfectionist justice is, admittedly, not compatible with *every* conception of freedom on offer within contemporary political theory. While it is not possible to examine all the conceptions of freedom that conflict with perfectionist justice, in this section I

---

[30] For this way of putting the critique, see Kramer, M., *Liberalism with Excellence*, pp. 59–62.

shall discuss one sophisticated and influential such conception: namely, the notion of full self-ownership that is central to libertarian theories of justice.

My argument will be that the incompatibility of perfectionist justice with full self-ownership should come as no embarrassment to the perfectionist because this conception of freedom is not independently plausible. Before seeking to substantiate this claim, though, one caveat is in order. A comprehensive assessment of the merits of libertarian full self-ownership is well beyond the scope of this work, which is primarily in dialogue with anti-perfectionist liberalism, not libertarianism. So the arguments that follow fall short of being fully developed, knock-down arguments and are instead intended simply to be sufficiently suggestive as to cast some doubt on the idea of full self-ownership.

The concept of self-ownership says that each individual enjoys a set of moral rights over her own person and powers. However, this concept is indeterminate and admits of different conceptions. Many political theories therefore accept some form of self-ownership. Perfectionist justice, for instance, recognizes some specification of the idea of self-ownership, as is clear from the fact that the first principle of perfectionist justice (namely, the equal basic liberties principle) includes the right to bodily integrity, among other rights. What is interesting and distinctive about libertarian political theories is that they are committed to *full* self-ownership. Full self-ownership assigns each person the strongest possible set of moral rights over her own person and powers, where this is understood to mean the most stringent and extensive set of moral rights over her own person and powers that is compatible with all other persons having the same set of rights.[31] This set of rights includes (i) the right to *control* the use of one's person and powers, (ii) the right to *compensation* if someone uses one's person or powers without consent and (iii) the right to *transfer* these rights to others by sale, rental, gift or loan.[32] In this regard, it is often said that 'to [fully] own oneself is to enjoy with respect to oneself all those rights which a slaveowner has over a complete chattel slave.'[33]

The idea of full self-ownership is often said to be highly appealing. It provides a simple and powerful explanation of many of our considered convictions about social justice, such as the conviction that it is wrong to sacrifice the rights of an individual for the sake of the greater good. In this way, the idea of full self-ownership accords well with the thought that, in Nozick's words, we are 'inviolate individuals, who may not be used in certain ways by others as means or tools or instruments or resources.'[34] Full self-ownership also has strongly anti-paternalistic

---

[31] This follows the influential delineation of full self-ownership in Cohen, G. A., *Self-Ownership, Freedom, and Equality* (Cambridge: Cambridge University Press, 1995), pp. 213–17.

[32] This representative statement is drawn from Vallentyne, P., Steiner, H. and Otsuka, M., 'Why Left-Libertarianism Is Not Incoherent, Indeterminate, or Irrelevant: A Reply to Fried', *Philosophy & Public Affairs* 33 (2005), pp. 203–4.

[33] Cohen, G. A., *Self-Ownership, Freedom, and Equality*, p. 214.

[34] Nozick, R., *Anarchy, State, and Utopia* (New York: Basic Books, 1974), pp. 333–4.

and anti-perfectionist implications. It implies, says Nozick, that the state 'scrupulously must be neutral between its citizens'.[35] This is because citizens who are subject to paternalistic or perfectionist laws and policies have a less extensive set of moral rights over their own lives than do citizens of a non-paternalistic or non-perfectionist state. Libertarians take these anti-paternalistic and anti-perfectionist implications to be among the principal attractions of full self-ownership.[36]

There are two main forms of libertarianism: so-called 'right-libertarianism' (whose advocates include Eric Mack, Jan Narveson and Robert Nozick) and so-called 'left-libertarianism' (whose advocates include Michael Otsuka, Hillel Steiner and Peter Vallentyne).[37] Both right-libertarians and left-libertarians subscribe to full self-ownership but they differ in that left-libertarians allow more scope for egalitarian considerations. More precisely, right- and left-libertarians differ in how they specify the conditions under which individuals can appropriate natural resources and thereby acquire rights of 'world-ownership'. Right-libertarians impose little or no moral restrictions on the appropriation of natural resources, whereas left-libertarians impose more stringent restrictions on such appropriation. The differences between these varieties of libertarianism need not detain us here; the important point is that, contrary to what is sometimes suggested, a commitment to full self-ownership does not necessarily entail a commitment to strong rights in worldly resources and so does not necessarily entail a rejection of redistributive taxation.

8.3.1 Three Implausible Implications

Despite its initial appeal, the doctrine of full self-ownership has several rather extreme or repugnant implications. Many are wary of full self-ownership because of Nozick's famous arguments from full self-ownership to the minimal state.[38] However, as I have just mentioned, left-libertarians such as Otsuka, Steiner and Vallentyne argue quite persuasively that full self-ownership is conceptually detachable from anti-egalitarianism. So, despite the fact that its incompatibility with redistributive taxation is arguably the most common reason for rejecting full

[35] Ibid., p. 33.
[36] But for an argument that the anti-paternalism of libertarianism is a weakness, not a strength, of the view, see Wall, S., 'Self-Ownership and Paternalism', *The Journal of Political Philosophy* 17 (2009), pp. 399–417.
[37] For the right-libertarians, see Mack, E., *Libertarianism* (Cambridge: Polity, 2018); Narveson, J., *The Libertarian Idea* (Peterborough: Broadview Press, 2001); Nozick, R., *Anarchy, State, and Utopia*. For the left-libertarians, see Otsuka, M., *Libertarianism Without Inequality* (Oxford: Oxford University Press, 2003); Steiner, H., *An Essay on Rights* (Oxford: Blackwell, 1994); Vallentyne, P., 'Left-Libertarianism as a Promising Form of Liberal Egalitarianism', *Philosophic Exchange* 39 (2009), pp. 56–71; Vallentyne, P., Steiner, H. and Otsuka, M., 'Why Left-Libertarianism Is Not Incoherent, Indeterminate, or Irrelevant'.
[38] See Nozick, R., *Anarchy, State, and Utopia*, especially pp. 171–2.

self-ownership, I shall not dwell on this particular alleged implication of full self-ownership here. Instead, I shall explore three implications that flow even more directly and constitutively from the core of the idea of full self-ownership: namely, that full self-ownership rules out enforceable duties of aid in cases of easy rescue, that it prohibits minor incursions or risks of incursions on other persons' bodies, and that it permits voluntary slavery.[39] My critique thus applies to libertarianism in both its left-wing and right-wing varieties, insofar as these three implications concern rights in personal resources ('self-ownership') rather than in worldly resources ('world-ownership').

A first extreme implication of full self-ownership, then, is that it rules out enforceable duties of aid in cases of easy rescue. Suppose that a small child is drowning in a shallow pond and that a passer-by could save the child's life at no risk to herself and at negligible cost. All the passer-by would need to do is to reach out and pull the child from the water. Defenders of full self-ownership must deny that the passer-by is under an enforceable moral obligation to assist the child. They must deny, that is, that the passer-by can be forced to save the child should she be unwilling to do so or that the passer-by can subsequently be punished for not saving the child. As Vallentyne says in this context, 'agents have no enforceable non-contractual obligation to provide personal services to others'.[40]

In response to this objection, defenders of full self-ownership are quick to point out that they can recognize that the passer-by has strong moral *reasons* to assist the child and perhaps even that the passer-by is under a moral *obligation* to assist the child.[41] All libertarians deny is that this obligation to assist the child is *enforceable*, in the sense that others may legitimately coerce the passer-by to assist the child. However, this response does not greatly blunt the force of the original objection from easy rescue. After all, what is so objectionable about the libertarian position is precisely the fact that it denies that individuals have enforceable obligations to assist others when those others are in dire need, when the cost of helping is miniscule and when there is no one else around to help.

A second and related extreme implication of full self-ownership is that it rules out minor incursions or risks of incursions on other persons' bodies. To illustrate this, Arneson imagines an individual who has several 'loose flakes of skin' on his arm that 'could somehow be used to save people from instant death'.[42] If full self-ownership obtains, then this individual is the sole rightful owner of his person, including these flakes of skin, and so it would be impermissible to force

---

[39] These are well-known objections to full self-ownership and so I claim no originality here. Indeed, my discussion of these objections draws quite heavily on the excellent critical discussion in Arneson, R., 'Self-Ownership and World-Ownership: Against Left-Libertarianism', *Social Philosophy and Policy* 27 (2010), pp. 168–94.

[40] Vallentyne, P., 'Left-Libertarianism: A Primer', in P. Vallentyne and H. Steiner (eds), *Left-Libertarianism and Its Critics: The Contemporary Debate* (New York: Palgrave, 2000), p. 4.

[41] See ibid., pp. 4–5.

[42] Arneson, R., 'Self-Ownership and World-Ownership', p. 184.

260 A PERFECTIONIST THEORY OF JUSTICE

him to yield the flakes, even if they are of no use to him and can save the lives of others. Yet as Arneson aptly says in this regard: 'nothing worth caring about in any sensible ideal of personal freedom is secured by the dogmatic and shrill insistence on the full property rights over each and every part of my body that the [full] self-ownership thesis affirms.'[43] Full self-ownership similarly prohibits an individual from engaging in activities that produce small amounts of pollution, such as mowing one's lawn, since these particles of pollution will fall upon the bodies of other persons without consent. Moreover, and relatedly, full self-ownership implies that activities that carry a *risk* of incursion on other persons' bodies, such as jogging in the city or driving a car, are impermissible. In these ways, full self-ownership appears to have implications that are extremely restrictive, even paralyzing.[44]

In response to this objection, some libertarians follow Nozick, who argues that minor incursions or risks of incursions on other persons' bodies can be permissible provided that the 'victims' of such incursions are appropriately compensated. Appropriate compensation is compensation that leaves the victim by her own lights no worse off than she would have been had there been no incursion. However, Nozick's compensation proposal does not eliminate the restrictive implications of full self-ownership in cases in which the victims of minor incursions do not accept any level of compensation for these incursions.[45] Suppose an individual has both colossal personal wealth and an extreme aversion to contamination, and as such refuses all offers of compensation from those who emit small amounts of pollution that falls on his skin or that enters his lungs. In this case, full self-ownership still appears to imply that this individual has an implausibly wide veto over the actions of his fellow citizens. In short, then, while compensation helps in cases in which individuals are willing to sell off their rights against minor incursion, it does not eliminate the fact that, in certain circumstances, full self-ownership has extremely restrictive, even paralyzing implications.

Finally, a third extreme implication of full self-ownership is that it permits permanent voluntary slavery. If each person has the most extensive possible set of moral rights over his own person and powers, including the right to transfer these rights to others by sale or gift, then it follows that an individual is entitled voluntarily to contract himself into permanent slavery, thereby making himself the full private property of another person.[46] An illustration of how this might occur is given by Otsuka, who imagines a group of individuals who agree to enter

---

[43] Ibid.

[44] For developments of this worry, see Railton, P., *Facts, Values, and Norms* (Cambridge: Cambridge University Press, 2003), ch. 7; Sobel, D., 'Backing Away from Libertarian Self-Ownership', *Ethics* 123 (2012), pp. 32–60.

[45] For a discussion of this problem as well as other problems with Nozick's compensation proposal, see Sobel, D., 'Backing Away from Libertarian Self-Ownership', pp. 38–49.

[46] For libertarians who permit voluntary slavery, see, for example, Nozick, R., *Anarchy, State, and Utopia*, pp. 58, 331; Vallentyne, P., Steiner, H. and Otsuka, M., 'Why Left-Libertarianism Is Not Incoherent, Indeterminate, or Irrelevant', p. 212.

a lottery that will determine who among them will 'become the (non-hereditary) lords, ladies, and other noble residents of [a collection of] manor houses' and who among them will 'become a (non-hereditary) serf or servant for life to the lord of lady of one or other of these manors instead'.[47] These individuals, we can suppose, 'find the prospect of becoming a wealthy, privileged aristocrat sufficiently attractive, even when weighed against the prospect of ending up a serf or servant', that they are willing to take this gamble.[48] So long as this shift towards a quasi-feudal arrangement occurs on the basis of free and informed consent, libertarians appear to have no grounds for saying that it represents a shift from a more to a less just arrangement. These implications follow quite straightforwardly from the core libertarian idea that individuals have the strongest possible set of rights to control the use of their own person and powers.

Again, libertarians have sought in various ways to defend this implication of full self-ownership. Vallentyne, for instance, explains that a 'well-informed decision to sell oneself into slavery (e.g., for a large sum of money to help one's needy family) is an exercise of autonomy'.[49] Indeed, 'under desperate conditions it may even represent an extremely important way of exercising one's autonomy'.[50] However, even if we grant for the sake of argument what Vallentyne says here about the alienability of basic rights under certain conditions, this does not rescue full self-ownership.[51] After all, the critic can accept that there can be very specific and unusual situations in which selling oneself into slavery is legitimate and even admirable. What the critic objects to is the libertarian's '*blanket* claim that each person *always* has an enforceable right to waive or alienate any of her rights over herself, even her entire set of personal autonomy and control rights, *for any reason at all or no reason*'.[52] So even if Vallentyne is correct that self-enslavement in exchange for a large sum of money to help one's needy family is a morally legitimate exercise of autonomy, how plausible is it that self-enslavement in exchange for, say, a chocolate bar is a morally legitimate exercise of autonomy?

Before continuing, I should make a clarification about the relationship between my criticisms of libertarian full self-ownership and my own positive views about social justice. I have tentatively argued against full self-ownership on the grounds that it offends against several of our considered convictions: it permits what should intuitively be prohibited, such as voluntarily selling oneself into permanent slavery, and it prohibits what should intuitively be permitted, such as

---

[47] Otsuka, M., *Libertarianism Without Inequality*, p. 116.

[48] Ibid.

[49] Vallentyne, P., 'Left-Libertarianism', p. 4.

[50] Ibid.

[51] For arguments that basic rights are inalienable, though, see, for example, Rawls, J., *Political Liberalism*, pp. 365–7; Freeman, S., 'Illiberal Libertarians: Why Libertarianism Is Not a Liberal View', *Philosophy & Public Affairs* 30 (2001), especially pp. 110–13, 131–5.

[52] Arneson, R., 'Self-Ownership and World-Ownership', p. 187 (emphases added).

262   A PERFECTIONIST THEORY OF JUSTICE

forcing a passer-by to save a drowning child in a case of easy rescue. But in pressing these objections I have not attempted to explain *why* voluntarily selling oneself into permanent slavery should be prohibited or *why* forcing a passer-by to save a drowning child in a case of easy rescue should be permitted. I have not, in other words, connected my objections to any particular *alternative* theory of justice or rights that might provide a vindication of or deeper rationale for the intuitions to which I have appealed. In particular, I have not connected these objections to the perfectionist conception of social justice articulated in Part II. These arguments against libertarian full self-ownership are in this way case-based rather than theory-based. Of course, this brings with it the risk that the relevant intuitions are not shared by everyone. Perhaps I am denying precisely what libertarians assert. But it does at least also mean that these arguments against libertarian full self-ownership are stand-alone arguments and are not tied to the success of any specific non-libertarian theory of justice.

8.3.2 Two Libertarian Responses

In addition to the more specific rejoinders considered when setting out the objections, libertarians can offer two general sorts of responses. The first is to deny that libertarianism is in fact committed to the extreme implications in question. The most common way to do this is to *weaken* or *qualify* full self-ownership. Here the libertarian 'slightly step[s] back from the full self-ownership thesis to endorse some version of the *near-full* self-ownership thesis: the thesis that every rational agent initially has a set of self-ownership rights that is "close" to full self-ownership rights (where "close" entails minor, circumscribed deviations, either in terms of stringency or in terms of extensiveness)'.[53] Near-full self-ownership might say, for instance, that although each individual has a very extensive set of moral rights over her person and powers, this set is not so extensive as to include the right to transfer oneself into slavery or the right to stand by in a case of easy rescue.

A clear example of this first strategy comes from Vallentyne, Steiner and Otsuka, who admit that full self-ownership has 'some rather radical implications'.[54] These implications, they continue, can be avoided by replacing full self-ownership 'in the

---

[53] Mazor, J. and Vallentyne, P., 'Libertarianism, Left and Right', in S. Olsaretti (ed.), *The Oxford Handbook of Distributive Justice* (Oxford: Oxford University Press, 2018), p. 134. For similar ideas, see Otsuka's defence of 'less than full' self-ownership (*Libertarianism Without Inequality*, p. 15); and Mack's suggestion that self-ownership rights need to be supplemented by an 'anti-paralysis postulate' (see Mack, E., 'Nozickian Arguments for the More-Than-Minimal State', in R. Bader and J. Meadowcroft (eds), *The Cambridge Companion to Nozick's Anarchy, State, and Utopia* (Cambridge: Cambridge University Press, 2011), pp. 112–14) and by 'elbow room' (see Mack, E., 'Elbow Room for Rights', in D. Sobel, P. Vallentyne and S. Wall (eds), *Oxford Studies in Political Philosophy, Volume 1* (Oxford: Oxford University Press, 2015), pp. 194–221).

[54] Vallentyne, P., Steiner, H. and Otsuka, M., 'Why Left-Libertarianism Is Not Incoherent, Indeterminate, or Irrelevant', p. 206.

strict sense' with full self-ownership 'in the looser sense'.[55] This looser conception of full self-ownership allows for exceptions 'when one or more of the [following] four conditions is satisfied': '(1) there is only a very small probability that [another person's action] will result in an incursion against oneself; (2) if there is an incursion, the harm to oneself will be trivial; (3) the harm was not reasonably foreseeable; and (4) the benefits to others of performing the action are enormous (e.g., the avoidance of social catastrophe)'.[56]

The move from full self-ownership to near-full self-ownership, however, brings with it at least two problems. The first is that near-full self-ownership still remains vulnerable to counterexamples. Admittedly, Vallentyne, Steiner and Otsuka's four exceptions provide grounds for holding that jogging in the city is permissible (because there is only a very small probability that this action will result in an incursion against others' bodies) and that taking lifesaving but unwanted flakes from a person's skin is permissible (because the harm to that person of doing so is trivial). But none of these four exceptions provides grounds for saying that self-ownership rights do not include the right to transfer oneself into slavery. Near-full self-ownership is thus still saddled with the repugnant implication that a society in which one half of the population voluntarily contract themselves to be the permanent slaves of the other half could nonetheless be a fully just society. Vallentyne, Steiner and Otsuka's exceptions also introduce new counterexamples, since they seem to imply that individuals lack rights where they should have them. In particular, condition (2) seems to imply that individuals lack rights over trivial items such as a sock or a pencil sharpener and thus that such items can be destroyed or stolen without violating the owner's rights.[57] This implication will be unacceptable to many within the libertarian tradition—'a tradition which holds that stealing a penny or a pin or anything from someone violates his rights [and which] does not select a threshold measure of harm as a lower limit', in Nozick's words—as well as to many non-libertarians.[58]

But even if the move to near-full self-ownership manages to secure extensional adequacy, a second problem remains. This is that the move to near-full self-ownership is not well-motivated and appears to be merely an ad hoc stipulation for fending off counterexamples. Is there a compelling rationale from within a libertarian framework for retreating from full self-ownership to near-full self-ownership? In this connection, it is striking that when Vallentyne, Steiner and Otsuka introduce their tweaks to full self-ownership, they do not explain what morally significant feature these four exceptions have in common. They do not, that is,

---

[55] Ibid., p. 207.

[56] Ibid.

[57] This criticism of Vallentyne, Steiner and Otsuka's conception of near-full self-ownership is made by Sobel in his 'Backing Away from Libertarian Self-Ownership', p. 52.

[58] Nozick, R., *Anarchy, State, and Utopia*, p. 75.

offer a rationale for why individual rights should deviate from full self-ownership in these specific ways, but not in other possible ways.[59]

This worry about the undermotivation of near-full self-ownership can be developed in any of several related directions. In one sense, it can be put as a worry about *coherence*. Here the concern is that once we *do* supply a rationale for the move to near-full self-ownership, this rationale will turn out to be in tension with the rationale for signing up to the idea of self-ownership in the first place. Many are initially attracted to the idea of full self-ownership because it promises a thoroughgoingly non-consequentialist account of individual rights. Nozick, for instance, explains that one of the attractions of libertarian conceptions of justice is that they take seriously 'the fact of our separate existence'.[60] 'They reflect the fact', he continues, 'that no moral balancing act can take place among us; there is no moral outweighing of one of our lives by others so as to lead to a greater overall social good. There is no justified sacrifice of some of us for others.'[61] By contrast, the best rationale for introducing Vallentyne, Steiner and Otsuka's four exceptions (and for favouring near-full self-ownership more generally) appears to be that doing so appropriately accounts for the importance of consequences and of the overall social good. So there may well be a conflict between the best rationale for qualifying the idea of full self-ownership (which is consequentialist in spirit) and the best rationale for subscribing to that idea in the first place (which is non-consequentialist in spirit). In this regard, Barbara Fried tellingly remarks that 'when the going gets tough, rights theorists tend to turn utilitarian.'[62]

In another sense, the worry about undermotivation can be put as a worry about *redundancy*. Here the concern is that even if it is possible to supply a rationale for the move to near-full self-ownership that is in keeping with the non-consequentialist spirit of self-ownership, it will be this rationale, rather than the idea of self-ownership, that does the fundamental explanatory work within

[59] This point is also made in Sobel, D., 'Backing Away from Libertarian Self-Ownership', p. 50. Why can't the achievement of extensional adequacy *itself* be the rationale for adopting these deviations from full self-ownership? Why, that is, can't it be that what justifies the shift from full self-ownership to near-full self-ownership is precisely the fact that such a shift brings libertarian theory into closer alignment with our intuitive judgements? To see the problem with this response, suppose that, faced with the objection that utilitarianism recommends pushing a large man into the path of a runaway trolley that is headed towards five unsuspecting workers, a utilitarian qualifies the principle of utility so that it does not apply to cases involving runaway trolleys. This qualification of the principle of utility is worryingly ad hoc. And the fact that this qualification of the principle of utility helps utilitarians achieve extensional adequacy does nothing to dispel this worry. Similarly, in order for the shift from full self-ownership to near-full self-ownership to avoid the charge of being ad hoc, gerrymandered or unmotivated, it needs to be justified by some rationale that is distinct from the mere fact that such a shift allows the libertarian to fend off pesky counterexamples. For this point in a different context, see Enoch, D., 'Why Idealize?', *Ethics* 115 (2005), pp. 766–9; Enoch, D., 'Idealizing Still Not Off the Hook: A Reply to Sobel's Reply', p. 3 (unpublished manuscript).

[60] Nozick, R., *Anarchy, State, and Utopia*, p. 33.

[61] Ibid.

[62] Fried, B., 'Does Nozick Have a Theory of Property Rights?', in R. Bader and J. Meadowcroft (eds), *The Cambridge Companion to Nozick's Anarchy, State, and Utopia*, p. 233.

a libertarian theory of justice. Suppose we say that full self-ownership should be rejected in favour of near-full self-ownership because the restrictive implications of full self-ownership undermine the very point of self-ownership rights, which are supposed to protect our nature as purposive beings with our own lives to lead in our own chosen way.[63] Or suppose we say that full self-ownership does not include the right to transfer oneself into slavery because to do so would undermine our status as free and equal citizens. The problem is that if we invoke in this way the further values of purposiveness or free and equal citizenship in order to explain in a more principled way how to balance the social good against individual rights, then the idea of self-ownership would become redundant—or, at the very least, would cease to play the kind of foundational role that is often taken to be a distinctive feature of libertarian theories of justice. Instead, what would ultimately determine the precise contours and detailed specification of individual rights would be the idea of purposiveness or free and equal citizenship.[64]

Having discussed the first general responsive strategy—which is to deny that libertarianism is in fact committed to the extreme implications in question by abandoning full self-ownership in favour of near-full self-ownership—let us consider the second sort of general response available to libertarians. Here the strategy is to accept that full self-ownership has various extreme or counterintuitive implications but to deny that this counts decisively against libertarianism.[65] There are various ways of pursuing this bullet-biting response. One way is to cast doubt on the reliability of moral intuitions, either as a general matter or specifically when elicited by far-fetched thought experiments. For instance, Jessica Flanigan says in this vein that 'the fact that self-ownership theory implies that nonvoluntary slavery and marital rape are morally impermissible would have been counted against the theory two hundred years ago. It could be that self-ownership theory is true and in two hundred years our descendants will view our acceptance of driving, polluting, inflicting risks on one another, and living in cities where we bump into people's bodies and assault them with noise and light as morally unacceptable'.[66] Another

---

[63] For a view along these lines, see Mack, E., 'Elbow Room for Rights'. For a critique, see Sobel, D., 'The Point of Self-Ownership', in D. Schmidtz and C. Pavel (eds), *The Oxford Handbook of Freedom* (Oxford: Oxford University Press, 2018), pp. 124–40.

[64] Admittedly, this would leave open the possibility that the idea of full self-ownership could still play some kind of downstream or heuristic role within libertarian theory. A view along these lines is suggested by Jason Brennan and Bas van der Vossen, who say that full self-ownership should be thought of as 'more of a conclusion than a premise'. See Brennan, J. and van der Vossen, B., 'The Myths of the Self-Ownership Thesis', in J. Brennan, B. van der Bossen and D. Schmidtz (eds), *The Routledge Handbook of Libertarianism* (Oxford: Routledge, 2019), p. 210. But then the real objection to perfectionism would lie elsewhere, and not in the idea of full self-ownership that is under consideration in this section.

[65] Of course, these two strategies are not mutually exclusive: libertarians can first soften the edges of full self-ownership by slightly qualifying that idea, and then insist that whatever counterintuitiveness remains is offset by the attractions of full self-ownership.

[66] Flanigan, J., 'Boundary Problems and Self-Ownership', *Social Philosophy and Policy* 36 (2019), p. 34.

266 A PERFECTIONIST THEORY OF JUSTICE

way of pursuing the bullet-biting response is to point out that fit with intuition is only one among a variety of theoretical virtues and that any extensional inadequacies are more than offset by the simplicity, parsimony and intrinsic appeal of the idea of full self-ownership. At the end of the theoretical day, libertarians may say, the benefits of the idea of full self-ownership are worth the costs. As Vallentyne, Steiner and Otsuka put this:

> Full self-ownership is both plausible in the abstract (we are fully in charge of our persons) and has a theoretical simplicity. To be sure, the plausibility of a principle does not depend solely on its theoretical attractiveness. It also depends on the plausibility of its concrete implications. Full self-ownership admittedly has some counterintuitive implications (e.g., the legitimacy of voluntary slavery and the absence of a legally enforceable duty to provide highly desirable personal services under certain circumstances). This, however, is true of all principles. A full defense of a principle requires a balancing of the abstract theoretical considerations with the plausibility of the concrete implications (e.g., as in reflective equilibrium). Our claim ... is that at least loose full self-ownership is justified by such a balancing procedure.[67]

In my view, however, full self-ownership does not strike the best balance between abstract theoretical considerations and the plausibility of concrete implications. Vindicating this impression is not straightforward. It is always difficult to say anything conclusive about which theory is the winner in reflective equilibrium once all the relevant considerations are tallied up. Indeed, since different people start with different priors, perhaps we should accept that there are multiple reflective equilibria, none of which can be shown to be superior to the others without begging the question. Still, let me make two remarks in support of the contention that full self-ownership does not strike the best balance between the competing considerations.

The first is that although the idea of full self-ownership is indeed plausible in the abstract and theoretically simple, the same is true of many of the leading ideas of alternative theories of justice, such as the idea of utility maximization that is central to utilitarianism, the idea of society as a fair system of social cooperation that is central to Rawls's conception of liberalism, the idea of equal concern and respect that is central to Dworkin's conception of liberalism, the idea of mutual independence that is central to Kantian liberalism, the idea of extinguishing the influence of brute luck on distribution that is central to luck egalitarianism, the idea of relating as equals that is central to relational egalitarianism, and, I daresay,

---

[67] Vallentyne, P., Steiner, H. and Otsuka, M., 'Why Left-Libertarianism Is Not Incoherent, Indeterminate, or Irrelevant', p. 208.

the idea of society as a fair striving for human flourishing that is central to perfectionist justice. In this sense, full self-ownership as the leading idea of libertarian theories of justice does not appear to possess a uniquely high level of intrinsic plausibility or theoretical simplicity, such that we should be especially forgiving of its counterintuitive implications.

The second remark is that the ways in which full self-ownership conflicts with our intuitive judgements seem to be quite serious. Full self-ownership conflicts not only with fairly weak or peripheral intuitions but also with some of our firmest considered convictions. Rawls explains that some considered convictions 'we view as fixed points: ones we never expect to withdraw, as when Lincoln says: "If slavery is not wrong, nothing is wrong".[68] Now while Lincoln and Rawls clearly have in mind here *non-voluntary* slavery, it is quite plausible that even the conviction that *voluntary* slavery is an injustice is a fixed point that we never expect to withdraw. It is, in other words, very difficult to believe that in, say, two hundred years we will become more, rather than less, sympathetic to the thought that justice is perfectly compatible with a quasi-feudal society structured by voluntarily contracted relations of mastery and slavery.

8.4 Pragmatic Concerns

The freedom-based objections to perfectionism that I have considered until now have been quite abstract and theoretical: these objections have contended that perfectionist laws and policies are incompatible with this or that conception of freedom. But there is another more pragmatic kind of freedom-based objection to perfectionism. Here the worry is that, even if perfectionist politics can *in principle* give the claims of freedom their due, we have learned from hard experience that *in practice* it does not. Any attempt to practically implement perfectionist justice, then, would risk the abuse of political power and the violation of individual liberties by incompetent, overzealous or corrupt state officials. Prudence thus dictates taking ideals of human flourishing off the political agenda, if only as a kind of prophylactic measure. Or so this objection goes.[69]

---

[68] Rawls, J., *Justice as Fairness* (Cambridge, MA: Harvard University Press, 2001), p. 29.

[69] For versions of this charge, see, for example, Ackerman, B., *Social Justice in the Liberal State* (New Haven, CT: Yale University Press, 1980), pp. 11–12, 361–5; Feinberg, J., *Harmless Wrongdoing: The Moral Limits of the Criminal Law, Volume 4* (Oxford: Oxford University Press, 1988), pp. 310–11; Kymlicka, W., 'Liberal Individualism and Liberal Neutrality', *Ethics* 99 (1989), pp. 900–2; Quong, J., *Liberalism Without Perfection*, pp. 35–6. For replies by perfectionists, see, for example, Raz, J., *The Morality of Freedom* (Oxford: Oxford University Press, 1986), pp. 427–9; Caney, S., 'Consequentialist Defences of Liberal Neutrality', *The Philosophical Quarterly* 31 (1991), pp. 457–77; Sher, G., *Beyond Neutrality*, ch. 5; Wall, S., 'Enforcing Morality', *Criminal Law and Philosophy* 7 (2013), pp. 470–1 (whose statement of this pragmatic objection I have followed quite closely); Wall, S., 'Moral Environmentalism', pp. 112–14; Sher, G., 'Perfectionism and Democracy', in R. Merrill and D. Weinstock (eds), *Political Neutrality: A Re-Evaluation* (New York: Palgrave Macmillan, 2014), pp. 144–58.

268 A PERFECTIONIST THEORY OF JUSTICE

This sort of suspicion of the misuse of state power has of course played an important role in the history of liberal thought, and remains influential in contemporary debates. Amy Gutmann says that 'the government should stay out of the business of making people virtuous because the virtue business, managed by the state, is bound to bankruptcy'.[70] Judith Shklar's 'liberalism of fear'—which holds that 'the original and only defensible meaning of liberalism' is 'to secure the political conditions that are necessary for the exercise of personal freedom'—is also firmly anchored in historical and sociological reflections about the cruelties of religious persecution and the abuses of state power.[71] Isaiah Berlin states that 'the search for perfection does seem to me a recipe for bloodshed, no better even if it is demanded by the sincerest of idealists, the purest of heart'.[72] And Bruce Ackerman likewise explains that one important motivation for anti-perfectionist liberalism is 'realism about the corrosiveness of power':

> [Certain] basic realities—imperial government, bureaucratic structure, burgeoning technologies—are fixtures of our age ... It is not enough, then, simply to muster up the philosophical courage needed to declare, with the appropriate 'Eurekas', that you have discovered the good for all humankind. You must also persuade yourself that an imperial, bureaucratic, and technologized government should be given the patent to make use of your discovery in the power plays of everyday life ... Good government, always precarious, can readily degenerate into an awful parody of itself—with hypocrites using the awesome powers of the bureaucratic state to spy, torture, and kill, merely to aggrandize themselves without any attention to the goods they profess to value ... Given these risks, surely the effort to save souls by governmental decree is a desperate gamble?[73]

There are two points to make in response to these pragmatic concerns. The first is that it is not enough to point out that the officials of a modern perfectionist state would wield tremendous and potentially corrupting power. After all, the officials of a modern anti-perfectionist liberal state would *also* wield tremendous and potentially corrupting power. We are all too familiar with instances of state officials being incompetent, corrupt or overzealous in the implementation of non-perfectionist laws and policies. An obvious contemporary example of this is the problem of police brutality and mass incarceration in the United States.[74] Even when ideals

[70] Gutmann, A., 'How Limited Is Liberal Government?', in B. Yack (ed.), *Liberalism Without Illusions: Essays on Liberal Theory and the Political Vision of Judith Shklar* (Chicago, IL: Chicago University Press, 1996), p. 66.

[71] Shklar, J., 'The Liberalism of Fear', in S. Young (ed.), *Political Liberalism: Variations on a Theme* (Albany, NY: State University of New York Press, 2004), p. 149.

[72] Berlin, I., 'The Pursuit of the Ideal', in *The Crooked Timber of Humanity: Chapters in the History of Ideas* (London: Pimlico, 2013), p. 19.

[73] Ackerman, B., *Social Justice in the Liberal State*, pp. 362–4, 369.

[74] For a powerful analysis of this, see Alexander, M., *The New Jim Crow: Mass Incarceration in the Age of Colorblindness* (New York: The New Press, 2010).

FREEDOM 269

of human flourishing are absent from the political agenda, in other words, the coercive power of the state is still at risk of being abused by hypocrites, bullies and fanatics. As Mill recognized, 'there is no difficulty in proving *any* ethical standard whatever to work ill if we suppose universal idiocy to be conjoined with it'.[75] So, taken at face value, pragmatic concerns seem to cast doubt on state action in general, rather than on perfectionist state action in particular, and thus seem to call for a minimal or night-watchman state.

To avoid this libertarian tilt, any pragmatic objection to perfectionism will need to be developed in a carefully comparative manner: it must demonstrate why we should expect perfectionist state officials to be *especially* prone to abuse their powers. But why is perfectionist statecraft at greater risk of backfiring than non-perfectionist statecraft? What is it about ideals of human flourishing in particular that makes their successful promotion by state officials especially unlikely? Anti-perfectionist liberals do not generally address this comparative question. They do not, for instance, provide detailed empirical evidence that the kinds of laws and policies that would be entailed by perfectionist justice (such as state support for the arts or restrictions on gambling) are more often abused by state officials than the kinds of laws and policies that would be entailed by anti-perfectionist liberal theories of justice (such as the establishment of prison facilities or the organization of democratic elections). Instead, anti-perfectionist liberals tend to make, as Ackerman does, rather speculative and rhetorical assertions from the armchair about the dangerousness of trying 'to save souls by governmental decree'. Of course, this is hardly surprising since political philosophers are often not best placed to broach these empirical complexities—complexities that fall more squarely within the domain of political scientists and sociologists.

Indeed, when one does consult the relevant empirical literature, it appears that political corruption and the abuse of power are determined by factors (such as press freedom, economic prosperity, gender equality, ethnic diversity, education and the rule of law) that are largely orthogonal to the question of whether the state's objectives have a perfectionist or non-perfectionist character.[76] Even the size of the state and the number of public officials—which would arguably be somewhat greater under perfectionism and which one might expect to be associated with corruption—do not seem to be reliable predictors of corruption and the abuse of power.[77] Under favourable conditions, then, moderate perfectionist laws and public policies—such as informative and educational public broadcasting, public funding of the arts, and the other proposals discussed in Chapter 6—look eminently feasible.

[75] Mill, J. S., *Utilitarianism* (Indianapolis, IN: Hackett, 2001), p. 24.
[76] See, for example, Dimant, E. and Tosato, G., 'Causes and Effects of Corruption: What Has Past Decade's Empirical Research Taught Us? A Survey', *Journal of Economic Surveys* 32 (2018), pp. 335–56.
[77] Ibid., p. 338.

So until a compelling version of this objection is forthcoming—one that is carefully comparative and empirically informed—it remains unclear why we should think that pragmatic concerns apply only or especially to perfectionist state action. For now, the only conclusion that can properly be drawn from these pragmatic objections is a very general one, namely that state officials of all kinds, perfectionist or non-perfectionist, should remain as vigilant as possible against the ever-present risks of heavy-handedness, error and abuse that attend the exercise of political power.

The second response is that even if perfectionist state officials are especially prone to abuse their powers, it does not straightforwardly follow that perfectionism fails as a conception of social justice. After all, it is entirely consistent to say that perfectionism articulates the right ideal or vision for politics but that, since this ideal is likely to backfire if entrusted to state officials in real-world settings, there should be some kind of moratorium on perfectionism.[78] The pragmatic objection thus seems to pose a challenge more to the *practical significance* of the perfectionist conception of justice than to its *truth*. This response is by no means a pyrrhic victory. After all, leading anti-perfectionist liberals such as Dworkin, Quong and Rawls have not generally been content to rest their case against perfectionism on pragmatic considerations. They have sought to argue that 'there are deep principled objections to perfectionism that do not depend on such empirical considerations [as the fallibility of government officials]'.[79] So even if perfectionism is especially likely to backfire in practice, its soundness at the level of moral principle or ideal theory would still be an important result—and one that would be troubling for many anti-perfectionist liberals.

Here the objector might contest the tenability of the distinction I have drawn between the 'truth' of the perfectionist conception of justice and its 'practical significance'—as well as the tenability of the related distinction between 'principled' and 'pragmatic' objections—on the grounds that the practical significance of a conception of justice bears directly on its truth. In particular, the objector might hold that the correct conception of social justice must be *feasible*.[80] This sort of feasibility constraint might be rooted in a conception of the role of political philosophy of the kind defended by Rawls, who, as we saw in Section 3.2, argues that 'political philosophy ... must be concerned, as moral philosophy need not be, with practical political possibilities'.[81] If there is a feasibility constraint of this kind, then

---

[78] This appears roughly to be the position of Raz in *The Morality of Freedom*, especially pp. 427–9.
[79] Quong, J., *Liberalism Without Perfection*, p. 35.
[80] For general discussions of the feasibility constraint, see, for example, Gilabert, P. and Lawford-Smith, H., 'Political Feasibility: A Conceptual Exploration', *Political Studies* 60 (2012), pp. 809–25; Weber, M. and Vallier, K. (eds), *Political Utopias: Contemporary Debates* (Oxford: Oxford University Press, 2017).
[81] Rawls, J., 'The Idea of an Overlapping Consensus', *Oxford Journal of Legal Studies* 7 (1987), p. 24.

it may be possible after all to infer the in-principle failure of perfectionism from its in-practice failure.

However, it is by no means obvious that there is in fact a feasibility constraint on conceptions of social justice.[82] After all, the difficulty or impossibility of creating an error-free criminal justice system does not appear to undermine the ideal that as a matter of justice there should be no convictions of the innocent and no acquittals of the guilty. Nor do feasibility constraints appear to apply to other normative ideals: unknowable truths are still truths, unattainable beauty is still beauty, superhuman strength is still strength.[83] Why, then, must ideals of justice be achievable? Why couldn't justice turn out to be hopelessly beyond our reach? Here too one might point to G. A. Cohen's well-known arguments that 'difficulties of implementation, just as such, do not defeat ... a conception of justice, since it is not a constraint on a sound conception of justice that it should always be sensible to strive to implement it'.[84] As with those who endorse the feasibility constraint, Cohen's rejection of this constraint appears to be rooted in a particular conception of the role of political philosophy: 'the question for political philosophy is not what we should do but what we should think, even when what we should think makes no practical difference'.[85] In short, perhaps perfectionism, despite its (supposed) infeasibility, does still offer the correct ideal or vision of what justice requires and of how things should be: 'the standards to which it holds people and institutions might be sound and true' and 'the fact that people will not live up to them ... is a defect of people, not of the theory'.[86]

Of course, nothing is stopping the relevant anti-perfectionist liberals from defending some version of the feasibility constraint against these challenges. But, while it is not possible to offer a full evaluation of the various potential specifications and defences of the feasibility constraint on social justice, let me spell out a general dilemma that anti-perfectionists would face here. When someone says that certain principles of justice are 'infeasible', they typically mean that the probability of their being successfully implemented is too low. But *how* low is too low? How low must this probability be in order for the principles to count as infeasible? On the one hand, anti-perfectionists may want to say that principles of justice are infeasible if there is even a *small chance* that they will not be successfully implemented. But, while perfectionism does admittedly violate this constraint, this is not a plausible constraint on social justice. This constraint makes social justice

---

[82] For rejections of the feasibility constraint on justice, see, for example, Cohen, G. A., *Rescuing Justice and Equality* (Cambridge, MA: Harvard University Press, 2008); Gheaus, A., 'The Feasibility Constraint on the Concept of Justice', *The Philosophical Quarterly* 63 (2013), pp. 445–64; Estlund, D., *Utopophobia: On the Limits (If Any) of Political Philosophy* (Princeton, NJ: Princeton University Press, 2019).

[83] This point is made in Gheaus, A., 'The Feasibility Constraint on the Concept of Justice', pp. 447–8.

[84] Cohen, G. A., *Rescuing Justice and Equality*, p. 271.

[85] Ibid., p. 268.

[86] Estlund, D., *Utopophobia*, p. 84.

too beholden to the contingencies and disappointments of the real world, and in fact seems equally to be violated by anti-perfectionist liberal conceptions of social justice. On the other hand, anti-perfectionists may want to say that the principles of justice are infeasible if there is a *high chance* that they will not be successfully implemented. But, while this is a much more plausible constraint on social justice, it is no longer clear that perfectionism violates this constraint. Plenty of contemporary states, after all, appear to have implemented moderate perfectionist laws and policies, such as support for the arts and restrictions on gambling, with reasonable success.

Anti-perfectionists thus face a dilemma between excessively strong interpretations of the feasibility constraint (which rule out perfectionism but which are not independently plausible as constraints on conceptions of social justice) and excessively weak interpretations of the feasibility constraint (which are more plausible as constraints on conceptions of social justice but which do not rule out perfectionism). And while I have not shown that it is impossible for anti-perfectionists to specify and defend a feasibility constraint that falls in the Goldilocks zone between these extremes, I hope to have indicated the empirical and normative difficulties in this vicinity—difficulties that anti-perfectionists who appeal breezily to pragmatic concerns have yet to acknowledge, let alone rigorously confront.

9

Paternalism

A traditional criticism of perfectionism is that it treats citizens as if they were children—as if they cannot be trusted to make sound decisions about how to spend their time and resources and are in need of the state to steer them, as a parent might do, towards worthwhile ways of life. Perfectionist laws and policies, in other words, are paternalistic or infantilizing. An objection of this kind stretches back at least to John Stuart Mill, who criticized the perfectionist policies of his day—such as restrictions on beer and spirit houses as a means of steering individuals away from insalubrious lifestyles—on the grounds that such policies are 'suited only to a state of society in which the labouring classes are avowedly treated as children or savages, and placed under an education of restraint, to fit them for future admission to the privileges of freedom'.[1] But this objection has recently been pressed in an especially direct and forceful way by Jonathan Quong, and it is this rendition of the paternalism objection that is the focus of this chapter.[2]

In this chapter, I first summarize Quong's argument (Section 9.1). Quong seeks to demonstrate the paternalism of perfectionism by arguing that perfectionists have no satisfactory answer to a 'simple but important' question: 'Why is state action necessary at all to achieve perfectionist objectives?'[3] Why wouldn't citizens be able to achieve human flourishing if left to their own devices with a fair share of resources (as defined by leading non-perfectionist theories of justice)? Quong considers various answers given by perfectionists to this question and finds nearly all to involve a negative judgement about the capacity of citizens to rationally pursue their own good—thus revealing 'perfectionism's true paternalist colours'.[4] I then consider (in Section 9.2) a recent attempt to provide a non-paternalistic justification for perfectionist state action—a justification for perfectionist state action that does not involve negative judgements about the capacity of citizens to rationally pursue their own good—and I argue that it does not succeed. Next, I offer (in Section 9.3) a more straightforward and hard-line response to Quong's argument, namely that there is nothing objectionable about assuming that citizens are not always disposed to make rational decisions about their own good—especially given that, as mounting evidence from the fields of social psychology and behavioural economics suggests, this assumption is true of all human beings.

[1] Mill, J. S., *On Liberty* (London: Penguin Books, 1985), p. 172.
[2] See Quong, J., *Liberalism Without Perfection* (Oxford: Oxford University Press, 2011), ch. 3.
[3] Ibid., p. 74.
[4] Ibid., p. 86.

A Perfectionist Theory of Justice. Collis Tahzib, Oxford University Press.
© Collis Tahzib (2022). DOI: 10.1093/oso/9780192847119.003.0010

9.1 Why Is Perfectionist State Action Necessary?

To show that perfectionism is objectionably paternalistic, Quong first defends what he calls a 'judgemental definition' of paternalism.[5] On this view, agent A acts paternalistically towards agent B when:

> Agent A attempts to improve the welfare, good, happiness, needs, interests, or values of agent B with regard to a particular decision or situation that B faces, [and] A's act is motivated by a *negative judgement* about B's ability (assuming B has the relevant information) to make the right decision or manage the particular situation in a way that will effectively advance B's welfare, good, happiness, needs, interests, or values.[6]

This definition of paternalism, says Quong, 'captures our sense that to treat someone paternalistically is to treat that person like a child in the specific sense of acting in that person's best interests because you believe, in this situation, the person lacks the ability to do so himself or herself'.[7] Quong clarifies that the main kinds of 'ability' referred to in this definition are 'practical reasoning, willpower, and emotion management'.[8] Thus, it is paternalistic for Adam to refrain from telling Beth about the release of a new movie because he judges that she lacks the reasoning ability to recognize that she ought to revise for her exam rather than see the movie. It is paternalistic for Cleo to refrain from telling Dan about the release of this movie because she judges that, while he would recognize that he ought to revise for his exam rather than see the movie, he lacks willpower and would succumb to the temptation to see the movie now. And it is paternalistic for Eva to refrain from telling Fred about the passing of his father because she judges that he is emotionally incapable of dealing with this information. By contrast, 'informational deficits' do not count as relevant inabilities.[9] So there is nothing paternalistic about alerting someone to the fact that a bridge is unsafe or trying to prevent someone who does not know that a bridge is unsafe from crossing it.

With this judgemental definition of paternalism in place, Quong seeks to demonstrate that perfectionism is paternalistic in this sense. He first notes that a central claim of perfectionist political theory is that state action is necessary to achieve perfectionist objectives. Joseph Chan, for instance, states that 'the state is often needed to provide conditions for worthwhile lives to flourish'.[10] Joseph

---

[5] Ibid., p. 80.
[6] Ibid.
[7] Ibid., p. 81.
[8] Ibid.
[9] Ibid., p. 82.
[10] Chan, J., 'Legitimacy, Unanimity, and Perfectionism', *Philosophy & Public Affairs* 29 (2000), p. 34.

PATERNALISM 275

Raz says that 'perfectionist ideals require public action for their viability. Anti-perfectionism in practice would lead not merely to a political stand-off from support for valuable conceptions of the good. It would undermine the chance of survival of many cherished aspects of our culture.'[11] And I have similarly claimed that taking seriously the idea of society as a fair striving for human flourishing between free and equal citizens requires that the state enact laws and policies that are conducive to flourishing ways of life, such as informative and educational public broadcasting and public funding for the arts.

In light of this, Quong argues that perfectionists have no satisfactory answer to a 'simple but important' question:

> A Simple Question: Why is state action necessary at all to achieve perfectionist objectives? Why would citizens be unable or unlikely to lead flourishing ways of life if left to their own devices with a fair share of resources (where a 'fair share' is defined by reference to the best non-perfectionist theory of justice)?[12]

Although 'perfectionists usually offer very little in the way of an answer to this question', Quong canvasses the most promising answers available to perfectionists and finds nearly all to involve 'negative assumptions about citizens' abilities to know and rationally pursue their own good', thus revealing 'perfectionism's true paternalist colours'.[13] In the rest of this section, I briefly summarize Quong's discussion of these answers to the question of why perfectionist state action is necessary.

The first and most obvious answer is that citizens are too *irrational* to make sound choices about how to spend their time and money. Chan appears to endorse this sort of answer when he says that 'what seems necessary to perfectionism is the claim that not all individuals are of equal ability to make correct judgements [about how to lead a flourishing life] and that sometimes the state or its representatives can make better judgements'.[14] On this view, perfectionist state action is required even after all have received their fair share of resources because some citizens will squander these resources on less worthy activities. Perfectionist policies are introduced to discourage this from happening. However, this answer is clearly paternalistic in the Quongian sense: it involves a negative judgement about citizens' ability to make sound decisions about how to lead a flourishing life.

A second answer to the question of why perfectionist state action is necessary is that citizens are too *weak-willed* to make sound choices about how to spend their time and money. Thomas Hurka, for instance, explains that the perfectionist state 'may believe that, although citizens have some tendency to seek out valuable

[11] Raz, J., *The Morality of Freedom* (Oxford: Oxford University Press, 1986), p. 162.
[12] See Quong, J., *Liberalism Without Perfection*, pp. 74, 85.
[13] Ibid., pp. 85–6.
[14] Chan, J., 'Legitimacy, Unanimity, and Perfectionism', p. 32.

activities, they also have other, less desirable impulses, for example, to engage in consumption or passive amusement' and thus state subsidies for worthy activities are designed 'to help more people's better tendencies actually guide their conduct'.[15] Similarly, Simon Caney says that 'sometimes the allure of worthless ways of life and the strenuous nature of some worthwhile forms of life may lead to the former driving out the latter'.[16] On this view, perfectionist state action is required even after all have received their fair share of resources not because some citizens are unable to discern the worthy from the unworthy but because some citizens lack the willpower to pursue what they rightly judge to be worthy. Once again, however, this view is paternalistic in the Quongian sense because it is premised on 'negative assumptions about citizens' abilities to know and rationally pursue their own good'.[17]

A third and more complex answer is that perfectionist goods are often *public goods* and that state action is required in order to overcome the collective action problems involved in the provision of public goods. A distinctive feature of public goods is that they are non-excludable: it is not possible to exclude people from accessing the good. This feature means that public goods are typically undersupplied in a free market of rational individuals because there is no incentive for rational individuals to pay for the good as opposed to free riding on the contributions of others.

To illustrate this argument, Quong considers an example of a perfectionist public good. He invites us to imagine a perfectionist view according to which 'people's lives go much better if they are able to appreciate and experience the following art form: firework displays set off in the sky above large cities'.[18] Quong explains that 'it is the combination of pyrotechnics and the night-time cityscape that makes this an aesthetically valuable experience' and so this 'could not be replicated in remote areas of wilderness that people could be forced to pay to enter'.[19] Since this firework display takes place in a public place from which individuals cannot permissibly be excluded, there is no incentive for individuals to pay to see it (as opposed to watching for free from their homes or the street), and so state action is necessary to overcome this market failure. Unlike the first two justifications for perfectionist state action, this public-goods-based justification looks non-paternalistic. It is not premised on a negative judgement about the competence or strength of will of individuals. Indeed, on the contrary, it takes off from the observation that individually rational decisions can produce collectively suboptimal outcomes.

---

[15] Hurka, T., *Perfectionism* (Oxford: Oxford University Press, 1993), p. 159.
[16] Caney, S., 'Consequentialist Defences of Liberal Neutrality', *The Philosophical Quarterly* 41 (1991), p. 460.
[17] Quong, J., *Liberalism Without Perfection*, p. 86.
[18] Ibid., p. 89.
[19] Ibid.

Quong accepts that this third answer to the question of why perfectionist state action is necessary is not guilty of paternalism. His objection to it is simply that it will 'rarely, if ever, serve as an appropriate defence of perfectionist subsidies since the subsidies usually called for by perfectionists almost never involve genuine public goods'.[20] Quong offers a list of standard perfectionist policies such as 'performance art, art galleries, public parks, works of literature, sights of cultural significance, educational programmes for adults, and athletic events'.[21] He explains that 'all of these goods can be (and often are) offered in ways that require payment at the point of consumption, which means that they lack the essential feature of non-excludability'.[22] Even forms of culture and education which require open or public spaces, such as carnivals and national parks, 'can often be provided in *enclosed* public spaces that people can be required to pay before entering'.[23] Of course, it might be the case that many people would *not* in fact pay for these perfectionist goods if they were required to do so at the point of consumption. But this just resurrects the original challenge. For the perfectionist now has to explain *why* it is the case that many people would not pay for these perfectionist goods at the point of consumption, in a way that does not reduce to the paternalistic claim that citizens are unable to make sound decisions about how to spend their time and resources.

A fourth answer to the question of why perfectionist state action is necessary is that in the absence of state support, worthy pursuits and activities would be *prohibitively expensive* for some citizens to access. Hurka, for instance, argues that sometimes there will only be 'few people' who pursue some valuable activity and that 'limited numbers may make this perfection more expensive than others that are intrinsically no better, but whose many practitioners permit economies of scale to be realized'.[24] But, as Quong notes, the problem with this kind of argument is that it just pushes back the question. Perfectionists now need to answer the question of *why* there is low market demand for worthy pursuits. Why is it that, even when a just background distribution of resources obtains (by the lights of leading non-perfectionist theories of justice), there will still be insufficient art aficionados to permit economies of scale to be realized for art galleries? To answer *that* question, perfectionists will presumably need to fall back on one of the other answers—for instance, that citizens are too irrational to recognize the value of going to art galleries, or that citizens are too weak-willed and so fall prey to low-brow temptations and passive forms of amusement. It is thus difficult to see how appeals to prohibitive cost can represent an independent answer to the simple but important question of why perfectionist state action is necessary.

---

[20] Ibid.
[21] Ibid.
[22] Ibid.
[23] Ibid., p. 90.
[24] Hurka, T., *Perfectionism*, p. 159.

278   A PERFECTIONIST THEORY OF JUSTICE

Pulling this together, Quong's argument is that all the most obvious and plausible rationales for perfectionist state action are guilty of paternalism, with only some minor exceptions (such as certain stylized public goods cases). To explain why we cannot expect the various components of human flourishing to be sufficiently realized via voluntary decisions against a background of full compliance with a promising egalitarian distributive theory, the perfectionist must assume that citizens will not make effective decisions about how to run their own lives. Only when coupled with this paternalistic assumption will perfectionist subsidies ever look preferable to simply letting resources remain with citizens to use as they see fit.

9.2 A Non-Paternalistic Justification for Perfectionist State Action?

Broadly speaking, there are two ways of defending perfectionism against Quong's objection from paternalism. The first is to deny that perfectionism is guilty of making negative assumptions about citizens' capacities by identifying a plausible non-paternalistic rationale for perfectionist state action. The second way of defending perfectionism against this objection is to accept that perfectionism is paternalistic (at least in the Quongian sense of making negative judgements about citizens' decision-making abilities) but to deny that there is anything particularly problematic about paternalism in this sense. I favour the second, more hard-line response, and I develop this response in Section 9.3. In this section, however, I consider and reject a recent version of the first, more concessive response.

The argument comes from Matthew Kramer, who invites us to consider a country, Civilitia, in which the state provides funding for grand annual 'gala festivities' that are open to all citizens free of charge and that are designed to foster 'the public good of fellowship or communal solidarity'.[25] Kramer explains that if the main purpose of these festivities were to provide an opportunity for entertainment, then Quong could rightly respond that this is an excludable good, since the festivals could be ticketed and individuals could be required to pay for admission. But since the main purpose of these festivities is to foster fellowship and communal solidarity, such a response is not available. After all, the perfectionist good realized by these festivals—namely, fellowship and communal solidarity—depends essentially on the festivals being free at the point of consumption. These festivals foster fellowship and communal solidarity precisely because they provide opportunities for Civilians to 'encounter one another as members of a community rather than as fellow customers' and precisely because all Civilitians 'know

---

[25] See Kramer, M., *Liberalism with Excellence* (Oxford: Oxford University Press, 2017), pp. 72–4.

that they have been fully entitled to attend as Civilitians'.[26] In these ways, the perfectionist value of the gala festivities is intimately bound up with their being free of charge. So 'although each of the festivals in Civilitia could be rendered exclusive, the foremost public good sought through the organizing of the festivals would thereby be undermined'.[27]

However, it is unclear that the provision of this single, highly stylized example of a perfectionist public good defeats Quong's general claim that public goods rationales will 'rarely, if ever, serve as an appropriate defence of perfectionist subsidies since the subsidies usually called for by perfectionists almost never involve genuine public goods'.[28] Quong, that is, could surely respond to Kramer's case by saying that even if the goods realized by Civilitian jubilees would be undermined by the imposition of admission fees, there is no reason to think that, *generally speaking*, the goods realized by perfectionist policies would be undermined by the imposition of admission fees.

Consider again in this regard Quong's list of standard perfectionist policies: 'performance art, art galleries, public parks, works of literature, sights of cultural significance, educational programmes for adults, and athletic events'.[29] It is difficult to see why these policies cannot achieve their purpose unless they are free at the point of consumption. Whereas Civilitian jubilees plausibly cannot achieve their purpose unless citizens 'encounter one another as members of a community rather than as fellow customers' and unless citizens 'know that they have been fully entitled to attend as [citizens]', this does not seem true of most of the items on Quong's list of standard perfectionist policies. Why can't educational programmes for adults, say, still achieve their main purpose—which is presumably to foster the intellectual enrichment of the citizenry—if they are ticketed and attendees are required to pay for admission? How is the good of intellectual enrichment tied to educational programmes being free at the point of consumption, in the way that the good of communal solidarity is tied to the gala festivities being free at the point of consumption?

Of course, the answer to these questions cannot be that, unless they are free, citizens would not *want* to spend their money on performance art, art galleries, educational programmes for adults, and so on. Perfectionists cannot say, for instance, that requiring payment for educational programmes for adults would undermine their purpose of fostering the intellectual enrichment of the citizenry by causing a collapse in attendance of such programmes. After all, that would resurrect the original charge of paternalism: it would raise the question of why citizens, when left to their own devices with a fair share of resources, cannot be expected to make sound decisions (by perfectionists' lights) about how to use their time and money. More

---

[26] Ibid., p. 73.
[27] Ibid.
[28] Quong, J., *Liberalism Without Perfection*, p. 89.
[29] Ibid.

280 A PERFECTIONIST THEORY OF JUSTICE

specifically, then, the question facing perfectionists who wish to deploy the public goods argument is this: why it is that the goods realized by perfectionist policies would in general be undermined by the imposition of admission fees, even if the imposition of such fees would have little or no effect on attendance?

In short, what needs to be provided is some systematic reason for thinking that most (or at least many) of the policies called for by perfectionists follow the model of Civilitian jubilees in the sense that they can only achieve their main purpose if they are free at the point of consumption.[30] In the absence of such a reason, it remains unclear what grounds there are for thinking that in the normal run of cases there exists a non-paternalistic justification for perfectionist state action.

9.3 Why Paternalism (in the Quongian Sense) Is Not Objectionable

My own suspicion is that the best answer to Quong's question about why perfectionist state action is necessary is likely to be pluralistic and to include both paternalistic and non-paternalistic elements. Among the non-paternalistic elements are: the need for the state to provide assurance to each citizen that others are doing their fair share towards the establishment and maintenance of social conditions conducive to flourishing ways of life; the need for the state to solve various coordination problems involving perfectionist externalities and perfectionist public goods; and the need for the state to resolve the indeterminacy between the different possible specifications of the perfectionist principles of justice through a public democratic determination of legal rights and duties. And among the paternalistic elements are the sorts of considerations mentioned in Section 9.1: the fact that citizens are not always able to discriminate effectively between more and less worthwhile activities and the fact that even when citizens are able to make such discriminations they do not always possess the willpower to pursue the worthier activities, which are often more strenuous and demanding. In combination, these sorts of factors will, I suspect, explain why state action is necessary to achieve perfectionist objectives.

In my view, then, perfectionists need not tie themselves in knots trying to show that they do not rely on 'negative assumptions about citizens' abilities to know and rationally pursue their own good'.[31] Perfectionists should instead offer a more straightforward and hard-line response to this objection, namely that the rationale for perfectionist state action does, at least partly, involve such assumptions but that

---

[30] For some interesting suggestions in this direction, see Billingham, P., 'Liberal Perfectionism and Quong's Internal Conception of Political Liberalism', *Social Theory and Practice* 43 (2017), pp. 87–8. One might also see Kramer's defence of aspirational perfectionism as providing a more systematic reason of this kind; I discuss aspirational perfectionism in Section 6.6.4.

[31] Quong, J., *Liberalism Without Perfection*, p. 86.

PATERNALISM 281

there is nothing particularly objectionable about proceeding on the basis of these assumptions—especially given that, as a growing body of evidence from the fields of social psychology and behavioural economics suggests, these assumptions are true of all human beings. In other words, perfectionists should argue that there is nothing objectionable about paternalism in the Quongian sense.[32]

An important challenge for anti-paternalists is the fact that there is now extensive empirical evidence that human beings are systematically and pervasively vulnerable to a catalogue of cognitive biases and failures of rationality.[33] To take just one of many possible examples, a study by Amos Tversky and Daniel Kahneman finds that when subjects are presented with what is by any measure the same option under two different descriptions or framings—for example, a medical procedure that has a 90 per cent chance of survival and a medical procedure that has a 10 per cent chance of death—they exhibit significant shifts of preference, thereby violating fairly uncontroversial principles of rational choice.[34]

Susceptibility to this catalogue of cognitive biases and failures of rationality is not unique to any specific social group but applies across human beings generally, including those recognized as experts in their fields. And 'debiasing' methods, such as warning subjects about the relevant biases before the experiment begins or offering them financial incentives to avoid errors, have been found to have little effect.[35] Susceptibility to bias and irrationality can thus be understood to be a deep and general fact about human beings even in ideal circumstances, and not simply an issue that arises in non-ideal circumstances. In light of this, one might wonder why we would cling to the demonstrably false assumption that citizens are always able 'to know and rationally pursue their own good'.[36] Far from being objectionable, isn't the assumption that citizens will not always make rational decisions about how to pursue their own good just plain common sense? Why should the state treat citizens as if they are disposed to make rational decisions about their own good, if there is every reason to believe that they are not in fact so disposed?

---

[32] Of course, an anti-perfectionist liberal might agree that there is nothing objectionable about paternalism in the Quongian sense but nonetheless argue that perfectionist justice should be rejected because it is paternalistic in some other (non-Quongian) sense. It is not possible to consider here whether perfectionism is guilty of paternalism in other possible senses, and if so whether this is objectionable, but for a wide-ranging recent defence of the view that there is nothing per se wrong with paternalism, see Hanna, J., *In Our Best Interest: A Defense of Paternalism* (Oxford: Oxford University Press, 2019).

[33] For some relevant empirical literature, see, for example, Thaler, R. and Sunstein, C., *Nudge: Improving Decisions About Health, Wealth, and Happiness* (New Haven, CT: Yale University Press, 2008); Ariely, D., *Predictably Irrational: The Hidden Forces That Shape Our Decisions* (New York: Harper Perennial, 2010); Kahneman, D., *Thinking, Fast and Slow* (New York: Farrar, Straus and Giroux, 2011).

[34] See Tversky, A. and Kahneman, D., 'The Framing of Decisions and the Psychology of Choice', *Science* 211 (1981), pp. 453–8.

[35] See, for example, Fischhoff, B., 'Debiasing', in D. Kahneman, P. Slovic and A. Tversky (eds), *Judgment Under Uncertainty: Heuristics and Biases* (Cambridge: Cambridge University Press, 1982), pp. 422–44.

[36] Quong, J., *Liberalism Without Perfection*, p. 86.

282   A PERFECTIONIST THEORY OF JUSTICE

There are at least three ways in which one might respond to this challenge.[37] The first option is to deny that these studies accurately describe human psychology and decision-making. Here one might argue, for instance, that this research is based largely on laboratory experiments which have low ecological validity and do not predict behaviour in real-world settings.[38] The second option is to accept that these studies accurately describe human psychology and decision-making but to deny that this constitutes evidence of 'irrationality' or 'bias' in any normatively signifi-cant sense. Here one might argue, for instance, that there are many conceptions of rationality, each of which posits different principles of reasoning and choice, and that the principles that human beings have been found to systematically violate are not in fact requirements of rationality properly conceived.[39] The third option is to accept that these studies accurately describe human psychology and decision-making, and to accept that this constitutes evidence of irrationality or bias, but to deny that this should lead us to abandon a commitment to anti-paternalism. To pursue this response, one might argue that showing respect to citizens requires treating them as if they are disposed to make rational decisions about their own good, *even if* there are good reasons to believe that they are not in fact so disposed. In what follows I will focus on this third line of response, since this is the response that Quong himself appears to favour.

To explore this third line of response, it is helpful to look further into Quong's account of the wrongness of paternalism. For Quong, paternalism is wrong be-cause it conflicts with what respect for the moral status of citizens requires. He explains that 'liberal political philosophy ought to begin with a moral or at least political conception of ourselves as free and equal. Following Rawls, we can char-acterize citizens as free and equal in virtue of their possession of two moral powers: a capacity for a sense of justice and a capacity for a conception of the good'.[40] The first moral power (a capacity for a sense of justice) is 'the capacity to understand, to apply, and to act from the public conception of justice'.[41] And the second moral power (a capacity for a conception of the good) is 'the capacity to form, to re-vise, and rationally to pursue a conception of one's rational advantage or good'.[42] What makes paternalism wrong is that it conflicts with this conception of moral status. It involves 'one person or group denying that another person or group has

[37] These three options are mentioned in Cholbi, M., 'Equal Respect for Rational Agency', in M. Timmons (ed.), *Oxford Studies in Normative Ethics* (Oxford: Oxford University Press, 2020), p. 184.

[38] See, for example, Koehler, J., 'The Base Rate Fallacy Reconsidered: Descriptive, Normative, and Methodological Challenges', *Behavioral and Brain Sciences* 19 (1996), pp. 1–17. For various responses, see the articles in 'Open Peer Commentary', *Behavioral and Brain Sciences* 19 (1996), pp. 17–53.

[39] See, for example, Gigerenzer, G., 'How to Make Cognitive Illusions Disappear: Beyond "Heuris-tics and Biases"', *European Review of Social Psychology* 2 (1991), pp. 83–115. For an interesting response, see Vranas, P., 'Gigerenzer's Normative Critique of Kahneman and Tversky', *Cognition* 76 (2000), pp. 179–93.

[40] Quong, J., *Liberalism Without Perfection*, p. 100.

[41] Rawls, J., *Political Liberalism* (New York: Columbia University Press, 2005), p. 19.

[42] Ibid.

the necessary capacity, in a given context, to exercise the second of the two moral powers: the capacity to plan, revise, and rationally pursue their own conception of the good'.[43] Similarly, Quong states that 'if [a law or policy] treats any person, or any class of persons, as if they lack, even temporarily, one of the two moral powers, it should be considered presumptively wrong'.[44] In this way, paternalistic laws and policies 'demean', 'denigrate' or 'disrespect' the moral status of citizens.[45]

Quong is aware, of course, that this not a factually accurate description of all citizens. 'We know that real people are not equal in terms of their capacity to realize the two powers described by Rawls', he notes, 'and so it [might seem] strange to require that we treat people *as if* they are.'[46] Why is it wrong to treat someone as if they lack the capacity to rationally pursue their own good, if they do in fact lack this capacity? In part, Quong's response to this challenge is to stress that he is only maintaining that paternalism is '*prima facie* or presumptive[ly]' wrong.[47] But this does not squarely address the challenge because it might seem strange to insist that there is *anything* wrong with treating people as if they lack a capacity that they really do lack. We are looking for an explanation of the *basis* for this wrong, not of its *magnitude*. Why is it *even presumptively wrong* to treat someone as if they lack the capacity to rationally pursue their own good, if they do in fact lack this capacity? Quong's more pertinent response thus seems to be that a certain sort of overestimation or benefit of the doubt is required by the conception of respect for moral status that is at the heart of the liberal project:

> Citizens must be treated as responsible moral agents, capable of responding to practical reasons, and capable of taking responsibility for their actions and the direction of their lives. This view of citizens as responsible moral agents is, I believe, a core element of liberalism. It is necessary to make sense of the rights

---

[43] Quong, J., *Liberalism Without Perfection*, p. 101.

[44] Ibid., p. 103.

[45] Ibid., pp. 101, 105. Other critics of perfectionism have appealed to similar ideas. Matthew Kramer suggests, as part of his critique of 'edificatory perfectionism', that paternalistic laws are objectionable because they bespeak a lack of 'respect for [citizens'] deliberative maturity' by 'treating them as untrustworthy in relation to their decisions about their own endeavours and lifestyles'. See Kramer, M., *Liberalism with Excellence*, pp. 200–1, 211–12, 217, 223, 231, 235. And Ruwen Ogien argues against perfectionism on the grounds that it is unnecessary, since people already 'naturally and inevitably aim at the best for themselves'. See Ogien, R., 'Neutrality Toward Non-Controversial Conceptions of the Good Life', in R. Merrill and D. Weinstock (eds), *Political Neutrality: A Re-evaluation* (New York: Palgrave Macmillan, 2014), pp. 97, 102–3. These arguments are, I believe, vulnerable to the same sort of objection developed in this section. In response to Kramer's argument—to give an illustration of how this generalization might go—we might naturally ask why respect for citizens' deliberate maturity requires treating them as if they are always trustworthy in relation to their decisions about their endeavours and lifestyles, if they are not in fact always trustworthy in relation to such decisions. In particular, why pick this specific conception of what respect for citizens' deliberative maturity requires over alternative conceptions of what such respect requires—for instance, a conception that says that respect for citizens' deliberate maturity requires treating them as if they are *often* (but not always) trustworthy in relation to their decisions about their endeavours and lifestyles?

[46] Quong, J., *Liberalism Without Perfection*, p. 102.

[47] Ibid.

284   A PERFECTIONIST THEORY OF JUSTICE

and freedoms to which all liberals are committed. By offering each person certain fundamental rights and liberties, liberalism affirms citizens' moral right to direct their own lives consistent with a similar right for others. This affirmation only makes sense if we attribute to citizens the moral powers necessary to direct their own life, and to act in ways consistent with the requirements of justice.[48]

So, at a first pass, Quong's account of the wrongness of paternalism appears to be as follows:

(P1) Respect for the moral status of citizens requires that the state treat them as if they have the capacity to rationally pursue their own good
(P2) Paternalistic laws and policies do not treat citizens as if they have the capacity to rationally pursue their own good
(C1) So, paternalistic laws and policies show disrespect for the moral status of citizens
(P3) Showing disrespect for the moral status of citizens is prima facie morally wrong
(C2) So, paternalistic laws and policies are prima facie morally wrong.

Before continuing, two initial comments on this argument are in order. The first concerns (P3). As mentioned above, Quong is at pains to stress that his claim is only that paternalism is '*prima facie* or presumptive[ly]' wrong.[49] There may well be cases, he says, when 'paternalistic policies, although disrespectful in terms of moral status and thus *prima facie* wrong, may nevertheless be justifiable all things considered'.[50] However, he presumably also wants to say more than the fairly uninteresting claim that the costs to moral status are so miniscule or slight that they are routinely outweighed by the benefits of perfectionist policies. To say that there is a sliver of a respect in which perfectionist policies are objectionable is not to say very much against perfectionism. Even if we cannot be very precise about such things, then, we can assume that Quong wants to say that insult to or disrespect of moral status is something that weighs fairly heavily on the decisional scales. Indeed, he does at one point speak of 'the *substantial* cost of denigrating citizens' moral status'.[51] So it seems reasonable to assume that, for Quong, showing disrespect for the moral status of citizens is a *fairly serious* moral wrong.

The second initial comment concerns (P2). Quong says that paternalistic laws treat citizens as if they lack 'the *capacity* to plan, revise, and rationally pursue their own conception of the good' and 'as if they lack the *ability* to make effective choices

---

[48] Ibid., pp. 315–16.
[49] Ibid., p. 102.
[50] Ibid., p. 103.
[51] Ibid. (emphasis added).

about their own lives'.[52] However, it seems more accurate to say that paternalistic laws treat citizens as if they lack the *disposition* or *propensity* to make rational choices about their own lives.[53] Consider a paternalistic state that passes laws to protect citizens from the allure of gambling. It is neither necessary nor plausible to suppose that this law is motivated by the belief that citizens *cannot* resist the temptation to gamble. Instead, what seems to motivate this law is the belief that citizens are *unlikely* to resist the temptation to gamble. So Quong's argument should be formulated in terms of propensities, dispositions or likely behaviour rather than capacities or abilities. This is important because doubting that someone is likely to act rationally is, at least on the face of it, less disrespectful than doubting that someone has the ability or capacity to act rationally—the former cuts less deep, in some sense, than the latter.

In light of these two points, a better formulation of Quong's argument for the wrongness of paternalism appears to be as follows:

(P1) Respect for the moral status of citizens requires that the state treat them as if they are disposed always to make rational decisions about their own good

(P2) Paternalistic laws and policies do not treat citizens as if they are disposed always to make rational decisions about their own good

(C1) So, paternalistic laws and policies show disrespect for the moral status of citizens

(P3) Showing disrespect for the moral status of citizens is fairly seriously morally wrong

(C2) So, paternalistic laws and policies are fairly seriously morally wrong.

In what follows, I challenge (P1). In particular, I argue that Quong has not explained why we should endorse this highly specific conception of what respect for the moral status of citizens requires over alternative possible conceptions of what respect for the moral status of citizens requires.

Quong does not consider whether there might be alternative conceptions of what respect for the moral status of citizens requires. He presents his conception of respect for moral status as if it were essential to or definitive of liberalism: he describes it as 'a core element of liberalism' and as a conception with which 'liberal political philosophy ought to begin'.[54] But in fact his conception of what respect for the moral status of citizens requires occupies only one point along a broad

[52] Ibid., pp. 101, 106 (emphasis added).
[53] This point is also made in Birks, D., 'Moral Status and the Wrongness of Paternalism', *Social Theory and Practice* 40 (2014), pp. 488–9; Enoch, D., 'What's Wrong with Paternalism: Autonomy, Belief, and Action', *Proceedings of the Aristotelian Society* 116 (2016), pp. 28–30; Kramer, M., *Liberalism with Excellence*, pp. 87–91; Billingham, P., 'Liberal Perfectionism and Quong's Internal Conception of Political Liberalism', pp. 86–7; Hanna, J., *In Our Best Interest*, p. 77–9.
[54] Quong, J., *Liberalism Without Perfection*, pp. 100, 316.

286 A PERFECTIONIST THEORY OF JUSTICE

continuum of possible conceptions of what such respect requires, many of which are compatible with liberalism. Consider, in this regard, the following list, the first entry of which corresponds to Quong's conception:

(R1) Respect for the moral status of citizens requires that the state treat them as if they are disposed *always* to make rational decisions about their own good

(R2) Respect for the moral status of citizens requires that the state treat them as if they are disposed *typically* to make rational decisions about their own good

(R3) Respect for the moral status of citizens requires that the state treat them as if they are disposed *often* to make rational decisions about their own good

(R4) Respect for the moral status of citizens requires that the state treat them as if they are disposed *sometimes* to make rational decisions about their own good

(R5) Respect for the moral status of citizens requires that the state treat them as if they are disposed *never* to make rational decisions about their own good.

Some of these views are clearly implausible. The fifth conception of respect for moral status, for instance, amounts to treating citizens as if they were children. But others among these conceptions are quite plausible. In particular, consider the third conception of respect for moral status. This conception does not 'treat citizens as if they were children' in any straightforward sense.[55] It does not threaten citizens' sense of themselves as 'responsible moral agents, capable of responding to practical reasons'.[56] Nor does it undermine 'the social bases of self-respect'.[57] These considerations, offered by Quong in support of (R1), seem to me to underdetermine the choice between (R1) and (R3), even if they do succeed in explaining why we should prefer (R1) to, say, (R5). So the availability of alternatives such as (R3) indicates that to reject (R1) is not, as Quong suggests, to deny the 'liberal conception of ourselves as free and equal'.[58] It is simply to deny a particular *interpretation* of free and equal liberal citizenship. In this way, (R3) can be understood to offer a rendering of the notion of free and equal citizenship that is found in the perfectionist ideal of society as a fair striving for human flourishing between free and equal citizens.

Importantly, this third conception of what respect for the moral status of citizens requires is compatible with putting in place some paternalistic laws and policies

[55] Ibid., p. 315.
[56] Ibid., pp. 315–16.
[57] Ibid., p. 103.
[58] Ibid., p. 107.

designed to protect citizens, as boundedly rational beings, against their own inevitable and occasional weaknesses of reason or will. Of course, these paternalistic laws and policies cannot be too extensive—for this would not treat citizens as if they are disposed often to make rational decisions about their own good. But the point remains that a state could enact plenty of paternalistic laws and policies without falling foul of this third conception of what respect for the moral status of citizens requires.

If (R1) is correct, then paternalistic laws and policies express disrespect for the moral status of citizens and so are fairly seriously morally wrong. Yet if (R3) is correct, then such laws are not disrespectful at all. If (R3) is correct, that is, then it is not just that paternalistic laws and policies, although disrespectful in terms of moral status and thus prima facie wrong, might be all-things-considered permissible; rather, there would be *nothing* disrespectful in terms of moral status about paternalistic laws and policies. So, in order to determine whether paternalism really is a fairly serious moral wrong, we need to adjudicate between these competing conceptions of what respect for the moral status of citizens requires. Is (R1) or (R3) more intuitively plausible?

Before trying to address this question, let me consider a possible challenge to this way of framing things. One might wonder why we should adopt the kind of coarse-grained, rule-based view of what constitutes respect for citizens that is implied by the formulations of (R1)–(R5). Shouldn't we instead assess each paternalistic action on a case-by-case basis? Consider an interpersonal analogue in which Abby paternalistically throws Ben's cigarettes into the bin. Wouldn't it be odd for Abby to say to Ben, 'My paternalistic treatment of you in this instance is nevertheless consistent with treating you with the respect that you are owed as my adult friend and colleague because my act in this instance is guided by a more general policy of treating you as being disposed *often* to make rational decisions for yourself'? Wouldn't it be much more natural to say that, in this instance, Abby does not treat Ben with the respect he is owed as her adult friend and colleague, even though, in many other instances, she does treat him with this level of respect? If Abby is guided by something like the rule (R3), then surely what she does is often treat Ben with the relevant respect, but sometimes not.[59]

It is unclear, however, that we can altogether avoid reliance on some general rule or principle about what constitutes respect for citizens. In the case of Abby and Ben, for example, we would be inclined to say that, in this instance, Abby does not treat Ben with the respect he is owed as her adult friend and colleague if we are inclined to accept something like (R1)—the view that respect for the moral status of individuals requires treating them as if they are disposed always to make rational decisions about their own good. If instead we are inclined to accept something like (R3), then it no longer looks as odd to say that instances of paternalistic treatment

---

[59] I thank Jonathan Quong for putting this objection to me.

can be consistent with respect, so long as those instances of paternalistic treatment are not too frequent. For those inclined to accept (R3), the fact that Abby's behaviour is guided by a more general policy of treating Ben as being disposed often to make rational decisions for himself is a morally significant fact—one that means that Abby does not treat Ben as a child, or threaten his sense of himself as a responsible moral agent, or undermine the bases of his self-respect. This is not to say that (R3) delivers the intuitively correct verdict in this case. Indeed, perhaps its implications in the case of Abby and Ben constitute a strike against (R3).[60] The point is just that case-by-case evaluations of paternalistic actions still seem to be informed, if only implicitly, by some general rule or principle, and so the important question remains that of whether (R1) or (R3) is the more intuitively plausible conception of respect.

Turning, now, to the matter of whether (R1) or (R3) is more plausible: this is a difficult question to answer, and I cannot do it justice here. Since (R1) appears to involve significant *overestimation* of citizens' abilities or dispositions, one way to begin to adjudicate between these conceptions of respect is to consider whether respecting others requires significant overestimation of this kind. Clearly, respect requires that we do not *underestimate* others. It is disrespectful to treat Mary as if she is incapable of doing brain surgery, if she can in fact do brain surgery. But does respect also go further than this, requiring that we significantly *overestimate* others? It is difficult to see why. Surely it is not disrespectful to treat Mary as if she is incapable of doing brain surgery, if she *cannot* in fact do brain surgery. Indeed, there may well be a sense in which significant overestimation of others is not just not required by respect but in fact positively disrespectful. Perhaps, that is, there is a sense in which it is disrespectful to treat Mary as if she is capable of doing brain surgery, if she cannot in fact do brain surgery—for such treatment would involve a kind of demeaning pretence or make-believe. This point is nicely brought out by Sarah Conly in some intriguing reflections on the relationship between respect and the estimation of others' abilities:

---

[60] Before one can draw this conclusion, though, two complications would need to be addressed. The first is that (R3) is a conception of respect meant to apply in the political context specifically, rather than in interpersonal contexts. This matters because paternalism that is disrespectful in the interpersonal context can often be respectful in the political context. Often, that is, it is wrong for a private individual to intervene in another person's actions for her own good, even though it is not wrong for the state and its officials to do so—in just the same way that it is often wrong for a private individual to intervene in another person's actions for the purpose of preventing harm to others (i.e. through acting as a vigilante), even though it is not wrong for the state and its officials to do so. (On this point, see, e.g., Hanna, J., *In Our Best Interest*, pp. 24–6.) The second complication is that Abby's paternalistic act is independently wrong: it involves the violation of Ben's property rights over his cigarettes. So, if we do feel intuitive pressure to say that, in this instance, Ben has not been treated with the respect he is owed, an alternative explanation of this intuition is available—an explanation that does not rely on the fact that, in this instance, Abby doubts that Ben is disposed to make a rational decision about his own good. If we replace Abby's paternalistic act (i.e. throwing Ben's cigarettes into the bin) with a paternalistic act that lacks any (other) wrong-making properties (e.g. a paternalistic offer), the intuition that Ben has been treated with disrespect (and indeed with a fairly seriously morally wrong sort of disrespect) becomes, I think, considerably weaker.

When someone accurately assesses my abilities ... and finds me lacking in some respects, it is very hard for me to argue that I have been ... disrespected ... It may, of course, take away from someone's consequence, in the eyes of others or in his own eyes, if it is pointed out that he doesn't have a particular quality that he thought he had. However, it is more demeaning to pretend to have a quality that you don't than to admit to not having one you might like to have. The story of the Emperor's new clothes is illustrative—the Emperor wouldn't have suffered embarrassment before all the people of the kingdom if he had admitted that he couldn't see the 'magic' clothes that the conmen tailors were trying to get him to accept ... What hurt him was pretending that he was one of the wise who were supposed to be able to see them ... Claiming to have a stature you don't is more disrespectful of self, and of one's real attributes, than is admitting to a lesser stature. It suggests that what you've got left when you eliminate the disputed property isn't worth much—but there is no reason to think this of people. We remain as we have been, as we have experienced ourselves, and have appreciated ourselves, and this is clearly valuable, whatever stature we may lose.[61]

I should stress that Conly's remarks do not perfectly dovetail with my contention that (R3) is a superior conception of respect to (R1). After all, the conception of respect that Conly appears to be defending is the view that respect requires treating citizens in line with an accurate assessment of their rational abilities and dispositions. So if citizens are in actual fact only *sometimes* disposed to make rational decisions about their own good, then Conly would presumably endorse (R4). In this sense, Conly does not endorse (R3), and she may well find (R3) still to be overly idealized, even if less idealized than (R1). Nonetheless, Conly's observations do lend support to the case for the superiority of (R3) to (R1) insofar as they suggest that respect does not require us to significantly overestimate others' abilities and that, if anything, such overestimation may in fact be disrespectful in an important sense.

In response, a defender of (R1) might argue that the requirement to treat citizens as if they are disposed always to make rational decisions about their own good is based not on some sort of demeaning pretence or make-believe reminiscent of the Emperor's new clothes but rather on an idea of *deference*. This view is defended by Michael Cholbi, who develops an account of the wrongness of paternalism very similar to that of Quong, and who argues that 'respect for rational agency requires deference toward agents even when they do not exercise that agency with full competence or capability'.[62] Deferring to others in this way establishes the kind

---

[61] Conly, S., *Against Autonomy: Justifying Coercive Paternalism* (Cambridge: Cambridge University Press, 2013), pp. 40–1.

[62] Cholbi, M., 'Paternalism and Our Rational Powers', *Mind* 126 (2017), p. 126. See also Cholbi, M., 'Equal Respect for Rational Agency'.

of 'distance' between individuals that is, for Kant, a mark of respect: 'if the principle of love bids friends to draw closer, the principle of respect requires them to stay at a proper distance from each other'.[63] As Cholbi explains more fully:

> Showing *deference* toward rational agents is an essential element of respecting rational agency, of seeing rational agency as establishing boundaries we have strong moral reasons not to trespass against. Such deference generates a high bar for the evidence needed to persuade us that someone's rational agency is faulty and thus helps to explain the general moral presumption against paternalistic intercessions in others' agency ... [Respect] asks us to discount or bracket evidence we may have concerning the competence of others' rational agency in order to respect them as rational agents. It may seem odd that a moral demand can have implications regarding our epistemic obligations—that a moral stance we take towards others can imply an epistemic stance we must take towards others. But there are instances in which our moral obligations require us to *forego* the pursuit of particular knowledge or information, such as when the right to privacy entails an obligation not to pursue certain evidence ... The deference involved in respecting rational agency generates obligations of a different epistemic kind, compelling us (at least to some degree) to *disregard* evidence concerning an agent's rational competence. It thus operates somewhat like legal obligations, imposed on judges, to set aside evidence resting on hearsay or acquired via coercion.[64]

I do not deny that a certain sort of deference is a constitutive feature of respect. What I find doubtful, though, is that the idea of deference entails (R1). To see this, it is helpful to observe that Cholbi's account of deference is indeterminate in an important respect. Cholbi explains that, once we are satisfied that an individual exceeds a minimal threshold of rational competence, showing deference towards that individual requires us to disregard, *at least to some degree*, evidence concerning his rational competence. But to what degree, exactly, should we disregard evidence concerning an individual's rational competence? Here again we can imagine a spectrum of possible conceptions of deference. For the sake of symmetry with (R1) and (R3), let us consider just two points along this spectrum:

(D1) Showing deference towards an individual requires us *always* to disregard evidence concerning that individual's rational competence

(D3) Showing deference towards an individual requires us *often* to disregard evidence concerning that individual's rational competence.

---

[63] Kant, I., *Practical Philosophy*, trans. and ed. M. Gregor (Cambridge: Cambridge University Press, 1996), p. 585.

[64] Cholbi, M., 'Paternalism and Our Rational Powers', pp. 146–8 (emphases in original).

PATERNALISM 291

Perhaps (D1) entails (R1)—at least in the sense that (D1) is compatible with (R1) and incompatible with (R3). But consider (D3). (D3) is a plausible interpretation of what it means to show deference towards an individual. Someone committed to (R3) sees rational agency as establishing boundaries we have strong moral reasons not to trespass against, accepts that moral demands can have implications regarding our epistemic obligations, and often (though not always) disregards evidence concerning others' rational competence. Importantly, however, (D3) does not entail (R1). After all, (D3) is compatible with (R3), since (D3) allows us to take into account evidence of other individuals' irrationality, so long as this does not occur too frequently. What this shows is that whether the idea of deference entails (R1) depends on whether (D1) or (D3) is the most intuitively plausible specification of deference.

Appealing to the idea of deference thus does little if anything to help us adjudicate between (R1) and (R3). It simply pushes the question back. Previously, we were asking: is (R1) the right conception of what respect for the moral status of citizens requires? In particular, is (R1) more or less plausible than alternative conceptions of what respect for the moral status of citizens requires, such as (R3)? Now, we are asking: is (D1) the right conception of what showing deference towards an individual requires? In particular, is (D1) more or less plausible than alternative conceptions of what showing deference towards an individual requires, such as (D3)? Much more would need to be said, then, in order to justify the claim that the requirement to treat citizens as if they are disposed always to make rational decisions about their own good is based not on pretence or make-believe but rather on an ideal of deference.[65]

In short, (R3) is attractive because it accommodates the advantages of (R1) without the kind of significant overestimation of citizens' abilities that does not seem to be necessary for showing respect for moral status and that may even be incompatible with showing such respect. Like (R1), that is, (R3) does not treat citizens

---

[65] Defenders of (R1) might instead be tempted to ground the requirement to treat citizens as if they are disposed always to make rational decisions about their own good in the idea of 'opacity respect', which is developed by Ian Carter. See Carter, I., 'Respect and the Basis of Equality', *Ethics* 121 (2011), pp. 538–71; see also the discussion in Hanna, J., *In Our Best Interest*, pp. 81–2. Again, I do not deny that treating citizens as opaque is, in some sense, a constitutive feature of respect. (But for the view that opacity respect is better regarded as a useful social norm rather than a fundamental moral principle, see, e.g., Arneson, R., 'Basic Equality: Neither Acceptable Nor Rejectable', in U. Steinhoff (ed.), *Do All Persons Have Equal Moral Worth? On 'Basic Equality' and Equal Respect and Concern* (Oxford: Oxford University Press, 2015), pp. 45–8.) Still, I suspect that my response to the attempt to ground (R1) in the idea of deference would apply to the attempt to ground (R1) in the idea of opacity respect: namely, that the idea of opacity respect is to some degree indeterminate and amenable to various possible interpretations and specifications, some of which entail (R1) but others of which do not, and that one would need to engage in a detailed comparative analysis of the intuitive plausibility of these various alternatives in order to justify the conclusion that (R1) is entailed by the idea of opacity respect. Rather than providing compelling independent reasons for the superiority of (R1) to (R3), in other words, the appeal to opacity respect also looks likely to simply push back the question of whether (R1) or (R3) is superior.

as if they are children, does not threaten citizens' sense of themselves as responsible moral agents, and does not undermine the social bases of citizens' self-respect. Moreover, like (R1), (R3) is compatible with a plausible specification of the sort of deference that seems to be constitutive of respect. But unlike (R1), which tells us to treat others as if they are, quite literally, superhumanly reliable practical reasoners, (R3) grows out of a more realistic and recognizable assessment of persons' powers of reason and will—which are considerable, but have identifiable limits.

Here one might object that, in saying that (R3) accommodates the advantages of (R1), I am assuming a binary picture: either we treat citizens as children or we don't, either we undermine the social bases of self-respect or we don't, and so on. But if we think of things as aligned along a spectrum, isn't it plausible to say that (R3) involves treating citizens *more* like children than (R1), but less so than (R5)? And if so, doesn't this consideration favour (R1) over (R3)?[66]

As a matter of linguistic or conceptual intuition, though, is not at all clear to me that (R3) does involve treating citizens more like children than (R1). Consider an analogy. Suppose I treat Alice either (a) as if she is disposed to give 100 per cent of her surplus income to charity or (b) as if she is disposed to give 90 per cent of her surplus income to charity. Do I really treat Alice as 'more' of a Scrooge in (b) than in (a)? In my view, it is more natural to say that in *neither* case I treat Alice as a Scrooge (to any extent). In both cases I treat her as an altruist; it is just that in (b) I treat her as an altruist who is slightly less disposed to give her surplus income to charity than in (a). It might, of course, be disrespectful to treat Alice as slightly less disposed to give her surplus income to charity; but it would not be disrespectful *because doing so treats her more like a Scrooge.* Similarly, suppose I treat Anton either (a) as if he is disposed to make rational decisions about his own good 100 per cent of the time or (b) as if he is disposed to make rational decisions about his own good 90 per cent of the time. Do I really treat Anton as 'more' of a child in (b) than in (a)? Again, it seems more natural to say that in *neither* case I treat Anton as a child (to any extent). In both cases I treat him as an adult; it is just that in (b) I treat him as an adult who is slightly less disposed to make rational decisions than in (a). As before, it might be disrespectful to treat Anton as slightly less disposed to make rational decisions (though for the reasons given in this section I doubt this); but it would not be disrespectful *because doing so treats him more like a child.* In other words, (R1) and (R3) both prescribe treating citizens so differently from the way in which children are typically treated that the contrast between these two conceptions of respect is not really illuminated by thinking about whether they involve treating citizens more or less like children. So while invoking the metaphor of the child might be helpful for adjudicating between, say, (R1) and (R5), after a certain point this metaphor ceases, I believe, to be at all helpful for adjudicating between conceptions of respect.

---

[66] I thank Jonathan Quong for putting this objection to me.

Clearly, these initial impressions do not come close to settling things. They do not vindicate the thought that respect for the moral status of citizens requires treating citizens as if they are disposed often to make rational decisions about their own good, rather than treating them as if they are disposed always to do so. The main point that I want to make here is just that there is much more work to do before we can be confident that paternalism in the Quongian sense is a fairly serious moral wrong. There is, I have suggested, a range of alternative and not implausible conceptions of what respect for the moral status of citizens requires, and until some reason has been given for picking Quong's specific conception of respect for moral status over these alternatives, it is unclear why we need to think that paternalistic laws and policies are fairly seriously morally wrong.

10
The Village Busybody

The objections to perfectionism that have been considered so far all claim that the objectionable feature of perfectionism consists in the way it treats citizens: that it imposes on them values that are subject to reasonable disagreement; that it threatens their freedom, autonomy or personal sovereignty; and that it makes negative, infantilizing judgements about their capacity to rationally run their own lives. But one might also critique perfectionism from a different direction: not by focusing on how it treats citizens but by focusing on the vices or unappealing characteristics of the perfectionist state itself. In particular, one might think that there is something meddlesome or snoopy about the outlook of the perfectionist state. In this vein, Martha Nussbaum argues that 'it is just nosy and impertinent for the state and its agents to inquire' too closely into citizens' values and choices, while Gerald Gaus speaks in this context of the 'difficult virtue of minding one's own business' and calls for 'the political rehabilitation of Ebenezer Scrooge'.[1]

This kind of objection has recently been pressed in an especially vigorous and sophisticated way by Matthew Kramer, who argues that the deeply objectionable feature of perfectionism consists not in the way it treats citizens but rather in the mentality that imbues the perfectionist state. Perfectionist regimes that seek the elevation and edification of the citizenry, argues Kramer, are guilty of a 'quidnunc mentality'—a mentality akin in important respects to that of a village busybody who distributes 'boxes of delicious homemade fudge' to 'inspire her fellow inhabitants to lead lives of propriety' and who in general meddles in matters that are none of her business.[2] Put differently, the perfectionist state violates a 'deontological ethic of self-restraint'.[3] What makes the activities of a perfectionist state illegitimate, on this view, is that such activities emanate from, and are animated by, an objectionable mentality—one that is redolent of the mentality of a village busybody, a curtain-twitcher or a Nosey Parker.

In this chapter I first spell out Kramer's quidnunc mentality objection (Section 10.1). I then argue (in Section 10.2) that the quidnunc mentality objection fails because it begs the question against perfectionism by assuming precisely what needs to be shown, namely that the edification of the citizenry falls outside

---

[1] Nussbaum, M., 'Perfectionist Liberalism and Political Liberalism', *Philosophy & Public Affairs* 39 (2011), p. 33; Gaus, G., 'On the Difficult Virtue of Minding One's Own Business: Towards the Political Rehabilitation of Ebenezer Scrooge', *The Philosopher* 5 (1997), pp. 24–8.
[2] Kramer, M., *Liberalism with Excellence* (Oxford: Oxford University Press, 2017), ch. 6, at p. 282.
[3] Ibid., p. 253.

A Perfectionist Theory of Justice. Collis Tahzib, Oxford University Press.
© Collis Tahzib (2022). DOI: 10.1093/oso/9780192847119.003.0011

the proper bounds of government. In other words, when Kramer says that the perfectionist state sticks its nose where it does not belong or meddles in matters that are none of its business, he already assumes that the state has no duty to promote the flourishing and edification of the citizenry; but he cannot help himself to this assumption because the question of whether the state has a duty to promote the flourishing and edification of the citizenry is precisely what is at stake in the debate between perfectionists and anti-perfectionist liberals. I then consider and reject two responses available to Kramer: that he has provided a substantive argument against the existence of perfectionist duties based on the idea of warranted self-respect and on the harm principle (Section 10.3); and that any perfectionist theory that evades the quidnunc mentality objection would be indistinguishable from leading forms of anti-perfectionist liberalism (Section 10.4). Finally, in an addendum, I offer some brief comments on a recent rejoinder by Kramer to a previously published version of this chapter (Section 10.5).

10.1 What Is the Quidnunc Mentality?

Though this chapter will focus on Kramer's quidnunc mentality argument in particular, it is worth briefly situating that argument within his broader views. Recall from Section 6.6.4 that Kramer draws a distinction between two forms of perfectionist political theory: 'edificatory perfectionism' (which is the form of perfectionism espoused by all contemporary perfectionists, including myself) and 'aspirational perfectionism' (which is Kramer's preferred form of perfectionism and which, he explains, 'has not heretofore been espoused by anyone').[4] Both views largely converge on the bottom line insofar as they both call for public policies that promote excellence in a range of areas of human endeavour.[5] However, they differ in their underlying justificatory structure and 'in the *rationales* that generate their respective verdicts on matters of public policy'.[6] Whereas edificatory perfectionists support perfectionist policies on the grounds that these policies promote the edification of the citizenry, aspirational perfectionists eschew this 'edificatory impulse' and instead support perfectionist policies on the grounds that 'the attainment of excellence by a society through the emergence of impressive feats within it is a necessary condition for the warrantedness of a robust sense of self-respect on the part of each individual who belongs to that society'.[7] Since the theory I defend qualifies, in Kramer's terminology, as an *edificatory*-perfectionist theory of justice and not an *aspirational*-perfectionist theory of justice, I will need to defend it against the quidnunc mentality objection that

---

[4] Ibid., p. 36.
[5] See ibid., pp. 49, 55, 278–9.
[6] Ibid., p. 49 (emphasis added).
[7] Ibid., p. 36.

Kramer has recently levelled against edificatory-perfectionist theories. In what follows, I will focus exclusively on edificatory perfectionism and so I will sometimes drop the qualification 'edificatory' for the sake of readability.

One of the most interesting and distinctive features of Kramer's quidnunc mentality objection to perfectionism is that it involves 'a change of perspective'.[8] To date, critics of perfectionism have generally adopted what Kramer calls a 'citizen-focused perspective' and have held that the illegitimacy of perfectionist politics derives from the way in which it treats citizens.[9] By contrast, Kramer adopts what he calls a 'government-focused perspective', according to which the illegitimacy of perfectionist politics derives from the mentality or outlook of a perfectionist system of governance and its state officials.[10] In the course of his analysis, he uses a variety of richly suggestive terms to evoke aspects of this mentality: officious, over-weening, prickly, heavy-handed, unaccommodating, overbearing, meddlesome, busybody, censorious, nosy and, of course, its official label 'quidnunc'.

This shift of perspective, says Kramer, is important for understanding what makes perfectionism 'always and everywhere morally wrong' and parallels a shift in his earlier work on the ethics of torture.[11] There he argues that any absolutist account of the wrongness of torture must refer not only to the interests, rights and dignity of the victim but also to the perpetrators of torture, who, by stooping to this atrocious practice, tarnish their moral integrity as well as the moral integrity of the system of governance on whose behalf they act. The perpetrator-focused perspective is necessary for explaining the absolute wrongness of torture because if we consider matters solely from the perspective of the victim, it is difficult to account for the wrongness of certain instances of torture, such as the torture of a victim who is physiologically incapable of experiencing pain. Similarly, there might be cases in which perfectionism is not disrespectful or otherwise problematic from the citizen's perspective and so the government-focused perspective is necessary for capturing what makes the 'drive for edification' always and everywhere wrong.[12]

But what, more precisely, *is* the quidnunc mentality and what makes it *wrongful*, as opposed to merely less than ideal? Here it is helpful to turn to the main analogy that Kramer uses to illustrate the quidnunc mentality, namely that of the village busybody. On Kramer's view, officials who uphold a perfectionist system of governance interact with their fellow citizens 'in broadly the same fashion in which a busybody of some village interacts with her fellow villagers'.[13] In seeking to promote the edification of citizens through elevating their tastes, refining their

---

[8] Ibid., p. 254.
[9] Ibid.
[10] Ibid.
[11] Ibid., pp. 254–64, at p. 255. See Kramer, M., *Torture and Moral Integrity: A Philosophical Enquiry* (Oxford: Oxford University Press, 2014), especially pp. 187–212.
[12] Kramer, M., *Liberalism with Excellence*, p. 264.
[13] Ibid., p. 276.

THE VILLAGE BUSYBODY 297

sensibilities or perfecting their characters, perfectionist state officials express the same cast of mind as that of a village busybody who 'keeps track of how her fellow residents behave' and who 'hectors or ostracizes anyone whom she believes to be falling significantly short', even though the relevant conduct of the residents 'affect[s] her only through her own sentiments of offendedness and gratification'.[14]

Kramer argues that the attitude of the village busybody is objectionable in two main ways, namely by being 'a form of self-aggrandizement and a form of self-abasement'.[15] Since so much of the prima facie intuitive force of this objection is bound up with Kramer's vivid and inimitable depictions of the pathologies of the village busybody, it is worth quoting at some length here:

> At the level of an individual, the quidnunc mentality is quite evidently a failure of self-restraint. It is both a form of self-aggrandizement and a form of self-abasement. It is a meddlesome form of self-aggrandizement because it takes for granted that one's fellows can rightly be prevailed upon—through coercion or through vehement exhortation—to modify patterns of behavior that are not legitimately of concern to anybody except the individuals themselves who engage in those patterns of behavior. Yet the quidnunc mentality also consists in self-abasement, since it makes one's own sense of satisfaction partly dependent on the responsiveness of one's fellows to one's officious badgering about their private pursuits. Instead of abiding by a live-and-let-live ethos, a busybody partly ties the success of her own life to her effectiveness in not letting other people lead their lives as they see fit. That is, the success of her own life partly hinges on the willingness of other people to desist from conduct that offends her (even though the conduct does not otherwise harm her or anybody else). In precisely that respect, one's possession of a quidnunc mentality is a manifestation of weakness.[16]

Moving back to politics, Kramer contends that similar points apply to the mentality that characterizes perfectionist governments:

> At the level of a system of governance, a quidnunc mentality that underlies various laws or policies is even more egregiously a failure of self-restraint. Again, it is both a form of self-aggrandizement and a form of self-abasement. It is a meddlesome form of self-aggrandizement because any laws or policies that emanate from it are aimed neither at preventing the infliction of harm by some people on others nor at fulfilling any of the further responsibilities [of government]. Rather, those laws or policies are aimed at prevailing upon people—coercively or enticingly—to abandon certain patterns of behavior that are not harmful to other people in any

[14] Ibid.
[15] Ibid., p. 277.
[16] Ibid.

significant ways. Furthermore, the overweeningness of the quidnunc mentality in that regard is integrally linked to the sense in which such a mentality is also a self-abasing manifestation of weakness. It is an outlook of self-abasingness because it presumes that the success of a system of governance is partly dependent on the willingness of citizens to alter their private pursuits in response to inducements by the system's officials. Instead of remaining confined to the dispensation of information and the maintenance of fair conditions for informed decisions by citizens about the aforementioned pursuits, a system of governance with laws or policies that stem from a quidnunc mentality will have tied the success of its endeavors partly to its effectiveness in not letting citizens arrive at disfavored decisions about the ways in which they should lead their lives ... A scheme of governance should not be dependent for its success on its prodding of citizens about their preferred lifestyles when no requirements of justice are at stake; a scheme of governance should not resemble a busybody whose equanimity hinges on the effectiveness of the similarly officious prodding in which she engages.[17]

In acting on the basis of a mentality that renders it 'both grandiosely presumptuous and demeaningly vulnerable', the perfectionist state violates a 'deontological ethic of self-restraint'—a wrong that 'tarnishes its moral integrity', that 'far-reachingly informs and taints' its relationship with the citizenry and that 'deprives [its edificatory-perfectionist laws] of moral legitimacy'.[18]

Before proceeding, three important clarifications are in order. The first is that this objection is not meant to be an accusation of error. Kramer clarifies that although 'most busybodies are indeed error-prone when they identify standards of propriety which they apply in their censorious judgments about the behavior of other people', the quidnunc mentality objection does not allege that the perfectionist state will make mistakes about what ways of life are worthy or unworthy.[19] Even if we assume that the perfectionist state will 'always be correct' in its judgements about worthiness and unworthiness, its interactions with citizens will still be both self-aggrandizing and self-abasing.[20]

The second clarification is that this objection is not limited to the perfectionist state's discouragement of unworthy activities through measures such as sin taxes and legal prohibitions ('the stick'); it also applies to its encouragement of worthy activities through measures such as subsidies, incentives, awards and educational programmes for adults ('the carrot'):

A busybody might berate or ostentatiously shun any of her fellow villagers who have not lived up to her standards of propriety, or she might instead regularly

---

[17] Ibid., pp. 277–8.
[18] Ibid., pp. 253, 277, 278.
[19] Ibid., p. 279.
[20] Ibid.

and conspicuously provide inducements—such as boxes of delicious homemade fudge—to her fellow villagers who have managed to live up to those standards. In either case, she is acting with the aim of influencing the lifestyles of other people beyond what is required of them as matters of justice and basic civility. She implements that aim in a more objectionably heavy-handed fashion when she pursues it through vilification and ostracism than when she pursues it through selective largesse, but her project is overweeningly officious in either case. It manifests her presumptuousness as she obtrudes her judgemental assessments upon the other residents of her village, and it likewise manifests her abject tendency to let her peace of mind depend on the choices of those residents concerning their pastimes and private ideals. Similarly, when an edificatory-perfectionist system of governance draws upon subventions and other affirmative means of encouragement to press citizens to improve their modes of living (beyond what is required of them as matters of justice), it partakes of the meddlesomeness of a busybody ... The officials in an edificatory-perfectionist system of governance exhibit the mentality of a quidnunc as they nosily judge that, in the absence of subsidies or other stimuli, too many citizens will lead lives that are insufficiently refined or wholesome or autonomous. Those officials dispense subsidies or apply other stimuli accordingly, just as the busybody in the village distributes her boxes of fudge to inspire her fellow inhabitants to lead lives of propriety. Like the busybody, the edificatory-perfectionist functionaries reveal their own impertinence and condescension as they take it upon themselves to elevate the citizens of their country into finer specimens of urbaneness.[21]

The third clarification is that, in attributing to perfectionist governments a quidnunc mentality, Kramer is not seeking to advance an empirical hypothesis about the actual mental states and self-understandings of the officials and functionaries of a perfectionist government.[22] The 'imputation of a quidnunc mentality to edificatory perfectionism is not an exercise in psychological speculation from one's armchair' but is instead 'the distillation of an outlook from which the drive for edification makes most sense'.[23] That is, the quidnunc mentality is meant to refer to a normative property that, 'at a high level of generality', would 'most credibly account for [the] decisions and behavior' of perfectionist state officials, whether or not they are conscious of it.[24] In this sense, Kramer's argument is in line with much jurisprudential literature on legal interpretation and legislative intent, according to which the attribution of an intention to a law or to a government involves not peering into the souls of legislators but

[21] Ibid., p. 282.
[22] Ibid., pp. 254, 269–70.
[23] Ibid., p. 254.
[24] Ibid., p. 270.

300   A PERFECTIONIST THEORY OF JUSTICE

rather trying, in light of a range of considerations, to make sense of a law and the objectives that most plausibly account for its having been adopted and sustained.[25]

10.2 How the Quidnunc Mentality Objection Begs the Question

As a preliminary to my principal argument, it is worth noting there are at least five ways in which one might criticize the quidnunc mentality objection.[26] First, one can question whether being self-aggrandizing and self-abasing in the Kramerian sense—that is, going beyond what is morally required of one and making one's sense of success dependent on the responsiveness of others to one's efforts to alter their private pursuits, respectively—accurately captures what it means to be self-aggrandizing and self-abasing in the ordinary morally significant senses of those terms. For instance, does an individual who feels more successful when he manages to persuade his neighbour to adopt a healthier, less calorific diet really thereby *abase* himself? If not, Kramer might be getting undue moral and rhetorical mileage out of evocative labels that do not fit the behaviour to which they are applied.

Second, even if Kramer captures what it means to be self-aggrandizing and self-abasing in the ordinary morally significant sense, one might wonder how the attitudes of self-aggrandizement and self-abasement are relevant to permissibility as opposed to character evaluation.[27] Why not say that village busybodies act permissibly yet possess flawed characters—in the same way that if someone donates money to a famine-relief charity on the basis of a Mrs Jellyby mentality, or with an attitude of self-congratulation, then while this shows that she has a flawed character, it does not make her donation impermissible?

Third, even if self-aggrandizement and self-abasement are relevant to permissibility, it is unclear why these vices are *so* great—and why manifesting them is *so* wrong—that they could form the basis of a deontological prohibition of the particularly stringent kind that Kramer seeks. Actions that involve self-aggrandizement and self-abasement are presumably all-things-considered permissible when something more important is at stake. Yet mightn't the importance of village busybodies' objectives—namely, the improvement of other people's lives—exceed in stringency considerations of self-aggrandizement and self-abasement, thereby generally rendering their actions all-things-considered permissible?

---

[25] See ibid., pp. 75–87.

[26] I thank Jeff McMahan for helping me to distinguish these five lines of criticism.

[27] For the view that individual intentions are irrelevant to moral permissibility, see, for example, Thomson, J. J., 'Self-Defense', *Philosophy & Public Affairs* 20 (1991), pp. 283–310; Scanlon, T. M., *Moral Dimensions: Permissibility, Meaning, Blame* (Cambridge, MA: Harvard University Press, 2008); di Nucci, E., *Ethics Without Intention* (London: Bloomsbury, 2014).

THE VILLAGE BUSYBODY   301

A fourth line of potential criticism concerns the extrapolation Kramer makes from individual vices to state vices. It is, after all, debatable whether the properties of self-aggrandizement and self-abasement can meaningfully be imputed to states through the kind of exercise in institutional interpretation and distillation that Kramer describes. Jeremy Waldron, for instance, is sceptical of the possibility of 'our being able to discern or attribute to [a legislature] any thoughts, intentions, motives, or beliefs', and he argues that 'beyond the meanings embodied conventionally in the text of the statute, there is no state or condition corresponding to "the intention of the legislature" to which anything else—such as what particular individuals or groups of legislators said, wrote, or did—could possibly provide a clue'.[28]

Fifth, even if states can as a conceptual matter be bearers of attitudes and mentalities, it is unclear that self-aggrandizement and self-abasement have the same moral status when understood as generalized supervenient properties imputed to a collective 'self' as they do when understood as actual psychological character flaws of a village busybody.[29] Given that state attitudes are not at all like individual attitudes, is it really plausible to suppose that they are deeply morally significant in the way that individual attitudes and intentions are sometimes thought to be?

Though I am sympathetic to some of these lines of argument, in this chapter I grant (i) that Kramer accurately captures the morally significant essence of self-aggrandizement and self-abasement, (ii) that these vices are relevant to permissibility, (iii) that they are of sufficient moral significance to ground a particularly stringent prohibition, (iv) that they can be applied meaningfully at the state level and (v) that they still retain their stringent-prohibition-grounding moral significance when applied to the state. Still, I argue that the quidnunc mentality objection fails because it begs the question against perfectionism.

The perfectionist outlook, recall, is supposedly *self-aggrandizing* because it is 'aimed neither at preventing the infliction of harm by some people on others nor at fulfilling any of the further responsibilities' of government such as maintaining public order or the provision of public education.[30] As Kramer elsewhere puts it, the outlook of the perfectionist state is self-aggrandizing because its 'laws and policies are not necessary for the fulfilment of the elementary moral responsibilities that are incumbent on any system of governance'.[31] Similarly, the perfectionist outlook is supposedly *self-abasing* because 'it presumes that the success of a system of

---

[28] See Waldron, J., *Law and Disagreement* (Oxford: Oxford University Press, 1999), ch. 6, at p. 142.

[29] For the view that the case for the irrelevance of *state* intentions to permissibility is even stronger than the case for the irrelevance of *individual* intentions to permissibility, see Enoch, D., 'Intending, Foreseeing and the State', *Legal Theory* 13 (2007), pp. 69–99; Brinkmann, M., 'Political Anti-Intentionalism', *Res Publica* 24 (2018), pp. 159–79. As Enoch puts this point: 'whatever reasons we have to be suspicious about [intention's] moral significance in general, we have *very* good reasons to believe it lacks intrinsic moral significance when applied to state action' (p. 69).

[30] Kramer, M., *Liberalism with Excellence*, p. 277.

[31] Ibid., p. 285.

302 A PERFECTIONIST THEORY OF JUSTICE

governance is partly dependent on the willingness of citizens to alter their private pursuits in response to inducements by the system's officials'.[32] Kramer elsewhere explains that the outlook of the perfectionist state is self-abasing because it makes its success 'dependent on choices that are none of its business'—choices about which it should not care, choices that should be beneath its notice.[33] As these statements indicate, the notion of a 'quidnunc mentality' is heavily moralized: it presupposes a variety of substantive moral claims.

The problem with this argument, however, is that perfectionists can argue, and have argued, that governments have duties of edification towards their citizens. Call this view *duty-based* edificatory perfectionism. Duty-based edificatory perfectionists regard the edification of the citizenry as one of the 'elementary moral responsibilities that are incumbent' on the state, as one of the 'further responsibilities' of government, as a matter of public rather than 'private' concern, and as the proper 'business' of the state. The charge of self-aggrandizement and self-abasement begs the question against duty-based edificatory perfectionism by *assuming* that perfectionist duties do not exist rather than *demonstrating* that perfectionist duties do not exist. So it is difficult to see how the quidnunc mentality argument is meant to persuade those who are not already persuaded of the falsity of duty-based perfectionism. For the quidnunc mentality argument to be persuasive, the non-existence of perfectionist duties would need to be the conclusion of the argument, not a premise. In other words, when Kramer says that the perfectionist state sticks its nose where it does not belong or meddles in matters that are none of its business, he already assumes that the state has no duty to promote the flourishing and edification of the citizenry; but he cannot help himself to this assumption because whether or not the state has a duty to promote the flourishing and edification of the citizenry is precisely what is at stake in the debate between perfectionists and anti-perfectionist liberals.[34]

Admittedly, it is rare for perfectionists to argue that the edification of the citizenry is required—either at the bar of justice or at the bar of some other moral value. As I explained in the Introduction, most perfectionists hold that perfectionist policies are permissible, or that they are legitimate, or that they are justified, or that there is a presumption in favour of them, or that there are reasons to pursue them—without going the extra step of saying that perfectionist policies are morally obligatory. But some perfectionists, notably Joseph Raz and Steven Wall, have defended the existence of edificatory-perfectionist duties. For Raz, 'governments are

---

[32] Ibid., p. 277.

[33] Ibid., p. 289.

[34] A similar response to the quidnunc mentality objection is briefly made in Sher, G., 'Confessions of a Quidnunc', *The American Journal of Jurisprudence* 63 (2018), pp. 54–5 and in Billingham, P. and Taylor, A., 'Liberal Perfectionism, Moral Integrity, and Self-Respect', *The American Journal of Jurisprudence* 63 (2018), p. 69, though these discussions do not consider the responsive strategies available to Kramer that are explored in Sections 10.3 and 10.4.

subject to *autonomy-based duties* to provide the conditions of autonomy for people who lack them.[35] 'The autonomy principle', he explains, 'permits and even *requires* governments to create morally valuable opportunities, and to eliminate repugnant ones.'[36] As Raz elsewhere puts it, the state '*should* act with discrimination to encourage the good and the valuable and to discourage the worthless and the bad'.[37] Similarly, Wall argues that 'political authorities *should* take an active role in creating and maintaining social conditions that best enable their subjects to lead valuable and worthwhile lives'.[38] He argues that by steering people towards worthy ways of life and away from unworthy ways of life, 'the government discharges its *duty* to promote and sustain social conditions that promote the flourishing of those subject to its authority'.[39]

Similarly, of course, in this book as a whole (and in Part II in particular) I seek to offer an extended argument in favour of perfectionist duties of justice. At the most general level, the argument is that society ought to be viewed for political purposes as a fair striving for human flourishing between free and equal citizens and that perfectionist principles of justice are the most appropriate principles for regulating a society conceived of in this way, as the choice of the parties in the perfectionist original position indicates. Moreover, the claim that states are under perfectionist duties of justice has been defended against the charges that such duties violate the public justification principle, that such duties unduly restrict freedom, and that such duties are objectionably paternalistic. An implication of this perfectionist conception of justice is that a society regulated by anti-perfectionist liberal principles of justice would fail to respect some of the moral rights of its citizens and that citizens of such a state could feel legitimately aggrieved that the state does not do more to sustain an environment that is conducive to their edification and upliftment. From this perspective, in other words, the anti-perfectionist liberal state is not a state that complies with 'a deontological ethic of self-restraint' but rather is a state that is derelict in its perfectionist duties—just as, from the perspective of anti-perfectionist liberalism, the libertarian state is not a state that complies with an ethic of self-restraint but rather is a state that is derelict in its egalitarian duties.[40]

If these substantive arguments in favour of perfectionist duties are sound, perfectionist state officials do not stick their nose where it does not belong and

---

[35] Raz, J., *The Morality of Freedom* (Oxford: Oxford University Press, 1986), p. 415 (emphasis added).

[36] Ibid., p. 417 (emphasis added).

[37] Raz, J., 'Liberalism, Skepticism, and Democracy', *Iowa Law Review* 74 (1989), p. 785 (emphasis added).

[38] Wall, S., *Liberalism, Perfectionism and Restraint*, p. 8 (emphasis added). See also Wall's arguments for the existence of perfectionist duties in Wall, S., 'Moral Environmentalism', in C. Coons and M. Weber (eds), *Paternalism: Theory and Practice* (Cambridge: Cambridge University Press, 2013), pp. 96–100.

[39] Wall, S., *Liberalism, Perfectionism and Restraint*, p. 224 (emphasis added).

[40] Kramer, M., *Liberalism with Excellence*, p. 254.

304   A PERFECTIONIST THEORY OF JUSTICE

do not meddle in matters that are none of their business. In such a case, laws and policies aimed at the promotion of human flourishing no more express self-aggrandizement and self-abasement—no more violate a deontological ethic of self-restraint—than do laws and policies aimed at the promotion of freedom and equality. It is thus one's prior view of the state's duties and its legitimate domain of activity that does all the real moral work in determining whether a quidnunc mentality is present. So, in order to successfully wield the quidnunc mentality objection, Kramer must engage the substantive question of whether states have moral duties to promote the flourishing and edification of the citizenry rather than merely presupposing a negative answer to this question.

Here Kramer might say that the charge of begging the question can be hurled in either direction in this debate, and that assuming the existence of edificatory-perfectionist duties simply begs the question in the opposite direction, namely against the proponent of the quidnunc mentality objection.[41] But, as I see it, to say this would be to subtly misdiagnose the dialectical situation. After all, and as alluded to above, edificatory perfectionists such as Raz and Wall have already provided what is, by Kramer's own admission elsewhere, 'elaborate' and 'extensive argumentation' in favour of perfectionist duties.[42] In referring to these arguments in response to the quidnunc mentality objection, the perfectionist is not *assuming* the existence of edificatory-perfectionist duties (which would indeed beg the question in the opposite direction). Rather, the perfectionist refers to these arguments as a way of *supporting* the existence of edificatory-perfectionist duties. The perfectionist recognizes, of course, that these elaborate and extensive arguments in support of the existence of perfectionist duties might ultimately fail.[43] But the perfectionist simply maintains that the proponent of the quidnunc mentality objection must *demonstrate* how they fail. To demonstrate such failure, the proponent of the quidnunc mentality objection would need either (i) to provide some specific reasons to reject the leading arguments in favour of duties of edification, or (ii) to provide some general reason to think that duties of edification do not exist, or ideally both. At this particular stage in the dialectic, then, it seems fair to say that, in the absence of supplementary arguments along these lines, the proponent of the quidnunc mentality objection looks especially vulnerable to the charge of begging the question.

---

[41] I thank Matthew Kramer for putting this point to me.

[42] See Kramer, M., *Liberalism with Excellence*, p. 62 and Kramer, M., 'One Cheer for Autonomy-Centered Perfectionism: An Arm's-Length Defense of Joseph Raz's Perfectionism Against an Allegation of Internal Inconsistency', *Argumenta* 1 (2015), p. 92.

[43] Indeed, though I do endorse edificatory-perfectionist duties, I have my doubts about some of Wall's arguments in favour of them. See Section 6.6.3; see also Tahzib, C., 'Perfectionist Duties', in D. Sobel, P. Vallentyne, and S. Wall (eds), *Oxford Studies in Political Philosophy, Volume 7* (Oxford: Oxford University Press, 2021), pp. 128–32.

10.3 A Substantive Argument Against Perfectionist Duties?

While Kramer does not engage in specific rebuttals of Raz's and Wall's arguments in favour of perfectionist duties, he has indicated that some general reason to doubt the existence of perfectionist duties is given in the course of part of his discussion in *Liberalism Without Excellence*:

> I there maintain that, outside the sway of the harm principle (the genuine harm principle [rather than Raz's perfectionist reformulation of it—CT]) and the preservation of a societal infrastructure, the measure of the ethical strength of a system of governance is given by what it can safely ignore and does ignore. An ethical eagle can and does safely ignore the chirping of the little birds. Since the ethical strength of a system of governance is a key constituent of the political and social and economic conditions under which everyone can be warranted in harboring an ample sense of self-respect, edificatory-perfectionist duties would run athwart a system's responsibility for bringing about those conditions.[44]

This argument—that the conditions of citizens' warranted self-respect depend on the ethical strength of government and that the ethical strength of government depends in turn on what it safely ignores—is developed too briefly in the relevant pages of *Liberalism with Excellence* to allow for a proper evaluation of its merits, and my understanding is that it will be explored in much greater depth in Kramer's book-in-progress *A Stoical Theory of Justice*. Nonetheless, let me comment specifically on the suggestion that this argument would rule out perfectionist duties.

For this argument to rule out perfectionist duties, it would have to be the case that perfectionist objectives (such as edification and flourishing) can be safely ignored by the state, whereas non-perfectionist objectives (such as freedom and equality) cannot. But why think this? Why think that the distinction between what can and cannot be safely ignored tracks the distinction between perfectionist and non-perfectionist objectives? Why do citizens' failures to achieve edification and flourishing count as the trifling and ignorable 'chirping of little birds', whereas citizens' failures to achieve freedom and equality do not? A lot here will hinge, I think, on what is meant by 'safely ignore'. In general, one is not just safe but safe *from* something. So a natural way of tackling the questions just posed is to ask: *in what sense, and from what threat*, could states remain safe while ignoring the failure of some citizens to lead edified and flourishing lives?

In response to this question, Kramer might argue that citizens' failures to achieve edification and flourishing can be safely ignored in the sense that they can be ignored *without thereby threatening harm to others*. By contrast, citizens'

---

[44] I thank Matthew Kramer for providing this elaboration (personal correspondence, 6 May 2019).

306 A PERFECTIONIST THEORY OF JUSTICE

failures to achieve, say, freedom and equality cannot be safely ignored in this sense. Something along these lines does seem to be playing a role in Kramer's argument; although he does not provide a full specification and defence of the Millian harm principle, he does make a number of passing references to it.[45]

But it is unclear that hitching the quidnunc mentality objection to the wagon of the harm principle will help Kramer here. To see why, it is worth noting that there are two main ways of conceptualizing harm: *moralized* accounts of harm and *non-moralized* accounts of harm. According to moralized accounts of harm, what is harmful is just a matter of what violates positive and negative duties. As Raz explains:

> One can harm another by denying him what is due to him. This is obscured by the common misconception which confines harming a person to acting in a way the result of which is that that person is worse off after the action than he was before. While such actions do indeed harm, so do acts or omissions the result of which is that a person is worse off after them than he *should* then be. One harms another by failing in one's duty to him, even though this is a duty to improve his situation and the failure does not leave him worse off than he was before. Consider a disabled person who has a legal right to be employed by any employer to whom he applies and who has fewer than four per cent disabled employees in his work force. If such an employer turns him down he harms him though he does not worsen his situation.[46]

Mill himself also appears to endorse a moralized account of harm. He agrees that actions or omissions that violate positive or negative duties count as harms, and that the prevention of such duty-violations can justify state action compatibly with the harm principle:

> There are also many positive acts for the benefit of others which he may rightfully be compelled to perform, such as to give evidence in a court of justice, to bear his

---

[45] See especially Kramer, M., *Liberalism with Excellence*, pp. 275–7. Elsewhere Kramer explains that edificatory-perfectionist policies 'demean the system of governance by tying the success of its operations partly to matters that would be beneath its notice if it concerned itself not with citizens' *harmless foibles* but with its own foremost responsibility' (Kramer, M., 'On Political Morality and the Conditions for Warranted Self-Respect', *Journal of Ethics* 21 (2017), p. 339, emphasis added). Kramer discusses some features of the harm principle in greater depth in another article, but there too he does not offer a full specification and defence of it. See Kramer, M., 'Legal Responses to Consensual Sexuality between Adults: Through and Beyond the Harm Principle', in C. Pulman (ed.), *Hart on Responsibility* (Basingstoke: Palgrave Macmillan, 2014), pp. 109–28. For other recent arguments that the harm principle rules out perfectionism, see Ogien, R., 'Neutrality Toward Non-Controversial Conceptions of the Good Life', in R. Merrill and D. Weinstock (eds), *Political Neutrality: A Re-evaluation* (New York: Palgrave Macmillan, 2014), pp. 103–6; Stanton-Ife, J., 'Must We Pay for the British Museum? Taxation and the Harm Principle', in M. Bhandari (ed.), *Philosophical Foundations of Tax Law* (Oxford: Oxford University Press, 2017), pp. 35–56.

[46] Raz, J., *The Morality of Freedom*, p. 416 (emphasis added).

fair share in the common defence or in any other joint work necessary to the interest of the society of which he enjoys the protection, and to perform certain acts of individual beneficence, such as saving a fellow creature's life or interposing to protect the defenceless against ill usage—things which whenever it is obviously a man's duty to do he may rightfully be made responsible to society for not doing. A person may cause evil to others not only by his actions but by his inaction, and in either case he is justly accountable to them for the injury.[47]

On the moralized view, if perfectionist duties exist, then a state that fails to promote the edification of the citizenry harms the citizenry and a citizen who fails to contribute (for example, through paying taxes) towards programmes aimed at the edification of her fellow citizens harms those other citizens.[48] Edificatory-perfectionist state action would then be compatible with the moralized harm principle. As Raz puts this point: 'a person who fails to discharge his autonomy-based obligations towards others is harming them, even if those obligations are designed to promote the others' autonomy rather than to prevent its deterioration.'[49] He further explains that 'the government has an obligation to create an environment providing individuals with an adequate range of options and the opportunities to choose them. The duty arises out of people's interest in having a valuable autonomous life. Its violation will harm those it is meant to benefit. Therefore its fulfillment is consistent with the harm principle.'[50]

Again, Kramer would of course deny that any such edificatory-perfectionist duties exist, and so he would deny that edificatory-perfectionist policies are consistent with the harm principle. But, as the foregoing discussion illustrates, if we adopt a moralized account of harm, inconsistency with the harm principle is not an independent argument against edificatory-perfectionist duties. To say that perfectionist policies are inconsistent with the harm principle, one must first have established that there are no perfectionist duties that we owe to one another. So the appeal to the moralized version of the harm principle is no less question-begging

---

[47] Mill, J. S., *On Liberty* (London: Penguin, 1985), p. 70. Mill relatedly says that when a person 'violate[s] a distinct and assignable obligation to any other person or persons, the case is taken out of the self-regarding class and becomes amenable to moral disapprobation in the proper sense of the term' (p. 148). Joel Feinberg, an influential defender of Mill's harm principle, similarly appears to endorse a moralized account of harm. Despite his slogan that harm is to be understood as a 'setback to interests', Feinberg recognizes that harm (at least for the purposes of the harm principle) cannot be defined without any reference to rights and duties, since some setbacks to interests do not violate rights (e.g. a setback to interest that is consented to or that is incurred in legitimate competition). Thus Feinberg ends up settling on a moralized conception of harm as a *wrongful* setback to interests. See Feinberg, J., *Harm to Others: The Moral Limits of the Criminal Law, Volume 1* (Oxford: Oxford University Press, 1984).

[48] In another context, Kramer concedes the possibility of a perfectionist account of harm along these lines, on the assumption (which he there grants *arguendo*) that edificatory-perfectionist duties exist. See Kramer, M., *Liberalism with Excellence*, p. 60.

[49] Raz, J., *The Morality of Freedom*, p. 417.

[50] Ibid., pp. 417–18.

than the original quidnunc mentality objection: like the quidnunc mentality objection itself, the claim that citizens' failures to lead edified lives could be safely ignored by the state without thereby harming others *already presupposes* the non-existence of perfectionist duties (at least, to repeat, if we are working with a moralized account of harm). Hitching the quidnunc mentality objection to the wagon of the moralized harm principle thus does not help because it fails to provide what is needed here: an independently persuasive, morally substantive argument against perfectionist duties.

It is important to note here that the passages from Raz quoted above do of course presuppose the existence of perfectionist duties, and so they too cannot constitute an independently persuasive, morally substantive argument *for* perfectionist duties. Those arguments are developed, extensively and elaborately, elsewhere in the work of duty-based edificatory perfectionists. The important point for our purposes is simply about the inability of the moralized harm principle to do dialectical work here one way or the other: this principle cannot rescue the quidnunc mentality objection by helping us to determine whether or not perfectionist duties exist, because on the moralized view judgements about harm are parasitic on prior judgements about what duties we owe to others. The moralized version of the harm principle, in other words, is conceptually downstream; it comes later in the day, only once the deep and difficult questions about the existence or non-existence of edificatory-perfectionist duties have been figured out.

Perhaps, then, we should look for a *non-moralized* account of harm—an account that does not simply define harm in terms of pre-existing rights and duties. Prominent among these non-moralized accounts of harm is the counterfactual account. According to a straightforward version of this counterfactual account of harm, A's action harms B if and only if it makes B worse off than B would otherwise have been. It is natural to wonder whether a counterfactual account of harm along these lines could be plugged into the harm principle to yield an independently persuasive argument against edificatory-perfectionist duties.

However, counterfactual accounts of harm notoriously fail to accommodate many of our pre-theoretical intuitions about harm. This can be shown by considering two kinds of cases.[51] The first kind involves *pre-emption*.[52] Suppose that A breaks one of V's legs, but that if A had not done this, then B would have broken both of V's legs. The counterfactual account entails that A does not harm V. After all, A's action does not make V worse off than V would otherwise have been: if A had not broken V's leg, then both of V's legs would have been broken. Yet intuitively it seems clear that A harms V. The fact that V would have been harmed to an

---

[51] For the remainder of this paragraph I closely follow Ben Bradley's discussion in 'Doing Away with Harm', *Philosophy and Phenomenological Research* 85 (2012), pp. 396–8; see also pp. 405–9.

[52] For a rejection of various ingenious recent attempts by counterfactual theorists of harm to overcome this problem, see Johansson, J. and Risberg, O., 'The Preemption Problem', *Philosophical Studies* 176 (2019), pp. 351–65.

even greater extent were it not for A's action seems irrelevant to whether A's break-ing of V's leg is harmful. The counterfactual account thus under-generates harm: it counts as harmless what seems clearly harmful. A second problem involves *failures to benefit*.[53] Suppose that C buys a coffee to give to D as a random act of kindness. Tempted by the smell of the coffee, though, C decides instead to drink it himself. The counterfactual account entails that C harms D by drinking the coffee. After all, D is worse off than she would have been if C had given D the coffee rather than drinking it himself. Yet intuitively it seems clear that C does not harm D. C merely fails to bestow a benefit on D, and merely failing to bestow a benefit on someone surely does not amount to harming that person. The counterfactual account thus over-generates harm: it counts as harmful what seems clearly harmless.

Moreover, even if there were an intuitively plausible non-moralized account of harm such as the counterfactual account, plugging this account into the harm prin-ciple would not yield an intuitively plausible principle of political morality.[54] The reason for this is that non-moralized accounts of harm allow for the possibility of non-wrongful harms (such as losses incurred in legitimate competition, and per-haps offence) and harmless wrongs. Harmless wrongs in particular pose problems for the harm principle because they are actions that do not harm others yet that still seemingly ought to be regulated by political authorities. Familiar examples, some of which are alluded to above in the passage from Mill, include voluntary self-enslavement, the failure to save a drowning child in a case of easy rescue, se-cretly recording the private actions of an individual who never discovers that this has occurred, the exploitation of someone's misfortune through a mutually ben-eficial transaction (such as offering a stranded backpacker an exorbitant fee for a lift home), and the destruction of the last member of a little-known species of flower whose extinction will have no adverse impact on others.[55] None of these actions is harmful to others—at least in the non-moralized counterfactual sense that none of these actions leaves others worse off than they would have been in the absence of the action. Indeed, in some of these cases, such as that of offer-ing the backpacker an exorbitant fee for a lift home, others are made better off than they would have been in the absence of the action. Yet it is difficult to believe

---

[53] For a recent attempt by a counterfactual theorist to overcome this problem by invoking the do-ing/allowing distinction, see Purves, D., 'Harming as Making Worse Off', *Philosophical Studies* 176 (2019), pp. 2629–56. This argument is criticized in Johansson, J. and Risberg, O., 'Harming and Failing to Benefit: A Reply to Purves', *Philosophical Studies* 177 (2020), pp. 1539–48.

[54] For further arguments to this effect, see Holtug, N., 'The Harm Principle', *Ethical Theory and Moral Practice* 5 (2002), pp. 364–77.

[55] For further examples of so-called 'harmless wrongdoing', see, for example, Woodward, J., 'The Non-Identity Problem', *Ethics* 96 (1986), pp. 809–11; Feinberg, J., *Harmless Wrongdoing: The Moral Limits of the Criminal Law, Volume 4* (Oxford: Oxford University Press, 1990); Gardner, J. and Shute, S., 'The Wrongness of Rape', in J. Horder (ed.), *Oxford Essays in Jurisprudence: Fourth Series* (Oxford: Oxford University Press, 2000), pp. 193–218; Ripstein, A., 'Beyond the Harm Principle', *Philosophy & Public Affairs* 24 (2006), pp. 215–45; Tadros, V., *Wrongs and Crimes* (Oxford: Oxford University Press, 2016), pp. 102, 201–3, 216–22, 292–8.

310   A PERFECTIONIST THEORY OF JUSTICE

that the state therefore cannot legitimately discourage or prohibit actions such as voluntary self-enslavement, Bad Samaritanism, unnoticed invasions of privacy, price gouging, and the destruction of a plant species. So once harm is conceptualized in non-moralized terms, the claim that harm to others is a necessary condition for the legitimacy of coercive state action is not a plausible principle of political morality.

In short, any attempt to supplement the quidnunc mentality objection with a harm-principle-based argument against edificatory-perfectionist duties would appear to face a dilemma: on the one hand, if the harm principle is construed in moralized terms, then it will be no less question-begging (and so no more independently persuasive) than the original quidnunc mentality objection; on the other hand, if the harm principle is construed in non-moralized terms, then it will struggle to track our intuitions about both the nature of harm and the legitimate sphere of coercive state action. While I have not shown that it is impossible to overcome this dilemma, I hope to have indicated the formidable difficulties confronting anyone who wishes to do so.

10.4 Indistinguishability Rides Again

At one point, Kramer considers the possibility of a version of the duty-based edificatory perfectionism outlined in Section 10.2—in particular, a version that takes autonomy to be a central component of human flourishing.[56] He says that 'autonomy-centered perfectionists' of this kind, for whom 'the nurturing of each individual's autonomy' is a 'matter of justice', may argue that the quidnunc mentality objection simply begs the question by assuming that the promotion of autonomy is not a proper responsibility of government.[57] 'A riposte of that kind', Kramer continues, 'could most promisingly be advanced in a Rawlsian guise' whereby autonomy is viewed as a 'primary natural good in Rawls's sense'.[58]

But the main problem with presenting edificatory perfectionism as a doctrine of justice, argues Kramer, is that it would become indistinguishable from leading non-perfectionist theories of justice:

> When the attainment of autonomy is taken to be a primary natural good ... and when opportunities to attain autonomy are taken to be distribuenda covered by the principles of justice that should apportion primary goods in any liberal-democratic society, the proponents of an autonomy-centered account of justice are not disagreeing with Rawlsians over the doctrine of liberal neutrality. Instead, at the very most, they are disagreeing with Rawlsians over the index of primary

[56] See Kramer, M., *Liberalism with Excellence*, pp. 289–96.
[57] Ibid., pp. 289–90.
[58] Ibid., p. 289.

natural and social goods ... Hence [the view] would not itself be perfectionist. It would be concerned with modifying or clarifying Rawls's thin theory of the good rather than with affirming that a system of governance can legitimately aim to promote some thicker conception(s) of the good.[59]

We have already considered, in Sections 6.5, 6.6 and 6.7, a generic form of the question of whether a perfectionist theory of justice might be indistinguishable from leading non-perfectionist theories of justice. But here we have an opportunity to reconsider the important matter of indistinguishability in the specific form in which Kramer presses the charge.

There are two main problems with Kramer's worry about indistinguishability. First, it is not clear why duty-based edificatory perfectionists would need to present their view in terms of primary goods. Kramer's argumentation is curious here because he himself states that duty-based edificatory perfectionism 'could most promisingly be advanced in a Rawlsian guise' before going on to critique such a view for being indistinguishable from Rawlsianism. But duty-based edificatory perfectionists such as Raz and Wall have not gone about defending their duty-based edificatory-perfectionist views in Rawlsian terms. Behind Wall's endorsement of edificatory-perfectionist duties, for instance, is not a Rawlsian picture in which autonomy is a primary good to be distributed in accordance with some distributive principle but rather a picture in which autonomy is a component of a flourishing life and the role of the state is to foster human flourishing:

> [Perfectionism] is the thesis that political authorities should take an active role in creating and maintaining social conditions that best enable their subjects to lead valuable and worthwhile lives. If autonomy is a central component of a fully good life, and if we ought to accept the general thesis of perfectionism, then it would follow that political authorities should take an active role in creating and maintaining social conditions that help their subjects realize this ideal.[60]

And while, unlike Raz and Wall, I have in Part II deployed a Rawlsian framework to argue for perfectionism, I have not argued that perfectionist goods such as moral, intellectual and artistic excellence are primary goods to be distributed in accordance with the difference principle or some other distributive principle (be it egalitarian, prioritarian, sufficientarian or otherwise). Rather, I have argued in favour of an additional and distinctively perfectionist principle of justice, one which seeks to establish an environment conducive to flourishing ways of life, and it is at this point that considerations of moral, intellectual and artistic excellence enter into the conception of justice. My argument in Part II, in other words, does

---

[59] Ibid., pp. 292–3.
[60] Wall, S., *Liberalism, Perfectionism and Restraint*, p. 131.

312 A PERFECTIONIST THEORY OF JUSTICE

not involve rejecting (or amending) Rawls's index of primary goods; what it rejects is the suggestion that justice is *exhausted* by the fair distribution of primary goods, since it calls, in addition, for the encouragement and promotion of flourishing ways of life.

The second problem with Kramer's indistinguishability argument is that, even if the only or best way to formally depict the difference between Rawlsians and duty-based edificatory perfectionists were in terms of a disagreement about the index of primary natural or social goods, it would not follow that duty-based edificatory perfectionism is indistinguishable from Rawlsianism or that it endorses liberal neutrality. This becomes particularly clear when we consider what Wall calls 'non-autonomy-based perfectionist political action'—that is, when we consider not just *autonomy-centred* duty-based edificatory perfectionism (the form of duty-based edificatory perfectionism that Kramer focuses on) but also other versions of duty-based edificatory perfectionism.[61]

To see this, consider an autonomy-unrelated example from Wall. Suppose that an edificatory-perfectionist state 'grants public subsidies to artists' in 'an effort to promote and stimulate appreciation of high art'.[62] The most natural way to understand Wall's point here, it seems to me, is that the role of the state is to promote human flourishing and thus that the state should promote appreciation of high art as a component of human flourishing. But even if, somewhat contrivedly, we read Wall as suggesting that appreciation of high art and other components of human flourishing should be understood as primary goods, as 'distribuenda covered by the principles of justice', it does not follow that Wall's view is indistinguishable from Rawlsianism or that it endorses liberal neutrality. After all, Rawlsians and defenders of liberal neutrality tend to eschew judgements of this kind in politics. Rawlsians and liberal neutralists, that is, tend to hold that 'the liberal state should not be in the business of deciding what constitutes a valuable or worthwhile life and trying to make sure that citizens live up to this ideal—that job should be left to citizens themselves'.[63] A disagreement about the index of primary goods, then, is not just a minor intramural matter for Rawlsians: it can conceal deep substantive disagreements between Rawlsians and edificatory perfectionists.

10.5 Addendum

As this book was going to press, Kramer provided a stimulating and instructive rejoinder to a previously published version of this chapter.[64] While the previously

---

[61] Ibid., p. 213.
[62] Ibid.
[63] Quong, J., *Liberalism Without Perfection*, p. 1.
[64] See Kramer, M., 'Looking Back and Looking Ahead: Replies to the Contributors', in M. McBride and V. Kurki (eds), *Without Trimmings: The Legal, Moral, and Political Philosophy of Matthew Kramer*

published version of this chapter differs from the present version in some of its details, its central argumentative thrust is substantially the same, and so it is worth making a few brief comments here on Kramer's recent rejoinder to the accusation that the quidnunc mentality objection begs the question against edificatory perfectionists.

Kramer begins his rejoinder by noting that 'even if the charge of begging the question were correct, it would not necessarily be damaging. Most arguments beg the question against sundry opposing arguments in one way or another, and thus the pivotal point to be ascertained is whether a specific way of begging the question is vicious or not'.[65] I agree that begging the question is not always a vice. Every argument begs the question with respect to *some* constituency of persons by making assumptions that are explicitly rejected by that constituency. Many of the most celebrated arguments in liberal political philosophy, for instance, no doubt beg the question against virulently racist outlooks, but that is nothing for the proponents of those arguments to be embarrassed about. Under what conditions, then, does an instance of begging the question count as 'vicious'? In my view, the viciousness of an instance of begging the question depends, at least in large part, on *contextual* factors: an argument begs the question in a vicious way if it begs the question against a constituency of persons that the argument is supposed to address and persuade. Assuming the correctness of this contextual account of the conditions under which an instance of begging the question is vicious, the quidnunc mentality objection does appear to beg the question in a vicious way. After all, what is being contended in this chapter is that the quidnunc mentality objection begs the question against edificatory perfectionists—which is presumably a constituency of persons that this argument is supposed to address and persuade. In other words, given the specific dialectical context in which the quidnunc mentality objection operates, it is not viciously question-begging for this argument to assume the falsity of, say, racist outlooks, but it *is* viciously question-begging for this argument to assume the non-existence of edificatory-perfectionist duties.

Still, this does not settle things, since Kramer contends that 'there is a clear-cut sense in which [his] critique of edificatory perfectionism does not beg the question'.[66] In other words, Kramer contends that there is a clear-cut sense in which he has given *arguments* for why edificatory-perfectionist duties do not exist, as opposed to merely assuming that edificatory-perfectionist duties do not exist.

Perhaps Kramer's most important argument against edificatory-perfectionist duties appeals to the harm principle: 'the fact that edificatory-perfectionist duties would morally require governmental measures that squarely violate the harm

---

(Oxford: Oxford University Press, 2022), pp. 491–508. For the previously published version, see Tahzib, C., 'Does Edificatory Perfectionism Express a Quidnunc Mentality?', in M. McBride and V. Kurki (eds), *Without Trimmings*, pp. 297–318.

[65] Kramer, M., 'Looking Back and Looking Ahead', p. 495.

[66] Ibid.

314 A PERFECTIONIST THEORY OF JUSTICE

principle is one strong reason for concluding that there are no such duties'.[67] Endorsing a moralized account of harm, Kramer notes my doubts (mentioned in Section 10.3) about the helpfulness of hitching the quidnunc mentality objection to the wagon of the moralized harm principle: namely, that to say that edificatory-perfectionist policies violate the moralized version of the harm principle is to already presuppose the non-existence of edificatory-perfectionist duties, and so is no less question-begging than the original quidnunc mentality argument. To this he offers the following very interesting response:

> [Tahzib] is suggesting that edificatory-perfectionist duties would lift themselves up by their own bootstraps into conformity with the harm principle simply through their own existence. Although the implementation of those duties would not avert or remedy the infliction of any non-moralized harm by anyone upon anyone else, and although the contravening of those very duties would be the only ostensible moralized harm averted or remedied by the implementation of them, Tahzib believes that that one element of ostensible moralized harm is sufficient to vindicate the consistency of edificatory-perfectionist duties with the Millian harm principle. Such a position is untenable, however ... Duties cannot bootstrap themselves into consistency with that principle simply by existing as such. *Instead, the genuine consistency of a duty D with the harm principle consists in the fact that the implementation of D will avert or remedy the infliction of some non-moralized harm by somebody on somebody else, or in the fact that the implementation of D will avert or remedy a transgression of some moral obligation(s) beyond D itself.* Since neither of those bases for the consistency of a duty with the harm principle is applicable to edificatory-perfectionist duties, those duties would be inconsistent with that principle and are thus non-existent as moral obligations.[68]

I disagree with the general account proposed by Kramer (and italicized above) of the conditions under which a duty is genuinely consistent with the harm principle. Irrespective of its implications for edificatory-perfectionist duties, this account makes it too difficult for moral duties to be reconciled with the harm principle. It seems to imply, for instance, that the state cannot prohibit voluntary self-enslavement, if selling oneself into slavery does not inflict non-moralized harm on anyone else and does not transgress moral obligations beyond the obligation itself not to sell oneself into slavery. The same goes for the other cases mentioned in Section 10.3 of wrongdoing that is harmless in the non-moralized sense: namely, the failure to save a drowning child in a case of easy rescue, secretly recording the private actions of an individual who never discovers that this has occurred, the

---

[67] Ibid., p. 502.
[68] Ibid., pp. 502–3 (emphasis added).

THE VILLAGE BUSYBODY 315

exploitation of someone's misfortune through a mutually beneficial transaction, and the destruction of the last member of a little-known species of flower whose extinction will have no adverse impact on others.

Instead, as I see it, the genuine consistency of a duty D with the harm principle consists in the fact that the implementation of D will avert or remedy the infliction of some non-moralized harm by somebody on somebody else, or in the fact that the implementation of D will avert or remedy a transgression of some moral obligation *that is supported on independent grounds*. This alternative general account of the conditions under which a duty is genuinely consistent with the harm principle avoids the bootstrapping problem, since it does not allow a duty D to lift itself up by its own bootstraps into conformity with the harm principle simply through asserting its own existence. But it does so without ruling out edificatory-perfectionist duties. After all, I have in Part II offered an extended argument for edificatory-perfectionist duties on the grounds that society ought to be viewed for political purposes as a fair striving for human flourishing between free and equal citizens and that perfectionist principles of justice are the most appropriate principles for regulating a society conceived of in this way, as illustrated by the choice of the parties in the perfectionist original position. If edificatory-perfectionist duties had not been supported on these sorts of independent grounds, it would indeed be objectionably bootstrapping to say that the moralized harm of violating edificatory-perfectionist duties is itself sufficient to vindicate the consistency of edificatory-perfectionist duties with the harm principle. But that is not what is going on. It is the argument from Part II, rather than the bare assertion that edificatory-perfectionist duties exist, that brings edificatory-perfectionist duties into conformity with the harm principle.

Beyond inconsistency with the harm principle, Kramer mentions some other arguments against edificatory-perfectionist duties. Kramer explains that the quidnunc mentality objection is not his only objection to edificatory perfectionism and that the fifth chapter of *Liberalism with Excellence* demonstrates the neglect by edificatory perfectionists of the content-independent value of freedom. As Kramer puts this, 'the drive for edification stifles freedom.'[69] He also explains that edificatory-perfectionist policies are not necessary for, and indeed are inimical to, 'the paramount moral responsibility incumbent on any system of governance [which] is a duty to bring about the political and economic and social conditions under which everyone within the jurisdiction of the system can be warranted in sustaining a high level of self-respect.'[70] These arguments—from the content-independent value of freedom and from the value of warranted self-respect—are meant to provide non-question-begging arguments against the existence of edificatory-perfectionist duties.

[69] Ibid., p. 498.
[70] Ibid.

However, if it is the values of freedom and warranted self-respect that do the fundamental work of explaining why edificatory-perfectionist duties do not exist, where does this leave the quidnunc mentality objection? Doesn't this make the whole machinery of the quidnunc mentality objection—the vices of self-aggrandizement and self-abasement, the village busybody analogy, and so on—superfluous? Hasn't the 'quidnunc mentality' become merely a way of describing an independently established conclusion—a poetic label that is applied once it has been worked out that edificatory perfectionism is wrong, but not a way of getting at what's wrong with edificatory perfectionism? This part of Kramer's rejoinder thus seems to me to raise broader questions about the role that the quidnunc mentality objection is supposed to play in the case against edificatory perfectionism—and in particular about the level of explanatory fundamentality at which the quidnunc mentality argument is supposed to operate.

Here one might wonder whether the quidnunc mentality argument, even if it is not explanatorily fundamental, can at least serve as an illuminating heuristic—a way of making vivid the force of other more fundamental arguments from freedom and warranted self-respect. But it is doubtful whether the quidnunc mentality argument can even play an illuminating heuristic role of this kind. To see this, we might note that the argument from inconsistency with the harm principle to the non-existence of edificatory-perfectionist duties is at least recognizably *internal* to the quidnunc mentality idea, since a core feature of village busybodies is that they concern themselves with others' harmless foibles and meddle in people's private pursuits. As such, the quidnunc mentality machinery may well be an illuminating way to represent the wrongness of actions that violate the harm principle. By contrast, it is unclear how the values of freedom and warranted self-respect fit within, or draw upon, the quidnunc mentality machinery. It is unclear, for instance, what the relationship is between freedom and warranted self-respect on the one hand and the vices of self-aggrandizement and self-abasement on the other. The quidnunc mentality machinery thus looks more likely to obscure than to illuminate the arguments from freedom and warranted self-respect. By appealing to the values of freedom and warranted self-respect, in other words, the case against edificatory perfectionism appears to have shifted onto very different ground from that of the quidnunc mentality objection.

Of course, these reflections do not by themselves show that edificatory perfectionism is in the clear. Kramer's other arguments against edificatory perfectionism must be rebutted on their own terms. I have sought to do this elsewhere: in Section 8.2 I defuse the freedom-based argument; and in Section 10.3 I suggest that the self-respect-based argument depends for its success on a harm-principle-based argument which, as I suggest there and in this section, is inconclusive. But what these reflections do show is that the quidnunc mentality objection is morally epiphenomenal: it cannot explain or even illuminate why edificatory perfectionism is illegitimate because it already assumes that the illegitimacy of edificatory perfectionism has been demonstrated by means of other very different sorts of arguments.

Conclusion

Many liberal thinkers, I explained in Part I, hold that the state should refrain from making and acting on judgements about the value or worthiness of the lives that citizens lead. These thinkers hold that the state should ensure that citizens treat each other in line with the dictates of liberal justice: it should ensure, that is, that basic rights are respected, that all citizens enjoy fair equality of opportunity and that resources are distributed in an appropriately equal way. But, beyond this, they say, the state should not try to elevate citizens' tastes, to refine their sensibilities or to perfect their characters. It should neither steer them towards activities and ways of life that it deems worthy nor steer them away from activities and ways of life that it deems unworthy. Different liberals, we have seen, arrive at this anti-perfectionist conclusion in different ways. Comprehensive liberals argue for anti-perfectionism on the basis of claims about autonomy or individuality, and political liberals argue for anti-perfectionism on the basis of claims about reasonable disagreement. And other liberals argue for anti-perfectionism on the grounds that there are no objective truths about human flourishing, or that there are such truths but they remain unknowable to us, or that there are knowable objective truths about human flourishing but their promotion by the state would be futile or even counterproductive.

Against the backdrop of these influential accounts of liberal political morality, I argued in Part II that the promotion by the state of flourishing ways of life is not only morally permissible but in fact required at the bar of justice. On this view, perfectionist laws and policies are not merely a legitimate complement to justice but an essential constituent of justice. While no single component of this perfectionist theory of justice carries the entire burden of justification—since 'justification is a matter of the mutual support of many considerations, of everything fitting together into one coherent view'—the theory is strongly shaped by certain fundamental ideas and conceptions, including notably the perfectionist conception of society and the provisional conception of human flourishing.[1] In particular, I contended that society ought to be viewed for political purposes as a fair striving for human flourishing between free and equal citizens, and I employed an original position heuristic in order to identify the principles of justice most appropriate for regulating a society conceived of in this way. These principles of justice include a principle that calls for the promotion of flourishing ways of life—where

---

[1] Rawls, J., *A Theory of Justice* (Cambridge, MA: Harvard University Press, 1971), p. 579.

A Perfectionist Theory of Justice. Collis Tahzib, Oxford University Press.
© Collis Tahzib (2022). DOI: 10.1093/oso/9780192847119.003.0012

this distinctively perfectionist principle is subject to the satisfaction of two lexically prior principles of justice (namely, the equal basic liberties principle and the fair equality of opportunity principle) and is to be intuitionistically balanced against the difference principle. I suggested, provisionally, and again for political purposes, that flourishing lives are to be thought of as lives rich in the enjoyment of moral, intellectual and artistic excellence. And, while acknowledging that high-level political theories do not straightforwardly yield particular practical outcomes, I began to consider what a concrete programme of law and public policy designed to foster the enjoyment of moral, intellectual and artistic excellence might look like.

Liberals have long been concerned that perfectionist politics simply amounts to some people imposing their will on others, and they have expressed this concern in a variety of related yet distinct ways: that perfectionist politics involves appeal to values and judgements that are subject to reasonable disagreement within modern pluralistic societies; that it is unduly restrictive of freedom, autonomy or personal sovereignty; that it is premised on the paternalistic belief that citizens are unable to make effective decisions about how to run their own lives when left to their own devices; and that it manifests a village busybody mentality that is at once self-aggrandizing and self-abasing. In Part III, I defended the perfectionist conception of justice against these forceful and impressive objections. While this discussion was largely defensive in posture, it introduced along the way certain novel ideas, such as the idea of a perfectionist conception of reasonableness as a competitor to the anti-perfectionist liberal conception of reasonableness that has hitherto dominated the literature on public reason and public justification.

Here is one way of summarizing many of these arguments. Anti-perfectionist liberalism maintains that there is there is an important *asymmetry* between liberal values such as freedom, equality and fairness and perfectionist values such as moral, intellectual and artistic excellence: it holds that the state should enthusiastically promote the former values but should scrupulously refrain from promoting the latter values. A central contention of this work is that this asymmetry is indefensible: there is no sound reason to exclude ideals of human flourishing from a conception of social justice. Many of the reasons that have been given for such exclusion—that perfectionist values are subject to reasonable disagreement, that perfectionist laws and policies unduly restrict individual freedom, that perfectionist laws and policies are premised on negative assumptions about the decision-making abilities of citizens, and so on—are untrue or, if true, then unobjectionable and indeed often equally true of anti-perfectionist liberalism. The asymmetry at the heart of anti-perfectionist liberalism, then, remains an asymmetry in search of a rationale.

CONCLUSION   319

Justicitis?

In concluding, I wish to comment on a big-picture question that one might have about this work, namely that of why we should think of perfectionism as a doctrine of *justice* as opposed to thinking of it in terms of some other concept. Even if perfectionist policies are a good idea, are they really required at the bar of justice in particular? Is a state that does not enact perfectionist policies, but that otherwise ensures that all citizens receive a fair share of rights, opportunities and resources, really thereby aptly characterized as (pro tanto) unjust? Isn't talk of a 'perfectionist theory of justice' simply a kind of category mistake?

A sharp way of putting this objection is that the very idea of a perfectionist theory of justice is a symptom of what Chandran Kukathas calls 'justicitis'—an unhealthy obsession with justice, to the point where all social, moral and even aesthetic values are eventually baked into the concept of justice.[2] In elaborating the malady of justicitis, Kukathas notes that in recent political philosophy there has been a proliferation of theories of justice and that there now appears to be a theory of justice for 'nearly every aspect of human existence'.[3] He says that 'we have made too many things matters of justice' and as a result 'justice has become an oversold theoretical and normative commodity'.[4] 'Oral health', Kukathas explains, 'is a matter of justice, if we are to believe the editor of a collection of papers, *Justice in Oral Health Care*, which includes a contribution on "Just Dentistry"'.[5] 'Water policy, the provision of public toilets, and access to the internet', he notes, have all also been theorized from the perspective of justice.[6] Kukathas explains that he does not 'wish for a moment to suggest that any of these issues is unimportant'.[7] 'But', he adds, 'I wonder whether they are matters of justice.'[8] So, even if state support for art galleries, say, is important and desirable, is this really the kind of thing that belongs under the rubric of justice? In treating perfectionist policies as integral components of justice, have I not 'succumbed to the temptation to make justice the measure of all things political'?[9]

To respond to this challenge, we need to distinguish between the *concept* of justice and the competing *conceptions* of justice.[10] There are many discussions

---

[2] See Kukathas, C., 'Justicitis', in N. Simsek, S. Snyder and M. Knoll (eds), *New Perspectives on Distributive Justice: Deep Disagreements, Pluralism, and the Problem of Consensus* (Berlin: De Gruyter, 2018), pp. 187–204.
[3] Ibid., p. 187.
[4] Ibid., pp. 187, 191.
[5] Ibid., p. 189.
[6] Ibid., p. 190.
[7] Ibid.
[8] Ibid.
[9] Ibid., p. 188.
[10] See Rawls, J., *A Theory of Justice*, pp. 5–6, whose use of the distinction between concepts and conceptions follows Hart, H. L. A., *The Concept of Law* (Oxford: Clarendon Press, 1961), pp. 155–9.

within political philosophy about conceptions of justice: about whether the correct conception of justice is utilitarian, liberal, socialist, libertarian, prioritarian, sufficientarian, luck egalitarian, and so on. What makes it the case that these theorists are all speaking about the same thing rather than speaking past each other? What makes these conceptions conceptions of justice as opposed to conceptions of some other normative concept? The answer must be that, despite their differences, there are certain general features that are shared by these different conceptions. The *concept* of justice, then, is specified by the general feature or features that differing conceptions of justice have in common.

Although there are far fewer discussions of the concept of justice than there are discussions of the various conceptions of justice, there are nonetheless some prominent attempts to identify the general feature or features common to all conceptions of justice.[11] One of the most well-known accounts of the concept of justice is given by John Rawls:

> What is just and unjust is usually in dispute. Men disagree about which principles should define the basic terms of their association. Yet we may still say, despite this disagreement, that they each have a conception of justice. That is, they understand the need for, and they are prepared to affirm, a characteristic set of principles for assigning basic rights and duties and for determining what they take to be the proper distribution of the benefits and burdens of social cooperation. Thus it seems natural to think of the concept of justice as distinct from the various conceptions of justice and as being specified by the role which these different sets of principles, these different conceptions, have in common. Those who hold different conceptions of justice can, then, still agree that institutions are just when no arbitrary distinctions are made between persons in the assigning of basic rights and duties and when the rules determine a proper balance between competing claims to the advantages of social life. Men can agree to this description of just institutions since the notions of an arbitrary distinction and of a proper balance, which are included in the concept of justice, are left open for each to interpret according to the principles of justice that he accepts. These principles single out which similarities and differences among persons are relevant in determining rights and duties and they specify which division of advantages is appropriate. Clearly this distinction between the concept and the various conceptions of justice settles no important questions. It simply helps to identify the role of the principles of social justice.[12]

[11] For helpful discussions, see, for example, Buchanan, A., 'Justice and Charity', *Ethics* 97 (1987), pp. 558–75; Baier, K., 'Justice and the Aims of Political Philosophy', *Ethics* 99 (1989), pp. 784–9; Vallentyne, P., 'Justice in General: An Introduction', in P. Vallentyne (ed.), *Equality and Justice: Justice in General* (London: Routledge, 2003), pp. xi–xviii; Olsaretti, S., 'Introduction: The Idea of Distributive Justice', in S. Olsaretti (ed.), *The Oxford Handbook of Distributive Justice* (Oxford: Oxford University Press, 2018), pp. 1–9.

[12] Rawls, J., *A Theory of Justice*, pp. 5–6.

CONCLUSION 321

Rawls's view here appears to be that a conception of justice, in order to be a conception *of justice*, must possess two features: it must offer a non-arbitrary specification of basic rights and duties, and it must offer a specification of the proper distribution of the benefits and burdens of social life. And the perfectionist conception of justice possesses precisely these features: it offers a non-arbitrary specification of basic rights and duties, one which attributes to citizens a right to social conditions promotive of and conducive to flourishing ways of life and which attributes to states a duty to establish and maintain such conditions; and it offers a specification of the proper distribution of the benefits and burdens of social life, one which affords special benefits to worthy ideals and activities. Of course, the substantive arguments for this view might fail, in which case perfectionist laws and policies are not, in the end, required by justice. But this would need to be shown by engaging with the substantive arguments; it cannot be assumed by conceptual fiat, since the view has the right general form to qualify as a conception of justice, at least if Rawls's account of the requisite form is correct.

It is unclear, then, what basis there is for saying that defenders of perfectionist justice must suffer from justicitis. It is true that when we zoom in, as Kukathas does, and consider the provision of art galleries or some other similarly specific matter such as public toilets or dentistry, it might seem strange to classify these things as matters of justice. But no doubt many policies that are bona fide matters of justice will look similarly strange when viewed at this level of specificity—when viewed, that is, in isolation from the package of policies of which they are a part and in isolation from the broader objectives to which they are intended to contribute. Art galleries, for instance, are part of a broader package of policies that are intended as a whole to support an environment that is conducive to morally, intellectually and artistically excellent ways of life. Viewed from this more general perspective, it no longer seems strange to say that the provision of an edifying social environment can fall under the rubric of justice and that the failure to provide such an environment can constitute a departure of at least some degree from full or perfect justice.

Perhaps Kukathas should be read as rejecting the two Rawlsian features that I have mentioned—a non-arbitrary specification of rights and duties and a specification of the proper distribution of the benefits and burdens of social life—as explanations of what it is that makes something a 'matter of justice'. But then Kukathas would owe us an alternative account of the concept of justice. Although he does not develop in detail such an account, Kukathas does express sympathy for what he calls the 'Humean story', according to which the 'purpose' of 'norms of justice' is 'to make human society possible'.[13] On this view, what makes something a matter of justice is that it is relevant to the very possibility of human society. For instance, norms of property, says Kukathas, are matters of justice because without

---

[13] Kukathas, C., 'Justicitis', pp. 192, 196.

some kind of distinction between mine and thine, human society would not be possible. And since human society obviously is possible without art galleries and other perfectionist policies, this account of the concept of justice would seem to imply that perfectionist policies do not after all fall under the rubric of justice.

The Humean story, however, is not a plausible account of the concept of justice. After all, it implies that once human society is up and running, no further questions can coherently be asked about the justice of its laws and policies (at least so long as those laws and policies do not threaten the possibility of human society). On the Humean account of the concept of justice, it appears that we cannot, for instance, say that a state that supports racial segregation is less just, other things equal, than a state that outlaws racial segregation, assuming that both states make human society possible. In general, the Humean account appears to have the implausible implication that states that differ with respect to the rights and duties they recognize or with respect to how they distribute the benefits and burdens of social life cannot differ with respect to justice, if those differences in rights and duties and the distribution of benefits and burdens do not affect the possibility of human society.

There is, then, no reason why perfectionist laws and policies cannot properly fall under the rubric of justice. The important question is not conceptual but substantive: it is whether the perfectionist theory of justice accords more closely with our considered convictions at all levels of generality and whether it expresses and embodies more intrinsically appealing ideals of society and of the person than rival theories. The preceding chapters provide my reasons for thinking that perfectionism is superior in this regard to its rivals and in particular to anti-perfectionist liberalism. Contrary to what dominant strands of liberal thought have long suggested, then, justice calls not merely for the protection of basic rights and for a suitably equal distribution of opportunities and resources; it also calls for the state to take a clear stand on the question of what constitutes a flourishing human life and to promote this ideal through its main social and political institutions.

References

Abbey, R. and Spinner-Halev, J., 'Rawls, Mill, and the Puzzle of Political Liberalism', *The Journal of Politics* 75 (2012), pp. 124–36.

Ackerman, B., *Social Justice in the Liberal State* (New Haven, CT: Yale University Press, 1980).

Ackerman, B., 'Neutralities', in R. B. Douglass et al. (eds), *Liberalism and the Good* (London: Routledge, 1990), pp. 29–43.

Ackerman, B., 'Should Opera Be Subsidized?', *Dissent* 46 (1999), pp. 89–91.

Adams, R., *Finite and Infinite Goods: A Framework for Ethics* (Oxford: Oxford University Press, 1999).

Alexander, M., *The New Jim Crow: Mass Incarceration in the Age of Colorblindness* (New York: The New Press, 2010).

Ariely, D., *Predictably Irrational: The Hidden Forces That Shape Our Decisions* (New York: Harper Perennial, 2010).

Aristotle, *The Politics*, trans. H. Rackham (Cambridge, MA: Harvard University Press, 1990).

Arneson, R., 'Paternalism, Utility, and Fairness', *Revue Internationale de Philosophie* 43 (1989), pp. 409–37.

Arneson, R., 'Primary Goods Revisited', *Noûs* 24 (1990), pp. 429–54.

Arneson, R., 'Human Flourishing Versus Desire Satisfaction', *Social Philosophy and Policy* 16 (1999), pp. 113–42.

Arneson, R., 'Rawls Versus Utilitarianism in the Light of *Political Liberalism*', in V. Davion and C. Wolf (eds), *The Idea of a Political Liberalism* (Oxford: Rowman & Littlefield, 2000), pp. 231–52.

Arneson, R., 'Liberal Neutrality on the Good: An Autopsy', in S. Wall and G. Klosko (eds), *Perfectionism and Neutrality: Essays in Liberal Theory* (New York: Rowman & Littlefield, 2003), pp. 191–218.

Arneson, R., 'Cracked Foundations of Liberal Equality', in J. Burley (ed.), *Dworkin and His Critics* (Oxford: Blackwell, 2004), pp. 79–98.

Arneson, R., 'Self-Ownership and World-Ownership: Against Left-Libertarianism', *Social Philosophy and Policy* 27 (2010), pp. 168–94.

Arneson, R., 'Neutrality and Political Liberalism', in R. Merrill and D. Weinstock (eds), *Political Neutrality: A Re-evaluation* (New York: Palgrave Macmillan, 2014), pp. 25–43.

Arneson, R., 'Political Liberalism, Religious Liberty, and Religious Establishment', in H. Dagan, S. Lifshitz and Y. Stern (eds), *Religion and the Discourse of Human Rights* (Jerusalem: The Israel Democracy Institute, 2014), pp. 117–44.

Arneson, R., 'Basic Equality: Neither Acceptable Nor Rejectable', in U. Steinhoff (ed.), *Do All Persons Have Equal Moral Worth? On 'Basic Equality' and Equal Respect and Concern* (Oxford: Oxford University Press, 2015), pp. 30–52.

Baier, K., 'Justice and the Aims of Political Philosophy', *Ethics* 99 (1989), pp. 771–90.

Barrett, L., *The Prime Minister's Christmas Card: Blue Poles and Cultural Politics in the Whitlam Era* (Sydney: Power Publications, 2001).

324 REFERENCES

Barry, B., 'John Rawls and the Priority of Liberty', *Philosophy & Public Affairs* 2 (1973), pp. 274–90.

Barry, B., *The Liberal Theory of Justice: A Critical Examination of the Principal Doctrines in A Theory of Justice by John Rawls* (Oxford: Oxford University Press, 1973).

Barry, B., *Justice as Impartiality* (Oxford: Oxford University Press, 1995).

Barry, B., 'Something in the Disputation Not Unpleasant', in P. Kelly (ed.), *Impartiality, Neutrality and Justice* (Edinburgh: Edinburgh University Press, 2000), pp. 186–257.

Barwise, P. and York, P., *The War Against the BBC* (London: Penguin Books, 2020).

Bauerlein, M. and Grantham, E. (eds), *National Endowment for the Arts: A History 1965–2008* (Washington, DC: National Endowment for the Arts, 2009).

Berlin, I., *The Crooked Timber of Humanity: Chapters in the History of Ideas* (London: Pimlico, 2013).

Billingham, P., 'Liberal Perfectionism and Quong's Internal Conception of Political Liberalism', *Social Theory and Practice* 43 (2017), pp. 79–106.

Billingham, P. and Taylor, A., 'Liberal Perfectionism, Moral Integrity, and Self-Respect', *The American Journal of Jurisprudence* 63 (2018), pp. 63–79.

Billingham, P. and Taylor, A., 'A Framework for Analyzing Public Reason Theories', *European Journal of Political Theory* (forthcoming).

Bird, C., 'Review of Matthew Kramer, *Liberalism with Excellence*', *Political Theory* 47 (2019), pp. 286–93.

Birks, D., 'Moral Status and the Wrongness of Paternalism', *Social Theory and Practice* 40 (2014), pp. 483–98.

Boettcher, J., 'Respect, Recognition, and Public Reason', *Social Theory and Practice* 33 (2007), pp. 223–49.

Bradford, G., 'Problems for Perfectionism', *Utilitas* 29 (2017), pp. 344–64.

Bradley, B., *Well-Being and Death* (Oxford: Oxford University Press, 2009).

Bradley, B., 'Doing Away with Harm', *Philosophy and Phenomenological Research* 85 (2012), pp. 390–412.

Bradley, B., *Well-Being* (Cambridge: Polity Press, 2015).

Brennan, J. and van der Vossen, B., 'The Myths of the Self-Ownership Thesis', in J. Brennan, B. van der Bossen and D. Schmidtz (eds), *The Routledge Handbook of Libertarianism* (Oxford: Routledge, 2019), pp. 199–211.

Brighouse, H., 'Neutrality, Publicity, and State Funding of the Arts', *Philosophy & Public Affairs* 24 (1995), pp. 35–63.

Brink, D., *Mill's Progressive Principles* (Oxford: Oxford University Press, 2013).

Brinkmann, M., 'Political Anti-Intentionalism', *Res Publica* 24 (2018), pp. 159–79.

Bruckner, D., 'Quirky Desires and Well-Being', *Journal of Ethics & Social Philosophy* 10 (2016), pp. 1–34.

Buchanan, A., 'Justice and Charity', *Ethics* 97 (1987), pp. 558–75.

Caney, S., 'Consequentialist Defences of Liberal Neutrality', *The Philosophical Quarterly* 31 (1991), pp. 457–77.

Caney, S., 'Thomas Nagel's Defence of Liberal Neutrality', *Analysis* 52 (1992), pp. 41–5.

Caney, S., 'Impartiality and Liberal Neutrality', *Utilitas* 8 (1996), pp. 273–93.

Caney, S., 'Liberal Legitimacy, Reasonable Disagreement, and Justice', *Critical Review of International Social and Political Philosophy* 1 (1998), pp. 19–36.

Carroll, N., 'Can Government Funding of the Arts Be Justified Theoretically?', *Journal of Aesthetic Education* 21 (1987), pp. 21–35.

Carter, I., *A Measure of Freedom* (Oxford: Oxford University Press, 1999).

Carter, I., 'Respect and the Basis of Equality', *Ethics* 121 (2011), pp. 538–71.

REFERENCES 325

Cavanagh, M., *Against Equality of Opportunity* (Oxford: Clarendon Press, 2002).

Chalmers, D., 'Verbal Disputes', *The Philosophical Review* 120 (2011), pp. 515–66.

Chambers, C., *Against Marriage: An Egalitarian Defence of the Marriage-Free State* (Oxford: Oxford University Press, 2017).

Chan, J., 'Legitimacy, Unanimity, and Perfectionism', *Philosophy & Public Affairs* 29 (2000), pp. 5–42.

Chan, J., 'Political Authority and Perfectionism: A Response to Quong', *Philosophy and Public Issues* 2 (2012), pp. 31–41.

Chan, J., *Confucian Perfectionism: A Political Philosophy for Modern Times* (Princeton, NJ: Princeton University Press, 2014).

Cholbi, M., 'Paternalism and Our Rational Powers', *Mind* 126 (2017), pp. 123–53.

Cholbi, M., 'Equal Respect for Rational Agency', in M. Timmons (ed.), *Oxford Studies in Normative Ethics* (Oxford: Oxford University Press, 2020), pp. 182–203.

Clarke, S., 'Contractarianism, Liberal Neutrality, and Epistemology', *Political Studies* 47 (1999), pp. 627–42.

Cohen, G. A., *Self-Ownership, Freedom, and Equality* (Cambridge: Cambridge University Press, 1995).

Cohen, G. A., *Rescuing Justice and Equality* (Cambridge, MA: Harvard University Press, 2008).

Cohen, J., 'Moral Pluralism and Political Consensus', in D. Copp, J. Hampton and J. Roemer (eds), *The Idea of Democracy* (Cambridge: Cambridge University Press, 1989), pp. 270–91.

Conly, S., *Against Autonomy: Justifying Coercive Paternalism* (Cambridge: Cambridge University Press, 2013).

Couto, A., *Liberal Perfectionism* (Berlin: De Gruyter, 2014).

Daniels, N., 'Health-Care Needs and Distributive Justice', *Philosophy & Public Affairs* 10 (1981), pp. 146–79.

de Marneffe, P., 'The Slipperiness of Neutrality', *Social Theory and Practice* 32 (2006), pp. 17–34.

de Marneffe, P., 'The Possibility and Desirability of Neutrality', in R. Merrill and D. Weinstock (eds), *Political Neutrality: A Re-evaluation* (New York: Palgrave Macmillan, 2014), pp. 44–56.

Devlin, P., *The Enforcement of Morals* (Oxford: Oxford University Press, 1965).

Dietrich, F., 'Liberalism, Neutrality, and the Child's Right to an Open Future', *Journal of Social Philosophy* 51 (2020), pp. 104–28.

Dimant, E. and Tosato, G., 'Causes and Effects of Corruption: What Has Past Decade's Empirical Research Taught Us? A Survey', *Journal of Economic Surveys* 32 (2018), pp. 335–56.

Di Nucci, E., *Ethics Without Intention* (London: Bloomsbury, 2014).

Dorsey, D., 'The Significance of a Life's Shape', *Ethics* 125 (2015), pp. 303–30.

Dorsey, D., 'Why Should Welfare "Fit"?', *The Philosophical Quarterly* 67 (2017), pp. 685–708.

Dworkin, R., 'The Original Position', in N. Daniels (ed.), *Reading Rawls: Critical Studies on Rawls' A Theory of Justice* (Stanford, CA: Stanford University Press, 1975), pp. 16–53.

Dworkin, R., 'Liberalism', in S. Hampshire (ed.), *Public and Private Morality* (Cambridge: Cambridge University Press, 1978), pp. 113–43.

Dworkin, R., *Taking Rights Seriously* (Cambridge, MA: Harvard University Press, 1978).

Dworkin, R., 'Neutrality, Equality, and Liberalism', in D. MacLean and C. Mills (eds), *Liberalism Reconsidered* (Totowa, NJ: Rowman and Allanheld, 1983), pp. 1–11.

326   REFERENCES

Dworkin, R., *A Matter of Principle* (Cambridge, MA: Harvard University Press, 1985).

Dworkin, R., 'Foundations of Liberal Equality', in G. Peterson (ed.), *The Tanner Lectures on Human Values* (Salt Lake City, UT: University of Utah Press, 1990), pp. 3–119.

Dworkin, R., 'Foundations of Liberal Equality', in S. Darwall (ed.), *Equal Freedom: Selected Tanner Lectures on Human Values* (Ann Arbor, MI: University of Michigan Press, 1995), pp. 190–306.

Dworkin, R., *Sovereign Virtue: The Theory and Practice of Equality* (Cambridge, MA: Harvard University Press, 2000).

Dworkin, R., 'Ronald Dworkin Replies', in J. Burley (ed.), *Dworkin and His Critics* (Oxford: Blackwell, 2004), pp. 337–95.

Easton, C., 'Two Types of Liberalism' (unpublished manuscript).

Ebels-Duggan, K., 'The Beginning of Community: Politics in the Face of Disagreement', *The Philosophical Quarterly* 60 (2010), pp. 50–71.

Eberle, C., *Religious Conviction in Liberal Politics* (Cambridge: Cambridge University Press, 2002).

Edmundson, W., *John Rawls: Reticent Socialist* (Cambridge: Cambridge University Press, 2017).

Eliot, T. S., *The Idea of a Christian Society* (London: Faber & Faber, 1939).

Enoch, D., 'Why Idealize?', *Ethics* 115 (2005), pp. 759–87.

Enoch, D., 'Intending, Foreseeing and the State', *Legal Theory* 13 (2007), pp. 69–99.

Enoch, D., 'Against Public Reason', in D. Sobel, P. Vallentyne and S. Wall (eds), *Oxford Studies in Political Philosophy, Volume 1* (Oxford: Oxford University Press, 2015), pp. 112–44.

Enoch, D., 'What's Wrong with Paternalism: Autonomy, Belief, and Action', *Proceedings of the Aristotelian Society* 116 (2016), pp. 21–48.

Enoch, D., 'Idealizing Still Not Off the Hook: A Reply to Sobel's Reply' (unpublished manuscript).

Estlund, D., *Democratic Authority: A Philosophical Framework* (Princeton, NJ: Princeton University Press, 2008).

Estlund, D., *Utopophobia: On the Limits (If Any) of Political Philosophy* (Princeton, NJ: Princeton University Press, 2019).

Feinberg, J., *Harm to Others: The Moral Limits of the Criminal Law, Volume 1* (Oxford: Oxford University Press, 1984).

Feinberg, J., *Harmless Wrongdoing: The Moral Limits of Criminal Law, Volume 4* (Oxford: Oxford University Press, 1990).

Feldman, F., *Pleasure and the Good Life: Concerning the Nature, Varieties and Plausibility of Hedonism* (Oxford: Oxford University Press, 2004).

Finnis, J., *Natural Law and Natural Rights* (Oxford: Oxford University Press, 2011).

Fischhoff, B., 'Debiasing', in D. Kahneman, P. Slovic and A. Tversky (eds), *Judgment under Uncertainty: Heuristics and Biases* (Cambridge: Cambridge University Press, 1982), pp. 422–44.

Flanigan, J., 'Boundary Problems and Self-Ownership', *Social Philosophy and Policy* 36 (2019), pp. 9–35.

Fletcher, G., *The Philosophy of Well-Being* (London: Routledge, 2016).

Fowler, T. and Stemplowska, Z., 'The Asymmetry Objection Rides Again: On the Nature and Significance of Justificatory Disagreement', *Journal of Applied Philosophy* 32 (2015), pp. 133–46.

Fraser, R., 'Aesthetic Injustice' (unpublished manuscript).

Freeman, S., 'Illiberal Libertarians: Why Libertarianism Is Not a Liberal View', *Philosophy & Public Affairs* 30 (2001), pp. 105–51.

REFERENCES 327

Freeman, S., *Justice and the Social Contract: Essays on Rawlsian Political Philosophy* (Oxford: Oxford University Press, 2007).

Freeman, S., *Rawls* (London: Routledge, 2007).

Fried, B., 'Does Nozick Have a Theory of Property Rights?', in R. Bader and J. Meadowcroft (eds), *The Cambridge Companion to Nozick's Anarchy, State, and Utopia* (Cambridge: Cambridge University Press, 2011), pp. 230–52.

Galston, W., *Liberal Purposes: Goods, Virtues, and Diversity in the Liberal State* (Cambridge: Cambridge University Press, 1991).

Galston, W., *Liberal Pluralism: The Implications of Value Pluralism for Political Theory and Practice* (Cambridge: Cambridge University Press, 2002).

Gardner, H., 'Reflections on Multiple Intelligences: Myths and Messages', *The Phi Delta Kappan* 77 (1995), pp. 200–9.

Gardner, H., *Multiple Intelligences* (New York: Basic Books, 2006).

Gardner, J. and Shute, S., 'The Wrongness of Rape', in J. Horder (ed.), *Oxford Essays in Jurisprudence: Fourth Series* (Oxford: Oxford University Press, 2000), pp. 193–218.

Gaus, G., *Justificatory Liberalism: An Essay on Epistemology and Political Theory* (Oxford: Oxford University Press, 1996).

Gaus, G., 'On the Difficult Virtue of Minding One's Own Business: Towards the Political Rehabilitation of Ebenezer Scrooge', *The Philosopher* 5 (1997), pp. 24–8.

Gaus, G., *Contemporary Theories of Liberalism: Public Reason as a Post-Enlightenment Project* (London: Sage, 2003).

Gaus, G., 'Liberal Neutrality: A Compelling and Radical Principle', in S. Wall and G. Klosko (eds), *Perfectionism and Neutrality: Essays in Liberal Theory* (Oxford: Rowman & Littlefield, 2003), pp. 137–65.

Gaus, G., 'The Diversity of Comprehensive Liberalisms', in G. Gaus and C. Kukathas (eds), *Handbook of Political Theory* (London: Sage, 2004), pp. 100–14.

Gaus, G., 'State Neutrality and Controversial Values in *On Liberty*', in C. L. Ten (ed.), *Mill's On Liberty: A Critical Guide* (Cambridge: Cambridge University Press, 2008), pp. 83–104.

Gaus, G., 'Coercion, Ownership, and the Redistributive State: Justificatory Liberalism's Classical Tilt', *Social Philosophy & Policy* 27 (2010), pp. 233–75.

Gaus, G., 'A Tale of Two Sets: Public Reason in Equilibrium', *Public Affairs Quarterly* 25 (2011), pp. 305–25.

Gaus, G., *The Order of Public Reason: A Theory of Freedom and Morality in a Diverse and Bounded World* (Cambridge: Cambridge University Press, 2011).

Gaus, G., 'Sectarianism Without Perfection? Quong's Political Liberalism', *Philosophy and Public Issues* 2 (2012), pp. 7–15.

Gaus, G., 'On Theorizing About Public Reason', *European Journal of Analytic Philosophy* 9 (2013), pp. 64–85.

Gaus, G., 'The Good, the Bad, and the Ugly: Three Agent-Type Challenges to *The Order of Public Reason*', *Philosophical Studies* 170 (2014), pp. 563–77.

Gaus, G., 'On Being Inside Social Morality and Seeing It', *Criminal Law and Philosophy* 9 (2015), pp. 141–53.

Gaus, G., 'Public Reason Liberalism', in S. Wall (ed.), *The Cambridge Companion to Liberalism* (Cambridge: Cambridge University Press, 2015), pp. 112–40.

Gaus, G., 'Is Public Reason a Normalization Project? Deep Diversity and the Open Society', *Social Philosophy Today* 33 (2017), pp. 27–52.

George, R., *Making Men Moral: Civil Liberties and Public Morality* (Oxford: Oxford University Press, 1993).

Gheaus, A., 'The Feasibility Constraint on the Concept of Justice', *The Philosophical Quarterly* 63 (2013), pp. 445–64.

Gilabert, P. and Lawford-Smith, H., 'Political Feasibility: A Conceptual Exploration', *Political Studies* 60 (2012), pp. 809–25.

Goffman, E., *The Presentation of the Self in Everyday Life* (London: Penguin, 1990).

Greenawalt, K., 'On Public Reason', *Chicago-Kent Law Review* 69 (1994), pp. 669–89.

Guthman, E. and Allen, C. (eds), *RFK: His Words for Our Times* (New York: Harper Collins, 2018).

Gutmann, A., 'How Limited Is Liberal Government?', in B. Yack (ed.), *Liberalism Without Illusions: Essays on Liberal Theory and the Political Vision of Judith Shklar* (Chicago, IL: Chicago University Press, 1996), pp. 64–81.

Hampton, J., 'Should Political Philosophy Be Done Without Metaphysics?' *Ethics* 99 (1989), pp. 791–814.

Hanna, J., *In Our Best Interest: A Defense of Paternalism* (Oxford: Oxford University Press, 2018).

Hart, H. L. A., *The Concept of Law* (Oxford: Clarendon Press, 1961).

Hart, H. L. A., 'Rawls on Liberty and Its Priority', *University of Chicago Law Review* 40 (1973), pp. 534–55.

Heath, J., *The Machinery of Government: Public Administration and the Liberal State* (Oxford: Oxford University Press, 2020).

Heathwood, C., 'Desire-Fulfillment Theory', in G. Fletcher (ed.), *The Routledge Handbook of Philosophy of Well-Being* (London: Routledge, 2016), pp. 135–47.

Hendy, D., *Public Service Broadcasting* (Basingstoke: Palgrave Macmillan, 2013).

Higgins, C., *This New Noise: The Extraordinary Birth and Troubled Life of the BBC* (London: Faber & Faber, 2015).

Hinton, T. (ed.), *The Original Position* (Cambridge: Cambridge University Press, 2015).

Hollingdale, J. R., *Nietzsche: The Man and His Philosophy* (Baton Rouge, LA: Louisiana State University Press, 1965).

Holtug, N., 'The Harm Principle', *Ethical Theory and Moral Practice* 5 (2002), pp. 364–77.

Hooker, B., 'The Elements of Well-Being', *Journal of Practical Ethics* 3 (2015), pp. 15–35.

Horton, J., 'Why Liberals Should Not Worry About Subsidizing Opera', *Critical Review of International Social and Political Philosophy* 15 (2012), pp. 429–48.

Huggett, R., *Physical Geography: The Key Concepts* (Oxford: Routledge, 2010).

Hurka, T., 'Critical Notice of Vinit Haksar, *Equality, Liberty and Perfectionism*', *Canadian Journal of Philosophy* 13 (1983), pp. 449–70.

Hurka, T., 'Why Value Autonomy?', *Social Theory and Practice* 13 (1987), pp. 361–82.

Hurka, T., *Perfectionism* (Oxford: Oxford University Press, 1993).

Hurka, T., 'Indirect Perfectionism: Kymlicka on Liberal Neutrality', *Journal of Political Philosophy* 3 (1995), pp. 36–57.

Hurka, T., 'Book Review of George Sher's *Beyond Neutrality: Perfectionism and Politics*', *Ethics* 109 (1998), pp. 187–90.

Hurka, T., 'Nietzsche: Perfectionist', in B. Leiter and N. Sinhababu (eds), *Nietzsche and Morality* (Oxford: Oxford University Press, 2007), pp. 9–31.

Hurka, T., 'On "Hybrid" Theories of Personal Good', *Utilitas* 31 (2019), pp. 451–62.

Jacobsmeier, M., 'Public Opinion on Government Funding of the Arts in the United States: Demographic and Political Factors', *International Journal of Cultural Policy* 27 (2021), pp. 463–84.

James, A., 'Constructing Justice for Existing Practice: Rawls and the Status Quo', *Philosophy & Public Affairs* 33 (2005), pp. 281–316.

Johansson, J. and Risberg, O., 'The Preemption Problem', *Philosophical Studies* 176 (2019), pp. 351–65.

Johansson, J. and Risberg, O., 'Harming and Failing to Benefit: A Reply to Purves', *Philosophical Studies* 177 (2020), pp. 1539–48.

Kagan, S., 'Well-Being as Enjoying the Good', *Philosophical Perspectives* 23 (2009), pp. 253–72.

Kahneman, D., *Thinking, Fast and Slow* (New York: Farrar, Straus and Giroux, 2011).

Kant, I., *Practical Philosophy*, trans. and ed. M. Gregor (Cambridge: Cambridge University Press, 1996).

Kelly, P. (ed.), *Impartiality, Neutrality and Justice: Re-reading Brian Barry's Justice as Impartiality* (Edinburgh: Edinburgh University Press, 2000).

Kim, S., *Public Reason Confucianism: Democratic Perfectionism and Constitutionalism in East Asia* (Cambridge: Cambridge University Press, 2016).

King, N., *The Excellent Mind: Intellectual Virtues for Everyday Life* (Oxford: Oxford University Press, 2021).

Klosko, G., 'Rawls's "Political" Philosophy and American Democracy', *The American Political Science Review* 87 (1993), pp. 348–59.

Klosko, G., *Democratic Procedures and Liberal Consensus* (Oxford: Oxford University Press, 2000).

Klosko, G., 'An Empirical Approach to Political Liberalism', in S. Young (ed.), *Political Liberalism: Variations on a Theme* (Albany, NY: State University of New York Press, 2004), pp. 129–48.

Kniess, J., 'Justice in the Social Distribution of Health', *Social Theory and Practice* 45 (2019), pp. 397–425.

Koehler, J., 'The Base Rate Fallacy Reconsidered: Descriptive, Normative, and Methodological Challenges', *Behavioral and Brain Sciences* 19 (1996), pp. 1–17.

Koppelman, A., 'Neutrality and the Religion Analogy', in K. Vallier and M. Weber (eds), *Religious Exemptions* (Oxford: Oxford University Press, 2018), pp. 165–83.

Kramer, M., 'Legal Responses to Consensual Sexuality between Adults: Through and Beyond the Harm Principle', in C. Pulman (ed.), *Hart on Responsibility* (Basingstoke: Palgrave Macmillan, 2014), pp. 109–28.

Kramer, M., *Torture and Moral Integrity: A Philosophical Enquiry* (Oxford: Oxford University Press, 2014).

Kramer, M., 'One Cheer for Autonomy-Centered Perfectionism: An Arm's-Length Defense of Joseph Raz's Perfectionism Against an Allegation of Internal Inconsistency', *Argumenta* 1 (2015), pp. 79–95.

Kramer, M., *Liberalism with Excellence* (Oxford: Oxford University Press, 2017).

Kramer, M., 'On Political Morality and the Conditions for Warranted Self-Respect', *Journal of Ethics* 21 (2017), pp. 335–49.

Kramer, M., 'Replies to the Symposium Articles on *Liberalism with Excellence*', *The American Journal of Jurisprudence* 63 (2018), pp. 133–73.

Kramer, M., 'Looking Back and Looking Ahead: Replies to the Contributors', in M. McBride and V. Kurki (eds), *Without Trimmings: The Legal, Moral, and Political Philosophy of Matthew Kramer* (Oxford: Oxford University Press, 2022), pp. 363–552.

Kraut, R., 'Desire and the Human Good', *Proceedings and Addresses of the American Philosophical Association* 68 (1994), pp. 39–54.

330 REFERENCES

Kraut, R., 'Politics, Neutrality, and the Good', in E. Paul, F. Miller and J. Paul (eds), *Human Flourishing* (Cambridge: Cambridge University Press, 1999), pp. 315–32.

Kraut, R., *What Is Good and Why: The Ethics of Well-Being* (Cambridge, MA: Harvard University Press, 2007).

Kugelberg, H., 'Can Local Comparative Judgements Justify Moderate Perfectionism?', *Philosophia* 50 (2022), pp. 595–604.

Kugelberg, H., 'Civic Equality as a Democratic Basis for Public Reason', *Critical Review of International Social and Political Philosophy* (forthcoming).

Kukathas, C., *The Liberal Archipelago: A Theory of Diversity and Freedom* (Oxford: Oxford University Press, 2003).

Kukathas, C., 'Justicitis', in N. Simsek, S. Snyder and M. Knoll (eds), *New Perspectives on Distributive Justice: Deep Disagreements, Pluralism, and the Problem of Consensus* (Berlin: De Gruyter, 2018), pp. 187–204.

Kymlicka, W., 'Liberal Individualism and Liberal Neutrality', *Ethics* 99 (1989), pp. 883–905.

Kymlicka, W., *Liberalism, Community and Culture* (Oxford: Oxford University Press, 1989).

Kymlicka, W., *Contemporary Political Philosophy: An Introduction* (Oxford: Oxford University Press, 2002).

Laborde, C., *Liberalism's Religion* (Cambridge, MA: Harvard University Press, 2017).

Lamont, M., *Money, Morals, and Manners: The Culture of the French and the American Upper-Middle Class* (Chicago, IL: The University of Chicago Press, 1992).

Larmore, C., *Patterns of Moral Complexity* (Cambridge: Cambridge University Press, 1987).

Larmore, C., 'Political Liberalism', *Political Theory* 18 (1990), pp. 339–60.

Larmore, C., *The Morals of Modernity* (Cambridge: Cambridge University Press, 1996).

Larmore, C., 'The Moral Basis of Political Liberalism', *The Journal of Philosophy* 96 (1999), pp. 599–625.

Larmore, C., 'Political Liberalism: Its Motivations and Goals', in D. Sobel, P. Vallentyne and S. Wall (eds), *Oxford Studies in Political Philosophy, Volume 1* (Oxford: Oxford University Press, 2015), pp. 63–88.

Leib, E., *Friend v. Friend: The Transformation of Friendship—And What the Law Has to Do with It* (Oxford: Oxford University Press, 2011).

Leib, E., 'Friendship and the Law: A Response', *The New Republic*, 22 February 2011.

Leland, R. J., 'Civic Friendship, Public Reason', *Philosophy & Public Affairs* 47 (2019), pp. 72–103.

Leland, R. J. and van Wietmarschen, H., 'Political Liberalism and Political Community', *Journal of Moral Philosophy* 14 (2017), pp. 151–75.

Li, Z., *Political Liberalism, Confucianism, and the Future of Democracy in East Asia* (New York: Springer, 2020).

Lippert-Rasmussen, K., 'Rawls and Luck Egalitarianism', in J. Mandle and S. Roberts-Cady (eds), *John Rawls: Debating the Major Questions* (Oxford: Oxford University Press, 2020), pp. 133–47.

Lister, A., 'Public Justification and the Limits of State Action', *Politics, Philosophy & Economics* 9 (2010), pp. 151–75.

Lister, A., *Public Reason and Political Community* (London: Bloomsbury, 2013).

Lister, A., 'Public Reason and Perfectionism: Comments on Quong's *Liberalism Without Perfection*', *Philosophy and Society* 25 (2014), pp. 12–34.

Lloyd, S. A., 'Relativizing Rawls', *Chicago-Kent Law Review* 69 (1994), pp. 709–35.

REFERENCES   331

Locke, J., *An Essay Concerning Human Understanding*, ed. P. Nidditch (Oxford: Clarendon Press, 1975).

Locke, J., *Second Treatise of Government and a Letter Concerning Toleration* (Oxford: Oxford University Press, 2016).

Lott, M., 'Restraint on Reasons and Reasons for Restraint: A Problem for Rawls' Ideal of Public Reason', *Pacific Philosophical Quarterly* 87 (2006), pp. 75–95.

Macedo, S., *Liberal Virtues: Citizenship, Virtue, and Community in Liberal Constitutionalism* (Oxford: Clarendon Press, 1990).

MacIntyre, A., *After Virtue* (Notre Dame, IN: University of Notre Dame Press, 1984).

Mack, E., 'Nozickian Arguments for the More-Than-Minimal State', in R. Bader and J. Meadowcroft (eds), *The Cambridge Companion to Nozick's Anarchy, State, and Utopia* (Cambridge: Cambridge University Press, 2011), pp. 89–115.

Mack, E., 'Elbow Room for Rights', in D. Sobel, P. Vallentyne and S. Wall (eds), *Oxford Studies in Political Philosophy, Volume 1* (Oxford: Oxford University Press, 2015), pp. 194–221.

Mack, E., *Libertarianism* (Cambridge: Polity, 2018).

Macleod, C., 'Liberal Neutrality or Liberal Tolerance?', *Law and Philosophy* 16 (1997), pp. 529–59.

Macleod, C., 'Neutrality, Public Reason and Deliberative Democracy', in R. Merrill and D. Weinstock (eds), *Political Neutrality: A Re-evaluation* (New York: Palgrave Macmillan, 2014), pp. 159–77.

Mang, F., 'Liberal Neutrality and Moderate Perfectionism', *Res Publica* 19 (2013), pp. 297–315.

Matravers, M., 'What's "Wrong" in Contractualism?', in P. Kelly (ed.), *Impartiality, Neutrality and Justice: Re-reading Brian Barry's Justice as Impartiality* (Edinburgh: Edinburgh University Press, 2000), pp. 108–19.

Mazor, J. and Vallentyne, P., 'Libertarianism, Left and Right', in S. Olsaretti (ed.), *The Oxford Handbook of Distributive Justice* (Oxford: Oxford University Press, 2018), pp. 129–51.

McCabe, D., *Modus Vivendi Liberalism: Theory and Practice* (Cambridge: Cambridge University Press, 2010).

McGinn, C., 'Reasons and Unreasons', *The New Republic*, 24 May 1999, pp. 34–8.

McKenna, M., 'Where Frankfurt and Strawson Meet', *Midwest Studies in Philosophy* 29 (2005), pp. 163–80.

Mendus, S., *Toleration and the Limits of Liberalism* (London: Macmillan, 1989).

Metz, T., 'Respect for Persons and Perfectionist Politics', *Philosophy & Public Affairs* 30 (2001), pp. 417–42.

Mill, J. S., *On Liberty* (London: Penguin Books, 1985).

Mill, J. S., *Utilitarianism* (Oxford: Oxford University Press, 1998).

Miller, D., 'What's Wrong with Religious Establishment?', *Criminal Law and Philosophy* 15 (2021), pp. 75–89.

Moran, J., *Armchair Nation: An Intimate History of Britain in Front of the TV* (London: Profile Books, 2013).

Mulhall, S. and Swift, A., *Liberals and Communitarians* (Oxford: Blackwell Publishing, 1996).

Nagel, T., 'Rawls on Justice', *The Philosophical Review* 82 (1973), pp. 220–34.

Nagel, T., 'Moral Conflict and Political Legitimacy', *Philosophy & Public Affairs* 16 (1987), pp. 215–40.

Nagel, T., *Equality and Partiality* (Oxford: Oxford University Press, 1991).

Narveson, J., *The Libertarian Idea* (Peterborough: Broadview Press, 2001).

332 REFERENCES

Nathan, D., 'Liberal Principles and Government Support for the Arts', *Public Affairs Quarterly* 8 (1994), pp. 141–51.

Neal, P., 'Dworkin on the Foundations of Liberal Equality', *Legal Theory* 1 (1995), pp. 205–26.

Neal, P., *Liberalism and Its Discontents* (New York: New York University Press, 1997).

Neufeld, B., 'Shared Intentions, Public Reason, and Political Autonomy', *Canadian Journal of Philosophy* 49 (2019), pp. 776–804.

Nozick, R., *Anarchy, State, and Utopia* (New York: Basic Books, 1974).

Nozick, R., *Philosophical Explanations* (Oxford: Clarendon Press, 1981).

Nussbaum, M., 'Perfectionist Liberalism and Political Liberalism', *Philosophy & Public Affairs* 39 (2011), pp. 3–45.

Ogien, R., 'Neutrality Toward Non-Controversial Conceptions of the Good Life', in R. Merrill and D. Weinstock (eds), *Political Neutrality: A Re-evaluation* (New York: Palgrave Macmillan, 2014), pp. 97–108.

Olsaretti, S., 'Introduction: The Idea of Distributive Justice', in S. Olsaretti (ed.), *The Oxford Handbook of Distributive Justice* (Oxford: Oxford University Press, 2018), pp. 1–9.

Otsuka, M., *Libertarianism Without Inequality* (Oxford: Oxford University Press, 2003).

Pallikkathayil, J., 'Neither Perfectionism Nor Political Liberalism', *Philosophy & Public Affairs* 44 (2016), pp. 171–96.

Pallikkathayil, J., 'Resisting Rawlsian Political Liberalism', *Philosophy & Public Affairs* 45 (2017), pp. 413–26.

Pallikkathayil, J., 'Disagreement and the Duties of Citizenship', *American Philosophical Quarterly* 56 (2019), pp. 71–82.

Parfit, D., *Reasons and Persons* (Oxford: Oxford University Press, 1984).

Pateman, C. and Mills, C., *Contract and Domination* (Cambridge: Polity, 2007).

Patten, A., 'Liberal Neutrality: A Reinterpretation and Defense', *The Journal of Political Philosophy* 20 (2012), pp. 249–72.

Peter, F., 'Epistemic Foundations of Political Liberalism', *Journal of Moral Philosophy* 10 (2013), pp. 598–620.

Pettit, P., 'Rawls's Political Ontology', *Politics, Philosophy & Economics* 4 (2005), pp. 157–74.

Pettit, P., 'Can Contract Theory Ground Morality?', in J. Dreier (ed.), *Contemporary Debates in Moral Theory* (Oxford: Blackwell, 2006), pp. 77–96.

Pogge, T., 'Is Kant's *Rechtslehre* a "Comprehensive Liberalism"?', in M. Timmons (ed.), *Kant's Metaphysics of Morals: Interpretative Essays* (Oxford: Oxford University Press, 2002), pp. 133–58.

Policy Research and Planning Department of the Arts Council of England, *International Data on Public Spending on the Arts in Eleven Countries* (London: Arts Council of England, 1998).

Posner, E., 'Huck and Jim and Law', *The New Republic*, 21 February 2011.

Purves, D., 'Harming as Making Worse Off', *Philosophical Studies* 176 (2019), pp. 2629–56.

Putnam, R., *Bowling Alone: The Collapse and Revival of American Community* (New York: Simon & Schuster, 2000).

Quong, J., 'Disagreement, Asymmetry, and Liberal Legitimacy', *Politics, Philosophy & Economics* 4 (2005), pp. 301–30.

Quong, J., *Liberalism Without Perfection* (Oxford: Oxford University Press, 2011).

Quong, J., '*Liberalism Without Perfection*: A Précis', *Philosophy and Public Issues* 2 (2012), pp. 1–6.

Quong, J., '*Liberalism Without Perfection*: Replies to Gaus, Colburn, Chan, Bocchiola', *Philosophy and Public Issues* 2 (2012), pp. 51–79.

REFERENCES 333

Quong, J., 'On the Idea of Public Reason', in J. Mandle and D. Reidy (eds), *The Blackwell Companion to Rawls* (Oxford: Wiley Blackwell, 2013), pp. 265–80.

Quong, J., 'Justification vs. Proof', in J. Mandle (ed.), *The Cambridge Rawls Lexicon* (Cambridge: Cambridge University Press, 2014), pp. 390–1.

Quong, J., '*Liberalism Without Perfection*: Replies to Lister, Kulenović, Zoffoli, Zelić, and Baccarini', *Philosophy and Society* 25 (2014), pp. 96–122.

Quong, J., 'What Is the Point of Public Reason?', *Philosophical Studies* 170 (2014), pp. 545–53.

Quong, J., 'Disagreement, Equality, and the Exclusion of Ideals: A Comment on *The Morality of Freedom*', *Jerusalem Review of Legal Studies* 14 (2016), pp. 135–46.

Quong, J., 'On Laborde's Liberalism', *Criminal Law and Philosophy* 15 (2021), pp. 47–59.

Railton, P., 'Facts and Values', *Philosophical Topics* 14 (1986), pp. 5–29.

Railton, P., *Facts, Values and Norms* (Cambridge: Cambridge University Press, 2003).

Ramakrishnan, K., 'Treating People as Tools', *Philosophy & Public Affairs* 44 (2016), pp. 133–65.

Rawls, J., *A Theory of Justice* (Cambridge, MA: Harvard University Press, 1971).

Rawls, J., 'Fairness to Goodness', *Philosophical Review* 84 (1975), pp. 536–54.

Rawls, J., 'Kantian Constructivism in Moral Theory', *The Journal of Philosophy* 77 (1980), pp. 515–72.

Rawls, J., 'Justice as Fairness: Political not Metaphysical', *Philosophy & Public Affairs* 14 (1985), pp. 223–51.

Rawls, J., 'The Idea of an Overlapping Consensus', *Oxford Journal of Legal Studies* 7 (1987), pp. 1–25.

Rawls, J., 'The Domain of the Political and Overlapping Consensus', *New York University Law Review* 64 (1989), pp. 233–55.

Rawls, J., *John Rawls: Collected Papers*, ed. S. Freeman (Cambridge, MA: Harvard University Press, 1999).

Rawls, J., *Justice as Fairness: A Restatement* (Cambridge, MA: Harvard University Press, 2001).

Rawls, J., *Political Liberalism* (New York: Columbia University Press, 2005).

Rawls, J., *Lectures on the History of Political Philosophy* (Cambridge, MA: Harvard University Press, 2007).

Raz, J., *The Morality of Freedom* (Oxford: Clarendon Press, 1986).

Raz, J., 'Liberalism, Skepticism, and Democracy', *Iowa Law Review* 74 (1989), pp. 761–86.

Raz, J., 'Facing Diversity: The Case of Epistemic Abstinence', *Philosophy & Public Affairs* 19 (1990), pp. 3–46.

Reidy, D., 'Reciprocity and Reasonable Disagreement: From Liberal to Democratic Legitimacy', *Philosophical Studies* 132 (2007), pp. 243–91.

Reith, J., *Broadcast Over Britain* (London: Hodder and Stoughton, 1924).

Richards, J., 'Equality of Opportunity', in A. Mason (ed.), *Ideals of Equality* (Oxford: Blackwell, 1998), pp. 52–78.

Ripstein, A., 'Beyond the Harm Principle', *Philosophy & Public Affairs* 24 (2006), pp. 215–45.

Ripstein, A., *Force and Freedom: Kant's Legal and Political Philosophy* (Cambridge, MA: Harvard University Press, 2009).

Ripstein, A., 'Form and Matter in Kantian Political Philosophy: A Reply', *European Journal of Philosophy* 20 (2012), pp. 487–96.

Rorty, R., *Objectivity, Relativism, and Truth: Philosophical Papers* (Cambridge: Cambridge University Press, 1991).

Rosati, C., 'Internalism and the Good for a Peron', *Ethics* 106 (1996), pp. 297–326.

Rosati, C., 'The Story of a Life', *Social Philosophy and Policy* 30 (2013), pp. 21–50.

Rudisill, J., 'The Neutrality of the State and Its Justification in Rawls and Mill', *Auslegung* 23 (2000), pp. 153–68.

Ryan, A., 'Mill in a Liberal Landscape', in J. Skorupski (ed.), *The Cambridge Companion to Mill* (Cambridge: Cambridge University Press, 1998), pp. 497–540.

Sandel, M., 'The Procedural Republic and the Unencumbered Self', *Political Theory* 12 (1984), pp. 81–96.

Sandel, M., *Liberalism and the Limits of Justice* (Cambridge: Cambridge University Press, 1998).

Sangiovanni, A., 'Justice and the Priority of Politics to Morality', *The Journal of Political Philosophy* 16 (2008), pp. 137–64.

Sarch, A., 'Internalism About a Person's Good: Don't Believe It', *Philosophical Studies* 152 (2011), pp. 161–84.

Sarch, A., 'Multi-Component Theories of Well-Being and Their Structure', *Pacific Philosophical Quarterly* 93 (2012), pp. 439–71.

Scanlon, T. M., *What We Owe to Each Other* (Cambridge, MA: Harvard University Press, 1998).

Scanlon, T. M., *Moral Dimensions: Permissibility, Meaning, Blame* (Cambridge, MA: Harvard University Press, 2008).

Schouten, G., *Liberalism, Neutrality, and the Gendered Division of Labor* (Oxford: Oxford University Press, 2019).

Schwartz, A., 'Moral Neutrality and Primary Goods', *Ethics* 83 (1973), pp. 294–307.

Sheppard, S., 'The Perfectionisms of John Rawls', *Canadian Journal of Law and Jurisprudence* 11 (1998), pp. 383–416.

Sher, G., *Beyond Neutrality: Perfectionism and Politics* (Cambridge: Cambridge University Press, 1997).

Sher, G., 'Perfectionism and Democracy', in R. Merrill and D. Weinstock (eds), *Political Neutrality: A Re-evaluation* (New York: Palgrave Macmillan, 2014), pp. 144–58.

Sher, G., 'Confessions of a Quidnunc', *The American Journal of Jurisprudence* 63 (2018), pp. 49–61.

Shklar, J., 'The Liberalism of Fear', in N. Rosenblum (ed.), *Liberalism and the Moral Life* (Cambridge, MA: Harvard University Press, 1989), pp. 21–38.

Sinopoli, R., 'Liberalism and Contested Conceptions of the Good: The Limits of Neutrality', *The Journal of Politics* 55 (1993), pp. 644–63.

Sobel, D., 'Backing Away from Libertarian Self-Ownership', *Ethics* 123 (2012), pp. 32–60.

Sobel, D., *From Valuing to Value: A Defense of Subjectivism* (Oxford: Oxford University Press, 2017).

Sobel, D., 'The Point of Self-Ownership', in D. Schmidtz and C. Pavel (eds), *The Oxford Handbook of Freedom* (Oxford: Oxford University Press, 2018), pp. 124–40.

Southwood, N., *Contractualism and the Foundations of Morality* (Oxford: Oxford University Press, 2010).

Stanton-Ife, J., 'Must We Pay for the British Museum? Taxation and the Harm Principle', in M. Bhandari (ed.), *Philosophical Foundations of Tax Law* (Oxford: Oxford University Press, 2017), pp. 35–56.

Steiner, H., *An Essay on Rights* (Oxford: Blackwell, 1994).

Stemplowska, Z., 'Should I Be Proud of *Liberalism with Excellence*? On the Collective Grounds of Self-Respect', *The American Journal of Jurisprudence* 63 (2018), pp. 81–91.

Strawson, P. F., 'Freedom and Resentment', *Proceedings of the British Academy* 48 (1962), pp. 187–211.

Strawson, P. F., 'Freedom and Resentment', in G. Watson (ed.), *Free Will* (Oxford: Oxford University Press, 2003), pp. 72–93.

Sypnowich, C., *Equality Renewed: Justice, Flourishing and the Egalitarian Ideal* (London: Routledge, 2017).

Tadros, V., *Wrongs and Crimes* (Oxford: Oxford University Press, 2016).

Tahzib, C., 'Pluralist Neutrality', *The Journal of Political Philosophy* 26 (2018), pp. 508–32.

Tahzib, C., 'Perfectionism: Political not Metaphysical', *Philosophy & Public Affairs* 47 (2019), pp. 144–78.

Tahzib, C., 'Does Social Trust Justify the Public Justification Principle?', *The Journal of Applied Philosophy* 38 (2021), pp. 461–78.

Tahzib, C., 'Is Anti-Sectarianism a Desideratum of a Public Reason View?', *Public Affairs Quarterly* 35 (2021), pp. 228–46.

Tahzib, C., 'Perfectionist Duties', in D. Sobel, P. Vallentyne and S. Wall (eds), *Oxford Studies in Political Philosophy, Volume 7* (Oxford: Oxford University Press, 2021), pp. 124–60.

Tahzib, C., 'Do the Reactive Attitudes Justify Public Reason?', *European Journal of Political Theory* 21(2022), pp. 423–44.

Tahzib, C., 'Does Edificatory Perfectionism Express a Quidnunc Mentality?', in M. McBride and V. Kurki (eds), *Without Trimmings: The Legal, Moral, and Political Philosophy of Matthew Kramer* (Oxford: Oxford University Press, 2022), pp. 297–318.

Taylor, A., 'Public Justification and the Reactive Attitudes', *Politics, Philosophy & Economics* 17 (2018), pp. 97–113.

Taylor, F. and Barresi, A., *The Arts at a New Frontier: The National Endowment for the Arts* (New York: Plenum Press, 1984).

Thaler, R. and Sunstein, C., *Nudge: Improving Decisions About Health, Wealth, and Happiness* (New Haven, CT: Yale University Press, 2008).

Thomson, J. J., *The Realm of Rights* (Cambridge, MA: Harvard University Press, 1990).

Thomson, J. J., 'Self-Defense', *Philosophy & Public Affairs* 20 (1991), pp. 283–310.

Turner, J., 'Politics, Truth, and Respect', in D. Sobel, P. Vallentyne and S. Wall (eds), *Oxford Studies in Political Philosophy, Volume 7* (Oxford: Oxford University Press, 2021), pp. 100–23.

Tversky, A. and Kahneman, D., 'The Framing of Decisions and the Psychology of Choice', *Science* 211 (1981), pp. 453–8.

Vallentyne, P., 'Left-Libertarianism: A Primer', in P. Vallentyne and H. Steiner (eds), *Left-Libertarianism and Its Critics: The Contemporary Debate* (New York: Palgrave, 2000), pp. 1–20.

Vallentyne, P., 'Justice in General: An Introduction', in P. Vallentyne (ed.), *Equality and Justice: Justice in General* (London: Routledge, 2003), pp. xi–xviii.

Vallentyne, P., 'Left-Libertarianism as a Promising Form of Liberal Egalitarianism', *Philosophic Exchange* 39 (2009), pp. 56–71.

Vallentyne, P., Steiner, H. and Otsuka, M., 'Why Left-Libertarianism Is Not Incoherent, Indeterminate, or Irrelevant: A Reply to Fried', *Philosophy & Public Affairs* 33 (2005), pp. 201–15.

Vallier, K., *Liberal Politics and Public Faith: Beyond Separation* (New York: Routledge, 2014).

Vallier, K., 'On Jonathan Quong's Sectarian Political Liberalism', *Criminal Law and Philosophy* 11 (2017), pp. 175–94.

Vallier, K., *Must Politics Be War? Restoring Our Trust in the Open Society* (Oxford: Oxford University Press, 2019).

Vallier, K. and Muldoon, R., 'In Public Reason, Diversity Trumps Coherence', *The Journal of Political Philosophy* 29 (2021), pp. 211–30.

Van Schoelandt, C., 'Justification, Coercion, and the Place of Public Reason', *Philosophical Studies* 172 (2015), pp. 1031–50.

Van Wietmarschen, H., 'Political Liberalism and Respect', *The Journal of Political Philosophy* 29 (2021), pp. 353–74.

Vranas, P., 'Gigerenzer's Normative Critique of Kahneman and Tversky', *Cognition* 76 (2000), pp. 179–93.

Waldron, J., 'Theoretical Foundations of Liberalism', *The Philosophical Quarterly* 147 (1987), pp. 127–50.

Waldron, J., *Law and Disagreement* (Oxford: Oxford University Press, 1999).

Waldron, J., 'Liberalism, Political and Comprehensive', in G. Gaus and C. Kukathas (eds), *Handbook of Political Theory* (London: Sage, 2004), pp. 89–99.

Wall, S., *Liberalism, Perfectionism, and Restraint* (Cambridge: Cambridge University Press, 1998).

Wall, S., 'Is Public Justification Self-Defeating?', *American Philosophical Quarterly* 39 (2002), pp. 385–94.

Wall, S., 'Perfectionist Politics: A Defense', in T. Christiano and J. Christman (eds), *Contemporary Debates in Political Philosophy* (Oxford: Blackwell, 2009), pp. 99–117.

Wall, S., 'Self-Ownership and Paternalism', *The Journal of Political Philosophy* 17 (2009), pp. 399–417.

Wall, S., 'Neutralism for Perfectionists: The Case of Restricted State Neutrality', *Ethics* 120 (2010), pp. 232–56.

Wall, S., 'Enforcing Morality', *Criminal Law and Philosophy* 7 (2013), pp. 455–71.

Wall, S., 'Moral Environmentalism', in C. Coons and M. Weber (eds), *Paternalism: Theory and Practice* (Cambridge: Cambridge University Press, 2013), pp. 93–114.

Wall, S., 'Perfectionism', in G. Gaus and F. D'Agostino (eds), *The Routledge Companion to Social and Political Philosophy* (London: Routledge, 2013), pp. 342–52.

Wall, S., 'Subjective Perfectionism', *The American Journal of Jurisprudence* 63 (2018), pp. 109–31.

Wall, S., 'The Good Society', in S. Olsaretti (ed.), *The Oxford Handbook of Distributive Justice* (Oxford: Oxford University Press, 2018), pp. 195–212.

Watson, L. and Hartley, C., *Equal Citizenship and Public Reason: A Feminist Political Liberalism* (Oxford: Oxford University Press, 2018).

Weber, M. and Vallier, K. (eds), *Political Utopias: Contemporary Debates* (Oxford: Oxford University Press, 2017).

Weinstock, D., 'Neutralizing Perfection: Hurka on Liberal Neutrality', *Dialogue* 38 (1999), pp. 45–62.

Weithman, P., *Why Political Liberalism? On John Rawls's Political Turn* (Oxford: Oxford University Press, 2010).

Weithman, P., 'In Defence of a Political Liberalism', *Philosophy & Public Affairs* 45 (2017), pp. 397–41.

Wendt, F., *Compromise, Peace and Public Justification: Political Morality Beyond Justice* (London: Palgrave Macmillan, 2016).

Wendt, F., 'Rescuing Public Justification from Public Reason Liberalism', in D. Sobel, P. Vallentyne and S. Wall (eds), *Oxford Studies in Political Philosophy, Volume 5* (Oxford: Oxford University Press, 2017), pp. 39–64.

Wilkinson, T., 'Against Dworkin's Endorsement Constraint', *Utilitas* 15 (2003), pp. 175–93.

Wilson, J., *The Works of James Wilson, Volume 1*, ed. R. McCloskey (Cambridge, MA: Harvard University Press, 1967).

Wolf, S., 'Moral Saints', *The Journal of Philosophy* 79 (1982), pp. 419–39.

Wolff, J., 'Fairness, Respect, and the Egalitarian Ethos', *Philosophy & Public Affairs* 27 (1998), pp. 97–122.

Wolff, R. P., *Understanding Rawls: A Reconstruction and Critique of A Theory of Justice* (Princeton, NJ: Princeton University Press, 1977).

Wolterstorff, N., *Understanding Liberal Democracy: Essays in Political Philosophy* (Oxford: Oxford University Press, 2012).

Wong, B., 'Is It Sectarian for a Rawlsian State to Coerce Nozick? On Political Liberalism and the Sectarian Critique', *Philosophia* (forthcoming).

Woodard, C., 'Hybrid Theories', in G. Fletcher (ed.), *The Routledge Handbook of Philosophy of Well-Being* (London : Routledge, 2015), pp. 161–74.

Woodward, J., 'The Non-Identity Problem', *Ethics* 96 (1986), pp. 804–31.

Young, S., 'The Concept of Political Liberalism', in S. Young (ed.), *Political Liberalism: Variations on a Theme* (Albany, NY: State University of New York Press, 2004), pp. 1–23.

Index

Abbey, Ruth 22 n. 7, 29 n. 49
Ackerman, Bruce 34 n. 1, 41, 43, 44, 126–7, 139 n. 41, 156 n. 2, 157, 161, 242, 267 n. 69, 268, 269
Anti-perfectionist liberalism
  about reasons for state action, not consequences of state action 171
  analysis of distinction between perfectionism and 1, 19, 22, 174–5, 176, 206
  comprehensive-liberal variant of 19–33
  expressions of support for, by various political liberals 44–5
  as generalization of idea of religious toleration 37, 43–4, 54, 217
  importance of not setting up a straw man of 172–4
  political-liberal variant of 34–59
  present state of debate between perfectionism and 4–5
  tendency of proponents of, to falsely generalize from crude or excessively sectarian versions of perfectionism 25 n. 22, 117–19, 145–6
  as term of art serving classificatory purposes 22, 174
  thumbnail description of 1, 19
Anti-sectarianism
  general explanation of Anti-Sectarian Desideratum 233–6
  possible arguments for Anti-Sectarian Desideratum rejected 236–43
  as pro tanto good within some bounds 244 n. 122
  as threshold or constraint 236, 237–8, 243–6
  as underlying motivation for public reason project 14, 45, 216–17, 233, 236–8, 243–6
Aristotelian Principle *see* Rawls, John
Arneson, Richard
  on autopsy of anti-perfectionist liberalism 4
  on cheap thrills 152–3
  on comprehensive perfectionism and principled secularism 217 n. 68
  on difference principle and lexical priority 100
  on Dworkin's challenge model of ethics 31 n. 64

on list of objective goods 134–5, 148, 149 n. 63
on objections to full self-ownership 259–61
on political liberalism and bar of rational acceptability 119
Aspirational perfectionism *see* Kramer, Matthew
Athletic excellence 141, 142, 147, 211 n. 54
Autonomy *see* freedom

Baier, Kurt 68 n. 24, 320 n. 11
Barry, Brian
  on Aristotelian Principle 179 n. 73
  on impermissibility of perfectionism 44
  on lexical priority 100
  on multiple components of income and wealth 140
  on scepticism as basis for anti-perfectionism 107 n. 69, 127–8, 129
  on scope of public justification principle 41 n. 38
BBC 165–7
Berlin, Isaiah 36 n. 8, 268
Billingham, Paul
  on consensus/convergence distinction 197 n. 4
  on Kramer's argument from warranted self-respect to aspirational-perfectionist policies 187
  on possibility of perfectionist internal conception 209 n. 46, 218
  on question-begging nature of quidnunc mentality argument 302 n. 34
  on structural looseness of perfectionist public reason 226–8
  on weightiness of content-independent value of freedom 254 n. 25
Bradford, Gwen 148 n. 62, 150 n. 64
Bradley, Ben 148, 149 n. 63, 308–9
Brighouse, Harry 176 n. 59, 180 n. 77
Broad-and-enduring-appeal criterion 206 n. 34, 229–32
Bruckner, Donald 105–7
Burdens of judgement
  applicable to questions of justice 45, 118–19
  general explanation of 39–40

INDEX

Caney, Simon 117 n. 96, 119 n. 100, 129 n. 12, 206–8, 223 n. 79, 267 n. 69, 276
Carroll, Noël 156, 161, 176 n. 59, 181 n. 86
Carter, Ian 253 n. 23, 291 n. 65
Challenge model of ethics
  anti-perfectionist implications of 32–3, 252
  compatibility of perfectionist justice with 252, 256
  sketch of 30–3, 252
Chan, Joseph
  on Confucian conception of human flourishing 10, 131–2
  free-standing conception of human flourishing of 132 n. 19
  on human flourishing as purpose of living together 76
  as non-duty-based perfectionist 6
  paternalistic justification for perfectionist state action 275
  on public justifiability of perfectionism 206–8
Cholbi, Michael 282, 289–90
Civic friendship 48, 200, 201–5, 211, 214, 215
Cohen, G. A. 114 n. 89, 257, 271
Comprehensive liberalism
  characterized and distinguished from political liberalism 10, 20–3
  Dworkin's challenge model of ethics 30–3, 252
  Kant and Mill as exemplars of 10, 20 n. 1, 21, 30, 34, 35, 36 n. 8, 37, 38, 51, 54
  Kantian liberalism 23–6
  Millian liberalism 26–30, 251
  subject to reasonable disagreement 21, 34–5, 37–9, 45, 48, 49, 54, 236
  as term of art serving classificatory purposes 20, 22
Conly, Sarah
  on argument from subjectivism to anti-perfectionist liberalism 126–7 n. 2
  on insusceptibility of perfectionist values to state promotion 156–7
  on relationship between respect and estimation of others' abilities 288–9
Constructivist approach to public reason
  general explanation of perfectionist application of 209–10
  objection that, preaches to the converted 211–13, 241
  see also empirical approach to public reason, perfectionist public reason, public justification, reasonable citizen and reasonable disagreement
Content-independent value of freedom see freedom and Kramer, Matthew

Contractualist devices see perfectionist original position, perfectionist public reason, public justification and Rawlsian original position
Convivia see Kramer, Matthew
Couto, Alexandra
  on list of objective goods 134–5, 148, 149 n. 63
  as non-duty-based perfectionist 6
Crib test see enjoyment of moral, intellectual and artistic excellence

de Marneffe, Peter 99 n. 45, 174 n. 57
Degradia 87–8
Devlin, Patrick 249–50, 251, 252
Dorsey, Dale 136 n. 35, 144 n. 56
Dworkin, Ronald
  on argument from intergenerational fairness to perfectionist policies 180–2
  on challenge model of ethics 30–3, 252
  on endorsement constraint 32, 136 n. 35, 137 n. 39, 252
  on impermissibility of perfectionism 44, 180
  on objective-list conceptions of human flourishing 136
  on redundancy of original position 120 n. 106
  on scheme for classifying political theories 77
  shift from political liberalism to comprehensive liberalism 30 n. 52
  uncharitable invocation of Falwell's perfectionism by 145–6, 201

Eberle, Christopher 52, 201–5
Edificatory perfectionism see Kramer, Matthew
Empirical approach to public reason
  critique of 208, 212
  general explanation of perfectionist application of 206–7
  see also constructivist approach to public reason, perfectionist public reason, public justification, reasonable citizen and reasonable disagreement
Endorsement constraint see Dworkin, Ronald
Enjoyment of moral, intellectual and artistic excellence
  arbitrariness of three excellences 130, 147–51
  as conception adopted for political purposes 11, 13, 130, 134, 135, 137, 205, 211, 215, 318
  and the crib test 148, 150, 248 n. 3
  diversity of forms of 135, 138, 150–1, 158, 160
  as elitist or ideological 150–1
  enjoyment as necessary condition 130, 135–7, 141, 151–5

340 INDEX

Enjoyment of moral, intellectual and artistic excellence (*Continued*)
  excellence as necessary condition 130, 137, 141, 151–5
  excessive abstractness of three excellences 138–41
  as fundamental idea within perfectionist theory of justice 12, 210–11, 220–1, 242, 317
  informs perfectionist definition of reasonable citizen 210–11, 220–1, 242
  (in)susceptibility of, to state promotion 137, 156–7, 159, 160–70
  interpretations of excellences need not be built into foundations of theory and can be assigned to legislative stage 139, 141, 232
  provisionality of conception of human flourishing as 13, 130, 139, 141–7, 154–5, 211 n. 54
  satisfies plausible specification of public justification principle 132, 133, 134, 142, 146, 211 n. 54, *see also* perfectionist public reason
  specific interpretations of three excellences 118, 135, 138–41, 150–1, 158–9, 160, 164–5, 168, 199, 210, 225–33
Enoch, David 48, 129, 200, 264 n. 59, 285 n. 53, 301 n. 29
Estlund, David 217, 271
Excellence *see* enjoyment of moral, intellectual and artistic excellence
Exchange branch of government *see* Rawls, John

Fair striving for human flourishing *see* perfectionist conception of society
Fair system of social cooperation *See* Rawlsian conception of society
Falwell, Jerry 145–6, 147, 201–5
Feasibility constraint on justice 15, 270–2
Feinberg, Joel 267 n. 69, 307 n. 47, 309 n. 55
Feldman, Fred 148, 150, 248 n. 3
Fletcher, Guy 129 n. 10, 136 n. 35, 144 n. 56, 148 n. 60, 148 n. 62, 149 n. 63
Fowler, Timothy 117–18 n. 96, 228 n. 89
Freedom
  as basis of objection to perfectionism 14, 247–72
  compatibility of perfectionist justice with several conceptions of 14, 247, 250–6
  conception of, found within perfectionist theory of justice 247, 248–50
  Dworkin's challenge model of ethics 30–3, 252

  incompatibility of perfectionist justice with, as full self-ownership 14, 247, 256–8
  Kantian conception of, as mutual independence 23–6
  Kramer on content-independent value of 253–4, 315–16
  libertarian conception of, as full self-ownership 256–67
  Millian conception of, as individuality 26–30, 251
  Quong on perfectionist subsidies and autonomy intrusion 254–6
Freeman, Samuel 46 n. 69, 91 n. 5, 104 n. 56, 176, 261 n. 51

Galston, William 21 n. 4, 51, 52 n. 108, 53, 71, 240
Gaus, Gerald
  on anti-sectarianism within public reason theory 233, 234 n. 98, 235, 237, 238, 241
  on deeply objectionably characteristic of perfectionism 198
  on definition of reasonable citizen 42–3, 56, 242 n. 119
  on disrespect involved in imposing laws on unreasonable 240–1 n. 115
  on libertarian tilt of public justification principle 45–6, 197 n. 4, 225 n. 81
  on minding one's own business 294
  on reactive attitudes as rationale for public justification principle 49 n. 85, 56–9
  on scope of public justification principle 41 n. 38
  tendentious characterization of violators of public justification principle by 202
Good life *see* human flourishing
Grass-counter 104–7, 111, 118, 128, 152, 157, 207

Hampton, Jean 68 n. 24, 70
Hanna, Jason 142 n. 54, 281 n. 32, 285 n. 53, 288 n. 60, 291 n. 65
Harm principle
  as basis of objection to perfectionism 305–10, 313–16
  compatibility of perfectionism with 307–8, 314–15
  Kramer on, and problem of bootstrapping 314–15
  as mid-level principle, not explanatorily fundamental principle 243, 308
  Mill on 26–7, 243, 306–7
  moralized definition of harm 243, 306–8, 310, 314–15

INDEX   341

non-moralized counterfactual definition of
 harm 243 n. 120, 308–10, 314–15
Hart, H. L. A. 93 n. 16, 100, 319 n. 10
Human flourishing
 Aristotelian conceptions of 132
 Christian conceptions of 131
 Confucian conceptions of 131–2
 desire for and knowledge of, stipulated
  into parties in perfectionist original
  position 102–10, 111–12
 as enjoyment of moral, intellectual and artistic
  excellence 13, 130, 135–7
 objective-list conceptions of 134–5
 reasonable disagreement about Christian,
  Confucian and Aristotelian conceptions
  of 10–11, 13, 123, 130, 132–3, 134, 139,
  211, 214, 216, 217
 see also enjoyment of moral, intellectual and
  artistic excellence; scepticism about human
  flourishing *and* subjectivism about human
  flourishing
Hurka, Thomas
 on Aristotelian conception of human
  flourishing 132
 on asymmetrical hybrid conceptions of
  human flourishing 154
 as comprehensive perfectionist 10, 214
 on consequentialist perfectionism 77 n. 64
 on end of period of neutralist liberalism 4
 paternalistic justifications for perfectionist
  state action 275–6, 277
 on perfectionism and in-principle guarantee
  of liberal institutions 250
 on relationship between having options and
  expansiveness of agency 253

Ideal of conscientious engagement *see* Eberle,
 Christopher
Ideal theory 39, 179, 270–2, 278, 281
Indistinguishability of perfectionism and
 anti-perfectionist liberalism
 extensional 14, 128, 157–8, 170–2, 175–89,
  193–4
 general explanation of 170–2
 intensional 14, 128, 157–8, 170–2, 189–94
 Kramer on 310–12
Individuality *see* freedom *and* Millian liberalism
Internal conception *see* constructivist approach
 to public reason

James, Aaron 68–9 n. 24, 79
Justicitis 319–22
Justificatory constituency *see* reasonable citizen

Justificatory disagreement versus foundational
 disagreement *see* Quong, Jonathan

Kagan, Shelly 136 n. 37, 154 n. 75
Kantian liberalism
 anti-perfectionist implications of 24–6
 sketch of 23–6
Kennedy, Robert 82–3
Klosko, George 34 n. 1, 54 n. 116, 235
Kramer, Matthew
 on all-purpose versatility of entitlement to
  primary goods 108
 on argument from warranted self-respect
  and harm principle to non-existence of
  edificatory-perfectionist duties 305–10,
  315–16
 on argument from warranted self-respect to
  aspirational-perfectionist policies 184–9
 on distinction between edificatory perfectionism and aspirational perfectionism 6 n. 16,
  184–5, 253 n. 21, 295
 on indistinguishability of duty-based
  perfectionism and anti-perfectionist
  liberalism 310–12
 on neglect by edificatory perfectionists of content-independent value of
  freedom 253–4, 315–16
 on neglect by edificatory perfectionists of
  deontological value of freedom 253 n. 23,
  283 n. 45
 on non-paternalistic justification
  for perfectionist state action
  (Convivia) 278–80
 on quidnunc or village busybody mentality of
  edificatory perfectionism 143, 294–316
 on Quong's autonomy-based objection to
  perfectionist subsidies 256
 see also quidnunc mentality
Kraut, Richard
 on Aristotelian conception of human
  flourishing 132
 on icicle-smasher 104
 setting up of straw man of anti-perfectionist
  liberalism by 172–4
Kugelberg, Henrik 49 n. 83, 208 n. 42
Kukathas, Chandran 64 n. 1, 319–22
Kymlicka, Will 44–5, 104 n. 56, 120 n. 106, 126
 n. 1, 136 n. 35, 137 n. 39, 267 n. 69

Larmore, Charles
 on anti-sectarianism within public reason
  theory 235
 on political liberalism as liberalism come of
  age 34–5, 39, 45, 216

342 INDEX

Larmore, Charles (*Continued*)
  on political liberalism as middle ground
    between Hobbesian modus vivendi and
    comprehensive liberalism 51
  on reasonable disagreement about ideals of
    autonomy and individuality 37–9
  on respect as rationale for public justification
    principle 49–53, 200
  on scope of public justification principle 41
    n. 38
Leib, Ethan 161–4
Lexical priority *see* perfectionist principles of
  justice *and* Rawls, John
Liberal neutrality
  neutrality of justification, not neutrality of
    consequences 171
  perfectionist justice incorporates restricted
    neutrality principle 115–16, 133, 217–18
  versus terminology of 'anti-perfectionist
    liberalism' 1 n. 1
  see also anti-perfectionist liberalism
Libertarianism 14, 45–7, 64–5, 101, 124, 225
  n. 81, 227, 244 n. 122, 247, 255, 256–67,
  269, 303
Lister, Andrew
  on civic friendship as rationale for public
    justification principle 48 n. 80, 200
  on laws against murder not a matter of
    on-balance judgement 240
  on modus vivendi as alternative to public
    reason liberalism 201–2
  on possibility of perfectionist internal
    conception 209 n. 46
  on public justification and fundamentally
    alien values 226
Lloyd, S. A. 68–9 n. 24, 71, 73 n. 48
Locke, John 2, 45, 127, 137

Macedo, Stephen 41, 242
MacIntyre, Alasdair 37, 38 n. 18
Mack, Eric 258, 262 n. 53, 265 n. 63
Macleod, Colin 181 n. 86, 206 n. 35
Mang, Franz 206–8
Mediocria 88, 188
Millian liberalism
  anti-perfectionist implications of 26–30
  compatibility of individuality with
    perfectionist justice 251, 256
  sketch of 26–30, 251
  subject to reasonable disagreement 21, 34–5,
    37–9, 45, 48, 49, 54
  see also harm principle
Modus vivendi liberalism 48, 51, 201–2
Moral powers of citizens *see* Rawls, John

Muldoon, Ryan 5, 212, 235
Mulhall, Stephen 10 n. 30, 37 n. 15, 55 n. 122,
  214 n. 58

Nagel, Thomas 34 n. 1, 41, 48, 108 n. 73, 126
  n. 1, 199, 222 n. 77
National Endowment for the Arts (NEA) 168–9
Neal, Patrick 68–9 n. 24, 252–3 n. 20
Neutrality *see* liberal neutrality
Non-perfectionist rationales *see* indistinguishability of perfectionism and anti-perfectionist
  liberalism *and* perfectionist law and public
  policy
Nozick, Robert 64, 124, 189, 242, 257, 258, 260,
  263, 264
Nussbaum, Martha 2, 4 n. 9, 34 n. 1, 48 n. 79,
  294

Ogien, Ruwen 157 n. 4, 283 n. 45, 306 n. 45
Opus Dei: Political Not Metaphysical 216,
  244–5
Original position *see* perfectionist original
  position *and* Rawlsian original position
Otsuka, Michael 257, 258, 260–1, 262–5, 266–7

Pallikkathayil, Japa
  on alternatives to public justification 48 n. 76,
    199–200 n. 9, 202–3 n. 22
  on anti-perfectionist implications of Kantian
    liberalism 24 n. 19, 25
  invocation of crude or excessively sectarian
    version of perfectionism by 25 n. 22, 145–6
    n. 57
Parfit, Derek 134–5, 136 n. 37, 148, 149 n. 63
Paternalism
  as basis of objection to perfectionism 15,
    273–93
  non-paternalistic justification for perfectionist
    state action 278–80
  paternalistic justifications for perfectionist
    state action 275–8, 280
  in the Quongian sense is not morally
    wrong 15, 273, 280–93
  Quong's judgemental definition of 274
Perfectionism
  about reasons for state action, not
    consequences of state action 171
  analysis of distinction between anti-
    perfectionist liberalism and 1, 19, 22,
    174–5, 176, 206
  defined by two commitments 131
  as denoting a position in political theory, not
    ethical theory 132 n. 21

distinction between comprehensive perfectionism and political perfectionism 10–11, 133–4, 213–18
list of main objections to 3–4, 19–20, 318
present state of debate between anti-perfectionist liberalism and 4–5
as term of art serving classificatory purposes 22, 174
terminology of 'liberal perfectionism' 248
Perfectionist conception of society
fundamental organizing idea within perfectionist theory of justice 12, 63, 74–5, 77, 220–1, 242, 249, 317
general explanation of, as fair striving for human flourishing 74–7
as helping to bring convictions into reflective equilibrium 86–88, 221
informs perfectionist definition of reasonable citizen 210–11, 220–1, 242
informs perfectionist original position and principles of justice 89, 97, 102, 121–2, 121–2, 248–9, 254
as interpretation of ideas in public political culture 77–86, 221
as subject of overlapping consensus 84–6
Perfectionist definition of reasonableness *see* perfectionist public reason
Perfectionist law and public policy
expressive harms of 159–60
implementation of, cannot be settled from armchair as depends on empirical contingencies 157, 164, 167, 169, 170
(in)susceptibility of perfectionist values to state promotion 137, 156–7, 159, 160–70
laws and policies promotive of artistic excellence 13–14, 157, 168–9, 170
laws and policies promotive of intellectual excellence 13, 157, 164–7, 170
laws and policies promotive of moral excellence 13, 157, 160–4, 170
non-perfectionist rationales for 3, 14, 157–8, 170–94, 221, *see also* indistinguishability of perfectionism and anti-perfectionist liberalism
Perfectionist original position
argument for perfectionist principles of justice in 110–16
as heuristic device 121–5
informed by perfectionist conception of society 89, 97, 102, 121–2
less illuminating than Rawlsian original position 122–5
redundancy of 120–5
specification of menu of principles in 97–101

specification of parties in 101–10
strains of commitment on dissenters 115–16
strains of commitment on worst-off 113–15
thinness of stipulations in 102–3, 109–10, 122–3
see also perfectionist principles of justice
Perfectionist principles of justice
extreme and Nietzschean account of 98–9, 117
informed by perfectionist conception of society 89, 97, 248–9, 254
moderate and mixed account of 99–100
principle of perfection subordinated to lexically prior principles 12–13, 99–100, 115–16, 117, 146 n. 58, 248–50, 317–18
quite strongly egalitarian 113–15, 151 n. 67
stated 12–13, 99–100
see also perfectionist original position
Perfectionist public reason
arguments within, involve plausible interpretation and balance of abstract values 210, 225–33
general explanation of 14, 198–9, 205–13, 224
goes beyond Rawls's thin theory of the good 205–6
illustrative cases of citizens (Anna, Barry, Callum) deemed unreasonable by 88, 218–19
indicates flexibility and generalizability of public reason framework 205, 231–2, 246
informed by perfectionist conception of society and provisional conception of human flourishing 210–11, 220–1, 242
leaves intact underlying motivations of public reason project 211 n. 54, 213–18, 236–8, 243–6
more sectarian than rival public reason views 199, 233–43
motivations for marriage of perfectionism and constructivism 213–18
practical-necessity-based argument against 221–4
precise content of, not fixed prior to actual democratic debate 232
still leaves ample room for reasonable disagreement about human flourishing 115, 132–3, 145–6, 211, 214, 216–18
structural looseness of 199, 226–33
too sectarian 199, 217, 229, 231, 237–8, 243–6
see also constructivist approach to public reason, empirical approach to public reason, public justification, reasonable citizen *and* reasonable disagreement

344 INDEX

Perfectionist theory of justice
aptly describable as version of liberal perfectionism 248
built atop Rawls's justice as fairness 100–1
disallows religious perfectionism 115, 133, 145–7, 217–18
employs Rawlsian methodology 8–11, 63, 89, 213–18, 311–12
generates perfectionist duties of justice, not merely permissions 6–8, 223–4, 303, 315, 317
incorporates restricted neutrality principle 115–16, 133, 217–18
is form of free-standing political perfectionism, not comprehensive perfectionism 10–11, 13, 130, 134, 147, 205, 210–11, 213–18
only needs to provide illuminating general framework, not highly specific or determinate verdicts 119–20, 138–41, 158, 230–1, 232
see also enjoyment of moral, intellectual and artistic excellence; perfectionist conception of society; perfectionist law and public policy *and* perfectionist principles of justice
Pettit, Philip 64 n. 3, 122 n. 113
Political liberalism
anti-perfectionist implications of 35–6, 42–7, 197–8
characterized and distinguished from comprehensive liberalism 10, 20–3
as liberalism come of age 34–5, 39, 45
as term of art serving classificatory purposes 22
Pragmatic concerns
are relevant to practical significance of perfectionist theory, not its truth 15, 270–2
as basis of objection to perfectionism 14, 247, 267–72
do not apply especially to perfectionism 15, 268–70
Primary goods
abstractness of 139–41
fair distribution of, not exhaustive of justice 99, 311–12
general explanation of 91–2, 205–6
not perfectionist values 172–5, 205–6
not purely empirical generalizations 107–8
Provisional conception of human flourishing *see* enjoyment of moral, intellectual and artistic excellence
Public goods 276–7, 278–80
Public justification
as basis of objection to perfectionism 14, 35–6, 197–246

compatible with perfectionism *see* perfectionist public reason
consensus versus convergence models of 41 n. 35, 197 n. 4
flexibility and generalizability of framework of 205, 231–2, 246
general explanation of 40–7
as heuristic device, not explanatorily fundamental principle 241–3
intuitively sectarian policies can pass test of 228, 230 n. 90
libertarian tilt of 45–7, 197 n. 4, 225 n. 81
necessary but not sufficient condition of legitimacy 230 n. 90
praises of, sung by political liberals 41–2
rationales for principle of 47–59, 200, 215
scope of principle of 41 n. 38
sincerity requirement on 230 n. 90
sketch of possible argument against 47–8, 199–205
versus alternative models of political justification 47–8, 51–2, 199–205, 240
weightiness of principle of 48, 53, 199–200
see also constructivist approach to public reason, empirical approach to public reason, perfectionist public reason, reasonable citizen *and* reasonable disagreement
Public political culture *see* perfectionist conception of society *and* Rawlsian conception of society
Public reason *see* public justification

Quidnunc mentality
applies to affirmative as well as prohibitive measures 298–9
as basis of objection to perfectionism 15, 294–316
constituted by self-aggrandizement and self-abasement 297–8, 300–4, 316
five preliminary criticisms of objection from 300–1
general explanation of 15, 295–300
and harm principle 305–10, 313–16
as illuminating heuristic 316
is a normative property, not a matter of psychological speculation 299–300, 301
objection from, begs question against duty-based perfectionism 15, 294–5, 301–4, 307–8, 313–16
objection from, does not assume perfectionist states promote incorrect conception of good life 143, 298

violates deontological ethic of self-restraint 294, 297, 298, 303, 304

Quong, Jonathan
  on anti-sectarianism within public reason theory 236
  on applicability of burdens of judgement to questions of justice 119 n. 100
  on definition of reasonable citizen 42–3, 46–7, 117–18 n. 96, 209, 220, 222
  on distinction between foundational and justificatory disagreement 117–18 n. 96, 226 n. 83
  on egalitarian justice as rationale for public justification principle 49 n. 83, 200
  on empirical approach versus constructivist approach (internal conception) to public reason 42, 206 n. 34, 208, 209, 212
  on framing of neutrality-perfectionism debate 7, 171
  on autonomy-based argument against perfectionist subsidies 254–6
  on full political status of unreasonable 219
  on irrelevance of beliefs of real people to public justification 209, 244–5
  on paternalism-based argument against perfectionism 15, 273–93
  on political liberalism and wholehearted participation in the liberal project 21, 35, 45
  on practical-necessity-based argument against perfectionist definition of reasonableness 222–4
  on pragmatic objections to perfectionism 267 n. 69, 270
  on public-justification-based argument against perfectionism 35–6, 42–3, 46–7, 222
  on 'the reasonable' as technical term 219
  on scope of public justification principle 41 n. 38
  on stability and subject of overlapping consensus 85
  on unclear rationale for marriage of perfectionism and constructivism 213–14
  see also paternalism

Railton, Peter 128 n. 8, 135–6, 260 n. 44
Rawls, John
  on argument from unanimous consent and equality to perfectionist policies 3, 177–80, 190–1
  on Aristotelian Principle 177–9
  on burdens of judgement 39–40

on classification of Millian liberalism as anti-perfectionist 28–9
on concept of justice versus conceptions of justice 319–21
on conception-based political theories 77
on embedding ideals into principles of justice 192
on exchange branch of government 177–9
on fact of reasonable disagreement 12, 36–40, 118–19, 197
false generalization from crude or excessively sectarian version of perfectionism by 117–19, 145–6 n. 57
on family of reasonable liberal conceptions of justice 46, 210, 226–7, 231
on four-stage sequence 139 n. 42
on ideology 72 n. 44
on impermissibility of perfectionism 44, 117, 177, 190–1
on inalienability of basic rights 261 n. 51
interpretive and contextualist aspects of later writings of 68–72
on justification as a matter of mutual support of many considerations 12, 317
on Kant and Mill as comprehensive liberals 20 n. 1, 34
on lexical priority 93, 100
on methodology 8–11, 68–72, 138
on Nietzschean perfectionism 98–9, 117
on overlapping consensus 54, 69, 84–6, 107
on perfectionist values as especially controversial 116–20
on political virtues 173
on practical-necessity-based argument against perfectionist definition of reasonableness 222
on primary goods 91–2
on public reason and school prayer 230 n. 90
on reasonableness as deliberately loose category 47–8, 199, 222
on reciprocity 96, 112–13
on reflective equilibrium 72–3, 267
on relationship between political liberalism and wars of religion 22, 37, 54, 201
on role of political philosophy 69–70, 270
on scepticism as basis for anti-perfectionism 107, 126 n. 1
on scope of public justification principle 41 n. 38
on sincerity requirement on public reason 230 n. 90
on stability as rationale for public justification principle 53–6
on strains of commitment 97, 113, 114

346 INDEX

Rawls, John (*Continued*)
  on two moral powers of free and equal
    citizens 67, 282
  two principles of justice of, (justice as fairness)
    stated 93
  on use of abstract conceptions 67, 74
  on veil of ignorance 90–2, 103–4, 109–10
  on weightiness of public justification
    principle 48, 53, 200
  see also Rawlsian conception of society *and*
    Rawlsian original position
Rawlsian conception of society
  general explanation of, as fair system of social
    cooperation 64–8
  as helping to bring convictions into reflective
    equilibrium 72–3, 220
  informs anti-perfectionist definition of
    reasonable citizen 209, 220
  informs Rawlsian original position and
    principles of justice 90
  as interpretation of ideas in public political
    culture 68–72, 220
Rawlsian original position
  argument for Rawlsian principles of justice
    in 94–7
  as heuristic device 121
  informed by Rawlsian conception of
    society 90
  specification of menu of principles in 92–3
  specification of parties in 91–2
  thinness of stipulations in 109–10, 122–3
Raz, Joseph
  on compatibility of perfectionism and harm
    principle 306–8
  as comprehensive perfectionist 214
  on freedom's lack of content-independent
    value 253
  as liberal perfectionist 248
  on perfectionist duties 7, 302–4, 311
  on political theory and radical criticism 72
  on pragmatic objections to perfectionism 267
    n. 69, 270 n. 78
Reactive attitudes 49, 56–9
Reasonable citizen
  anti-perfectionist definitions of 42–7, 117–18
    n. 96, 209, 220, 221–4
  perfectionist definition of 14, 205–13, *see also*
    perfectionist public reason
  technical term, not worked out by colloquial
    use of term 'reasonable' 219
  unreasonable citizens still enjoy full political
    status 219

see also constructivist approach to public
  reason, empirical approach to public
  reason, perfectionist public reason,
  public justification *and* reasonable
  disagreement
Reasonable disagreement
  about Christian, Confucian and Aristotelian
    conceptions of human flourishing 10–11,
    13, 123, 130, 132–3, 134, 139, 211, 214, 216,
    217
  about comprehensive liberalism 21, 34–5,
    37–9, 45, 48, 49, 54, 236
  about good life and human flourishing
    generally 12, 36–40, 42–7, 115–16, 116–20,
    197–8, 214–15
  about justice 45–7, 118–19, 210, 225, 226–7
  about religion 37, 41, 43–4, 115, 133, 145–7,
    207, 216, 217, 244–5
  general explanation of 36–40
  technical definition of, must remain in
    contact with folk concept of 216, 238, 244,
    245
  versus terminology of 'reasonable
    pluralism' 36 n. 8
  see also reasonable citizen
Reasonable pluralism *see* reasonable
  disagreement
Reflective equilibrium *see* Rawls, John
Respect
  competing conceptions of what, requires in
    regard to estimating rational powers of
    citizens 15, 273, 282–93
  deference and 289–91
  expressed by ideal of conscientious
    engagement 52, 202–5
  opacity and 291 n. 65
  as rationale for Anti-Sectarian
    Desideratum 234, 240
  as rationale for public justification princi-
    ple 48, 49–53, 200, 201–5, 211, 214, 215,
    240
Ripstein, Arthur 23–6, 309 n. 55
Rosati, Connie 136 n. 35, 144 n. 56

Sandel, Michael 37, 38, 117–18 n. 96
Sarch, Alexander 136 n. 35, 154 n. 75
Scanlon, T. M. 120 n. 106, 300 n. 27
Scepticism about human flourishing
  argument from, to anti-perfectionist
    liberalism 107 n. 69, 126–8
  Barry on 107 n. 69, 127–8, 129
  criticized 129, 138–9

INDEX 347

disavowal of, by anti-perfectionist
liberals 107, 126 n. 1
Sectarianism *see* anti-sectarianism
Self-ownership *see* freedom
Self-respect
detrimental effect of perfectionist policies
on 159–60
Kramer's argument from warranted, to
aspirational-perfectionist policies 184–9
Kramer's argument from warranted, to
non-existence of edificatory-perfectionist
duties 305–10, 315–16
paternalism and social bases of 286, 288, 292
as primary good 91, 102, 108, 109, 115, 139,
140, 174, 205
Sher, George
on abstruseness of his perfectionist theory 133
n. 29
on analysis of distinction between
perfectionism and anti-perfectionist
liberalism 175
on Aristotelian conception of human
flourishing 132
on compatibility of perfectionist legislation
and liberal rights 250
as comprehensive perfectionist 10, 214
on far-reaching practical upshots of
perfectionist values 170
as non-duty-based perfectionist 6
perfectionist theory of, viewed from Rawlsian
perspective 8–9
on question-begging nature of quidnunc
mentality argument 302 n. 34
on weightiness of content-independent value
of freedom 254 n. 25
Sobel, David 128 n. 8, 137 n. 38, 152, 154–5 n.
75, 260, 263–4, 265 n. 63
Social trust 48, 56, 200, 201–5, 211, 214, 215
Spinner-Halev, Jeff 22 n. 7, 29 n. 49
Stability
as consideration in favour of justice as fairness
in original position 96–7
as rationale for Anti-Sectarian
Desideratum 234, 238–9
as rationale for public justification
principle 48, 53–6, 214
can be realized (for the right reasons) by
perfectionist justice 84–6
Steiner, Hillel 257, 258, 260 n. 46, 261, 262–5,
266–7

Stemplowska, Zofia 117–18 n. 96, 185–6 n. 103,
228 n. 89
Strains of commitment *see* perfectionist original
position *and* Rawls, John
Strawson, Peter 56–9
Subjectivism about human flourishing
argument from, to anti-perfectionist
liberalism 126–8
Bruckner's defence of, criticized 105–7
disavowal of, by anti-perfectionist
liberals 107, 126 n. 1
general form of, criticized 128–9, 138, 193
Swift, Adam 10 n. 30, 37 n. 15, 55 n. 122, 214 n.
58

Taylor, Anthony 57, 59 n. 145, 187, 197 n. 4, 254
n. 25, 302 n. 34
Thomson, Judith Jarvis 120–1 n. 106, 300 n. 27

Vallentyne, Peter 257, 258, 259, 260 n. 46, 262–5,
266–7, 320 n. 11
Vallier, Kevin
on anti-perfectionism as desideratum of
public reason theories 5
on anti-sectarianism as desideratum of public
reason theories 216, 233 n. 95, 235, 236–7,
241
on consensus/convergence distinction within
public reason 41 n. 35, 197 n. 4
on perfectionist public reason as reductio ad
absurdum of constructivist approach 212
n. 56
on redundancy and stipulativeness of
constructivist approach 212–13 n. 57, 241
on social trust as rationale for public
justification principle 48 n. 82, 56, 200
Value pluralism 36 n. 8, 217 n. 69
Van Schoelandt, Chad 212 n. 58, 241 n. 116, 245
n. 123
Veil of ignorance *see* Rawls, John
Village busybody *see* quidnunc mentality

Waldron, Jeremy 21 n. 2, 34 n. 1, 41–2, 301
Wall, Steven
on alternatives to public justification 48 n. 76,
199–200 n. 9
on argument from equality and fairness to
perfectionist policies 114 n. 88, 182–4
on classifying theories of well-being as
subjective, objective and hybrid 137 n. 38
as comprehensive perfectionist 214

348 INDEX

Wall, Steven (*Continued*)
  on excellence devoid of enjoyment 152
  on expressive harms of perfectionist
    policies 159 n. 5
  as liberal perfectionist 248
  on perfectionist duties 7, 302–4, 311–12
  on pragmatic objections to perfectionism 267
    n. 69
  on restricted neutrality principle 115, 133,
    217

on subjective perfectionism 131 n. 13
on two defining commitments of
  perfectionism 131
on weightiness of public justification
  principle 48 n. 78, 200 n. 11
Weithman, Paul 34 n. 1, 48 n. 81, 49 n. 84, 55 n.
  119
Wendt, Fabian 48 n. 78, 55, 84 n. 75, 200 n. 11,
  202–3 n. 22
Wilson, James 82–3